BOOK WEBSITE

ABBREVIATIONS

ANOVA	Analysis of variance
APA	American Psychological Association
CI	confidence interval
df	degrees of freedom
COS	Center for Open Science (cos.io)
DFY	don't fool yourself
DV	dependent variable
ES	effect size
ESCI	Exploratory Software for Confidence Intervals
H_0	null hypothesis
H_1	alternative hypothesis
IQR	inter-quartile range
IV	independent variable
LL	lower limit of a CI
MoE	margin of error (length of one arm of a CI)
MoE_{av}	average of the two arm lengths of an asymmetric CI
NHST	null hypothesis significance testing
NOIR	levels of measurement: nominal, ordinal, interval, ratio
OS	Open Science
OSF	Open Science Framework (osf.io)
Q1	first quartile
Q2	second quartile, median
Q3	third quartile
RCT	randomized control trial
SD	standard deviation
SE	standard error
UL	upper limit of a CI

SYMBOLS

α	Type I error rate (alpha)
β	Type II error rate (beta)
β	slope of a standardized regression line, standardized regression weight
δ	population ES, Cohen's δ (delta)
η^2	proportion of variance, in ANOVA (eta squared)
μ	population mean (mu)
μ_0	μ specified in the null hypothesis
μ_1	μ specified in the alternative hypothesis
Π	population proportion (upper case pi)
ρ	population Pearson's correlation (rho)
Σ	addition (upper case sigma)

σ	population SD (sigma)
σ^2	population variance
ϕ	phi coefficient
χ^2	chi-square
ω^2	proportion of variance, in ANOVA (omega squared)
A	first IV in a factorial design
a	intercept of a regression line
B	second IV in a factorial design
b	slope of a regression line, regression weight
C	level of confidence
d	sample ES, Cohen's d
$d_{unbiased}$	unbiased estimate of δ
$F(df_1, df_2)$	test statistic used in ANOVA
i	integer, used as an index
k	number of levels of an IV
M	sample mean
M_t	trimmed mean
N, n	sample size
p	p value, in NHST
P	proportion
r	Pearson's correlation
s	sample SD
s^2	sample variance
s_{av}	standardizer for Cohen's d, paired design
s_p	pooled SD
s_t	SD for trimmed data set
t	variable, often with t distribution
$t_{.95}(df)$	.95 critical value of t for stated df
V	variance
X	dependent variable
X	integer, numerator of a proportion
$\hat{Y}$	regression prediction of Y
z	variable, often with normal distribution
$z_{.95}$	z for central .95 area under normal distribution
?	$.05 < p < .10$
*	$.01 < p < .05$
**	$.001 < p < .01$
***	$p < .001$

Introduction to the New Statistics

This is the first introductory statistics text to use an estimation approach from the start to help readers understand effect sizes, confidence intervals (CIs), and meta-analysis ("the new statistics"). It is also the first text to explain the new and exciting Open Science practices, which encourage replication and enhance the trustworthiness of research. In addition, the book explains null hypothesis significance testing (NHST) fully so students can understand published research. Numerous real research examples are used throughout. The book uses today's most effective learning strategies and promotes critical thinking, comprehension, and retention, to deepen users' understanding of statistics and modern research methods. The free ESCI (Exploratory Software for Confidence Intervals) software makes concepts visually vivid, and provides calculation and graphing facilities. The book can be used with or without ESCI. Other highlights include:

- Both estimation and NHST approaches are covered, and full guidance given on how to easily translate between the two.
- Some exercises use ESCI to analyze data and create graphs including CIs, for best understanding of estimation methods.
- Videos of the authors describing key concepts and demonstrating use of ESCI provide an engaging learning tool for traditional or flipped classrooms.
- In-chapter exercises and quizzes with related commentary allow students to learn by doing, and to monitor their progress.
- End-of-chapter exercises and commentary, many using real data, give practice for analyzing data, as well as for applying research judgment in realistic contexts.
- *Don't fool yourself* tips help students avoid common errors.
- *Red Flags* highlight the meaning of "significance" and what p values actually mean.
- Chapter outlines, defined key terms, sidebars of key points, and summarized take-home messages provide study tools at exam time.
- www.routledge.com/cw/cumming offers for students: ESCI downloads; data sets; key term flashcards; guides; tips for using IBM's SPSS and R for analyzing data; and videos. For instructors it offers: tips for teaching the new statistics and Open Science; additional assessment exercises; answer keys for homework and assessment items; question bank for quizzes and exams; downloadable slides with text images; and PowerPoint lecture slides.

Designed for introduction to statistics, data analysis, or quantitative methods courses in psychology, education, and other social and health sciences, researchers interested in understanding the new statistics will also appreciate this book. No familiarity with introductory statistics is assumed.

Geoff Cumming is professor emeritus of La Trobe University and has been teaching statistics for over 40 years.

Robert Calin-Jageman is a professor of psychology and the neuroscience program director at Dominican University and has been teaching and mentoring undergraduate students for nine years.

Introduction to the New Statistics

Estimation, Open Science, and Beyond

Geoff Cumming

Robert Calin-Jageman

Routledge
Taylor & Francis Group

NEW YORK AND LONDON

Front cover: Artwork is from *Treasure* by Claire Layman (www.clairelayman.com), and is used with her generous permission.

First published 2017
by Routledge
711 Third Avenue, New York, NY 11107

and by Routledge
2 Park Square, Milton Park, Abingdon, Oxon OX14 4RN

Routledge is an imprint of the Taylor & Francis Group, an informa business

© 2017 Taylor & Francis

Library of Congress Cataloging in Publication Data
Names: Cumming, Geoff. | Calin-Jageman, Robert.
Title: Introduction to the new statistics : estimation, open science, and beyond / Geoffrey Cumming and Robert Calin-Jageman.
Description: New York : Routledge, 2017. | Includes bibliographical references.
Identifiers: LCCN 2016007814 (print) | LCCN 2016008456 (ebook) |
ISBN 9781138825529 (pbk.) | ISBN 9781138825512 (hardback) |
ISBN 9781315708607 (eBook)
Subjects: LCSH: Estimation theory–Textbooks. | Mathematical statistics–Textbooks. | Confidence intervals–Textbooks.
Classification: LCC QA276.8 .C86 2017 (print) |
LCC QA276.8 (ebook) | DDC 519.5–dc23
LC record available at http://lccn.loc.gov/2016007814

ISBN: 978-1-138-82551-2 (hbk)
ISBN: 978-1-138-82552-9 (pbk)
ISBN: 978-1-315-70860-7 (ebk)

Typeset in Meridien LT Std
by Out of House Publishing

GC: For my grandchildren: Tom, Lachie, Odin, Pippa, Lucy, Erin, Zoe, and any who may follow.

RC-J: For Irina, Tavi, and Emilia, and for the many students who've made teaching these topics such a pleasure.

Brief Contents

Detailed Contents

Preface

This book is about how you can use limited data to draw reasonable conclusions about how the world works. Put more formally, this book is about *inferential statistics,* the art of using information from a *sample* to estimate what might be true about the world as a whole.

Inferential statistics is an exciting and powerful field! It's how physicians can test a new drug on a limited number of patients and then estimate how well the drug might work for the general public. It's how psychologists can test a new therapy on a limited number of clients and then estimate how well the therapy is likely to work for all patients with the same disorder. It's how pollsters can survey a limited number of likely voters and then estimate how much support there is for a candidate in an upcoming election. All this and so much more: It's no exaggeration to say that inferential statistics is at the very heart of our civilization's expanding ability to understand, predict, and control the world around us. This book will help you learn this amazing set of skills for yourself. With some work, you'll soon be able to make sound estimates from limited data, and you'll also be able to understand and critically assess the attempts of others to do so.

We hope this sounds enticing, but you may have heard that inferential statistics is dull, impenetrable, and confusing. Well—it doesn't have to be. This book teaches what we call the *new statistics,* an approach that we believe is natural and easy to understand. Here's an example. Suppose you read in the news that "Support for the President is 68%, in a poll with a margin of error of 3%." Does that seem particularly confusing? Hopefully not. You can immediately understand that the poll was conducted with a sample of voters, not by surveying everyone in the whole country. Then the pollsters applied inferential statistics to the results from the sample to determine that 68% is our best *estimate,* and that we can be reasonably confident that support in the whole population is within 68% ± 3%, which is the 95% *confidence interval* (CI). That, in a nutshell, is the *estimation approach* to inferential statistics, a key component of the new statistics. Of course, there's a lot to understand to be able to use estimation for yourself. We'll discuss issues like how to select the sample, how big the sample should be, and how to calculate and understand the *margin of error.* We'll also emphasize combining results from multiple studies, an approach called *meta-analysis,* which is a second key component of the new statistics. The important point for now is that the new statistics is not something you need be afraid of—learning from this book will take effort (see *Making the Most of This Book,* below), but we believe it will be easier and more intuitive than the way inferential statistics was taught in the past.

Although inferential statistics is very powerful, it can only lead to sound estimates if the data are collected and analyzed without *bias.* For example, you obviously couldn't trust poll data if certain types of voters were excluded or if the poll asked leading questions. Therefore, this book teaches not only inferential statistics, but also some approaches for minimizing bias while conducting research. Specifically, we emphasize *Open Science,* an evolving set of practices intended to reduce bias by increasing the openness of research and thus ensuring that research results are accurate, and worthy of our trust. Open Science emphasizes the stating of research plans and predictions in advance. Then, after you conduct the study, it emphasizes sharing materials, posting data publicly for others to analyze and use, and conducting replications to double-check your own work and the work of others. It's basically the old scientific method updated for the internet age—it's an exciting development that's leading researchers in many disciplines to change the ways they have traditionally worked. We introduce Open Science in Chapter 1, then throughout the book we discuss Open Science and other ways to limit bias.

Before we begin, you may be wondering: If this book teaches the new statistics, then what was the "old statistics"? In many fields, a more traditional type of inferential statistics, known as null hypothesis significance testing (NHST), has dominated. In Chapter 6, we'll explain this approach in detail. And throughout the book, we'll help you understand how to translate back and forth between estimation and NHST, so that when you read research conducted using NHST you'll easily be able to understand it using the estimation approach we take in this book. As you'll see, the estimation and NHST approaches are built on the same foundations and often lead to similar conclusions. We believe, however, that the estimation approach is not only easier to learn but also helps researchers make better judgments from their data. And this isn't just our opinion. An increasing number of journals and professional organizations are urging researchers to avoid problems with NHST by using the new statistics. This textbook is the very first of its kind to help beginning students learn the new statistics and Open Science practices. We hope you'll be excited to know, then, that working your way through this book will help put you right at the forefront of best research practices.

If You Are a Student

Especially if you are starting your first statistics course, welcome, and we hope you find it rewarding. As we've said, we hope you find estimation a natural way to think about research and data. We also hope that you'll find the section *Making the Most of This Book* helpful.

We hope you come to feel at least some of the passion we have for statistics. It's great to see a beautiful picture that makes clear what some data are telling us! Statistics is not really about mathematics, but about what data reveal, and examining pictures of data is usually the best approach. Perhaps this gives us new insights into the world, or how people think and behave. Welcome to the world of research, statistics, and informative pictures.

If You Are a Researcher or Instructor

You are probably very familiar with NHST and appreciate how well established it is. Between the two of us, we've taught NHST for almost 50 years and understand the challenges of changing. We believe, however, that all of us should carefully consider statistical reform issues, and decide how best to proceed in our own research areas and with our own students. Perhaps the new statistician's greeting will appeal: "May all your confidence intervals be short!"

Although adjusting the way you've been teaching statistics may seem daunting, we believe the work you put in will benefit your students tremendously. Not only should the new statistics be easier for your students to learn and use, but making the change should better prepare your students for a research world that's rapidly adopting Open Science practices. As an example of evolving standards, consider the new guidelines for authors introduced in 2014 by the leading journal *Psychological Science*. The editorial explaining the changes is at tiny.cc/eicheditorial and the new guidelines include this statement:

> *Psychological Science* recommends the use of the "the new statistics"—effect sizes, confidence intervals, and meta-analysis—to avoid problems associated with null-hypothesis significance testing (NHST). Authors are encouraged to consult this *Psychological Science* tutorial [Cumming, 2014, available from tiny.cc/tnswhyhow] by Geoff Cumming, which shows why estimation and meta-analysis are more informative than NHST and how they foster development of a cumulative, quantitative discipline. Cumming has also prepared a video workshop on the new statistics [available from tiny.cc/apsworkshop]. (From: tiny.cc/pssubguide accessed 1 July 2016.)

Psychological Science also encourages researchers to adopt Open Science practices, and offers badges to recognize preregistration of research plans, open materials, and open data (tiny.cc/badges). An editorial published in December 2015 (tiny.cc/lindsayeditorial) drew on Geoff Cumming's work to help justify further steps the journal was taking to increase the reproducibility of research it would accept for publication. Other journals and professional associations are making similar moves.

We are excited to work with you and your students to prepare for a future in which estimation and Open Science are the norm in our fields. We invite you also to consider the following section, *Making the Most of This Book*.

Intended Audience

This book assumes no previous statistical knowledge. It is designed for use in any discipline, especially those that have used NHST, including psychology, education, economics, management, sociology, criminology and other behavioral and social sciences; medicine, nursing and other health sciences; and biology and other biosciences. If you are teaching or studying in any such discipline, then this book is intended for you. We hope it serves you well.

KEY FEATURES OF THIS BOOK

An Estimation Approach Based On Effect Sizes and Confidence Intervals: The New Statistics

We're convinced that the new statistics, meaning estimation based on confidence intervals (CIs), is a better approach to data analysis. We believe it's easier for students to understand and more informative for researchers. Moreover, it's becoming widely used so it's vital that students and researchers understand it and can use it with their own data. We assume no previous statistical knowledge and focus on estimation from the very start, explaining it in simple terms, with many figures and examples. We also explain the traditional approach (NHST, null hypothesis significance testing) in Chapter 6 and use it alongside estimation in the subsequent chapters—with ample guidance for easy conversion back and forth between the two approaches.

Meta-Analysis, From the Very Start

Meta-analysis combines results from several studies and is a key component of the new statistics. It allows us to draw quantitative conclusions from a research literature, and these are what we need for evidence-based practice. We introduce meta-analysis in Chapter 1, then in Chapter 9 we explain it in a highly accessible way using the simple forest plot, without any formulas. This is the first introductory textbook to do so.

Open Science, From the Very Start

This is the first introductory textbook to integrate Open Science all through. The new statistics and Open Science are closely linked, and together are the way of the future.

Open Science promotes openness and replicability. Journals, funding bodies, and professional associations are revising their policies in accord with new Open Science standards. The basic ideas, including preregistration and open data, are easy for students to grasp. We discuss them throughout the book, with many examples—including examples of student research projects, which are often part of a highly valuable world-wide replication effort.

Promotion of Effective Learning and Studying Techniques

Recent research on how students study has identified how learning can be strikingly more efficient; for example, by having students work with meaningful examples and express things in their own words, and by asking them to keep retrieving earlier material. We've used these findings to guide the design of the book and the way we use numerous real research examples. We explain the effective learning techniques in the section *Making the Most of This Book*.

Compatible with Traditional or Flipped Classrooms

This book and all the materials provided at the website are designed to support effective learning, whether the course is organized along traditional lines or is based on a flipped classroom, in which students undertake assigned work with the book and its materials before coming to class.

Promotes Critical Thinking and Statistical Judgment

We emphasize careful critical thought about every stage of conducting research, rather than focusing on calculations. We provide essential formulas and many examples of data analysis, but our discussion of the numerous real research examples aims to develop students' deep understanding and confidence in making their own statistical judgments. The use of ESCI (Exploratory Software for Confidence Intervals) simulations, and guidance from the instructional videos, help students develop a deeper understanding and greater confidence in their own statistical judgment.

SUPPORTIVE PEDAGOGY

- Each chapter starts with pointers to what it contains, and closes with summary *take-home messages*. These summarize key points of the chapter, provide an overview, and serve as a study tool.

- Often in the text the student is asked to *pause, reflect, and discuss* intriguing issues. Research shows this is an effective learning technique, so we often ask students to write about a topic or discuss it with another student, to encourage critical thinking. These are also useful as prompts for class discussion or activities.

- Definitions of *key terms* are set off from the text. Many terms and expressions are also defined in the *Glossary* near the end of the book, which provides students with a quick reference and study tool. Lists of abbreviations and symbols appear at the very start of the book, and a list of selected formulas at the very end.

- *Exercises* and *quizzes* are placed throughout each chapter. Answers and our commentary, including much discussion of conceptual issues, are at the end of the chapter to allow students to test their understanding and quickly obtain feedback about their progress.

- ▶
  Sidebars in the margins are visual markers highlighting key issues and points. This makes it easier for the reader to gain an overview and to find key points when reviewing for exams.

- Some of the exercises use the *ESCI software* (see below), for interactive learning and a visual grasp of concepts.

- We highlight common pitfalls, or things to watch out for. We call these *Don't fool yourself* (DFY) points, in recognition of Richard Feynman's sage advice that "The first principle is that you must not fool yourself". We hope these will help students avoid making such errors.

- In considering the NHST approach to data analysis, we explain important cautions that students always need to keep in mind, including troubles with the meaning of "significance" and what p values can and cannot tell us. These are the five *Red Flags*.

- There are *end-of-chapter exercises*, which often use real data sets and allow students to analyze real data as well as practice research judgment in realistic contexts. Our answers and commentary for these exercises are at the end of the book.

SOFTWARE SUPPORT

ESCI (Exploratory Software for Confidence Intervals) is the free software that goes with the book and is available for download on the book's website. You can readily use the book without ESCI, but it's designed to help by presenting statistical concepts vividly and interactively. Watch out for the dance of the means, dance of the CIs, and dance of the *p* values. You can use ESCI to analyze your own data, especially to calculate confidence intervals and create graphical depictions of your results. See the *Appendix* for more about ESCI. At the book website (see below) there are also guides for using the book with other software, in particular R and IBM's SPSS.

SUPPLEMENTAL RESOURCES ON THE BOOK WEBSITE

The book's website is: www.routledge.com/cw/cumming For easy typing, use tiny.cc/itns. The website is an integral part of the learning package we offer.

For Students:

- Reading guides that provide chapter-by-chapter guidance for making best use of the book and materials.
- Free download of ESCI, which runs under Microsoft Excel.
- Downloadable data sets, including those used in end-of-chapter exercises.
- Model manuscripts showing how to report your research in APA format.
- Glossary flashcards for practice and exam preparation.
- Guides for using other statistical software—in particular R and SPSS—for analyzing your own data and example data discussed in the text, and for answering end-of-chapter exercises.
- Videos that explain important concepts. Many of the videos show how to use ESCI to see concepts and analyze data.

For Instructors:

- An Instructor's Manual, which includes guidance for instructors teaching the new statistics, including additional reading suggestions and sample syllabi.
- Additional homework exercises (with solutions for instructors).
- Complete Powerpoints for each chapter, plus in-class activities with answer keys.
- Quiz and test bank questions.
- Downloadable images from the text.

CONTENTS

Here's a brief outline of what each chapter contains. The sequence is what we feel is best, but chapters can easily be used in a different order, in accord with the preferences of different instructors.

Chapter 1 introduces the process of asking research questions and using data to provide answers. It mentions Open Science and introduces many research and statistical concepts informally and intuitively.

Chapter 2 introduces further fundamental research ideas, says more about Open Science, and explains many terms.

Chapter 3 describes basic descriptive statistics, introduces the ESCI software, and uses ESCI to illustrate a number of ways to picture data.

Chapter 4 discusses the normal distribution and explains the basics of sampling. It uses ESCI simulations to explore sampling variability.

Chapter 5 explains CIs and effect sizes, and describes four ways to think about and interpret CIs. It also introduces the *t* distribution.

Chapter 6 discusses *p* values, NHST, and their close links with estimation.

Chapter 7 discusses the independent groups design for comparing two treatments. It describes both estimation and NHST approaches, including the *t* test for independent groups. It also introduces the standardized effect size measure, Cohen's *d*.

Chapter 8 describes the paired design, also taking both estimation and NHST approaches, including the paired *t* test. It discusses Cohen's *d* for the paired design.

Chapter 9 introduces meta-analysis using a visual approach based on forest plots, and provides many examples to illustrate its importance.

Chapter 10 has more on Open Science, then takes two approaches to planning studies: first, by finding *N* to achieve a desired precision of estimation and, second, by using statistical power.

Chapter 11 discusses Pearson correlation, *r*, and describes applications, including its value for meta-analysis.

Chapter 12 discusses linear regression, and explains how regression relates to correlation.

Chapter 13 uses proportions to analyze frequencies and discuss risk, and also introduces chi-square.

Chapter 14 takes a contrasts approach to analyzing one-way designs, and introduces one-way analysis of variance (ANOVA).

Chapter 15 continues the contrasts approach with two-way factorial designs, including discussion of interactions, and introduces two-way ANOVA.

Chapter 16 brings together earlier discussions of Open Science, and sketches a number of future directions, including longitudinal studies and big data.

The *Appendix* explains how to download and use ESCI, with numerous hints for getting the most out of the software. Look here to find which ESCI page you need to explore a concept, or to carry out calculations on your own data.

ACKNOWLEDGMENTS

GC: Numerous colleagues and students have contributed to my learning that has led to this book. I thank them all. Mark Burgman, Fiona Fidler, and Tim van Gelder are valued colleagues who have assisted in many ways. Eric Eich and Steve Lindsay, successive editors-in-chief of *Psychological Science*, and Alan Kraut and other leaders of the *Association for Psychological Science*, have guided and encouraged my work, and have also provided outstanding leadership toward better research practices. My treasured colleague Neil Thomason continues to provide inspiration, wonderful ideas, and an unswerving commitment to sound argument and clear communication. This book is way better because of his efforts. I'm grateful for the sustained dedication, intellectual rigor, and good humor of all members of the group Neil led to critique drafts, especially John Campbell, Keith Hutchison, Larry Lengbeyer, Michael Lew, Erik Nyberg, and Yanna Rider. At home I'm forever grateful to Lindy for her enduring support and encouragement.

RC-J: My contributions to this book would not have been possible had I not been fortunate enough to co-teach methods and statistics for the past eight years with outstanding and dedicated colleagues: Tracy Caldwell, Tina Taylor-Ritzler, Kathleen O'Connor, and most especially Rebecca Pliske, who mentored us all. Thanks for the many discussions, beers, and tears spent together pushing each other to do even better for our students.

Together we warmly thank Gabrielle Lehmann and Sarah Rostron for their painstaking work. We also thank the many researchers whose data we use, both those who provided their data openly to the world and those who kindly provided data in response to our request. We thank Gideon Polya for the artistry of his drawings and for his generosity in creating such a broad range to fit the book. We are grateful to the reviewers of draft chapters, who gave us valuable guidance that improved the book in numerous ways. Some remain anonymous; reviewers who agreed to be named were: Dale Berger, Claremont Graduate University; Bruce Blaine, Saint John Fisher College; Karen Brakke, Spelman College; Stephanie DeLuca, Virginia Tech; Thomas Faulkenberry, Tarleton State University; Franklin Foote, University of Miami; Catherine Fritz, University of Northampton (U.K.); Jon Grahe, Pacific Lutheran University; Rink Hoekstra, Groningen University (The Netherlands); S. Jeanne Horst, James Madison University; Fred Li, National Chai-yi University of Taiwan; Kevin Matlock, Humboldt State University; Christopher Nave, Rutgers University-Camden; Carrol Perrino, Morgan State University; Ed Purssell, King's College London; Robert Rieg, Aalen University (Germany); William Roweton, Chadron State University; Christopher Sink, Old Dominion University; Susan Troncoso Skidmore, Sam Houston State University; Jorge Tendeiro, Groningen University (The Netherlands); Patrizio Tressoldi, Università di Padova (Italy); Meg Upchurch, Transylvania University; Michael Van Duuren, University of Winchester (U.K.); Jordan Wagge, Avila University; Meg Waraczynski, University of Wisconsin-Whitewater. We warmly thank Toby Cumming, David Erceg-Hurn, Chuck Huber, Ryne Sherman, and others named at the book website, who developed valuable materials to go with this book—all are free downloads from that website. We thank David Erceg-Hurn again, for assistance with Chapter 16. We are greatly indebted to Debra Riegert, senior editor, and Rebecca Pearce, our development editor, both at Routledge, and Tom Moss Gamblin, our copy editor, for their outstanding support and professionalism. After that long list of wise advisors we must say that any remaining errors and weaknesses are all our own work. Please let us know of any you discover. Finally, thank you for joining us on this exciting journey of helping to shape how research will be done. May this book serve you well on that journey.

ABOUT THE AUTHORS

As you can see on the front cover, there are two of us, but we have decided, starting with the next section *Making the Most of This Book*, to write as if we were one, and to use "I" often. A particular "I" may refer to either of us, but usually it's both. We hope this gives a more informal and personal tone, which is how we both like to discuss ideas with students.

Geoff Cumming is professor emeritus at La Trobe University, Melbourne, and the author of *Understanding The New Statistics: Effect Sizes, Confidence Intervals, and Meta-Analysis*, published by Routledge in 2012. He has taught statistics for more than 40 years at every level, from introductory to advanced. His statistics tutorial articles have been downloaded more than 370,000 times. See: tiny.cc/errorbars101 and tiny.cc/tnswhyhow. The *Association for Psychological Science* has published six videos of his highly successful workshop on the new statistics (see: tiny.cc/apsworkshop). His main research interests are the investigation of statistical understanding and promotion of improved statistical practices. A Rhodes Scholar, he received his Doctorate degree in experimental psychology from Oxford University.

Robert Calin-Jageman is a professor of psychology and the neuroscience program director at Dominican University. He has taught statistics and mentored students in psychological science for nine years, publishing with 16 undergraduate co-authors (so far). His research focuses on how memories are formed and forgotten. He has also been active in exploring the replicability of psychological science and promoting Open Science. He received his PhD in biological psychology from Wayne State University.

Making the Most
of This Book

While writing this book I've been fascinated by recent research on practical ways that people can learn more efficiently. Before saying more about that, I invite you to consider the common learning techniques listed in Table 0.1 and record how often you use each strategy and how effective you judge each to be. If you like, have a guess at the third column—what research tells us.

 Throughout the book, I use this little picture when I'm asking you to pause and do something. It really is worth giving it a try before reading on.

Table 0.1 Learning Techniques

Technique	How often you use it	How effective you think it is	How effective research finds it to be
1. Reread the textbook.	_____	_____	_____
2. Highlight key points.	_____	_____	_____
3. Write summaries.	_____	_____	_____
4. Study one topic thoroughly before moving on.	_____	_____	_____
5. Use tests, including self-tests. Ask and answer questions, alone or in a group.	_____	_____	_____
6. Retrieve material from memory, even when not fully mastered and retrieval is difficult. Correct any errors.	_____	_____	_____
7. Move on to the next topic before mastering the current topic. Try to figure out the next thing for yourself.	_____	_____	_____
8. Practice reflection: Identify important ideas, invent examples, and make links with earlier material.	_____	_____	_____
9. Distribute study activities over time. Retrieve material later, then again after a delay. Then again.	_____	_____	_____
10. Interleave study activities. Mix things up. Study a range of different topics; use a variety of activities.	_____	_____	_____

If you skipped to here, I urge you to go back to the table and think about all the items on the left, and how useful you think they are.

Research on how students study and learn has in recent years found startling results. There's good evidence that most of us can do way better. Before I go on, here's an analogy: I recently read an article (tiny.cc/runfast) about a long-distance runner who learned from a coach how to breathe differently: more from the diaphragm and in a different rhythm. It took effort and practice, but with the new technique he shattered his previous personal best for the marathon.

I found that story intriguing and instructive, because it just goes to show that even something you already think you are good at (like breathing!) can be drastically improved through science. Well, according to a range of research from psychology, it's the same for study skills.

I'll summarize a few of what I see as important lessons from the research, then I'll revisit Table 0.1, and suggest some first steps you can take.

Get Motivated and Engaged

Of course, anyone learns better if they feel engaged, and see the material as relevant for themselves. I'll do my best to explain why I believe statistics are so important. There will be numerous real world examples that will help you see that statistics are part of all our lives, and persuade you that they really matter—to you, me, and all of us. That's one reason I find them so fascinating. I'll also try to provide lots of interesting, even enjoyable activities. I invite you to seek reasons relevant to you for getting engaged and I hope you find that statistical understanding helps not only in your studies, but also in the wider world. Unfortunately, reports in the media and discussions of current affairs often invoke research findings, but draw unjustified conclusions. Distortions and misleading claims can be tricky to spot, but basic statistical understanding can be a great help—you can enjoy using your data detective skills.

Thinking of a different approach to motivation, you no doubt appreciate that finding the right friends to work with can help—in person or in cyber-space. I'll often invite you to pause and reflect on some issue; you may find that discussion with others is a good strategy.

I've seen many students at first skeptical about statistics and their own abilities who become absorbed by the challenges of understanding research and drawing conclusions from data. I hope you also can become absorbed by these challenges.

Spend Time on Task

Who would have guessed it? We need to put in the hours. Motivation and engagement help us find the time, and keep up the concentration. Working with others may help. If rewards work for you, then allow yourself coffee, chocolate, or a walk on the beach when you finish a chapter, or master a tricky idea—whatever it takes to keep up the motivation and put in the time.

Seek ways to keep motivated and engaged, to help you put in the time.

Build Your Statistics Confidence

For years I asked students at the start of my introductory course to rate their attitude towards statistics on a scale from "no worries" to "blind panic". Then I'd invite especially the blind panic students to extra lunchtime meetings where we discussed any statistical questions they cared to ask. They were usually reassured to find others who shared their concerns, and also that working through the basics, with many pictures, led them to feel increasingly confident. If you are initially anxious, I hope the many examples and pictures in this book, and the interactive simulations we'll use in ESCI, will similarly reassure you and help you build your confidence. Maybe find some others with initial doubts, and work at it together.

Use the Most Effective Learning Techniques

Before reading on, if you haven't written down your responses for the blanks in Table 0.1, please do so now. One of the main messages of this section is that it's highly valuable to think and do, as well as read. My request that you think about your response for all the blanks in the table is a first go at that.

Surveys suggest that enormous numbers of students, perhaps the majority, rely on 1–4 in the table. However, research indicates that these techniques are generally not the most effective use of time. They often give the illusion of understanding—you seem to be working hard, focusing on the material, and grasping it. However, the learning is often superficial and won't persist because it's not sufficiently elaborated and integrated with prior knowledge, or linked with examples and practical application.

By contrast, 5–10 have been found effective for achieving learning that's deep and enduring. One key idea is *retrieval*, which means closing the book and trying to bring to mind the main points, and maybe writing some bullet points in your own words. You could practice now for this section. Then open the book and check. It's fine if you miss lots and make mistakes—the great value is retrieval itself, even when you only partly grasp something. Come back to it, retrieve again, and enjoy doing way better!

In other words, a valuable learning activity is to work at retrieving something, even if it's only half-learned, half-understood. Persist, do your best, compare with the correct answer, then come back later and retrieve again. It can be difficult working with not-quite-understood material, but it's effective, even if it doesn't seem so at the time. Researchers who study retrieval suggest that achieving a difficult retrieval actually changes your brain and makes you smarter. In summary, the slogan is: "Don't read again, retrieve again".

If you are a runner, maybe think of retrieval as the studying equivalent of diaphragm breathing—a great way to do better that, with a bit of effort, anyone can learn, but which most people don't appreciate.

I summarize 5–10 in the table as "Make it your own". Take any new idea and express it in your own words, make a picture, link it back to things you know already, think up an example, then a crazy example, try explaining it to someone else—do whatever helps to make it your own. Then later test yourself—do your best to retrieve it. Then tomorrow retrieve it again.

Change a Fixed Mindset to a Growth Mindset

A further key idea is the distinction between a *fixed mindset* and a *growth mindset*. Carol Dweck and colleagues have demonstrated that helping students adopt a growth mindset can be a highly effective way to help them learn better and achieve more. Here's how Dweck describes the two mindsets:

> In a fixed mindset students believe their basic abilities, their intelligence, their talents, are just fixed traits. They have a certain amount and that's that.... In a growth mindset students understand that their talents and abilities can be developed through effort, good teaching and persistence. They don't necessarily think everyone's the same or anyone can be Einstein, but they believe everyone can get smarter if they work at it. (Carol Dweck, tiny.cc/dwecktalk)

I've mentioned three important ideas about learning.
...before reading on, you may care to close the book and practice retrieval...

▶ Many students rely on rereading and highlighting, but these strategies may give only superficial learning that won't last.

▶ Work at a challenging retrieval to change your brain and get smarter.

▶ ■ Don't read again, retrieve again.
■ Make it your own.

▶ Fixed mindset: The belief that my capabilities are more or less fixed, whatever I do.
Growth mindset: The belief that effort, persistence, and using good techniques can help me learn more successfully and become more capable.

- Retrieval is valuable, even when it is difficult, even when you don't fully grasp the material.
- To "make it your own" by elaboration, discussion, or in any other way can be highly effective.
- Adopting a growth mindset can motivate effective learning efforts.

Reflect on how the three relate, and how you might make use of them. Explain your thinking to someone else.

Make It Stick

Make it stick: The science of successful learning is a great book by Brown, Roediger, and McDaniel (2014). It describes the research findings on effective learning, and uses real stories to make the main recommendations intuitive and vivid. You may find reading the book helpful. For a start, you could try one or more of the following:

- Browse the book's website, at makeitstick.net At the "About" tab, find a paragraph that summarizes the main message. At the "Contents" tab go to a page for each chapter with a one-paragraph summary and a box with a brief version of that chapter's story. Which is your favorite story? (Mine is about Michael Young, the Georgia medical student.)
- Watch this video: tiny.cc/misvideo

Writing Take-Home Messages

Each chapter in this book ends with take-home messages, and towards the end of each chapter I'll encourage you to write your own, before reading mine. Make that part of your doing, not just reading.

 Here's a first chance to write your own take-home messages. Think (or look) back over this *Making the Most of This Book* section, and choose what, for you, are the main points. I've written four, but you can write as few or as many as you wish.

Pause, write, discuss, before reading on…
It really is worth closing the book and bringing to mind what you think are the main messages.

No, don't read on yet…

Take-Home Messages

■ **Find ways to engage.** Find whatever strategies work for you to find motivation, to relate statistical ideas to your own interests, and to keep engaged—so you can keep putting in the time. Work with others if it helps.

■ **Make it your own.** Use a mix of activities—asking and answering questions, discussing, writing in your own words, using the software, applying the ideas—as you seek to make sense of it all, and to make the material your own.

■ **Retrieve and retrieve again.** Retrieve again, rather than read again. Retrieval that's challenging can give good learning, change your brain, and make you smarter. Then retrieve again later, then again later.

■ **Adopt a growth mindset.** Use good learning techniques, seek guidance, and persist, and you will learn and become more capable.

1

Asking and Answering Research Questions

A large part of science is asking questions, then trying to find data that can help answer them. In this chapter I'll use an everyday example to illustrate the general idea of asking and answering questions. I'm hoping you'll find the example pretty intuitive—you may discover that you already have a good idea of how data can show us how the world works.

This chapter introduces:

- A simple opinion poll that illustrates how data can help answer a research question
- The scientific research process, from asking questions to interpreting answers
- Pictures that help us understand data
- Basic ideas of *population* and *sample*, and of *estimate* and *margin of error*
- The idea of a *confidence interval*, a vital part of the answer to our research question
- *Open Science*: An approach to research that tackles some of the ways that data can mislead, and emphasizes the need to think carefully about every stage of the research process
- The value of *replication* studies that repeat research to check its accuracy, and of *meta-analysis* to combine results from a number of similar studies

Words in italics, like *population*, are terms I'll define later. For the moment, read them as normal English words, although you could, if you wished, consult the Index or Glossary at the back of this book. Also, be sure to explore the book's website, which has lots of goodies, including videos. Make it a favorite or bookmark: www.routledge.com/cw/cumming or, for easy typing: tiny.cc/itns

A SIMPLE OPINION POLL

Here's the example—a simple opinion poll. You read this in the news:

Public support for Proposition A is 53%, in a poll with a 2% margin of error.

Let's say Proposition A proposes a law requiring serious action on climate change by reducing the use of fossil fuels and switching to renewable energy. Soon there will be a state-wide vote to determine whether the proposition becomes law. You and your friends have set up a website explaining why the proposition is a great idea, and are eager to know the extent of support for it among likely voters. Therefore, our question is:

What's the support for Proposition A in the population of people likely to vote?

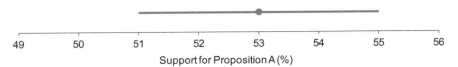

Figure 1.1. Support for Proposition A, in percent, as reported by the poll. The dot marks the point estimate, and the two lines display the margin of error (2%) either side of the dot. The full interval, from 51% to 55%, is the 95% confidence interval.

The poll's answer is:

Estimated support in the population of likely voters is 53±2%.

This result from the poll is displayed in Figure 1.1. Does this make you happy? Probably yes, because estimated support is greater than 50%, so the proposition is likely to pass, although perhaps only by a small margin.

A Thumbnail Sketch of Research

Here's a slightly fuller account of the poll example, which illustrates a common way research proceeds.

1. Ask a research question. *What's the support for Proposition A in the population of people likely to vote?*
2. Design a study to collect data that can answer the question. *Design a poll that will ask a sample of intending voters about their support for Proposition A.*
3. Carry out the study and collect the data. *Choose a sample of intending voters and ask them about their support for the proposition.*
4. Apply statistical analysis to picture and describe the data, and provide a basis for drawing conclusions. *Calculate that 53% of people in the sample say they support the proposition. Use knowledge of the poll design, especially the size of the sample, to calculate from the data that the margin of error is 2%, and therefore the confidence interval extends from 51% to 55%. Prepare Figure 1.1.*
5. Draw conclusions about what the data tell us in answer to our original question. *We take the 53% as the best estimate the data can give us of support in the population of likely voters, and the 2% margin of error as indicating the uncertainty in that estimate. In the figure, the dot marks the best estimate, and the confidence interval indicates the range of uncertainty.*
6. Interpret the results, give a critical discussion of the whole study, and prepare a report. Think about the next study. *Most likely, the true level of support among intending voters is within the interval from 51% to 55%, therefore the proposition is likely to be approved—although it may not be.*

Of course, that's a mere sketch of the research process. You may have many questions: "How do we choose the sample?", "How large a sample should we use?", "How do we calculate the margin of error?", "How should we interpret the 95% confidence interval in Figure 1.1?" We'll discuss answers to these and many other relevant questions throughout this book.

Where in the process do you need to know about statistics? Most obviously at Step 4, to calculate the confidence interval. However we need statistical understanding at every single one of the steps, from formulating the question and designing a study, to interpreting the results and making a critical evaluation of the whole study. Throughout the book, whatever statistical idea we're discussing, always bear in mind the whole research process. Statistical ideas are needed at every stage.

Perhaps the most amazing thing about statistics-based research is that the process sketched above permits us to study just a relatively small sample of people, and yet draw conclusions that might apply broadly, in some cases to the whole world! Statistical techniques give us a sound basis for analyzing sample data and making inferences—drawing conclusions—that sometimes apply very broadly. Yes, there's always uncertainty, but our analysis can tell us *how much* uncertainty. That's the magic of statistics.

Scientists have used more fully developed versions of this framework—my thumbnail sketch above—and statistical understanding to discover much of what we know about people and the world. Among a vast number of examples, such research has told us about

- how effective cognitive-behavior therapy can be for depression;
- how much ice mass the Greenland icecap is likely to lose in the next two decades; and
- the extent that having more friends can lead to improved learning in elementary school.

You may not wish to be a researcher, although you may have the chance to participate in worthwhile research as part of your course. In any case, to appreciate how such knowledge was gained requires statistical understanding. Beyond that, to be a critically aware citizen means being able to understand data reported about society and our immediate world, and to know what searching questions to ask. Statistical understanding is essential for that.

Conducting research properly can be tricky—Chapter 2 is about lots of ways we can fool ourselves. We'll see examples where wrong statistical choices cost lives, and poor research practices cause widespread misconceptions about what's true in the world. It's essential to use the best research and statistical practices we can, and to use them correctly. And always to think carefully about what any data really tell us.

Intuitions About the Poll

I invite you now to think informally and intuitively about the poll example. Here are some points worth thinking about:

- Our question is about the whole *population*, meaning all people likely to vote on the proposition.
- The poll couldn't ask everyone, or even most people, in the population, so it took a *sample* from the population, and asked people in the sample whether they supported the proposition.
- If the sample was chosen in a fair and unbiased way, it's probably representative of the population, so we can take the sample results as a reasonable *estimate* of support in the population.
- There is some unknown *true* level of support in the population. Our best *point estimate* of that is 53%, the support the poll found in the sample.

We use results from a sample to *estimate* something about a population.

The *point estimate* is the best single value the data can give us for what we're estimating about the population.

▨ We calculate the *margin of error* (2%) as the likely greatest error in the point estimate. In other words, 53% is unlikely to be more than 2% away from the true value.

▨ Most likely the true value of support in the population lies in the range 53±2%, or [51, 55]. That's the full extent of the interval displayed in Figure 1.1.

If at least some of those points match your intuitions, well done! You are well on the way to appreciating the basic logic of research that asks and seeks to answer questions of this kind.

We call that range of values, [51, 55], our *95% confidence interval*, abbreviated as "CI." It's an interval inside which the true value is likely to lie, which means we can say:

We are 95% confident the interval [51, 55] includes the true level of support in the population.

The 95% CI extends from 51% to 55%, so the *margin of error* (2%) is half the length of the CI, as Figure 1.1 illustrates. The "95%" means we are not guaranteed that the CI includes the true value. However, most likely it does, assuming that the poll was carried out well—later there's much more on what it means to carry out studies well. You might be dissatisfied with "most likely"—we would prefer to be certain. However, research studies rarely, if ever, give definitive answers to our questions, so we must be willing to think about uncertainty and not fool ourselves by looking for certainty. The great value of a CI is that it *quantifies* uncertainty—its length is a measure of the extent of uncertainty in our point estimate.

We can also say that the CI tells us how *precise* our estimate is likely to be, and the margin of error is our measure of precision. A short CI means a small margin of error and that we have a relatively precise estimate—the 53% is likely to be close to the population value. A long CI means a large margin of error and that we have low precision—the 53% may be further from the true value.

The curve in Figure 1.2 illustrates how *plausibility* or *likelihood* varies across and beyond the interval. Values around the center of the CI, say around 52% to 54%, are the most plausible, the most likely, for the true value in the population. Values toward either end of the CI are progressively less plausible, and values outside the interval even less so. The further a value lies outside the CI the more implausible it is. In other words, values near the point estimate are relatively good bets for where the true value lies, and values progressively

▶ The *95% confidence interval* (CI) is a range of values calculated from our data that, most likely, includes the true value of what we're estimating about the population.

▶ The *margin of error* is half the length of the 95% CI, and the likely greatest error in the point estimate.

▶ The margin of error is our measure of the *precision* of estimation. A small margin of error means a short CI and a precise estimate.

▶ Figure 1.2 illustrates how values near the center of a CI are most *plausible* for the true population value, and how plausibility decreases toward the ends of the CI and then beyond the CI.

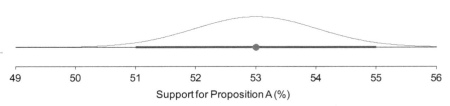

Figure 1.2. Same as Figure 1.1, but with the addition of the smooth curve that pictures how likelihood varies across and beyond the 95% CI. Likelihood, or plausibility, is represented by the height of the curve above the CI and the fine horizontal line.

further away from the point estimate are progressively less good bets. In other words again, the likelihood that a point is the true value is greatest for points near the center of the interval and drops progressively for points further from the center.

Note in particular that there's nothing special about the endpoints of the CI. Always keep in mind the smooth likelihood curve of Figure 1.2, which applies to just about any CI and illustrates how likelihood, or plausibility, varies across and beyond the interval.

Why 95%? Good question. You might occasionally come across other CIs, perhaps 90% or 99% CIs, but 95% CIs are by far the most common. It's almost always best if we agree on which CI to use, so I recommend we follow convention and use 95% CIs, unless there are very strong reasons for using something different. I'll routinely use 95% CIs, so if I mention a CI assume 95% CI unless I say otherwise.

Estimates and Estimation

We can refer to a CI as an *interval estimate* because it's an interval containing the most plausible values for the population value, as illustrated in Figures 1.1 and 1.2. The main approach to data analysis in this book is based on point and interval estimates, and you won't be surprised to hear that this general approach is referred to as *estimation*. It's a highly informative way to analyze data. I hope you'll find it a natural and easily understood way to report results and draw conclusions from data.

> The CI is our *interval estimate* of the population value of interest.

To use estimation, what type of research questions should we ask? We could ask "Is Proposition A likely to pass?" but this suggests a yes-or-no way of thinking about the world, and that a yes-or-no answer would be sufficient. However, we're much less likely to fool ourselves if we think about the world in a *quantitative* way, and therefore ask quantitative questions, such as "What's the extent of support?" or "How great is the support?" Such questions call for quantitative answers, in terms of percent support, which are more informative and therefore preferable. Using estimation, we should always express research questions in quantitative rather than yes-or-no terms. We should ask "To what extent...?", "How much...?", or similar questions, then appreciate the quantitative, informative answers.

> Express research questions in estimation terms. Ask, for example, "How much...?", or "To what extent...?"

Making Your Interpretation

A couple of paragraphs back I said that, after calculating point and interval estimates, we need to "draw conclusions from data". After reporting a CI, you should give us your interpretation—what do the values mean, in the context of the study? In our example, what might you say about the poll result? We can summarize the result as "53% support, 95% CI [51, 55]". What do those values imply, considering the impending vote on Proposition A?

> *I'll often ask you questions like that. You can read straight on and see my answer, but it's much better to look away and think of your own. Write it down! Even better—call a friend for a chat before you write. I'll use the pause and think logo, as below, to suggest a good moment for you to pause, think, discuss, and write. But be encouraged to pause, chat, and write whenever you like. Often is good.*

 So, have you written down your answer?

As I explained earlier, in "Making the Most of This Book", research tells us that learning is much better if you write things in your own words, even if you feel you are making a wild guess.

▶ The *limits* of a CI are its two endpoints.

Think of the campaigns for and against the proposition. Think of what 51% and 55%, the *limits* of the CI, might mean—"limits" is what we call those two endpoints of a CI.

▶ Use judgment to interpret the point estimate and CI, in the particular context.

You might suggest that a 2% margin of error is not bad—we'd always like a smaller margin of error, meaning higher precision, but the result we have is useful. You might say the CI indicates that all plausible values for the true level of support in the population are greater than 50%, so we can feel confident the proposition will pass. However, you might also worry that a strong "No" campaign has been running, and there's enough time for a few percent of voters to be persuaded to change their minds—the poll suggests that such a small change could tip the result. You'd therefore encourage your friends to make a final effort to keep support high, perhaps by stepping up your social media campaign. The important point is that how you interpret the result requires you to think about the context and implications. You need to consider both the point estimate and the CI, then go beyond those mere numbers and give your judgment of what they mean in the particular situation. One aim of this book is to help you build your confidence to acknowledge uncertainty and make interpretations based on judgment.

FURTHER INTUITIONS

Here are some questions to test your intuitions further:

If we ran the poll again, with a new sample, but using the same procedure and as close as possible at the same time, what's the likely result?

 Pause... think... call... chat... write...

Instead of my answer, here's another question:

Suppose we ran the poll again, with a much larger sample, what do you think is likely to happen to the margin of error? With a much smaller sample? Which result is most useful?

 Hint: Think of an enormous sample. A tiny sample. It's often a good strategy to think of extreme cases.

▶ *Sampling variability* is variability in results caused by using different samples.

For the first question you probably quickly appreciated that a second poll would be very unlikely to give exactly the same point estimate. However, it's likely to give a similar estimate, not too far from 53%. Most likely, it will give a value in the interval [51, 55], which is our 95% CI from the original poll. *Sampling variability* is the name we give to the variation caused by using different samples. It's the variation from poll to poll—when we assume they are all carried out at the same time and in the same way, but using different samples. The CI gives us a good idea of the extent of sampling variability.

▶ Larger sample, shorter CI; smaller sample, longer CI— all else remaining the same. A sample four times as large gives a CI about half as long.

For the second question, a much larger sample is likely to give a result that's closer to the true value in the population, meaning its CI will be shorter, its estimate more precise. In fact, if we used a sample four times as large, the CI would probably be about half the length. On the other hand, a smaller sample is likely to give us a longer CI.

Do we prefer our 95% CIs to be long or short?

 If you like, reward yourself (chocolate? coffee?) for taking a break to think about the question.

That's an easy one: short, of course. A short CI means our sample estimate is most likely very close to the true value—the margin of error is smaller, the precision is greater. That's good news. That's why we go to the expense and trouble of running a poll with a large sample—to get a smaller margin of error, meaning a short CI.

From now on I'm going to refer to the margin of error as MoE, which I pronounce as "MO-ee", although you can say it as you wish. So MoE is half the length of a 95% CI, and MoE is our measure of precision.

MoE stands for margin of error.

 Quiz 1.1

1. A company is interested in how satisfied its customers are. To help find out, 50 customers are randomly selected to take part in a survey. Which of the following is true?
   a. The 50 customers surveyed are the sample, all the company's customers are the population.
   b. Whatever result is found in the sample will be exactly the same in the population.
   c. The company would be better off sampling only 10 customers, as this would produce less uncertainty about overall customer satisfaction.
   d. All of the above.
2. A confidence interval (CI) expresses
   a. a range of plausible values for what is most likely true in the population.
   b. our uncertainty about what is true in the population.
   c. the fact that results from a sample may not perfectly reflect the population, due to sampling variability.
   d. all of the above.
3. You read a poll result that says "62±4% of likely voters support the referendum". What is the ±4% part?
   a. This is the point estimate for referendum support.
   b. This is the population for referendum support.
   c. This is the margin of error (MoE).
   d. This is the sample size.
4. If the poll in Question 3 was conducted well, which of these results would be most *unlikely*?
   a. The referendum passes with 66% support.
   b. The referendum passes with 63% support.
   c. The referendum passes with 61% support.
   d. The referendum passes with 55% support.
5. We calculate a CI from the sample / population and use it to tell us about the sample / population. Half the length of the CI is called the _____, with abbreviation _____.
6. If *N*, the sample size, is made four times as large, the CI length will be about _____ what it was before, the precision will be lower / higher, and the researcher is likely to be more / less happy.
7. Make for yourself at least three further quiz questions, then give your answers. Swap with a friend.

Next, some exercises. It's so important to be thinking and doing, not just reading, that I've included exercises throughout the text. These in-chapter exercises often introduce new ways of thinking about what we've been discussing, or even new concepts. They are not just there for practice, but often play an important part in the main discussion,

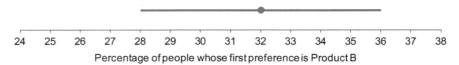

| 24 | 25 | 26 | 27 | 28 | 29 | 30 | 31 | 32 | 33 | 34 | 35 | 36 | 37 | 38 |

Percentage of people whose first preference is Product B

Figure 1.3. First preference for your product (Product B), marked by the dot, with 95% CI.

so please be encouraged to read and think about them all. You'll find my commentary and the answers at the end of each chapter.

1.1 Your company has decided to branch out into beauty products and has produced Invisible Blemish Cream. (I didn't invent that name—who cares about blemishes you can't see?!) A survey assessed people's first preference when given a choice of your company's cream and three competing products. For the test, the products were given the neutral labels A, B (your cream), C, and D. Figure 1.3 displays the results.

   a. What is the point estimate of the first preference for your product? The interval estimate? The margin of error?
   b. What is the population? Who would you like to have in the sample?
   c. Make two statements about the level of first preference for your product in the population.

1.2 If people chose randomly, you would expect 25% first preference for your product. Is your product more strongly preferred than this? Why or why not?

1.3 How could you achieve a CI about half as long as that shown in Figure 1.3?

CAREFUL THINKING ABOUT UNCERTAINTY

In later chapters we'll discuss important ideas raised by this poll example, including sampling, point estimates, and CIs, and how to use sample data to make conclusions about a population. We'll see definitions and formulas, and discover how to calculate 95% CIs. But for now I want to continue our informal discussion.

It's vital when reading a result like "53% with a 2% margin of error", or seeing a picture like Figure 1.1, to appreciate immediately that the result—the percentage support in the sample—could easily have been different. The CI gives us an idea of how different it might have been, if all details of the poll remained the same but we'd happened to choose a different sample. Sampling variability is one source of uncertainty with our results, and statistical procedures—calculating the CI—quantifies that for us.

However, beyond sampling variability there's virtually always additional uncertainty, which is much harder to pin down. It can have different causes in different situations, and usually there's no statistical formula to quantify it. We need careful critical thought to identify problems that might be contributing additional uncertainty.

▶ Beyond sampling variability there may be uncertainty arising from incomplete or biased reporting, or other causes.

Thinking of the poll example, here's one problem that could be contributing additional uncertainty. The news website where we read the poll result reported only this single poll, but perhaps there were other polls taken at the same time that it didn't report? If so, did it report the largest or best, or were the results we saw *selected*—by which I mean chosen to reflect some preference or bias? Other polls may have given different results, and our news source may have chosen to report just this particular poll because it liked its message. If a news source *selects* what to report from a number of results, then we can't draw confident conclusions from what it does report. There's an unknown amount of extra uncertainty and we can no longer be 95% confident the CI based on the poll results includes the true value. We need to seek out the most trustworthy news sources, seek out any other poll results, and note any signs of bias in a particular news source. In general, we need to think carefully and critically about any results, especially by asking:

> *Do we have the full story, or were these results selected in some way that might give a misleading message?*

If we suspect such selection, we can't draw confident conclusions.

You might also ask how the sample of people to be polled was obtained—we need to have confidence that it's likely to be reasonably representative of the whole population of intending voters. You could also be thinking that a poll result can be influenced by the wording of the question people are asked, by the communication channel used—phone or email or face-to-face—and especially by the proportion of people in the sample who cannot be contacted or refuse to respond. These are all good thoughts. Reputable polling companies have refined their procedures to minimize all these problems, but we still need to be alert to such additional ways that poll results may be uncertain. To help us assess the results, we need to have full details of the poll, including information about how it was conducted, what questions were asked, how the sample was chosen, and how many of the people in the sample answered the questions. In general, to have confidence in any data we need to ask:

> *Do we have full details about how the data were collected?*

THE REPLICABILITY CRISIS AND OPEN SCIENCE

Those two questions (*Were the results selected in a way that might mislead? Do we have full information?*) mark our first encounter with *Open Science*, a central idea that we'll meet often in this book. We can only have full confidence in conclusions from research when a number of Open Science requirements are met, and these questions express two of those.

The first two requirements for *Open Science* are: (1) avoid misleading selection of what's reported, and (2) report research in full detail.

"Open Science" comprises a number of practices designed to improve research. It has emerged only in the last few years and is still developing. It has largely been prompted by the *replicability crisis*—the alarming discovery that a number of widely known and accepted research findings cannot be replicated. In other words, when researchers repeat the earlier studies that reported the findings in question, they get clearly different results. In one dramatic example, a company wanting to develop new cancer therapies examined 53 findings from cancer research that looked promising. The company first attempted to confirm each finding by running a *replication* study, meaning a study designed to be as similar as possible to the original study that reported the promising result. In only 6 of the 53 cases (Begley & Ellis, 2012) could they confirm the main findings. That's terrible! It seems that some well-accepted research findings are simply wrong.

A *replication* is a repeat of an original study, similar to the original but with a new sample.

Similar, although happily less extreme, results have been reported in psychology and other disciplines. Here's an example from psychology. Gorn (1982) published evidence that even unobtrusive music, perhaps in a supermarket, can markedly influence consumer preference. The finding has been cited hundreds of times and is routinely included even in recent textbooks on consumer psychology. The first large and careful attempt at replication was by Vermeulen et al. (2014), who reported three studies that together suggested the effect was either zero or very much smaller than reported by Gorn, and of little, if any, practical import. Students, teachers, and psychologists working in marketing have been misled by the original results for several decades.

The *replicability crisis* is the realization that some published findings can't be replicated and therefore are almost certainly wrong.

Open Science

Open Science addresses the crisis by aiming to reduce the chance that incorrect research results are obtained and reported. I've mentioned two of its requirements—to avoid selection in what's reported, and to report research in full detail. We'll meet further requirements in later chapters, but another aim of Open Science is to encourage replication. Rarely, if ever, can a single study give a definitive answer to a research question, and so we should look for a replication study that found similar results before starting to have confidence in any finding.

Why "open"? Good question. The idea is that, as much as possible, full information about every stage of research should be openly available. In particular, the data and full details of the data analysis should be available, so other researchers can repeat the original data analysis as a check, or analyze the data in a different way. Sometimes, for privacy or other reasons, data can't be openly available, but where possible it should be. Having full information also allows other researchers to conduct a replication study, confident that it's as similar as possible to the original.

A good summary of a number of Open Science requirements is the question I asked earlier: "Do we have the full story?" We can now add "Seek replication." as another Open Science guideline.

Two Open Science slogans are:

• Do we have the full story?
• Seek replication.

Suppose we have results from an original study and a number of replication studies. The results look broadly similar, but of course are not exactly the same—for a start, sampling variability will cause them to vary. Fortunately, there are statistical tools that allow us to combine the results and provide a basis for overall conclusions. I'm referring to meta-analysis, our next topic.

META-ANALYSIS

One great thing about estimation is that it can be extended beyond a single study. If we have results from two or more similar studies, we can use *meta-analysis* to combine the results. Usually, meta-analysis gives an overall CI that's shorter than the CI for any of the single studies. That's reasonable because adding further information from additional studies should reduce our uncertainty about where the population average lies, and reduced uncertainty corresponds to a shorter CI.

Use *meta-analysis* to combine results from two or more studies on the same or similar questions.

We'll discuss meta-analysis more fully in Chapter 9, but here I'll report a meta-analysis of our original poll (Poll 1) and two further polls that I'm supposing were taken at a similar time, asking the same or a similar question. Figure 1.4 shows the result of Poll 1, the same as in Figures 1.1 and 1.2, and

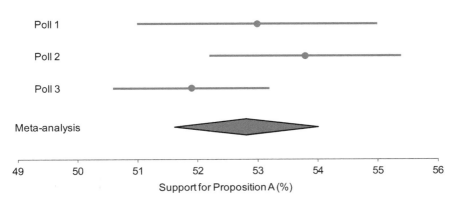

Figure 1.4. A forest plot showing the result of Poll 1, the original poll as in Figures 1.1 and 1.2, and two further polls, together with the result of a meta-analysis of all three polls. For each poll, the point estimate and 95% CI are displayed. The diamond is the 95% CI that is the result of the meta-analysis.

also the results of Polls 2 and 3. For each poll we have the point estimate and 95% CI. I applied meta-analysis to combine the three results, and obtained 52.8% as the overall point estimate, with CI of [51.6, 54.0]. That result is pictured as the diamond in Figure 1.4. That figure is our first example of a *forest plot*, which displays individual study results and uses a diamond to show the results of a meta-analysis. We'll see later that the diamond shape is a revealing way to picture a CI, but for the moment just note that the diamond indicates a special CI, a CI that is the result of a meta-analysis.

A *forest plot*, such as Figure 1.4, shows point and interval estimates for individual studies, and displays the meta-analysis result as a diamond.

Just to be sure, say in words what those numbers found by the meta-analysis represent. How are they pictured by the diamond?

 Hint: Point and interval estimates?

Yes, 52.8%, the overall point estimate, is our best single estimate of support in the population of intending voters. We are combining, or integrating, evidence from the three studies, and so it makes sense that the overall estimate (52.8%) lies well within the range of the three separate estimates, as marked by the three large dots in Figure 1.4. The 95% CI, the interval estimate given by the meta-analysis, is [51.6, 54.0], meaning that after considering all three studies we can be 95% confident this interval includes the true level of support in the population. This interval is shorter than the other CIs, as we expect for the result of a meta-analysis, which, after all, is based on the results from all three studies. As usual, a short CI is good news.

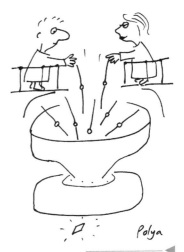

Meta-Analytic Thinking

Partly because of the rise of Open Science, researchers now increasingly appreciate the crucial importance of replication. Well-conducted replications make a vital contribution to building a research literature that includes fewer wrong findings, and therefore deserves our trust. Once we have an original study and at least one replication study, we can use meta-analysis to integrate the results.

Replication and meta-analysis are so important that we should adopt *meta-analytic thinking*. That's thinking that prompts us to watch out for any

Meta-analytic thinking is the consideration of any study in the context of similar studies already conducted, or to be conducted in the future.

opportunity for meta-analysis to help. It prompts us to think of any study as one contribution, to be combined where possible with earlier studies, replications, and other related studies yet to come. We should adopt meta-analytic thinking whenever we review, plan, or interpret research.

It's time to step back and look in a general way at the estimation approach we've been using.

A STEP-BY-STEP PLAN FOR ESTIMATION

Here's my suggested list of the important steps in an estimation approach to asking and answering research questions. It's a slight expansion of my thumbnail sketch earlier in this chapter.

1. State the research question. Express it as a "how much" or "to what extent" question.
   What's the support for Proposition A in the population of people likely to vote?
2. Identify the measure that's most appropriate for answering that question.
   The percentage of likely voters who express support.
3. Design a study that uses that measure and gives us good point and interval estimates to answer our question.
   Choose a sample of intending voters and ask them about their support for the proposition.
4. After running the study, examine the data, calculate point and interval estimates, and make a figure.
   See Figures 1.1 and 1.2. In answer to our question, the poll found a point estimate of 53%, with CI of [51, 55].
5. Interpret these, using judgment in the research context.
   See the section "Making Your Interpretation".
6. Report the study, making sure to state there was no selective reporting of just some of the results, and giving full details of every aspect of the study.
   These are two Open Science requirements.
7. Adopt meta-analytic thinking throughout. Seek other similar studies and, if appropriate, conduct a meta-analysis. Consider conducting a replication.
   Figure 1.4 shows results from two further similar polls and meta-analysis of the three polls.

Polya

This list is not meant to be a comprehensive guide to conducting good research, but it does express many of the important steps. We'll expand and refine the list in later chapters.

In the course of discussing the poll example we've encountered a number of important ideas in an informal way. I've introduced many terms, again informally. If you feel you are beginning to understand the whole estimation approach to finding out about the world, then give yourself a big pat on the back: You are well on the way to understanding research and statistics.

? Quiz 1.2

1. You see the result of a poll. What are three additional things you need to know before you can understand the result?
2. A poll found 66% support for a proposition, with margin of error of 4%. What is the CI? If the poll were repeated, with a second sample of the same size, what result would you expect?
3. A replication study
   a. uses the same sample as the original study.
   b. most likely gives exactly the same result as the original study.
   c. is usually a waste of time.
   d. is similar to the original study but with a new sample.
4. A forest plot displays for each study a dot that marks _____ and a line that marks _____. The diamond represents _____.
5. What are two important slogans for Open Science?_____
   _____
6. It is important not only to replicate results but also to combine the data across replications to determine the overall pattern of results. Which is the correct term for this?
   a. Repli-analysis.
   b. Meta-analysis.
   c. Under-analysis.
   d. Repeato-analysis.
7. Make further quiz questions, some on material from near the start of the chapter. Swap with a friend.

Looking Ahead

Our poll was perhaps the simplest possible estimation study—it estimated just a single percentage. In future chapters we'll discuss many more studies, which address various types of research questions. For all of them we'll take the estimation approach that I've introduced in this chapter, and our step-by-step plan will be a useful guide. Here are a few words about several of the studies that we'll discuss:

Two separate groups of participants. To what extent do you learn more from lectures if you use a pen rather than a laptop to take notes? This study compared the quality of notes taken, and amount learned from the lecture, for two separate groups of students, one for each method of note-taking. We'll discuss this study further in Chapter 2, then again in later chapters.

A single group of participants, measured twice. How effective is a computer-based method called *argument mapping* in improving students' critical thinking ability? Scores on a critical thinking test were compared before and after a single group of students had learned and practiced the argument mapping method. There's more on this in Chapter 8.

The correlation between two variables. To what extent do people in large cities tend to walk faster than people in towns or small villages? Walking speeds were observed for people in cities, towns, and villages in various countries around the world, and then used to assess the correlation, or relationship, between observed walking speed and the population size of the city, town, or village. We'll discuss correlation in Chapter 11.

In the next five chapters we'll discuss some further fundamentals of research (Chapter 2), graphs to help us explore our data and statistics that summarize data (Chapter 3), and a number of steps that lead to the calculation of confidence intervals (Chapters 4 and 5), with a look in Chapter 6 at an alternative to estimation—a second approach to analyzing data and drawing conclusions about a population. Then we'll have the tools we need to discuss and analyze studies of the types I described just above.

I now invite you to revisit this chapter, and discuss with other learners anything you find particularly interesting, or puzzling, or surprising.

 I'll close the chapter with take-home messages. You can look ahead to see what I've written, but it's much more useful if you write yours first. What are the major points so far? What's worth remembering? I suggest you try writing a list, then sleep on it, discuss with others, then revise your list. Then you can compare it with my list—and give yourself extra points for including any important items I've left out.

After your first go at writing some take-home messages, try these exercises—which may suggest more items for your list.

1.4 Draw a picture of a CI and use it to explain (a) point estimate, (b) interval estimate, (c) MoE.

1.5 Make up two interesting exercises involving CIs. Swap with a friend, or post to your discussion group. Discuss everyone's answers. How about a prize for the most interesting exercise?

1.6 Search the web for examples of different ways that CIs are pictured in figures reporting data. Do you have a preference?

1.7 Revise again your list of take-home messages. Scan through the chapter again, looking for anything further that's important enough to include. I have 10 items on my list, but your list can have whatever number you think best.

Finally, a quick reminder that it's worth visiting the book website—have you made a favorite or bookmark? It's at www.routledge.com/cw/cumming but for easy typing you can use tiny.cc/itns Incidentally, I use tiny.cc shortenings for some links in later chapters, for easy typing and so that I can, if necessary, update where they point, after the book is published. At the book website there's a list of those shortenings and the full links.

Reporting Your Work

An essential part of the research process is reporting your work—presenting or publishing your results so that others can learn from the data you have collected. Because this is so important, you'll find a section like this one at the end of most chapters with pointers for this vital step. You'll also find example manuscripts on the book website that you can use as a model.

To get us started, here are four basic principles to follow in reporting your work. They may seem a bit vague for the moment, but you'll see how they work in practice as you move through the book. In the last chapter of the book, Chapter 16, there's a recap of these principles plus, for each, bullet points that we've encountered along the way.

Tell the full story. Give a complete account of your research process and the data you collected. Don't selectively report results.

Provide sufficient detail. Include all the details necessary for someone else to replicate your work. Include all the data necessary for someone else to incorporate your results into a meta-analysis. Share your data online, if possible.

Tell the full story is our main guideline for reporting research.

Show the data. Whenever possible, provide figures that show your key findings. Prefer figures that show all the data rather than just summary statistics.

Interpret the point estimate and CI. Focus your conclusions and interpretation on the point estimate and confidence interval.

Choose a style and format that is appropriate for your audience. To help with this, these sections provide tips for following the APA Style laid out in the *Publication Manual of the American Psychological Association* (APA, 2010). APA style is the most commonly used style for writing manuscripts in a very wide range of disciplines. In fact, you'll notice that I've tried to make this book consistent with APA style, so examples you encounter in the text and the end-of-chapter exercises will, in many cases, provide further examples of APA style in action. Keep in mind, though, that these pointers are not a comprehensive treatment of APA style; you'll still need to consult the *Manual* when writing your own reports.

Even though APA style is our focus, that doesn't mean you should always follow its conventions. If you are using this book for a class, be sure to follow the assignment guidelines carefully. In addition, keep in mind that APA style is intended primarily as a pre-publication format, for manuscripts that will be submitted to a journal for transformation into more readable form. If your work is going direct to readers, you should adapt accordingly. For example, in this book I don't always follow exact APA referencing style—I might write Chaix et al. rather than several researchers' names, as specified by APA, when there's no ambiguity and to avoid cluttering the text, especially when we're discussing that study for several pages.

If you'd like to work seriously on your writing, or just read about how to be a great writer, try *The Sense of Style* by Steven Pinker (2014)—would you believe, it's beautifully written.

 ## Take-Home Messages

- Think in a quantitative, not a yes-or-no way. State research questions in estimation terms: "How much...?", "To what extent...?"

- An outline of the research process is provided by the seven-step plan for estimation. Refer to the listing of the seven steps.

- Point estimates and interval estimates provide quantitative, informative answers to research questions.

- A confidence interval (CI) is our interval estimate, and is a range of values calculated from data that most likely includes the true population value we are estimating.

- We can say we're 95% confident our 95% CI includes the true population value. Values near the center of the CI are most plausible for the true value, and plausibility decreases with increasing distance from the center of the CI.

- Use judgment and knowledge of the research context to interpret the results— the point and interval estimates. A figure is usually helpful.

- Open Science requires (a) avoidance of possibly misleading selection of results to be reported, (b) fully detailed reporting of research, and if possible (c) replication with an eye to meta-analysis.

- Meta-analysis combines results from two or more studies on the same or similar research questions, and is likely to give more precise estimates.

- Meta-analytic thinking considers any study in the context of past similar studies and with the expectation that replications are likely to be valuable.

- Using simple examples, pictures, and estimation suggests that learning about research methods and statistics need not be scary or mysterious, but is actually absorbing, highly useful, and even fun. (I didn't say that earlier, and you may not agree, but my aim is to persuade you it's true.)

Polya

End-of-Chapter Exercises

Answers to all end-of-chapter exercises are at the back of the book.

1) A study estimated the percentage decrease in pain ratings following 60 minutes of guided relaxation. The result was 34% [19, 49].

   a. What is the point estimate of the decrease? The interval estimate? The 95% CI? MoE?

   b. Make two statements about what the CI tells us. Give your interpretation of the results.

   c. Considering Open Science, what concerns do you have?

2) Suppose the result from the pain study had instead been 13% [−3, 29]. Answer all the same questions.

3) You are considering a replication of the pain study of Exercise 1 above.

   a. Supposing you want MoE from the replication to be about half of MoE from the original study, describe your replication study.

   b. Invent the results of such a replication. Compare with the original results.

   c. Suppose you meta-analyze those two sets of results. Suggest roughly what results the meta-analysis might give, and interpret those.

   d. What's the value of replication and meta-analysis?

 Answers to Quizzes

Quiz 1.1

1) a; 2) d; 3) c; 4) d; 5) sample, population, margin of error, MoE; 6) half, higher, more; 7) Questions don't need to be complicated, but it's best to choose things you find somewhat tricky.

Quiz 1.2

1) Are there other similar polls? Information about the sample—how was it chosen, how large? How was the poll conducted—what questions, what procedure? 2) [62, 70], most likely a point estimate within the first CI; 3) d; 4) the point estimate, the CI, the result of the meta-analysis; 5) Do we have the full story? Seek replication; 6) b; 7) It's worth using quizzes to review the whole chapter.

 Answers to In-Chapter Exercises

1.1 a. 32%, marked by the solid dot; the 95% CI, which is [28, 36]; 4%, the length of either arm, or half the full CI length; b. All potential purchasers of the cream; potential purchasers; c. We are 95% confident the interval from 28% to 36% includes the true first preference in the population for Product B, and values inside the CI are plausible for the true level of first preference, whereas values outside are relatively implausible.

1.2 The whole CI lies above 25%, so all plausible values for the true first preference are greater than 25%. Most likely our product is more strongly preferred than that.

1.3 Use a sample four times as large.

1.4 Refer to Figure 1.1. a. The point estimate is 53%, the solid dot, and is our best single estimate of the true value in the population; b. The interval estimate, the 95% CI, is the interval from 51% to 55%, marked by the line; c. MoE, the margin of error, is 2%, and is the length of either segment of the line, and half the length of the CI.

1.5 You might choose a current media report that includes—or should include—data, then ask how knowing the CI would help us understand what's really going on. Once you are aware of sampling variability, as signaled by a CI, you begin to notice how often people mention only the point estimate, for example an average or a percentage, with no mention that there's often considerable uncertainty in that value.

1.6 I found pictures like those in this chapter, or with little crossbars at the ends, and others that pictured a CI as a narrow stripe, without a dot in the middle or crossbars at the ends. I also saw the diamond, as in Figure 1.4. Often CIs are reported only as numbers in text, with no picture. But pictures with CIs are so informative, so cool. An easy search that presents many pictures is for "pictures of confidence intervals".

2

Research Fundamentals: Don't Fool Yourself

It can be wonderfully exciting to discover new and perhaps surprising things about how the world works—that's the fascination of research. Research can also be hard work, and there are lots of things we need to think about to avoid jumping to unjustified conclusions. A good scientist is always questioning, always skeptical, always looking for error and thinking carefully about alternative explanations.

This chapter is about fundamental research concepts. I'll summarize its main theme with a quotation. Richard Feynman, the famous physicist—also bongo drummer—wrote:

> The first principle is that you must not fool yourself and you are the easiest person to fool.

That's our first Don't-Fool-Yourself, or DFY, statement.

 DFY: Don't fool yourself, and you are the easiest person to fool.

This chapter is about not fooling ourselves. I'll define lots of terms and discuss lots of cautions, but don't let all that distract you from the excitement of research and thrill of new discovery.

You might be wondering why I keep referring to carrying out research, and to you as a researcher, when you may be feeling very new to it all and not (yet) planning a career in research. There are several reasons. First, research has become important in many, many fields: Corporations carry out market research, human resource offices conduct surveys of employee satisfaction, schools conduct trials to evaluate new teaching technologies, hospitals help enroll patients in clinical studies, governments conduct studies to evaluate policy changes, and so much more. You could easily be involved in planning, conducting, and interpreting research in your future career—perhaps often. In addition, as a citizen and consumer you will often encounter issues and choices for which understanding research will be invaluable, even essential. In such cases, it's often helpful to take the researchers' perspective—how did they see their work, how did they choose what to report and how to report it?

Research has become such an important part of society that more and more students—undergraduate as well as graduate—are participating in real research projects, so you may have such a chance before too long. The pen–laptop study (Mueller & Oppenheimer, 2014), which I mentioned at the end of Chapter 1, is a nice example of research by a student, Pam Mueller, that quickly became famous. Who knows where your class project may lead!

I'll mention that pen–laptop study a few times in this chapter. When you take notes in a lecture, is it better to write notes on paper, or type them on your laptop? What's the difference, in terms of quality of notes, and the amount you understand and remember? Before reading on, write down your thoughts.

Here's our agenda for the chapter, all with the theme of not fooling ourselves:

- Using a sample to make inferences about a population
- Basic concepts, including experimental and non-experimental research
- The measure that provides our data, and its reliability and validity
- Four levels of measurement, which have this acronym: NOIR
- Three problematic types of selection; planned and exploratory analysis
- Open Science: Do we have the full story?

INFERENCE FROM SAMPLE TO POPULATION

In the poll in Chapter 1 we used the results from a *sample* of people to make an *inference*, or conclusion, about the *population* of all intending voters. The main goal of this book is to explain techniques of *statistical inference* that justify doing that—using a sample to reach a conclusion about a population. There's almost always uncertainty, and ways we can easily fool ourselves, but inference is a bit of magic at the heart of most research. *Estimation* is the main statistical inference technique we'll discuss, then in Chapter 6 I'll describe an alternative approach.

I'll now define some basic terms, many of which I used informally in Chapter 1. From here on, I'll generally mark important terms by making them bold and italic the first time they are defined or explained. I'll continue to use plain italics for general emphasis. Note that the Index and Glossary can also help you find information about terms.

> *Statistical inference* is a set of techniques for drawing conclusions from a sample to the population the sample came from. *Estimation* is our favored approach to statistical inference.

Figure 2.1 illustrates the idea. The population of interest is at left, and the sample of N people chosen for the sample at right.

From now on, I'll usually refer to the average by its slightly more technical name, the *mean*.

> The *mean* is simply another name for the average.

The *sample mean* (M, or sometimes $\bar{X}$) is a *sample statistic* that is the average of the sample data. It's our point estimate of the *population parameter*, the population mean, μ.

It's vital to be clear about the distinction between a sample and the underlying population it came from. The population is usually large, even extremely large, whereas the sample is a manageable number of people taken from the population. To help make the distinction clear, for the sample we use Roman letters and refer to *sample statistics*, such as the sample mean, M. (Some books use $\bar{X}$, rather than M, for the sample mean.) For the population, we use Greek letters and refer to *population parameters*, such as the population mean, μ (Greek mu).

I've been talking about a population and sample of people, but we may be interested in other populations, of school classes, or companies, or rabbits—whatever our research question refers to. However, to keep things simple I'll continue to refer to people.

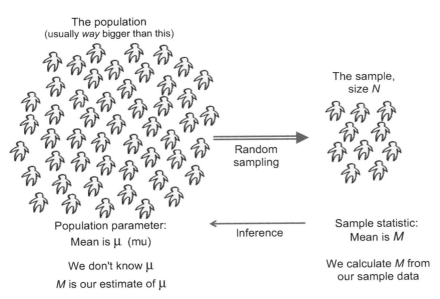

Figure 2.1. A population on the left, random sampling to obtain the sample shown on the right, and inference from the sample to the population. Sample mean, M, is our point estimate of population mean, μ.

A **population** is a usually very large set of people about which we are interested in drawing conclusions.

A **sample** is a set of people selected from a population.

In a moment I'll discuss how we should select the sample, but first a couple more definitions. The first step in data analysis is usually to calculate *descriptive statistics* from the data, for example the sample mean, to summarize the sample data.

A **descriptive statistic** is a summary number, such as the sample mean, that tells us about a set of data.

We also calculate from the data *inferential statistics*, which are designed to tell us about the population—for example, a confidence interval (CI), which is a range of values that most likely include the population mean.

An **inferential statistic**, such as a CI, is calculated from sample data and tells us about the underlying population.

Random Sampling

A sample is useful to the extent that it tells us about the population, which means that it needs to be *representative* of the population. How should we choose the sample so it's representative? The best strategy is usually to seek a *random sample*, meaning one that's generated by a process of *random sampling*. In Figure 2.1, that's the label on the arrow from population to sample. Random sampling requires that

Using a *random sample* is usually the best way to obtain a sample likely to be *representative* of the population.

- every member of the population has an equal probability of being chosen; and
- all members of the sample are chosen independently, meaning separately— the choice of one sample member has no influence on whether another is chosen.

> A *random sample* is chosen from the population such that all population members have the same probability of being chosen, and all sample members are chosen independently.

If for your study you wanted a random sample of students at your college, you might obtain a complete list of all such students, then choose a sample of, say, $N = 50$ by using some random selection method. You might, for example, put all the names on separate slips of paper in a box, stir well, and pull out 50 names. More practically you could use a table of random numbers (search online for this) to select 50 names from the list. Can you see any practical difficulties with using such a random sample of 50 students in your study?

 You know this logo is a reminder to pause, think, find someone for a discussion, and have a coffee. Then write down your thoughts.

What if you can't obtain access to a full list of enrolled students? Even if you can choose a sample randomly, what if you can't contact all of the chosen 50, or if some decline to participate or drop out halfway through the study? In practice it's rarely possible to meet the two requirements of random sampling, and you are likely to have to use a *convenience sample*, meaning the students who were willing to sign up to your online request then actually showed up on the day, or who agreed to participate when you asked in a large lecture class for volunteers, or who particularly like the flavor of ice cream you are offering as a reward.

> A *convenience sample* is a practically achievable sample from the population.

We have a dilemma. Using CIs for inference relies on the assumption of random sampling, but usually we have to use a convenience sample. What should we do? First, we should come as close as possible to meeting the requirements for random sampling. Second, it's usual to make the assumption in order to calculate CIs, and then make a judgment as to whether it's reasonable to draw conclusions about a particular population.

The key question is the extent to which we judge our sample to be reasonably representative of a population. If, for example, our research question concerned political attitudes and our convenience sample was all psychology students, it probably wouldn't be wise to generalize the result to students majoring in, say, law, who may have different political attitudes. Or to students in another country with a quite different culture. If we're doubtful about how representative our sample is of a population, any conclusion needs to be correspondingly tentative. As usual, we can't escape careful thought and judgment.

▶ If random sampling is in doubt, we need to judge a sample to be reasonably representative of a population before using inferential statistics to reach a conclusion about that population.

I said that calculation of a CI requires the assumption of random sampling. More formally, I can say that calculation of inferential statistics requires statement of a *statistical model*, which is a set of assumptions. One assumption of our statistical model is random sampling. We'll meet other assumptions of the model in Chapters 4 and 5.

> A **statistical model** is a set of assumptions. Random sampling is one assumption in the statistical model we use for calculation of inferential statistics.

In summary, sampling is a central issue. Advanced books describe more complex ways to sample from a population, but in this book we'll rely on random sampling. Be aware, however, of the practical difficulties of achieving random samples, and the need to make a judgment as to whether it's reasonable to apply a conclusion to a particular population.

Ignoring the random sampling assumption and not considering carefully how representative our sample is of the population is a major way to fool ourselves.

> *DFY: Don't let statistical inference fool you: It relies on a statistical model. Our model includes the assumption of random sampling, which is often not achievable. If it isn't, use judgment before applying a conclusion to a particular population.*

2.1 Figure out a good way to understand and remember all the definitions we are encountering. Make flash cards and use them again and again? Invent an example for each definition? Form a group and test each other? For suggestions, revisit the *Making the Most of This Book* section near the start of this book.

MAKING COMPARISONS

The Chapter 1 poll asked one question about support for the proposition, but more often we want to make comparisons. How much has support for our candidate increased since the last poll? How much less depressed are those treated with an antidepressant compared with those not treated? How much better is critical thinking in 16-year-olds than in 10-year-olds? These are all research questions that require comparisons between different sets of measurements.

Let's define some more terms. I'll refer again to the pen–laptop study as an example. To make a comparison, a study needs at least two *variables*. First is the *independent variable* (IV), the pen-or-laptop variable, which defines the two conditions we wish to compare. The IV can take two values or *levels*, Pen and Laptop. Levels are also referred to as *conditions* or *treatments*.

> The **independent variable** (IV) is the variable whose values are chosen or manipulated by the researcher.

> **Levels** are the different values taken by the independent variable, for example, Pen and Laptop. Levels are also called **conditions**, or **treatments**.

Sometimes one of the conditions is chosen to provide a baseline, or starting point, for a comparison, in which case we can refer to it as the *control condition*. For example, if our research question asks about the effect of a low-fat diet, then the conditions might be usual diet and low-fat diet. The usual diet is the baseline, or control condition. As you'd guess, a *control group* is simply a group that experiences the control condition.

> A *control condition* is the condition that provides a baseline or starting point for a comparison. A *control group* is a group that experiences the control condition.

The first important variable is the IV. The second is the measure that provides the data sought, such as some measure of the quality of the notes taken by the student. This is the *dependent variable* (DV), so called because it depends on the participants' behavior.

> The *dependent variable* (DV) is the variable that's measured in the study and provides the data to be analyzed.

Experimental and Non-Experimental Research

To make a comparison, how should we set up our study? There are several options. For pen–laptop, one option would be to simply find students who choose to write notes with a pen, and others who choose to use a laptop, then compare learning or memory scores for those two groups. We would be taking a *non-experimental* approach. Another option would be to *manipulate* the note-taking method to create two independent—meaning separate—groups or conditions. We could create a pen group and a laptop group by *randomly assigning* some students to use pen, and others to use laptop. Alternatively, we could ask the same students to use pen for one study session and laptop for another, *randomly assigning* each student to which order they will use. Either way, making a manipulation means we are taking an *experimental* approach. Experimental approaches have strengths and also weaknesses; the same is true for non-experimental approaches. Can you think of a few for each?

 Pause, discuss, reflect... Consider how easy each type of study might be to set up. Consider how convincing the result might be. Which would you prefer? Write down your thoughts.

The non-experimental approach is often easy and convenient, but the trouble is that the groups almost certainly differ in ways other than note-taking method. Perhaps some pen students can't afford a laptop. Perhaps some laptop students are more committed to their studies. We therefore can't conclude that any difference we observe was caused by the choice of pen or laptop; it could have been caused by any of the possible differences between the two groups, or perhaps several of those differences. We call those additional differences *confounds*. A confound is an unwanted difference between groups that limits the conclusions we can draw from a study. We say that interpretation of the study is *confounded* by the possible extra differences between the Pen and Laptop groups.

> A *confound* is an unwanted difference between groups, which is likely to limit the conclusions we can draw from a study.

The key feature of the experimental approach is that it uses random assignment to form the groups or conditions to be compared. Random assignment tends to even out all the other differences, meaning that it helps avoid confounds. It gives us groups or conditions that, most likely, differ in only one way—for example whether the student used pen or laptop, which is the experimental manipulation, the IV, that we're interested in. With groups that differ in only one way—the note-taking method—we can conclude that any difference we observe was, most likely, *caused* by use of pen or laptop. That's gold, because the aim of research is to investigate cause and effect—we'd love to discover what *causes* cancer, or depression, or better learning.

◀ If two groups or conditions differ on only one factor, then that factor is the likely *cause* of any observed difference between the two.

Experimental research uses random assignment of participants to groups or conditions—to the different levels of the IV that is being manipulated. It can justify a causal conclusion.

Non-experimental research uses pre-existing groups, not formed by random assignment or manipulation of the IV. It cannot justify a causal conclusion, because there could easily be confounds.

Random assignment is great, but often it isn't possible, for example if the IV is gender, or whether or not a couple is married, or whether or not a child has been exposed to a neurotoxin. But we can assign students randomly to the Pen or Laptop groups. Random assignment needs to be done strictly, using coin tosses, or a random number table, or computer assignment. It's not good enough, for example, to assign all the students who come on Monday to Pen and those on Thursday to Laptop. Such groups might differ in any number of other ways—perhaps the Monday folk are still recovering from the weekend, or Thursday is sports day and Thursday volunteers are the non-sporty types?

◀ *Random assignment* of participants to groups or conditions gives the best grounds for a conclusion of causality.

If our IV is gender, and so random assignment isn't possible, we can't conclude that gender is the cause of any observed difference. To investigate causality in non-experimental studies we need advanced techniques, many of them based on regression, the topic of Chapter 12.

Both experimental and non-experimental studies can be valuable, and often their data are analyzed in the same way—which is great news. We need to take care, however, when stating conclusions. An experimental study can justify concluding that using pen rather than laptop most likely caused increased learning. By contrast, for a non-experimental study we can say only that gender "is associated with" the observed difference, or that females "tend" to respond more quickly than males, without making any presumption about cause.

◀ Data analysis is often the same for an experimental and non-experimental study, but conclusions usually must be quite different: Only an experimental study can justify a causal conclusion.

 DFY: Don't let lack of random assignment fool you. Only experimental research, based on careful random assignment, can justify a causal conclusion. Be cautious about any causal conclusion you read—is it based on experimental research?

I've presented a blizzard of terms and definitions, but they cover issues at the core of research. It's worth reviewing the chapter to this point. One key idea is random sampling to obtain a sample of participants for our study, even if in practice we often have to make do with a convenience sample. A second key idea is the distinction between experimental and non-experimental research. Only experimental research may be able to justify a causal conclusion—which can make us very happy. The next major topic is measurement, and the nature of the variables we use.

2.2 Once again, work on good ways to learn all those definitions and fundamental concepts. Can social media help?

2.3 Suppose a study measures the word knowledge and number knowledge of four groups of children, who are, respectively, 3, 4, 5, and 6 years old.
   a. Is this an experimental or a non-experimental study?
   b. What is the IV and how many levels does it have?
   c. What is or are the DV(s)?

2.4 Suppose the study in 2.3 uses a random sample of children in a large urban school district.
   a. How might that sample have been chosen? Is random assignment to groups possible? Explain.
   b. Suggest two populations to which you think it would be reasonable to apply a conclusion from the study. Explain.
   c. Suggest two populations to which you think it would not be reasonable to apply such a conclusion. Explain.
   d. Suppose the study found differences between the group means on the DVs. Would it be reasonable to conclude that differences in age caused those differences? Explain.
   e. Do you have an experimental study? Explain.

2.5 Suppose you wish to evaluate the effectiveness of visual imagery of restful scenes in nature as a therapy for mild depression. Forty people with mild depression have agreed to participate.
   a. You decide to use independent groups. How would you form the groups? Why?
   b. What is your IV, and what is your DV?
   c. What type of conclusion could you draw? What assumption are you making? Is it reasonable? Explain.

? Quiz 2.1

1. Statistical inference uses the _____ mean, which has symbol _____, to tell us about the _____ mean, which has symbol _____.
2. If you have a random sample from a population, you know that
   a. the sample is a convenience sample.
   b. the researcher chose the people to include in the sample very carefully after seeing their data.
   c. people in the sample were chosen independently.
   d. the sample is an inconvenience sample.
3. The variable that a researcher manipulates is the _____ variable, abbreviation ___, and the variable the researcher measures is the _____ variable, abbreviation ___.
4. A study has independent groups that see a movie, or read a book, or listen to some songs. Participants then report their state of relaxation. What is the DV? What is the IV? What are the levels of the IV?

5. If you have random assignment of _____ to form two _____ groups, you can / cannot conclude that any difference you observe is most likely caused by the IV manipulation.
6. Using random sampling to obtain participants, and random assignment to form two groups, means that we have an experimental / a non-experimental study, and that the two groups are likely to differ in only one / more than one way.
7. Make some more quiz questions, swap with a friend, and compare answers.

MEASUREMENT

To measure the length of a table you reach for a tape measure and report the length as 110.4 cm. You hardly give it a thought, although, if I asked, you would say that doing it again would give very close to the same result, and that even using a different tape measure should give close to the same result. In psychology and other disciplines that study people, however, *measurement* is not so easy. To measure a person's anxiety, or the amount they learned from a lecture, we need to find relevant questions to ask and a way to score the answers that gives us an acceptable measure of anxiety or amount learned. In many cases there are well-established tests or instruments we could choose. For anxiety, one such as the State-Trait Anxiety Inventory (STAI; Spielberger et al., 1983), which is a set of 40 items such as "I am tense; I am worried", which the respondent rates on a four-point scale from "almost never" to "almost always". Higher scores indicate greater anxiety.

◄ *Measurement* is an important issue across science. Choose measures carefully.

We call anxiety the *construct* of interest. It's the underlying psychological characteristic we wish to study. The STAI score is the measure we use to *operationalize* anxiety, meaning that we take that score as our measure of anxiety. We say anxiety is *operationalized* as the STAI score. This acknowledges that the STAI score and the underlying construct of anxiety are different, and that we're using one as our measure of the other. We could say that length is our construct of interest and that we operationalize the length of the table as the reading on the tape measure.

> A **construct** is the underlying characteristic we wish to study. Anxiety, well-being, and confidence are examples of constructs.

> A measure **operationalizes** a construct if it provides a practical way of measuring that construct. For example, the STAI score operationalizes anxiety.

Can you think of a couple more constructs and measures that operationalize them?

I won't always insert the icon, but by now you know to pause and reflect, discuss and write. It's always better to put things in your own words.

What makes a good measure? Two basic features of a good measure are reliability and validity.

◄ Two basic features of a good measure are *reliability* and *validity*.

Reliability

Reliability refers to repeatability or consistency: If you measure again, are you likely to get the same or a very similar value? With the tape measure the answer

▶
Test-retest reliability is the extent that a measure gives the same result when repeated in the same situation.

is "Yes", but what about the measure of anxiety, or learning? Reliability can be measured in various ways, but the simplest is *test-retest reliability*, which is the extent to which two scores on the test are the same or similar, when they come from the same person and are taken under conditions as close as possible to the same. For example, you might assess a questionnaire measure of anxiety by giving it to a sample of 100 people, then giving it to them again a day later and assessing the closeness of the two sets of scores. In Chapter 11 on correlation we'll see one way to measure such closeness. Conditions can never be exactly the same for the second testing—levels of anxiety might vary from day to day—but when assessing reliability the researcher will make them as similar as possible.

> The **reliability** of a measure is its repeatability, the extent to which we get the same or a similar value if we measure again.

Validity

Validity refers to the extent a measure actually measures what we want it to measure. We can be confident that our tape measure does measure length, and not density or temperature. But does our questionnaire tap anxiety, rather than, say, arousal or introversion? One way to assess validity is to compare or correlate scores on the anxiety questionnaire with scores on a different, already well-established, measure of anxiety. (Again, there's more on how to do this in Chapter 11 on correlation.) Close correspondence between the two scores suggests our measure of anxiety has reasonable validity. Another approach is to investigate how well scores predict a relevant outcome. An example is a test of job aptitude, which is designed to predict later job performance. We could test a number of new employees on the aptitude test, then compare their scores with their later job performance. Again, close correspondence indicates good validity of the test for its purpose.

> The **validity** of a measure is the extent to which it measures what it is designed to measure.

In this book we'll usually assume our measures are reliable and valid. Yet again, judgment is required. If we suspect a measure does not have high reliability and validity we need to be very cautious in drawing any conclusions based on it, to avoid the syndrome of GIGO—garbage in, garbage out.

Time for another *Don't fool yourself* statement.

 DFY: Don't let a measurement fool you. The measure is not the same as the underlying construct. Consider how well the measure operationalizes the construct. Consider its reliability and validity.

2.6   a. Is the number of words in a term paper a reliable measure?
     b. Is it a valid measure of the academic quality of the paper?
     c. Suggest a better measure of the academic quality of a paper.
     d. Suggest how you could assess the reliability of that measure.
     e. Suggest how you could assess its validity.

Next is more on measurement: I'll consider four different types, or levels, of measurement.

FOUR TYPES OF MEASURE: NOIR

Length is a detailed and informative measure. Classifying someone as left- or right-handed is also a measure, but is, by contrast, a much less detailed measure—a dichotomy. It's useful to distinguish four different types, or *levels*, of measurement, which differ in their degree of detail. They can be summarized by the handy acronym: NOIR. This stands for *nominal, ordinal, interval,* and *ratio* levels of measurement, which are the four levels ordered from least to most detailed and informative. Let's take a look at each of these.

> The four levels of measurement are: **nominal**, **ordinal**, **interval**, and **ratio**, summarized as NOIR.

Nominal Measurement

Suppose you classify people as left- or right-handed. Those labels illustrate the simplest and most basic level of measurement—*nominal*, also referred to as *categorical* measurement. Similarly, if you label ice cream as strawberry, chocolate, vanilla, or coffee, the labels are a nominal, or categorical, measure. We can also refer to a measure having nominal or categorical *scaling*. The labels identify different categories, but are not quantitative and there's no notion of ordering—we're not saying that coffee flavor is larger or better than strawberry, just different. We might for convenience code strawberry as 1, chocolate as 2, vanilla as 3, and coffee as 4, but the numbers are arbitrary and their values mean nothing beyond labeling: We could have coded the flavors as 80, 70, 999, and −8. Using words emphasizes the categorical nature of nominal measurement. If we use numbers, we must be cautious because numbers suggest calculations, but in this case these would be meaningless or even misleading. The average of 1, 2, 3, and 4 is 2.5, but it makes no sense to say that the average ice cream flavor is 2.5. Whenever we calculate anything we need to think of what the numbers represent and whether it makes sense to do the calculation. Which leads us to an important warning.

 DFY: Don't let calculations and results fool you. Think about what the numbers represent: Does it make sense to manipulate them? Don't average the flavors!

We can't calculate a mean with nominal data, but are there other operations we can apply? Yes, we can count, and record the number, or *frequency*, of cases in a category. We might for example count how many of each flavor were sold last week—these are the frequencies for each flavor.

> With nominal data, all we can do is record the **frequency** of cases in each category.

A measure has **nominal** or **categorical** scaling if it comprises category labels, with no sense of order or quantity. For example, ice cream flavors.

Ordinal Measurement

An *ordinal* measure, meaning a measure with ordinal scaling, has order or rank, but no sense of distance between ranks. For example, after a race we may give medals to the runners who placed 1st, 2nd, and 3rd. These numbers represent the order of finishing, but say nothing about the margins between them. The first-place winner could have blown away the competition or could have won by a fraction of a second. Ordinal measures have some numerical meaning (1st is faster than 2nd in the race example) but this is limited solely to comparisons of greater and less than. At graduation, students may have a class rank; you might have consulted a list of rankings when choosing a college; and you may find yourself obsessively checking your favorite sports team's rank as the playoffs draw near. These are all ordinal measures. Can you think of some other examples?

▶ With ordinal data, we can arrange values in order, but can't calculate a mean.

With ordinal data, we can arrange values in order, but in general we can't calculate a mean. If I came 1st in yesterday's race and 3rd in today's, it doesn't make sense to say that, on average I came 2nd, because the differences between the different finishing positions could be small or large or anything at all, whereas calculating a mean assumes that all the differences between adjacent values in the ordering (between 1st and 2nd, and between 2nd and 3rd, etc.) are equivalent.

> A measure has **ordinal** scaling if it gives information about order, meaning that increasing numbers represent increasing (or decreasing) amounts of whatever is being measured. For example, a ranking of sports teams is an ordinal measure.

Interval Measurement

Each step forward through NOIR gives a measure that's more detailed and informative. Taking the next step, an *interval* measure has order, and also distance, which means we can add and subtract data values. Each unit interval on the scale is equivalent—it has the same size. For example, you could measure age by asking people to tell you their birth year, and you could put those numbers in order, from oldest respondent to youngest. In addition, you could subtract to find the distances between birth years: Someone born in 1946 (like me) is 50 years older than someone born in 1996 (perhaps like you). Calculation of differences works because each year is the same amount of time (let's not quibble about leap years), unlike with ordinal data where the difference between 1st and 2nd may not be the same as the difference between 2nd and 3rd.

However, for birth year, even though differences have meaning, ratios do not. The ratio between my birth year (1946) and 1996 would be 1946/1996 = 0.975. Does this mean I have 97.5% as much age as the person born in 1996? Clearly that doesn't make sense; why not? Because birth year is a measure on a relative scale, with all measurements made relative to a 0 point that was chosen purely because of its importance within Christianity. However, 0 is not an absolute zero point for the concept of time—different cultures anchor their calendars to different 0 points. Thus, your birth year doesn't represent your age in any absolute sense, but just the amount of time that passed between the "first" Christmas and your birth.

Another example with an arbitrary zero is longitude, which by international agreement is measured relative to Greenwich, England. We need to agree on an arbitrary reference point because there's no natural or absolute zero of longitude. Similarly, many psychological and educational variables lack a natural or absolute zero. It makes little practical sense to think of a person having zero intelligence, or zero extraversion. Can you think of other psychological variables that cannot be measured in absolute terms?

▶ With interval data, we can calculate means, but not ratios or percentages.

For interval data we have distance, meaning all unit intervals are of the same size. We can therefore calculate an average. However, without a true zero, it's not meaningful to calculate the ratio of two scores, or to express one as a percentage of another.

A measure has *interval* scaling if we are willing to assume that all unit intervals anywhere on the scale are equivalent. For example, birth year and longitude are interval measures.

Ratio Measurement

A *ratio* measure has a meaningful zero, as well as distance, so the measure represents absolute quantities of what's being measured. On a ratio scale, 0 represents a complete absence of whatever is being measured. For example, a person's height is a ratio measure, because zero height has physical meaning. It serves as a natural zero for measuring height, even though no person can have zero height. We not only have distance—a centimeter difference in height is the same amount of height anywhere on the scale—but we can also calculate meaningful ratios. A 204 cm basketballer is twice as tall as her daughter who is 102 cm tall.

Ratio measures are the most informative ones, and are common in the physical sciences: Distance, mass, and force are all ratio measures, because they all have a natural zero. The time taken to complete a task is also a ratio measure. But, as I mentioned above, in psychology and other human disciplines many variables lack a natural zero and so don't have ratio scaling.

Because it has distance and a true zero, a ratio measure permits us to calculate means, ratios, and percentages.

◀ With a ratio measure we can calculate means, ratios, and percentages.

A measure has *ratio* scaling if it has a meaningful zero, as well as distance. For example, length, mass, and the time taken to complete a task are all ratio measures.

Considering the Four Levels of Measurement

Table 2.1 summarizes the four levels. Suppose your measure is the number of items correct out of 100. What's the level of measurement?

Hmmm...

Level	Feature	Allowable operations	Examples
Nominal	Same/different	Count frequencies	Gender, ice cream flavors
Ordinal	Order	As nominal, plus: arrange in order	Ranking of colleges
Interval	Distance	As ordinal, plus: add and subtract, calculate mean	Birth year, longitude
Ratio	True zero	As interval, plus: calculate ratio and percentage	Height, mass, time to complete a task

Table 2.1 The Four Levels of Measurement, NOIR

If you suggested ratio, well done. It's probably reasonable to consider that an additional one item correct is pretty much equivalent whether it's an increase from 60 to 61, or 73 to 74; in addition, zero items correct is an absolute zero and so it makes sense to say that a score of 80 is twice a score of 40. Note that you could translate to letter grades, say A to E, which would be an ordinal measure—A is more than B, but it's probably not reasonable to assume that the distance from A to B is equivalent to the distance from B to C. That translation, however, from a ratio measure to an ordinal measure, is from a higher level (later in the NOIR sequence) to a lower level of measurement. It throws away information, which we should avoid where we can.

 DFY: Don't let translating a measure to a lower level fool you. Such a translation loses information, and should be avoided if possible. Prefer higher levels, where that's possible. In other words, prefer ratio to interval to ordinal to nominal.

A nominal measure, like gender, is often easy to identify. A nominal measure often serves as the IV in a study, as in our example in which pen–laptop is a nominal or categorical variable. At the other end of the NOIR scale, a ratio measure is also usually easy to identify—for example a participant's response time to a stimulus, or the number of items correct out of 100—and often serves as a study's DV. However, in the middle of the NOIR scale, considering ordinal and interval scaling, things often become tricky. Should we regard a variable as having ordinal or interval scaling? This question deserves its own section.

Ordinal or Interval Scaling?

The central question is: Do we have distance? Is one unit on the scale the same at all points on the scale? This is often a question for judgment in context, without a clear yes or no answer. Consider a type of self-report question often used in surveys. You've no doubt answered many such questions yourself.

Please mark X in one square to record your level of agreement with the statement. "Global warming presents a terrible threat to humanity."

Very strongly disagree	Strongly disagree	Disagree	Neutral	Agree	Strongly agree	Very strongly agree
☐	☐	☐	☐	☐	☐	☐
1	2	3	4	5	6	7

Items like that are called Likert ("LICK-ert" or "LIKE-ert") items. Likert items can give useful information, and people can often answer them quickly and reasonably easily, so they are widely used. Researchers usually score the answers by using the numbers I've placed under the response options; these numbers are usually not included in the version seen by respondents.

What type of measure are those numbers? Interval scaling would require even spacing between response items: The "distance" from "Strongly disagree" to "Disagree" would need to be equivalent, in some sense, to the distance from "Neutral" to "Agree", and to every other single step on the scale. That's not a statistical question, but a question about strength of agreement and how we can measure it. Do you think those two steps are equivalent, so have the same size? (Pause… discuss…)

Actually, the question is not what *we* think, but whether the respondents are using the scale in a way that reflects equal steps between each of the answer options. Assuming our respondents used the scale that way seems to me a strong and perhaps unrealistic assumption. Thus, some psychologists argue that responses on self-report scales should be regarded as ordinal. Many, though, are willing to make that assumption about how respondents use the scale, and therefore treat measurements from these scales as interval.

You may be wondering: Who cares? The answer matters because the interval assumption permits calculation of means, CIs, and other useful statistics. If we assume only ordinal scaling, we can use other statistics, as we'll discuss in Chapter 3, but these are generally less informative.

Researchers very often do calculate means for response data from Likert items. However, before doing so they should think carefully about the strong equal-steps assumption they are making—difficult though that is—and bear in mind that assumption when they report and interpret the mean.

Earlier I stated a DFY about always considering what numbers represent. Here's a more specific version:

Using the mean (or CI) requires interval *scaling, even though the equal-intervals assumption may seem unrealistic.*

 DFY: Don't let precise numbers fool you into believing they must mean something. When using a mean or other statistic that requires interval scaling, consider whether the equal-interval assumption is justified.

I'll end by saying that whether or not the interval assumption is appropriate is often a matter for careful judgment in context. Every stage of research is like that, which makes it all the more interesting.

2.7 Consider the numbers worn by basketball players.

    a. What's the level of measurement? Why?

    b. Suggest a way to assign those numbers so they have ordinal scaling.

2.8 A grade point average is calculated by translating A = 4, B = 3, etc. What assumption is necessary to justify that calculation? To what extent is it reasonable? Explain.

2.9 Consider the Likert item "Self-testing is a practical and effective method for students to improve their learning". Responses are scored from 1 = Very strongly disagree, to 7 = Very strongly agree. The mean response for a group of 50 students is 5.3.

    a. What level of scaling is required to justify calculation of that mean?

    b. What assumption does that require? Do you think it's reasonable? Explain.

? Quiz 2.2

1. If a measure operationalizes a construct, then we can be sure that
   a. the measure is reliable and valid.
   b. the measure helps us carry out research that involves the construct.
   c. we have an experimental study.
   d. All of the above.
2. Suppose a measure of happiness gives the result 3.5 for a person in a particular situation, then on another day again gives 3.5 for that same person in the same situation. That suggests the measure may be _____.
3. If a measure actually measures the construct we wish it to measure, we say it is a(n) _____ measure.
4. A variable with _____ scaling is also referred to as having categorical scaling. We <u>can / cannot</u> place different values of such a variable in order.
5. If a variable has ratio level of measurement, then
   a. we can order different values of the variable.
   b. we can calculate a mean, CI, and percentage.
   c. it has a true zero.
   d. All of the above.

6. If you are prepared to make the equal-interval assumption for a variable, you can assume it has _____ scaling and therefore you <u>can / cannot</u> calculate a mean. If not, it probably has _____ scaling and you <u>can / cannot</u> calculate a mean.
7. Question 7 is always the same: Make some more quiz questions and swap with a friend.

THREE PROBLEMATIC FORMS OF SELECTION

In Chapter 1, the two main Open Science points were "Do we have the full story?" and "Seek replication". I'm now going to expand a little, by considering three different ways that *selection* can be problematic for research. First, let's consider replication and selection of the studies that are available to us.

Replication and Selection of Studies

The first question to ask whenever you see a result is: Has it been replicated?

I mentioned in Chapter 1 that rarely, if ever, can a single study provide a definitive answer to a research question. The scientist, ever skeptical, needs to see one or more replications and then consider them all before reaching any conclusion. Note that not all replications are the same: There's a spectrum from a *close replication*, designed to be as similar as possible to an original study, through to a more *distant* replication that's designed to be a little different so it can extend the research in some interesting way—maybe it compares note-taking in two quite different disciplines, such as history and engineering.

> A *close* replication uses a new sample, but otherwise is as similar as possible to the original study. It's also called an *exact* or *literal* replication.

> A more *distant* replication is deliberately somewhat different from the original study. It's also called a *modified* or *conceptual* replication.

In practice, no replication is perfectly close. Even if conducted by the same researchers using the same procedure, some details are inevitably different—perhaps the weather, or what the participants had eaten for breakfast. However, if all studies give reasonably similar results, meta-analysis of the original study and the replications should give more precise estimates. It should also provide reassurance that the original result was not a fluke, a mere fluctuation caused by sampling variability.

> **!** **DFY: Don't let lack of replication fool you. Usually we need replications before we have confidence in a research finding.**

Selection of *studies* is the first problematic type of selection. If only a limited selection of relevant studies is available, we don't have the full story and meta-analysis may mislead.

In Chapter 1, I also mentioned that if the poll we discussed had been selected from a number of similar polls, we might be getting a biased impression. To have the full story we need to know about *all* studies on our research question. This means that replication by itself is not sufficient—in addition we need to know full details of *all* relevant replications that have been conducted. Unfortunately, journals are more likely to publish studies that "work"—that find large or striking results. This is an under-appreciated but damaging type of selection known as *publication bias*, and it often means that we don't have the full story because studies that "didn't work", that happened to find smaller or less striking results, are not published and thus not available. Therefore, meta-analysis of available studies is likely to give a biased result. One of the goals of Open Science is to ensure that *all* relevant studies are available. That's what we need in order to have the full story.

> **Publication bias** is the selection of which studies to make available according to the results they obtain. Typically, studies finding large or striking results are more likely to be published.

Selection of which studies are available—publication bias—is the first of three types of selection that are problematic. Replications must not only be carried out, but reported. Otherwise we don't have the full story, and meta-analysis of available studies could easily mislead.

 DFY: Don't let selection of studies fool you. All relevant studies must be available for us to have the full story. If publication bias means that some relevant studies are unavailable, even meta-analysis may give a biased result.

Full Reporting of a Study

The second problematic type of selection is straightforward: The report of a study must be fully detailed. Just as we can't evaluate a single study without the full context, we also can't evaluate a single variable or condition of a study if we lack the full context. For example, suppose a researcher examined how therapy influences depression. Because depression can be tricky to measure, the researcher used five different ways of measuring it—two self-report scales, one clinical diagnosis, one behavioral test, and one report from a close friend. Even if the therapy has absolutely no effect, sampling variability makes it unlikely that all five measures will obtain the exact same result. The danger is that the researcher may select by highlighting the measure that shows the best result and may dismiss or even fail to report the other four. As always, we need *all* relevant evidence to reach a justifiable conclusion—we need the full story.

Selection of what to report about a study is the second problematic type of selection. Fully detailed reporting is needed for us to have the full story, and also for close replication to be feasible.

Furthermore, suppose you want to conduct a close replication. You need to have full details about the original study, including participants, stimuli, and the procedure. That's another excellent reason why fully detailed reporting is so important.

 DFY: Don't let incomplete reporting of a study fool you. Fully detailed reporting is needed, to avoid being misled.

Planned and Exploratory Data Analysis

The third type of problematic selection is a bit more tricky to grasp. The basic idea is that you should state *in advance* which aspects of your data you will focus on. If you scan all possible differences or effects before selecting what to focus on, you may just be telling us about some random fluctuation.

I'll use a fictitious example to explain. Suppose you evaluate what you hope is a wonderful new way to support learning in high school. You have 10 improvement scores obtained in a wide range of areas, from sports to mathematics and science, to history, to music and art. Figure 2.2 shows what

I'm assuming are your results. You eagerly examine the 10 sets of scores and note considerable variability, but that history, say, shows a dramatic increase with the new approach. You triumphantly report that the new approach leads to greatly improved learning in history, and perhaps other areas. Do you see any problem here?

Discuss, ponder…

The trouble is that results always vary, so one of your 10 improvement score means is bound to lie somewhat higher than the others, even if only because of sampling variability. If you examine all 10 and focus on the highest, perhaps you are simply telling us which one happened to be highest; perhaps you are only telling us about sampling variability. You selected which result to focus on *after* seeing all the results.

If, instead, you had good reason to predict that your new approach is likely to be especially effective for history, and you tell us that *in advance*, then I'll be more impressed by Figure 2.2. You made a prediction in advance and this was confirmed by the data. That makes any researcher happy. (But maybe I'm skeptical and need convincing that you really did make the prediction in advance? We'll consider that problem shortly.)

A ***data analysis plan*** states, in advance of carrying out a study, the researcher's predictions and full details of the intended data analysis.

The vital distinction is between *planned* and *exploratory* data analysis. Each is valuable, but they are very different and must be distinguished clearly. Planned analysis requires that a *data analysis plan* be stated in advance. This is a document that states your predictions, describes what measures you will use, and gives full details of how you will analyze the data to evaluate your predictions. In other words, planned analyses are prespecified in such an analysis plan. Then you run the study, follow the stated plan to analyze the data, and report the results. Such *planned* analysis provides the most convincing conclusions.

Planned analysis is specified in advance and provides the best basis for conclusions.

If you don't state a data analysis plan in advance, you are carrying out *exploratory analysis*—also called *post hoc analysis*—which runs the risk of simply telling us which effect happened to be largest; it may only be telling us about sampling variability. However, after carrying out the planned analysis it can

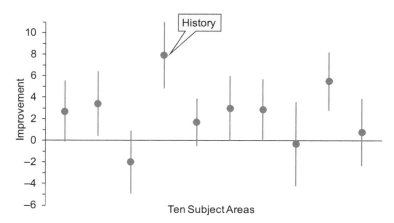

Figure 2.2. Means and 95% CIs for the improvement in scores in 10 different subject areas, from a fictitious evaluation of a new way to support learning in high school.

be highly illuminating to explore your data further—you may even discover some unexpected and important finding. Such a finding can only be a tentative suggestion, for possible further investigation, but just might lead to an important advance.

> *Exploratory* or *post hoc analysis* ("post hoc" is Latin for "after the fact") is not specified in advance. It risks merely telling us about sampling variability, but may provide valuable hints for further investigation.

If you don't use planned analysis, we say that you are *cherry picking* the result you prefer, or are *capitalizing on chance* by focusing on the result that happened to be largest. We could also say you are *chasing noise*, meaning you are just responding to random variability—noise—in the data.

Have you ever gazed up at the sky and daydreamed about shapes in the clouds? Clouds are more or less random, but it's often easy to see monsters or faces or what you will in the clouds. I call this human tendency *seeing a face in the clouds*. It's another way to think of cherry picking, of seeing patterns in randomness. We'd probably love to find some real effect in our data, but perhaps all we're seeing is a face in the cloud of randomness.

◄ A result predicted in advance is much more convincing than a result selected afterwards, which may be cherry picked.

> *Cherry picking*, or *capitalizing on chance*, or *seeing a face in the clouds*, is the choice to focus on one among a number of results because it is the largest, or most interesting, when it may be merely a random fluctuation. It's triumphantly reporting the history result in Figure 2.2, in the absence of a prior prediction.

Any report of research must provide full details of all data analyses, and make very clear which of the analyses were planned and which only exploratory. Only the planned analyses can justify firm conclusions.

 DFY: Don't be fooled by seeing a face in the clouds, by results that may be cherry picked. Distinguish carefully between planned and exploratory analysis.

To summarize, the three problematic selection issues are:

1. What selection of studies are published? We need to know about *all* relevant studies, especially for meta-analysis.
2. What's been selected to report about a study? Reporting must be fully detailed, or we may be misled, and replication may be difficult or impossible.
3. Which results have the researchers selected to focus on? If that selection occurs after seeing the data, we may have cherry picking. We may only be seeing a face in the clouds.

OPEN SCIENCE: DO WE HAVE THE FULL STORY?

All three selection problems, and especially the third—which requires a careful distinction between planned and exploratory analysis—have long been recognized by researchers. However, the replicability crisis I mentioned in Chapter 1 and the rise of Open Science have emphasized the importance of all three. They are all part of the fundamental Open Science question: Do we have the full story?

Open Science is a set of evolving strategies designed to make science more, well, open. Overcoming selection problems is a major aim. I'll briefly mention here two Open Science strategies; there will be more on Open Science in later chapters, especially Chapters 10 and 16.

Polya

Preregistration

How can we be sure that a research report is complete? How can I be sure that you really did nominate history in advance? The best strategy is *preregistration* of a research plan in advance, meaning that the plan was lodged at some secure website with a date stamp. The plan should describe in full detail all aspects of the planned study, and include a full data analysis plan.

> *Preregistration*, also called *registration in advance*, is the lodging in advance, at a secure website and with a date stamp, of a fully detailed research plan, including a data analysis plan.

The researcher conducts the study and analyzes the data in accordance with the plan, then, in the research report, provides a link to the preregistered plan. We can check what's reported against the plan, and be confident that we are getting the full story and that the reported analysis had indeed been planned in advance.

Preregistration is new for most researchers, but its use is increasing rapidly. We'll meet studies that were preregistered, and you'll be able to read preregistered plans for studies that are currently being conducted, which adds to the excitement of research—you can read about studies that will lead to some of the discoveries shortly to be reported.

 DFY: Don't let lack of preregistration fool you. Without preregistration, aspects of the study or its analysis may be missing from what's reported.

Open Materials and Data

Researchers should post online full details of their study, including the stimuli, measures, and any other materials they used. This allows anyone to consider the full context as they evaluate the results. It's also essential for anyone wishing to replicate the study.

Wherever possible, researchers should also post their full data online. This is important for future meta-analyses, and allows other researchers to check the data analysis, or run other analyses they think could be insightful. One way to do this is through the Open Science Framework (OSF, osf.io), a free website that makes it easy for researchers to share their data and materials. There's more on OSF in later chapters. As you complete the exercises in this book you'll notice that many of them use data that was made available from the OSF—so Open Science is also helping with statistics education!

2.10 You read about a large study that reports evidence that boys behave more aggressively than girls. What should you require before accepting the conclusion of a gender difference in aggressive behavior? Does the study provide evidence that gender causes the difference? Explain.

2.11 Another study mentioned it had measured many aspects of girls' and boys' behavior. It reported data and analyses only for two measures on which there were clear gender differences.
   a. Discuss the approach to reporting data and analysis.
   b. If many studies reported data and analyses only for measures that showed clear gender differences, is the published research literature likely to give an overestimate or underestimate of any difference between girls and boys?
   c. What's the solution to the issues raised in parts (a) and (b)?

2.12 A research team reports a study of a number of therapies for mild depression. Exploratory analysis suggests that visual imagery of restful scenes in nature may be helpful. The researchers decide to use independent groups to investigate further.
   a. Outline a good study the researchers might conduct.
   b. From an Open Science standpoint, what should the researchers do before starting data collection? Explain.

2.13 Preregistration requires the researcher to foresee what data analysis will be most appropriate. Is that always possible? What's a possible disadvantage of preregistration?

WHERE DO RESEARCH QUESTIONS COME FROM?

At the start of this chapter I mentioned the excitement of research. Let's revisit this excitement by asking where research questions come from. Often they come from previous research, plus a good idea about how to take the research further. Perhaps most excitingly, a research project can arise from sharp observation of everyday life experience. The pen–laptop research is a lovely example. Pam Mueller, who was at the time a graduate student, wrote:

> We began this line of research because we wanted to scientifically test some intuitions we'd experienced in real life. I was a teaching assistant for Prof. Oppenheimer's Psychology 101 course, and usually brought my laptop to class. But one day I found I had forgotten it. I used a notebook that day, and felt like I'd gotten so much more out of the lecture. I told him that, and a few days later, he had a complementary experience in a faculty meeting, where he'd been typing lots of notes, but found that he had no idea what the person had actually been saying.

Curious researchers are always thinking about what's going on around them. Also, it's a great habit when reading about a study to think of what the next study might be. What question would be most interesting to ask next? Can you think of an alternative explanation for the result, and a study that could test your idea? Sure, there are lots of ways of fooling ourselves, but also lots of scope for good ideas. Never stop thinking, discussing, and wondering.

When reading a research report, think what the next study might be.

 While you are wondering, start formulating your take-home messages. Bring to mind the terms and concepts we've encountered and the long list of DFYs. Think about measurement and different types of measures, the three types of selection issues, and faces in the clouds. Maybe post your first list of take-home messages on social media and ask for comments.

Quiz 2.3

1. A replication that's as similar as possible to the original study is called a(n) _____ replication. One that's somewhat different is called a(n) _____ or _____ replication.
2. If only selected studies are published, then
   a. meta-analysis is likely to give a biased result.
   b. meta-analysis is needed to fill in what's missing.
   c. fully detailed reporting of the published studies can compensate for what's missing.
   d. research is more efficient, because only important results are published.
3. The fundamental Open Science question is "Do we _____?"
4. Data analysis that is specified in advance is called _____ analysis; otherwise we are conducting _____ analysis. We can have greater confidence in results from _____ analysis.
5. Looking at the data, then reporting the result that is largest and most interesting, can be referred to as
   a. cherry picking.
   b. capitalizing on chance.
   c. seeing a face in the clouds.
   d. All of the above.
6. If you state in advance a detailed research plan for a study, you are _____ the study. The plan should / need not include a data analysis plan.
7. ...just a prompt to do what you always do at the end of a quiz.

2.14 Some professors provide detailed notes in advance and encourage students not to take their own notes during lectures, but instead to listen, question, and discuss. Suggest a study to investigate effects of this strategy.

2.15 Suggest a further study to follow up the original pen–laptop study.

2.16 Revise your list of take-home messages if you wish.

Have you discovered the quizzes, videos, and other stuff at the book website? Have a squiz at: www.routledge.com/cw/cumming

Reporting Your Work

The fundamental issues covered in this chapter will come up throughout your research report. So here are a few guidelines.

▪ Throughout the manuscript, be sure to match the language you use to the research design. For experimental research use causal language, for non-experimental research use relational language. This is true not only for describing your own work, but also for summarizing the work of others.

   • For experimental research, use phrases to indicate causation. For example, you can write that the independent variable affects the dependent variable, that it determines the dependent variable, that it produces an effect, or that it causes a change in the dependent variable. When writing about causation, keep in mind the tricky spelling of affect/effect: affect is usually a verb ("the variable affected the scores"), whereas effect is usually a noun ("the variable produced a large effect").

   • For non-experimental research we cannot draw causal conclusions, so instead we use phrases indicating a relationship *between* the variables being studied. You might for example write that one variable is *associated* with the other, that the variables are correlated, that as one changes the other tends to change, or that participants with a high score on one variable also tended to have high scores on another. Be sure to avoid any language that suggests a causal relationship.

- Your research report should be a complete account of your research process, without selection. It can actually help to state this at the end of the introduction, so that your reader is clear. For example you might state "This report describes all the studies we have so far conducted on this topic. For each study, all measures and conditions are described, and any participants excluded are noted."
- If you preregistered your research design, state this at the beginning of the Method section. Note and explain any deviations you made from the preregistered plan. Also note if you have posted the materials or data online and provide a link.
- As you describe each measure in the method section, note any information you have about the measure's reliability and validity. For established measures you may be able to cite a reference with this information.
- In the results section, make it very clear which analyses were planned and which were exploratory. If you did not make a clear plan in advance of viewing the data, then state that all analyses are exploratory.

Seek to make your research report publicly available, either in a peer-reviewed journal or in an online repository. For example, the OSF (osf.io) provides a free platform for posting materials, data, and research reports (more information about this is in Chapters 10 and 16).

◄ Let your reader know your report is the full story, and describe in full the Open Science practices you have adopted.

 ## Take-Home Messages

- "The first principle is that you must not fool yourself and you are the easiest person to fool." There are many ways to be fooled. Each *Don't fool yourself* (DFY) statement describes one.

- Fundamental concepts include *mean, sample, sample mean* (M), *sample statistic, population, population mean* (μ), *population parameter, descriptive statistic, inferential statistic*, and *statistical inference*.

- The *independent variable* (IV) is the variable that the researcher chooses or manipulates, and the *dependent variable* (DV) is the *measure* that provides the data.

- For a *random sample*, every *population* member must have the same probability of being chosen, and all sample members must be chosen independently.

- *Experimental research* requires random sampling, and groups or *conditions* that differ in only one way, which is usually best achieved by *random assignment* of participants. A conclusion of causality may be justified. *Non-experimental research* lacks random assignment and may have *confounds*. It cannot justify causal conclusions.

- *Reliability* of a measure refers to its repeatability. *Validity* refers to the extent to which it measures what we want it to measure.

- The four levels of measurement are, from least to most informative: *nominal, ordinal, interval*, and *ratio* (remember NOIR). Deciding the level of measurement requires judgment.

- A *close replication* is very similar to the original. A more *distant replication* can address additional research questions.

- Selective publication of studies can mislead, and bias meta-analysis. Selective reporting of only some aspects of a study can mislead, and make replication difficult.

- *Planned analysis* provides the best support for conclusions. *Exploratory analysis* risks cherry picking—seeing faces in the clouds—but may provide hints for further investigation.

- *Open Science* requires *preregistration* where possible, and open materials and data, where possible. Do we have the full story?

- Enjoy the fascination of research. Always be skeptical and thinking of alternative explanations. Try to think of what the best next study would be.

End-of-Chapter Exercises

1) Suppose you are tasked with finding out about the study habits of students at your school. Which of these approaches would provide a random sample of your intended population? Explain your decisions.

   a. You obtain a list of all student emails. For each email you roll a die with 6 sides. Any time you get a 1, that student's email is added to the list of participants to contact.

   b. You wait at your school's café. Every time a participant walks by you roll a die with 6 sides. Any time you get a 1, you invite that student to be in your study. Otherwise you don't approach the student.

   c. You invite all of your friends to be part of the study, and you ask each of them to randomly give you the email of another of their friends for you to contact.

   d. You obtain a list of all the psychology majors and randomly select half of these students to contact to be part of your study.

   e. You obtain from the registrar a list of all currently enrolled students. You use a table of random numbers to assign a random number from 1 to 10 to each student, and select all those assigned a 2 to be contacted for the study.

2) For each of the following, give the scale of measurement:

   a. Participants are asked about their political orientation and instructed to mark a 1 for conservative, a 2 for liberal, and a 3 for unsure.

   b. Participants are asked to mark their political orientation by rating themselves on a scale from 1 (*very conservative*) to 10 (*very liberal*).

   c. Participants are asked if they support or oppose 10 different political initiatives. The number of opinions deemed consistent with liberal policies is tallied, giving a score from 0 to 10 indicating the degree to which the participant agrees with liberal policies.

   d. Romantic interest in a potential partner is investigated by asking the participant to rate her or his interest on a scale of 1 (*not if we were the last two people on Earth*) to 7 (*you haunt my dreams*).

   e. Romantic interest in a potential partner by marking a photo of the partner as "hot" or "not".

3) How much do babies learn from electronic media? To investigate, 100 families with two-year-old children were surveyed. Parents indicated how many educational DVDs they owned. They also indicated how many different words their child knew from a set of early vocabulary words. It was found that children whose families own more educational DVDs are also rated as knowing more words.

   a. Is this an experimental study or a non-experimental study? How can you tell?

   b. From these results, it *could* be that owning more educational DVDs increases word knowledge. What are some other explanations for the finding?

   c. For number of DVDs owned, what is the measurement scale?

   d. The researchers asked the parents to report their child's word knowledge on two different days. They found that responses on day 1 were about the same as those on day 2. What are the researchers checking here?

   e. Who might be the intended population for this study? Does it seem likely that random sampling was used?

   f. For further thought: Would it be reasonable to assume this finding would apply to families with three-year-old children? To families in other countries? To families that speak other languages?

4) To what extent does thinking of money make you less egalitarian? Caruso, Vohs, Baxter, and Waytz (2013) reported five studies, in each of which participants were randomly assigned

to be subtly exposed to either images of money or control images. In every study, those exposed to money became less egalitarian than those not exposed. (Search for "meaning of egalitarian" if you wish.)

a. Are these experimental or non-experimental studies?

b. Although all five studies reported by Caruso et al. (2013) showed consistent effects, it turns out that four similar studies were conducted by those researchers but not reported, and that in each of those four there was little to no change in egalitarian attitudes (Rohrer, Pashler, and Harris, 2015). What issues does this raise in terms of selection? What is a meta-analysis of just the five *published* studies likely to find? What about a meta-analysis of all nine studies?

c. In one of the studies reported by Caruso et al. (2013), participants were asked eight questions about their support for egalitarian tax policies. When responses were averaged over all eight questions, those exposed to money had scores that were similar to those not exposed to money. However, when the data were examined question by question it was found that three of the questions did show somewhat less egalitarianism for the participants exposed to money. Does the item-by-item finding seem like a planned or an exploratory analysis? How would this finding need to be reported?

 ## Answers to Quizzes

Quiz 2.1

1) sample, M, population, μ; 2) c; 3) independent, IV, dependent, DV; 4) a measure of relaxation, the activity required of participants, seeing the movie/reading the book/listening to the songs; 5) participants, independent, can; 6) an experimental, only one; 7) It's worth the effort!

Quiz 2.2

1) b; 2) reliable; 3) valid; 4) nominal, cannot; 5) d; 6) interval, can, ordinal, cannot; 7) Treat yourself to an ice cream of your favorite flavor when you're fully done.

Quiz 2.3

1) close, more distant, conceptual (or modified); 2) a; 3) have the full story; 4) planned, exploratory, planned; 5) d; 6) preregistering, should; 7) It can be useful to ask about tricky things in earlier chapters.

Answers to In-Chapter Exercises

2.1 Repeated testing over an extended period of time is effective for learning. Best is testing that requires you to express ideas in your own words and explain them to others. Doing all this requires effort and persistence, but does pay off.

2.2 Experiment, to find what works for you and your friends. Mix it up, to keep things interesting. Make sure to revisit early things much later.

2.3 a. Non-experimental. b. The IV is age, with four levels (3, 4, 5, and 6 years). c. There are two DVs: measures of word and number knowledge.

2.4 a. To be a random sample it must be chosen randomly from all students, perhaps by random selection from a complete list of all students currently enrolled in the district. The groups differ by age, so children cannot be randomly assigned to the different groups. b. Conclusions could be applied to that school district, and probably to other urban school districts that are similar, for example having similar demographics, because the sample is likely to be reasonably representative of the population of children in such districts. c. It would not be reasonable to apply the conclusions to children in other districts that differ in important ways, for example by being rural or having quite different demographics, because the sample is not likely to be representative of such populations. d. For any population, no, because we don't have random assignment to groups. Such differences might have many causes. e. We don't have an experimental study because random assignment to groups is not possible, and groups may differ in more than one way.

2.5 a. Assign the participants randomly to the two groups, $N = 20$ in each, so we have an experiment and can most likely draw a causal conclusion for any difference we find. b. The experimental group would be trained to use visual imagery of restful scenes. The other group, the control group, may be trained to use visual imagery of some neutral scenes, perhaps houses or shops. The IV is type of scene: restful nature, or neutral. The DV is some measure of depression. c. To draw the conclusion that the different type of imagery causes any change in depression in the population of all mildly depressed people, we need to assume—in addition to random assignment to groups—that our 40 participants are a random sample from that population. That's probably unrealistic, but we may judge the group sufficiently representative of the population that we're willing to apply the conclusion to the population.

2.6 a. Number of words is a reliable measure of length, because if you count again you should get the same number. b. It's hardly a valid measure of quality. c. A better measure would be a professor's grade for the paper. d. To assess the reliability of a set of grades, ask the professor to grade the papers again, perhaps after a delay so she is less likely to remember particular papers, then examine how closely the two sets of grades match. e. For validity, we might match the professor's original grades against the grades assigned for the same set of papers by a more experienced professor.

2.7 a. Nominal, assuming that order or size of number does not provide meaningful information. b. If numbers were assigned so their order matched, for example, players' salaries, or points scored last year, or age, then the numbers would have ordinal scaling, and perhaps even interval or ratio scaling.

2.8 The distance assumption, meaning that the difference in achievement between A and B is assumed the same as that for each other single letter difference. I think the assumption is arguable. People are likely to have different views as to whether it's justified. Averages are very commonly calculated, however, so the assumption is being made, even if most people don't realize that it's necessary to justify calculating an average.

2.9 a. Interval scaling. b. This requires the distance assumption—that every unit interval on the scale represents the same difference in amount of agreement. Perhaps that assumption is a bit unrealistic, but it's very commonly made and I'm often prepared to make it.

2.10 Was the analysis planned and do we have full information about all analyses conducted? Could the result have been cherry-picked? We would also like to see replication. Groups of girls and boys differ in many ways. Random assignment is not possible, so there may be many causes contributing.

2.11 a. Probably the two were cherry-picked because they were the measures that showed differences; they may be faces in the clouds. b. Any particular effect varies from study to study because of sampling variability. If it's more likely to be reported when it happens to be large, and not when small, then a meta-analysis of the reported values is likely to overestimate the true effect size. Chapter 9 has more on that. c. An Open Science approach provides the best solution, especially by requiring preregistration where possible and fully detailed reporting.

2.12 a. As for Exercise 2.5, compare a group trained to use visual imagery of nature scenes with a group using imagery of neutral scenes. Allocate participants randomly to the two groups, so a causal conclusion may be justified. b. Before starting data collection, preregister the plan for the study, including analysis of the change in depression scores for the two groups, so this primary comparison is planned.

2.13 It's a joy and a frustration that research is unpredictable. Sometimes unforeseen results can open up exciting new research directions. Sometimes an analysis of data that was not foreseen can be highly revealing. The best strategy is to preregister a detailed plan and follow that carefully, but then to explore the data further if that looks interesting. The results of any such exploration might be faces in the clouds, but nonetheless may be valuable hints worth investigating in future studies. Preregistration takes effort and thought, but is important.

2.14 Use independent groups to compare traditional note taking by pen with the pre-prepared notes condition, with amount remembered as DV.

2.15 A follow-up study might compare note taking by pen with notes dictated (say, to a phone) by the student during the lecture—this study could use a video lecture seen by students individually, wearing headphones, so their dictation would not disturb surrounding students.

3

Picturing and Describing Data

Usually, the most exciting moment in research is when, for the first time, you have your data and are ready to use them to start answering your research questions. We'll discuss two approaches: data pictures and descriptive statistics. Both can be wonderfully revealing about your data. As usual, there are choices to make and careful thinking is essential.

This chapter discusses:

- Pictures of data that reveal the location, spread, and shape of a distribution
- Dot plots, frequency histograms, and the beautiful bell-shaped normal distribution
- Descriptive statistics for location: mean, median, and mode
- Descriptive statistics for spread: variance and standard deviation
- Descriptive statistics for individual data points: z scores and percentiles
- Good and bad pictures, and ways that pictures can mislead

This chapter also introduces ESCI ("ESS-key", *Exploratory Software for Confidence Intervals*), which runs under Microsoft Excel. Exploring ESCI pictures will, I hope, help make statistical ideas memorable and intuitive.

PICTURES OF A DATA SET

Most often, our data will be a sample from a population, in which case we'll want to make inferences about the population. We'll discuss statistical inference in Chapters 4 and 5, but the first step is to consider the data set itself, starting with one or more pictures.

My main example data set in this chapter is from the Laptop group in Study 1 of Mueller and Oppenheimer (2014). The researchers found that students on average remembered more after taking notes with pen than with laptop. They investigated further, and found that laptop notes tended to include more verbatim transcription from the lecture. By contrast, when using pens, students tended to express the material in their own words, rather than transcribing. The researchers suspected that such re-expression gives better learning than mere transcription. I'll discuss these comparisons of Pen and Laptop further in Chapter 7, but for now I'll simply use the Laptop transcription scores as an example data set. Figure 3.1 is a *stacked dot plot* of that data set. The colored dots represent the individual data points, which are stacked up where necessary so we can see every dot. The dependent variable is transcription score in percent —the percentage of a student's notes that was a verbatim transcription from the lecture. I'll use X as a general name for that dependent variable. The stacked dot plot is one way we can picture how the data points are distributed along the X axis; in other words it's a picture of the *distribution* of the data.

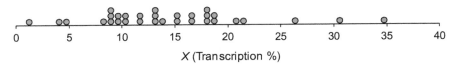

Figure 3.1. A stacked dot plot of the verbatim transcription data, in percent, for the Laptop group, with *N* = 31, from Study 1 of Mueller and Oppenheimer (2014).

The ***distribution*** of a set of data is the way the data points are distributed along the *X* axis.

When seeing such a distribution of data we should consider four major aspects:

1. **The Measure and the Scale.** That's *X*, which here is transcription score. Note the values on the *X* axis, and the full possible range of the scale, which is from 0 (no transcription) to 100 (completely copied).

2. **Location.** Where, overall, do the data lie? Eyeballing of Figure 3.1 suggests that the Laptop data points are centered around, roughly, 15%.

▶ *When seeing a data set, think of the **measure** (X), the **location** of the data, their **spread**, and the overall **shape** of the distribution.*

3. **Spread.** How dispersed or spread are the data points? Over what range? What's their variation or *dispersion*? The Laptop data range from, roughly, 0 to 35%, meaning that some students included very little transcription in their laptop notes, whereas others included up to around one-third of verbatim transcription from the lecture.

4. **Shape.** What's the shape of the whole *distribution* of data points? Is it *symmetric* or *asymmetric*? The distribution of Laptop data is a little heaped around its center and looks approximately symmetric.

With those four aspects in mind, what might the picture imply? What might it mean for note-taking that transcription scores were centered around, roughly, 15%—rather than around, say, 5% or 35%? Thinking of spread, did the students who gave particularly high transcription scores use a deliberate copying strategy, or were they just good typists? Did they generate longer notes than other students? Did the students with low scores learn better from the lecture? A data set can give answers, but also often prompts further interesting questions. That's one of the fascinations of research.

Figure 3.2 shows the stacked dot plots of six fictitious data sets. For each, write a few words about the location, spread, and shape.

 Time to pause, consult, write...

The data sets in A and B differ in location and also in spread. The data sets in A, B, and C are all approximately symmetric. Distributions like those three with a single overall peak are called *unimodal*. In contrast, the distribution in D has two main peaks and is *bimodal*. Asymmetric distributions, such as those in E and F, are said to be *skewed*. The distribution in E is *positively skewed*, or *skewed to the right*; that in F is *negatively skewed*, or *skewed to the left*. Remember that, for skew, "positive" or "to the right" refers to the tail, not the peak. All those descriptions refer to the general shape of the distributions, ignoring small local fluctuations in the heights of columns of dots. Imagine defocusing your eyes to get an overall impression of the distribution shape.

A ***bimodal*** distribution has two main peaks, as in Panel D of Figure 3.2.

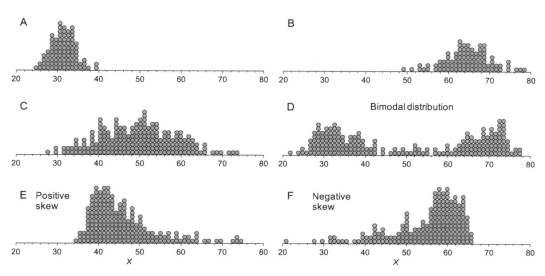

Figure 3.2. Stacked dot plots of six fictitious data sets to illustrate different distribution shapes. The distributions in Panels A, B, and C are all unimodal and approximately symmetric. The spread is relatively small in A, larger in B, and larger again in C.

A *unimodal* distribution has a single peak, as in all other panels of Figure 3.2.

Skew is asymmetry as in Panels E and F of Figure 3.2. Panel E illustrates *right* or *positive skew*; Panel F illustrates *left* or *negative skew*.

You should go beyond a simple description of shape to consider what the shape means, for your X in context. A bimodal distribution might suggest two subgroups of scores—perhaps, for example, the data set combines test scores from younger and older children. Positive skew, as in Panel E, is common when X is the time to complete a task: There's a minimum (around $X = 35$ in Panel E), which is a kind of lower boundary, and most people take only a little more time than that. However, some times are rather longer, perhaps because of a lapse of attention or an interruption. The negative skew in Panel F may also reflect a boundary. The data set might, for example, be scores on a test with 66 items, so a score above 66 is not possible. It's an easy test, so most people scored only a little below 66, but a few did poorly.

Interpret the location, spread, and overall shape of the distribution, for the particular X in context.

Dot Plots and Frequency Histograms

Almost always there's more than one way to picture a data set. Figure 3.3 presents four pictures of the Laptop data. Panel B is the same as Figure 3.1.

Panel A is a dot plot without stacking, so dots often overlap and can coincide if the same value occurs more than once. Panel B is a stacked dot plot, as in Figure 3.1. Points have been moved by tiny amounts left or right so they can be stacked in neat columns, so points are typically a tiny distance from their correct X value. However, this isn't a problem because we should use pictures to gain understanding of the whole data set rather than to read off exact values. A stacked dot plot is useful because it gives information about individual data points as well as the whole set.

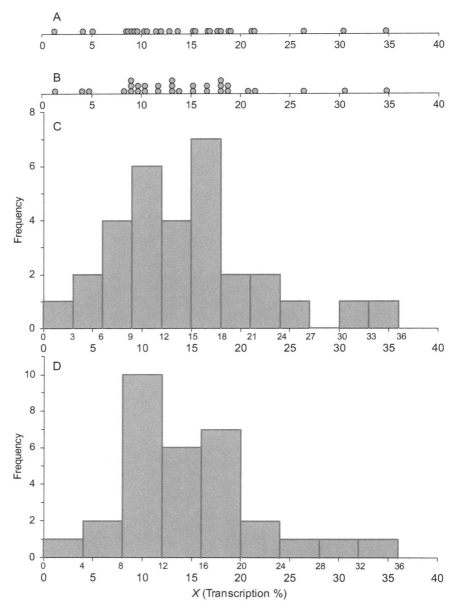

Figure 3.3. Four different pictures of the Laptop data in Figure 3.1. Panel A shows a simple dot plot, and Panel B a stacked dot plot, as in Figure 3.1. Panel C shows a frequency histogram with 12 bins, and D a similar histogram with 9 bins. The small numbers on the horizontal axis mark bin boundaries.

Panel C shows a *frequency histogram* of the same data set, using 12 *bins*, each of width 3. The relevant portion of the *X* axis is divided into 12 equal-width intervals, or bins, then the number, or *frequency*, of data points in each bin is represented by the height of the column. The bin boundaries are marked by the small numbers, so the first bin is from 0 to 3, the next from 3 to 6, and so on. The height of the first column is 1, because only one data point falls in that bin as the stacked dot plot shows. How many data points lie between 6 and 9? Can you find the answer in two places?

Both Panels B and C tell us that 4 data points lie between 6 and 9. Bin boundaries should be convenient numbers (e.g., 6, rather than 9.123). Panel D is a frequency histogram with 9 bins of width 4, with bin boundaries of 0, 4, 8, … The different overall shapes of C and D reflect the different numbers of bins, and how data points happen to fall into the bins.

How many bins should we use? Good question, and the answer is that—as so often—there's no clearly right answer and judgment is needed. Too few bins and details of the shape may be lost; too many and the overall shape may not be so clear. The histograms in Panels C and D are probably both reasonable choices, although Panel C may have too many bins. Another reasonable choice would be 7 bins with the natural boundaries of 0, 5, 10, …

The general message of Figure 3.3 is that there are many ways to picture a data set, and different pictures can give different impressions. Therefore, when examining any figure we should be thinking of how else the data could be represented, to avoid fooling ourselves.

◄ A *frequency histogram* shows the overall shape of a data set, but its appearance depends on the bin boundaries and number of bins.

DFY: Don't let any one particular picture fool you. A different picture may give a different impression. Consider other ways the data set might be pictured.

Thinking back, what did we already have in mind when considering any data set?

 Recall our discussions of Open Science.

You could ask whether we have the full story, because if we don't, and are seeing only selected data, we might be getting a misleading impression. Second, do we sufficiently understand how the data were collected and what they are measuring? Those are Open Science questions; now we have one more: How else might this data set be pictured, and how might that change our understanding?

 Would you prefer to see the stacked dot plot or one of the frequency histograms?

Frequency histograms are used more often, and can do a good job of representing very large data sets in a simple way. Remember, however, that the choice of number of bins can change histogram shape, especially for small data sets. I generally prefer a stacked dot plot because it gives information about every data point as well as overall shape.

◄ A *stacked dot plot* gives information about every point in a data set and also shows the overall shape.

USING THE ESCI SOFTWARE

To enable us to play around with pictures like those in Figure 3.3 I'll introduce the ESCI ("ESS-key") software, which runs under Microsoft Excel. Many of the exercises in this book involve using ESCI to explore statistical concepts—these are marked with an ESCI logo. These exercises are integral, so you shouldn't skip over them. I aim, however, to include enough figures so you can follow along even if you're not in front of a computer. As usual, challenge yourself to think, question, and reflect, and focus as much as you can on the statistical ideas, not the details of the software.

esci 3.1 Load and run **ESCI intro chapters 3–8**, which is a free download from the book website at: www.routledge.com/cw/cumming; the Appendix can assist.

esci 3.2 Click the bottom tab to go to the **Describe** page. Compare with Figure 3.4. *If you don't see the data shown in that figure, scroll right to see the yellow areas, then click the button at red 11 to load the Laptop data.*

esci 3.3 Find red 1 (the bold red 1 near the top left), and read the popout comment (hover the mouse near the little red triangle). If you wish, type to change any of the three labels. Start by clicking near the left end of the white cell and end with the Enter key. Note that the **Units** label appears on the *X* axis and in a few other places.
The bold red numbers (1, 2, ...) give a suggested sequence for looking around the page, but feel free to explore as you wish.
*   If you ever seem to be in an ESCI mess, look for some helpful popout comments. The Appendix may help. Or experiment with the checkboxes, spinner, and other on-screen controls—you won't break anything. Or you can close ESCI (don't Save), and start again.*

esci 3.4 Use the spinner at red 6 to change the number of bins. Click slowly to allow the display to change. Choose 9 bins to match Figure 3.3D.
This needs Excel macros. If you get an error message, you may not have enabled macros. See the Appendix.

esci 3.5 Click and unclick the checkbox at red 8 and watch the dot plot. What's going on? The popouts should help.

esci 3.6 Type a new value in any cell below red 2 to replace the current value (end with Enter) and see the dot plot and frequency histogram update. (To get back to the original data set, retype the original value, or scroll right and click the button at red 11 to reload the Laptop data. Or close ESCI—don't Save—and open it again.)

esci 3.7 Scroll down the list of data points below red 2 and type some additional values below the original 31. Do the figures update as you expect?
*ESCI is not intended to be a full data analysis application, and has no facilities for loading or saving data sets. To save a data set, you need to save the **ESCI intro chapters 3–8** file with a new name—add something to the filename to indicate it contains your data set.*

esci 3.8 If a data point lies exactly on a bin boundary, does ESCI place it in the bin to the left or the right? Perform an experiment to find out.
You could type in a new data point, with value equal to a bin boundary, then see which column in the frequency histogram changes.
*   In general, simply explore and see what happens. To get back to Figure 3.4, Exit (don't Save) and reopen ESCI.*

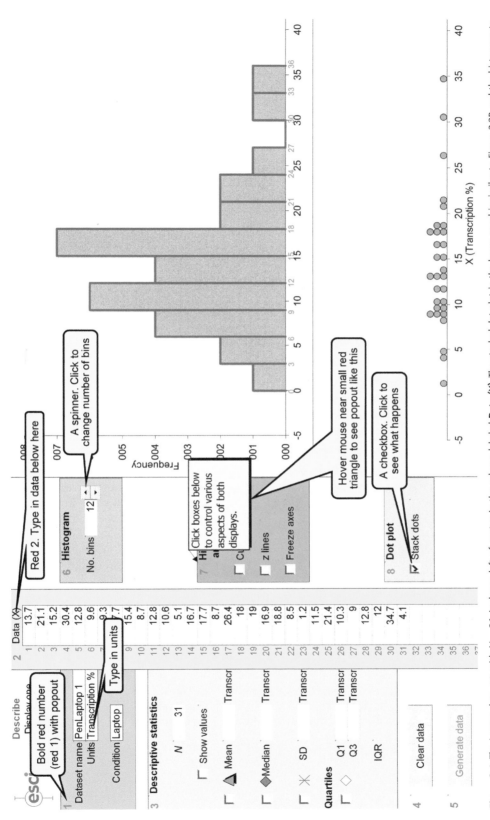

Figure 3.4. The Laptop data set, with $N = 31$, is shown left of center, in the column labeled **Data (X)**. The stacked dot plot in the lower panel is similar to Figure 3.3B and the histogram to Figure 3.3C. The callouts with rounded corners point to some features of the display. Adapted from the **Describe** page of **ESCI intro chapters 3–8**.

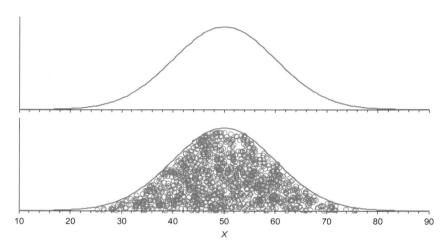

Figure 3.5. Two pictures of a normal distribution. In the lower panel, open dots represent some of the data points in the distribution.

esci 3.9 To clear all data, click the **Clear data** button at red 4, then **OK**. You can type in any new data you wish.

3.10 Suggest a redesign of a histogram so it shows graphically how many dots are in each bin.

THE NORMAL DISTRIBUTION

▶

The **normal distribution** is a bell-shaped distribution that's important in statistics and sometimes occurs, approximately, in the world.

The attractive smooth bell-shaped curve in Figure 3.5 is probably the most widely known shape for a statistical distribution. It's the *normal distribution*. We'll discuss it further in Chapter 4, but I want to introduce it briefly here. Think of it as an extremely large, or even infinite, set of potential data points. The lower panel shows the idea: The data points are piled most deeply around the center, and become progressively less deep as we move away from the center. The two thin tails extend to infinity in both directions, getting ever thinner, but most of the action usually happens in the central area shown in the figure. The curve is symmetric around its midpoint, which is $X = 50$ in the figure. Other normal distributions have different midpoints and scales, but all have the characteristic bell shape.

The normal distribution is important in the theory and practice of statistics and also sometimes occurs, at least approximately, in the world—as we'll discuss in Chapter 4. Many statistical models assume the population of interest is normally distributed and that the sample data are a random sample from that normal distribution. I usually make those assumptions in this book, although in Chapter 16 we consider techniques that don't require them all.

Quiz 3.1

1. We've looked at three different ways to picture the distribution of a set of scores: A(n) _____ _____ shows a dot for each data point but similar data points can overlap; a(n) _____ _____ shows a dot for each data point, but with dots stacked up so as not to overlap; and a(n) _____ shows a bar indicating the frequency of scores within a certain bin or range.
2. When looking at a data picture, four important features to note are the _____, _____, _____, and _____.
3. A distribution spread out over a wide range indicates diversity / similarity in scores.
4. A distribution with two prominent peaks is called unimodal / bimodal. What might this say about the set of scores?
5. A distribution that stretches much further to the right has positive / negative skew. What might this say about the set of scores?
6. The normal distribution
   a. is symmetric, meaning both tails are similar, without skew.
   b. has one peak.
   c. is often assumed true in a population of interest.
   d. All of the above.
7. In your own quiz questions, include some about earlier chapters.

DESCRIPTIVE STATISTICS: MEASURES OF LOCATION

Examining one or more pictures should give you an overall impression of your data. Then you may want to text your friends some brief information about your findings. For this you need descriptive statistics, which are numbers that summarize important aspects of the data. We'll focus on descriptive statistics for location and spread, two of the aspects you considered when inspecting data pictures.

Usually, the most informative descriptive statistic is a measure of location, which tells us where, overall, the data lie. Location is also referred to as the *central tendency* of the data set. The mean is the most familiar measure of central tendency, and we'll also consider the *median* and the *mode*.

The Mean

As you know, the mean is the simple average. Suppose last week I counted the number of calls I received on successive days, Monday to Friday. The first column of numbers in Table 3.1 is those counts. I have 5 data points, which I can refer to as $X_1, X_2, \ldots X_5$. In general, we can refer to a set of N data points as $X_1, X_2, \ldots X_i, \ldots X_N$, so X_i is a general symbol for any individual data point, and the index i can take any value from 1 to N.

Day	X_i	$(X_i - M)$	$(X_i - M)^2$
Monday	7	−1	1
Tuesday	9	1	1
Wednesday	14	6	36
Thursday	7	−1	1
Friday	3	−5	25
Total	40		64

Table 3.1 My Phone Calls Last Week

As you expect, my sample mean, M, is calculated as the total of my data divided by N, so $M = 40/5 = 8.0$. In general,

$$M = \frac{X_1 + X_2 + \ldots + X_i + \ldots + X_N}{N}$$

We can also write that as

The mean, M.

$$M = \frac{\sum X_i}{N} \tag{3.1}$$

where Σ (Greek upper case sigma) signals addition, and $\sum X_i$ indicates that we add all the X_i, meaning all our data points from X_1 to X_N.

If you are following along in ESCI, near red 3 click the checkbox to the left of **Mean**. (Note that "near red 3" or even "at red 3" can refer to anywhere in the colored area that has red 3 at the top.) The sample mean should be marked by a green triangle and vertical line in both the histogram and the dot plot—which should look like Figure 3.6. I use a triangle because the mean is the balance point of the data. Imagine the data points are basketballs and the X axis is a long beam that itself has no weight and rests just on the triangle. If the triangle is at the mean, the beam will balance. Which balls have most influence, which have hardly any influence?

> Imagine how the beam would tip if you shifted a ball slightly, or removed it from the beam.

The *mean* is the balance point of a data set and is strongly influenced by very low and very high points.

The extreme data points, at around 1 or 35, have most influence—the largest tendency to tip the beam. Remove either of those points and you need to move the mean considerably to regain balance. Data points very close to the mean have very little influence. You could add an additional data point exactly at the mean without altering the balance—or the mean. The further a data point is from the mean, the greater its pulling power on where the mean is, so the mean is especially sensitive to very low or high data points. That's particularly true for small data sets—for large data sets, any individual data points have smaller influence.

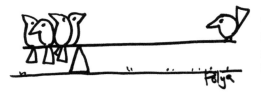

At red 3, click beside **Show values** to see the value of the mean reported as 14.5%. (Rounded from 14.519. I'll often round a value read from the screen.) Recall that calculating a mean requires interval scaling—the equal-interval assumption—as

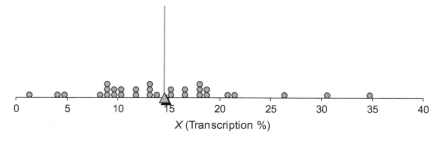

Figure 3.6. A stacked dot plot of the Laptop data, as in Figure 3.1. The sample mean is the balance point, marked by the triangle and vertical line.

we discussed in Chapter 2. Our next measure of location does not require that assumption.

The Median

The *median* is a measure of location that requires only ordinal scaling. The median is the value on the X axis below and above which half of the data points lie. The Laptop data set has $N = 31$ data points, so to find the median we arrange the 31 points in order, then count along from the lowest to find the 16th value, which is the median, because 15 data points lie below this value and 15 lie above. In Figure 3.6, count dots from the left (or right) to find the 16th. It's one of the vertical pile of 3, which are in fact three data points all equal to 12.8. (You could check that by examining the data values below red 2.) So 12.8% is the median of the Laptop data set, a little to the left of the mean at 14.5%.

> The *median* is the value on the X axis below and above which half of the data points lie.

For another example of a median, I clicked the **Generate data** button at red 5 to make a data set. I saw the dialog box shown in Figure 3.7. The four radio buttons on the left allow us to choose the shape of the distribution from which ESCI will take a random sample of N data points. I clicked **Skew right** and **Go**. I got a frequency histogram and dot plot for a new data set with $N = 100$ points. I clicked below red 3 to mark the **Median** in the figures with a pink diamond and a vertical line. The dot plot on my screen resembled Figure 3.8.

With $N = 100$, to find the median we could count from the lowest value to find the 50th and 51st values, then average these two. In my data set shown in Figure 3.8 the median is 48.1, as marked by the diamond and vertical line. (My mean is 50.5.) If you are following along in ESCI, your data set no doubt looks a little different and your mean and median are also a little different from mine.

> To find the median, order the data, then count halfway through the data points. If N is even, average the two middle values.

The distribution has positive skew, which is what I requested by choosing **Skew right** in the dialog box, as shown in Figure 3.7, to instruct ESCI to generate data from a distribution with right skew.

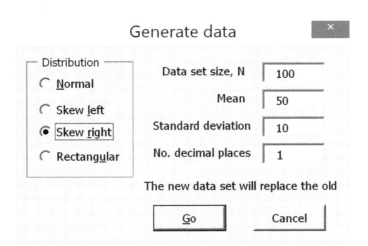

Figure 3.7. Dialog box displayed when the **Generate data** button is clicked. Choose characteristics of the distribution from which N data points will be randomly sampled.

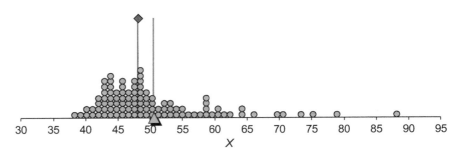

Figure 3.8. A data set generated by ESCI with $N = 100$ and right skew. The mean is marked by the triangle and vertical line, and the median by the diamond and vertical line.

To find the median we only need to arrange the data points in order then count. We need ordinal scaling to justify ordering the values, but not interval scaling, so using the median allows us to avoid the interval scaling assumption.

You might be thinking that averaging the 50th and 51st values requires interval scaling. Strictly, you are correct, but in practice those two values are usually very close together, and the averaging of the two middle values is such a small part of finding a median that we don't worry too much about needing the equal-interval assumption for this final small step. When N is odd there is a single middle value—as with our example above with $N = 31$—so no averaging is needed.

Looking at Figure 3.8, consider what happens to the median if you slide (in your mind's eye) any of the dots to the left of the diamond further left, or pile them up very close to the diamond. There's no change to the median, provided they all remain to the left of the original median. Similarly, bring some of the far distant points to the right back in toward the center, or shift them even further to the right: again, no change to the median. The mean is strongly influenced by outliers—meaning points considerably lower or higher than most others, as I discuss below—but the median is not influenced at all by how far any point is to the left or right of the median. All that matters is where the middle value in the data set falls.

> The median requires only *ordinal scaling* and is not influenced by how far points are to the left and right of the median.

In Figure 3.8, the few values in the long right tail pull the mean higher, so it's higher than the median. Mean higher than median is a strong sign we have positive skew in a data set; mean lower than median indicates negative skew. For the Laptop data, the mean of 14.5 is a little higher than the median of 12.8, reflecting the small positive skew shown in Figure 3.6.

> Extreme points pull the mean, but not the median. Mean greater than median indicates right skew; mean less than median left skew.

Keep pictures like Figure 3.6 and 3.8 in your head. They can help you associate any mean with the balance of balls on a beam—so outliers can easily pull the mean up or down—and any median with the middle of a collection of dots.

The Mode

Our third descriptive statistic for location is the *mode*, which is the most frequent data value. Recall our discussion in Chapter 2 of nominal measurement and ice cream flavors: If the highest frequency, meaning the largest number of sales last week, was for chocolate, then chocolate is the mode of the distribution of sales. Chocolate was the modal flavor last week.

> The *mode* is the most frequent data value, and requires only nominal scaling.

The mode requires only nominal scaling, and it makes sense as a rudimentary descriptive statistic of a set of frequencies, such as the ice cream sales data. For a frequency histogram, as in Figure 3.3, the mode is the bin with the highest frequency. That may make little sense, however, because it can change merely by changing the number of bins: For Figure 3.3C the mode is the 15–18 bin, whereas for D it's the 8–12 bin.

We've already met a common use of the mode, to describe distributions as unimodal or bimodal, depending on whether they have one or two peaks.

In summary, our three descriptive statistics for location, or central tendency, are:

- The mean, which requires interval scaling. It's sensitive to extreme points.
- The median, which requires ordinal scaling. It reflects only whether points are above or below it, and not how far above or below they are.
- The mode, which requires only nominal scaling. A common use is as a count of the major peaks in a distribution.

3.11 In Figure 3.6, what would happen to the mean and the median if you shifted the highest data point down to 20? Up to 40?

 In **Describe**, click to display the mean and median in the figures. Find the highest value below red 2 and change it to 20, then 40, to test your predictions.

3.12 Think of two data points you could add to the Laptop data set to achieve the following. Explain in each case:

a. The mean changes but the median does not.
b. Both the mean and median change.
c. The mean doesn't change but the median does.
d. Neither the mean nor the median changes.

 In **Describe**, type in two new values below the data at red 2 to test any of your predictions if you wish.

3.13 Consider that every person has a certain number of friends. (Choose some definition of "friend".) Let X be a variable that is that number, so X can take values of 0, 1, 2, … What do you think is the mean of X? The median? Are they likely to differ? Explain.

DESCRIPTIVE STATISTICS: MEASURES OF SPREAD

The Standard Deviation

We'd like a descriptive statistic that tells us generally how spread or dispersed the data points are. Our first choice is the *standard deviation* (SD), which seems a bit complicated but has desirable statistical properties. Think of the SD as being, very roughly, a measure of how far a typical data point lies from the mean. To calculate the SD, we first calculate the *variance*, which is a slightly strange property of a data set that's also commonly used because it has valuable statistical properties. The variance, V, is

$$V = \frac{\sum (X_i - M)^2}{N - 1}$$

(3.2)   The *variance*, V.

and the SD, for which we use the symbol s, is simply the square root of the variance, $s = \sqrt{V}$. Therefore, the formula for s is

▶ ——————
The *standard deviation*, s.

$$s = \sqrt{\frac{\sum (X_i - M)^2}{N - 1}} \qquad (3.3)$$

Here are the steps to apply that formula, referring to my phone data in Table 3.1:

1. Calculate M, which for us is $M = 8.0$.
2. For each X_i, calculate its *deviation* from the mean, which is $(X_i - M)$, as in the second column of numbers in the table.
3. Square those deviations, as in the rightmost column in the table, then add to find the total $\sum (X_i - M)^2 = 64.0$. Why do we square? That's a good question, which I'll discuss shortly.
4. Divide by $(N - 1) = 4$ to find the variance, $V = 16.0$. Why $(N - 1)$ and not N? Another good question, and I'll discuss that shortly also.
5. Take the square root to find $s = 4.0$.

I conclude that my mean number of calls last week, Monday to Friday, was $M = 8.0$ calls, and the standard deviation was $s = 4.0$ calls.

> The *deviation* of a data point, X_i, is its distance from the mean, which is $(X_i - M)$.

▶ ——————
The *standard deviation* is a measure of the spread of data points. It's the square root of the *variance*. SD is very strongly influenced by very low and very high points.

The SD is calculated from the squared deviations, which are the values shown in the rightmost column of Table 3.1. The total of that column, which is 64.0, comes very largely from the two data points (for Wednesday and Friday) that lie furthest from the mean—the two data points that have particularly large deviations. Our s is strongly influenced by the Wednesday and Friday data points, which illustrates how the squaring magnifies the influence of any data point that is relatively far from the mean. The value of s is even more strongly influenced by extreme values than is the mean.

Figure 3.9 illustrates the standard deviation for the Laptop data: The upper cross at left is one SD below the mean, and the cross at right is one SD above the mean. The standard deviation is $s = 7.29$ transcription percentage points. You might be thinking that the great majority of data points are closer than one SD from the mean, so the SD is hardly a "typical" distance from M. That's a good thought. As I mentioned above, the squaring means that points a great distance from M have an especially large influence, so the SD is often larger than we might first guess. In general, the variance and SD are very strongly influenced by low or high points.

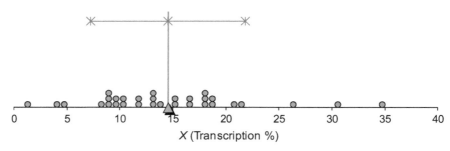

Figure 3.9. Same as Figure 3.6 but with cross symbols and line segments marking a distance one SD above and one SD below the mean. The SD is $s = 7.29$.

Why do we square? I said I'd discuss the squaring in Equations 3.2 and 3.3, but it's not essential to know the details—if your eyes glaze over, skip ahead to **Unbiased estimates**. First, why don't we simply average the deviation scores? If you average the $(X_i - M)$ values in Table 3.1, you'll obtain 0. The result is always 0, because the mean is chosen so the negative and positive deviations balance. Another possibility is to ignore whether the deviations are negative or positive, regard them all as positive and find the average. However, we rarely do that. Instead, we square the deviations to find the variance, because unlike the two other possibilities I just mentioned, it has a very valuable statistical property. That valuable property is that often you can *add* variances, as I'll now illustrate.

Suppose to get home you wait for a bus, then travel home on the bus. Total time to get home is waiting time plus travel time:

Time to get home = Waiting time + Travel time

From day to day there is variability in both those times. It turns out that not only do times add, but the variances also add. The variance of the total time to get home equals the variance of the waiting time plus the variance of the travel time:

Variance(Time to get home) = Variance(Waiting time) + Variance(Travel time)

However, adding those variances requires the important assumption that waiting time and travel time are independent, meaning that waiting and travel time are separate and don't influence each other. That may be unrealistic—if there's heavy rain, for example, both are likely to be long—but if they are independent we can add variances. For variables that are independent, variances add. Standard deviations don't add. That's why variance is highly useful, and is the basis for a number of widely used statistical techniques, including one called, would you believe, "analysis of variance", ANOVA for short.

◄
Variances add, when variables are independent.

Unbiased estimates. There's one further tricky thing I raised earlier. Why do Equations 3.2 and 3.3 have $(N-1)$, and not simply N, in the denominator? Because, as statisticians tell us, using $(N-1)$ in Equation 3.2 gives an *unbiased* estimate of population variance. An unbiased estimate is given by a formula that, on average, gives an accurate estimate of the population value. If we take a large number of samples, the average of their values of V will be very close to the variance of the population. Using N instead of $(N-1)$ would give *biased* estimates—on average a little smaller than the population variance. Incidentally, for the mean, you'll be pleased to know that Equation 3.1 gives an unbiased estimate of the population mean.

An ***unbiased*** estimate is given by a formula that on average gives a value equal to the population value.

Usually we consider our data set to be a sample from a population, so want the variance we calculate to be a good estimate of population variance. We prefer an unbiased estimate, so we choose Equation 3.2. Most statistical software including ESCI does that. Once we have the variance, Equation 3.3 tells us to take the square root to find the standard deviation, which is $s = \sqrt{V}$.

What are the units of M, s, and V? The mean, as marked in Figures 3.6 and 3.9, is in transcription percentage points. We square the deviations to find the variance, V, of the transcription scores, so V is in units of (transcription percentage points, squared). We take a square root to find s, which is, therefore, back in transcription percentage points, and can be shown as a distance on the X axis, as in Figures 3.6 and 3.9. Because it's a squared measure, variance is hard to picture and can be hard to think about.

? Quiz 3.2

1. Consider the mean, median, and mode as measures of location.
   a. Which is calculated as the sum of scores divided by the number of scores?
   b. Which is defined as the most common score?
   c. Which is the most sensitive to outliers?
   d. Which can be used with nominal data?
   e. Which can be used with ordinal, but not nominal, data?
   f. Which requires the assumption of interval scaling?
2. How is the variance of a set of scores calculated?
3. The standard deviation is the _____ of the variance.
4. On the first exam of the semester, nearly everyone in the class scored over 90%. The second exam was much harder, with scores ranging from 30% to 90%. Which exam would have the larger standard deviation?
5. On the final exam for the semester, $s = 0$. What does this tell you about the diversity of scores in the class? Can you think of two different ways this could happen?
6. What is an unbiased estimate? Give two examples.
7. I'm sure you don't need more reminders to make your own questions.

DESCRIPTIVE STATISTICS: INDIVIDUAL DATA POINTS

A descriptive statistic can summarize the data set, as we've seen for measures of location and spread. It can also tell us about where an individual data point sits in the whole data set, and this can matter, as you may have experienced. For example, scoring a low mark on a test can be discouraging, but if you learn that your mark is a lot higher than the mean for the class, you'll probably be much encouraged. First I'll consider individual data points that are extreme.

Outliers

Points that are very low or very high, relative to most of the other data points, are *outliers*. There's no good or widely agreed criterion for deciding which points are sufficiently atypical to be identified as outliers. We'll use the term informally for points that look extreme.

An *outlier* is a data point that is extreme, relative to others in a data set.

Removal of outliers can be useful. For example, surveys usually include a small number of respondents who enter outrageous responses as a type of joke. Including such non-compliant responders can distort our conclusions. On the other hand, removing data is a form of selection, and can easily lead to biased or flawed understanding. Ideally you should remove outliers only if (i) you can specify an objective standard for identifying which responses are not valid, and (ii) the rules for removing outliers were made in advance of seeing the results, as part of a planned analysis. In any case, you should always report what outliers were removed, why they were removed, and when this decision was made. Recognize that outliers may be telling us something important, so consider what that might be.

An alternative approach, if you suspect you might obtain outliers, is to state in advance that you will use descriptive statistics that are relatively insensitive to outliers, for example the median rather than the mean. A further approach is to report two analyses, the first of all the data and the second without the outliers.

z Scores

Now for an extremely useful measure of where an individual data point lies in a distribution or data set. It uses the standard deviation as a measuring unit: We note that a particular data point, or *X* value, is a certain number or multiple of standard deviations below or above the mean. This number is called the *z score* of that point. In Figure 3.9, for example, a data point at about *X* = 22% would line up with the right hand cross symbol, and would therefore be 1 SD above the mean. So *z* = 1 for such a point. In Figure 3.10, vertical lines mark values of *X* that are various numbers of SDs away from the mean. We call those vertical lines *z lines* because they mark *z* = 0 (the mean), *z* = −1 (at a distance of one standard deviation below the mean), *z* = 1, and so on. A *z* score can be calculated for any data point or *X* value, and *z* lines displayed for any data set or distribution.

> A ***z score*** is the distance of a data point, or an *X* value, from the mean, in standard deviation units.

For example, to calculate the *z* score for *X* = 34.7%, the highest data value in the Laptop data set, find how far it is from *M* then divide by *s*. The formula is:

$$z = \frac{X - M}{s} \qquad (3.4)$$

◄ Calculate *z* from *X*.

For *X* = 34.7%, the formula gives *z* = (34.7% − 14.5%)/7.29% = 2.77, which reflects what we can see in Figure 3.10: The rightmost data point is almost 3 SDs above the mean. To go in the other direction, use

$$X = M + zs \qquad (3.5)$$

◄ Calculate *X* from *z*.

If *z* = −1.00, then *X* = 14.5% − 1.00 × 7.29% = 7.2%, which is the position of the first *z* line to the left of the mean in Figure 3.10.

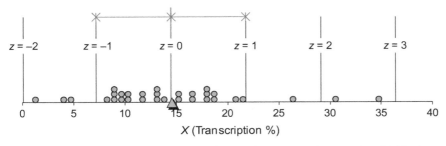

Figure 3.10. Same as Figure 3.9 but with vertical lines marking *X* values that are 1, 2, and 3 SDs above the mean, and 1 and 2 SDs below the mean. These *z* lines mark *z* scores, as indicated by the labels. The *z* score at the mean is 0, as labeled.

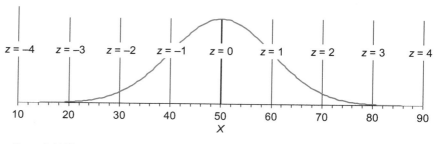

Figure 3.11. The same normal distribution shown in Figure 3.5, but with z lines.

The Laptop data set in Figure 3.10 has the majority of its points between $z = -1$ and $z = 1$ (they lie within 1 SD of the mean) and only a few points lie beyond $z = -2$ and $z = 2$ (they lie more than 2 SDs from the mean). That pattern is roughly true for many, but far from all data sets.

Figure 3.11 shows a normal distribution, as in Figure 3.5, with z lines. Most of the area under the curve lies between $z = -1$ and $z = 1$ (within 1 SD of the mean) and only small areas lie beyond $z = -2$ and $z = 2$ (more than 2 SDs from the mean). Areas indicate the relative numbers of data points available, so a random sample of data from a population with a normal distribution is likely to have a majority of data points within 1 SD of the mean, and only a few that are more than 2 SDs from the mean. That's as we observed for the Laptop data, so perhaps it's reasonable to assume that those data were a random sample from a normally distributed population of potential transcription scores. In Chapter 4 there will be more about z scores and sampling from normal distributions.

Here are two things to note about z scores:

> In many, but far from all, data distributions, a majority of points are within 1 SD of the mean, and only a few are more than 2 SDs from the mean.

- Because they are based on the mean and standard deviation, z scores require interval scaling.
- We can calculate z scores for any distribution or data set for which we know the mean and standard deviation. They don't apply *only* to normal distributions.

Finally, reflect on how incredibly useful z scores can be—they provide a standardized way of thinking about individual scores. We can compare two z scores, even when they were calculated from different X variables. Consider depression, for example, which is often measured using the Beck Depression Inventory (BDI), with scores ranging from 0 (not at all depressed) to 63 (extremely depressed). Another frequently used measure is the Quick Inventory of Depressive Symptomology (QUIDS), with scores ranging from 0 (not at all depressed) to 16 (extremely depressed). We can't compare scores directly—16 is only mild depression on the BDI, but extreme on the QUIDS. However, if Jack's depression score is $z = 1.5$ and Jill's is $z = 0$, then we can compare, and conclude that Jill is around average whereas Jack is definitely depressed. We can compare, even without knowing whether BDI or QUIDS was used with Jack, or with Jill. There's lots more about these types of comparisons in Chapters 7 and 8.

3.14 Make up a cover story to tell us what the data in Table 3.2 represent. Find the mean, *M*, then fill in all the cells marked with two dots. Use Equations 3.2 and 3.3 to calculate variance, *V*, and standard deviation, *s*.

X_i	$(X_i - M)$	$(X_i - M)^2$
6	..	..
7	..	..
3	..	..
10	..	..
7	..	..
9	..	..
Total ..		..

Table 3.2
Calculating a
Standard Deviation

 3.15 Type the data set of Table 3.2 into ESCI and check the M and s you calculated above were correct.

    a. Calculate z for the largest X value in Table 3.2.

    b. What X would have $z = 1$?

3.16 Consider the data set comprising the digits from 0 to 9. Find the mean, median, and SD. What's the z score of 7?

3.17 With the Laptop data as in Figure 3.6, what two extra data points could you add without changing the mean or the SD?

esci   Use ESCI to test your prediction. (To load the Laptop data, scroll right and click at red 11 in the **Describe** page.)

esci 3.18 a. Clear all the checkboxes at red 3. Click at red 5 to generate a data set. Examine the dot plot and histogram, and guess the mean and SD. Ask a friend to guess, then click at red 3 to display values, and markers in the pictures. How did you both do?

    b. Repeat. Try small and large data sets. (To set N, change the value in the dialogue box shown in Figure 3.7). Try left and right skew. Make it a competitive game.

    c. Do you prefer estimating mean and SD from the dot plot, or the histogram? Why?

    d. Do you make consistent over- or underestimates? Suggest why.

Percentiles

Next is a measure that requires only ordinal scaling. To find the median we order the data, then count 50% of the way from the left. The median can be called the 50th *percentile* of the data set. Do the same for any other percentage to find X that is that percentile of the data. The largest data value is the 100th percentile. Figure 3.12 illustrates the idea: A cursor marks the 25th percentile, and data points to the left (25% of all data points) are red.

In **Describe**, generate a data set of your choice, perhaps with N at least 100. Click **Cursor** at red 7 to see a red vertical cursor in the dot plot and a large slider below. Use the slider to move the cursor and note the red percentage value displayed on it. Experiment—can you figure out what's going on?

Dots in the dot plot that are to the left of the cursor are displayed red in Figure 3.12. Move the slider to the right and see more red. The cursor in the dot plot moves in small steps, usually corresponding to data point by data point. The red percentages tell us which *percentile* of the data set the current cursor position represents. A percentile is the value of X below which the stated percentage of data points lie. Use the slider to position the cursor in the dot plot to mark any percentile you wish to find. Is the median indeed the 50th percentile?

A *percentile* is the value of X below which the stated percentage of data points lie.

Quartiles

The *first quartile*, with label Q1 or Q_1, is another name for the 25th percentile, meaning that 25% of the data points lie below Q1. Similarly, the *third quartile*, or Q3, is another name for the 75th percentile. Of course, 75% of the data points lie below Q3. As you probably guessed, the second quartile, Q2, is simply the median. Below red 3, click **Show values** to see the values of Q1 and Q3. Click at **Median** and **Quartiles** to see the quartiles marked as in Figure 3.13. Move the cursor to check that the quartile lines are where they should be.

> The *first quartile*, or Q1, is the 25th percentile and the *third quartile*, or Q3, is the 75th percentile.

Quartiles, like percentiles, require only ordinal scaling. We can think of Q1 as the median of the half of the data set that lies below the median. Similarly, Q3 is the median of the half of the data set above the median. We can use the first and third quartiles to give us an indication of the spread of the data in our data set. The *interquartile range* (IQR) is simply the interval from the first to third quartiles. Perhaps I could have introduced the IQR earlier, in the section *Descriptive Statistics: Measures of Spread*, but it's here because it's based on quartiles, which more naturally fit in this section. For the data set in Figure 3.13, the IQR extends from 44.5 to 53.4, which is the interval between the two fine vertical lines in the figure.

> The *interquartile range* (IQR) extends from Q1 to Q3, and is an indicator of the spread of points in a data set.

Finally, I should mention the simplest descriptive statistic for spread. It's the *range*, which is simply the interval from the lowest to the highest data point. The range also could fit in the earlier section about spread, but is here because it's based on individual data points. For the data set in Figure 3.13, the range is from 38.4 to 88.4, which are the values of the leftmost and rightmost dots in the figure.

> The *range* is the interval from the lowest to the highest point in a data set.

A problem with the range is that it's dependent only on the two extreme points in a data set, so is extremely sensitive to any outliers. Perhaps we should ignore some of the points at the two ends of the distribution? That's a good thought, and is what the IQR does: The IQR is the range of the core of the data set, after we've removed the bottom 25% and top 25% of data points. It's therefore not sensitive to outliers, or how points might be distributed in the lower or upper tails of the distribution of points. On the other hand, it tells us only about the middle 50% of the data.

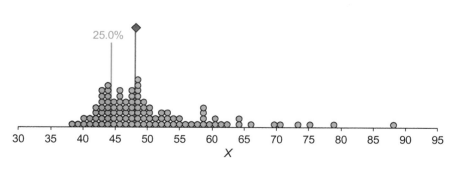

Figure 3.12. The data set shown in Figure 3.8. The diamond and vertical line mark the median. A percentile cursor is shown at 25%.

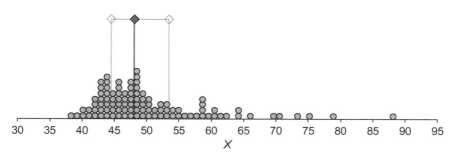

Figure 3.13. The same data set as in Figure 3.12, but with fine vertical lines marking Q1 and Q3, the first and third quartiles. The interquartile range (IQR) is the interval between the two fine vertical lines.

Removing the lower and upper 25% of points to obtain the IQR is an example of *trimming*, which refers to removal of a selected proportion of data points from the two ends of the distribution. The range is calculated after 0% trimming (no points removed) and the IQR after 25% trimming, meaning 25% from each end of the distribution. Of course, other trimming strategies are possible, reflecting different decisions about how much of the two tails to ignore. An extreme case is the median, which is what's left after 50% trimming. In Chapter 16 we'll consider 20% trimming, which turns out often to be a good choice.

◀
Trimming refers to removal of a stated percentage of the data points from the two ends of the distribution.

CHOOSING DESCRIPTIVE STATISTICS

We've seen descriptive statistics that summarize a data set—think mean, median, and standard deviation—and others that position a particular data point in the set—think z score and percentile. So our aims should be the first consideration when choosing descriptive statistics.

Even so, often there are options. The commonest question is probably: mean or median? The two statistics convey different information, and sometimes it may be useful to report both. We need to think carefully (as usual) about what message a particular statistic is giving. For example, suppose X in Figure 3.8 is annual income in thousands of dollars. A politician wanting an upbeat message might boast that average income is around $50,000, whereas an opposing politician might say times are not so easy, with income only around a median of $48,000. To make the contrast more striking, type an additional data point of 1000 into ESCI, for an Internet entrepreneur with an income of $1,000,000, and see the mean leap to about $59,000, while the median is virtually unchanged.

The mean and SD are by far the most widely used descriptive statistics, even though they require interval scaling and the assumption of equal intervals is often questionable. The median is widely used, especially with skewed data sets. Percentiles, quartiles, and the IQR should probably be used more often than they are. Those measures, and the median, can be used with data having ordinal scaling, but they can also, of course, be used with data having interval scaling. Most of our common statistical techniques, including the calculation of CIs, are based on means and SDs. These techniques are usually the most informative, and are what I'll almost always use in this book, but we need to keep in mind that they assume interval scaling.

◀
The mean and SD are the most commonly used descriptive statistics, and what we'll usually choose. But they require interval scaling.

In practice, researchers will often simply do whatever is customary in their research field, which for Likert items and GPA, for example, is usually to assume interval scaling. Therefore, when we read their reports containing means, SDs, and CIs, we need to bring to mind the interval scaling assumption as we think about what their results mean.

We need to understand any numbers we elect to feed in to the computer, and need to think about what lies behind any data picture or summary statistics we read in a research report. Only then can we understand what's going on, and draw justified conclusions.

3.19 a. Invent your own data set of a dozen numbers. Find the median, first and third quartiles, IQR, and range.
     b. Change the largest data point to a considerably higher value. What happens to the mean, SD, z lines, median, IQR, and range? Explain.

3.20 Many IQ tests are designed so that their scores have close to a normal distribution, with mean $= 100$ and SD $= 15$ in the general adult population. (The normal distribution extends to infinity in both directions, but we are not saying that negative IQ scores are possible. As usual, we pay most attention to the central part of the normal distribution, within, say, 3 or 4 SDs of the mean.) Suppose you had the IQ scores of a sample of 100 adults, randomly chosen from the general population. About where would you expect most of the scores to lie? Specify two intervals in which you would expect just a few scores to lie. Where would you expect to find very few or no scores?

3.21 In a data set with $N = 60$, how many points lie to the left of the 10th percentile? How many to the right of the 80th percentile? How many lie between Q1 and Q3? If your variable has interval scaling, would any of your answers change? Explain.

3.22 a. A teacher calculates the mean score for all students in the class, then notices that only 40% of the students scored higher than the mean. Is that possible? What is a likely shape of the distribution?
     b. It's not possible for everyone in the class to score above the class average, but what's the maximum number of students who could, and what would the distribution look like?

3.23 To measure happiness, you ask people: "In general, how happy are you these days, on a scale from 1 to 20, where 1 means as unhappy as you can imagine, and 20 means as happy as you can imagine." You collect happiness ratings from 30 people.
     a. Would it be reasonable to calculate the mean and SD of those 30 ratings? Explain.
     b. Suppose you calculated $M = 14.6$ and $s = 3.7$ for those 30 ratings. What assumption would you be making? How could you interpret that mean and SD?
     c. How else could you summarize your 30 ratings? What would be the best way to report your data set, with some statistics to describe it?
     d. If $M = 17.6$ and $s = 3.7$, what can you say about the shape of the distribution?

GOOD AND BAD PICTURES

Having discussed descriptive statistics, I want to close the chapter by returning to data pictures and considering a key question: What makes a good or bad picture? I could insert here some examples, but it's more fun to explore the numerous examples easily available online. Search for "misleading graphs" or similar. Wikipedia gives a good overview of bad graphs, at tiny.cc/wikimisgraph The best website is probably that of Michael Friendly of York University in Toronto: tiny.cc/mfdatavis At that site, the links on the left present laurels and give the thumbs-up to several collections of good graphs, and links on the right give the thumbs-down to collections of bad graphs.

There's no simple definition of "good" and "bad". As you'd expect, it's to some extent a matter for judgment in context and depends on your research questions. A good graph is informative and revealing, and doesn't mislead.

When examining any picture of data, here are some basic first questions to ask:

- What's the measure, in what units? What does any single data point represent?
- What are the axes? Check the label and units for each axis, and look for zero and for markings of equal intervals.
- How else could the same data set be pictured? How would that change the impression I'm getting?
- Behind the numbers, what does the data set tell us about what's going on in the world?

Here are a few things *not* to do, if you want to make a good graph:

- Change the vertical scale, perhaps omitting zero, to change the impression given by a series of data points. Almost flat becomes a dramatic increase, simply by changing the vertical scale.
- Omit some values on the horizontal scale, so it doesn't proceed in regular steps from left to right. This often happens with dates, or ranges of dates.
- Use pictographs (little pictures of people, cars, or other things) that expand in size to dramatize a change in amount. Using a pictograph twice as high gives the impression of a four-fold increase because the area of the larger pictograph is four times greater. Try 3-D for even greater exaggeration.

Such bullet point lists can only give starting points. Find and discuss lots of examples, good and bad. Keep copies of your favorites. Make your own bullet point lists. Playing with pictures and designing better ones can be highly entertaining—make it a party game.

Possibly the most widely known statistics book is *How to Lie with Statistics* by Darrell Huff (1954). It may be dated but it's still wonderful, with numerous examples of misleading graphs and ways to select or distort information to give the wrong impression. It's a book of things to look out for. Search for the book title and you'll easily find a full copy online that you can read, or even download and keep. You can even find both the U.S. and the British editions, which have different cartoons.

It's time for take-home messages. Look back over the whole chapter and make your own list, with pictures if you like. Sleep on it, and see if you can improve your list.

SAME DATA! Polya

3.24 Explore Michael Friendly's Data Visualization Gallery at tiny.cc/mfdatavis and choose your favorite graph, or graphs, that illustrate:

- the importance of seeing zero on the vertical axis;
- the importance of using a well-chosen, complete set of values on the horizontal axis;
- the danger of using small pictographs.

3.25 Choose three graphs you like, and explain to your friends why you chose these.

3.26 Go to tiny.cc/bbcdatavis and try the four questions. Discuss with your friends before clicking below each question to see an explanation.

3.27 Search on "pie charts" and choose two that illustrate how terrible pie charts can be. Can you find an example of a good pie chart?

3.28 Have these exercises suggested anything you should add to your list of take-home messages? Revise your list if you wish.

? Quiz 3.3

1. In Figure 3.13, which single point might you consider an outlier? Which three points might you consider to be outliers?
2. A z score is an individual score (*X*) minus the _____ and then divided by the _____.
3. Anna has taken four exams in her physics class. Her results are: Exam 1: $z = 1.1$; Exam 2: $z = 0.0$; Exam 3: $z = -0.8$; Exam 4: $z = 2.3$
   a. On which exam did Anna score exactly at the class mean?
   b. On which exam did Anna score below average?
   c. On which exam did Anna do the best?
4. In a data set with $M = 10$ and $s = 2$, what *X* score corresponds to $z = -1.5$? $z = 0.5$? $z = 3$? Does *X* have to be normally distributed?
5. The interquartile range is the range of scores between Q__ and Q__. The interquartile range is a measure of spread that is <u>more/less</u> sensitive to outliers than the standard deviation.
6. Q1 is another name for the ____ percentile, Q2 for the ____, and Q3 for the ____ percentile.

↗ Reporting Your Work

Descriptive statistics often form the heart of the results section when reporting your work. Here are some key points to keep in mind.

- The shape of a distribution is important (roughly normal, skewed, etc.). But it takes a good bit of data (at least 100 cases) to get a good sense of the shape of a variable's distribution. If you have fewer cases than this, it's probably best not to make judgments about shape.
- As usual, it's best if your readers can see the data. However, you usually can't include a dot plot or histogram for every single variable collected. As you'll see in later chapters, many of the graphs used for complex analysis provide all the information in a dot plot plus more.

▶──────
Use figures and descriptive statistics to help provide the full story of your data.
──────

- Although data pictures are really useful, so are good descriptive statistics. For every measure collected, you should provide a measure of location and a measure of spread. Typically, these will be the mean and standard deviation, but use your judgment and consider other descriptive statistics, especially if you have outliers or strong skew. If you have a complex study with lots of measures, a table of descriptive statistics can efficiently summarize a tremendous amount of information.
- When interpreting descriptive statistics, be sure to consider not only the mean but also the spread of the variable, as both are important.
- Remember to think about the scale of measurement for the variables you collected and to select appropriate descriptive statistics. Don't report the mean gender of your participants!

> ▦ In APA style, Roman letters serving as statistical symbols are italicized, so use *M* for sample mean, *s* for sample standard deviation, *N* for overall sample size, and *n* for any subsample or subgroup being summarized. However, Greek letters serving as statistical symbols are not italicized, so use μ (not *μ*) for the population mean. Be sure the sample size for any descriptive statistic is clear.
>
> ▦ For each measure, consider the number of decimal places that could be meaningful and then round appropriately. For example, you would probably report an exam grade average as *M* = 85% or 85.3%, not as *M* = 85.292% because the extra digits almost certainly suggest greater precision than your data justify. In other words, too many decimal places may mislead and not be useful for drawing conclusions. Be sure to round *only* at the stage of reporting your statistics, never during calculations.
>
> No sample write-ups yet; these start in Chapter 5, when we can integrate various measures and CIs.

Take-Home Messages

■ Pictures of data can be highly revealing. Bring to mind other ways to picture the same data, which might give a different impression.

■ A *frequency histogram* can give a good overview, especially of a large data set. A *stacked dot plot* provides an overview and also information about individual data points. *Descriptive statistics* can be indicated on both types of data picture.

■ An asymmetric distribution has *skew*—positive skew if the longer tail is to the right, and negative skew if to the left.

■ The *normal distribution* is a symmetric bell-shaped distribution that's important in the theory of statistics and also sometimes occurs, approximately, in the world.

■ *Take-home picture:* Figure 3.5, showing two views of a normal distribution.

■ The *mean* is the balance point of a data set and is strongly influenced by low and high values, especially *outliers*.

■ The *median* is the center point, below and above which 50% of the data points lie; it's not influenced by how far out the extreme points are.

■ With positive skew the mean is greater than the median. *Take-home picture:* Figure 3.8, showing a stacked dot plot with mean and median.

■ The *standard deviation* is calculated from squared deviations of data points from their mean, and is greatly influenced by low and high values. The *variance* is the square of the standard deviation.

■ A *z* score is the distance of a point from the mean, expressed in standard deviation units. Lines at *z* = ... −1, 0, 1, ... are *z* lines and can be displayed for any data set.

■ A *percentile* is the point on the *X* axis below which the stated percentage of the data points lie. The first and third *quartiles*, Q1 and Q3, are the 25th and 75th percentiles. The interval between Q1 and Q3 is the *interquartile range*, IQR.

■ The mean and standard deviation require interval scaling. The median, quartiles, and percentiles require only ordinal scaling.

■ Pictures of data can reveal or mislead. Design pictures carefully. Watch out for ways that pictures can deceive. Think of what lies behind the picture and any descriptive statistics reported.

End-of-Chapter Exercises

1) Let's practice calculating descriptive statistics. Table 3.3 contains a set of ACT scores from a sample of college students. The ACT is a standardized college-readiness exam taken by many U.S. students; scores can range from 1 to 36.

Table 3.3 ACT Scores for Exercise 1.

Student	ACT	$(X_i - M)$	$(X_i - M)^2$
1	26		
2	24		
3	28		
4	31		
5	20		
6	27		
7	18		
8	17		
9	21		
10	29		
11	24		
Total			

a.   Location: Calculate the mean (M), median, and mode for this sample.

b.   Spread: Calculate the standard deviation (s), range, and interquartile range for this sample. For s, fill in the two columns on the right in Table 3.3, then use the formula to calculate s yourself.

2)   Now let's *look* at some distributions of data (ESCI will help you with this, or you may have other software you like to use). From the book website, load the **College_Survey_1** data set. This is a large data set containing data from a wide-ranging survey of college students. You can read the code book for the data file to get a better sense of the different variables measured.

a.   Visualize the distribution of positive affect scores (Positive_Affect). Students rate how often they experience each of 10 positive emotions, using a scale from 1 (*not at all*) to 5 (*extremely*), then the score is the average of the 10 ratings. To use ESCI, follow these steps:

  • In **Describe**, click at red 4 to clear data.
  • Switch to the data set, select the Positive_Affect data, and copy to the clipboard.
  • Switch back to **Describe**, click to select the top data cell at red 2, and use Paste Special/Values to enter the column of data.
  • At **Units** near red 1, click near the left of the blank cell and type "Pos Affect" or similar, press Enter.
  • If you wish to have easy future access to the positive affect data, save the ESCI file with a new name.

  Describe the distribution you see, noting the location, spread, and shape, and the number of major peaks.

b.   Visualize and describe the distribution of student age. Note the skew and the high outliers. Note the mean and median and explain why they differ. Would it make sense to delete outliers? Explain.

c.   Visualize the distribution of exercise scores, which are calculated as 9×strenuous + 5×moderate + 3×light, where students report the number of times per week they engage in strenuous, moderate, and light exercise. There is an extreme outlier. What would that extreme value mean? Would it make sense to delete it? Explain. If you do delete it, what happens to the standard deviation? Test your prediction.

d. Visualize the distribution of Raven scores (Raven_Score), which are the proportion correct on a short 8-item IQ test. Next, visualize the distribution of GPA. Compare the two distributions. Why might they differ in shape?

e. In this data set, Gender is coded as female = 1 and male = 2. ESCI calculates that the mean is $M = 1.28$ for Gender. Does this make sense? How might you better summarize gender in this sample?

3) Continuing with the same data set as in Exercise 2, let's put some individual scores in context:

a. One female participant achieved a score of .875 on the Raven measure. What is her z score?

b. The same female participant has a GPA of 3.9. What is her z score for GPA? On which measure (GPA or Raven) is she more unusual?

c. One participant scored a 2 for Positive Affect and a 2 for Negative Affect. Even though these raw scores are the same, they are very different within the context of the whole study. Express both as z scores and percentiles. Which score is more unusual?

d. A z score of more than 3 or less than −3 is sometimes considered an outlier. By this standard, would the participant who is 59 qualify as an outlier for age? Would the participant who reported an exercise score of 1,810 qualify as an outlier for exercise?

4) Let's look at some data about religious beliefs. The **Religious_Belief** data set on the book website has data from a large online survey in which participants were asked to report, on a scale from 0 to 100, their belief in the existence of God.

a. First, sketch the distribution you think this variable will have. Consider the relative frequencies of people you expect to strongly believe in God (high end of the scale), to strongly *not* believe in God (low end of the scale), or to be unsure (middle of the scale).

b. Now make a picture of these data and describe it in words.

c. Does the mean do a good job representing this data picture? Does the median? The mode? Why do all these measures of location seem to fail?

? Answers to Quizzes

Quiz 3.1

1) Dot plot, stacked dot plot, frequency histogram; 2) measure, location, spread, shape; 3) diversity; 4) bimodal, there may be two subgroups; 5) positive, there may be a boundary just below the lowest score; 6) d.

Quiz 3.2

1) a. mean, b. mode, c. mean, d. mode, e. median, f. mean; 2) The difference between each score and the mean is calculated, then each result is squared, then all the squared deviation scores are summed, then the sum is divided by $(N − 1)$; 3) square root; 4) The second, because the standard deviation measures spread, which is much larger for that exam; 5) $s = 0$ means that all scores were the same; perhaps the test was extremely easy, so everyone scored 100%, or was extremely hard, so everyone scored 0%. Other scores are also possible, for example if everyone cheated from the same cheat sheet; 6) An unbiased estimate is given by a formula that, on average in the long run, gives an accurate estimate of the population value. Sample mean and variance are unbiased estimates of population mean and variance.

Quiz 3.3

1) the highest point, about 88; the three highest points, about 75, 79, 88; 2) mean (M), standard deviation (s); 3) a. Exam 2; b. Exam 3; c. Exam 4; 4) 7, 11, 16, no; 5) Q1, Q3, less; 6) 25th percentile, median, 75th percentile.

Answers to In-Chapter Exercises

3.5 As you click and unclick, many of the dots move a tiny amount left or right, so they line up neatly in columns when stacked.

3.8 ESCI places it in the bin to the left.

3.10 One possibility is to combine the two displays, so we see both dots and columns, although that would be messy. Better might be to mark fine horizontal lines across each column to indicate frequency more pictorially: A column representing a frequency of 5, for example, would be divided by horizontal lines into a stack of 5 small rectangles.

3.11 No change to the median. Shift to 20 and the mean decreases to 14.04; to 40 and the mean increases to 14.69. (If you know about Excel, you may have expected the Undo command would allow you to reverse any change to a data value. However, the **Describe** page needs to use macros to update the figures, so the Undo command is not available after changes to data values. Sorry!)

3.12 a. A value just below the median and another just above it; b. Two values both considerably above, or below, the mean and median; c. Two values both at the mean; d. This last one is tricky: We need one value some distance below the mean and another the same distance above the mean—and the two points added must be on opposite sides of the median.

3.13 I'll let you guess a value for the mean. The distribution is likely to be positively skewed, because 0 is a lower boundary. If so, many people have a moderate number of friends but a few have many friends, and the mean will be greater than the median.

3.14 The completed table is Table 3.4.

Table 3.4 Calculating a Standard Deviation

X_i	$(X_i - M)$	$(X_i - M)^2$
6	−1	1
7	0	0
3	−4	16
10	3	9
7	0	0
9	2	4
Total 42		30

The mean is $M = 7.0$, variance is $V = 30/(6 - 1) = 6.0$, and SD is $s = \sqrt{6} = 2.45$.

3.15 a. $z = 1.22$; b. $X = 9.45$

3.16 4.5, 4.5, 3.03, 0.83

3.17 Type in an additional point 1 SD below the mean and another point 1 SD above the mean, and find that the mean is unchanged and the SD remains the same or changes by only a tiny amount.

3.18 a–d. I prefer the dot plot. Every time I do this task I remind myself how valuable it is to think of the mean as the balance point. Even so, with skew I often don't place the mean sufficiently far into the longer tail. Also, I often underestimate the SD, and need to learn how to increase my first guess to get a more accurate estimate of SD.

3.19 a. If the values are $X_1, X_2, ..., X_{12}$, then Q2, the median, lies half way between X_6 and X_7; Q1 lies half way between X_3 and X_4; Q3 lies half way between X_9 and X_{10}; IQR is the interval from Q1 to Q3; Range is the interval from X_1 to X_{12}; b. If X_{12} is made much larger, the mean, SD, and range will increase, while the median and IQR won't change; the z lines will be more widely spaced and $z = 0$ will be higher.

You may be wondering about how to place Q1 and Q3 when N is not neatly divisible by 4. If $N = 9$, or 10, then Q1 should be between X_2 and X_3, but where exactly? ESCI uses an Excel function that interpolates between the two values. Other software may use slightly different interpolation—choice of a formula for interpolation is rather arbitrary. In practice it's not worth worrying about exactly how it's done. Placing the quartile half way between the two values is usually a simple and acceptable strategy.

3.20 Think of Figure 3.11, but with a different X axis of IQ scores. The mean is at 100, and the $z = 1$ line is at 115 (i.e., one SD above the mean) and the $z = -1$ line is at 85. The curve is highest around 100, so we expect most scores around 100, in particular between about 85 and 115. A few scores would lie a little further out from the mean, a bit below 85 and above 115. Very few would be even further out, say around 50–60 or 140–150.

3.21 Six points (10% of 60) lie to the left of the 10th percentile, and 12 to the right of the 80th percentile (48, which is 80% of 60, lie to the left). Half the points, which is 30, lie between the first and third quartiles. No, answers wouldn't change. Percentiles require only ordinal scaling, but can just as easily be used with interval scales.

3.22 a. By definition, 50% of students score above the class median. If the score distribution is positively skewed, the mean will be greater than the median, so less than 50% of students will score higher than the mean. Only 40% scoring above the median is quite possible and suggests considerable positive skew; b. If one student has a very low score and all other students score the same, then the mean will be a little below their common score. All but one student will score above the mean. So it's not possible for everyone to score above the mean, but almost everyone can, just!

3.23 a. Calculating the mean and SD requires the equal-interval assumption, so we have an interval scale. Many researchers do make this assumption and calculate the mean and SD for rating scales such as this happiness scale, although we can doubt whether the difference in happiness represented by the change from 10 to 11 is really equivalent to the difference represented by the change from 2 to 3, or from 18 to 19; b. To calculate these values of M and s, we'd be making the equal-interval assumption. To interpret the values of M and s I would describe the scale fully and present a dot plot of the 30 ratings, with M and s illustrated as in Figure 3.9. I would explain the mean in terms of the amount of happiness corresponding to its position on the scale, and would similarly describe s as an interval on the scale and a corresponding step in amount of happiness. I would note that I'm assuming interval scaling, and would make some remarks about whether that seems reasonable. In general, I'm prepared to adopt common practice and assume interval scaling in such cases, but the issue is arguable; c. An alternative would be to present the dot plot and report the median, Q1, and Q3 to summarize, along with some remarks about only needing to assume ordinal scaling; d. The M of 17.6 is close to the maximum, 20, which is a boundary. So s as large as 3.7 must reflect many points considerably below the mean. There must be considerable negative skew.

3.24 The site is a gold mine of good and poor examples. Bullet points can be useful summary statements, but there are exceptions to most. There's no substitute for inspecting and thinking about lots of examples.

3.25 A good data picture is informative, conveys an accurate and fair message, and is quickly and easily understood by readers. It should be as simple as possible, and also look appealing.

3.26 The questions address basic issues in the design of good data pictures.

3.27 It's hard to find examples where a pie chart is the best picture, and some authorities advise never using pie charts. Go to tiny.cc/ediblepie for an interesting example.

4

The Normal Distribution and Sampling

Take a sample, then use the sample results to draw conclusions about the world—well, the particular population at least: As you know, that's statistical inference, the foundation of most research. Sampling, the first step, is our main business in this chapter. Then, in Chapter 5, we'll go on to the second step by discussing CIs. In this chapter, we'll start with more about the normal distribution, and then mostly we'll discuss samples and sampling. Watch out for the dance of the means, and the mean heap. Here's the plan for this chapter:

- Continuous distributions, z scores, and areas and probabilities
- The normal distribution
- The population and a random sample
- Sampling: Dance of the means and the mean heap
- A measure of sampling variability: The standard error
- Some statistical magic—the central limit theorem

To understand statistics it helps to appreciate dancing, and the dance of the means is our first dance. It illustrates sampling variability, which is a central idea that's vital to grasp intuitively. People usually underestimate sampling variability, so they often don't grasp how much uncertainty there is in data. Here we'll discuss our measure of sampling variability, the *standard error*; then, in Chapter 5, we'll use the standard error to calculate what we really want, the CI.

CONTINUOUS DISTRIBUTIONS

Figure 3.5 illustrated the smooth curve of the normal distribution and how we can think of such a curve as a pile of an extremely large number of potential data points. The variable X in that figure is a *continuous variable*, meaning it can take any value in some range—it's not restricted to taking separate, discrete values. By contrast, the number of eggs in a bag is a *discrete variable*, which can take only the distinct values 0, 1, 2, …, assuming we have no broken fractions of an egg. The continuous variable X might measure time to carry out a task, or the weight gained by a baby in a month. In practice we can only measure such variables to a certain accuracy—perhaps the weight gain is recorded as 173.2 g or 173.3 g—but, in principle, variables like time, length, and weight can take any (positive) value, so they are continuous.

> A *continuous variable* is a variable that can take any of the unlimited number of values in some range.

> A *discrete variable* is a variable that can take only distinct or separated values.

The smooth normal distribution curve of Figure 3.5 is the *probability distribution* of the continuous variable X. Figure 4.1 pictures a different probability distribution, which has positive skew, a longer tail to the right. Such a curve might picture the population of times that different people take to complete today's crossword—distributions of times often have positive skew. Instead of marking X values on the horizontal axis, the figure displays z lines and marks z scores on that axis, which we can call a z *axis*.

> The *probability distribution* of a continuous variable is a smooth curve, as in Figure 4.1.

Areas under the curve correspond to probability. *Probability* runs from a minimum of 0, meaning impossible, to 1, meaning certain, and probability distribution curves are designed so the total area under the curve is 1—after all, a study will certainly give us *some* results. We might for example judge that roughly 40% of the total area under the curve in Figure 4.1 lies between $z = -1$ and the mean, which implies that the probability is roughly .40 that a randomly chosen time to complete the crossword has a z score between -1 and 0. We could, alternatively, write that as "40%", that being an acceptable way to express a probability. Figure 4.1 also indicates that hardly any values are lower than $z = -2$, whereas a small proportion of values lie more than 2 SDs above the mean, and some even 3 SDs above it.

> Areas under a probability distribution correspond to *probability*. The total area under the curve is 1.

The height of the curve represents *probability density*, which is the label on the vertical axis. Probability density indicates how high the probability is "piled up" at various points along the z axis—in this case, piled highest between $z = -1$ and the mean, and decreasing smoothly to left and right. Don't be too concerned about probability density—treat it simply as a label on the axis, since we won't be using it further. The vital thing is that area under the curve represents probability. Now let's return to the normal distribution.

THE NORMAL DISTRIBUTION

In Chapter 3 and the section above we saw how z scores and z lines can be used with any data set and any variable, whatever the shape of its distribution. However, one common use of z is to represent the normal distribution in Figure 4.2, which is the *standard normal distribution*, with mean of 0 and SD of 1. We use z as the name of a variable that has this distribution—but we need to state clearly that's how we're using z, because z scores can also be used with any other shape of distribution.

> The *standard normal distribution* has mean of 0 and SD of 1. It's usually displayed on a z axis.

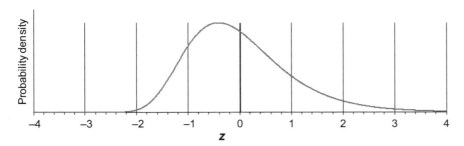

Figure 4.1. A probability distribution with positive skew. The vertical lines are z lines and the numbers on the z axis are z scores, in standard deviation units.

z Scores, Probabilities, and Areas

Figure 4.2 shows the approximate percentages of data points that lie in various z intervals, for any normal distribution. Distributions other than normal will almost certainly have different percentages—different areas—as Figure 4.1 illustrated. The normal curve is symmetric about the mean, and therefore the percentages are the same below and above the mean, as Figure 4.2 reports. About 34% of values lie between the mean and $z = -1$, and another 34% between the mean and $z = 1$. Some 2.5% lie in the left tail, below $z = -2$, and the same percentage above $z = 2$. About 95% of values lie within 2 SDs of the mean, as indicated by the shaded area. Of course, 50% of values lie to the left of the mean and 50% to the right. We can just as easily think of the percentages and areas in Figure 4.2 as probabilities: For example, the probability a randomly chosen z will lie between −1 and 0 is about .34.

IQ scores, which came up in Exercise 3.20, are a widely-known example of a variable that's set up to be approximately normally distributed. They are usually scaled to have a mean of 100 and SD of 15. Therefore a person scoring 115 would have a z score of 1, because 115 is 1 SD above the mean. That person would score higher than about 84% of the population of people to whom the distribution applies.

Can you figure out where that 84% came from? Make up a couple more simple examples of IQ scores, z scores, and percentages.

 Just a reminder. Pause, ponder, ask yourself questions, challenge your friends—and do these good things often.

You could think of the person scoring 115 as being at the $z = 1$ point in Figure 4.2. Add all the percentages to the left and get 84%, or simply add 50% (all the distribution to the left of the mean) and 34% for the distribution between the mean and $z = 1$. Another way of saying the same thing is to note that the person is at the 84th percentile of the distribution of IQ scores. As further examples you might observe that roughly 2/3 of people are likely to score between 85 and 115 and only about 2.5% of people above 130.

What about the thin tails? About 0.13% of data points lie below $z = -3$ and, of course, 0.13% above $z = 3$, which corresponds to an IQ score of 145. That means we expect on average about 1 person in 770 to score above 145. However, whenever we apply a statistical distribution like the normal distribution to a real-life example such as IQ scores we need to be cautious about the tails, because distributions often don't represent the real world very well at the extremes. As I mentioned in Chapter 3, of course IQ scores can't be negative,

Any normal distribution has about 68% of values within 1 SD of the mean, and about 95% within 2 SDs of the mean.

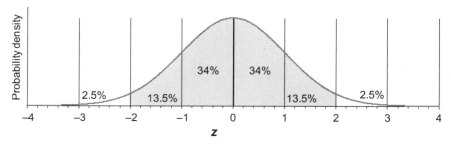

Figure 4.2. The normal distribution on a z axis. The percentages are approximate and refer to areas between the z lines, except that 2.5% refers to the whole tail area beyond $z = -2$ (left tail) and likewise beyond $z = 2$ (right tail). The shaded area between $z = -2$ and 2 is approximately 95% of the total area. The areas indicate probabilities.

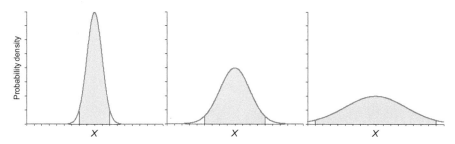

Figure 4.3. Three normal distributions, shown with the same units on the vertical and horizontal axes. The SD doubles from the distribution on the left to the one in the middle, and doubles again to the curve on the right. In every case, the shaded area extends from $z = -2$ to $z = 2$ and therefore marks about 95% of the area under the curve. The total area under each curve is 1.

even though the normal distribution continues left to minus infinity, as well as right to infinity.

You may be wondering what I mean by "between 100 and 115": Am I including or excluding 100 and 115? That's a good thought. IQ scores are typically given as whole numbers, with no decimal places—in other words IQ score is a discrete variable, taking only distinct values, like 94, 95, 96, and so on. Yet I'm referring to IQ scores, represented by X, as if they were continuous. For the moment, let's keep things simple by assuming X is continuous and ignore the fact that IQ scores are usually considered discrete. I'll come back to this issue.

The normal distribution is expressed by a mathematical function that's a little complicated, but requires only the mean and SD to specify the curve in full. To say that a bit more technically, the normal distribution is a *two-parameter* distribution: State the mean and SD, which are the two *parameters*, and the distribution is fully specified. Figure 4.3 pictures three normal distributions with different SDs. The SD doubles in size from the distribution on the left to the one in the middle, and doubles again to the curve on the right. In each case the central area between $z = -2$ and $z = 2$ is shaded, so about 95% of the area under each curve is shaded. In each case the total area under the curve is 1, corresponding to total probability of 1, or 100% of the data points. With the changing SDs, the heights need to change correspondingly, to maintain that fixed area under the curve. So the height halves from the distribution on the left to the one in the middle, and halves again to the curve on the right, and the area of shading is the same in each case.

The three curves in Figure 4.3 may look a little different, but they are all normal distributions. The relations between z and area, or probability, expressed in Figure 4.2 apply to all of them, as well as to every other normal distribution.

> The mean and SD are the two *parameters* that fully specify a normal distribution.

Polya

z Scores and X Scores

I hope you found it easy to swap back and forth between IQ scores, or X, and z scores, by keeping in mind that a z score is the distance from the mean, in units of the SD. In the previous chapter we used Equations 3.4 and 3.5 to translate from X to z, and from z to X. However, with normal distributions we usually have in mind a population. We follow the convention and use Greek letters for the *population parameters*, so the population mean is μ (mu) and SD is σ (lower case sigma). The corresponding *sample statistics* are mean, M, and standard deviation, s, and we usually use M as our estimate of μ, and s as our

> *Sample statistics are mean, M, and standard deviation, s. Corresponding population parameters are mean, μ, and standard deviation, σ.*

estimate of σ. Thinking of populations we can use μ and σ rather than M and s to calculate z scores, so Equation 3.4 becomes

▶ Calculate z from X.

$$z = \frac{X - \mu}{\sigma} \qquad (4.1)$$

If $X = 85$, then $z = (85 - 100) / 15 = -1$ as we expect. Equation 3.5 becomes

▶ Calculate X from z.

$$X = \mu + z\sigma \qquad (4.2)$$

If $z = 1.50$, then $X = 100 + 1.5 \times 15 = 122.5$, which we'd probably report as 122.

Do we need to make any assumptions about the scale of measurement if we want to use z scores?

(I know you are reaching for the coffee, your bike, or your cellphone. I said I wasn't going to mention such things so often.)

· We need to assume interval scaling because we are using the mean and SD. If we are willing to assume only ordinal scaling we should not be using the mean, SD, or z scores.

? ## Quiz 4.1

1. A normal distribution
   a. is symmetrical, meaning both tails are similar, without skew.
   b. has one mode.
   c. is defined by two parameters: the mean, μ, and the standard deviation, σ.
   d. All of the above
2. Geo takes a statistics exam and scores exactly at the class average. What is Geo's z score?
   a. < 0
   b. 0
   c. > 0
   d. We can't tell.
3. On the next exam, Geo's teacher tells him that he has $z = 3$. Should Geo be happy?
   a. Yes, this means he did much better than average.
   b. No, this means he did much worse than average.
   c. Sort of— it means he is again around average.
   d. Trick question, you can't turn exam scores into z scores.
4. Which of the following is true about the standard normal distribution?
   a. The total area under the curve is −1.
   b. The mean is 1, the standard deviation is 0.
   c. About 95% of all scores fall within 2 SDs of the mean.
   d. All of the above.
5. What is the difference between a discrete variable and a continuous variable? Give an example of each.
6. We often use a <u>sample / population</u> statistic, represented by a <u>Roman / Greek</u> letter, to estimate the <u>sample / population</u> parameter, represented by a <u>Roman / Greek</u> letter.
7. Just one last reminder!

Finding z Scores and Probabilities

Very often we'll work with populations that we assume are normally distributed. One reason for this is that many common statistical methods require this assumption, although in Chapter 16 we'll discuss other possibilities. A second reason is that a fair number, although far from all, of the variables we encounter in the world have approximately a normal distribution—I'll discuss that remarkable fact later in this chapter. Fortunately, in many cases it's reasonable to use statistical methods based on normal distributions, even for populations that are only approximately normally distributed.

We need a way to translate accurately between z scores and area or probability. We'll use such translations to help calculate CIs and other good things. Some statistics books provide tables that do the job, or you can use Excel or other software, or an online calculator. Here we'll use the **Normal** page of ESCI.

4.1 Find the z score for an IQ of 60, and the IQ score for a z score of 1.2.

4.2 With Figure 4.2 in mind, state at least three approximate rules about normal distributions that express how z scores relate to areas—or probabilities or percentiles. Choose rules you think it would be handy to remember.

esci 4.3 Open **ESCI intro chapters 3–8** and go to the **Normal** page. Read any labels and popout comments of interest, and explore the controls. Can you figure out what's going on? If you like, look for the red numbers.

esci 4.4 If necessary, below red 3 click the checkbox on, and type in 100 as the mean and 15 as the SD of X. Type in a brief label for the units if you wish.

esci 4.5 Click at red 2 to show the **Mean line**, and at red 1 select **Two tails** and **Areas**. Use the big slider at the bottom to shift the cursors until the **Two tails** area is .05, meaning 5%. When I did all that I saw Figure 4.4.

esci 4.6 Note the z axis at the bottom and corresponding X axis above. What z score gives that upper tail area of .025? What can you say about the approximate values in Figure 4.2? It's $z = 1.96$ that gives that upper tail area, as Figure 4.4 illustrates. The left cursor is at $z = -1.96$ and the area of the two tails is .05; the remaining area, between $z = \pm 1.96$, is .95, or 95%. That 1.96 value of z comes up often, so it's worth remembering. Mention it casually at parties to make sure everyone knows you are a statistics groupie.

esci 4.7 As you move the slider, you can focus on z displayed at the bottom, or X at the top. The z and X values of the cursor positions are shown under the figure. Select **One tail** at red 1. What proportion of randomly chosen people are likely to score at least 120 on the IQ test? What proportion between 70 and 80? For the moment, assume X to be a continuous variable.

> The area under a normal distribution to the right of $z = 1.96$ is .025, and to the left of $z = -1.96$ is also .025. The area between $z = -1.96$ and $z = 1.96$ is .95. So 95% of values in a normal distribution are within 1.96 SDs of the mean.

Hint: It's often useful to make a sketch of a normal curve and shade in the area of interest. You may need to use ESCI twice, to find two areas, which you need to write down and add or subtract.

esci 4.8 Make up a few more questions about values and probability, and use ESCI to find the answers. You could use a different X variable, with different mean and SD. Swap with friends.

Let's return to the issue of IQ score as a discrete variable. We can think of an underlying continuous variable, X, that can take any value, which is then rounded to the nearest integer as the IQ score. (An integer is a number like 0, 1, 2, −15, or 107, with no fractional part.) Then we could for example calculate the probability a person will score 100 by finding the area under the curve between the X values of 99.5 and 100.5, because any X value in that interval is rounded to an IQ score of 100.

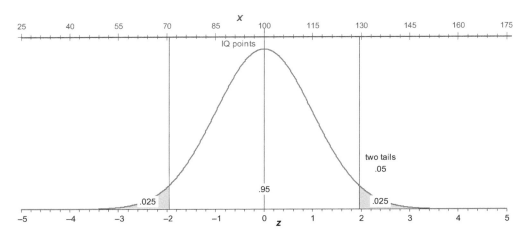

Figure 4.4. A normal distribution with both X and z axes, where X displays IQ scores. The cursors are positioned at $z = 1.96$ and $z = -1.96$ to give two tails with total area of .05. From the **Normal** page of ESCI.

esci 4.9 Find that probability—that a randomly chosen person will give an IQ score of 100.

esci 4.10 What's the probability a person scores between 100 and 115, first excluding those two values from the interval of interest, then including both?

esci 4.11 One international grading system for students' academic performance calculates GPAs on a scale from 1 to 7. Suppose in a particular college the students' GPA values are approximately normally distributed, with mean of 4.7 and SD of 0.8. What proportion of students are likely to score at least 4? What proportion less than 3?

esci 4.12 That GPA scale extends only from 1 to 7, yet the normal distribution extends from minus infinity to plus infinity. What about the upper tail of the normal distribution corresponding to GPA scores greater than 7?

POPULATION AND SAMPLES

We're getting closer to pictures of sampling variability. The next step: Consider a population having a normal distribution, and samples taken from that population. We'll shift from IQ scores to a new example. Suppose you are investigating the climate change awareness of college students in your country. You decide to use the Hot Earth Awareness Test (HEAT), which is a well-established survey—actually, I just invented it—that asks questions about a respondent's knowledge, attitudes, and behavior in relation to climate change. You plan to test a sample of students to estimate the mean HEAT score for students in your country.

Now we do some statistical assuming. Suppose there's a large population of students in your country, and their HEAT scores are normally distributed with mean of μ and SD of σ. You take a random sample of N students from that population, obtain their scores, and calculate the mean, M, and standard deviation, s, of your sample. You'll use M as your point estimate of μ. Later you'll calculate a CI to tell us the precision of your estimate—how close M is likely to be to the unknown μ.

Our statistical model assumes a normally distributed population and random sampling. This is the model we need in Chapter 5 to calculate CIs. The assumptions are:

- *Normality.* This strong assumption about the population distribution is often but not always reasonable.
- *Random sampling.* Recall that there are two vital aspects:
  1. Every member of the population must have an equal probability of being sampled; and
  2. All members of the sample must be chosen independently.

You should always keep these assumptions in mind, and judge how closely they are met in a particular situation. It's probably reasonable to assume at least approximate normality of HEAT scores. You will probably need to use a convenience sample of students, but, as we discussed in Chapter 2, you should aim to come as close as practical to random sampling, and judge how representative your sample is of the population.

Always keep in mind the distinction between population and sample. We know *M* and *s* for our sample, although repeating the experiment would of course give different *M* and *s*—that's sampling variability. We don't care about our *M* and *s*, except to the extent they are useful as estimates of the unknown population parameters μ and σ.

Now comes a critical moment. I've said that μ and σ are unknown. However, to use a simulation to explore sampling we need to assume particular values for μ and σ. Working with the computer, there are fundamental differences from the usual situation of a researcher:

1. For a simulation we need to assume a population distribution—usually normal—with stated values of μ and σ.
2. We'll simulate taking many, many samples.

In real life, in stark contrast, the researcher doesn't know μ and σ, can only hope the population is approximately normal, and usually takes only one sample. However, computer simulations can be highly revealing, even if they are different from carrying out real-life research.

◀ Our *statistical model* assumes a normally distributed population and random sampling from the population.

◀ We use sample statistics *M* and *s* as point estimates of population parameters μ and σ.

◀ In simulation, unlike in real-life research, (i) we specify μ, σ, and the shape of the population; and (ii) we take many samples.

 4.13 Open the **CIjumping** page. Have a look around. At red 2 click **Population**, and below red 1 make sure the **Normal** button is selected. Use the sliders to adjust μ and σ. As you change σ, the vertical scale changes so the curve always has a convenient height.

4.14 Set μ = 50 and σ = 20. (The manual for the HEAT test suggests these values are typical.) At red 2 click **Fill random** and see most of what's in Figure 4.5. ESCI can't display the infinite number of dots under the curve that, notionally, make the population of potential HEAT scores, but you get the idea. We'll assume the population of HEAT scores in your country is normally distributed, with μ = 50 and σ = 20, so ESCI is now displaying that population.

4.15 Click the **Clear** button near red 3—nothing happens, but we're getting set. Click near red 4 so **Data points** is clicked on, and unclick both **Sample means** and **Dropping means**. Yes, still nothing, but now a dramatic moment: We're about to take our first random sample.

4.16 Use the spinner near red 4 to select your sample size, perhaps *N* = 20 or whatever you choose. Take a deep breath, then click the **Take sample** button. You should see a scatter of *N* points just below the curve, as in Figure 4.5. They are the data points of our sample. That's our simulated

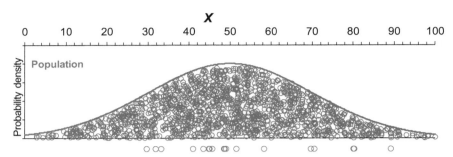

Figure 4.5. A normally distributed population with $\mu = 50$ and $\sigma = 20$, and, below, a scatter of points that's a single random sample, $N = 20$, of HEAT scores taken from the population. From **CIjumping**.

equivalent of finding a random sample of N students and testing them on the HEAT.

esci 4.17 Take more samples. You might try the **Run-Stop** button. The scatters of data points for successive samples vary greatly—they appear to be dancing wildly. As we'll discuss, randomness is intriguing and weird, and sample-to-sample variation is often large.

esci 4.18 Watch your samples carefully. Do you observe that the sampled points in the long run are about equally often below and above μ? That they tend to cluster fairly close to μ, but values further from μ are quite common? That just occasionally you get an extreme point? Those features of sampled values follow directly, of course, from the shape of the population, and our sampling, which we assume gives every data point in the population an equal chance of being chosen.

SAMPLING: THE MEAN HEAP AND DANCE OF THE MEANS

The next important idea is the *sampling distribution of the sample mean*, and to discuss this we'll need some pictures of sampling variability. Imagine taking lots of independent samples from a population—we'll do that in a moment. The means of those successive samples vary, but they tend to cluster around the population mean, μ. A collection of many such sample means forms a distribution in its own right, called the sampling distribution of the sample mean. If we could take an infinite number of samples, their infinite number of means would form a normal distribution, thus demonstrating that the sampling distribution of the sample mean is normal. It's an excellent question why this sampling distribution is normal in shape—more on that shortly.

> The *sampling distribution of the sample mean* is the distribution created by the means of many samples.

As I mentioned, always distinguish carefully between playing around on the computer with simulations of many experiments, and running and analyzing a single experiment in real life. One vital lesson from computer simulations is that any data we obtain from a real experiment could easily have been different—perhaps very different—if we'd happened to take a different sample. That's sampling variability, which is often disappointingly large. Simulations can help us build good intuitions about the extent of sampling variability, and how it depends on N and other factors.

In the exercises that follow, I'll keep thinking of X as representing HEAT scores, but you can, if you wish, make up your own interpretation of X and the sampling of X values. Perhaps X represents the time, in seconds, to carry out some dexterity task, and you take samples of six-year-old children and measure the time they take to complete the task. Or X could be the number of seeds in the large seed pod of a particular type of tree, and to take a sample you find N seed pods in the forest.

esci 4.19 We'll now work towards generating pictures like those in Figure 4.6.

    a. Click the **Clear** button and click near red 4 so **Sample means** and **Dropping means** are both clicked on. Take a sample. The sample mean appears as a green dot just below the scatter of data points.

    b. Near red 4, values are shown for M and s, the sample statistics for the latest sample you've taken. Compare these with the values we've chosen for their population counterparts, μ and σ.

esci 4.20 Click **Take sample** a few times. The means drop down the screen, as in Figure 4.6. Watch the values bounce around, and compare them with the μ value you set. Each click is equivalent to running an experiment, meaning you take a new sample of size N, obtain the HEAT scores for those N students, then calculate M and s. Click **Run-Stop** and watch the sample means dance down the screen. It's the *dance of the means*, as in Figure 4.6, which illustrates the extent of variation or bouncing around of the mean, from sample to sample. Imagine (or play on your computer) your choice of backing music for the dance. It's sampling variability in action: Enjoy!

The *dance of the means* is my name for a sequence of sample means falling down the screen.

esci 4.21 Click **Run-Stop** to stop the dance, then **Clear**. Now think about two predictions: First, if you change N, what will happen to the dance? Will larger N give a wider, more frenzied dance—the means tending to vary side-to-side more—or a narrower, more restrained dance? What about smaller N? Make your predictions—write them down. The two halves of Figure 4.6 illustrate the dance for different values of N. Are your predictions consistent with what that figure shows?

esci 4.22 Second, what would happen if you increase or decrease σ? Any change to the width of the dance? Which way would it change? Lock in your predictions.

esci 4.23 Try, say, two different values of N, and two of σ, to test your predictions. Which change—a different N or a different σ—tends to make more difference?

esci 4.24 Click **Mean heap** near red 5 to see dancing means collect into a heap of green dots, as Figure 4.7 illustrates. This is the sampling distribution of the mean, which I call the *mean heap*. It's another picture of sampling variability. Run the simulation to build up a good-sized heap. (Not quite time for a quick coffee!) Do this for at least two very different values of N, and keep track of how wide the heap appears: Record for each N your eyeball estimate of the SD of the mean heap. (To help estimate an SD, recall the rule of thumb that about 95% of the values in a normal distribution lie within 2 SDs of the mean.) Figure 4.7 shows the mean heap for two values of N. Should we prefer a narrow or a wide mean heap? Translate your conclusion into advice for a researcher who is considering what size sample to take.

The *mean heap* is my name for the sampling distribution of the sample mean. It's a pile of green dots that represent sample means.

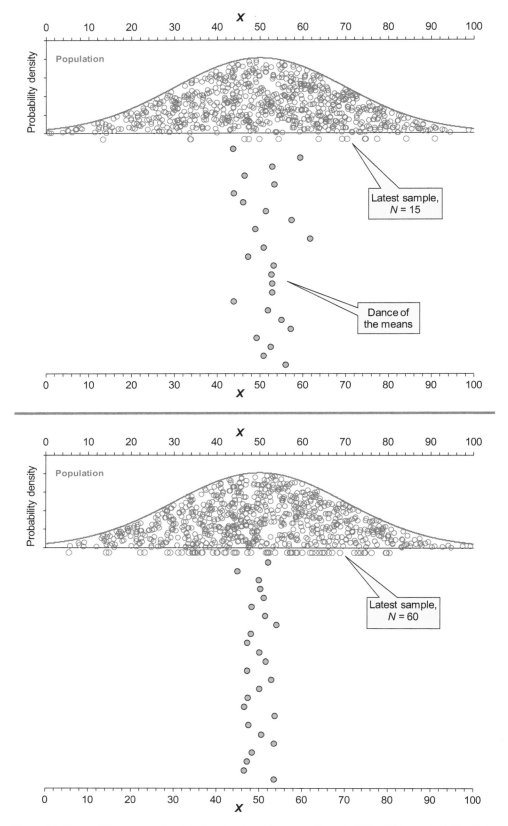

Figure 4.6. Dance of the means—the dots dropping down the screen. Upper half: N = 15. Lower half: N = 60. In each case the population distribution is displayed at the top, and the latest sample appears as the scatter of N data points in a horizontal line just below.

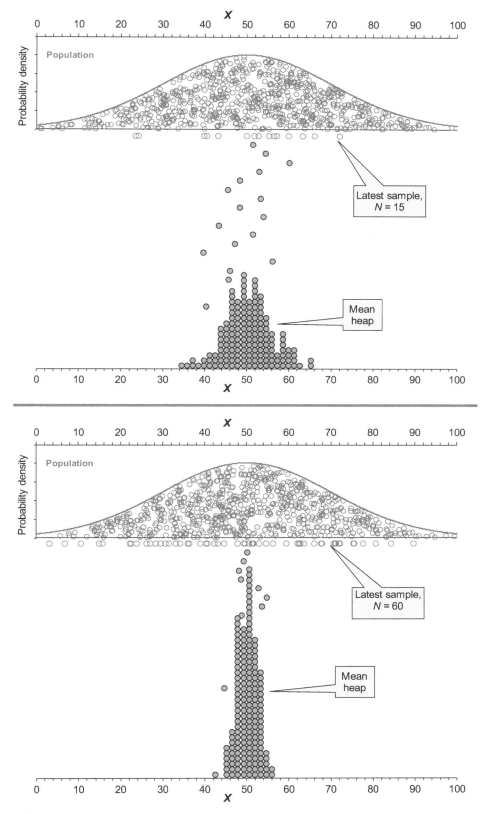

Figure 4.7. The mean heap, in each case after taking 175 samples. Most means are in the heap, a few are still dancing down. Upper half: $N = 15$, and my eyeball estimate of the SD of the mean heap is about 5. Lower half: $N = 60$, and the SD of the mean heap looks to be about 3.

Take an infinite number of samples: The distribution of their means is the *theoretical sampling distribution of the sample mean*. (The mean heap is my name for the *empirical sampling distribution of the sample mean*.)

4.25 Click **Sampling distribution curve** near red 5. The normal distribution displayed on the mean heap, as in the lower panel of Figure 4.8, is the *theoretical sampling distribution of the sample mean*. We can compare that with the mean heap, which is the *empirical sampling distribution of the sample mean*—the heap of the means we've taken so far. The curve is the distribution theoretically predicted from knowing μ, σ, and N. (In ESCI, the curve is scaled vertically so it fits to the mean heap. Take more samples, and the mean heap and sampling distribution curve both grow higher—but not wider; the SD of the sampling distribution remains the same.)

? Quiz 4.2

1. The use of confidence intervals for estimating population parameters from sample statistics depends on two important assumptions. What are they?
2. To conduct random sampling,
   a. participants must be selected in groups and all members in the population must have an equal chance of selection.
   b. participants must be selected in groups and some portions of the population must be given a higher chance of being selected.
   c. participants must be selected independently and all members in the population must have an equal chance of selection.
   d. participants must be selected independently and some portions of the population must be given a higher chance of being selected.
3. The _____ is the distribution created by the means of many samples.
4. From exploring the dance of the means, you know that
   a. due to sampling variability, any given sample might provide a poor estimate of the population mean.
   b. even though individual sample means dance around, the distribution of sample means is normally distributed around the population mean.
   c. the larger the sample size, the less sample means dance around the population mean.
   d. All of the above.
5. The larger the value of σ, the <u>more / less</u> sample means tend to vary from the population mean.
6. The theoretical sampling distribution of the sample mean is a <u>normal / non-normal</u> distribution that has <u>larger / smaller</u> spread than the population distribution.

THE STANDARD ERROR

A chant: "The *standard error* is the standard deviation of the sampling distribution of the sample means."

Here comes the next important idea: The SD of the sampling distribution of the sample mean is important, and so is given a name: It's called the *standard error* (SE). The SE summarizes the breadth or spread of the mean heap—or its curve. It's a measure of sampling variability. Yes, the SE is a particular case of an SD. That continues to confuse many people, so you can feel a tiny bit smug when you understand. It's worth making a chant. Dismay your friends at parties by intoning: "The standard error is the standard deviation of the sampling distribution of the sample mean." You can easily explain by pointing to the mean heap, and the vital distinction between population and sample—between the normal distribution in the upper panel (the population) and that in the lower panel (the sampling distribution of the mean) in Figure 4.8.

The *standard error* is the standard deviation of the sampling distribution of the sample mean.

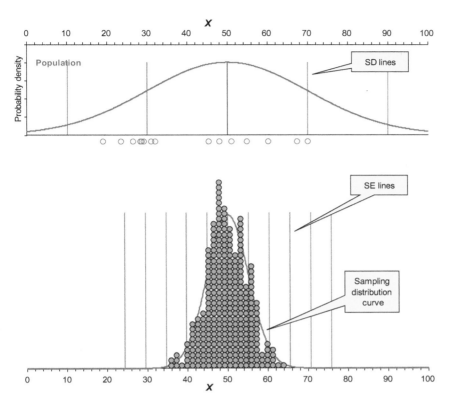

Figure 4.8. The upper panel displays the population distribution, with lines marking SD units, showing $\sigma = 20$. Below is the mean heap of 300 sample means. The superimposed curve is the theoretical sampling distribution of the mean, with lines marking standard error (SE) units. In this example, $N = 15$ and $SE = \sigma/\sqrt{N} = 20/\sqrt{15} = 5.16$.

Happily, the formula is reasonably simple. Here it is:

$$SE = \frac{\sigma}{\sqrt{N}}$$ (4.3)

Formula for SE.

where, as usual, σ is population SD and N is sample size. Here I'm still assuming we know σ, and therefore can use that formula. In practice we hardly ever know σ, and in Chapter 5 we'll find how to drop the assumption that σ is known.

The SE formula is vital, and one you need to explore and remember. Informally, think of the SE as telling us roughly how far from the population mean the sample means are likely to fall.

esci 4.26 Click **SE lines** near red 5 and see vertical lines marking SE units across the sampling distribution curve, as in the lower panel of Figure 4.8. Do these look as though they are the z lines marking SD units of that normal distribution?

esci 4.27 Near red 5 find **Curve SE** and note its value. The popout comment explains that it's the SE of the sampling distribution curve. Does it change if you take further samples? Explain.

4.28 Click **SD lines** near red 2 (if necessary, click **Population** and unclick **Fill random**). SD lines for the population curve are displayed, as in the upper panel of Figure 4.8. Compare these with the SE lines for the sampling distribution curve in the lower panel. In each case you can regard the lines as z lines for the respective normal distributions. (To see the sampling distribution curve more clearly, unclick **Sample means** near red 4.)

▶
A formula to remember is $SE = \sigma/\sqrt{N}$. The SE varies inversely as the square root of sample size.

The sampling distribution of the mean is normally distributed—as the curve on the mean heap illustrates—with mean μ and SD of $\sigma/\sqrt{N}$. Therefore, $SE = \sigma/\sqrt{N}$, which is Equation 4.3, a vital formula to remember. Post it to your social media site, for safe-keeping? The mean heap and its curve are centered symmetrically under the population. The SD of that curve is smaller than that of the population—by a factor of $\sqrt{N}$. As I said, the SE is a particular case of an SD. Note how I'm deliberately talking about SE and SD all at once—not trying to confuse you, but to warn you that people often don't speak or write clearly about the SE. Just remember that our chant says it all: "The SE is the SD of the sampling distribution of M." Here's an even simpler version: "The SE is the SD of the mean heap."

▶
To halve the SE, we need N that's four times as large.

If N is made four times bigger, $\sqrt{N}$ becomes twice as large, so the SE should be halved. Compare the lower halves of Figures 4.6 and 4.7, for which $N = 60$, with the upper halves, for which $N = 15$. Does the lower dance seem about half as varied, half as wide as the upper? The lower mean heap about half as wide as the upper? Unfortunately, to halve the amount of variation we need to take a sample four times as big. That's bad news for researchers trying to make precise estimates because, as we'll see, the SE determines precision. A broad mean heap signals a large SE and imprecise estimates. Perhaps you are reminded of the approximate guideline in Chapter 1, that using N four times as large is likely to give a CI about half as long? If so, well done—that's a great intuition, because CI length depends heavily on the SE.

We like greater precision, so we like a restrained, narrow dance of the means, a narrow mean heap, a small SE and, therefore, a large N. When I ask my classes "What do you want for your birthday?", they know to answer immediately "Big N!"

 4.29 Use the values of σ and N that you set, which are shown near red 1 and red 4, to calculate SE. Check that the value shown at **Curve SE** is correct.

 4.30 Suppose HEAT scores have population mean 50 and SD of 20 in your country. For samples with $N = 30$, what is the SE? Use the formula to calculate it, then use ESCI to check. Describe the sampling distribution of the mean.

4.31 That's a typical textbook problem. Invent and solve a few more. Swap with a friend.

4.32 Someone asks "What's a standard error?" How do you respond?

 4.33 Make up some exercises for discovery learning of the $SE = \sigma/\sqrt{N}$ relation. You could suggest first making predictions, or guesstimates, of the SE of the mean heap (and the sampling distribution curve) for a few widely separated values of N of your own choosing. Turn off **Sampling distribution curve**, then, for each of those N values, take at least 50 samples and eyeball the SD of the mean heap—which, as you know, is the SE. See Figure 4.8. Compare those eyeballed estimates with the ESCI values near red 5 for the **Mean heap SE**, which is the SE of the displayed mean heap. What does a sketched graph of those SE values against N look like? How accurate were the original predictions? Find someone who doesn't know about SE to try out your exercises.

We've come a long way on our journey towards calculating CIs. We've seen a dance and a heap, both of which are pictures of sampling variability. We've discovered the SE, which is a measure of sampling variability, and have a formula for calculating it. Now for some magic, before we jump to the next chapter for MoE and CIs. Do you recall the excellent question asking why the sampling distribution of the mean is normal in shape?

SOME STATISTICAL MAGIC: THE CENTRAL LIMIT THEOREM

Why do statisticians choose the normal distribution as a statistical model? Because of the *central limit theorem*, which is a central result in theoretical statistics. Consider this example: Suppose T is the time it takes you to get home from your workplace or campus, and therefore T is the sum (i.e., total) of the times it takes for all the components of the journey. Perhaps these are: T_1, time to walk from your desk to the elevator; T_2, waiting time until an elevator arrives; T_3, time the elevator takes to deliver you to the ground floor; ... lots more components, including T_i, time spent traveling on the bus; ... T_N, time taken to unlock the door of your home and step inside. Therefore,

$$T = T_1 + T_2 + T_3 + \ldots T_i + \ldots T_N$$

Each of the T_i is likely to vary from day to day, and will influence how T, the sum of all the T_i, varies from day to day. Let's assume that all the T_i are independent, meaning that they don't influence each other on any particular day. That assumption may not be realistic—for example, on a wet day many are likely to be longer—but for now we'll assume independence anyway. The central limit theorem says this amazing thing: The distribution of T, the total time, is approximately normal. Most remarkably, this is the case almost regardless of the distributions of the various T_i! The times for the components of my journey may vary in all sorts of different ways, but, provided they are all independent, their sum is approximately normally distributed. The normal distribution appears out of thin air, and therefore represents some fundamental aspect of the universe.

The theorem also states that the more components there are to be added—the larger N is—the closer the distribution of T to the normal. Also, the theorem applies if T is the mean, rather than the sum, of the T_i—which isn't too surprising, because the mean is just the sum divided by N.

The upper panel of Figure 4.8 shows the population of HEAT scores and the lower panel, a heap of sample means. The central limit theorem tells us that the sampling distribution in the lower panel is approximately normal—*for virtually any shape of population in the upper panel*! A bit of statistical magic. Our sampling has been from a normal population, but the central limit theorem tells us that the mean heap and the sampling distribution curve (in the lower panel) will be close to normal, even if our population (upper panel) has some quite different shape, perhaps a totally weird shape. Also, with larger N (samples of larger size), the curve is even closer to normal.

The *central limit theorem* states that the sum, or the mean, of a number of independent variables has, approximately, a normal distribution, almost whatever the distributions of those variables.

Sampling From Non-normal Populations

Let's take samples from populations having some non-normal shapes. First we'll explore a *rectangular distribution*, also referred to as a uniform distribution.

 4.34 Click **Clear**, then at red 1 click **Rectangular** to select that population shape. Display it in the upper panel, perhaps filled with dots. Can you think of a variable likely to have this population shape?

 4.35 With N of 20 or more, take samples—let it run for a bit—and observe the shape of the mean heap. Click **Sampling distribution curve** and compare that curve with the mean heap.

 4.36 Now try a very small value of N. How well does the sampling distribution curve fit the mean heap? In what ways does it not fit well? What happens if you use $N = 1$? Explain.

With moderate or large N, the heap of means looks to be normally distributed, even though all data points were sampled from a population with a distribution that's nothing at all like normal. The smooth bell shaped curve appears by magic from thin air! Yes, that's the central limit theorem in action.

> For larger samples (larger N) the sampling distribution of the sample mean is closer to normally distributed, with mean μ and standard deviation of $\sigma/\sqrt{N}$.

When you click to display the sampling distribution curve in the lower panel, ESCI uses the population values you chose for μ and σ, and sample size N, to calculate a normal curve for display, with mean μ and standard deviation of $\sigma/\sqrt{N}$. It does this whatever the shape of the population. Therefore, if that sampling distribution curve appears to fit the mean heap of sample means coming from a rectangular population, we have an illustration of the central limit theorem, and also evidence that Equation 4.3 for the SE applies for a rectangular as well as a normal population.

When the population is not normally distributed, the sampling distribution is only approximately normal, but the ESCI simulations show that the approximation is surprisingly good for the rectangular distribution. Figure 4.9 shows what ESCI gave me when I took 550 samples with $N = 3$. Even for N as tiny as 3, much smaller than we ever wish to use in our research, the sampling distribution curve looks to fit the heap of means very well. For larger N, the fit is even closer.

One reason the sampling distribution here is a close approximation to the normal is that the population is symmetric. If the population has a skewed distribution, the sampling distribution is typically not so well approximated by the normal—at least not for smaller N. Skewed distributions come in numerous different shapes, but ESCI includes just one. It's skewed to the right and you can choose the degree to which it is skewed.

 4.37 Repeat the last three exercises for a skewed population distribution. At red 1 click **Skew**, then use the spinner to specify the amount of skew. Observe the shape for all the values available, from 0.1 to 1. Do Exercises 4.34–4.36 for small skew and for large skew.

Figure 4.10 shows what ESCI gave me when I took 400 samples of size $N = 6$, from a skewed population, with skew spinner set to 0.7. As usual, I used $\mu = 50$ and $\sigma = 20$. In the lower panel, compare the normal sampling distribution curve and the mean heap: The heap looks to be closer to normal in shape than the population, but is still positively skewed. Its peak is

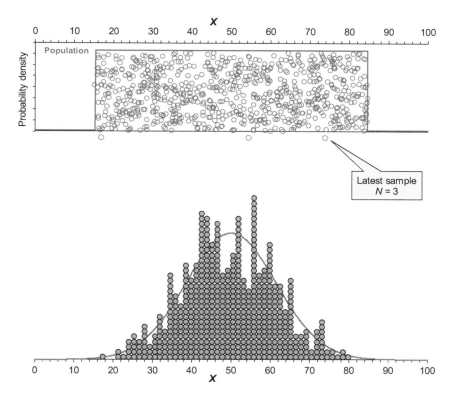

Figure 4.9. Sampling from a population with a rectangular distribution. The lower panel displays the means of 550 samples of size $N = 3$. The latest sample is the 3 dots just below the population. The curve is the normally distributed sampling distribution calculated using $\mu = 50$, $\sigma = 20$, and $N = 3$, so the curve has mean of 50 and SD of $20/\sqrt{3} = 11.55$.

a little to the left of the mean of the sampling distribution curve and it has dots on the right, suggesting a tail to the right. The left tail of the curve, however, looks to be empty of sample means. Even so, the fit of the curve to the mean heap is not terrible. With N even smaller than 6, the mean heap is more different from normal, and with larger N, as we'd always hope, the normal sampling distribution is a better approximation to the mean heap. With a smaller amount of skew, the fit will also be closer.

It's an important conclusion that sampling distributions of the mean are often normal, or closely approximated by a normal distribution, at least unless samples are very small. It's important because much of the standard statistical theory that underlies CIs and other aspects of statistical inference assumes that sampling distributions are normal. Yes, we often assume that populations are normal, which guarantees that the sampling distribution of the mean is normal. But even if a population departs somewhat from normal, the sampling distribution is likely to be close to normal—thanks to the central limit theorem. And having a normal *sampling* distribution is often the crucial thing for our statistical techniques. It implies, for example, that we can routinely use Equation 4.3 in most common situations.

Polya

Thanks to the central limit theorem, the sampling distribution of sample means is often close to normally distributed, even for non-normal populations.

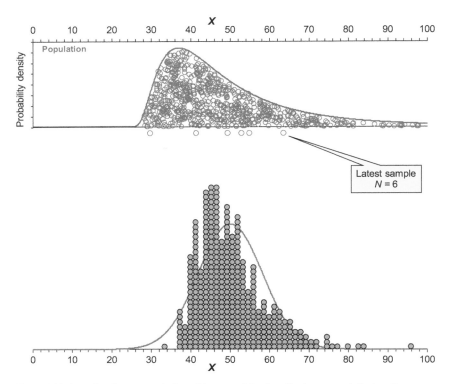

Figure 4.10. Sampling from a population with strong right skew. The lower panel displays the means of 400 samples of size $N = 6$. The curve is the normally distributed sampling distribution calculated using $\mu = 50$, $\sigma = 20$, and $N = 6$, so the curve has mean of 50 and SD of $20/\sqrt{6} = 8.16$.

That's the good news, but we still need to be alert for cases in which the sampling distribution may not be close to normal. One case to watch for is the combination of strong skew and small samples. Chapter 16 has more on these issues, but until then I'll generally assume the central limit theorem gives us sampling distributions that are sufficiently close to normal for us to use the standard methods for estimation. These are coming soon.

The Normal Distribution in the World

Thanks to the central limit theorem, many—although far from all—variables in the world have, approximately, a normal distribution.

Think of my "journey home" example, in which total time T is approximately normally distributed, even though it's the sum of many components that differ greatly. The individual components may have all sorts of different distributions, but, if they are independent, the central limit theorem can do its work. It turns out that quite a few variables in the world have approximately a normal distribution, probably because they are a bit like T. Suppose the length of an adult's arm, or the time it takes a penguin egg to hatch, are determined by the addition of lots of independent influences—maybe various genes, food habits, temperature and other environmental factors, perhaps some random influences, and so on—then we can expect arm length or egg hatching time to be approximately normally distributed. Provided enough of the influences are independent, and that they add to give total length or hatching time, then the central limit theorem applies. No doubt mere addition of independent influences is much too simplistic a biological model, but the idea probably does explain why the normal distribution often appears in nature, at least approximately. The central limit theorem and the normal distribution do seem to express some basic aspects of how the natural world functions.

Enjoy and marvel at the central limit theorem, which gives meaning to the beautiful normal curve, and links it firmly to real life. It's also the basis for most of what we'll do in statistics.

It's nearly time for MoE and CIs, but they deserve a new chapter. So it's time to write your take-home messages for this chapter. To help you think back over this chapter and to give a couple of hints about Chapter 5, here are a few more exercises.

4.38 What's the total area under a normal distribution and what does it represent? How much of it lies within 3 SDs of the mean?

4.39 Remarkably, scores on a number of standard tests of IQ have for decades been increasing at an average rate of about 3 points per decade, meaning an increase of 15 points, a full SD, over the last 50 years (Flynn, 2012). This is the Flynn effect, named for the New Zealand scholar James Flynn. Therefore, if an IQ test is to remain current, and continue to give a mean of 100 in the general adult population, it needs to be revised periodically. Later versions will need to be more difficult, so a person at the population mean still scores 100. Suppose we have 2005 and 2015 versions of an IQ test, each with mean 100 and SD of 15 in the general adult population at the date the version was published. Assuming an increase of 3 points per decade, we would expect someone who now scores 100 on the 2015 version to score higher on the 2005 version, also taken now. How much higher? Why?

4.40 With the same assumptions, consider testing people from the general adult population in 2015.

a. What proportion of these people would you expect to score above 100 on the 2015 version? (Assume IQ score is a continuous variable.) What proportion above 130?

b. If the same people were also tested in 2015 on the 2005 version, what proportion would you expect to score above 100 on that old version? Above 130? Compare your answers for the two versions.

c. What thoughts do you have about testing with the 2005 version? What additional assumption are you making?

4.41 In the United States, a capital offender with mental retardation can avoid the death penalty. Scoring below 70 on an IQ test is often regarded as an important part of the evidence for mental retardation. If you are the defense lawyer for such an offender, would you wish them to be tested by a recently-revised test, or an old version? Explain.

4.42 Consider IQ scores with population mean = 100 and SD = 15. If $N = 36$, what is the SE? How large a sample would you need for the SE to be no more than 2?

4.43 A news report of a study claims that 45% of children show signs of a food allergy, almost double the figure of 20 years earlier. How would you respond?

4.44 What do you want for your birthday? Why?

4.45 With a normally distributed population in ESCI, take a large number of samples. Examine the mean heap, then turn on the sampling distribution curve and SE lines.

    a. About what proportion of the sample means fall within 2 SEs of the overall mean? About what proportion of samples would you expect to have a sample mean that's within $2 \times SE$ of the population mean, μ? Explain.

    b. If you did the same investigation of sampling with a non-normal population, would your answers change? Try it if you like. Explain.

4.46 Look back over the chapter. Perhaps the figures prompt useful memories. Revise your list of take-home messages if you wish.

? Quiz 4.3

1. Sample means tend to be normally distributed around the true population mean. The standard deviation of the distribution of sample means is
   a. the SE.
   b. z.
   c. X.
   d. the MoE.
2. What is the formula for the SE?
3. The SE gets smaller as _____ increases or as _____ decreases.
4. The _____ states that the sum or mean of many independent variables will tend to be normally distributed.
5. We find that all / many / few / no variables in psychology and biology have normal distributions, perhaps because the phenomena studied in these fields are often the sum of lots of independent factors.
6. For the SE to be halved, N needs to be _____ times smaller / larger. If N is 9 times larger, the SE will be larger / smaller by a factor of _____.

⌂ Take-Home Messages

■ The probability distribution of a *continuous variable* X is a smooth curve that plots probability density against X, as in Figures 4.1 and 4.2. Areas under the curve represent probability, and the total area under the curve is 1.

■ The *standard normal distribution* has mean 0 and standard deviation 1. *Take-home picture*: Figure 4.2, which shows some approximate areas under the normal curve: About 34% of cases lie between $z = 0$ and $z = 1$, and about 95% within 2 SDs either side of the mean. The **Normal** page of ESCI provides accurate areas for any z score of a normal distribution.

■ *Sample statistics* are mean M and standard deviation s, and *population parameters* are mean μ and standard deviation σ. Equations 4.1 and 4.2 (also Equations 3.4 and 3.5) allow translation in either direction between X values and z scores.

■ We often use a *statistical model* that assumes random sampling from a normally distributed population.

■ *Take-home movie*: The dance of the means, as in Figure 4.6, which illustrates the extent of sampling variability.

■ The *mean heap* is a nickname for the empirical sampling distribution of the sample means. After a notionally infinite number of samples it becomes the theoretical sampling distribution, which is illustrated in ESCI by the sampling distribution curve. *Take-home picture*: The mean heap, as in Figures 4.7 and 4.8.

- For a normally distributed population, the sampling distribution of the sample means is normally distributed with mean μ and standard deviation of $\sigma/\sqrt{N}$, as in Figure 4.8.

- The SD of the sampling distribution is called the *standard error* (SE), which prompts the chant, "The standard error is the standard deviation of the sampling distribution of the sample mean." More briefly, "The SE is the SD of the mean heap." The formula $SE = \sigma/\sqrt{N}$ is a vital one to remember.

- The *central limit theorem* states that the sum, or mean, of a large number of variables that are independent has, approximately, a normal distribution, pretty well whatever the distributions of those variables.

- Even for non-normal populations, the sampling distribution of the mean is often approximately normally distributed, thanks to the central limit theorem. For larger sample sizes (i.e., larger N), the sampling distribution becomes closer to normal.

- Sampling distributions are not always very close to normally distributed, for example when the population is strongly skewed and N is small.

- The central limit theorem can explain why quite a few, although far from all, variables occurring in nature are approximately normally distributed.

 ## End-of-Chapter Exercises

1) For a standardized exam of statistics skill, scores are normally distributed: $\mu = 80$, $\sigma = 5$. Find each student's z score:
   a. Student 1: $X = 80$
   b. Student 2: $X = 90$
   c. Student 3: $X = 75$
   d. Student 4: $X = 95$

2) For each student in Exercise 1, use ESCI to find what percent of students did better. (Assume X is a continuous variable.)

3) Gabriela and Sylvia are working as a team for their university's residential life program. They are both tasked with surveying students about their satisfaction with the dormitories. Today, Gabriela has managed to survey 25 students; Sylvia has managed to survey 36 students. The satisfaction scale they are using has a range from 1 to 20 and is known from previous surveys to have $\sigma = 5$.
   a. No mathematics, just think: which sample will have the smaller SE: the one collected by Gabriela or the one collected by Sylvia?
   b. When the two combine their data, will this shrink the SE or grow it?
   c. Now calculate the SE for Gabriela's sample, for Sylvia's sample, and for the two samples combined.
   d. How big a sample size is needed? Based on the combined SE you obtained, does it seem like the residential life program should send Gabriela and Sylvia out to collect more data? Why or why not? This is a judgment call, but you should be able to make relevant comments. Consider not only the SE but the range of the measurement.

4) Rebecca works at a nursing home. She'd like to study emotional intelligence amongst the seniors at the facility (her population of interest is all the seniors living at the facility). Which of these would represent random sampling for her study?
   a. Rebecca will wait in the lobby and approach any senior who randomly passes by.
   b. Rebecca will wait in the lobby. As a senior passes by she will flip a coin. If the coin lands heads she will ask the senior to be in the study, otherwise she will not.

    c.   Rebecca will obtain a list of all the residents in the nursing home. She will randomly select 10% of the residents on this list; those selected will be asked to be part of the study.

    d.   Rebecca will obtain a list of all the residents in the nursing home. She will randomly select 1% of the residents on this list; those selected will be asked to be part of the study.

5) Sampling distributions are not always normally distributed, especially when the variable measured is highly skewed. Below are some variables that tend to have strong skew.

    a.   In real estate, home prices tend to be skewed. In which direction? Why might this be?

    b.   Scores on easy tests tend to be skewed. In which direction? Why might this be?

    c.   Age of death tends to be skewed. In which direction? Why might this be?

    d.   Number of children in a family tends to be skewed. In which direction? Why might this be?

6) Based on the previous exercise, what is a caution or warning sign that a variable will be highly skewed?

 ## Answers to Quizzes

Quiz 4.1

1) d; 2) b; 3) a; 4) c; 5) A continuous variable can take on any value within its range; a discrete variable can only take on distinct values. For example, height is a continuous variable, but number of car accidents is a discrete variable; 6) sample, Roman, population, Greek.

Quiz 4.2

1) normal distribution of the variable being studied and random sampling of participants; 2) c; 3) sampling distribution of the sample mean; 4) d; 5) more; 6) normal, smaller.

Quiz 4.3

1) a; 2) $SE = \sigma/\sqrt{N}$; 3) N, σ; 4) central limit theorem; 5) many; 6) 4, larger, smaller, 3.

Answers to In-Chapter Exercises

4.1   −2.67, 118

4.2   About 34%, or one third, between $z = 0$ and either $z = -1$ or $z = 1$; about 95% between $z = -2$ and $z = 2$; about 2.5% in either tail, beyond $z = -2$ or $z = 2$; about 5% total outside $z = \pm2$.

4.6   1.96. The approximate values in Figure 4.2 are usefully close to accurate.

4.7   .092, .068 (If you prefer to think in percentages, 9.2% and 6.8%.)

4.9   Click **Two tails** and position the cursors as close as possible to $X = 99.5$ and 100.5. The area between, which is the answer, is reported as .026.

4.10   Sketch a picture. Find areas for 99.5, 100.5, 114.5, and 115.5. Add or subtract areas to find the answers: .32 and .36.

4.11   .81, using 4.0 as the cursor position; .017, using 3.0 for the cursor.

4.12   It's important to bear in mind any such limitation on the applicability of the normal distribution. However, if fit is questionable, it's probably in the far tails that fit is most in doubt, and what happens in the far tails of a distribution often doesn't matter much in practice. With mean of 4.7 and SD of 0.8, just .002 of values under the normal curve lie above 7.0 and only .0002 beyond 7.5, so for practical purposes the lack of perfect fit of the upper tail—which represents impossible GPA scores—is unlikely to be a problem.

4.19   b. Compare M and s, which are different for each sample and shown near red 4, with μ and σ shown near red 1.

4.21   Larger N gives smaller sampling variability, M values generally closer to μ, less bouncing around, more sober dance. Smaller N the reverse.

4.22   Larger σ means broader spread in the population, so larger sampling variability, M values generally bouncing around more, and a more drunken dance.

4.23 That depends of course on the sizes of the changes to N and σ, but generally changes to σ have more dramatic effects.

4.24 Narrow. Larger N gives a narrower heap. This indicates smaller sampling variability, which is more desirable.

4.26 Observe that about one third of the area under the curve lies between the mean and one SE either lower or higher, and about 95% of the area lies within 2 SE lines below and above the mean. In other words, check that the lines in relation to the curve appear as in Figure 4.2. Similar proportions of dots in the mean heap should lie in the various intervals defined by the SE lines, which are the z lines of the sampling distribution curve. So the lines do appear to be z lines marking SD units for this normal distribution.

4.27 It doesn't change as we take more samples, because the SE is the SD of the curve in the lower panel, which doesn't change its spread as we take more samples.

4.29 Use $SE = \sigma/\sqrt{N}$.

4.30 3.65. The sampling distribution of the mean is normal, with mean $= \mu = 50$ and SD $=$ SE $= 3.65$.

4.32 You could state one of our chants, while pointing to the mean heap. Explain that the SE is the SD of that heap of sample means.

4.33 There's lots of evidence that it can be a good learning strategy—for yourself or someone else—to first make predictions, then find what happens, then compare and draw lessons. A graph of SE against N would show SE dropping slowly as N increases: N four times larger means SE half the size.

4.34 Random numbers chosen from an interval, often between 0 and 1, should have a rectangular distribution because every value in the interval should have the same chance of occurring. The last two digits of the phone numbers, or license plates, of your friends are likely to be more or less random, and so have a rectangular distribution.

4.35 It fits remarkably well, although of course means cannot fall outside the range of the distribution, so the tails, or extreme tails, of the sampling distribution are empty.

4.36 It still fits quite well, although once again the tails are empty. With $N = 1$, each "sample" comprises a single point, so the heap of "means" is just a heap of points, and in the long run this will match the population shape, which here is a rectangular distribution.

4.37 Distributions of response time—the time it takes to complete some task—are often found to be positively skewed, perhaps as in Figure 4.1. The distribution of personal or household income is an example with strong right skew, because most incomes are low or medium and relatively few are high. Values from 0.1 to 1 specify skew that ranges from just visibly different from normal, to very strongly skewed. The sampling distribution normal curve is a closer fit to the mean heap for less skew and/or larger N; the mean heap is more clearly non-normal for more skew and smaller N. With $N = 1$, again the sampling distribution will in the long run be the same as the population distribution. (The distribution with skew of 0.7 is what the **Describe** page uses when you click the **Generate data** button to ask for a data set with right skew. For left skew it uses a mirror image of that distribution.)

4.38 The total area is 1, which represents total probability, or certainty. Use **Normal** to find that almost all of the area, actually 99.7% of it, lies within 3 SDs of the mean.

4.39 We expect them to score 3 points higher, because the earlier test was easier by 3 points.

4.40 a. Testing in 2015 on the 2015 version, 50% should score above 100. I used **Normal** to find that 2.3% should score above 130; b. Testing in 2015 on the 2005 version, we expect anyone on average to score 3 points higher on the old version, so anyone scoring over 97 on the new version should score over 100 on the old version. The **Normal** page tells us that 57.9% score over 97 on the new and thus over 100 on the old. For 130 on the old I entered 127 into **Normal** and found 3.6% as the answer. Comparing 50% with 57.9% and 2.3% with 3.6% suggests that even fairly small shifts in the mean—just 3 points—can shift the percentages considerably. The most dramatic change is in the tail proportions—there is more than a 50% increase (from 2.3% to 3.6%) in the percentage of people scoring above 130; c. We're assuming random sampling from the whole adult population, and that the average increase of 3 points per decade is the same at every level across the distribution. Flynn (2012) discussed these and many other related issues, including likely causes of the effect. I've given answers assuming IQ is a continuous score, although you can easily use the **Normal** page to find percentages assuming IQ scores are integers. For example, to find the percentage of people scoring above 100, enter $X = 100.5$ and find 48.7% score higher.

4.41 A person is likely to score higher on an old test, so you would want your client tested on the latest reputable test available, which would give the best indication of their status now and, incidentally, the lowest score. If that test were a number of years old, you could argue that the score obtained in testing today should be reduced by 0.3 points for each year since the test was revised and published. If no adjustment were made, a person with mental retardation could be executed merely because they were tested with an outdated test. A current test should give 2.3% of the population scoring below 70, but a ten year old test, used today, would give only 1.4% of the population scoring below 70—to find that value I entered 67 into the **Normal** page. See Flynn (2012, Chapter 4) for a fascinating discussion, or search online for "Flynn effect and the death penalty". Understanding z scores and the normal distribution can be a life-or-death issue!

4.42 $SE = \sigma/\sqrt{N} = 15/\sqrt{36} = 2.5$. Set $SE = 2$ and the same formula gives $2 = 15/\sqrt{N}$, and therefore $N = (15/2)^2 = 56.25$. Choose $N = 57$, the next highest integer, and SE will be a little less than our target of 2. Later we will use this logic to find how large an experiment we need to run to achieve precision as high as we would like.

4.43 You would want to know full details of the studies on which the percentages were based. What were the populations of children, and how were the samples drawn? What size samples? What definition of food allergy was used and how were children in the samples assessed? How precise were the estimates of the percentage having an allergy? You would be particularly concerned that such characteristics were comparable for the two studies, otherwise it may not make sense to compare the old and new estimates. Think of further Open Science issues: You would also want to know whether either study had been selected from a number of available studies because of its results—perhaps a particularly low estimate 20 years ago, and a particularly high one now.

4.44 Big N, because larger samples give more precise estimates and thus better answers to our research questions.

4.45 a. About 95% of sample means should fall within 2 SEs of the overall mean, because the sampling distribution is normally distributed, its SD is the SE, and one of the characteristics of any normal distribution is that about 95% of values lie within 2 SDs of the mean. The mean of the sampling distribution is μ, the population mean, and therefore about 95% of the sample means should lie within $2 \times$ SE below or above μ; b. With a non-normal population, if the normal sampling distribution curve is a good fit to the mean heap, then same answer. In other cases, for example if we have a strongly skewed population and very small N, the percentage could be different.

5

Confidence Intervals and Effect Sizes

This is the chapter in which a trumpet fanfare announces a more detailed discussion of CIs. At one level, most people have a reasonable idea what a CI tells us, as we discussed in Chapter 1. However, at a deeper level CIs are tricky and it's fascinating as well as important to try to understand them well. In this chapter I discuss four ways to think about and interpret CIs. Here's the agenda:

- Errors of estimation and MoE
- Trumpets for CIs, and the dance of the CIs
- The *t* distribution
- An interlude on randomness
- Effect sizes
- Four ways to think about and interpret CIs

These are all ideas at the heart of estimation, and, therefore, at the heart of this book. We'll see more dancing and, as usual, pictures and simulations will help us develop good statistical intuitions.

DISCUSSING CIS INFORMALLY

I started Chapter 1 with this example: "You read this in the news:

"Public support for Proposition A is 53%, in a poll with a 2% margin of error."

We summarized the result as "53% support, 95% CI [51, 55]". Figure 5.1 pictures that, with some labels as reminders. Our point estimate of the true level of support in the population of likely voters is 53%. We can refer to the line segments either side of the mean as *error bars*. Each error bar has length MoE, the margin of error. The two error bars together picture the 95% CI. The total length of the CI is twice the MoE, and the ends are the lower and upper limits. I'll discuss the two curves in a moment.

Error bars are the line segments either side of the mean in a picture of a CI. The length of each error bar is MoE.

While discussing CIs informally, I made statements such as:

- We can be 95% confident the interval [51, 55] includes the true value of support in the population.
- MoE, which is 2%, is the largest likely error of estimation, so our point estimate (53%) is most likely no more than 2% away from the true value.
- If we repeat the poll, using the same procedure but with a new sample, we'll quite likely get a result in the original CI, although we may not.

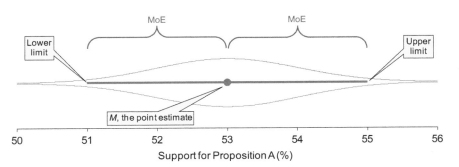

Figure 5.1. The result of the poll example in Chapter 1, with error bars to picture the 95% CI. Same as Figure 1.1, with addition of labels and cat's-eye picture.

The *cat's-eye picture* indicates how the plausibility, or likelihood, that a value is the true value is greatest near *M* and decreases out to the limits of the CI, and beyond.

Now for the curves. The upper curve in Figure 5.1 is the same curve as in Figure 1.2, which indicates how likelihood, or plausibility, varies across and beyond the CI. The lower curve is simply the mirror image of the upper curve, and the two curves make the *cat's-eye picture* of a CI. That picture is fattest in the middle, which tells us that values around 52% to 54% are the most likely for the true level of support in the population, and that lower and higher values get progressively less likely, or less plausible, the further they are from *M*. I can add a fourth informal statement about our CI:

▪ The cat's-eye picture illustrates how the plausibility, or likelihood, that any particular value is the true value is greatest near the point estimate and decreases smoothly out to the limits of the CI, and in fact beyond those limits.

Later in this chapter I'll develop statements like those into the four ways to think about CIs—which are our basis for estimation. Use any of those four to help you interpret any CI you read about or calculate. Now let's pick up the discussion from Chapter 4. First we need to discuss estimation error.

Polya ## ESTIMATION ERROR AND MOE

Look back at Figure 4.8. We were sampling from a population distribution of HEAT scores, assumed to be normally distributed with $\mu = 50$ and $\sigma = 20$. Using $N = 15$, we calculated the SE to be $\sigma/\sqrt{N} = 20/\sqrt{15} = 5.16$, assuming $\sigma = 20$ is known. Later we'll discuss a technique that allows us to drop that last, rather unrealistic assumption, which is good news, because in practice we rarely know σ. SE lines are displayed in the lower panel of Figure 4.8. Exercise 4.45 asked what proportion of sample means in a mean heap like that displayed in the figure would fall within 2 SEs of μ. Equivalently, what area under the sampling distribution curve lies between 2 SEs below and above the mean? Consider Figure 4.8 as you choose your answer.

Just a quick reminder. I'm hoping you are now strongly in the habit of pausing, discussing, and writing whenever I ask questions in the text. Or any other time.

The answer is about .95, or 95%, because that's the proportion of area within 2 SDs of the mean of any normal distribution, and the SE is the SD of the sampling distribution. Again, I'm taking every opportunity to use SE and SD in the same sentence, so you can feel good about understanding what others might find confusing. Remember our chants!

 With the display of Figure 4.8 on my screen in **CIjumping**, near red 5 I clicked **±MoE around** μ, and near red 7 I clicked μ **line**. I saw the display in Figure 5.2, which has green vertical lines placed approximately 2 SEs either side of μ = 50. I'll call those lines the *MoE lines*. There's a green stripe at the bottom between them.

What is the *z* score corresponding to *exactly* 95% of the area under a normal distribution? We know that it's approximately 2, but what is it more accurately? (Think, consult,…) Knowing that number shows you are a real statistics groupie.

It's 1.96, because 95% of the area under any normal distribution lies within 1.96 SDs either side of the mean. The MoE lines are placed to enclose 95% of the area under the sampling distribution curve so that, in the long run, 95% of sample means will fall between the MoE lines. The MoE lines are therefore positioned 1.96 × SE either side of μ—just inside the SE lines that are 2 SEs below and above the mean.

Now we need to focus on *estimation error*. Each dot in the mean heap is a value of *M*, the sample mean. How good an estimate of μ is it? The center of the mean heap is at μ, and the sample means, shown by the green dots, generally fall a little to the right or left of μ. The distance away they fall is (*M* − μ), the *estimation error*, which is different for every sample. The mean heap, and the sampling distribution curve, illustrate that (i) most means fall fairly close to μ, so have small estimation errors; (ii) many fall a moderate distance away; and (iii) just a few fall in the tails of the sampling distribution, signaling large estimation errors.

> The **estimation error** is (*M* − μ), the distance between our point estimate based on the sample, and the population parameter we are estimating.

We defined MoE, the *margin of error*, as the largest likely estimation error. We usually choose "likely" to mean 95%, so there's a 95% chance the estimation error is less than MoE, and only a 5% chance we have been unlucky and our sample mean *M* falls in a tail of the sampling distribution. Because the MoE lines in Figure 5.2 mark the central 95% of the area under the curve, they are at a distance of MoE below and above μ. The 95% of means that fall between the lines have estimation error less than MoE. As we discussed above, the lines are positioned 1.96 × SE from μ. Recall the formula for SE, assuming σ is known. Putting it all together, we can state that

The *margin of error* (MoE) is the largest likely estimation error. Choosing "likely" to mean 95%, the MoE is 1.96 × SE.

$$\text{MoE} \;=\; 1.96 \;\times\; \text{SE} \;=\; 1.96 \;\times\; \frac{\sigma}{\sqrt{N}} \tag{5.1}$$

This is the MoE when σ is assumed known.

The trumpets are very close, but let me first invite you to use ESCI to explore MoEs and estimation errors.

 5.1 At ESCI's **CIjumping** page, click near red 5 to display the mean heap, sampling distribution curve, and SE lines. Take samples using μ = 50, σ = 20, and *N* = 15. Near red 5 click **±MoE around** μ and near red 7 click μ **line**. Your screen should resemble Figure 5.2.

5.2 What percentage of green dots do you expect will fall beyond the MoE lines to the left? Beyond them to the right? Explain.

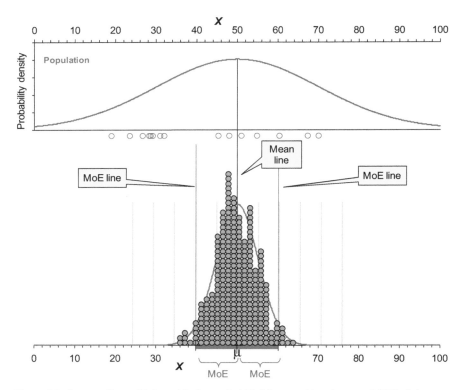

Figure 5.2. Same as Figure 4.8, but with the vertical MoE lines marking the central 95% of the area under the sampling distribution curve. Mean, μ, is also marked with a vertical line. The stripe at the bottom between the MoE lines extends a distance of MoE either side of the mean μ = 50, where MoE = 1.96 × SE = 1.96 × 5.16 = 10.12 (assuming σ = 20 is known). In the long run, 95% of sample means will fall between the MoE lines.

esci 5.3 Click **Dropping means** near red 4, run the simulation, and watch how often a mean falls outside the MoE lines to the left or right.

a. Still assuming $N = 15$, state an interval of HEAT values that should in the long run include 95% of sample means.

esci 5.4 Now consider $N = 36$. Calculate MoE. Set $N = 36$ near red 4 and take samples.

a. Are the MoE lines positioned about where you would expect?

b. Again state an interval that in the long run should include 95% of sample means.

c. Make sure **±MoE around μ** is clicked on, and note the MoE value shown near red 5. Check that it's the same as you calculated.

esci 5.5 How would you expect MoE to change for different σ? Test out your prediction. For any value of σ you try, observe about how many green dots fall outside the MoE lines.

Imagine now a big drum roll…

CALCULATING A CI: SOUND THE TRUMPETS!

Keep an eye on Figure 5.2 or ESCI as you read this paragraph. For 95% of means the estimation error is less than MoE, meaning that $|M - \mu|$ < MoE. (The vertical bars mean *absolute value*, so $|M - \mu|$ is the positive value of the difference, ignoring any minus sign. The absolute value is never less than zero.) In other words most values of M are close to μ, where "close to" means "less than MoE away from". When we run ESCI simulations we assume μ is known, and observe lots of values of M. By contrast, in real life as researchers we don't know μ—we want to estimate it—and have only one observed value of M. Even so, MoE can help us enormously. Considering our single M, where do we think μ lies? Yes, most likely close to our M. In fact within MoE of our M would be our best bet, likely to be correct for 95% of M values. If we make an interval extending MoE below and above our M, that interval is likely to include μ, which is what we're trying to estimate. What do you think we might call such an interval?

For 95% of samples, $|M - \mu|$ < MoE, meaning that for most samples M is close to μ. Therefore in most cases μ is close to M.

Did that previous paragraph make the slightest sense? The argument it presents is at the heart of estimation, and important enough to consider in more detail. The ESCI simulations we've been using require us to assume μ and σ are known. Figure 5.3, by contrast, shows all we know as typical researchers: our single sample of $N = 15$ data points and their mean. Whenever you see a data set, as in Figure 5.3, first imagine in your mind's eye the population, and recognize you don't know its μ or σ. You usually don't even know whether it's normally distributed, although here we're assuming it is. Next, visualize the dance of the means and the mean heap. We have a single green dot, but it's randomly chosen from the infinite dance. The width of the dance—the amount the means bounce around from side to side—or the width of the mean heap, would tell us how far our M might be from the μ we want to estimate.

We use our M to estimate μ, and we know most values of M are close to μ. Therefore, for most samples μ is not far away from our M, in fact, within MoE of our M. If we mark out an interval extending MoE either side of our M, for most samples we'll include μ. Sound the trumpets! As I'm sure you've guessed, that interval is the *confidence interval* (CI).

We define the interval $[M - \text{MoE}, M + \text{MoE}]$ as the CI. In 95% of cases, that interval will include the unknown population mean μ. That's the interval we want, and the reason for trumpets. The formal definition is:

> The 95% **confidence interval** (CI) is an interval calculated from sample data that's one from an infinite sequence, 95% of which include the population parameter. For example, the CI on the sample mean is $[M - \text{MoE}, M + \text{MoE}]$. In the long run, 95% of such intervals include μ.

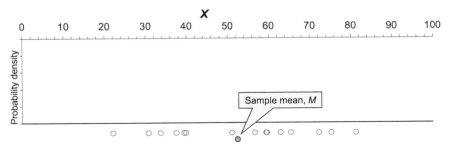

Figure 5.3. All a researcher knows: A single sample of $N = 15$ data points and their mean, $M = 52.5$.

Recall Equation 5.1, which stated that MoE = $1.96 \times SE = 1.96 \times \sigma/\sqrt{N}$. Therefore the 95% CI is:

This is the 95% CI when σ is assumed known.

$$\left[M - 1.96 \times \frac{\sigma}{\sqrt{N}}, M + 1.96 \times \frac{\sigma}{\sqrt{N}} \right] \qquad (5.2)$$

For eyeballing purposes, you can use 2 in place of 1.96.

As a first example, consider Figure 5.2. MoE is 10.12 and therefore if we observe $M = 52.50$, which is the sample mean in Figure 5.3, we can calculate our 95% CI to be [52.50 − 10.12, 52.50 + 10.12], which is [42.38, 62.62]. It easily includes $\mu = 50$, because our M did not fall in either of the tails outside the MoE lines.

For statistics groupies: $z_{.95} = 1.96$, meaning 95% of the area under the normal curve lies between $z = -1.96$ and $z = 1.96$. Also $z_{.99} = 2.58$.

We've been using the fact that any normal distribution has 95% of its area between $z = -1.96$ and $z = 1.96$. I'll write that as $z_{.95} = 1.96$, where the ".95" refers to the area captured by that value of z below and above the mean of a normal distribution. Can you use ESCI's **Normal** page to find the value of $z_{.99}$?

Simply click to select **Two tails** and **Areas**, and move the cursors until the central area is .99, to find $z_{.99} = 2.58$. That's important enough to be another number for the statistics groupies, worth remembering.

? ## Quiz 5.1

1. Although samples can help us understand a population, the sample mean is not always equal to the population mean. The difference between the sample mean and the population mean is known as _____.
2. The _____ is the typical or standard amount of estimation error, whereas the _____ of _____ is the largest likely estimation error.
3. For a 95% CI we find the MoE by multiplying the standard error by 1.96. Where does the 1.96 come from?
4. Once we know the MoE, the CI is found by simply _____.
5. Which of the following is (or are) true?
   a. Sample means tend to be normally distributed around the true mean. That is, most sample means will be relatively close to the true population mean, some will be further away on either side, and even fewer will be quite far away on either side.
   b. The SE is the standard deviation of the normal distribution of sample means around the true mean.
   c. The MoE is based on the SE and indicates the furthest distance most sample means will fall from the population mean.
   d. A 95% CI gives boundaries around the sample mean that indicate the largest estimation error likely, given the sample characteristics.
6. A 95% CI is one of a(n) _____ sequence, ____ % of which include the sample / population mean.

The *level of confidence*, or *confidence level*, is the 95 in "95% CI". It specifies how confident we can be that our CI includes the population parameter μ.

Level of Confidence, C

We can label the 95 as the *level of confidence*, C, because it specifies how confident we can be that a CI includes μ. It's also referred to as the *confidence level*. As you probably know we almost always choose C = 95, but other values are possible and you can use ESCI to experiment with them. In Equations 5.1 and 5.2, the 1.96 value is actually $z_{.95}$, so for the 99% CI we would simply replace that with $z_{.99}$, which is 2.58. More generally, for the C% CI we would use $z_{C/100}$, and write the C% CI as:

This gives the C% CI when σ is assumed known.

$$\left[M - z_{C/100} \times \frac{\sigma}{\sqrt{N}}, M + z_{C/100} \times \frac{\sigma}{\sqrt{N}} \right] \qquad (5.3)$$

And therefore:

$$\text{MoE}_C = z_{C/100} \times \frac{\sigma}{\sqrt{N}} \qquad (5.4)$$

> This gives the MoE for a $C\%$ CI, σ assumed known.

where MoE_c is of course MoE for a $C\%$ CI.

You might have noticed a problem: MoE is calculated from σ but, you ask, how can we do that when we don't know σ? You're correct, but as a first step we'll keep assuming σ is known and use it to calculate MoE and the CI. Later I'll introduce a way to avoid that assumption about knowing σ. OK, formula overload—time for some ESCI play.

esci 5.6 Near red 5 click **±MoE around** μ, and red 7 click μ **line**. With $N = 15$, take samples. Compare with Figure 5.4, upper panel. Do you have any means beyond MoE? What percentage would you expect in the long run?

esci 5.7 The green stripe at the bottom has length $2 \times$ MoE. We place a line of that length over each sample mean, to mark an interval extending MoE either side of the mean. Near red 6 click **Known** and **CIs**, and there they are. Run the simulation and enjoy the *dance of the CIs*. Music? Compare with Figure 5.4, lower panel.

> The *dance of the confidence intervals* is the sequence of CIs for successive samples, as in Figure 5.4, lower panel.

esci 5.8 A CI *includes* μ, or *captures* μ, every time, unless the sample mean falls outside the MoE lines. Run the simulation and watch. What percentage of CIs will in the long run miss μ? What percentage will miss to the left? To the right?

esci 5.9 Unclick **±MoE around** μ to remove the MoE lines. Near red 7, in the purple area, click **Capture of** μ. (μ **line** must also be clicked on.) The CIs all change color. If a CI doesn't capture μ, it's red. Do you have any red CIs? Explain what a red CI means.

esci 5.10 Run the simulation, enjoy the dance of the CIs to your favorite music, and watch **Percent capturing** μ near red 7. What happens near the start of a run? What happens after a minute or two? After 10 minutes? After an hour or more?

esci 5.11 Run it again with a very small value of N, and then with $N = 100$, the maximum ESCI allows. What can you say about the extent of bouncing around? Does the length of a single CI tell you anything about the bouncing, the width of the dance?

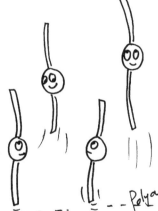

How should we interpret a CI? The dance of the CIs gives the basic answer. Our CI is one of an infinite sequence of possible CIs generated from the infinite sequence of possible samples, any one of which we might have obtained in our experiment. In the long run, 95% of those CIs will capture μ, and 5% will miss and be red in ESCI.

It's a basic CI slogan: "It might be red!" We can be 95% confident that our CI captures μ, but it might be red. In your lifetime of calculating and reading and considering numerous 95% CIs, around 95% will include the population parameters they estimate, and 5% will be red. In other words, on average 19 out of 20 will include the parameter and just 1 will miss and be red. Occasionally you'll find an opinion poll report such as "Support for the proposition was 53%, plus or minus 2%, 19 times out of 20"—this is what that last comment is referencing.

> For any CI, bear in mind "*It might be red!*" It might be one of the intervals that doesn't capture μ, although in real life we'll never know.

It's a great convenience that ESCI can display in red the CIs that miss μ. Alas, in real life CIs don't come in color: You can never be sure whether any particular CI should be red or not.

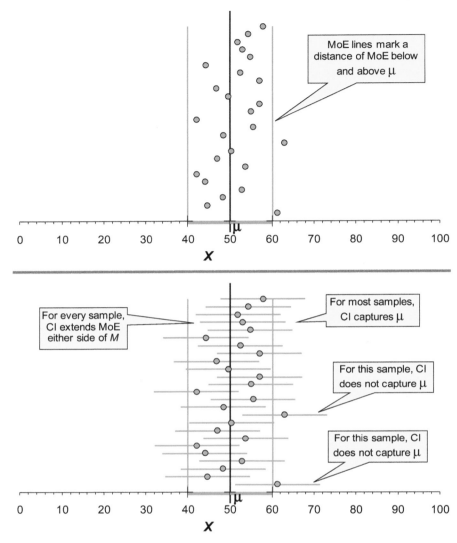

Figure 5.4. Dance of the means for $N = 15$, with the same dance in the two panels. A vertical line marks $\mu = 50$. In each half of the figure a stripe at the bottom extends MoE either side of μ, and the green MoE lines are displayed. Most means fall between those lines, just two happen to fall outside them. In the lower half, error bars of length MoE either side of each mean are displayed: These are the 95% CIs, and this is the dance of the CIs. Most CIs capture μ; only for the two means falling outside the MoE lines does the CI fail to include μ.

5.12   What would you expect if we change C, the level of confidence? Would 99% CIs be shorter or longer than 95% CIs? For higher confidence of capturing μ, would you need a smaller or a larger net? What about 90% or 80% CIs? Note down your predictions.

▶
For larger
C, the CI is
longer, for
smaller C it is
shorter. A 99%
CI is longer
than a 95% CI.

esci   5.13   Near red 6 is the spinner to set C. Read the popout. Change C and test your predictions. Does it make sense that CIs sometimes change color as you change C? Explain. (*Note:* The spinner will give you values up to 99, but you can type in values up to 99.9. Type in a value, then press Enter.)

5.14 Play around with *C*. Think back to Figure 4.8, the mean heap, and MoEs and the percentage of the mean heap the MoE lines include. Any surprises as you vary *C*?

5.15 Suppose you take a sample of *N* = 25 IQ scores and observe *M* = 106.6.

  a. Calculate the 95% CI for the mean of the population from which the sample came. Use σ = 15, as usual for IQ scores. What might you conclude?

  b. Calculate the 99% CI. Compare the lengths of the two intervals. What might you conclude?

 5.16 These are typical textbook problems. Invent a few more, as varied as you can, and swap with a fellow learner. Perhaps use HEAT scores because they fit conveniently on the **CIjumping** *X* axis, so you can use ESCI to check your answers.

In Chapter 1 we discussed how estimation can answer many research questions. Since then you have played with simulations of sampling and calculated your first CIs. You therefore know the fundamentals of estimation and the main job of the book is done. From here on, we investigate how to use those fundamentals of estimation in different situations. You can feel very positive about reaching this point. Reward yourself with more **CIjumping**!

The next step is to find a way to avoid assuming σ is known, so we can calculate CIs for realistic situations. For this we need the *t* distribution.

THE *t* DISTRIBUTION

Refer back to Figure 5.2. For any *M*, we can consider a *z* score that tells us where that sample mean falls in the sampling distribution. We need Equation 4.1—here it is again:

$$z = \frac{X - \mu}{\sigma} \qquad (4.1)$$

Calculate *z* from *X*.

Apply that to our latest *M* in Figure 5.2. The *z* we want refers to the sampling distribution curve, which is a normal distribution with mean μ and SD of SE = σ/√*N* . Therefore,

$$z = \frac{M - \mu}{\sigma/\sqrt{N}} \qquad (5.5)$$

Calculating *z* for sample mean *M*.

Does that make sense? The MoE lines mark where that *z* equals ± $z_{.95}$, which is ±1.96.

Now suppose we don't know σ, as is usually the case. Our best information about σ will be *s*, the SD of our sample. We'll need to use our *s* to estimate σ, so we can calculate a CI for μ. Rather than using the *z* score for our sample, which needs σ, I'll define a value of *t* instead. This is calculated in the same way, but uses *s* in place of σ:

$$t = \frac{M - \mu}{s/\sqrt{N}} \qquad (5.6)$$

Calculating *t* for sample mean *M*.

Does *z* vary from sample to sample? Does *t*?

Yes and yes! Of course z varies, because M varies. In a sense t varies more, because t depends on both M and s, and both of these vary from sample to sample. Perhaps that makes it not so surprising that the distribution of t is a bit more complicated than the distribution of z, which is, of course, the normal distribution.

The statisticians tell us that t, as defined by Equation 5.6, has what they call a *t distribution*, sometimes called "Student's t distribution". There's actually a whole family of t distributions, and to select the one we need we have to specify a parameter called the *degrees of freedom* (df). In our situation there are $(N-1)$ degrees of freedom, so we specify $df = (N-1)$.

What's this weird "degrees of freedom" number? Please hold that question for a moment while we use ESCI to see some t distributions. I promise to come back to it.

▶ The quantity defined by Equation 5.6 has a *t distribution*, with $df = (N-1)$ degrees of freedom.

▶ $t_{.95}(df)$ defines the central 95% of the area under the t distribution with df degrees of freedom.

esci 5.17 Open ESCI's **Normal and t** page, unclick all checkboxes, click at red 1 on t, and watch what happens to the red curve as you play around with the df spinner near red 1. You are visiting the family of t distributions.

esci 5.18 At red 1 click on t and z. What are the two curves? Again change df. What happens? Describe the t distribution in relation to the normal, and describe how that relation changes with df.

esci 5.19 We used $z_{.95}$ to refer to the value of z that defines the central 95% of the area under a normal curve. We'll use $t_{.95}(df)$ to refer to the t value that defines the central 95% of the area under the t distribution with the stated df. Set $df = 14$, click **Two tails** at red 2, click **Areas**, and move the large slider to find $t_{.95}(14)$. Compare with Figure 5.5. Find $t_{.99}(14)$.

esci 5.20 Find $t_{.95}(3)$, $t_{.95}(9)$, $t_{.95}(29)$, and $t_{.95}(59)$. Compare with $z_{.95}$. Is that what you would expect? Compare the pattern of $t_{.95}(df)$ values with what you observed about the shape of the different t distributions in Exercise 5.18.

esci 5.21 Many statistics textbooks include tables that allow you to look up values of $z_{C/100}$ and $t_{C/100}(df)$. Instead, I provide ESCI's **Normal and t** page. You could, if you like, make up your own table of $t_{.95}(df)$ values, for $df = 1, 2, 3 \ldots$

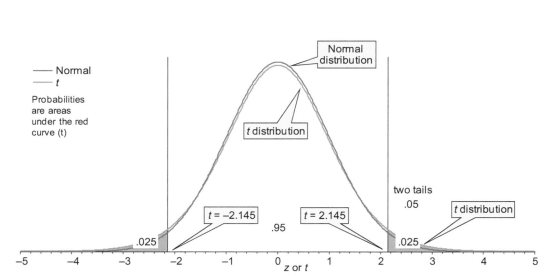

Figure 5.5. The t distribution (red line) with $df = 14$, and the normal distribution (blue line). The cursors are set to $t = \pm2.145$, which gives the two red shaded tail areas each of .025 and the central area of .95. Therefore $t_{.95}(14) = 2.145$. From **Normal and t**.

5.22 If you know about Excel, you may care to investigate the functions NORM.S.INV() and T.INV(), which allow you to find $z_{C/100}$ and $t_{C/100}(df)$, respectively. However, be careful because the formats of the two functions are a little different: compare "=NORM.S.INV(.975)" and "=T.INV(.975,14)".

5.23 What does the Guinness brewery in Dublin have to do with the history of the *t* distribution? Why is that sometimes called "Student's *t* distribution?" Search on "William Gosset" to find out.

Degrees of Freedom

I'll give three answers to the question about degrees of freedom. First is the "trust me" non-answer: You have seen in ESCI that the *t* distribution changes shape with *df*, especially when *df* is small or very small. We therefore need to specify *df* so we know which *t* distribution to use. For a single sample, $df = (N - 1)$. In other situations I'll provide the formula for the appropriate *df*, which is usually strongly dependent on *N*. So *df* is simply a number we need to know so we can choose the appropriate *t* distribution for our situation.

My second answer is that we expect *s* to be a good estimate of σ when *N* is large, in which case *df* is large and you have seen that the *t* distribution is similar to the normal. The larger *N* is, the closer *t* is to normal, and the closer $t_{.95}(df)$ is to $z_{.95}$. Therefore, we can think informally of *df* as an indicator of how good an estimate or approximation we have—the larger *df* is, the better *s* is as an estimate of σ and the closer we are to the normal distribution, which requires that we know σ. Large *df* is good, just as large *N* is good.

Now for my third answer, but if your eyes glaze over it's OK to skip to the next section. The number of degrees of freedom is the number of separate, *independent* pieces of information we have that relate to the question at hand. For example, suppose I tell you I'm thinking of 4 numbers and their mean is 7.0. If I tell you 3 of the numbers, I'm giving you fresh information, but once you know those 3, you can figure out the fourth, because you know the mean. Given the mean, there are only 3 degrees of freedom in my set of 4 numbers. Now consider *s* as an estimate of σ. The *df* tells us how many independent pieces of information *s* provides. Recall Equation 3.3 for *s*:

$$s = \sqrt{\frac{\sum (X_i - M)^2}{N - 1}} \qquad (3.3)$$

> This formula gives the standard deviation, *s*.

> The number of **degrees of freedom**, *df*, is the number of separate, relevant pieces of information that are available.

The addition is of a number of terms, all like $(X_i - M)^2$. In fact, *N* terms are added, one for each data point. Each of these provides information about σ because each is a measure of how far away a particular X_i is from the sample mean. However, as in my example with 4 numbers, calculating *M* from those *N* data points, X_1 to X_N, uses up one degree of freedom and so, even though we add *N* terms in the course of calculating *s*, they provide only $(N - 1)$ separate pieces of information. Once *M* has been calculated, only the first $(N - 1)$ of the $(X_i - M)^2$ terms are free to vary, then the Nth term is set by the requirement that X_1 to X_N have mean *M*. Therefore, $df = (N - 1)$. Incidentally, *s* having $(N - 1)$ degrees of freedom for the estimation of σ is related to why $(N - 1)$ appears in Equations 3.2 and 3.3. In general, the larger *df* is—the larger the amount of relevant information we have—the closer *t* is to normal, and the happier we are. Now back to CIs, the reason for all this *t* and *df* business.

CIs When σ is not Known

Almost always in practice we don't know σ, so need to use s, the SD of our sample. To calculate CIs and MoE we use Equations 5.3 and 5.4, but with $t_{C/100}(df)$ in place of $z_{C/100}$ and s in place of σ. Making those substitutions gives us the C% CI when σ is not known:

This is the C% CI when σ is not known.

$$\left[M - t_{C/100}(df) \times \frac{s}{\sqrt{N}}, M + t_{C/100}(df) \times \frac{s}{\sqrt{N}} \right] \tag{5.7}$$

And therefore:

This is the MoE for the C% CI, σ not known.

$$\text{MoE}_C = t_{C/100}(df) \times \frac{s}{\sqrt{N}} \tag{5.8}$$

Usually we want the 95% CI, for which

This is the MoE for the 95% CI, σ not known.

$$\text{MoE} = t_{.95}(df) \times \frac{s}{\sqrt{N}} \tag{5.9}$$

Let's watch those formulas in action.

esci **5.24** Click back to **CIjumping**. Still assuming μ = 50 and σ = 20, take samples with $N = 15$ and display the dance of the means. Near red 6 make sure $C = 95$ and that **Assume σ is: Known** is selected. Click **CIs**. Near red 7 click **μ line** and **Capture of μ**. Take more samples and enjoy the dance of the CIs. Compare with the upper half of Figure 5.6. What can you say about the lengths of the CIs? Explain.

esci **5.25** Stop the dance and select **Assume σ is: Unknown**. Compare with Figure 5.6, lower half. Click on and off a few times and watch carefully. If we drop the assumption that σ is known we are being much more realistic. MoE for each sample is now calculated using that sample's s to estimate σ. What can you say about the lengths of the CIs? Explain.

5.26 Every sample has its own s, so the CIs vary in length from sample to sample. What would happen for $N = 10$, or even smaller? Would s vary more or less, from sample to sample? Would s typically be a better or worse estimate of σ? Would you expect CI length to vary more, or less, from sample to sample? What about $N = 100$? Lock in your predictions.

esci **5.27** Experiment to test your predictions. Eyeball the amount of variation in CI length with very small N, and large N. Compare and explain.

5.28 Recall the Pen–Laptop study we discussed in Chapters 2 and 3.

a. For the Laptop group, $N_2 = 31$, and for transcription scores, $M_2 = 14.52$ and $s_2 = 7.29$, as Figures 3.6 and 3.9 illustrated. (I'm referring to Laptop as Group 2, for consistency with the discussion of the whole study in Chapter 7.) Calculate the 95% CI, of course without knowing σ.

b. Do the same for the Pen group, for which, as we'll see in Chapter 7, $N_1 = 34$, and for transcription scores, $M_1 = 8.81$ and $s_1 = 4.75$.

5.29 Suppose the Pen group had $N_1 = 136$ and happened to obtain $M_1 = 8.81$ and $s_1 = 4.75$ as before.

a. How does this value of N_1 compare with the first value? How do you expect the CI with this new N_1 to compare with the first CI? Explain.

b. Calculate the CI using this new N_1. Compare with the first CI. Comment.

5.30 Invent a few more textbook problems like those, as varied as you can, and swap with a friend. Compare answers and discuss.

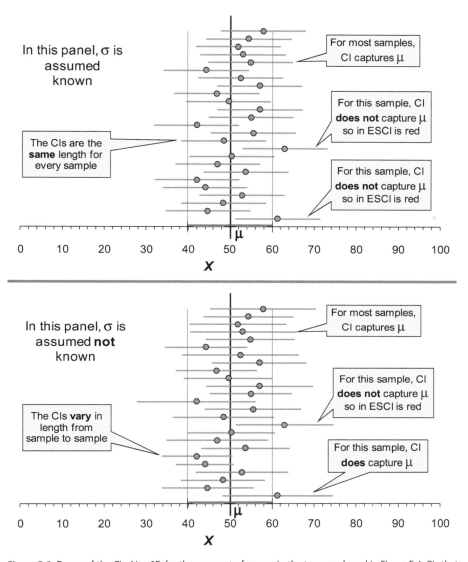

Figure 5.6. Dance of the CIs, *N* = 15, for the same set of means in the two panels and in Figure 5.4. CIs that miss μ are red. Upper panel: Assuming σ is known, all CIs are the same length. Lower panel: That assumption is dropped and each CI is calculated using *s* for that sample, so the CIs vary in length. Whether a CI captures μ or not may change when the assumption about σ changes, as here for the bottom sample.

After all these simulations we should once again remind ourselves what a researcher typically knows: just the data from one study, as in Figure 5.3. Now, however, the researcher can calculate the CI, as in Figure 5.7. I mentioned earlier that, when seeing a data set, we should think about what population lies behind the data, and the dance of the means. Now we can add thinking about the dance of the CIs. As before, we always need to be aware of what we easily could have obtained instead. The dance of the CIs reminds us that our CI could have been different, perhaps very different. And that it just might be … what color?

Yes, it could be one of the 5% in the dance that are red, although we'll never know.

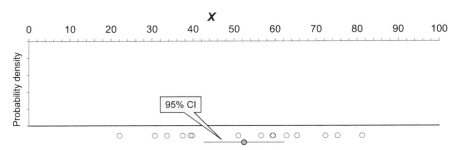

Figure 5.7. All a researcher knows: The data points of a single sample with $N = 15$, as shown in Figure 5.3, but now the 95% CI has been calculated, using s.

5.31 Figure 5.7 is the same as Figure 5.3, but now we have calculated the 95% CI, using s from our data points. Focus on that CI. What two aspects of the dance of the means does our CI tell us about?

RANDOMNESS

Before discussing different ways to think about CIs, I'd like to say a few more words about randomness. In Chapter 2 I talked about seeing faces in the clouds—our mind's eye wants to find meaning even in random swirls of clouds. People generally have poor intuitions about randomness. As well as seeing patterns where there are none, they make predictions when there's no basis to predict. Poor judgments like those help keep casinos in business. **CIjumping** can't show you how to win at the casino, but it can illustrate a few of the pitfalls.

The dances in ESCI illustrate the random bouncing around we expect from sampling variability.

 5.32 Set $C = 95$. Select **Assume σ is: Known**, so the CIs are all the same length. Make sure μ capture is indicated by color. Run the simulation, enjoy the dance of the CIs to your favorite music, watch for red CIs and watch **Percent capturing** μ near red 7. What happens to that percentage near the start of a run? What happens after a few minutes? After an hour?

5.33 Do it all again without assuming σ known, so the CIs vary in length. Use a very low value of N, and also $N = 100$. If you like, try different values of C.

In the short run, a random sequence is likely to appear lumpy, with enticing fragments of patterns. Beware faces in the clouds!

Watching those dances, do you see patterns? Just as we see faces in clouds, do the means or CIs dancing down the screen suggest glimpses of runs, or alternations, or other brief patterns? We can't help but see patterns in randomness—it seems that we're just wired that way. Beware: It's very easy to be misled by such apparent patterns in data that are actually random.

In the short term, randomness is lumpy, weird, surprising, totally unpredictable. Short-term lumpiness explains why early in a run, after taking a small number of samples, the percent capturing μ is likely to differ a bit from C, and to fluctuate, perhaps a lot. Further into a run it's likely to be closer to C and to fluctuate progressively less.

In the long run, true randomness looks very different: The percentage of samples for which the CI captures μ becomes close and eventually extremely close to *C*, and there is very little or no fluctuation. And that's true for any *N*, any *C*, and whether or not you assume σ is known. Yes, the formulas for CIs predict extremely well how random sampling behaves—in the long run.

There is no memory in the sequence. Whether or not any CI captures μ is entirely independent of any other. The effect of any early clumps simply gets diluted by the large number of following samples, so the overall percentage capturing is eventually very close to *C*.

In the long run, a random sequence gives an overall outcome very close to what we expect.

You may be thinking that ESCI is just a computer program, so the samples can't be truly random. You are right, but the software random number generator that ESCI uses gives numbers that are, for planet Earth, as close to random as we are likely to get. I'm happy to regard the dances as truly random.

So there's the fascination of randomness—it's ever surprising, locally lumpy, yet in the long term entirely predictable. Lumps in the randomness—faces in the clouds—can be enticing, and suggestive of differences or patterns. Beware—try not to be caught by interpreting a pattern that most likely is merely a lump in the randomness.

5.34 Suggest three areas in everyday life in which we could expect to see local lumpiness and long-term regularity, just as a random process would give us.

5.35 Casinos often have an electronic display near each roulette table to let you know the last dozen or more results given by that particular wheel. Why do they do this? Does it help the gambler?

EFFECT SIZES

Interpretation of CIs is not far away, but first I need to introduce a slightly awkward term. An *effect size* (ES) is the amount of anything that's of research interest. Typically, it's what our dependent variable measures in a study. Some examples are the percentage of verbatim transcription in a student's notes, the difference between the weights I can lift with my left and right hands, and the time it takes to solve a crossword. The term is awkward because "effect" might suggest there has to be an identified cause, but that's not necessary. We can calculate verbatim transcription score without considering any particular cause. Similarly, the mean systolic blood pressure of a group of children, the number of companies that failed to submit tax returns by the due date, and the ratio of good to bad cholesterol in a diet are all perfectly good effect sizes.

Effect size (ES) is the amount of anything that's of research interest.

The *population ES* is simply the true value of an effect in the population. The *sample ES* is calculated from the data, and is typically used as our best point estimate of the population ES. It's often referred to as an *ES estimate*.

We calculate from our data the *sample effect size* (*ES*), and use this as our estimate of the *population ES*, which is typically what we would like to know.

A *population effect size* is the true value of an effect in the population.

A *sample effect size*, or *effect size estimate*, is calculated from sample data.

Thinking back to our step-by-step plan for estimation near the end of Chapter 1, our research question (Step 1) typically asks about a population ES (*What's the support for Proposition A in the population of people likely to vote?*). Step 2 requires us to identify the measure that's most appropriate for answering that question (*The percentage of likely voters who express support is …*). We can now restate Step 2 as requiring us to state the sample ES we need to answer our research question. We'll use that sample ES as our point estimate of the population ES specified in Step 1. Of course, we'll also provide the CI, our interval estimate.

Often the research question asks about a difference, in which case the effect size we want is a difference. So the Pen–Laptop ES is the difference between the two group mean transcription scores, and the corresponding interval estimate is the CI on that difference.

Note that people use "effect size" to refer to the measure (*The ES we'll use is the percentage of likely voters.*) and also to a particular value (*The ES was 53%.*). Usually that won't cause a problem, but be aware of the two possible meanings of ES. Sometimes I'll refer to an "effect size measure" if that seems clearer. Often it takes careful thought to choose the most appropriate ES measures when designing a study.

5.36 Study Figure 5.7 again. That's all a researcher knows. That's all that's available for the report of a study. Whenever you see such a figure you should bring to mind two underlying things to illuminate how you think about the results. What are they? *Hint*: Look back to Figure 5.3 and the discussion of that.

5.37 In Figure 5.7, what's the sample ES? The population ES? In each case, do we know it, or do we wish to know it?

? Quiz 5.2

1. State whether each of the following statements is true or false.
   a. Although we typically calculate a 95% CI, we can calculate CIs for any level of confidence desired.
   b. Compared to a 95% CI, a 99% CI will be longer.
   c. For a given level of confidence, we find the z score corresponding to our selected percentage of cases in the normal distribution, then use that z to help calculate the MoE.
2. When the population standard deviation is not known, we must estimate it using the sample standard deviation. Then, when calculating a CI we use ___ rather than ___ to help find the MoE.
3. The t distribution is more complex than the z distribution—it depends on the _____ of _____. For small sample sizes, the t distribution is <u>wider / narrower</u> than the z distribution.
4. Randomness is
   a. lumpy, meaning that clusters and runs of scores can occur.
   b. sometimes easy to mistake for patterned or meaningful data.
   c. in the long run, going to give us what we expect.
   d. All of the above.
5. A(n) _____ is the amount of something that's of research interest.
6. In practice, we <u>know / don't know</u> the population ES, and we <u>know / don't know</u> the sample ES. So we use the <u>sample / population</u> ES to estimate the <u>sample / population</u> ES.
7. Time for chocolate or coffee—as soon as you've invented a few of your own quiz questions, and swapped with a friend.

INTERPRETING EFFECT SIZES AND CONFIDENCE INTERVALS

Back to CIs at last. In Chapter 1 I made statements like: "The poll estimated support in the population to be 53% [51, 55]". Here I'll discuss how to interpret such CIs, but I included the previous short section on ESs because a CI is only as useful as the point estimate it tells us about. The effect size is the best single answer to our research question that our data can provide. Therefore, interpretation should refer, first, to the ES estimate (the 53%) and then to the CI, although we usually discuss the two together.

It may seem surprising, but even the experts are not fully agreed on how best to interpret CIs. Of the four ways to think about CIs that I'll describe, only the first is endorsed by everyone. The others each attract quibbles or criticism from one expert or another. However, all four interpretations are, in my view, reasonable and I recommend using any or all of them, as seems most illuminating in a particular situation. After I've discussed the four, Table 5.1 provides a summary.

CI Interpretation 1: Our CI Is One From the Dance

It's always correct to think of our CI, which is [51, 55], as one from the notionally infinite sequence of intervals we'd obtain if the experiment were repeated indefinitely. Each interval is one randomly chosen from the dance of the CIs. Seeing your interval, have in your mind's eye the dance of similar intervals. If your interval is short, most likely the dance is quite narrow; the longer your interval, the wider the dance is likely to be. Most likely your interval captures the parameter you wish to estimate, but, by chance, you may have an interval that doesn't include the parameter, and which ESCI would show in red. Never forget: "It might be red!"

Interpretation 1 of a CI. Our CI is one from the *dance*—a notionally infinite sequence of repeats of the experiment. Most likely it captures the parameter we're estimating, but "It might be red!"

Some strict scholars will say *only* that our CI is randomly chosen from a dance, 95% of which include μ. They permit no comments about our particular interval. In practice, however, we need to interpret what we have—our single interval. Is that justified? My answer is that yes, it's reasonable to interpret our CI, but on one important condition: It only makes sense if our CI is likely to be representative of the whole dance. It usually is, but I can think of two cases in which our CI is not likely to tell us truly about the dance. Can you think of one?

Hint: Look back at Exercises 5.26 and 5.27, which asked about the variation in CI length for different values of *N*. What happened for very small samples?

Select **Assume σ is: Unknown** and choose a small *N*, say *N* = 4. Watch the dance of the CIs, as illustrated by Figure 5.8. CI length varies enormously—some intervals are more than 5 times longer than others. Therefore, the length of any one interval—for example, the CI we calculated from our data—may not give us a good idea of the uncertainty. That CI may not be representative of the dance, and a repeat of the study may give a CI with a *very* different length. We need *N* of at least, say, 6 to 8 to be reasonably happy about interpreting a CI.

If *N* is less than about 6 to 8, CI length may be a very poor indicator of precision and the width of the dance. Such a CI may mislead.

I mentioned that there is a second problematic case. Think back to our discussion of Open Science. We need reassurance that the result we see has not been selected from a larger set of results on our question of interest. If the study had been run several times it would be misleading if we were given only the shortest CI, or only the result with the largest ES. Our CI would not be representative of its dance because it has been selected, rather than coming randomly from the dance.

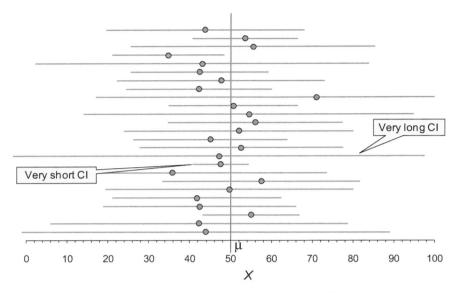

Figure 5.8. The dance of the CIs when σ is not assumed known and N = 4. CI length varies dramatically from sample to sample.

If we don't have very small N, at least 6 to 8, and if our CI hasn't been selected in some possibly misleading way, then I recommend we go ahead and interpret our CI. It's likely to give us a good idea of the whole dance. The following three ways to interpret a CI all focus on our interval. We must, however, always remember that our CI is one from the dance. It might not include μ. *It might be red!*

▶ If *N* is at least 6 to 8 and our CI has not been selected in a way that might mislead, then interpret our interval.

CI Interpretation 2: The Cat's-Eye Picture Helps Interpret Our Interval

Bear in mind the cat's-eye picture, as shown in Figure 5.9. Focus on the 95% CI in the middle; I'll refer to the others later. The cat's-eye picture tells us how plausibility, or likelihood, varies smoothly, being greatest around the center at *M* and dropping away towards either limit and beyond. There's no step at the CI limits, so we shouldn't take much note of whether a value falls just inside or just outside a CI.

▶ *Interpretation 2* of a CI. The cat's-eye picture shows how plausibility is greatest near the center of the CI, and decreases smoothly towards and beyond either limit. The CI includes values that are most plausible for μ.

Consider the lower panel of Figure 5.2 and the sampling distribution curve it shows on the mean heap. This curve tells us that, in most cases, *M* is close to μ. Now consider the cat's-eye curves in Figure 5.9. The cat's-eye pictures are fattest at *M*, which tells us that, most likely, the unknown μ lies close to *M*. The two figures give us the same message, just expressed differently. Figure 5.2 tells us that most means fall close to μ and progressively fewer means fall at positions further away from μ. Correspondingly, the cat's-eye curves tell us that, most likely, μ is close to *M*, and likelihood drops progressively for values of μ farther away from *M*, out to the limits of the CI and beyond. To put it another way, the cat's-eye picture in Figure 5.9 is fattest around *M*, which tells us that our best bet for where μ lies is close to *M*. It also illustrates how bets for μ get progressively worse as we consider values further from *M*.

I'm not saying that researchers should necessarily include cat's-eye pictures in their research reports, but you should be able to see them in your mind's eye

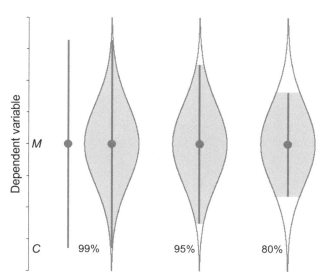

Figure 5.9. The cat's-eye picture, for CIs with various levels of confidence, *C*, as indicated at the bottom, all for the same data set. Each CI spans *C*% of the total area between the curves. In each case this area is shaded. At left are two different pictures of the 99% CI.

whenever you see a CI. Imagine the cat's eye on our result of 53% [51, 55]—do you see Figure 5.1 in your mind's eye? You might say that values around 52% to 54% are most plausible for μ, because they are near the center of the CI, and the likelihood for other values being μ decreases gradually in both directions, out to and beyond the limits of the CI. And always remember… What color did I mention?

Yes, even CIs with cat's-eye pictures might be red.

I find the cat's eye highly revealing about what a 95% CI is telling us, so I see it as a beautiful picture. I hope you can share the feeling.

For Exercise 5.28 you probably calculated that, for Laptop, the mean transcription score was 14.5% [11.8, 17.2]. It may be tempting to say "the probability is .95 that μ, the mean Laptop transcription percentage in the population, lies in that 95% CI", but I recommend avoiding probability language, which may suggest μ is a variable, rather than having a fixed value that we don't know. However, it's acceptable to say "we are 95% confident our interval includes μ", provided we keep in mind that we're referring to 95% of the intervals in the dance including μ. I'm also happy to say "most likely our CI includes μ" and "values in the interval are the most plausible for μ".

Substantive interpretation of the CI should start with the point estimate in the center (14.5, or roughly 15), and also consider the two ends of the interval (roughly 12 and 17). The *lower limit* (LL) is a likely lowest estimate, or lower bound, for μ, and the *upper limit* (UL) is a likely highest estimate, or upper bound, for μ.

So, for substantive interpretation we should consider what it means to say that around 15% of the notes are verbatim transcriptions from the lecture. We also need to consider that the population value could plausibly be as low as around 12% or as high as around 17%—or even a little beyond those values. That sounds complicated when described in words, but the cat's-eye picture can help. In Chapter 7 we'll consider also how this Laptop mean compares with the Pen mean.

The *lower limit* (LL) of our interval is a likely lower bound for μ, and the *upper limit* (UL) a likely upper bound.

Make a substantive interpretation of values in our CI, especially the point estimate and the limits. Bear the cat's eye in mind.

CI Interpretation 3: MoE Gives the Precision

▶————
Interpretation 3 of a CI. The MoE of a 95% CI indicates precision, and is the maximum likely estimation error.
————

A third approach to CI interpretation focuses on MoE and the quality of information a result gives us. MoE indicates how close our point estimate is likely to be to μ; it's the largest likely error of estimation, and MoE of a 95% CI is our measure of the precision of our experiment. Take care: It's easy to get tangled up in language about precision, because our measure of precision is MoE of a 95% CI, but *increased* precision means a *shorter* MoE, and an *increase* in MoE (perhaps because we used smaller N) means *lower* precision.

In Chapter 1, MoE for the poll result was 2%. We discussed the precision of the poll, as indicated by this MoE, and how we might achieve higher precision. A focus on precision can be helpful especially when planning a study—how large a sample should we use, to obtain some desired precision? Chapter 10 is about research planning and makes much use of MoE as our measure of precision. It thus uses this Interpretation 3 of CIs.

CI Interpretation 4: Our CI Gives Useful Information About Replication

In Chapter 1, I asked what's likely to happen if we ran the poll again, just the same but with a new sample. I said that such a close replication would be likely to give a similar result, quite likely in the range [51, 55], which is the 95% CI from the original poll. We can think of that original CI as predicting where the mean of a close replication experiment is likely to land. I'll refer to such a mean as a *replication mean*, and so we can say that a CI is a *prediction interval* for a replication mean. The CI tells us how close a replication mean is likely to be to the original mean.

A *replication mean* is the mean obtained in a close replication.

Let's investigate a HEAT example with ESCI.

 5.38 In **CIjumping**, set up the dance of the CIs, with a normal population. Click near red 8 in the tan area to select **Capture of next mean**. You should see something like Figure 5.10, which is what I obtained with samples of size $N = 20$, and σ assumed not known. Think of each CI as predicting where the mean of the following sample will lie—that's the mean displayed just above it.
   a. Focus on the short diagonal pink lines. Explain in your own words what they are telling us.

5.39 Suppose your study estimated the mean HEAT score as 57.4 [48.2, 66.7]. What mean would you expect a replication to give? Your original result happens to be the bottom CI in Figure 5.10. Eyeball the next mean, just above it in the figure. Is it captured by your CI? Does the CI on that next mean (second from the bottom) capture the mean next above it? Explain.

(esci 5.40 Note the **percent capturing next mean** near red 8 and read the popout. Clear, then slowly take a dozen or so single samples and watch the percent capturing. What's going on?

(esci 5.41 Run the dance for a few minutes, and note the percent capturing. Do this for σ known, and for σ not known. For σ not known, try a couple of values of N.

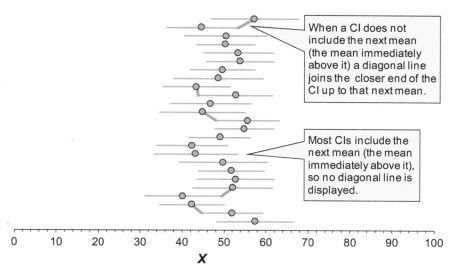

Figure 5.10. Dance of the 95% CIs on HEAT means, assuming a normally distributed population with μ = 50 and σ = 20, and using *N* = 20. The 95% CIs were calculated with σ assumed not known. When a CI does not capture the next mean—the mean immediately above it—a diagonal pink line joins the closer limit of the CI up to that next mean.

You know that 95% of CIs in the dance will, in the long run, capture μ. Here we are considering something quite different. We are identifying whether a CI includes the next replication mean, which is the mean immediately above it in the dance—the *next mean*. When the next mean is *not* captured by a CI, ESCI displays a pink diagonal line joining the closer limit of the CI up to that next mean. When, as usual, the CI captures the next mean, no line is displayed.

Figure 5.10 displays 25 means, so there are 24 predictions by a CI of the next mean. Five pink diagonal lines are displayed because in 5 cases the CI does not capture its next mean; in the other 19 cases the CI captures. Therefore, percent capturing is 19/24 = 79.2%. In your experiments, I expect you found percentages around 80–85%.

Perhaps you expected 95%? We're asking, however, not whether a CI captures a fixed μ, but a moving target—the next mean. Both the CI and next mean bounce around with sampling variability, so we should expect percent capture of less than 95%. What's the percent capture in the long run? Almost always about 83%.

On average, a 95% CI has about a .83 chance of capturing the next mean; that's about a 5 in 6 chance. It's an 83% prediction interval for where the result of a close replication will fall. That's an important thing a CI does: It gives us information about the future, by telling us what's likely to happen on replication. It's likely—although certainly not guaranteed—that a replication of the poll would give a mean in the interval [51, 55].

I've discussed four ways to interpret a CI. In Chapter 6 I'll describe a fifth. To close this section, Table 5.1 summarizes the four interpretations we've seen so far. In the next section I'll discuss, in terms of cat's eyes, how CI length changes with *C*, the level of confidence.

Interpretation 4 of a CI. A 95% CI has on average an 83% chance of capturing the mean of a replication experiment, so it's an 83% **prediction interval** for a replication mean.

Table 5.1 Four Ways to Interpret a 95% CI for μ	1	The dance	Our CI is a random one from an infinite sequence, the dance of the CIs. In the long run, 95% capture μ and 5% miss, so our CI might be red.
	2	Cat's-eye picture	Interpret our interval, provided N is not very small and our CI hasn't been selected. The cat's-eye picture shows how plausibility, or likelihood, varies across and beyond the CI—greatest around M and decreasing smoothly further from M. There is no sharp change at the limits. We're 95% confident our CI includes μ. Interpret points in the interval, including M and the lower and upper CI limits.
	3	MoE	MoE of the 95% CI gives the precision of estimation. It's the likely maximum error of estimation, although larger errors are possible.
	4	Prediction	A 95% CI provides useful information about replication. On average there's a .83 chance (about a 5 in 6 chance) that a 95% CI will capture the next mean.

CI LENGTH, MOE, AND LEVEL OF CONFIDENCE, C

▶ The *C%* CI spans *C%* of the total area of the cat's-eye picture.

Flip back to Figure 5.9, which illustrates how CI length changes with *C*, the level of confidence. It shows the cat's-eye picture on 99%, 95%, and 80% CIs. All the CIs are calculated for the same data. The percentages shown are also the percentage of the area between the curves that is spanned by the particular CI. Those areas are shaded in the figure. For the 95% CI, does the shaded area look to you to be about 95% of the total area? For the 80% CI, about 80% of the total area? For the 99% CI we can hardly see the tiny unshaded areas at each end, beyond the limits of the CI, but they are there. I included a second copy of the 99% CI so you can see its length more easily.

▶ The *tragedy of the error bar* is my name for the unfortunate fact that error bars don't automatically announce what they represent. We need to be told.

Figure 5.9 uses the same error bar graphic to represent CIs of different levels of confidence. Of course, unless we are told *C*, we can't make any sense of the interval. In addition, researchers commonly use error bars also to represent other quantities. It's best to use error bars to represent a CI with *C* = 95, but error bars may represent a CI with any other level of confidence, or they might be picturing standard deviations or standard errors, or something else entirely. These are fundamentally different quantities, telling us very different things. Of course, unless we know what error bars represent we can't interpret. It's extremely unfortunate that we don't have graphical conventions to make clear what error bars are picturing. Even worse, figures including error bars often neglect to state what the bars represent. That's terrible! I call the problem the *tragedy of the error bar*. When you include error bars in a figure, state clearly what they show, even when they just show 95% CIs—our usual choice. When you see error bars, look for a statement of what they mean. If there's no such statement, we simply can't interpret them.

▶ Always state what error bars in a figure represent. Whenever possible, use error bars to represent a 95% CI.

The curves in Figure 5.9 are the same for all the CIs in the figure. All that changes as we change *C* is the proportion of the area between the curves that's spanned by the bars. In other words, for a given data set, 99%, 95%, and 80% CIs don't give us substantively different information, they just report different fractions of the whole cat's eye. This means that, given a 95% CI, we can calculate the 99% CI for the same data if we wish, or indeed the CI with any other level of confidence.

To investigate, let's use the 95% CI in Figure 5.9 as a standard. Compared with this, how much longer do you judge the 99% CI to be, for the same data set? How much shorter do you judge the 80% CI to be? Write down your eyeballed answers, then we'll calculate.

Recall that, for any CI, total length is twice MoE. For the moment I'll assume σ is known, and use the basic formula:

$$\text{MoE}_C = z_{C/100} \times \frac{\sigma}{\sqrt{N}} \tag{5.4}$$

This gives the MoE for C% CI, σ assumed known.

5.42 The $\sigma/\sqrt{N}$ doesn't change if we change C. Therefore to calculate MoE, or CI length, for various values of C, we need to consider only $z_{C/100}$. Can you recall $z_{.95}$ and $z_{.99}$? They are two numbers for the statistics groupies, and what we need to find how much longer MoE for the 99% CI is than MoE for the 95% CI. In other words, how much longer MoE_{99} is than MoE_{95}. The ratio $z_{.99}/z_{.95}$ is the ratio of the two MoEs, which is the same as the ratio of the two CI lengths. If you need to, look back or use the **Normal** page to find $z_{.99}$ and $z_{.95}$, then find how much longer a 99% CI is than a 95% CI. Recall also Exercise 5.15 and my answer to that.

5.43 Do the same for an 80% CI.

In Figure 5.9, compare MoE_{99} and MoE_{95}. To my eye, MoE_{99} is about one-third longer than MoE_{95}. In other words, a 99% CI is about one-third longer than a 95% CI. Why so much longer? The 99% CI must span 99% of the area between the curves, but the cat's-eye picture is quite narrow just beyond the limit of the 95% CI. Therefore the 99% CI has to be considerably longer, to span sufficient (i.e., 99%) of the total area. Now compare the 80% CI with the 95% CI. To my eye, MoE_{80} is about one-third shorter than MoE_{95}. In other words, the 80% CI is about one-third shorter than the 95% CI.

In summary, Figure 5.9 illustrates that, compared with the 95% CI,

- the 99% CI is about one-third longer;
- the 80% CI is about one-third shorter.

These simple relationships are worth remembering. They are usually most valuable for helping us translate from a CI reported with some C other than 95, into what we'd prefer—the equivalent 95% CI. You can also use them for approximate eyeballing of CIs with other values of C. For example, a 90% CI will be intermediate in length between the 80% and the 95% CIs. A 99.9% CI will be even longer than the 99% CI—in fact, about two-thirds longer than the 95% CI. If you like, make that an additional bullet point to remember.

One final comment. To prepare Figure 5.9, I assumed σ known, as we did for Exercises 5.42 and 5.43. The cat's-eye curves are normal distributions. Assuming σ is not known, the curves would be t distributions. However, unless N is very small, say 10 or less, the changes would not be great. I'm suggesting the approximate guidelines above for building intuitions and for eyeballing, rather than for accurate calculations. Therefore, I'm happy to recommend these pictures and guidelines as sufficiently accurate for general use.

Just to recap, whenever you see a CI, you should bear in mind a number of things, four of which are:

- A CI is calculated assuming a statistical model. Our model assumes random sampling and a normally distributed population.
- Our CI is one from a dance, and could easily have been different. Visualize sample means with CIs dancing down the screen, with music if you like.
- However we interpret our CI, "It might be red!"
- Provided our CI was not selected in a way that might mislead, and N is not very small, then it's reasonable to interpret our single interval. Use any or all of Interpretations 2–4.

It's almost time for take-home messages. We started this chapter with estimation error and MoE, and touched on dances, CIs, t, randomness, then the four interpretations and various levels of confidence. Perhaps play the dance of the CIs as inspiration while a group of you discuss your take-home messages.

? Quiz 5.3

1. The cat's-eye image is useful when thinking about a CI because:
   a. Even though the whole range of the CI is plausible, the middle of the range is most likely and the end the least likely.
   b. Even though the whole range of the CI is plausible, the end of the range is most likely and the middle is the least likely.
   c. Even though the whole range of the CI is plausible, the middle of the range and the ends of the range are equally likely.
   d. CIs, like cat's eyes, always come in pairs.
2. Any given CI you calculate is one from the dance of the CIs. Why is this important to keep in mind?
3. In the long run, we expect about 95% of CIs to capture the population mean. However, this depends on the assumption that
   a. The data have not been selected in a way that could bias the sample mean.
   b. Random sampling was used.
   c. The variable measured is normally distributed.
   d. All of the above.
4. Even though we expect 95% of CIs to capture the population mean, we only expect ___% to capture the mean of a close replication.
5. When you make a figure that has error bars, it's vital always to _____.
6. Compared with a 95% CI, the 99% CI for the same data is about _____ shorter / longer, and the 80% CI is about _____ shorter / longer.

5.44 Choose a CI or two, from Chapters 1 or 2, or somewhere else, and interpret them in each of the four ways. Which seem to you best?

5.45 Find, on the Internet or elsewhere, three examples of results reported with a CI, perhaps in research reports, news media, or science magazines. Identify for each CI what interpretation is given, and which of my four it best matches. Use another of the four to make your own interpretation.

5.46 Think of the dance of the means, the mean heap, and the dance of the CIs. Are you dreaming about them yet? You are sufficiently familiar with them when they come up in your dreams.

5.47 Suppose the mean reduction in anxiety is reported as 8.0 points on an anxiety scale, 99% CI [2.0, 14.0]. What, approximately, is the equivalent 95% CI? The equivalent 80% and 99.9% CIs?

5.48 Revise your own take-home messages from this chapter.

Reporting Your Work

With your new knowledge of CIs plus your understanding of descriptive statistics (Chapter 3), you're ready to write basic results sections.

- For variables where a mean makes sense, report the mean with a CI, almost always the 95% CI. Report the CI immediately following its mean. State the units after the mean, but don't repeat them for the CI.
- In APA format, a CI is reported in brackets with a comma between the lower and upper ends of the interval. This is preceded by the confidence level and the abbreviation for confidence interval. Strange but true: In APA style "CI" is not italicized because it is regarded as an abbreviation rather than a statistical symbol. Also a bit odd is the fact that the abbreviation is not marked with periods (it's CI, not C.I.). Here's an example:

```
Average age was typical for a college sample: M = 21.6 years,
95% CI [20.6, 22.6].
```

- In interpreting your results, always focus on the CI, as well as the point estimate from the sample. Be sure your conclusions acknowledge the full range of uncertainty within the CI. For very large samples, the CI may be so short as to need no comment. When the CI is long, be sure your conclusions are appropriately tentative.
- Remember from Chapter 3 that the spread of your measures deserves as much attention as the location. Any mean reported should be accompanied by a measure of spread (usually the standard deviation) and the sample size should also be stated.
- Report statistics using a reasonable number of decimal places (see Chapter 3). For each measure, be consistent in the number of decimal places used to report its mean, CI, and standard deviation.

Here are three examples:

For most variables, use text or tables to provide the mean, the 95% CI on the mean, and the standard deviation. For example: $M = 450$ ms, 95% CI [435, 465], $s = 77$ ms.

```
Happiness ratings covered the full range (1-7, s = 1.2). The
average level of happiness was moderate (M = 3.8, 95% CI [3.6,
4.0]). The short CI indicates the population mean is likely
moderate.

There was considerable variation in recall scores (s = 15.1%),
but no participant remembered more than 80% of the material.
The average in the sample was fairly low (M = 32.6%, 95% CI
[21.8, 43.3], N = 10). The CI is fairly long, however, and is
consistent with anywhere from poor up to moderate levels of
recall.

For females, there was tremendous variability in resting heart
rate, with participants varying from 52 up to 94 bpm at rest
(s = 10 bpm). The average heart rate in the sample was 74
bpm, 95% CI [70, 78], n = 27. This CI is somewhat long, but
indicates the average resting heart rate for females in this
age group is likely to be somewhere in the 70s for bpm.
```

Take-Home Messages

- The 95% CI extends MoE either side of M, so is [$M - $ MoE, $M + $ MoE]. Assuming σ is known, the 95% CI is

$$\left[M - z_{C/100} \times \frac{\sigma}{\sqrt{N}}, M + z_{C/100} \times \frac{\sigma}{\sqrt{N}} \right]$$

- Dropping the unrealistic assumption of known σ, we use s as an estimate of σ, and the CIs vary in length from sample to sample—and more so for smaller N. We need the t distribution with degrees of freedom $df = (N - 1)$. The 95% CI is

$$\left[M - t_{.95}(N-1) \times \frac{s}{\sqrt{N}}, M + t_{.95}(N-1) \times \frac{s}{\sqrt{N}} \right]$$

- *Take-home movie:* The dance of the CIs, as in Figure 5.6. In the long run, 95% of intervals in the dance include μ, while 5% miss μ and are red.

- Randomness, as in the dances, is endlessly intriguing, but beware seeing faces in the clouds. Expect surprises and lumpiness in the short term but, in the very long term, very close to 95% of CIs capturing μ.

- An *effect size* (ES) is the amount of anything of research interest, for example a mean, median, percentage, or difference between two means. We typically use a sample ES as our point estimate of the population ES. Routinely interpret ESs and the CIs on those ESs.

- *Interpretation 1* of a CI: *One from the dance.* Our CI is defined to be one from an infinite sequence of replications, 95% of which will include μ. Our CI is one from the dance, but "It might be red!"

- If *N* is not very small, and our CI not misleadingly selected from a number of results, then our CI is likely to be representative of its dance and it's reasonable to interpret our interval. The remaining three ways to interpret CIs do this.

- *Interpretation 2* of a CI: *Cat's-eye picture.* I'm 95% confident my CI includes μ. The cat's-eye picture shows how plausibility, or likelihood, varies across and beyond the CI: greatest around the center, then smoothly decreasing to the limits and beyond. Our CI is a range of values that are most plausible for μ.

- *Take-home picture:* The cat's-eye picture, as in Figure 5.9, especially for a 95% CI.

- *Interpretation 3* of a CI: *MoE gives the precision.* MoE of the 95% CI, the largest likely *error of estimation*, is our measure of *precision*. Small MoE means high precision and good estimates; large MoE means poor precision.

- *Interpretation 4* of a CI: *Information about replication.* A 95% CI is, on average, an 83% prediction interval for the next mean, obtained as the result of a close replication. CIs give useful information about replication.

- Error bars are used to represent various different quantities. That's the *tragedy of the error bar*. Every figure with error bars must state what the bars represent. Routinely use error bars to report 95% CIs.

- CIs with different values of *C* span corresponding percentages of the area of the cat's-eye picture. A 99% CI is about one-third longer than the 95% CI, and the 80% CI is about one-third shorter.

End-of-Chapter Exercises

1) A student wants to know the average ACT score at her college (the ACT is a standardized college-readiness exam taken by many U.S. students). She surveys 9 students; Table 5.2 shows the data.

Table 5.2 ACT Data (*N* = 9) for Exercise 1

Student	ACT
1	26
2	34
3	21
4	26
5	23
6	24
7	15
8	18
9	21

a. Nationally, for ACT scores, $\sigma = 5$. Using this knowledge, calculate MoE and the 95% CI for this sample to estimate the average ACT score at this college.

b. Later, this student finds out from a college administrator that the true ACT mean at the college is $\mu = 22$. Has this sample done a good job estimating that true mean?

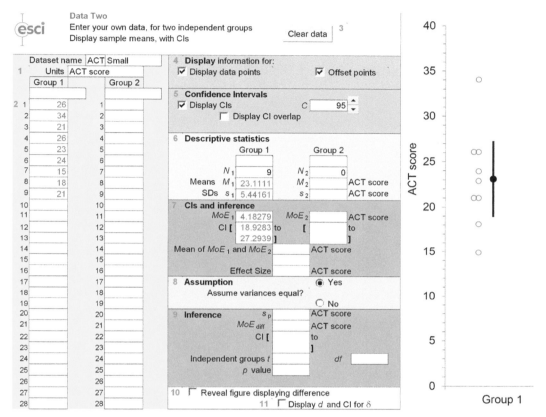

Figure 5.11. ACT scores ($N = 9$) have been entered near red 2 at left. The figure shows individual data points (open dots), mean, and 95% CI. Values for mean and CI are shown near red 6 and 7. From **Data two**.

c. Suppose the student hadn't known σ, but instead used the sample s. Would the CI become shorter or longer (assume that s will come out to be close to σ)? Check your prediction by re-calculating MoE and the 95% CI using the sample s. Be sure to use a t value as a multiplier to obtain MoE, rather than z.

d. If the student were to collect more data, would the CI become shorter or longer? How much more data would need to be collected to make the CI about half as long?

e. Open **Data two** and look around. For Group 1, near red 2, type in the nine ACT values in Table 5.2. Type labels at red 1. (Click towards the left in the white box to select it, so you can type in a label.) Your screen should resemble Figure 5.11. Play around with the display options at red 4 and 5 if necessary. Check that the values shown near red 6 for mean and SD match what you calculated. Check that the values for MoE and the CI shown near red 7 match yours.

2) Let's examine some more ACT scores. Load the **College_Survey_1** data set from the book website. This contains real data from a large student survey (as used for exercises at the end of Chapter 3). Use ESCI to help you explore this data set, or some other software if you

prefer. If using ESCI, the **Data two** page is useful for the exercises in this chapter. First, in the file with the data for this question, select the column of ACT values in the data set, and copy. Then switch to ESCI, select the first data cell near red 2, and use Paste Special/Values to paste the ACT scores as the data for Group 1. Type labels at red 1.

a. This sample contains 215 ACT scores. Do you expect the CI to be short or long? (Note that only the first 100 data points in a data set are displayed in the figure as dots. See the popouts near red 4.)

b. As I mentioned above, it turns out that the true average ACT score for this school is known: $\mu = 22$. Has this sample provided an accurate estimate of the population parameter?

c. Some CIs won't capture the true mean (some CIs are red!). However, in several years of helping students conduct surveys like this, the samples *almost always* have mean ACT scores that are higher than the college mean. Why might this be? Does it help to know that this survey uses a convenience sample? Does it matter that students self-report their ACT scores?

3) Continuing with the same data set:

a. To what extent are students doing well, on average, at this school? Calculate M, MoE, and a 95% CI for GPA, which is measured on a scale with maximum 4.0. Interpret your result.

b. To what extent are students happy at this school? Calculate M, MoE, and a 95% CI for the Subjective Well-Being Scale, a common measure related to happiness, which has a scale from 1 to 7. Does your conclusion for this school match with Diener and Diener's claim (1996) that "most people are happy"?

c. To what extent do students at this school feel wealthy relative to others? Calculate M, MoE, and a 95% CI for Self-Reported Wealth, which was measured on a scale from 1 (*well below average*) to 5 (*well above average*). Interpret your result.

4) Replication is important! The year after the student survey you analyzed in Exercises 2 and 3, a second survey was administered containing many of the same measures.

a. Based on your results for GPA, Subjective Well-Being, and Wealth, predict what you would expect for this second sample.

b. Load **College_Survey_2** which contains the data from the second survey. For each of these three variables calculate M, MoE, and 95% CI. Interpret each result.

c. Have the results replicated well across these two surveys?

Just as important as calculating a CI is interpreting it. Exercises 5 and 6 present reports of CIs, each with a number of alternative interpretations or statements. Give your comments on each. As usual, be prepared to use your judgment.

5) Anxiety was measured on a scale from 1 to 5 in a random sample of city dwellers. We found $M = 3.50$, 95% CI [3.25, 3.75].

a. The probability is .95 that the mean level of anxiety in the city lies between 3.25 and 3.75.

b. Such a short CI indicates that there's little variability in anxiety amongst city dwellers.

c. City dwellers are moderately anxious.

d. This CI is too long to be useful; more data must be collected.

6) April wants to know to what extent business majors are politically conservative. She asks 9 business majors to complete a measure of political conservatism on a scale from 1 to 10,

with 10 being most conservative. She finds $M = 8.0$, [6.0, 10.0]. This supports April's notion that business majors tend to be conservative, but the CI is long. April decides to collect more data to narrow the CI.

    a.   As more data are collected the CI will shorten, and stay centered around 8.

    b.   As more data are collected the CI will shorten, and the center change to a value within the original CI.

    c.   As more data are collected, the CI will shorten, and the center change to a value outside of the original CI.

    d.   Trick question—as more data are collected the CI will actually get longer.

? Answers to Quizzes

Quiz 5.1

1) estimation error; 2) standard error, margin, error; 3) 1.96 is $z_{.95}$, and 95% of the area under a normal distribution lies between $z = -1.96$ and $z = 1.96$; 4) calculating $M - \text{MoE}$ and $M + \text{MoE}$ as the lower and upper limits of the CI, respectively; 5) All four are true; 6) infinite, 95, population.

Quiz 5.2

1) All are true; 2) s, σ; 3) degrees, freedom, wider; 4) d; 5) effect size; 6) don't know, know, sample, population.

Quiz 5.3

1) a; 2) because 95% of CIs capture μ, while 5% miss and are red—ours may be red; 3) d; 4) 83; 5) State what the error bars represent; 6) one-third, longer, one-third, shorter.

Answers to In-Chapter Exercises

5.2   In the long run, 95% should fall between the lines and therefore, using the distribution curve's symmetry, we would expect 2.5% in either tail.

5.3   a. Use the mean of the sampling distribution curve $\pm$ MoE, which is approximately $\mu \pm 2 \times$ SE; by eyeball from Figure 5.2 this gives an interval approximately from 40 to 60. Using SE = 5.16, as we calculated a little earlier, the interval is from 39.7 to 60.3.

5.4   b, c. SE = $20/\sqrt{36}$ = 3.33, still assuming $\sigma = 20$ is known, so MoE is $1.96 \times$ SE = 6.53. The interval is from 43.47 to 56.53.

5.5   Smaller σ gives smaller MoE. In any case we expect about 5% of green dots to fall outside the MoE lines, about equal numbers in the left and right tails.

5.6 &

5.8   Again, 5%, about equally often (i.e., 2.5% each) to the left and the right.

5.9   CIs are red if they don't include μ, meaning M falls farther than MoE from μ.

5.10   The percent of 95% CIs capturing typically bounces around a lot near the start of a run, then settles down. It then continues to vary, but slowly gets less variable and closer and closer to 95%. After many thousands of samples have been taken, it will be very close to 95%.

5.11   Small N: long CIs, wide bouncing, frenetic dance; large N: short CIs, narrow bouncing, restrained dance. The length of our interval—of any single interval from the dance—gives a reasonable idea of the amount of bouncing, of the width of the dance.

5.12   Larger C, for example 99 rather than 95, means we wish to be more confident of capturing μ, so we'd better throw out a larger net. MoE needs to be larger so that more of the mean heap is within the MoE lines. MoE is calculated using a larger value of z, corresponding to .99 rather than .95. Larger C gives longer CIs, smaller C gives shorter CIs.

5.13   Change C and a different percentage of CIs will include μ, so some will need to change color. In every case, $(100 - C)\%$ of CIs will, in the long run, be red.

5.14 We expect in the long run that C% of means will fall between the MoE lines, meaning within MoE of μ. But there may be some short-run surprises—lumps in the randomness, faces in the clouds.

5.15 a. MoE = 1.96 × 15/$\sqrt{25}$ = 5.88, so the 95% CI is [106.6 − 5.88, 106.6 + 5.88], or [100.7, 112.5]. We can interpret that interval, for example by saying that values in the interval are plausible for the mean of the population the sample came from. We are 95% confident that interval includes the population mean; b. For 99%, as above, but use 2.58 in place of 1.96, so the CI is [106.6 − 7.74, 106.6 + 7.74], or [98.9, 114.3]. We are 99% confident that interval includes the population mean. We might say that interval is the range of all values that are at least somewhat plausible for the population mean. The 99% interval is longer than the 95% interval; the ratio is 2.58/1.96 = 1.32, so the 99% CI is about 32% or one-third longer than the 95% CI. That's a general finding that we'll revisit later in this chapter.

5.18 The red curve is t, the blue is normal. For large df the two curves are almost the same, but as df decreases they get more and more different, with t being lower at the center and having progressively fatter tails. Like the normal, the t curves are all symmetric and centered at 0, but for very small df the curves are considerably different.

5.19 $t_{.95}(14)$ = 2.14, and $t_{.99}(14)$ = 2.98. Read the popout at red 5 and figure out what the values below the slider are telling you. That's where to find very accurate values, given to many decimal places.

5.20 $t_{.95}(3)$ = 3.18, $t_{.95}(9)$ = 2.26, $t_{.95}(29)$ = 2.05, and $t_{.95}(59)$ = 2.00, so $t_{.95}(df)$ quickly approaches $z_{.95}$ = 1.96 as df increases, as we would expect given our observations of the t curves in Exercise 5.18.

5.21 Here's a table for the first ten values of df.

df	1	2	3	4	5	6	7	8	9	10
$t_{.95}(df)$	12.7062	4.3027	3.1824	2.7764	2.5706	2.4469	2.3646	2.3060	2.2622	2.2281

5.22 NORM.S.INV(.975) = 1.9600. More generally, use NORM.S.INV(0.5+C/200). T.INV(.975,14) = 2.1448. More generally, use the same approach but include the degrees of freedom: T.INV(0.5+C/200,DF).

5.23 William Gosset worked for the Guinness Brewery in Dublin. To analyze data from his experiments with small sample sizes he developed the fundamentals of what became the t distribution, but his employer only permitted him to publish his results under a pseudonym. He chose "Student".

5.24 All CIs are the same length because MoE for every interval is calculated from σ, which is assumed known and doesn't change.

5.25 Each sample has its own value of s, and so the calculated CI length will differ for each. When you click, some intervals get a bit longer, some a bit shorter. Occasionally, an interval changes color because it changes from including to not including μ, or vice versa—note the bottom interval in the upper and lower halves of Figure 5.6.

5.26 When we assume σ is not known, the variation in s from sample to sample will be greater for small N than for larger N, and so CI length will vary more from sample to sample for small N. With small N, there will be more change when you click between **Known** and **Unknown** for σ. Small samples typically give more variable and less precise estimates of σ. Try N = 5, or even 3 or 2.

5.27 As usual, large N is best. Very small samples, especially those with N < 10, have values of s that bounce around a great deal, so their CI lengths also bounce around a lot. Such small samples often give a very poor indication of the extent of uncertainty: If N is very small, we can't put great trust in CI length. What do you want for your birthday? Big N!

5.28 a. Laptop: mean transcription score was 14.52 [11.85, 17.19]; b. Pen: 8.81 [7.15, 10.47].

5.29 a. The sample size is four times as large so we expect the CI to be about half as long, by our approximate guideline, also considering the formula for a CI; b. For N_1 = 34, CI length is 10.47 − 7.15 = 3.32. For N_1 = 136, the CI is [8.01, 9.62] and so CI length is 9.62 − 8.01 = 1.61, which is half, as expected.

5.31 The position of our CI—where its M is—tells us approximately where the dance is located, and the length of our CI tells us approximately how much bouncing there is in the dance, how wide the dance is.

5.32–

5.33 All the same as 5.10, except that percent of CIs capturing μ settles down at C%.

5.34 Performance in many sports: A higher ranked golfer is more likely to win, but on a particular hole or a particular day performances often go against that long term probability. The weather: January is reliably hotter than March in the Southern Hemisphere—the opposite in the Northern Hemisphere—but individual days in either month often go against the long-term average. The stock market: During several years of economic growth, the market may rise year by year, but show large day-by-day fluctuations. None of those examples shows pure randomness—there are no doubt numerous causal factors contributing to what we observe—but the short-term haphazard bouncing around, despite long-term steady differences, is consistent with randomness playing an important role, which is often not sufficiently appreciated.

5.35 Many gamblers believe they can spot patterns and trends and they bet accordingly. They see patterns in randomness, faces in the clouds. On the basis of recent results, they believe a wheel may be running hot, or about to get hot. Casinos provide the recent record of each wheel to support such fallacious beliefs, and thus encourage gamblers to keep betting, and—on average—losing.

5.36 Bring to mind (i) the population—we don't know its μ or σ but we wish to estimate them—and (ii) the dance from which our single result came.

5.37 The sample ES is M, the mean of our sample, whose value we know. The population ES is the population mean μ, which we don't know, would like to know, and will estimate.

5.38 a. The pink lines appear only when the next mean does not fall within the CI just below. The line then joins whichever limit of the CI is closer to the mean just above it.

5.39 A replication would be quite likely, but certainly not guaranteed, to give a mean within [48.2, 66.7]. The second bottom mean appears to be about 52, and it is captured by the bottom CI. The second bottom CI doesn't capture the mean just above it, so a diagonal line is displayed.

5.40 The percent capturing next mean is the percentage of CIs for which the next mean does fall within the CI just below; these are the cases *without* diagonal lines.

5.41 Cumming and Maillardet (2006) reported that, in the long run, percent capturing when σ is known is 83%, for any N. When σ is not known, the percent capturing is, perhaps surprisingly, a little higher for very small N, but, for practical purposes, always think of 83%.

5.42 See my comments on Exercise 5.15.

5.43 From **Normal**, $z_{.80} = 1.28$, so $z_{.80}/z_{.95} = \mathbf{1.28/1.96} = 0.65$, so an 80% CI is about two-thirds as long as a 95% CI. In other words, an 80% CI is about one-third shorter than a 95% CI, as we might eyeball from Figure 5.9.

5.44 You could seek examples of how I use each of the four interpretations by scanning Chapter 1 and this chapter. For Interpretation 1 you could also refer to the dance of the CIs, and note that our CI might be red. Do you agree with my preferences, which I note in comments on the next exercise?

5.45 You may find a CI is reported, but, in discussion of the results, is not interpreted or even referred to. That's unfortunate, because the CI provides essential information about the precision of the point estimate, which is usually the main result, of most interest to others. Interpretation 2 is often most useful, but Interpretation 4 can sometimes give a useful perspective, and fits with meta-analytic thinking.

5.46 I wish you sweet dancing dreams.

5.47 $MoE_{99} = 6.0$, half the length of the 99% CI. So MoE_{95} is about 4.5—check that increasing 4.5 by one-third gives MoE_{99}. So the 95% CI is approximately [3.5, 12.5]. The 80% CI is about [5, 11] and the 99.9% CI about [0.5, 15.5].

p Values, Null Hypothesis Significance Testing, and Confidence Intervals

You may have noticed, in books or research reports, expressions like these:

"The result was significant, $p < .05$."

"We rejected the null hypothesis of no difference, and concluded there was a statistically significant increase, at the .01 level."

Such statements reflect *null hypothesis significance testing* (NHST), which is the traditional approach to statistical inference in many disciplines. You need to know about NHST, which is mainly based on what are called *p values*, at least so you can understand research reports that use them. Fortunately, there are many close links between NHST—including *p* values—and estimation based on confidence intervals, and many of the statistical formulas they need are very similar. So keep firmly in mind what you know about CIs as we discuss NHST.

Here's our agenda for this chapter:

- The basics of NHST and *p* values
- *p* values and the normal distribution
- *p* values and the *t* distribution
- Translating from a CI to *p*, and from *p* to a CI
- Four cautions about NHST and *p* values: The four red flags
- NHST decision making: The alternative hypothesis, and Type I and Type II errors

THE BASICS OF NHST AND *p* VALUES

What I'm calling NHST is actually a mixture of two quite different approaches, one developed by Sir Ronald Fisher, and the other by Jerzy Neyman and Egon Pearson, who famously disagreed with Fisher. Salsburg (2001) tells that and many other fascinating stories about the early days, but I'll keep it simple by discussing just the mixture, which is what researchers mainly use in practice.

Let's return to the poll example of Chapter 1, which estimated support for Proposition A as 53% [51, 55]. Figure 6.1 shows that result, with the cat's eye on the 95% CI. Recall that the CI and its cat's eye tells us that values around 53% are most plausible for the true level of support, values towards and beyond the limits are progressively less plausible, and values well beyond the CI, such as 50% and 56%, are relatively implausible, although not impossible. As always, you have in the back of your mind that our CI may be red. Now let's consider NHST and *p* values. We use a three-step process.

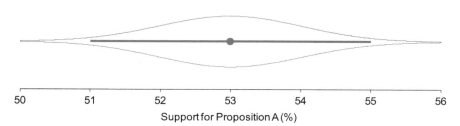

Figure 6.1. The result of the poll example in Chapter 1, with 95% CI and cat's-eye picture.

1. *State a null hypothesis.* The *null hypothesis* is a statement about the population that we wish to test. It specifies a single value of the population parameter that serves as a reference or baseline value, to be evaluated. Here we would probably choose 50% as our *null hypothesis value*, so our null hypothesis is the statement that "there is 50% support in the population"—the level to be exceeded for the proposition to pass. Often a null hypothesis states that there has been no change, or that an effect is zero.

   The *null hypothesis* states, for testing, a single value of the population parameter.

2. *Calculate the p value.* Calculate from the data the p value, which we can think of informally as measuring the extent to which results like ours are unlikely, IF the null hypothesis is true. (A little later I'll say how we define "results like ours".) The "IF" is vitally important: To calculate a p value, we assume the null hypothesis is true. A p value therefore reflects both the data and the chosen null hypothesis. For our poll result, and a null hypothesis of 50% support in the population, the p value turns out to be .003, which indicates that results like those found by the poll are highly unlikely, IF there's really 50% support in the population. It's therefore reasonable to doubt that null hypothesis of 50% support. More generally, we can say that a small p value throws doubt on the null hypothesis.

   The smaller the p value, the more unlikely are results like ours, IF the null hypothesis is true.

3. *Decide whether to reject the null.* NHST compares the p value with a criterion called the *significance level*, often chosen to be .05. If p is less than that level, we doubt the null hypothesis. In fact we doubt it sufficiently to *reject* it and say we have a *statistically significant* effect. If p is greater than the significance level, we *don't reject* the null hypothesis and can say we have a *statistically nonsignificant* effect, or that we didn't find statistical significance. Note carefully that we say the null hypothesis is "not rejected", but we *don't* say the null hypothesis is "accepted". Sorry about the multiple "nots"; I'm afraid they come with the NHST territory.

   NHST compares p with the *significance level*, often .05. If p is less than that level, we reject the null hypothesis and declare the effect to be *statistically significant*.

   The significance level, often .05, is the criterion for deciding whether or not to reject the null hypothesis. Strictly, the significance level should be chosen in advance of seeing the data; we could call that approach *strict NHST*. However, most researchers in practice do not nominate in advance the significance level they intend to use. Instead they compare the p value with a small number of conventional significance levels, most commonly .05, .01, and .001, as Figure 6.2 illustrates. Finding $p = .017$, for example, justifies rejecting the null hypothesis at the .05 level, whereas finding $p = .006$ justifies rejecting at the .01 level. The researcher uses the smallest value that permits rejection, because rejecting at a lower level (.01 rather than .05) provides a more convincing outcome. The researcher tailors the conclusion to where p falls in relation to the set of values, and therefore might conclude:

   Strict NHST requires the significance level to be stated in advance. However, researchers usually don't do that, but use a small number of conventional significance levels.

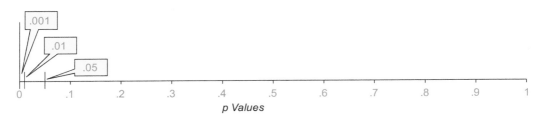

Figure 6.2. The three most commonly used significance levels, .05, .01, and .001, shown on a scale representing the possible range of *p* values from 0 to 1.

- If $p > .05$: "The null hypothesis was not rejected, $p > .05$."
- If $p < .05$ (but $p > .01$): "The null hypothesis was rejected, $p < .05$." Or "…rejected at the .05 level."
- If $p < .01$ (but $p > .001$): "The null hypothesis was rejected, $p < .01$." Or "…rejected at the .01 level."
- If $p < .001$: "The null hypothesis was rejected, $p < .001$." Or "…rejected at the .001 level."

The researcher may also make corresponding statements about statistical significance, such as: "The effect was statistically significant at the .05 level." Or "…was highly statistically significant, $p < .001$."

> The **significance level** is the criterion for deciding whether or not to reject the null hypothesis. If the *p* value is less than the significance level, reject; if not, don't reject.

▶ A lower significance level (.01 rather than .05) requires a smaller *p* value, which provides stronger evidence against the null hypothesis.

Researchers strongly prefer a lower significance level, because that provides a more convincing conclusion. Why? Think of the definition of the *p* value: A smaller *p* tells us that results like ours are less likely, IF the null hypothesis is true. The smaller the *p*, the more surprising are results like ours, IF the null is true. Therefore, a smaller *p* value gives us stronger reason to doubt the null; it provides stronger evidence against the null. To use a lower significance level (e.g., .01 rather than .05) we need a smaller *p* value. Therefore, a lower significance level provides stronger evidence against the null, more reason to doubt the null, and a more convincing conclusion.

Most researchers probably think of *p* values in terms of the evidence they provide against the null: The smaller the *p*, the stronger the evidence and the more confident they can feel in rejecting it. That's why you might hear researchers say things like "$p < .001$, which provides very strong evidence against the null hypothesis."

▶ If using NHST, report the *p* value itself ($p = .14$), not only a relative value ($p > .05$).

Anyone who uses NHST should report the *p* value itself: $p = .30$ or .04 or .007, and not merely $p > .05$, $p < .05$, $p < .01$. This provides more complete information, while also allowing readers to compare with any significance level they choose.

Now let's consider how to translate from CIs.

Using a Confidence Interval for NHST and *p* Values

NHST is usually carried out by calculating the *p* value directly, with no reference to a CI. Fortunately, however, if we have the CI there are easy ways to translate between estimation and *p* values. Choosing the .05 significance level, the basic relation between a 95% CI and the *p* value is illustrated in Figure 6.3 and can be stated as follows:

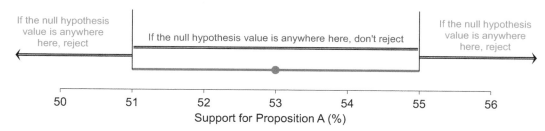

Figure 6.3. Same poll result as in Figure 6.1, but now indicating whether a null hypothesis should be rejected or not, at the .05 significance level, depending on whether the null hypothesis value lies outside or inside the 95% CI.

- If the null hypothesis value lies *outside* the 95% CI, the *p* value is *less* than .05, so *p* is less than the significance level and we reject the null hypothesis.
- Conversely, if the null hypothesis lies *inside* the 95% CI, the *p* value is *greater* than .05, so we don't reject.

Using .05 as the significance level, we simply note whether the null hypothesis value is inside or outside. Outside and we reject the null hypothesis and conclude the effect is statistically significant; inside and we don't reject. Could we reject a null hypothesis that support in the population is 50.5%? What about 60%? What about 52%? Consider where those values lie in Figure 6.3.

> For the .05 significance level, reject the null hypothesis if its value lies outside the 95% CI; if inside, don't reject.

I suspect you were right—you probably said we can reject the first two null hypotheses because the values stated are both outside the CI in Figure 6.3. And we can't reject the third because it lies inside the CI.

Later I'll talk about the translation from CIs to *p* values in more detail, and we'll see how to use significance levels other than .05.

Figure 6.3 suggests that *p* = .05 when the null hypothesis value is at one of the limits of the CI. What's *p* for other null hypothesis values? Figure 6.4 shows the idea—how, approximately, *p* varies for null hypothesis values at various positions inside and outside the CI. A null hypothesis of 50%, where the cat's eye is thin, well outside the CI, gives *p* = .003. That's strong evidence against that null hypothesis. By contrast, consider a null hypothesis of 52%. If that's the true level of support in the population, obtaining support around 53% in the poll is quite likely, so the *p* value is large, in fact *p* = .33. At 52%, the cat's eye is fairly fat. That's the pattern: Where the cat's eye is fat, *p* is large and gives no evidence against that null hypothesis value. As we consider values further from 53% and the cat's eye becomes thinner, the *p* value becomes smaller and gives progressively stronger evidence against those values as the null hypothesis.

> The further our sample result falls from the null hypothesis value, the smaller the *p* value and the stronger the evidence against the null hypothesis.

You've probably already seen the parallel: Plausibility, as indicated by the cat's eye, changes inversely with strength of evidence, as indicated by the *p* value. The *p* value gives no evidence against highly plausible values—around 52% to 54% where the cat's eye is fattest. And *p* gives progressively stronger evidence against values that are progressively less and less plausible, as we move further from 53% and beyond the CI, and as the cat's eye gets progressively thinner. Again the cat's-eye picture is wonderfully revealing: You can read it in terms of plausibility, or *p* values and strength of evidence. Everything ties together, as we'd hope.

> The cat's eye illustrates how strength of evidence varies inversely with plausibility of values, across and beyond the CI.

Consider the null hypothesis that support in the population is 51.5%. What can you say about the plausibility of that value? What would you guess the *p* value is for our poll results and that null hypothesis? What evidence do we have against that null hypothesis?

Approximate *p* values:

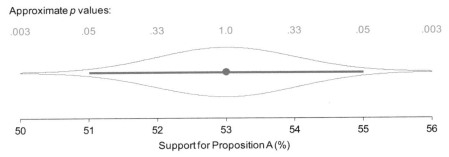

Figure 6.4. Same as Figure 6.1, but with approximate *p* values shown for different null hypothesis values. For example, the null hypothesis that support in the population is 52% gives *p* = .33.

 Those questions go a little beyond what I've discussed, but Figure 6.4 should help. Can you find someone to call or chat with?

At 51.5% the cat's eye still has some fatness, so this value is somewhat plausible as the true value, even if not as plausible as values closer to 53%. The *p* value lies between .05 and .33; it's actually .14, which provides virtually no evidence against the null hypothesis of 51.5%. I hope you are getting a feel for the way plausibility, the *p* value, and the strength of evidence all tie together. The key is always to keep the cat's-eye picture in mind.

Now for a couple of exercises, then we'll start calculating *p* values.

6.1   Consider a null hypothesis value of 54.5%.

   a. What can you say about the *p* value for our poll results?
   b. What could you conclude about 54.5% as a possible true level of support?

6.2   Do the same for the null hypothesis that support in the population is 57%.

? Quiz 6.1

1. The null hypothesis
   a. is a statement we wish to test using NHST.
   b. specifies a single value for the parameter we are interested in.
   c. is rejected when the *p* value obtained is very low.
   d. All of the above
2. In the NHST approach, *p* is the probability of obtaining results like ours IF the null hypothesis is true. What values can *p* take?
   a. Minimum of 0, maximum of 1.
   b. Minimum of −1, maximum of 1.
   c. Minimum of 0, no maximum at all.
   d. Trick question—there is no minimum or maximum for *p* values.
3. When *p* is very small (close to 0) it means we have obtained results that are likely / unlikely if the null hypothesis is true.
4. In the NHST approach, once a *p* value is obtained it is compared to the significance level, which is usually set at .05. If *p* < significance level,
   a. the null hypothesis is not rejected.
   b. the null hypothesis is rejected.
   c. the result is not statistically significant.
   d. something has gone horribly wrong in your research.

5. If the 95% CI contains the null hypothesis value, the corresponding _p_ value will be greater than / less than .05 and the NHST decision will be to reject / not reject the null hypothesis.
6. For a null hypothesis value at a point where the cat's eye is very thin, the _p_ value is large / medium / small and the evidence against the null hypothesis is strong / medium / weak / very weak.

_p_ VALUES AND THE NORMAL DISTRIBUTION

This is a notable moment: the calculation of our first _p_ value. It might not deserve trumpets, but let's have a drum roll. First, a couple of symbols. I'll refer to the null hypothesis as H_0, and the null hypothesis value as μ_0. I'll calculate the _p value_ for a HEAT example. As in Chapter 5 for CIs, I'll first use a statistical model based on the normal distribution that assumes σ is known, then a second model based on _t_ that doesn't require that assumption. The _p_ value is defined as the probability of obtaining the observed result, or more extreme, IF the null hypothesis is true.

> The **_p value_** is the probability, calculated using a stated statistical model, of obtaining the observed result or more extreme, IF the null hypothesis is true.

Note the shift from my earlier informal description of the _p_ value that referred to "results like ours". "Like ours" becomes "ours or more extreme". The "more extreme" refers to any possible result that's further than the observed result from what H_0 would predict—any possible result that would give stronger evidence against H_0 than our result does. Why include more extreme results in the _p_ value? Good question. It's tricky, but the idea is that we want the _p_ value to reflect all possible results that are at least as questioning of the null hypothesis as our result, that are at least as surprising if the null hypothesis is true.

We'll investigate the HEAT scores of students at College Alpha, and compare these with the population mean for students generally. I'll assume HEAT scores in the population of all college students are normally distributed with μ = 50 and σ = 20. Our null hypothesis is that the mean HEAT score for the population of all students at College Alpha is the same as the mean of the population of all students, namely 50. So our null hypothesis value is 50, and I'll write the null hypothesis as H_0: μ = 50. You test N = 30 students from that college and calculate M = 57.8, so the mean HEAT for your sample of 30 students is 7.8 points above the null hypothesis value we're examining. The _p_ value is the probability that a study like ours would obtain M that's 57.8 or more, or 42.2 or less, IF H_0 is true (i.e., μ = 50).

Where did that 42.2 come from? Yes, it's the same 7.8 points below 50 as our result is above, so values below 42.2 are just as extreme as values above our result of 57.8. When, like now, we're assuming σ is known, the sampling distribution of M is normal, so the _p_ value we seek is the area under both tails of that normal distribution. We need to find the _z_ score corresponding to our result, IF H_0 is true, then inspect the normal distribution to find the tail areas that will give us the _p_ value.

From Chapter 4 we know that the sampling distribution of the sample mean, M, is a normal distribution with mean μ and standard deviation of SE = $\sigma/\sqrt{N}$. Therefore, to calculate a CI when σ is known, in Chapter 5 we chose a statistical model based on the normal distribution. We do the same here. To find the _z_ score we want we can use the following formula from Chapter 5:

The null hypothesis is H_0, and the null hypothesis value is μ_0.

Use _z_ to calculate the _p_ value when we are willing to assume σ is known.

▶
z score for
the sampling
distribution of M

$$z = \frac{(M - \mu)}{\sigma/\sqrt{N}} \tag{5.5}$$

When H_0 is true, the population mean is μ_0. Insert that into Equation 5.5 to obtain:

▶
z score when H_0
is true

$$z = \frac{(M - \mu_0)}{\sigma/\sqrt{N}} \tag{6.1}$$

For our example, $z = (57.8 - 50)/(20/\sqrt{30}) = 2.136$. This z is a measure of how far $M = 57.8$ is from $\mu_0 = 50$, in SE units; it's a measure of how far our result deviates from what H_0 would suggest. The p value is the probability of obtaining this amount of deviation or even more, in either direction, IF H_0 is true.

Figure 6.5 shows the standard normal distribution with cursors at $z = 2.136$ and -2.136 to define the two tail areas we want. To make that figure, at the **Normal** page I clicked **Two tails** and **Areas**, and used the large slider to position the cursor. The total area of those two shaded tails is .0327. Our p value is therefore .0327, which I'll round to .03. So $p = .03$ is the probability of obtaining $z = 2.136$ or more, or -2.136 or less, in any normal distribution. Equivalently, .03 is the probability of obtaining M of 57.8 or more, or 42.2 or less in our example, IF the true mean is 50. What does that p value tell us about our null hypothesis?

A p value of around .03 says that, IF H_0 is true, there's only about a 3% chance of getting M of 57.8 or more extreme, and so this p provides some evidence against H_0. If we use NHST decision making, the fact that $p < .05$ leads us to reject the hypothesis that the mean HEAT score for College Alpha students is 50, the same as for students generally, and instead conclude the population mean for College Alpha students is greater than 50. We've found a statistically significant difference. In a moment there's an exercise that considers the CI for our result.

Here's a step-by-step summary of how we found and interpreted that p value:

1. We identified our sample result ($M = 57.8$) and our null hypothesis (H_0: $\mu = 50$).
2. We focused on the difference, or discrepancy, between that result and the null hypothesis value. Our difference was $(57.8 - 50)$.

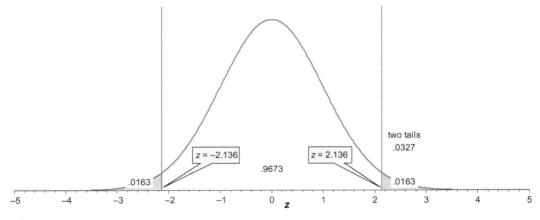

Figure 6.5. The standard normal distribution with cursors at $z = 2.136$ and -2.136. The two shaded tails have total area of .0327. From the **Normal** page.

3. We used a formula (Equation 6.1) to calculate from that difference the value of a *test statistic*, IF H_0 were true. We calculated that $z = 2.136$.
4. We consulted the distribution of the test statistic, *z*, to find the two tail areas corresponding to that value of the test statistic. Figure 6.5 tells us that the total area is .03 (after rounding); this is our *p* value.
5. We interpreted the *p* value, using the NHST or strength of evidence approach.

> A ***test statistic*** is a statistic with a known distribution, when H_0 is true, that allows calculation of a *p* value. For example, *z* is a widely used test statistic that has the standard normal distribution.

In future chapters we'll use some version of that step-by-step process to calculate the *p* value for various different dependent variables and various different study designs.

6.3 Considering Open Science, what questions should we ask about the College Alpha study?
6.4 Suppose we had obtained $M = 54.6$ in our HEAT study, with $N = 30$.
   a. Calculate the *p* value, assuming $\sigma = 20$ is known.
   b. Recall that MoE is half the length of a CI. Calculate MoE and the 95% CI for our result, still assuming $\sigma = 20$ is known.
   c. Compare the formula you used to find MoE and the formula you used for the *z* that gave you the *p* value.
   d. Compare the information provided by the CI and by the *p* value.
esci 6.5 a. Suppose you had used a sample of $N = 100$ College Alpha students, and happened to get the same $M = 54.6$. Calculate the *p* value and CI, and interpret. Compare with your original smaller study.
   b. Make up at least three more such exercises, which give a wide range of *p* values. Swap with friends.

p VALUES AND THE *t* DISTRIBUTION

If we drop the assumption that σ, the population SD, is known, we can follow the same step-by-step process as before to find the *p* value. The only difference is that, as in Chapter 5 when we calculated CIs without assuming σ is known, we need a statistical model based on the *t* distribution rather than the normal. Our test statistic is *t*, not *z*, and we refer to the *t* distribution to find the tail areas that give us the *p* value. As before, our null hypothesis is $H_0: \mu = 50$ and our sample of $N = 30$ students gave a mean HEAT score of $M = 57.8$. We also need to know that the standard deviation for our sample was $s = 23.5$. As before, the *p* value is the probability that a study like ours would obtain *M* that's 57.8 or more, or 42.2 or less, IF H_0 is true.

In Chapter 5, our formula for *t* was:

$$t = \frac{(M - \mu)}{s/\sqrt{N}}$$

(5.6)

t for the sampling distribution of *M*, using *s*

This is the same as Equation 5.5 for z, but with s in place of σ because we don't know σ and therefore must use the sample standard deviation, $s = 23.5$, as our best estimate of σ. There are $df = (N - 1) = 29$ degrees of freedom.

When H_0 is true, the population mean is μ_0. Insert that into Equation 5.6 to obtain

▶ *t* when H_0 is true

$$t = \frac{(M - \mu_0)}{s/\sqrt{N}} \tag{6.2}$$

▶ Use *t* and *s*, the sample SD, to calculate the *p* value when σ is not known.

For our example, $t = (57.8 - 50)/(23.5/\sqrt{30}) = 1.818$. This t is a measure of how far $M = 57.8$ is from $\mu_0 = 50$, in SE units; it's a measure of how far our result deviates from what H_0 would suggest. The p value is the probability of obtaining this amount of deviation or even more, in either direction, IF H_0 is true.

Figure 6.6 shows the t distribution with $df = 29$ and cursors at $t = 1.818$ and -1.818 to define the two tail areas we want. To make the figure, at the **Normal and t** page I clicked *t*, **Two tails**, and **Areas**, and used the slider to position the cursor. The total area of the two shaded tails is .0794. Our p value is therefore .0794, which I'll round to .08. So $p = .08$ is the probability of obtaining $t = 1.818$ or more, or -1.818 or less, in the t distribution with $df = 29$. Equivalently, .08 is our calculation of the probability of obtaining M of 57.8 or more, or 42.2 or less, IF the true mean is 50. What does that p value tell us about our null hypothesis?

A p value of around .08 says that, if H_0 is true, there's about an 8% chance of getting M of 57.8 or more extreme, and so this p provides very little, if any, evidence against H_0. If we use NHST decision making, with $p > .05$ we could not reject the hypothesis that the mean HEAT score for College Alpha students is 50, the same as for students generally. (Note that, as usual, we speak of not rejecting the null hypothesis, and *not* of accepting it. A sample mean of 57.8 is definitely *not* evidence the population value is 50.) We found no statistically significant difference. Again there's an exercise in a moment, but consider what you can already say about the CI, calculated using *t*. Where does it fall in relation to 50, our null hypothesis value?

Using *z* and *t*, our two p values are only a little different, .03 and .08 respectively. However, they happen to fall on opposite sides of .05, so NHST

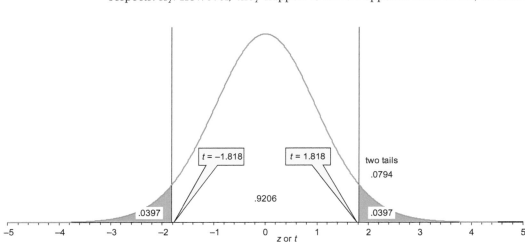

Figure 6.6. The *t* distribution with $df = 29$ showing cursors at $t = 1.818$ and -1.818. The two shaded tails have total area of .0794. From **Normal and t**.

with that significance level gives two different conclusions. Why do the two *p* values differ, despite our using the same sample mean, $M = 57.8$, in both cases?

The main difference, of course, is that the two are based on different statistical models. If we think it's reasonable to use the population value of $\sigma = 20$ for students at College Alpha, then we choose a normal distribution model and use *z* to calculate the *p* value. If we consider students at that college to be notably different from the whole college population to which the HEAT refers, then we might prefer to avoid assuming $\sigma = 20$ for students at College Alpha, choose a *t* distribution model, and use *s* and *t* to calculate the *p* value (or CI). As so often, it's a matter of your informed judgment. We will generally prefer to use a population value of σ, if available, rather than use our sample *s* as an estimate of σ, especially if *N* is small and therefore our *s* may not be a good estimate of σ.

◀ When it's reasonable to assume σ is known, do so, and use *z* to calculate the CI and/or *p* value. If not, use *s* to estimate σ and calculate *t*.

 6.6 Suppose again that we had obtained $M = 54.6$ in our HEAT study, with $N = 30$, and that $s = 14.3$.

   a. Calculate the *p* value, without assuming σ is known.
   b. Calculate the 95% CI for our result, still without assuming σ is known.
   c. Compare the formula you used to find MoE and the formula for the *t* you used to find the *p* value.
   d. Compare the information provided by the CI and the *p* value.

6.7 Suppose you had used a sample of $N = 100$ College Alpha students, and happened to get the same $M = 54.6$ and $s = 14.3$. Calculate the *p* value and CI, and interpret. Compare with your original experiment.

6.8 If you used a sample of $N = 400$ College Alpha students, would the sample *s* be a better or less good estimate of σ than *s* when $N = 30$? Why?

   a. Make up at least three more exercises like the last two, which give a wide range of *p* values. Swap with friends.

We've now seen how to calculate *p* values for a single group study, either with σ assumed known or without that assumption. The formulas for calculating *p* were very similar to those for calculating CIs, thus illustrating again the close links between *p* values and estimation. In future chapters we'll see many more examples of those links. Next I'll explore those links by discussing how we can translate back and forth between CIs and *p* values.

TRANSLATING BETWEEN 95% CIS AND *p* VALUES

From a 95% CI to a *p* Value

In Chapter 5 I discussed four ways to interpret a CI. Figure 6.3 illustrates a fifth way: Note whether the null hypothesis value μ_0 is outside or inside the CI to know whether $p < .05$ or $p > .05$. Here I'll go further and consider how to eyeball a *p* value, given a 95% CI and a null hypothesis value μ_0. Translation to *p* is my least favored way to interpret a CI, because it ignores much of the useful information a CI provides. However, I include this fifth approach partly because it broadens our options for thinking about a CI, but mainly because it's a stepping stone to the following section, which considers the valuable translation in the reverse direction: See a *p* value and mean, and eyeball the CI.

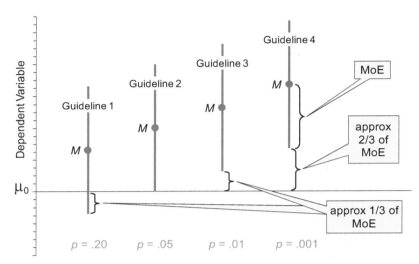

Figure 6.7. Four sample means with 95% CIs, all of the same length. The null hypothesis value is μ_0, often zero. The *p* value is shown below each CI. The labels indicate four approximate guidelines for eyeballing the *p* value from where the CI falls in relation to μ_0.

Figure 6.7 displays four sample means with 95% CIs, all of the same length, and four guidelines for *p* values. The null hypothesis value of μ_0 is marked by the horizontal line. The *p* value is shown at the bottom for each sample. First, note that the simple rule displayed in Figure 6.3 holds: The first CI, on the left, includes μ_0 and so *p* > .05. The third and fourth CIs, on the right, do not include μ_0 and so *p* < .05. The second CI illustrates the borderline case and Guideline 2: When a limit of the CI falls at μ_0, then *p* = .05.

That's a start, but we can do better. Above I noted also that the further a CI falls from μ_0, the more our data throw doubt on the null hypothesis and the lower the *p* value. The four CIs in Figure 6.7 are, from left to right, successively further above μ_0 and so we would expect the *p* value to decrease from left to right—as it does. I chose the four sample means to illustrate four cases that are easy to remember as guidelines to help eyeballing the *p* value, for any 95% CI on means.

Below are the four guidelines that the figure illustrates from left to right. Guideline 2 in the list below is exact and the others are approximate, but close enough for practical purposes. Recall that MoE is the length of one arm of a CI, as labeled in the figure.

> If a 95% CI falls so that μ_0 is about one-third of MoE beyond a limit, *p* = .01, approximately—Guideline 3 in Figure 6.7. The figure also illustrates three further guidelines to assist with eyeballing a *p* value.

1. If a 95% CI falls so μ_0 is about 1/3 of MoE back from a limit of the CI, then *p* = .20, approximately. (Guideline 1 on the left in Figure 6.7.)
2. If a 95% CI falls so that μ_0 is at a limit, then *p* = .05.
3. If a 95% CI falls so that μ_0 is about 1/3 of MoE beyond a limit, then *p* = .01, approximately.
4. If a 95% CI falls so that μ_0 is about 2/3 of MoE beyond a limit, then *p* = .001, approximately.

Note that it doesn't matter whether the CI falls above or below μ_0—the guidelines are the same. Of course, most cases we'll see in practice lie somewhere in between the cases illustrated in Figure 6.7, so we'll need to interpolate between the two cases that come closest. That's fine, because the aim is to eyeball a rough estimate of the *p* value, not to replace the calculation we'd need if we want an accurate *p* value.

Of course you can use the same guidelines when a CI is reported in text rather than shown in a figure. Perhaps you read that "the decrease in mean response time was 32 ms [10, 54]." You wish to estimate the *p* value for testing the null hypothesis of zero change, meaning $\mu_0 = 0$. First, note that 0 is not in the CI, so we know $p < .05$. Then sketch—or see in your mind's eye—the CI and how it falls in relation to zero. Compare with Figure 6.7, note that our CI falls between the two rightmost cases, meaning *p* is between .01 and .001, perhaps around .005. Again, note that we're happy for our eyeballing to be rough—the aim is a ballpark idea of the *p* value, not an exact calculation.

Figure 6.8 provides a further illustration of how the *p* value changes depending on where a 95% CI falls in relation to μ_0. Imagine moving *M* and the CI up and down, and eyeballing the *p* value. The short dotted lines labeled with *p* values move up and down with the CI, and mark our four guidelines.

 6.9 Open the **CI and p** page of **ESCI intro chapters 3–8**. Explore as you wish. Use the big slider to move the heavy blue 95% CI up and down in relation to the fixed μ_0 value. Try clicking on **Small hints**. Compare with Figure 6.8.

 6.10 Make up games or challenges to practice reading *p* values, given a 95% CI and μ_0. For example, turn off the *p* value (red 2) and all hints, move *M*, eyeball *p*, then turn on the *p* vale to check your accuracy. Go for speed and competition.

6.11 For each of the 95% CIs in Figure 6.9, estimate the *p* value.

6.12 You read that "the increase in mean reading age was 2.3 months [−0.5, 5.1]." What is the approximate *p* value, for the null hypothesis of zero increase?

If a 95% CI falls so μ_0 is at a limit (i.e., exactly at one end of the CI), then $p = .05$. Suppose a 99% CI falls so μ_0 is at a limit, what do you think the *p* value would be?

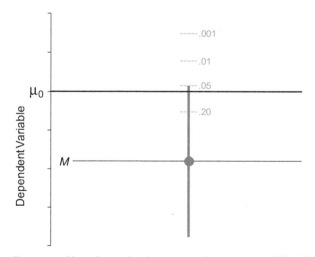

Figure 6.8. An illustration of how the *p* value changes according to where a 95% CI falls in relation to the null hypothesis value, μ_0. When μ_0 is just inside the 95% CI, as illustrated, $p = .07$. The short dotted lines and their *p* value labels provide hints for eyeballing. From the **CI and p** page, with **Small hints** turned on.

...Pause, think, discuss...

What about a 90% CI?

If you guessed that a 99% CI falling so μ_0 is at a limit gives a *p* value of .01, give yourself a pat on the back. For a 90% CI, the *p* value is .10. You probably see the pattern: For a *C*% CI, if μ_0 is at a CI limit, $p = (1 - C/100)$. Check that formula works for 95% CIs.

6.13 We saw in Chapter 5 that a 99% CI is about one-third longer than a 95% CI. Explain how that observation relates to our Guideline 3.

One final note: The guidelines in Figure 6.7 are based on large samples and the normal distribution, but are sufficiently accurate, for practical purposes, unless *N* is very small, say less than about 10. So feel encouraged to use these guidelines for any CIs on means.

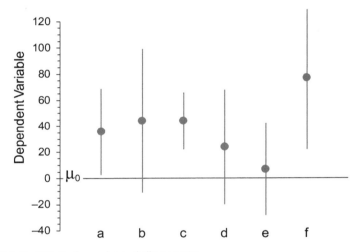

Figure 6.9. Six 95% CIs, for *p* value eyeballing practice.

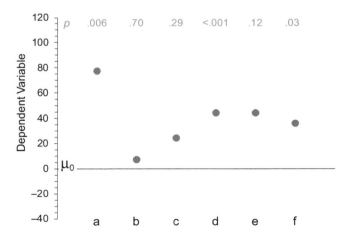

Figure 6.10. Six means, with their *p* values shown at the top, for eyeballing practice of the 95% CI on each mean.

From a Mean and a *p* Value to a 95% CI

If you are given a mean and a *p* value, and also know the null hypothesis value, then you can run the guidelines in Figure 6.7 backwards to eyeball the 95% CI on that mean. That's useful, because you can then interpret the result in terms of an effect size estimate (the mean) and the uncertainty of that estimate (the eyeballed CI). In practice, eyeballing the CI, even roughly, usually emphasizes that there's considerable uncertainty—the CI is often long—whereas seeing only the *p* value might give a misleading impression of certainty.

Given *M*, the *p* value, and μ$_0$, use the guidelines in Figure 6.7 to eyeball the approximate 95% CI.

Figure 6.10 displays six means and, at the top, their *p* values. Can you sketch or eyeball the CIs now, before I give a couple of hints? Very rough is OK.

 Pause, discuss ... As usual it's worth trying it yourself. Best is to make up a couple more examples.

Here's a simple way you could approach the task:

- If *p* = .05, the CI extends exactly from the mean to μ$_0$. Otherwise, there are two possibilities:
  1. *p* > .05, and the CI must extend past μ$_0$. The larger the *p*, the further the CI extends past μ$_0$.
  2. *p* < .05 and the CI extends only part way towards μ$_0$. The smaller the *p*, the shorter the CI in relation to μ$_0$.

Following even just those basic rules often gives useful insight, but you can go further:

- If *p* > .05, consider Guideline 1 in Figure 6.7. Note whether the *p* value is larger or smaller than .2 and eyeball the CI to be longer or shorter, respectively, than that in Figure 6.7. Remember: The larger the *p*, the further the CI extends past μ$_0$.
- If *p* < .05, consider Guidelines 3 and 4 in Figure 6.7. Note where the *p* value falls in relation to .01 and .001, and eyeball the CI accordingly to be longer or shorter than those in Figure 6.7. Remember: The smaller the *p*, the shorter the CI in relation to μ$_0$.

For example, consider (a) in Figure 6.10. The *p* value of .006 lies between .01 and .001, so the CI we want falls between the two rightmost cases in Figure 6.7. I'm eyeballing the mean as about 75 and the CI as extending down to about 25. Therefore my eyeballed CI extends from 25 up to 125, which is the same distance (50) above 75 as 25 is below. My eyeballed result is thus 75 [25, 125]. The accurate value is 77 [22, 132], so my eyeballed CI is easily good enough to give useful insight. It tells us there's wide uncertainty—the true value could plausibly be anywhere between, roughly, 25 and 125. That's an important message: Yes, the small *p* value of .006 provides quite strong evidence against μ$_0$ = 0, but if we think only of the *p* value we may not be sufficiently aware of the wide uncertainty remaining.

If *p* > .05, the 95% CI extends past μ$_0$, and the larger the *p*, the further it extends. If *p* < .05, the CI doesn't extend as far as μ$_0$, and the smaller the *p*, the shorter the CI.

Even a rough, ballpark idea of the CI provides guidance about uncertainty. Bringing to mind the approximate CI may be the best way to interpret a *p* value. Note, especially, that *p* around .05 tells us that the CI extends from *M* to close to μ$_0$, as in Figure 6.7, Guideline 2.

Eyeballing the CI may be the best way to interpret a *p* value. If *p* is around .05, the CI extends from *M* to close to μ$_0$.

6.14 Sketch and write as numbers your eyeballed CIs for the remaining five cases in Figure 6.10. Rough is OK.

6.15 You read that "the increase in mean reading age was 2.3 months, which was statistically significantly greater than zero, *p* = .03." What is the approximate 95% CI?

The next section discusses one of this book's most important messages, which I'll describe as a number of *red flags*.

Quiz 6.2

1. In NHST, the test statistic is used to obtain a *p* value by determining the probability of obtaining
   a. the observed result, *or more extreme*, if the null is true.
   b. the observed result, *or less extreme*, if the null is true.
   c. the observed result *exactly*, if the null is true.
   d. the observed result *approximately*, if the null is true.
2. With a sample test statistic z = 1, which panel in Figure 6.11 represents the associated *p* value?

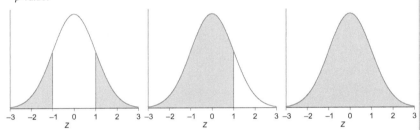

Figure 6.11. Three distributions of the z test statistic.

3. Use ESCI to calculate the *p* values for each test statistic:
   a. z = 1
   b. z = −1
   c. z = 3
   d. t(20) = 2
   e. t(50) = 2
   f. t(30) = −1
4. For the question above, which of these results would lead to rejecting the null hypothesis with a significance level of .01?
5. When testing a null hypothesis about a population mean, you need to calculate a *test statistic* that you will use to obtain a *p* value. Which of the following statements is (or are) true?
   a. Calculate a z score if you know σ, the population SD; otherwise calculate a *t* score.
   b. Calculate a z score if the data includes negative numbers, otherwise calculate a *t* score.
   c. Calculate a z score if you reject the null, otherwise calculate a *t* score.
6. A new training procedure gives a mean increase in performance of 8 points, 95% CI [1, 15]. Roughly, what is the *p* value to test the null hypothesis of zero change? Would you reject the null hypothesis at the .05 level? At the .01 level? At the .001 level?

FOUR NHST AND *p* VALUE RED FLAGS

Whenever you read about *p* values or NHST, these cautions should automatically pop up in your mind. I'll describe four here, and there's a fifth in Chapter 7.

Beware Dichotomous Thinking

If there's uncertainty in data—as there virtually always is—we should be wary of any conclusion that gives a false sense of certainty. The world is usually not black-and-white, but numerous shades of gray, so a dichotomous conclusion is likely to be inappropriate and too readily give a sense of certainty. A major disadvantage of NHST is that it prompts *dichotomous thinking* by giving a dichotomous conclusion—we reject or do not reject the null hypothesis; we conclude there is or is not a statistically significant effect.

Dichotomous thinking focuses on two mutually exclusive alternatives. The dichotomous reject-or-don't-reject decisions of NHST tend to elicit dichotomous thinking.

In contrast, *estimation thinking* focuses on quantitative information, which is usually far more useful. For example, consider a new therapy for anxiety. NHST addresses the question "Is there an effect?" and concludes that the therapy does or does not have a statistically significant effect, which is a yes/no answer to the question. However, an estimate of the size of the likely reduction in anxiety provides much better guidance for practical decision making about whether or not to use the therapy. A good way to prompt such useful quantitative answers is to express research questions in estimation terms: "How large is the effect?" rather than "Is there an effect?"

Estimation thinking focuses on "how much", by focusing on point and interval estimates.

Recall Step 1 in the step-by-step plan in Chapter 1:

1. State the research question. Express it as a "how much" or "to what extent" question.

What's the support for Proposition A in the population of people likely to vote?

When you read an aim that prompts a yes/no answer ("Does the therapy work?"), automatically reword it in your head as an estimation question. Often that's easy: Just add "to what extent" at the start. Expressing our research aims as estimation questions may be the key step toward adopting an estimation approach to research.

Express research questions in estimation terms.

> Beware dichotomous conclusions, which may give a false sense of certainty. Prefer estimation thinking. Express research aims as "how much" or "to what extent" questions.

Red Flag 1

Beware the Ambiguity of the "S" Word, "Significant"

The danger here is that "statistically significant" too easily suggests an effect is large or important. After all, the dictionary tells us that "significant" means "important" or "noteworthy". However, an effect can be of no importance, but highly statistically significant—simply use a very large *N*. Conversely, an effect can easily be highly important, but not even close to statistically significant. Therefore "significant", the "S" word, can be highly misleading: When used statistically, "significant" does *not* imply "important".

"Significant", the "S" word, can be highly misleading. A large or important effect might not be statistically significant; a trivial effect may be highly statistically significant.

As an example of how the S word can be dangerously ambiguous, consider the common fallacy I call the *slippery slope of significance*: In the data analysis section of an article, you read that "there was a statistically significant decrease in anxiety, *p* = .03". However, in the discussion the authors state that "anxiety was significantly reduced", which suggests that the reduction was substantial or important. The ambiguous S word silently morphs from its statistical to its everyday meaning. Discussing an effect size as large or important requires justification based on informed judgment, whatever the value of *p*. Seeing

I refer to the following fallacy as the *slippery slope of significance*: An effect is found to be statistically significant, is described, ambiguously, as "significant", then later is discussed as if it had been shown to be important or large.

the S word should automatically trigger your "ambiguous S word" red flag. In particular, beware the slippery slope of significance.

To avoid ambiguity, add "statistical" in front of the S word whenever that's the intended meaning. For other meanings, replace "significant" by "important", "notable", "large", or some other suitable word.

Researchers need to be especially careful when writing for the general public, or explaining their findings to the media. Journalists love to highlight that a result is "significant". Avoid using the S word when describing your results, and watch out for a journalist who adds it in anyway. Of course, make sure an especially large red flag pops up whenever you see the S word in any media report of a research result.

> "Significant" is a dangerously ambiguous word when used by itself. Say "statistically significant", or use a different word.

Red Flag 2

Beware the dangerously ambiguous S word. Say "statistically significant", or use a different word. Beware the slippery slope of significance.

6.16 Find uses of the S word in reports of research, in the media, or online. Reword to make clear which meaning is intended. Bonus points if you can find an example of the slippery slope of significance.

Beware Accepting the Null Hypothesis

Using NHST decision making, we reject H_0 when $p < .05$. If $p > .05$ we don't reject. That seems simple, but the danger is that failing to reject H_0 can easily lead to believing H_0 is true. First, we must be careful to say "H_0 was not rejected" rather than "H_0 was accepted". Second, we must be vigilant for any hint that "no sign of a difference" becomes "the difference is zero". Think of the many long CIs we've seen. Failing to reject H_0 merely tells us that μ_0 is somewhere within the CI, and provides no grounds for thinking that μ_0 is the true value. In other words:

"Not rejecting H_0 is not sufficient reason to conclude that H_0 is true."

Sentences with multiple "nots" are hard to read, but that's what we need here. Read that statement aloud a few times, faster and faster…

> I refer to the following fallacy as the *slippery slope of nonsignificance*: An effect is found to be statistically nonsignificant, then later discussed as if that showed it to be non-existent.

Here's another common fallacy: the *slippery slope of nonsignificance*. The data analysis states: "Because $p > .05$, we couldn't reject the null hypothesis of no difference in the levels of anxiety in the two groups." That's fine, but later, in discussing the results we see: "The treatment made no difference to the children's level of anxiety…." The statistically nonsignificant difference quietly became no difference, which a reader is likely to think of as a zero difference. Whenever a null hypothesis is not rejected, your "don't-accept-H_0" red flag should pop up to remind you of the danger of accepting the null hypothesis.

What, you might ask, if an effect is actually zero? Good question. The best approach is to estimate the size of the effect. If the CI is close to zero—perhaps zero is inside the interval, or perhaps not—and *all* values in the interval are very small, or negligible, you might be willing to conclude that, for practical purposes, the effect is around zero. That's usually as close as we can come to accepting a null hypothesis—to concluding that H_0 is true—and we didn't use NHST.

6.17 a. Suppose the result of our poll was 53% in a poll with margin of error of 4%. Test the null hypothesis of 50% support in the population. Describe how a researcher using NHST might report that result, (i) falling into the trap of accepting H_0, and (ii) avoiding that trap.

b. Interpret a result of 50.2% with a margin of error of 1%.

A large *p* value provides no evidence that the null hypothesis is true. Beware accepting the null hypothesis. Beware the slippery slope of nonsignificance.

Red Flag 3

Beware the *p* Value: What a *p* Value Is, and What It's Not

As you know, the *p* value indicates strength of evidence against H_0. It's the probability of getting our observed result, or more extreme, IF the null hypothesis is true. However, it's a common error to think the *p* value is something very different: the probability that H_0 *is* true. Unfortunately the *p* value can't tell us that, and believing it does is the *inverse probability fallacy*. Consider the striking difference between:

> The *inverse probability fallacy* is the incorrect belief that the *p* value is the probability that H_0 is true.

- *Probability 1.* The probability you speak English, IF you are reading this book (close to 1, I would think); and the reverse:
- *Probability 2.* The probability you will read this book, IF you speak English. (Even if one million people read this book—I wish!—that's still a probability close to 0, because so many millions of people in the world speak English.)

Here's another example of the same distinction. Compare:

- *Probability 3.* The probability of getting certain results, IF H_0 is true (that's our *p* value); and the reverse:
- *Probability 4.* The probability H_0 is true, IF we've obtained certain results. (We'd like to know that but, alas, *p* can't tell us.)

In both of these examples, the two probabilities are fundamentally different, with the second being the reverse of the first. It's worth reading them all again, to fully grasp that the relation between 3 and 4 is the same as the relation between 1 and 2.

Probability 3 is the *p* value that often is easily calculated when we assume H_0 is true. Probability 4 refers to truth in the world, and in a sense it must be either 0 (H_0 is false) or 1 (H_0 is true), but we don't know which. Probabilities 1 and 2 obviously have very different values. Probabilities 3 and 4 might be just as different. They are certainly not referring to the same thing.

Here's another way to think about the *p* value. Suppose you run an experiment to investigate whether your friend can use the power of her mind to influence whether a coin comes up heads or tails. You take great care to avoid trickery—consult a skilled conjurer to discover how difficult that is. Your friend concentrates deeply then predicts correctly the outcome of all 10 tosses in your trial. I can tell you that the *p* value is .001, the probability she would get all 10 correct, IF the null hypothesis of a fair coin and random guessing were true. Are you going to reject H_0, and buy her the drink she bet you? Or will you conclude that most likely she's just had a very lucky day? Sure, .001 is very small, but you find her claimed power of the mind *very* hard to accept. That's our dilemma: Either H_0 is true and a very unlikely event has occurred as the tiny *p* value indicated, or H_0 is not true. It's relevant to note the *p* value as we consider those two possibilities, but *p* doesn't tell us the probability that your friend is merely guessing. That's the dilemma, which NHST side-steps by using conventions that .05 or .01 are reasonable *p* values for rejecting H_0, thus resorting to a mechanical rule that takes no account of the situation.

Some statistics textbooks say that *p* measures the probability that "the results are due to chance"; in other words, the probability that the null hypothesis is correct. However, that's wrong, and merely a restatement of the inverse probability fallacy. Jacob Cohen, a distinguished statistics reformer, wrote that a *p* value "does not tell us what we want to know, and we so much want to know what we want to know that, out of desperation, we nevertheless believe that it does!" (Cohen, 1994, p. 997). In other words, we want to know whether H_0 is true (Probability 4 above), but *p* does *not* measure that—it measures the probability of obtaining certain results IF H_0 is true (Probability 3). In desperation we believe that *p* measures the probability H_0 is true (Probability 4)—wrong!—and, unfortunately, some textbooks perpetuate the error.

The *p* value is *not* the probability the results are due to chance. That's another version of the inverse probability fallacy.

> **Red Flag 4** Beware any suggestion that the *p* value is the probability that H_0 is true. In other words, the *p* value is *not* the probability that our results are due to chance.

6.18 What is the probability that a person is an American citizen, IF they are a member of the U.S. Congress? What is the probability a person is a member of the U.S. Congress, IF they are an American citizen? Explain why the two are different.

6.19 Call your answers to 6.18 Probabilities 5 and 6. Use them to explain how Probabilities 3 and 4 are different things, and might well have different values.

We've seen four red flags (there's a fifth to come, in Chapter 7):

1. The *dichotomous thinking* red flag. Be wary of black-and-white hypotheses or conclusions, which may give a false sense of certainty. Use estimation thinking and ask "how much" questions.

2. The *ambiguous S word* red flag. "Significant" is ambiguous—which meaning is intended? Avoid using the word, or say "statistically significant". Beware the slippery slope of significance.

3. The *don't-accept-H_0* red flag. Not rejecting H_0 is not sufficient reason to conclude that it's true. Beware the slippery slope of nonsignificance.

4. The *what the p value isn't* red flag. The *p* value is a tricky probability, IF H_0 is true; it's *not* the probability that H_0 is true, or that results are due to chance.

I hope your red flags are beginning to pop up and wave automatically, whenever you encounter any red flag triggers. I also hope that using estimation will reduce your red flag count.

NHST DECISION MAKING

To give a more complete picture of NHST, I need to discuss some additional topics. However, you could skip this whole section, and come back to it when, in Chapter 10, we discuss statistical power—which uses many of the concepts I'll now introduce. Here's the list:

- NHST decision making: Not only H_0, the null hypothesis, but also H_1, the alternative hypothesis
- The two possible errors: Type I and Type II errors
- A courtroom analogy for NHST decision making and the four possible outcomes
- An optional extra: How the p value, and the alternative hypothesis, may be one-tailed or two-tailed

Next comes a new concept, then a few slightly complicated steps as I describe how NHST decision making works. At the end I'll describe a courtroom analogy that I hope helps it all make sense. At any point, you might find it helpful to skip ahead and read the short courtroom analogy section, then come back.

The Alternative Hypothesis

So far we've considered only the single hypothesis, H_0, and have rejected H_0, or failed to reject it. The first new concept is the *alternative hypothesis*, with symbol H_1. NHST assumes that H_0 and H_1 do not overlap and that just one is true. Informally, think of it like this:

Informally, the alternative hypothesis, H_1, states "There is an effect."

- H_0: There's no effect.
- H_1: There is an effect.

> The *alternative hypothesis* is a statement about the population effect that's distinct from the null hypothesis.

It's common for NHST to use

- the null hypothesis H_0: $\mu = 0$, and
- the alternative hypothesis H_1: $\mu \neq 0$.

In other words, either the effect is zero, or it isn't.

The NHST Decision Rule

Recall strict NHST decision making, which requires the significance level to be chosen in advance. I'll refer to that significance level as α (Greek lower case alpha). NHST rejects H_0 if $p < \alpha$, and does not reject if $p \geq \alpha$. Recall our study that examined the HEAT scores of a sample of students at College Alpha. We used H_0: $\mu = 50$. We can now state an alternative hypothesis, which is H_1: $\mu \neq 50$. We found (using t) that $p = .08$. Choosing $\alpha = .05$, we note that $p \geq \alpha$ and so we don't reject H_0. We conclude that the mean HEAT score of College Alpha students is not statistically significantly different from 50, the mean in the general student population.

The strict NHST significance level chosen in advance is α, and the decision rule is: Reject H_0 when $p < \alpha$; otherwise don't reject.

6.20 Suppose we had found $p = .02$, what would we have decided? State your conclusion in good NHST language.

Table 6.1 The Four Possibilities for NHST Decision Making

		State of the world	
		H_0 is true, and $\mu = 0$ There's no effect	H_1 is true, and $\mu \neq 0$ There is an effect
Decision	$p \geq \alpha$, don't reject H_0	**Correctly don't reject H_0** ☺ No sign of an effect	**Type II error (rate = β)** ☹ Don't reject H_0 when it's false False negative: We missed the effect
	$p < \alpha$, reject H_0	**Type I error (rate = α)** ☹ Reject H_0 when it's true False positive: Wrongly claim an effect	**Correctly reject H_0** ☺ We found the effect!

Type I and Type II Errors

Given the assumption that either H_0 or H_1 is true, there are two possible states of the world: Either there's no effect and H_0 is true, or there is an effect and H_1 is true. In addition, there are two decisions we can make: Reject H_0, or don't reject H_0. Therefore, there are four possibilities, as illustrated by the four main cells of Table 6.1.

There are two cells we'd be happy to occupy, because our decision would be correct: In the top left cell, there's no effect, H_0 is true, and we correctly don't reject it. In the bottom right, there is an effect, H_1 is true, and we correctly reject H_0.

The other two cells are errors, which are called *Type I* and *Type II* errors:

▶ There are four possibilities for NHST decision making. Two would make us happy, two are errors.

A **Type I error** is the rejection of H_0 when it's true, as in the bottom left cell in Table 6.1.

▶ A *Type I error*, or **false positive**: We reject when we shouldn't.

A Type I error is a *false positive*. We shout "There's an effect!", but alas we're wrong. If we reject the null hypothesis that $\mu = 50$ for College Alpha students when that is indeed their population mean HEAT score, then we are making a Type I error.

A **Type II error** is failing to reject H_0 when it's false, as in the top right cell in Table 6.1.

▶ A *Type II error* is a **false negative**, or *miss*: We don't reject when we should.

A Type II error is a *false negative*, also called a *miss*. There is an effect, but we missed it. If we don't reject the null hypothesis that $\mu = 50$ for College Alpha students when their population mean HEAT score is *not* 50, then we are making a Type II error.

6.21 If you choose $\alpha = .01$ and obtain $p = .03$, what do you decide? Which cells in the table could you be in?

- ▨ Describe and name each of those cells.
- ▨ Do you ever know which single cell you are in? Explain.
- ▨ Can you ever be sure whether to be happy or sad? Explain.

6.22 Suppose you choose $\alpha = .05$ and obtain $p = .03$. Answer Exercise 6.21 for these values.

6.23 What's α, what's p, and how are they different?

Next comes a crucial point about α, and what it tells us about Type I errors.

The Type I Error Rate, α, and What It Means

What's the probability we'll make a Type I error when H_0 is true? When H_0 is true, we'll be unlucky and get $p < .05$ on just 5% of occasions in the long run. That's the definition of the p value. Choosing $\alpha = .05$, those 5% of occasions are when $p < \alpha$ and we reject H_0. Therefore α is the *Type I error rate*—the probability that we make a Type I error when the null hypothesis is true.

> The **Type I error rate**, α, is the probability of rejecting H_0 when it's true. It's also called the **false positive rate**. (Consider the bottom left cell in Table 6.1.)

$$\alpha = \text{Probability (Reject } H_0, \text{ WHEN } H_0 \text{ is true)} \qquad (6.3)$$

◀ Type I error rate, α.

It's vital to remember "WHEN H_0 is true" (same as "IF H_0 is true") for α, just as we must remember it for p values. Both α and a p value are probabilities that assume H_0 is true, and both can be misunderstood in the same way. Recall the warning about any statement like "The p value is the probability that H_0 is true." (Wrong!) Here we must beware any statement that α is the probability that H_0 is true, or the probability there's no effect. (Both wrong!)

◀ The Type I error rate, α, is the probability of rejecting H_0 when it is true. It is *not* the probability that H_0 is true.

Whenever you see α or a p value, say to yourself "assuming the null hypothesis is true."

6.24 Suppose you choose $\alpha = .05$. When the null hypothesis is true, what percentage of the NHST decisions you make will be false positives? Do we ever know whether the null hypothesis is true?

The Type II Error Rate, β, and What It Means

I'll now define the *Type II error rate*, which we refer to as β.

> The **Type II error rate**, β, is the probability of failing to reject H_0 when it's false. It's also called the *false negative rate*, or *miss rate*. (Consider the top right cell in Table 6.1.)

$$\beta = \text{Probability (Don't reject } H_0, \text{ WHEN } H_1 \text{ is true)} \qquad (6.4)$$

◀ Type II error rate, β.

To calculate a p value and consider α, the Type I error rate, we needed a null hypothesis that states a single value, such as $H_0: \mu = 0$. Similarly, to use Equation 6.4 to calculate β, the Type II error rate, we need an alternative hypothesis that states a single value. For our College Alpha example we might choose:

- $H_0: \mu = 50$ for the population of College Alpha students.
- $H_1: \mu = 60$.

Why 60? We might choose 60 because we know it has an especially strong environmental awareness program. Even so, it's artificial to suppose that the population mean is either exactly 50 or exactly 60, but using those hypotheses at least allows calculation of Type II as well as Type I error rates.

Using $H_1: \mu = 60$, β calculated using Equation 6.4 is the probability we'll miss the difference from 50, IF the College Alpha mean really is 60. Here we must note carefully that β is *not* the probability that H_1 is true—it's a probability that *assumes* H_1 is true. Whenever you see β or any mention of Type II errors, say to yourself "assuming H_1 is true", or "assuming there is an effect of exactly that size".

◀ The Type II error rate, β, is the probability of failing to reject H_0 when H_0 is false (i.e., H_1 is true). It is *not* the probability that H_1 is true.

A Courtroom Analogy to NHST Decision Making

After that blizzard of Greek letters, definitions, and sentences with lots of negatives (e.g., "don't reject", "false negatives"), here's the courtroom analogy. Earlier I described the dilemma of a researcher using NHST: Given a small *p* value, which indicates that our results are rather extreme, then either H_0 is true and an unlikely event has occurred, or H_0 is not true. Compare that with the dilemma in a courtroom. Suppose you are on a jury and hearing evidence about a defendant accused of a crime. If the person is innocent, the evidence you hear seems unlikely to have occurred, so you conclude there's fairly strong evidence of guilt. You are aching to know the truth—the accused either did or did not commit the crime—but you and the jury must decide, given only the evidence you've heard, whether to cry "guilty", or to let the initial strong presumption of innocence stand. You know that, whichever decision you make, you might be wrong.

> An analogy: A jury decides "guilty" or it doesn't; NHST rejects H_0 or doesn't reject.

There are strong parallels between the courtroom and NHST. In both cases there are two possible states of the world (the accused is not guilty or guilty; H_0 true or not), and a decision is required, despite uncertainty. Also, there is an initial presumption (the accused is innocent; H_0 is true) and a deliberate bias to reject that presumption only if the evidence is sufficiently strong—in the courtroom case, beyond reasonable doubt. There are two possible decision errors, one of which is regarded as more serious than the other. Here's the parallel:

	Researcher's Dilemma	Jury's Dilemma
Possible states of world	Effect exists, or it doesn't.	Accused is guilty, or not.
Initial presumption	H_0 true: No effect.	Not guilty.
Basis for deciding	Small *p* value.	Evidence, beyond reasonable doubt.
Decision possibilities	Reject H_0, there is an effect *or* don't reject H_0, and initial presumption stands.	Guilty *or* not guilty, and initial presumption stands.
Correct outcomes	Reject H_0 when effect exists. Don't reject H_0 when no effect.	Guilty person jailed. Innocent person walks free.
More serious error	False positive. Reject H_0 when there's really no effect.	False conviction. Innocent person jailed.
Less serious error	Miss. Don't reject H_0 when there is an effect.	Miss a conviction. Guilty person walks free.

When you encounter NHST ideas, think back to the courtroom analogy if you find that's helpful.

6.25 a. What's the courtroom equivalent of H_1?
  b. What courtroom outcome corresponds to a Type I error? Explain.
  c. What corresponds to a Type II error? Explain.

What Influences Type I and Type II Error Rates?

In the courtroom, suppose we decide to require even stronger evidence before deciding "guilty". What will happen to the two error rates—the numbers of guilty people who walk free and innocent people who are jailed? That's worth pondering… write down your thoughts.

The equivalent for the researcher is to choose smaller α, perhaps .01 rather than .05, so stronger evidence is required before we can reject H_0 and conclude there is an effect. What will happen to the Type I and Type II error rates?

Well, small α means we require stronger evidence before rejecting H_0, which means we'll be less likely to make Type I errors (less likely to convict the innocent); on the other hand, with a higher standard of evidence we'll also miss more effects that do exist (let more guilty people go free). In other words, smaller α means fewer Type I errors, but also more Type II errors.

Scientific progress is best if we can minimize both errors, but the two tend to trade off. For a given study, we can set smaller α so we make fewer Type I errors, but at the expense of more Type II—that's fewer false positives but more misses. Or we can choose larger α for the opposite pattern: More false positives, but we identify more effects when they do exist. Fortunately, there's a way out of this dilemma: Run a larger study. Other things remaining the same, for a stated Type I error rate (α), a larger N will give us a smaller Type II error rate (β), which is good news. With very large studies, you can even require a higher standard of evidence by reducing the Type I error rate (choosing smaller α) while still maintaining a quite low Type II error rate—again, all other things remaining the same. What do you want for your birthday? Big N! We'll discuss Type II error rates and choice of N as part of research planning in Chapter 10.

> Choose smaller α for fewer Type I errors, at the cost of more Type II. Fewer false positives, but more misses.

NHST tradition is to set a smallish α, usually .05, to limit the risk of false positives, and to test a single null hypothesis of no effect. The trouble is that it takes effort and judgment to specify a single H_1 value and consider β, and so NHST is often used without attention being paid to these critical factors—meaning we can't know what the Type II error rate might be. Therefore, if you read that H_0 was not rejected, bring to mind the risk of a Type II error—perhaps there's a real effect that was missed? Recall Red Flag 3 and make sure not to accept the null.

> Traditional NHST considers only H_0 and rejects it or not, with little or no idea of the risk of missing an effect by making a Type II error.

Finally in this section on the two errors, consider an important difference between them. The researcher chooses α, but what determines β? We've already seen two influences. If all other things remain the same:

- The two errors trade: Smaller α means larger β, and larger α means—you guessed it—smaller β.
- For a stated α, larger N gives smaller β.

The research design, for example independent groups or paired as we'll discuss in Chapters 7 and 8, influences β, and there's one more crucial influence. What difference do you think H_1 makes to β? In our College Alpha example, consider H_1: $\mu = 65$ rather than H_1: $\mu = 60$. Would you expect more or fewer Type II errors for a mean of 65 for the College population rather than 60?

> Type II error rate, β, is influenced by the research design, α, N, and the effect size stated by H_1.

 Ponder, call, discuss...

For a larger difference between H_0 and H_1, it will be easier to obtain statistical significance, meaning fewer Type II errors. The larger the effect, the easier it is to find. Therefore, other things remaining the same, we can say this:

- When H_1 states a larger effect (more different from the null hypothesis value), β is smaller.

One-Tailed *p* Values and One-Sided Hypotheses

These are two optional extra NHST concepts. First, one-tailed *p* values. To calculate the *p* value for the sample HEAT mean of $M = 57.8$ we included as "extreme" both values greater than 57.8 and values less than 42.2. However, if College Alpha has an especially strong environmental awareness program we might consider such low values as unbelievable and irrelevant—you may feel that, if the college mean is not 50, it can only be greater. If so, you could define "extreme" as only values greater than 57.8, in which case our *p* value is

$$p = \text{Probability } (M \geq 57.8, \text{ IF } H_0 \text{ true})$$

▶ When using means, one-tailed *p* is half of two-tailed *p*.

This is a *one-tailed p* value, whereas *p* that includes values above 57.8 and below 42.2 is called *two-tailed*. Working with means, the two tails have equal areas, and so one-tailed *p* is half of two-tailed *p*.

> A *one-tailed p* value includes values more extreme than the obtained result in one direction, that direction having been stated in advance.

> A *two-tailed p* value includes values more extreme in both positive and negative directions.

▶ One-tailed *p* includes values more extreme than the observed result only in the direction specified by the one-sided, or directional, alternative hypothesis, H_1.

If NHST tests H_0: $\mu = 50$ against the alternative H_1: $\mu \neq 50$, the alternative includes departures from H_0 in both directions, so requires two-tailed *p*. If we regard negative departures from H_0 as unbelievable, or beyond the scope of our research, we need the *one-sided*, or *directional*, alternative H_1: $\mu > 50$ and one-tailed *p*.

> A *one-sided*, or *directional*, alternative hypothesis includes only values that differ in one direction from the null hypothesis value. For example, H_1: $\mu > 50$.

If we've decided to use that one-tailed alternative, what do we do if we find $M = 41$, which is surprisingly far from 50, but in the "wrong", or unpredicted direction? We would simply not reject H_0, because rejecting it means deciding in favor of the directional hypothesis H_1: $\mu > 50$, which for $M = 41$ would be silly. We'd probably also plan a further study using a two-tailed alternative (or even H_1: $\mu < 50$) to explore the unexpected finding.

In our HEAT example we found two-tailed $p = .08$ and did not reject H_0. Had we predicted the direction in advance and used a directional alternative hypothesis, we would have calculated one-tailed $p = .04$ and could have rejected H_0. Does it make sense that $M = 57.8$ gives two different conclusions, depending merely on choice of H_1? That's worth thinking about, but is correct. The point is that our result, $M = 57.8$, is in the correct, or predicted direction. It's consistent with one-sided H_1 and this consistency provides a bit more evidence against H_0 and in favor of H_1.

The key requirement is that you must choose H_1 in advance of conducting the study, and only choose a one-tailed alternative if you have a very good reason. It's totally unacceptable to calculate, for example, $p = .06$, two-tailed, then claim that you really meant to use a one-tailed alternative, so one-tailed $p = .03$ and you can declare statistical significance. No! Any report that includes *p* values should state whether they are two-tailed or one-tailed. When a report states a one-tailed p value there might be doubt as to whether a directional alternative had actually been specified in advance, especially if one-tailed p is just less than .05. To be fully convinced we'd like to see a preregistered data analysis plan that included specification of the directional H_1.

One-tailed p values are justifiable in some situations, but generally I prefer to keep life simple by always using two-tailed p. That's what ESCI does and what I do throughout this book. Of course, another option is to use estimation and CIs, and not use p values at all.

Consider using one-tailed p only when there are strong reasons for specifying a directional H_1 in advance.

Quiz 6.3

Linda runs a study to compare donations to a charity prompted by the door-in-the-face technique with those prompted by a standard donation request. She will use NHST, using $\alpha = .05$ and the null hypothesis that donations are the same regardless of type of request. (Have you heard of the door-in-the-face technique? You can find out more at tiny.cc/doorinface).

1. What would be a Type I error for this study?
   a. The null hypothesis is true but Linda rejects it. That is, the door-in-the-face technique is *not* better, but Linda comes to think that it is.
   b. The null hypothesis is false, but Linda fails to reject it. That is, the door-in-the-face technique *is* better, but Linda remains skeptical.
   c. The null hypothesis is true, but Linda fails to reject it. That is, the door-in-the-face technique is *not* better, and Linda remains skeptical about it.
   d. The null hypothesis is false but Linda rejects it. That is, the door-in-the-face technique *is* better, and Linda comes to think that it is.
2. What would be a Type II error for this study? Choose again from a, b, c, and d.
3. Linda finds $p = .001$ for the comparison of donation amounts. She thus decides to reject the null hypothesis. In this case, what types of errors does Linda need to worry about?
   a. Linda might be making a Type I error, but she doesn't need to worry about a Type II error.
   b. Linda might be making a Type II error, but she doesn't need to worry about a Type I error.
   c. Linda could be making either a Type I or a Type II error.
   d. No need to worry about any kind of error: The p value is very small, so Linda is almost certainly correct. (Hint: This is *not* the right answer!)
4. If I choose smaller α, then β will be _____, and there will be more _____ errors, but fewer _____ errors.
5. When interpreting NHST results, it is important to remember that
   a. statistically significant ($p < \alpha$) does not necessarily mean the finding is important, large, or meaningful.
   b. just because the null is not rejected does not mean you should accept the null as true.
   c. p is not the probability that H_0 is true, it is the probability of obtaining your results or more extreme if H_0 is true.
   d. All of the above.
6. If you state α and H_0, but not H_1, could you make a Type I error? Do you know the Type I error rate? If so, what is it? Could you make a Type II error? Do you know the Type II error rate? If so, what is it?
7. Text your own quiz questions to your friends, and ask for theirs.

NHST and p Values in Context

In this chapter we've mainly discussed p values and NHST, but remember that estimation almost always provides the most complete and best basis for interpretation and drawing conclusions. You need to know about p values and NHST to read the literature, and sometimes you may wish to supplement full estimation reporting with p values and comments. However, especially as meta-analysis, replication, and other Open Science concepts gain widespread attention and support, I suspect that reliance on NHST will wane. That would be a beneficial development.

It's time now to write your take-home messages. We've calculated *p* values, translated back and forth between 95% CIs and *p* values—bring to mind a figure picturing some important relationships. We discussed four red flags, then explored researcher and jury decision making, and a few new NHST ideas and terms.

6.26 A researcher chooses $\alpha = .01$ and calculates $p = .004$.
   a. What does the researcher decide?
   b. What error might the researcher have made? Can you calculate the probability the researcher has made that error? If so, what is that probability? Explain.

6.27 A jury decides that a defendant is not guilty.
   a. What's the NHST equivalent of this decision?
   b. Which two cells in Table 6.1 could we be in? Explain.
   c. If the defendant is actually guilty, what's the probability the jury would make that decision? (Hint: It's a Greek letter.) Explain.

6.28 A researcher chooses $\alpha = .01$ and is keen for β to be small. Describe two ways the researcher could achieve that aim. Which of the two would you recommend, and why?

6.29 Revise your take-home messages if you wish.

⌁ Reporting Your Work

Although we're discussing NHST approaches in this chapter, it is still best to focus any research report on point and interval estimates. It is ok, though, to supplement this with NHST information. If you do so, you should always report:

▦   whether the analysis is planned or exploratory, unless this is already clear;
▦   the basic descriptive statistics for the measure you are analyzing (usually mean, standard deviation, and sample size);
▦   a figure, if possible, and state in the figure caption what error bars represent—95% CIs;
▦   the information required for the estimation approach (the 95% CI);
▦   the test statistic used to generate a *p* value (test statistics introduced in this chapter are *z* and *t*);
▦   the degrees of freedom (if any) for the test statistic (for *t*, for example, there is always an associated degrees of freedom)—the degrees of freedom are usually included in parentheses after the symbol for the test statistic;
▦   the *p* value itself; and
▦   an interpretation focused on the point estimate and CI.

For the *p* values you should give exact values, usually rounded to two decimal places. There are two exceptions to this rule. First, if *p* is very very small, it's best to just write $p < .001$ rather than give an exact value with lots of zeros in front. Second, if *p* is between .02 and .001, it can be a good idea to report three decimal places.

Another rule for APA formatting: Do not use a leading zero to report statistics which cannot exceed 1. So we report $p = .02$ rather than $p = 0.02$ because *p* values cannot be greater than 1.

Below are three examples of how you might write up NHST results in APA style. Note, as usual, that the focus is on explaining the conclusion drawn from the analysis—you don't have to write a statistics textbook to explain the concepts behind *p*, H_0, and so on. What is important, though, is that it is clear what variable you are analyzing and what groups you are comparing.

▶ _____
Report an exact ($p = .03$) rather than relative ($p < .05$) value. Give two decimal places, or three for values less than .02. State $p < .001$ rather than stating exact very small values.

Improvement in depression scores averaged 17.1 points (95% CI [8.5, 25.7], *s* = 18.9, *N* = 21). This CI is consistent with anywhere from moderate to very large average relief from depression. Moreover, this improvement in scores is statistically significant relative to the null hypothesis of no improvement (*t*(20) = 4.15, *p* < .001). Although there was considerable variation in improvement, only 6 participants showed no change or worsened; the rest showed at least some improvement.

Those who drank Neuroaid scored close to the national average of 100 on the IQ test (*M* = 101, 95% CI [98, 104], *s* = 15, *N* = 84). The CI indicates that it is unlikely that the drink produces more than a 4-point benefit in IQ, and is also consistent with no improvement or even a very small decline in IQ. Given a null hypothesis of performance at the national average, this result is not statistically significant (*z* = 0.61, *p* = .54).

Although this was not a planned analysis, we did note during exploration that participants enrolled in the music education class scored well on the ACT (*M* = 26, 95% CI [22.4, 29.6], *s* = 5, *N* = 10). The CI is quite long, but the mean was statistically significantly greater than the national average of 21 (*t*(9) = 3.16, *p* = .01). This suggests that music education could be somewhat associated with better college readiness, but an independent replication is needed to investigate this possibility further.

 # Take-Home Messages

The Basics of NHST and *p* Values

- The three-step NHST process: State the null hypothesis, H_0; calculate the *p* value assuming H_0 is true; then reject the null if *p* is less than the significance level (often .05) and otherwise don't reject.

- The null hypothesis value, μ_0, is the value that H_0 states to be true. It's often zero, in which case H_0: $\mu = 0$, but other values may be chosen.

- The *p value* is the probability of obtaining the observed result, or more extreme, IF H_0 is true. The lower the *p* value, the stronger the evidence against H_0, and the more we should doubt it.

- For a single-sample study, if σ is known use *z* given by Equation 6.1 to find the *p* value. If σ is not known, use *t* given by Equation 6.2 to find the *p* value. Report exact rather than relative *p* values.

Translation Between a 95% CI and a *p* Value

- Use the way a 95% CI falls in relation to μ_0 and the approximate benchmarks in Figure 6.7 (a *take-home picture*) to eyeball the approximate *p* value. For example, if μ_0 falls 1/3 of MoE beyond a limit, *p* is about .01. Also, given the *p* value, *M*, and μ_0, use the same patterns to eyeball the approximate 95% CI.

Four Red Flags

- *Red Flag 1.* Beware dichotomous conclusions, which may give a false sense of certainty. Prefer estimation thinking. Express research aims as "to what extent" questions.

- *Red Flag 2.* Beware the dangerously ambiguous S word ("significant"). Beware the slippery slope of significance, in which a statistically significant difference is unjustifiably discussed as large or important.

■ *Red Flag 3.* Beware accepting the null hypothesis. Beware the slippery slope of nonsignificance, in which failing to reject H_0 leads later to a statement that an effect is zero.

■ *Red Flag 4.* The *p* value is the probability of obtaining our result, or more extreme, IF H_0 is true. Beware the inverse probability fallacy: *p* is not the probability our results are due to chance.

NHST Decision Making

■ NHST can test H_0 against the alternative hypothesis, H_1. Strict NHST requires the significance level, most commonly $\alpha = .05$, to be stated in advance.

■ A *Type I error*, or *false positive*, is rejection of H_0 when it's true; the Type I error rate is α. A *Type II error*, or *miss*, is not rejecting H_0 when it's false. The Type II error rate is β. See the four main cells in Table 6.1.

■ If there are excellent reasons for specifying in advance a directional alternative hypothesis, such as $H_1: \mu > 0$, you could consider using a one-tailed *p* value.

 End-of-Chapter Exercises

These exercises will give you practice using the NHST approach. Remember, though, that it would be better to use the estimation approach: The CI provides all the information necessary to test any null hypothesis and gives a much better sense of the precision with which the research question has been answered.

1) Andrew is studying the extent to which Neuroaid influences IQ. He has 16 students drink Neuroaid and then take an IQ test which has a national average of 100 with $\sigma = 15$. His null hypothesis is that IQ after Neuroaid is also 100 ($H_0: \mu_{\text{Neuroaid}} = 100$). Given a significance level of .05, which of the following findings would be statistically significant?
   a. $p = .5$
   b. $p = .01$
   c. $p = .99$
   d. $z = 2.5$ (use ESCI to look up the *p* value)
   e. $z = -2.5$
   f. $z = 0$
   g. The sample mean is 106, 95% CI [98.5, 113.5]
   h. The sample mean is 115, 95% CI [107.5, 122.5]

2) Maria is studying the extent to which a first-year workshop on study skills helps students get more out of college. She asks 268 seniors to take a critical thinking test: Half took the study skills workshop during their first year, half did not. Using NHST, Maria obtains $t(266) = 2.19$, $p = .03$. Which of the following point estimates and confidence intervals for the difference ($M_2 - M_1$) between these two group means make sense and are consistent with that *p* value?
   a. $(M_2 - M_1) = 2.6$, 95% CI [−3, 8.2]
   b. $(M_2 - M_1) = 2.6$, 95% CI [0.3, 5]
   c. $(M_2 - M_1) = 0$, 95% CI [−3, 3]
   d. $(M_2 - M_1) = 2.6$, 95% CI [1.7, 3.5]

3) To what extent might an online chemistry class lead to better learning than a traditional chemistry course? You administer a standardized final to a sample of 36 students and obtain an average score of 82.0. Nationally, the average on this exam is 80, with an SD of 12, for a traditional course. Use NHST to test the null hypothesis that the online chemistry course has the same mean as a traditional course (that $\mu_{\text{online}} = \mu_{\text{national}} = 80$). Use a significance level of .05.

a.   What test statistic will you calculate, z or t? Why?
b.   Calculate the test statistic (it's z!). What is its value?
c.   Use ESCI to look up the p value for this test statistic.
d.   Based on the p value obtained, is this a statistically significant result? Will you reject the null hypothesis?
e.   Calculate the 95% CI for the difference between your online sample mean and the national average. Does the CI support a similar conclusion? Why might you prefer to know the CI rather than just the p value?
f.   Since this is not a statistically significant difference, can you therefore conclude that an online chemistry course is just as effective as traditional chemistry courses? *Hint:* Think about the four red flags.
g.   Write up an APA-formatted results section reporting your analysis.

4) Lauren is designing a study and will use the NHST approach with a significance level of .05 ($\alpha = .05$).
a.   If the null hypothesis is true, what is Lauren's chance of nevertheless rejecting the null hypothesis, making a Type I error?
b.   If the null hypothesis is not true, what factors influence Lauren's risk of making a Type II error?
c.   What can Lauren do to reduce the risk of a Type I error? What is a drawback of this strategy?
d.   What is the *best* way to reduce the risk of Type II error?

5) Does learning a new skill require a regular sleep pattern? Stickgold, James, and Hobson (2000) trained 11 participants on a new skill. That night all participants were sleep deprived. The data are (−14.7, −10.7, −10.7, 2.2, 2.4, 4.5, 7.2, 9.6, 10, 21.3, 21.8)—or download them from the book website (**Stickgold** data set). The data are the changes in learning scores from before training to after: 0 represents no change, positive scores represent improvement, and negative scores represent decline. Use NHST, test against the null hypothesis of no change (H_0: $\mu_{sleep\_deprived} = 0$). Use $\alpha = .05$. Data set courtesy of DataCrunch (tiny.cc/Stickgold)
a.   What test statistic will you calculate, z or t? Why?
b.   Calculate the test statistic (it's t!).
c.   Use ESCI to lookup the p value.
d.   Is this a statistically significant result? Will you reject the null hypothesis?
e.   Stickgold, James, and Hobson write that those sleep deprived show "no significant improvement" and therefore conclude that learning *requires* sleep. Which red flag about NHST does this call to mind?
f.   Calculate the 95% CI for change in learning scores. Does the evidence support the notion that no learning occurs during sleep deprivation?
g.   Write up an APA-formatted results section reporting your analysis.

? Answers to Quizzes

Quiz 6.1

1) d; 2) a: p is a probability and therefore can only range between 0 (no chance) and 1 (certain); 3) unlikely; 4) b; 5) greater than, not reject; 6) small, strong.

Quiz 6.2

1) a; 2) The panel on the left; 3) a. $p = .32$, b. $p = .32$, c. $p = .003$, d. $p = .06$, e. $p = .05$, f. $p = .33$; 4) Only result c, with $z = 3$, which gives $p = .003$; none of the other test statistics given produce $p < .01$ (the significance level), so none of these would lead to rejecting the null hypothesis; 5) a; 6) $p = .03$, yes, no, no.

Quiz 6.3

1) a; also, note that c and d are not errors, but correct decisions! 2) b; 3) a; 4) increased, Type II, Type I; 5) d; 6) Yes, yes, α, yes, no.

 ## Answers to In-Chapter Exercises

6.1   a. Between .33 and .05, actually .14; at the .05 significance level, we don't reject that null hypothesis; b. The cat's eye suggests this value is somewhat plausible.

6.2   a. 57% is a great distance beyond the CI limit, so *p* is extremely small; at the .05 significance level, we reject that null hypothesis and conclude that support is statistically significantly lower than 57% (we'll see later that we could also reject at much lower significance levels); b. The cat's eye is extremely thin and so 57% is highly implausible.

6.3   Do we know the full story? For example, are there any other similar studies? Are the results we have selected in any way? We want full details of what was done, and reassurance in particular that the assumption of random sampling is reasonable.

6.4   a. Equation 6.1 gives $z = 4.60/3.651 = 1.260$, for which $p = .2077$, rounded to .21; b. Equation 5.1 gives MoE $= 1.96 \times 20/\sqrt{30} = 7.157$, so the CI is [47.44, 61.76]; c. Very similar, except that for the CI we use a critical value of z (i.e., 1.96) and for *p* we calculate z and find the corresponding tails area, which is the *p* value; d. The CI gives us a range of relatively plausible values for the true mean; the *p* value of .21 indicates only that we can't reject the null hypothesis.

6.5   a. Equation 6.1 gives $z = 2.3$, for which $p = .02$. Equation 5.1 gives a CI of [50.68, 58.52]. The *p* value is consistent with the null hypothesis value a little outside the CI, and means we can reject the null at the .05 level. The larger sample gives, for the same *M*, a smaller *p* value and shorter CI.

6.6   a. Equation 6.2 gives $t = 4.6/(14.3/\sqrt{30}) = 1.762$, the $df = 29$, and so $p = .0886$, rounded to .09; b. Equation 5.8 gives MoE $= 2.045 \times 14.3/\sqrt{30} = 5.34$, so the CI is [49.26, 59.94]; c. Very similar, except that for the CI we use a critical value of t with $df = 29$ (i.e., 2.045) and for *p* we calculate t and find the corresponding tails area, which is the *p* value; d. The CI gives us a range of relatively plausible values for the true mean; the *p* value of .09 indicates only that we can't reject the null.

6.7   Equation 6.2 gives $t = 3.217$, with $df = 99$, and $p = .002$. MoE $= 1.984 \times 14.3/\sqrt{100} = 2.84$, so the CI is [51.76, 57.44]. The *p* value indicates strong evidence against the null hypothesis of 50, which is consistent with the CI being considerably above 50, and allows us to reject the null at the .01 level. The much shorter CI indicates a more precise estimate than before.

6.8   The much larger sample gives a much more precise estimate of *s*, just as it gives a much more precise estimate of the population mean.

6.9   My favorite is **Small hints**, but play with **Large hints** if you would like to see how CI length changes with *C*, the level of confidence.

6.11 The accurate values are, from **a** to **f**: .033, .12, <.001, .29, .70, .006.

6.12 About .11.

6.13 In Figure 6.7, focus on the (95%) CI second from right, and note that its *p* value is .01. Imagine extending it by one-third of MoE both upward and downward, which makes it approximately a 99% CI. The lower limit would be at μ_0, which means, because it's a 99% CI, that $p = .01$, and this accords with Guideline 3.

6.14 Cases **a** to **f** in Figure 6.10 are the same as cases **f** to **a** (i.e., order is reversed) in Figure 6.9. In Figure 6.10, from **a** to **f** the means and CIs are 77 [22, 132], 7 [−28, 42], 24 [−20, 68], 44 [22, 66], 44 [−11, 99], 36 [3, 69].

6.15 [0.2, 4.4]

6.16 When the statistical meaning is intended, insert "statistically". Otherwise replace with a synonym. If you can't tell which meaning is intended, there's a problem.

6.17 a. The result is 53% [49, 57], which includes 50% and so we can't reject that null hypothesis. (i) The poll found no statistically significant difference from 50%, or, worse, there was no difference from 50%. (ii) The null hypothesis of 50% could not be rejected; b. The second result is 50.2% [49.2, 51.2] so the null hypothesis is not rejected. The CI is very short and includes 50% so we might conclude that the true value is 50% or very close to 50%; for practical purposes, voters are split about 50–50.

6.18 That's 1, because being an American citizen is a requirement for members of Congress. Choose a random American citizen and there's only an extremely tiny chance he or she is a member of Congress, so the second probability is close to 0. The two are quite different conditional probabilities and there's no reason to expect them to be equal or even similar.

6.19 Probability 5 is 1; Probability 6 is close to 0. To get the two we simply swapped which of the two events "is an American citizen" and "is a member of Congress" comes after IF. The two Probabilities 3 and 4 are similarly a swap of which event, "getting certain results" or "H_0 is true", comes after the IF, so there is no reason to expect the two to be equal or even similar.

6.20 $p = .02$ means that $p < \alpha = .05$ and so we reject the null hypothesis and conclude that the mean for the college is statistically significantly greater than 50, assuming the M for our sample was greater than 50. You might be thinking that $H_1: \mu \neq 50$ and, therefore, if we reject H_0 we should conclude that the mean for College Alpha is different from 50, rather than greater than 50. Strictly, you are correct. However, virtually all researchers take a pragmatic approach and draw a directional conclusion, meaning that if $M > 50$ they conclude that rejecting H_0 justifies a conclusion that the true value is statistically significantly *greater* than 50.

6.21 Don't reject H_0. Either of the top two cells. If H_0 is really true (top left cell) the decision is correct: No sign of an effect. If H_0 is false, H_1 is true, and we've made a miss (Type II error, top right cell). We never know which of those two cells we're in, because we never know whether H_0 or H_1 is true—which implies that, in general, we can never know exactly which cell we are in, so can never be sure whether to be happy or sad.

6.22 Reject H_0, either of the bottom two cells. If H_0 true (bottom left), false alarm, Type I error. If H_0 false, correct rejection, bottom right cell. As before, we never know which of the two cells we're in.

6.23 Using strict NHST, α is the significance level chosen in advance, often .05 or perhaps .01 or .001. It's also the Type I error rate. The p value is calculated from the data and is the probability of obtaining our result or more extreme IF the null is true. So the two are quite different, one being chosen, the other calculated. We reject the null if $p < \alpha$ and otherwise don't reject.

6.24 5%; no.

6.25 a. For H_0, the equivalent is to assume innocent, and so for H_1 it's guilty; b. A Type I error corresponds to wrongly rejecting H_0, which is finding an innocent person guilty; c. A Type II error corresponds to failing to reject H_0 when it's false, which is letting a guilty person walk free.

6.26 a. $p < \alpha$, and so decide to reject H_0; b. This decision is a Type I error IF H_0 is actually true. We can't calculate the probability that error has occurred. All we know is that IF H_0 is true, the probability is α (the Type I error rate) that we would obtain $p < \alpha$, and therefore make a Type I error. But we never know whether H_0 is true.

6.27 a. H_0 is that the defendant is not guilty, so the jury's decision corresponds to not rejecting H_0; b. We are in one of the top two cells, because we are not rejecting H_0; c. If the defendant is actually guilty, the jury has made a Type II error. The probability of this occurring, IF the defendant is guilty, is β, the Type II error rate. Usually we don't know the value of β.

6.28 (i) Use very large N, or (ii) choose H_1 that specifies a population parameter that is very different from H_0, so IF H_1 is true the result is likely to be sufficiently far from the H_0 value for H_0 to be rejected. So β will be small, as wanted. However, such an H_1 may be unrealistic and not of practical interest, whereas (i) gives a more informative study, so should be our preference.

7

The Independent
Groups Design

Researchers often wish to investigate the difference between two conditions—between note-taking with pen and laptop, for example. This chapter considers the design that compares the conditions by using separate, *independent*, groups of participants. Then in Chapter 8 we'll consider a second approach: the *paired* design, in which a single group of participants contributes data for both conditions.

This chapter starts with the basics for independent groups: The estimation approach, which focuses on the difference between the two means—our effect size—and its CI. Then I'll introduce a different way to express that effect size, using a *standardized* effect size measure called *Cohen's d*. Cohen's d is a wonderfully useful measure that allows us to compare results across many different types of study. Finally, I'll discuss a second approach to data analysis, based on NHST and *p* values. Here are the key points:

- The independent groups design
- The CI on the difference between the two means
- Cohen's *d*, a standardized effect size measure
- Interpreting *d* and the CI on *d*
- Using *p* values and NHST with independent groups
- The dance of the *p* values, an intriguing picture of variability, and Red Flag 5

THE INDEPENDENT GROUPS DESIGN

In the *independent groups design*, each participant is tested on only one of the two conditions being compared.

To compare note-taking with pen and laptop, Mueller and Oppenheimer (2014) used two independent groups, with random assignment of students to the two conditions. This is the *independent groups design*, in which the performance data with pen are independent of the data with laptop because they come from different groups of students. It's an experiment, which justifies a conclusion that any difference observed was most likely caused by the Pen–Laptop IV. The study found that students learned more after taking notes in longhand than after typing notes. The researchers wondered whether writing encouraged expression of concepts in the student's own words, whereas typing encouraged relatively mindless transcription that led to relatively poor learning. To investigate, the researchers devised a *transcription score*, the percentage of notes that was verbatim transcription from the lecture. As in Chapter 2, transcription score is the dependent variable I'll discuss here.

The first step is to examine the data. Figure 7.1 presents individual data, which show wide variation in both groups. As we calculate descriptive and inferential statistics, always bear in mind the underlying individual data. Don't let a pattern of means fool you—individuals may not follow the overall trend.

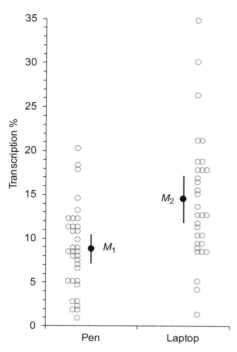

Figure 7.1. The Pen–Laptop transcription data for independent groups. Open dots are data for individual students. Group means M_1 and M_2, with 95% CIs, are displayed.

 DFY: Don't let a mean or pattern of means fool you. Behind any mean may be individual data points that show large variability.

The CI on the Difference

Our question is "What's the difference in mean transcription scores between Pen and Laptop?" The corresponding effect size is the difference between the two group means, $(M_2 - M_1)$. I'm calling Pen the first group and Laptop the second, so M_1 is the Pen mean and M_2 the Laptop mean, and $(M_2 - M_1)$ is (Laptop mean – Pen mean). I'll therefore be discussing the (Laptop – Pen) difference between means. Why not (Pen – Laptop)? Some textbooks and software use $(M_1 - M_2)$, which is the same difference but reversed in sign. Either approach is fine, but be consistent and report clearly which you are using. This book and ESCI use $(M_2 - M_1)$.

Polya

    To evaluate our effect size—the difference between the two group means—we want Figure 7.2, which displays not only the difference, but the 95% CI on that difference. It uses a difference axis, with zero lined up with M_1, and marks the $(M_2 - M_1)$ difference with the small solid triangle lined up with M_2. The difference is about 6. The CI on the difference extends from about 2 to about 9—values on the difference axis corresponding to the limits of the CI on the triangle. Unfortunately, it's very common for research reports to present only the separate means and CIs, as in Figure 7.1, but if our research question is about the difference—as it usually is—then we need to focus on the difference and its CI. The difference axis helps us do that.

◀ With two independent groups, the ES of interest is usually $(M_2 - M_1)$, the difference between the two group means. Focus on that difference and its CI.

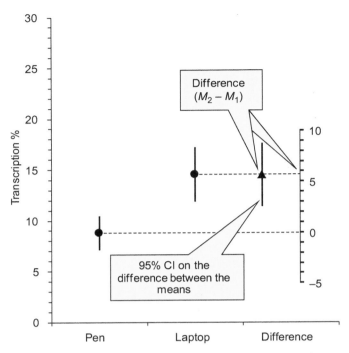

Figure 7.2. Pen–Laptop group means and CIs, with the difference and its 95% CI shown on the difference axis at right. The triangle marks the difference of the sample means, ES = $(M_2 - M_1)$, which looks to be around 6.

Table 7.1 presents statistics for the data shown in Figures 7.1 and 7.2. We'll use these to calculate the difference and its CI as our point and interval estimates of the population mean difference. Our statistical model for calculating those estimates has three assumptions:

- *Random sampling.* Both samples of data are random samples from the respective populations. Equivalently, we obtain a random sample of students, then use random assignment to form the independent groups.
- *Normal populations.* Both Pen and Laptop populations are normally distributed.
- *Homogeneity of variance.* The variances of the Pen and Laptop populations are equal. Equivalently, the two population SDs are the same. "Homogeneity" here means "sameness" or "equality".

I discussed random sampling in Chapter 2, and emphasized the importance of random assignment to groups, which we have here. However, the students participating in the study are a convenience sample, so when drawing conclusions about a population we need to consider how representative the sample is likely to be of that population.

Is it reasonable to assume normally distributed populations? The dot plots in Figure 7.1 both have some clumping around the center and don't look to have strong skew, and therefore look similar to the many samples from normal distributions that we've seen in **CIjumping**. We thus have no strong reason to doubt the second assumption of our model. I'll say more about the homogeneity of variance assumption in a moment.

		Pen		Laptop	
N	N_1	34	N_2	31	
Mean	M_1	8.81	M_2	14.52	
SD	s_1	4.75	s_2	7.29	
MoE	MoE_1	1.66	MoE_2	2.67	

Table 7.1 Statistics for the PenLaptop 1 Groups

7.1 Identify how Figures 7.1 and 7.2 represent each of the values in Table 7.1. Eyeballing the figures, do the values look about right?

Now for the calculations. The difference itself is simply

$$(M_2 - M_1) = 14.52 - 8.81 = 5.71$$

Our basic CI formula from Chapter 5 is that a CI is [M – MoE, M + MoE]. To calculate the 95% CI on a single mean, when σ is not known, we used

$$MoE = t_{.95}(df) \times s \times \left(\frac{1}{\sqrt{N}}\right) \quad (5.9)$$

t component, which makes it a 95% CI

Variability component

Sample size component

MoE for the CI on a single mean.

For the CI we seek on our ES, the difference, we need a similar formula. I've labeled three components in Equation 5.9, to help me explain the CI on the difference. Let's consider the three components.

The t component for the difference is $t_{.95}(df)$, where each group contributes to df, and so df for the difference between independent means is

$$df = (N_1 - 1) + (N_2 - 1) = (N_1 + N_2 - 2) \quad (7.1)$$

df for the difference between independent means.

The variability component for the difference needs to reflect variability in both the Pen and Laptop populations, as estimated by our s_1 and s_2, which are the SDs of the two groups. Table 7.1 tells us that their values are 4.75 and 7.29 respectively. Our statistical model assumes that the two populations—the populations of Pen and Laptop scores—have the same SD, which I'll call σ. Equivalently, I can say the two populations have the same variance, σ^2. This is the third assumption of our model, the *homogeneity of variance* assumption. Often, but not always, it's reasonable to make this assumption, and we'll make it here.

The next step is to combine, or *pool*, s_1 and s_2 to calculate s_p, the pooled SD, which is our best estimate of σ. Here's the formula:

To calculate MoE for the difference between two independent means, we often assume the two underlying populations have the same variance. That is, we assume **homogeneity of variance**.

$$s_p = \sqrt{\frac{(N_1 - 1)s_1^2 + (N_2 - 1)s_2^2}{N_1 + N_2 - 2}} \quad (7.2)$$

Pooled SD for independent groups.

The group standard deviations, s_1 and s_2, measure the spread *within* each group. The pooled standard deviation, s_p, is a type of weighted average of s_1 and s_2, and so s_p is called the *pooled SD within groups*. It's the variability component we need for calculating the CI.

The sample size component for the difference is $\sqrt{\frac{1}{N_1} + \frac{1}{N_2}}$, which reflects the sizes of both our Pen and Laptop samples, as we'd expect.

Now we can follow the pattern of Equation 5.9 above to combine the three components for the difference to get

$$\text{MoE}_{\text{diff}} = t_{.95}\left(N_1 + N_2 - 2\right) \times s_{\text{p}} \times \sqrt{\frac{1}{N_1} + \frac{1}{N_2}} \qquad (7.3)$$

- *t* component, which makes it a 95% CI
- Variability component
- Sample size component

▶

MoE for the CI on the difference between two independent means.

where MoE_{diff} is MoE for the 95% CI on the difference between independent means.

▶

In a number of common cases, MoE is based on three components: a *t* component reflecting *df* and the level of confidence *C*, a variability component reflecting population SD, and a sample size component.

Now we'll calculate. The first term is $t_{.95}(N_1 + N_2 - 2) = t_{.95}(63)$, and ESCI **Normal and t** tells us that $t_{.95}(63) = 2.00$. Applying Equation 7.2 to the values reported in Table 7.1 gives $s_{\text{p}} = 6.09$. This lies between $s_1 = 4.75$ and $s_2 = 7.29$, as we'd expect for a pooled estimate based on both s_1 and s_2. The third component is $\sqrt{\frac{1}{N_1} + \frac{1}{N_2}} = 0.248$. Putting those values into Equation 7.3, we get $\text{MoE}_{\text{diff}} = 2.00 \times 6.09 \times 0.248 = 3.02$. Our CI on the difference is therefore $[5.71 - 3.02, 5.71 + 3.02]$, so we can state that the difference is 5.71 [2.69, 8.73], in transcription score percentage points. This is the difference and CI pictured at right in Figure 7.2.

If you followed all that discussion, give yourself a pat on the back. That's about as complicated as it gets in this book. The main idea is that CI length reflects three main influences, via the three components on the right in Equation 7.3: Our choice of *C* (usually 95), the variability, and the sample size(s). In a moment some questions about those three, but practice a few calculations first.

7.2 Follow the discussion above to calculate for yourself the CI on the difference.

▨ Use ESCI **Normal and t** to find $t_{.95}(df)$.
▨ Use the values in Table 7.1 to calculate s_{p} and the sample size component, then the CI.

7.3 How does the *t* component change for a 90% CI? What effect does that have on the CI?

7.4 If variability in the population increases, what happens to the variability component? What happens to the CI? Explain.

7.5 Consider the third component. If one sample size is increased, what happens to the component? What happens to the CI?

▶

The CI on the difference between independent means is a little longer than either of the CIs on those two means.

Now consider Figure 7.2 and note that the CI on the difference is a little longer than either of the CIs for the groups. For independent groups, this is always the case because variability in the difference between the means, $(M_2 - M_1)$, reflects contributions from the variability in each of M_1 and M_2, and therefore is larger. In other words, the uncertainty in the difference is greater than the uncertainty in either mean. I'll explain how the formulas make this happen but, if your eyes glaze over, it's OK to skip the following paragraph.

Compare Equation 5.9 for MoE for a single sample mean, and Equation 7.3 for MoE for the difference between independent means. The first components—the critical values of *t*—are similar, and close to the same if sample sizes are large. The variability components are similar, in each case being an estimate of population SD. The difference comes in the sample size component, which is $\sqrt{\dfrac{1}{N_1}} = 0.17$ to calculate the CI on the Pen mean and $\sqrt{\dfrac{1}{N_2}} = 0.18$ for the CI on the Laptop mean. For the CI on the difference, it's $\sqrt{\dfrac{1}{N_1} + \dfrac{1}{N_2}} = 0.25$, which is a little larger than either $\sqrt{\dfrac{1}{N_1}}$ or $\sqrt{\dfrac{1}{N_2}}$. Therefore, the CI on the difference is longer than the CIs on either of the group means.

If you had only Figure 7.1, could you eyeball the difference and the CI on the difference? Yes you could, although sketching something like Figure 7.2 might be easier than creating the figure in your mind's eye. Here are the steps:

◄
For independent means, if you see the two means and CIs, you can eyeball the CI on the difference.

- Sketch the difference axis, with zero lined up with M_1 and the difference itself (marked in Figure 7.2 by the solid triangle) lined up with M_2.
- Sketch the CI on the difference, making it a little longer than the CIs for the independent group means.
- Interpret the difference and its CI, with reference to the difference axis.

Note that we're talking about the difference between two *independent* means, the means of two independent groups. If the groups are not independent, the situation is quite different, as we'll discover in Chapter 8. The key point is that, for independent groups, the CI on the difference will be a little longer than the CIs on the group means.

ESCI for the CI on the Difference

Figure 7.3 shows how ESCI analyzes and pictures the data shown in Figures 7.1 and 7.2. Examine Figure 7.3, or ESCI itself, as I again step through what we need for the independent groups design.

esci 7.6 Open **Data two** in **ESCI intro chapters 3–8**. If you don't see the PenLaptop 1 data, scroll right and click at red 14. Your screen should resemble Figure 7.3.
- Explore the page and figure out what's going on. As usual, you could elect to follow the red numbers. Note the popouts. What does **Offset points** near red 4 do?
- Identify where all the values in Table 7.1 are shown.

esci 7.7 Use this ESCI page as you wish. Change some data points and observe how the figure and CIs change. You could click at red 3 to clear the data then type in your own. To reload the PenLaptop 1 data, scroll right and click at red 14.

esci 7.8 Click at red 10 to reveal a second figure like Figure 7.2.
- Find where s_p, $\mathrm{MoE}_{\mathrm{diff}}$, and the CI on the difference are shown. Verify that the values we calculated are correct.

Note, incidentally, that **Data two** doesn't display cat's-eye pictures on any of the CIs. I hope by now you can bring to mind a cat's-eye picture if you wish. That's a great skill to have, and worth practicing, for example while working through this chapter.

Our calculations have relied on our statistical model, including the assumption of homogeneity of variance. Next I'll discuss this assumption and a way to avoid it.

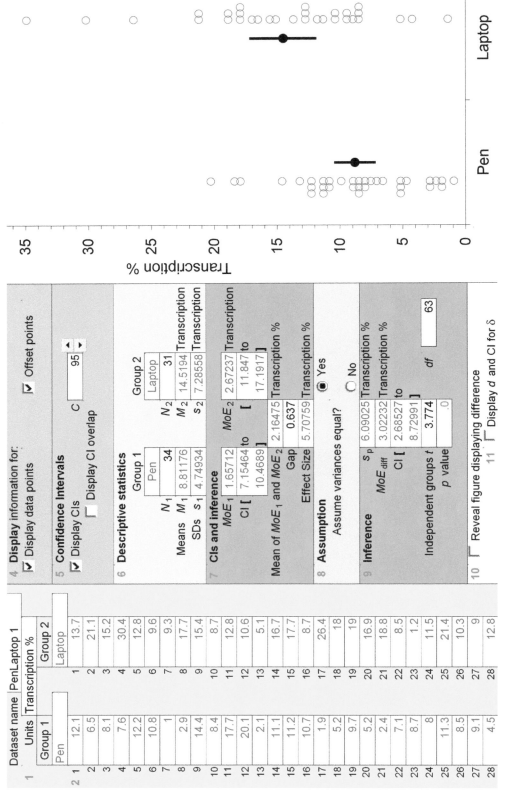

Figure 7.3. The figure on the right is the same as Figure 7.1. Near red 6 are descriptive statistics for the separate groups, near red 7 information about the separate CIs, and near red 9 information about the CI on the difference. From **Data two**.

The Assumption of Homogeneity of Variance and How to Avoid It

Click **Yes** at red 8 to assume homogeneity of variance, and instruct ESCI to use Equations 7.2 and 7.3, which rely on that assumption. If you click **No** you will see MoE for the difference and the CI change a little. ESCI is now using the Welch (also called the Welch–Satterthwaite) method, which is a good approximate method for calculating MoE and the CI for a difference, without assuming the two population variances are equal. It's a bit complicated, so just leave it to ESCI. It makes little difference which method you use—**Yes** and **No** give similar results—unless the two sample SDs are considerably different, *and* the two sample sizes also differ. In any case, when reporting the CI, mention which method you used to calculate it.

◀ The homogeneity of variance assumption is likely to be problematic only if the two group standard deviations are considerably different, and the two sample sizes are also considerably different.

 7.9 Explore the effect of making or not making the homogeneity of variance assumption. Try changing some of the data values in the Laptop group so you have even more very low data points and very high data points. Note how different the two *s* values now are, and observe what difference clicking **Yes** or **No** at red 8 makes to MoE_{diff} at red 9. Watch the change in the figure on the right in ESCI, with the difference axis.

 7.10 Delete at least half the data points in one of the groups, so N_1 and N_2, as well as the two *s* values, are considerably different. Again observe the effect of clicking **Yes** or **No**. What do you need to change about the data before clicking back and forth makes much difference to MoE_{diff}?

 7.11 When you click **No**, what happens to *df*? Read the popout for *df*.

Interpretation and Discussion

Our main result is that mean transcription scores for Pen and Laptop were 8.8% and 14.5% respectively. (I'm judging that one decimal place is plenty when reporting and discussing these results.) On average, Laptop scores were 5.7 percentage points [2.7, 8.7] greater than Pen scores, or more than half as much again as Pen scores. The CI suggests the population difference could plausibly be anywhere between about 3 and 9 points higher for Laptop. The CI is not very long, with MoE of around 3, so precision is reasonable.

In those brief comments I've referred to values in our interval and to MoE, so I've used Interpretations 2 and 3 of a CI, as we discussed back in Chapter 5. You could use other interpretations if you wish.

 Can you suggest a few more issues that deserve comment? Thinking, discussing...

We could note the wide spread of scores in each group, suggesting that the extent of students' verbatim note-taking varied considerably. We could comment on the assumptions we're making, and Open Science issues we discussed in Chapter 2. We could also suggest further research questions prompted by the result. For example, we might ask the extent to which students with less transcription in their notes learned better and remembered more.

7.12 Table 7.2 reports the summary statistics for PenLaptop 2, a second study from Mueller and Oppenheimer (2014), which also used independent groups. Use Equation 7.2 to calculate s_p. Explain what s_p is and compare it with s_p for PenLaptop 1.

Table 7.2 Statistics for the PenLaptop 2 Study

		Pen		Laptop
N	N_1	48	N_2	103
Mean	M_1	6.88	M_2	12.09
SD	s_1	4.22	s_2	5.52
MoE	MoE_1	1.23	MoE_2	1.08

7.13 Use Equation 7.3 to calculate MoE for the CI on the difference. What assumption are you making? Does it seem reasonable? Compare with PenLaptop 1.

esci 7.14 To load the PenLaptop 2 data set, scroll right and click at red 15. Compare what ESCI reports with the values in Table 7.2.

    a. Also compare your answers to Exercises 7.12 and 7.13 with what ESCI reports.

ESCI also offers an alternative approach: The **Summary two** page provides figures and carries out the calculations, given just the summary information shown in Table 7.2 about this independent groups study.

esci 7.15 Open the **Summary two** page. If necessary, near red 1 type a label for the units, and the values from Table 7.2 for N, M, and s for each group. Your screen should resemble Figure 7.4.

    a. Check that the values in the table for MoE_1 and MoE_2 agree with those on your screen.

esci 7.16 Eyeball the difference between the means and the CI on the difference. Make a sketch.

    a. Click near red 6 to reveal a second figure that shows the difference and its CI on a difference axis. How similar was your sketch?

> ## ? Quiz 7.1
>
> 1. In a study with two independent groups, which of these is usually the research question?
>   a. To what extent are the group means different?
>   b. Is the difference between the two groups 0?
>   c. Are the groups actually the same?
>   d. What is the p value?
> 2. When calculating a CI for the difference between two group means we usually assume that
>   a. both groups represent random samples.
>   b. in each group the scores being compared come from normally distributed populations.
>   c. the population variance is the same for both groups.
>   d. All of the above.
> 3. The variability component for the CI on the difference is the _____ standard deviation, with symbol _____, which is calculated from the two group _____.
> 4. For the comparison of two independent groups, what is the formula for degrees of freedom?
> 5. The CI for the difference between two group means is shorter / longer than the CIs for the means of the two single groups.
> 6. For the PenLaptop 1 study, what is the DV we are discussing? What level of measurement are we assuming for the DV? What is the IV? How many levels does it have and what are they? What level of measurement are we assuming for the IV?
> 7. Now it's your turn, although it's probably best not to work alone.

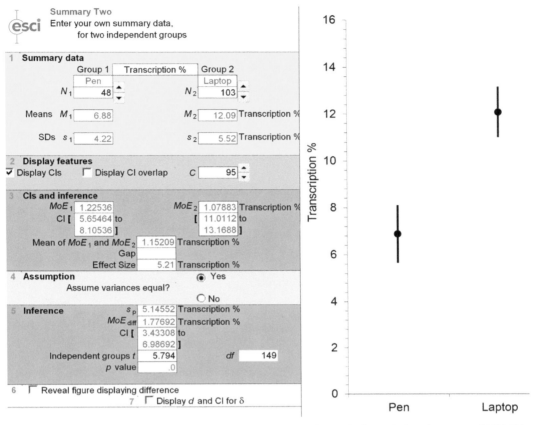

Figure 7.4. Summary statistics for the PenLaptop 2 study, as shown in Table 7.2. The figure displays the mean and 95% CI for each group. From **Summary two**.

So far we've expressed effect sizes in the units of the dependent variable, for example transcription score. Often, however, it's valuable to express effect sizes in other ways. The independent groups design is a good context to introduce the most important of these: Cohen's *d*.

A STANDARDIZED EFFECT SIZE MEASURE: COHEN'S *d*

Now for a bit of measurement magic—a way to compare results even when they're measured on different scales. Consider an example. Many studies show that when students get enough sleep they do better—Diekelmann and Born (2010) reviewed some of the research. Students do better in mathematics, in Spanish, and in sports, and may even play the violin more musically. To understand the effects of good sleep we need to compare, but how can we compare the number of mathematics problems solved with times to run 400 m? Scores on the Spanish exam with ratings of musicality? I'm happy to report that there is a solution, an effect size measure called *Cohen's d*. Using *d* we can make those comparisons, and also do other clever things, as we'll discover.

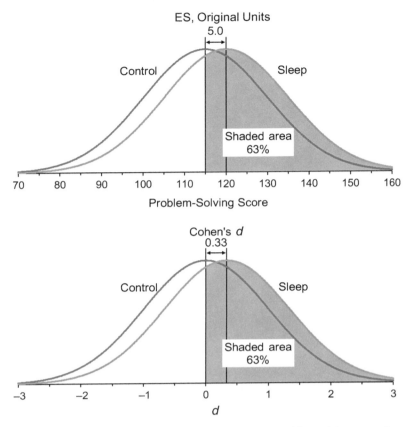

Figure 7.5. Two pictures of supposed distributions of mathematics problem-solving scores after normal sleep (Control curve) and good sleep (Sleep curve). The upper panel shows an average score difference of 5.0. The curves are normal, with SD = 15. Below, the same distributions represent values of Cohen's d, and the ES is d = 0.33. The shaded areas show that 63% of scores after good sleep are greater than the Control mean.

Let's consider a test of mathematics problem solving, and suppose that students on average solve 5.0 more problems after good sleep. I'd like some idea of what 5.0 means. Is it a big improvement, or hardly worth the effort? One approach is to consider the 5.0 against the distribution of scores of all the students. That's the ingenious strategy of Cohen's d, which expresses the 5.0 as a number of standard deviations, like a z score.

Figure 7.5 illustrates the idea. In the upper panel the Control curve is a normally distributed population of scores after normal sleep, with SD = 15. The Sleep curve is the same, but shifted up by 5.0 points. The effect size is 5.0 *original units*, meaning units of the problem-solving test.

Original units are the units of the dependent variable, in which the data are originally expressed.

The lower panel shows the same curves, but labeled in units of the standard deviation, which are the units of Cohen's d. We'll see in a moment that the effect size is d = 0.33. We saw normal curves like this in Chapter 3 and in **Normal and t**, labeled as z scores. Cohen's d is a number of SDs and is described as a *standardized ES measure*.

> Cohen's *d* is a *standardized effect size measure*, which is expressed in standard deviation units.

To convert from original units, use the basic formula for *d*, which is:

$$d = \frac{\text{Effect size in original units}}{\text{An appropriate standard deviation}} = \frac{\text{ES}}{\text{SD}} \qquad (7.4)$$

◀ Basic formula for Cohen's *d*.

The SD we choose is called the *standardizer*, and is the unit in which *d* is expressed. Here the SD is 15, as in the upper panel of Figure 7.5, and Equation 7.4 tells us that $d = 5/15 = 0.33$, as in the lower panel. The two means differ by 5.0 in original units, or one-third of a standard deviation.

◀ Cohen's *d* is an original-units ES divided by a standard deviation.

> The *standardizer* for Cohen's *d* is the standard deviation chosen as the unit for *d*. It's the denominator in Equation 7.4.

We can use Equation 7.4 to calculate *d* for an improvement in exam marks in Spanish, musicality ratings of violin performances, or even times to run 400 m. Cohen's *d* is a common metric for the differences in all those diverse abilities, which allows us to make the seemingly impossible comparisons I first described. In Chapter 9 we'll see that *d* also enables us to use meta-analysis to combine results from studies that used measures with different original units. Yes, *d* is a valuable tool.

Other Names for *d*

You may come across other names for Cohen's *d*. In medicine, what I'm calling *d* is referred to as the *standardized mean difference*, or *SMD*, which is a nice descriptive term for *d*. Another term for a standardized ES is *Hedges' g*, but, unfortunately, it's not used consistently. Sometimes it refers to what I'm calling *d*, sometimes to other quantities, so I suggest it's best avoided. My recommendation is to use "*d*".

Calculating *d* for Independent Groups

Let's calculate *d* for independent groups and use it to compare the results of two studies. Damisch et al. (2010) investigated the possible effect of superstition on performance. Their first study (Damisch 1) used a golf-putting task. Students in the experimental group were told they were using a lucky ball; those in the control group were not. Mean performance was 6.4 successful putts out of 10 in the experimental group, but only 4.8 in the control group—a remarkable difference of 1.67 [0.10, 3.24]. To interpret their result, the researchers suggested that invoking luck increased their participants' self-efficacy, which is a person's belief in their capability to succeed in a particular situation, and that this led to the better putting performance.

Aruguete et al. (2012) followed up the Damisch result by investigating a different way to increase self-efficacy. After checking that the great majority of their students had religious beliefs, they attempted to increase self-efficacy by reminding participants of their religious faith before they undertook a reasoning task. Their first study (Aruguete 1) used a reasoning task and compared an experimental group who were reminded of their faith with a control group who heard no mention of faith. Mean number of reasoning items correct was 16.1 in the control group and 16.4 in the experimental group, so being reminded of faith led to an increase of just 0.32 [−1.19, 1.83] items correct.

Table 7.3 reports summary results for the two studies, which used completely different dependent variables—number of successful golf putts and number of reasoning items correct—as in the second column of the table. We need d to compare the results.

For each study, as standardizer for d we need an estimate of population SD, which we'll calculate from the data. The usual approach is to assume homogeneity of variance and use as standardizer the pooled SD for the groups, s_p, calculated using Equation 7.2. Substitute in that equation the values from Table 7.3 for Damisch 1 to obtain the value of s_p shown in the table:

> To calculate d for independent groups, we usually assume homogeneity of variance and use s_p, the pooled SD, as standardizer.

$$s_p = \sqrt{\frac{(14-1)\times 2.15^2 + (14-1)\times 1.88^2}{14+14-2}} = 2.02$$

The ES in original units is the $(M_2 - M_1)$ difference. Substitute in Equation 7.4 to obtain our formula for Cohen's d for independent groups:

> Cohen's d for independent groups.

$$d = \frac{(M_2 - M_1)}{s_p} \tag{7.5}$$

For Damisch 1 the $(M_2 - M_1)$ difference is 1.67, so Equation 7.5 gives $d = 1.67/2.02 = 0.83$. Our standardizer, the measurement unit for d, is the population SD on the putting task, and our best estimate of that SD is 2.02. Our observed ES is 0.83 of those estimated units.

Let's see what ESCI has to offer, and also find d for Aruguete 1.

esci 7.17 Open **Summary two**. Near red 1 type in labels for the units and group names, and the summary data for Damisch 1 from Table 7.3. If you label the experimental group "Lucky", your screen should resemble Figure 7.6.

a. Find the two values you need and calculate Cohen's d.
b. Look around and see all that ESCI has calculated and displayed. Make sure **Yes** is selected at red 4. Reveal a figure displaying the difference and its CI.

esci 7.18 Type labels and data for Aruguete 1 into **Summary two**. Explain what the two figures tell us.

esci 7.19 Use the values in Table 7.3 to calculate d for Aruguete 1. Since two later examples use **Summary two** for Aruguete 1, you may care to save the whole ESCI file with a new name, so you can reopen this page and see Aruguete 1 when you need to.

7.20 Compare d for Damisch 1 and Aruguete 1. We don't have CIs yet, but what are your thoughts at this stage?

Table 7.3 Data for Studies Investigating the Effect of Superstition and Religious Faith on Performance

Study	Original units	Control group Mean (SD) M_1 (s_1)	N	Experimental group Mean (SD) M_2 (s_2)	N	Difference $(M_2 - M_1)$	Pooled SD s_p	95% CI on the difference
Damisch 1	Number of successful putts	4.75 (2.15)	14	6.42 (1.88)	14	1.67	2.02	[0.10, 3.24]
Aruguete 1	Number of reasoning items correct	16.11 (4.59)	71	16.43 (4.49)	70	0.32	4.54	[−1.19, 1.83]

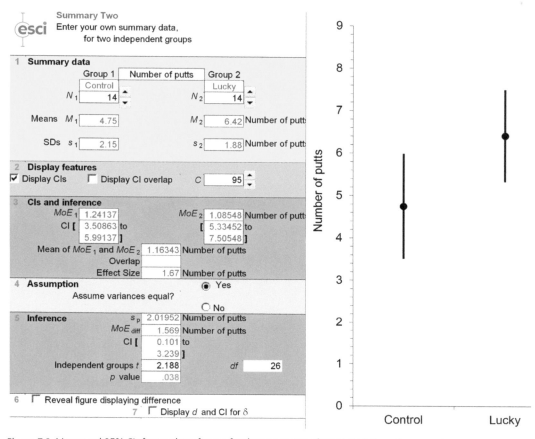

Figure 7.6. Means and 95% CIs for number of putts, for the two groups of Damisch 1. From **Summary two**.

7.21   Switch to the **Data two** page, where you should see the PenLaptop 1 data. Figure 7.7 shows part of the data analysis. Find the two values you need and calculate Cohen's *d*. Explain what it tells us.

Sampling Variability and *d*

Consider a close replication of Damisch 1 or of Aruguete 1. Would you expect the ES in original units to be different? The SD estimate we use as standardizer? The value of *d*?

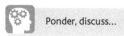   Ponder, discuss...

Sampling variability means that all the means and SDs will almost certainly be different on replication. Therefore, both the numerator and denominator—both the top and the bottom—of Equation 7.5 will be different, so our calculated *d* will be different. There's a dance of the $(M_2 - M_1)$ values and a dance of the s_p values, so values of $d = (M_2 - M_1)/s_p$ are likely to bounce around even more. The answers to my three questions are yes, yes, and especially yes. Always think of *d* as a ratio, and remember that sampling variability usually contributes to both the top and bottom of the ratio.

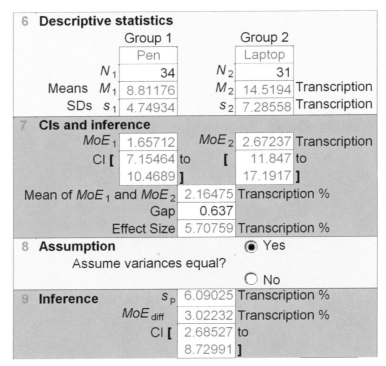

6	**Descriptive statistics**				
		Group 1		Group 2	
		Pen		Laptop	
	N_1	34	N_2	31	
Means	M_1	8.81176	M_2	14.5194	Transcription
SDs	s_1	4.74934	s_2	7.28558	Transcription
7	**CIs and inference**				
	MoE_1	1.65712	MoE_2	2.67237	Transcription
	CI [	7.15464 to	[	11.847 to	
		10.4689]		17.1917]	
	Mean of MoE_1 and MoE_2		2.16475	Transcription %	
	Gap		0.637		
	Effect Size		5.70759	Transcription %	
8	**Assumption**		⦿ Yes		
	Assume variances equal?				
			○ No		
9	**Inference**	s_p	6.09025	Transcription %	
	MoE_{diff}		3.02232	Transcription %	
	CI [		2.68527 to		
			8.72991]		

Figure 7.7. Part of the data analysis of the PenLaptop 1 data. From **Data two**.

Choosing a Standardizer

Choice of meters or feet makes a big difference to the number expressing someone's height. Similarly, choice of standardizer can greatly influence d. Let's discuss that choice; there are two major issues.

▶ ─────
To interpret d, we need to know the standardizer. Always state what standardizer was used to calculate d.

First, do we know a relevant population SD? For the mathematics problem-solving example, I assumed we knew a population SD—perhaps the test is widely used and the test manual reports that the SD is 15 in some relevant reference population, such as all college students. Anyone calculating d for scores on that test will use 15 as standardizer, so all will be using the same measurement unit, which is great. If, however, the problem-solving test, like most college tests, was simply a convenient collection of problems assembled for a single use, we don't know a population SD, and must use s_p as standardizer. Our d will depend not only on the original-units ES, but also on the value of s_p for our data. In short, if a relevant population SD is known, use it. If not, as for the two studies in Table 7.3, we are forced to use an estimate calculated from data, and d will reflect that estimate as well as the ES.

Second, what's the best population to choose? Suppose you read reports of two studies that assessed the influence of good sleep on problem solving by mathematics majors. One used students at Harvard and the other students at Noname College. Suppose each found an average 5.0 advantage after good sleep. Think about the two populations—mathematics majors at the two colleges. Do you think they have the same or different spread of mathematical ability? Because Harvard students are highly selected, I suspect their scores vary less than scores from the probably much more diverse students at Noname. Perhaps s_p for the Harvard study was 10, but for Noname was 20, in which case $d = 5.0/10 = 0.5$ for Harvard, but $d = 5.0/20 = 0.25$ for Noname. In original units, the effect size of good sleep is the same for the two colleges, but in standardized units it's very different. Two values of s_p may differ because of sampling variability, but also, as in this example, because they estimate different SDs in different populations.

To compare the two results we'd prefer a standardizer we could use for both—ideally the SD for all students across the country. If that's not available, we might use original units rather than d. However, if different tests were used at Harvard and Noname we have to use d, based in each case on that college's s_p. Unfortunately, we wouldn't know to what extent a difference in values of d reflects a real difference in the effect of sleep, or a difference in spread of mathematical ability in the two colleges.

Again the message is that d is a ratio, and we need to think about the denominator, which is the standardizer, as well as the numerator, which is the original-units ES. Choice of standardizer is important, so it's essential to state for any d what standardizer was used. Otherwise we can't make sense of d. Next I'll discuss CIs for d.

◄ If a relevant population SD is known, use it as standardizer for *d*. If not, use an estimate calculated from data.

> ### ❓ Quiz 7.2
>
> 1. Cohen's *d* enables comparison across studies that use different measures; it is a(n) _____ effect size measure.
> 2. Cohen's *d* is calculated by dividing a(n) _____ expressed in _____ by an appropriate _____.
> 3. If there is no difference between two groups, $M_1 = M_2$, and Cohen's *d* will be _____.
> 4. For two independent groups, it's most common to use _____ as the standardizer, in which case we need to assume _____.
> 5. Although s_p is commonly used as the standardizer for Cohen's *d*, it's important to be thoughtful about this, because
>   a. different participant populations can have different levels of variation, which can lead to big differences in the *d* that is calculated.
>   b. sometimes the population SD is known, and it may make more sense to use that rather than an estimate calculated from the data.
>   c. Both a and b.
> 6. The population SD of the HEAT is 20. A change in mean HEAT score of 5 is equivalent to $d =$ _____. A change of $d = -0.8$ corresponds to _____ on the HEAT.

Confidence Intervals on *d*

A value of *d* is our point estimate but, as usual, we'd like the CI as well. To calculate a CI on *d* for independent groups, our statistical model requires random sampling, a normally distributed population, and homogeneity of variance. So in this section we'll need to make those assumptions.

The population equivalent of *d* is called δ (Greek lower case delta), in line with the convention that Greek letters represent population parameters (notably μ and σ). In our first example, $d = 0.33$ is our point estimate of δ, the standardized ES for good sleep in the population of all students, which is measured in units of the population standard deviation, σ. We'd like a CI for δ, but note that we can refer to that interval as "the CI on *d*" or "the CI for δ". They refer to the same interval and both are correct.

◄ To calculate a CI on *d* we need to assume (i) random sampling from (ii) a normal population and (iii) homogeneity of variance.

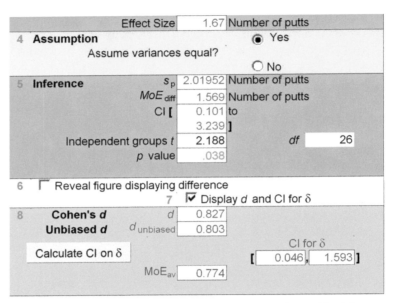

Figure 7.8. Data analysis for Damisch 1 as in Figure 7.6, but including the panel for *d*. From **Summary two**.

CIs on *d* are tricky to calculate and a little asymmetric.

Unfortunately, calculating the CI on *d* is tricky. We'll leave the details to ESCI, but you need to click a button to initiate calculation, which can take a second or two to complete. Also, the CI on *d* is slightly asymmetric, meaning the upper MoE (the distance from *d* to the upper limit of the CI) and the lower MoE are slightly different.

7.22 Figure 7.8 shows data analysis for Damisch 1, the same as Figure 7.6 but with a panel for *d* at red 8. Note *d* and the CI for δ, and interpret.

 7.23 In **Summary two**, set up for Damisch 1 as you did for Exercise 7.17. Click at red 7 to reveal the panel for *d*. Click the button near red 8 to trigger calculation of the CI for δ. You should see Figure 7.8.

■ Read the popout at red 8, which states some restrictions on when ESCI can calculate a CI.

■ Note the value reported below red 8 of MoE$_{av}$ and read the popout.

7.24 What would happen to the CI if one or both of the sample sizes were larger? Smaller? Why?

■ Test your predictions by adjusting N_1 or N_2 near red 1.

 7.25 Follow Exercise 7.18 to set up for Aruguete 1, or reopen the file with these data that you saved. Find the CI on that *d*. Interpret.

7.26 As you did in Exercise 7.20, compare *d* for Damisch 1 and Aruguete 1, but now consider the CIs as well.

Removing Bias in *d*

We usually calculate *d* because we want to estimate population effect size, δ. Unfortunately, whenever the standardizer is an estimate (for example, s_p), *d* is a biased estimate—it tends to overestimate δ, especially with small samples. An adjustment to *d* gives an unbiased estimate, which I call $d_{unbiased}$.

The extent of bias depends on the degrees of freedom of the standardizer. The larger the *df*, the smaller the bias, and for *df* = 50 or more, *d* and $d_{unbiased}$ hardly differ. ESCI makes it easy to routinely use $d_{unbiased}$, and that's my recommendation.

So, you ask, should I have been using $d_{unbiased}$ rather than *d* when discussing the examples for which we had no population SD and therefore used s_p? Yes, that would have been better. Unfortunately, many research reports don't make clear whether bias has been removed from the *d* values they discuss. If *df* is 50 or more, that hardly matters. For smaller *df* that's poor practice, and leaves us in doubt about what the values are telling us. You should, of course, always make clear whether you are reporting *d* or $d_{unbiased}$. For the CI there's no problem, because ESCI gives us the CI for δ, which is the best interval estimate of δ, whether we choose to use *d* or $d_{unbiased}$ as our point estimate.

Routinely use $d_{unbiased}$, although for df of 50 or more, d and $d_{unbiased}$ hardly differ.

7.27 In Figure 7.8, or on your **Summary two** page, find the values for *d* and $d_{unbiased}$ near red 8, also the value of *df* near red 5. By what percentage does *d* exceed $d_{unbiased}$? What does that tell us?

7.28 Set up for Aruguete 1 in **Summary two**, as you did for Exercises 7.18 and 7.25. For this example, what's the *df*, and what's the extent of bias in *d*?

7.29 What results for Damisch 1 and Aruguete 1 would you now report? Would you give the same interpretation as you gave in Exercise 7.26? Explain.

THINKING ABOUT VALUES OF COHEN'S *d*

I keep saying that we should interpret *d* and its CI in context, but what does that mean? I'll mention a few things to consider, then bring it all together. I'll refer to *d*, but the discussion applies equally to $d_{unbiased}$.

Overlap Pictures of *d*

Whatever we are measuring, if the two distributions are at least roughly normal, then Figure 7.5 illustrates *d* = 0.33. The two distributions overlap considerably. Figure 7.9 shows comparisons about which you may already have intuitions: The difference in mean weight between American women and men (*d* = 0.81) and the same for height (*d* = 2.26). The normal curves are an approximation. How do the pictures strike you?

I was surprised that *d* for height was much larger than *d* for weight. However, to understand *d*, always remember it's a ratio and that the standardizer matters. In round numbers, men are, on average, 13 kg heavier than women, but the pooled SD is as large as 16 kg, so *d* is 13/16, or about 0.8. Men and women's mean weights differ by less than one SD—mainly because the SD is so large. For height, there's a 14 cm mean difference, but the pooled SD is only 6 cm, so *d* is 14/6, which is more than 2, so men and women's mean heights differ by more than two SDs—mainly because the SD is so small. Yes, size of standardizer does matter. The very large *d* for height means that around 99% of men are taller than the average woman, but, even so, the two distributions overlap noticeably, and we all know many cases of a woman taller than a man.

There are two lessons here. First, consider the standardizers and, second, keep overlap pictures in mind. Such pictures tell us that even when *d* is large there's overlap—even with a large mean difference, many individuals go against the trend.

Consider overlap pictures. Even when d is large there's overlap, and many individuals go against the trend.

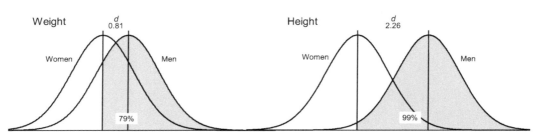

Figure 7.9. Pictures to illustrate d for differences between American men and women: weight on the left, height on the right. The curves represent roughly the distributions of weight and height. The percentages refer to the shaded areas and are the percentages of men with values greater than the women's mean.

Effect Sizes in Original Units

▶ ———
Thinking in terms of original units is often a good way to make sense of a value of d.

I discussed the weight and height values of d by referring to the original units – kilograms and centimeters. Thinking of both effect size and standardizer in terms of original units helps appreciation of those two different components of d. It can also make the discussion more concrete, if the original units are familiar. Thinking in terms of original units should often be the first approach to consider when interpreting results.

The Standardizer and Reference Population

▶ ———
Choose the most relevant reference population, then use the SD of that population—or an estimate of it—as standardizer for d.

One lesson of the weight and height example was the importance of considering the standardizer. A second aspect of the choice of standardizer is choice of reference population, which I illustrated with the Harvard and Noname example. If you suspect the two colleges have different SDs, then comparing values of d based on those different SDs could easily be misleading. As I said before, it's probably better, if possible, to find a single reference population, perhaps all college students in the country, and use the SD of that population—or an estimate of it—as standardizer for both colleges. In any case, we need to consider the reference population when interpreting d. That's another aspect of the vital question: d is a number of SD units, but the units are based on the SD of what?

Cohen's Reference Values for d

▶ ———
Cohen suggested 0.2, 0.5, and 0.8 as values for small, medium, and large effects, but recommended interpretation of d in context whenever possible.

When distinguished statistical reformer Jacob Cohen introduced d, he suggested that $d = 0.2$, 0.5, and 0.8 might for psychology be considered small, medium, and large effects, respectively. Figure 7.10 pictures these three values. He offered his reference values reluctantly and said that they provided a "conventional frame of reference which is recommended for use only when no better basis… is available" (Cohen, 1977, p. 25). Even so, his reference values have become widely used.

Values of d in Different Disciplines

What size effects do researchers study? In any discipline, of course, there's a wide range, but knowing what's typical may help us interpret our d values.

Psychology. Richard, Bond, and Stokes-Zoota (2003) reviewed evidence from more than 25,000 studies in social psychology. They found the average ES was about $d = 0.4$. About 30% of effects had $d < 0.2$, meaning

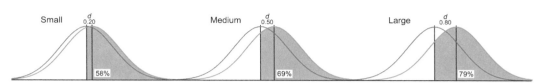

Figure 7.10. Reference values for small, medium, and large values of *d*, as suggested by Cohen (1977). The percentages refer to the shaded areas.

small or less than small in Cohen's terms. Only around 17% had *d* > 0.8, meaning large. I suspect that ESs studied in at least some other areas in psychology are similar.

Education. Visible Learning is a landmark book by John Hattie (2009) that reviewed more than 800 meta-analyses. Average *d* was 0.40 for the influence on learning over one school year of numerous variables, including a wide range of teaching innovations. Hattie recommended that, in the context of school learning, it's reasonable to regard *d* = 0.2 as small, 0.4 as medium, and 0.6 as large.

Medicine. Rutledge and Loh (2004) discussed ESs in medicine. They reported that taking aspirin routinely can decrease the risk of heart attack, with *d* = 0.03, and that being fit can reduce mortality in the next 8 years by *d* = 0.08. These look like tiny effects, but can really matter: Taking aspirin could avoid hundreds of heart attacks each year in a large city. Many common treatments and recommendations to change behavior to improve health are prompted by values of *d* between about 0.05 and 0.2.

> In terms of Cohen's benchmarks, many researchers in psychology and education study effects around "small", and in medicine many life-saving effects are small or tiny.

Pharmacology. Whenever I talk about small values of *d*, my colleague Michael Lew reminds me that in his discipline, pharmacology, researchers typically study effects for which *d* is greater than 5. Yes, it's vital to consider any *d* in its context.

The reviews of Richard et al. (2003), Hattie (2009), and Rutledge and Loh (2004) suggest that, for psychology, education, and especially medicine, reference values rather lower than Cohen's may often be appropriate.

Interpreting *d* and its CI in Context

To summarize so far, we should make our judgment of what *d* means in the particular situation, perhaps considering

> Use judgment to interpret values of *d* in context. Where relevant, consider original units, the standardizer and reference population, overlap of distributions, other results, and reference values.

- effect sizes in original units,
- the standardizer and reference population,
- the overlap picture for our *d*,
- values typical for our discipline, and
- perhaps, Cohen's or Hattie's reference values.

That's a long list, but thinking of the particular context usually prompts even further questions; for example, how difficult was it to achieve the effect? What's the cost-benefit? How big a practical difference does it make? What are the theoretical implications? How does it compare with previous research? Consider any of those questions that are relevant, as you use your judgment to interpret *d*.

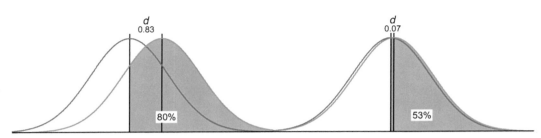

Figure 7.11. Overlapping curves to illustrate, on the left, $d = 0.83$ as in Damisch 1, and, on the right, $d = 0.07$ as in Aruguete 1. From **d picture**.

7.30 For Damisch 1 you probably calculated $d = 0.83$, and for Aruguete 1, $d = 0.07$. Figure 7.11 shows overlapping curves to illustrate those two values of d. Again compare the ESs for Damisch 1 and Aruguete 1, in light of Figure 7.11.

esci 7.31 Open **d picture**. Use the slider to set d, and click at red 2 to see an area shaded. Choose $d = 0.83$ and you should see curves like those on the left in Figure 7.11.

    a. Explore. Use this page to illustrate overlap for any d you are interested in.

7.32 Recall that IQ scores are usually scaled so the population mean is 100 and SD is 15. Suppose in an independent groups study the IQ means are 115 and 125 for the control and experimental groups respectively.

    a. What are the z scores for the two means?

    b. What is d? What's the relation between z and d?

Now I want to turn from Cohen's d to consider an additional approach to analyzing an independent groups study, based on NHST and p values. But first, a quiz.

? Quiz 7.3

1. A CI on d is an interval estimate of the _____ in the _____, for which the symbol is ____.
2. When interpreting Cohen's d it is important to remember that
   a. Cohen's suggestions for small, medium, and large effects are only general rules of thumb.
   b. what counts as a small, medium, or large effect varies quite a bit by field.
   c. it is probably best to consider an effect size relative to other similar findings in the field.
   d. All of the above.
3. The further Cohen's d is from 0, the more / less the distributions of the two groups overlap.
4. In a review of thousands of social psychology experiments, the average effect size was about $d =$ ____.
5. d slightly _____-estimates δ, and therefore $d_{unbiased}$ is a little _____ than d.
6. Cohen's d is expressed in units of the _____, which is the numerator / denominator in the formula for d, and is the _____ of a suitable reference population, or a(n) _____ of that.

NHST AND p VALUES

My recommended approach is to use estimation, but here I'll discuss another possibility that's based on the same statistical model. It uses NHST to test the null hypothesis of no difference between the group means. The *p* value for that difference is what's needed for an *independent groups* t *test*. In Chapter 6 we used Equation 6.2 to calculate *t* for a single sample when μ_0 is the null hypothesis value. Here is that equation again, in a slightly rewritten form:

$$t(df) = \frac{(M - \mu_0)}{s \times \left(\frac{1}{\sqrt{N}}\right)}$$

(6.2)

Effect size — Variability component — Sample size component

t for a single group.

with $df = (N - 1)$. Again I've labeled three components.

Our null hypothesis is zero difference between the group means, so the effect size is the $(M_2 - M_1)$ difference. Equation 7.1 tells us that $df = (N_1 + N_2 - 2)$. Equations 7.2 and 7.3 guide me to use s_p as the variability component and $\sqrt{\frac{1}{N_1} + \frac{1}{N_2}}$ as the sample size component. Entering all that into the equation just above gives

$$t(N_1 + N_2 - 2) = \frac{(M_2 - M_1)}{s_p \times \sqrt{\frac{1}{N_1} + \frac{1}{N_2}}}$$

(7.6)

t for independent groups.

where s_p is calculated using Equation 7.2 and we are assuming homogeneity of variance.

For the PenLaptop 1 data in Figure 7.1 and Table 7.1 we know that $df = 63$, $(M_2 - M_1) = 5.71$, $s_p = 6.09$, and $\sqrt{\frac{1}{N_1} + \frac{1}{N_2}} = 0.248$. Substitute in Equation 7.6 and we get $t(63) = 5.71/(6.09 \times 0.248) = 3.78$. To find the *p* value corresponding to this value of *t*, I opened ESCI **Normal and t**. I selected *t* and clicked **Two tails** and **Areas**, then set $df = 63$, moved the large cursor to $t = 3.78$ and observed the two tails area to be .0004, which we write as $p < .001$. I conclude that the *p* value for testing the null hypothesis that the population means of Pen and Laptop are the same is $p < .001$. Note in Figure 7.3 that **Data two** reports near red 9 the values of *df*, *t*, and *p*. Check that these match the values I've calculated above. (As usual, we're not concerned if there are tiny differences attributable to rounding errors.) Recall that if software reports a *p* value of 0, we take that to mean $p < .001$, the smallest value we report.

As usual, I chose two tails so the *p* value would be the probability of results like ours, or more extreme in either direction, if the null hypothesis is true.

Compare this *p* value of $< .001$ with how the CI on the difference falls in relation to zero on the difference axis in Figure 7.2. Relative to its length, the CI is a long way from zero, which corresponds to a *p* value close to zero. The data provide very strong evidence that the Laptop population mean is greater than the Pen population mean. Our independent-groups *t* test has found the difference to be highly statistically significantly greater than zero.

The *independent groups* **t** *test* uses a *p* value to test the null hypothesis of zero difference in an independent groups study.

Earlier, using estimation, we considered the CI on the difference, rather than a *p* value. Advantages of the estimation approach include that it focuses attention on the ES, and the CI is more informative than a *t* test about the extent of uncertainty.

Table 7.4 Data for an Independent Groups Study Comparing HEAT Scores at Two Colleges

College A	College B
63	41
66	56
49	39
50	74
84	66
74	45
57	51
79	46
	38

7.33 Refer back to Table 7.2. Use the formulas in this section to calculate the p value for the difference between Pen and Laptop.

   a. What assumption are you making? Is it reasonable?

   b. Compare your p value with that reported in Figure 7.4. Interpret.

   c. Consider the figure you saw when completing Exercise 7.16. Compare your interpretations for the p value and the CI on the difference.

7.34 Table 7.4 presents data from an unrealistically small HEAT study comparing independent groups of students.

   a. Use Equations 3.1 and 3.3 to calculate M and s for each group.

   b. Use Equation 5.9 to calculate the CIs on the two means.

7.35 Calculate the ES, s_p, and the CI on the difference, assuming equality of the two population SDs. Interpret.

   a. Calculate the p value to assess the null hypothesis of no difference between Colleges A and B. What can you conclude?

   b. Compare with the CI on the difference. Explain.

7.36 Type the data in Table 7.4 into **Data two**. Click to display the individual data points, and again to see the figure with a difference axis. Confirm all the values you calculated.

   a. Compare the CI on the difference with the two separate CIs.

OVERLAP OF CIS ON INDEPENDENT MEANS

I want to describe a handy way to think about a figure that shows independent means with their CIs. Figure 7.12 shows four changed versions of the PenLaptop 1 results, with four different supposed Laptop means. The labels at the top describe how the two CIs relate: Do they overlap, just touch, or is there a gap?

From left to right, do we have stronger or weaker evidence of a population difference? Would the p value increase or decrease?

Those questions are worth reflection. Think of the Pen CI as a range of values plausible for the Pen population mean, and ditto for Laptop: In each case, what does that suggest about the evidence for a difference?

Ponder, call, discuss...

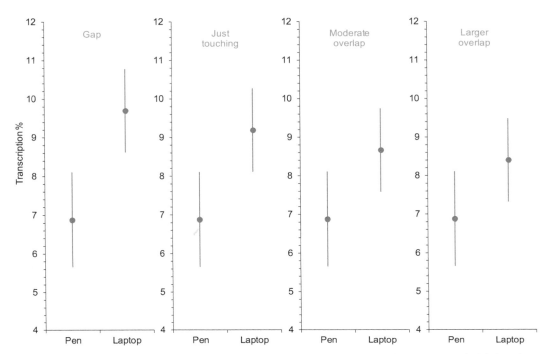

Figure 7.12. Four changed versions of the PenLaptop 1 results, with four different supposed Laptop means. The labels at the top describe how the two CIs relate.

The farther apart the two means, the stronger the evidence of a difference and the smaller the *p* value. From left to right the evidence becomes weaker and the *p* value larger. In fact, there is an approximate relation between the amount of overlap or gap, and the *p* value. Figure 7.13 adds lines to mark overlap or gap, and a statement of the approximate *p* values.

In the leftmost panel, all the plausible Pen values are lower than all the plausible Laptop values, so there's very strong evidence of a population difference and *p* is very small. In the rightmost panel, the two ranges of plausible values overlap considerably, so there's little or no evidence of a difference and *p* is large. It so happens that 95% CIs just touching corresponds approximately to *p* = .01, and moderate overlap to *p* = .05. I'll summarize by stating the *overlap rule*.

For independent CIs, the smaller the overlap (or larger the gap), the smaller the *p* value and greater the evidence of a population difference.

The Overlap Rule for CIs on Independent Means

Here's the overlap rule for independent means:

- If the two 95% CIs just touch, *p* is approximately .01. There's a moderate amount of evidence of a population difference.
- If the two 95% CIs overlap moderately, *p* is approximately .05. There's a small amount of evidence of a population difference.

By "overlap moderately" I mean overlap as in the third panel of Figure 7.13, by about half of MoE. The two means must be *independent*—in Chapter 8

The *overlap rule*: If independent CIs just touch, *p* is about .01; if they overlap moderately, *p* is about .05.

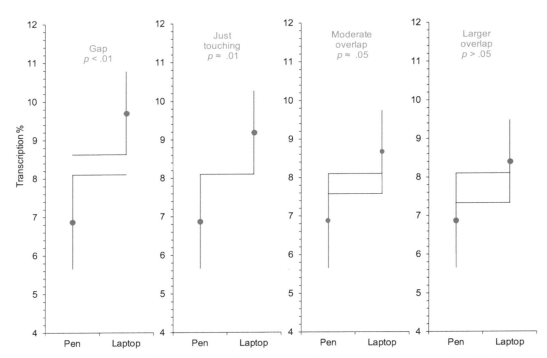

Figure 7.13. Same as Figure 7.12, but with horizontal lines to mark overlap or gap, and approximate *p* values stated— assuming independent groups.

we'll see that the situation is totally different when they are not. To be reasonably accurate, the rule also requires that the sample sizes are at least about 10 and that the two CIs are not very different in length. See Cumming and Finch (2005) for more about overlap, as well as a general introduction to CIs.

Does it seem surprising that CIs overlapping moderately provide some evidence of a difference? Imagine cat's-eye pictures on both CIs: Only the thin ends overlap, not the fat central bulges, so maybe the rule is not so surprising?

Regard the rule as rough but handy. Amaze your friends by nonchalantly stating a conclusion about the population difference, when all you're given is means and CIs. IF the means are independent, that is. Did I mention that independence is essential?

esci 7.37 Open **Summary two** and type in from Table 7.1 the PenLaptop 1 mean, SD, and *N* for each group. Type in different values for M_2 and watch as the amount of overlap changes. Note the *p* value shown near red 5.

  a. Click at red 2 to **Display CI overlap**, and note the value of **Overlap** (or Gap—ESCI tells you which) near red 3. Read the popouts. Change any of M_1, M_2, s_1, or s_2, and watch overlap or gap, and *p* change.

  b. When overlap is exactly .5, what is *p*? When overlap is exactly 0, what is *p*? What can you conclude about the overlap rule?

7.38 Click at red 7 to see *d*. Click to calculate the CI for δ. Why can't you see a *p* value to go with that CI? Because the *p* value for testing the null hypothesis of zero difference is the same, whether we are using original units or *d*. Simply use the *p* value near red 5, which we noted in the previous exercise.

   a. Click at red 6 to see the second figure. Change M_2 so that $p = .05$ and note something special about the CI on the difference. Click to calculate the CI for δ. Is it special in the same way? Explain.

Now I want to discuss a further red flag, perhaps the biggest red flag of all, and a strong reason for using estimation rather than NHST and *p* values.

BEWARE THE ENORMOUS VARIABILITY OF *p*: THE DANCE OF THE *p* VALUES

We've seen the dance of the means and dance of the CIs. We know that there are strong links between CIs and *p* values, so is there a dance of the *p* values? Figure 7.14 shows 25 simulated replications, assuming the population mean is μ = 10 as marked by the dashed line. The means and CIs dance as we expect.

Now consider the *p* values for testing the null hypothesis of 0 as marked by the solid vertical line. These are shown at left. You can check any *p* value by noting where its CI falls in relation to 0: The farther to the right a CI falls, the smaller the *p* value. The *p* values are marked using the star convention: * if $p < .05$, and ** if $p < .01$, and *** if $p < .001$. CIs that just overlap zero, so $.05 < p < .10$, are marked "?" to indicate they are close to statistical significance.

Now consider the column of *p* values—they vary dramatically! It seems our study could give us almost any *p* value—in the figure, *p* ranges from a low of $< .001$ up to .67. The *dance of the p values* is indeed very wide.

Think of running a study and obtaining a randomly chosen one of the 25 results in the figure. Would your CI tell us anything about the whole dance? Yes, it would: Its length would give us a reasonable idea of the amount of bouncing around in the dance of the means. However, if we could see only the *p* value, would that tell us anything about the dance? No, it would tell us very little because the *p* values range so widely.

The trouble is that a *p* value is a single value that gives no hint of the extent of uncertainty, whereas CI length gives information about uncertainty. Despite the strong links between CIs and *p* values, my conclusion is that a CI is much more informative than a *p* value—which tells us very little indeed. Alas, we really shouldn't trust any *p* value.

> By convention, stars are used to indicate strength of evidence against H_0: *** marks $p < .001$, ** marks $.001 < p < .01$, and * marks $.01 < p < .05$.

> The *dance of the p values* is very wide; a *p* value gives only very vague information about the dance.

> A *p* value gives no indication of uncertainty, whereas a CI is much more informative.

Beware the enormous variability of the *p* value. A single *p* value gives only very vague information. A replication study can easily give a *very* different *p* value. A *p* value is not to be trusted.

Red Flag 5

Especially at this point, look on the book website for videos relevant to our discussion—here, the dance of the *p* values.

INTERPRETING THE INDEPENDENT GROUPS DESIGN

Let's return to the main topic of this chapter, the independent groups design, and consider interpretation. Recall the definition from Chapter 2:

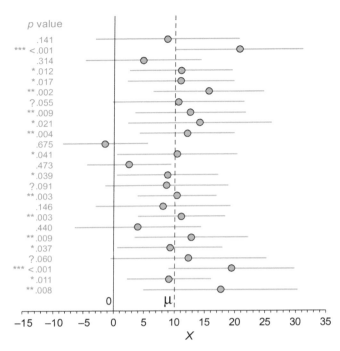

Figure 7.14. Dance of the 95% CIs, with $\mu = 10$ as marked by the dashed line. At left is the dance of the p values for testing the null hypothesis of 0, as marked by the solid line.

> *Experimental* research uses random assignment of participants to groups or conditions—to the different levels of the IV that is being manipulated. It can justify a causal conclusion.

▶────────
Random assignment to groups ensures experimental research and can justify a causal conclusion.
────────

If the independent groups we compare are two pre-existing groups, such as groups of students who themselves prefer to use pen or laptop, then we have non-experimental research. We can calculate and interpret the CI for the difference between the two groups, but we cannot make causal conclusions. Alternatively, we could use random assignment, in this case to separate pen and laptop groups. This should give groups that on average differ in only one way, which is the IV manipulation. It's experimental research and, therefore, we can conclude that, most likely, the pen–laptop manipulation caused whatever difference we observed in the DV.

Of course, here as in all other cases, our interpretation will also depend on our assessment of the reliability and validity of the dependent variable, and all the Open Science issues: Are the comparisons planned or exploratory, has there been any selection of participants or results, and so on. The question "Do we have the full story?" should automatically spring to mind.

It's time for take-home messages. Reflect, discuss, then write yours. Our main topic has been the independent groups design, and we encountered the importance of the CI on the difference. We've seen several bits of *d* magic. Do you have a lucky golf ball and would it help anyway? Recall the frenetic dance of the *p* values and a large red flag.

Polya

? Quiz 7.4

1. To compare two independent groups, the estimation approach focuses on the CI for the mean difference between groups. Considering NHST to compare two independent groups:
   a. NHST uses the same basic information as the CI: an effect size, a variability component, and a sample size component.
   b. NHST typically tests the null hypothesis that the difference between the groups is zero ($H_0: \mu_{diff} = 0$).
   c. Unlike the estimation approach, the NHST approach yields a p value which is then used to make a yes/no decision about the null hypothesis.
   d. All of the above.
2. Once a t value is calculated, a p value can be obtained. Think back to Chapter 6 on the NHST approach, then state what the p value represents.
3. When the 95% CI for the difference between two means includes 0, this means that p will be less than / greater than .05 and the result will / will not be judged statistically significant.
4. The more the CIs for independent groups overlap, the smaller / larger the p value and the weaker / stronger the evidence against the null hypothesis.
5. Both p values and CIs dance due to sampling variation. The dance of the p values, however, is more / less erratic than the dance of the CIs, and thus a single p value can tell you more / less about the dance as a whole.
6. When the 95% CIs on the means of two independent groups just touch, the p value is about _____; when they overlap considerably, p is _____; and when they overlap moderately, p is about _____.

7.39 You read a study claiming that wearing a red shirt makes a person feel more confident and assertive, with $p = .01$. A second researcher replicates the study as closely as possible, reports $p = .42$, and claims that the effect can't be real because it did not replicate. A third researcher then replicates the study as closely as possible, finds $p = .08$, and also claims that the effect can't be real.
   a. What should we conclude? If you wish to research the issue yourself, what should you do?
7.40 Watch the dance of the p values video again. Summarize the similarities and differences between the dance of the p values and the dance of the CIs.
7.41 Revisit your take-home messages. Revise and extend the list if you wish.

Reporting Your Work

Comparing groups is at the heart of most research projects, so being able to report and interpret group comparisons is indeed a wonderful skill to have. It will take some practice, as there is a lot of information to convey to the reader. For research questions about group differences your report will typically include:

- whether the comparison is planned or exploratory, unless this is already clear;
- basic descriptive statistics for both groups;
- the group difference, (M_2-M_1) and its CI;
- a standardized effect size estimate ($d_{unbiased}$ is best), preferably with its CI—in your Method section, make clear how your standardized effect size was calculated (which denominator was used);
- a figure if possible, preferably one like ESCI produces that shows all the raw data and which emphasizes the estimated group difference and its CI. State in the figure caption what error bars represent—95% CIs;

◼ an interpretation of the group difference that considers not only the point estimate but also the CI. You can focus on the group difference in original units or the standardized group difference, whichever you feel will be easier for readers to understand. Be sure, though, that the language in your conclusion is consistent with the research design (causal for experimental, relational for non-experimental).

▶ Compare two groups by focusing on the difference between the means (in original units and/ or standardized) and its CI.

Although figures (i.e., graphs) are ideal for showing group comparisons, they are not ideal for extracting data for meta-analysis. So including a figure does not replace the need to report the relevant statistics in the text, a table, or the figure caption.

Here are some examples. Each is based on analysis of a motor skill task that produces scores on a percentage scale.

The first planned analysis found that scores in the power condition ($M = 32.6\%$, $s = 14.8\%$, $n = 68$) were very slightly higher than in the control condition ($M = 31.0\%$, $s = 14.7\%$, $n = 83$). Relative to other findings in the field, the difference in performance was very small ($M_{power} - M_{control}$) = 1.6%, 95% CI [-3.2, 5.4], $d_{unbiased}$ = 0.11, 95% CI [-0.21, 0.43]). The CI is fairly short, indicating that the effect of power on performance is, most likely, no more than moderate in size.

The participants in this sample had a much wider range of ages than in the study we replicated. Although this was not a planned analysis, we also assessed the effect of power on motor skill when restricting the analysis to only those participants younger than 30. In this restricted sample, scores in the power condition ($M = 37.4\%$, $s = 14.1\%$, $n = 29$) were somewhat higher than in the control condition ($M = 34.5\%$, $s = 14.5\%$, $n = 42$). The difference in performance was moderate ($M_{power} - M_{control}$) = 3.0%, 95% CI [-4.0, 9.8], $d_{unbiased}$ = 0.20, 95% CI [-0.27, 0.68]). The CI is long, and is consistent with power producing a small detriment, no change, up to a large benefit. This exploratory analysis, then, does not provide clear evidence of a benefit of power in younger participants.

Motor skill for men ($M = 33.8\%$, $s = 12.8\%$, $n = 62$) was a little higher than for women ($M = 29.7\%$, $s = 15.8\%$, $n = 89$). The difference in performance may seem small in terms of raw scores ($M_{men} - M_{women}$ = 4.0%, 95% CI [-0.7, 8.8]), but the standardized effect size was moderate ($d_{unbiased}$ = 0.28, 95% CI [-0.05, 0.61]) relative to the existing literature. However, both CIs are quite long, and are consistent with anywhere from no advantage up to a large advantage for men. More data are required to estimate more precisely the degree to which gender might be related to motor skill.

For complex studies, writing out all this information for each dependent variable can become overwhelming. Fortunately, a table can provide a very efficient way to summarize lots of comparisons, although of course you'll still need to write your interpretation as text. Here's a link to an example you can use as a model, although note that units should not be stated again with the values of CI limits inside the square brackets: tiny.cc/statextable

 Take-Home Messages

◼ An independent groups study focuses on ($M_2 - M_1$), the difference between two sample means. This can be displayed with its CI on a difference axis, as in Figure 7.2, which is a *take-home picture*.

◼ Assuming homogeneity of variance, the CI on the difference is calculated using s_p, the pooled SD for the two groups. To avoid the assumption, use the Welch approximate method. The CI on the difference is a little longer than either of the two separate CIs.

- The CI on the difference is based on a *t* component, a variability component, and a sample size component. Use Equation 7.3.

- Cohen's *d* allows comparison of results obtained using different original measures. It's an ES in original units divided by a suitable SD—the *standardizer*—so *d* is a number of standard deviations. The population ES is δ, which is a number of σ units.

- If a suitable population SD is available, use it as the standardizer. If not, we usually assume homogeneity of variance and use s_p, the pooled SD within groups. Always state what standardizer was used.

- The CI for δ (the same as the "CI on *d*" and "CI on $d_{unbiased}$") is tricky to calculate, but important.

- Prefer $d_{unbiased}$ to *d*, although for *df* of 50 or more there's little difference.

- Use judgment to interpret values of *d* or $d_{unbiased}$, and the CI for δ, in context. Consider ESs in original units, the standardizer and reference population, the extent of overlap of distributions, previous research, cost-benefit, and practical and theoretical implications.

- If appropriate in context, consider reference values for small, medium, and large effects, for example 0.2, 0.5, and 0.8 as suggested by Cohen for psychology, or 0.2, 0.4, and 0.6 as suggested by Hattie for education.

- The independent groups *t* test assesses the null hypothesis of zero difference. To calculate *t* use Equation 7.6, which needs the ES, $(M_2 - M_1)$, and the variability and sample size components.

- Given independent means and CIs, we can use the overlap rule: If the CIs just touch, *p* is around .01 and there's some evidence of a difference. If they overlap moderately, *p* is around .05 and there's a small amount of evidence of a difference.

- *Red Flag 5*. A close replication can easily give a very different *p* value. The dance of the *p* values is very wide and a *p* value gives only very vague information about the dance. A *p* value is not to be trusted. CIs are much more informative.

- Random assignment to groups gives experimental research and can justify a causal conclusion.

End-of-Chapter Exercises

1) To what extent does a professor's presentation style influence students' perceptions of learning? Carpenter et al. (2013) asked students to watch a video of a professor giving a lecture fluently or haltingly, then to predict the percentage of the presented information they would remember on a quiz 10 minutes later. Table 7.5 shows the results. Use Equation 7.3 to calculate the difference, and its CI, between the fluent and halting groups for predicted learning.

Table 7.5 Summary Statistics for Students' Predictions of Amount Remembered

	Fluent	Halting
M	48%	25%
s	23%	21%
N	21	21

a. Is the assumption of equal variance reasonable? Explain.

b. What is *df*?

c. Look up the critical value of *t*.

d. Calculate s_p.

e. Almost there—calculate the sample size component.

f. Now calculate MoE_{diff}.

g. Calculate the 95% CI for the difference between the two groups.

h. Just as important as calculating the CI is interpreting it. Given that the two groups have means that are 23 percentage points apart, what does the CI tell you?

i. Type the values into **Summary two** and check your calculations.

2) Let's get some more practice calculating a CI for the difference between two means. Continuing the example, Carpenter et al. (2013) also gave participants a quiz to measure their actual learning. Table 7.6 shows the result.

Table 7.6 Summary Statistics for Students' Amount Remembered

	Fluent	Halting
M	26%	22%
s	22%	26%
N	21	21

a. Follow the same steps as in Question 1 to calculate the 95% CI on the difference.

b. Based on these results, Carpenter et al. (2013) claimed that presentation style (fluent or halting) does not impact learning at all, even though students think it will. Based on the CI you calculated, do you agree? Explain.

3) We often have to make numerical estimates (e.g., How many people will come to my party? What's a reasonable price to pay for a new car?). Jacowitz and Kahneman (1995) wanted to know how much our estimates can be influenced by subtly changing the context of the question. Specifically, they asked participants to make numerical estimates, but provided either a high or low *anchor*. For example, they asked participants to estimate how many babies are born in the United States each day, but provided some with the fact that the answer is more than 100 (low anchor) and others with the fact that the answer is less than 50,000 (high anchor). To what extent do these anchors influence the estimates provided? Load the **Anchor_Estimate** data set from the book website. This file has data from a large, multi-lab replication of this classic study (Klein et al., 2014a, 2014b). The file has data from just one of the labs that helped conduct the replication. Provided are the data from three different estimation tasks (number of babies born in the U.S./day, population of Chicago, and height of Mount Everest).

a. For number of babies born/day, use ESCI to make a figure showing estimates for the high and low anchors.

b. Looking at the descriptive statistics provided by ESCI, does it seem reasonable to assume equal variance in both groups? Use the option in ESCI to choose an appropriate method of calculating the CI on the difference.

c. Write an APA-style summary of this finding, incorporating the descriptive statistics (*M* and *s* for each group), the difference and its CI, and a standardized effect size estimate (Cohen's *d*). Include an interpretation of the overall result.

d. Optional: Repeat steps a–c for the other two estimation tasks.

4) Some researchers claim that moral judgments are based not only on rational considerations but also on one's current emotional state. To what extent can recent emotional experiences

influence moral judgments? Schnall et al. (2008) examined this question by manipulating feelings of cleanliness and purity and then observing the extent that this changes how harshly participants judge the morality of others. In Study 1, Schnall et al. asked participants to complete a word scramble task with either neutral words (neutral prime) or words related to cleanliness (cleanliness prime). All students then completed a set of moral judgments about controversial scenarios (Moral_judgment is the average of 6 items, each rated on a scale from 0 to 9, high meaning harsh). The data from this study are in the **Clean_Moral** data set available on the book website. This file also contains data from a replication of the original (Johnson, Cheung, & Donnellan, 2014).

    a. Examine the data from the original study. Make a figure and interpret the difference between the two means.

    b. Based on the data from the original study, Schnall et al. (2008) concluded that activating intuitions about cleanliness can reduce the severity of moral judgments. Do you agree or disagree with this interpretation? Explain.

    c. Based on the data from the original study by Schnall et al. (2008), what would you expect for the replication attempt by Johnson, Cheung, and Donnellan (2014)—which had group sizes of 106 and 102? Write down your prediction before looking at the data.

    d. Examine the data from the replication study. Make a figure and interpret the difference between the two means.

    e. Is the replication study consistent with the finding in the original study? To what extent?

    f. Considering both studies, to what extent do you think manipulating cleanliness influences moral reasoning?

5) To what extent do men and women differ in their attitudes towards mathematics? To investigate, Nosek et al. (2002) asked male and female students to complete an Implicit Association Test (IAT)—this is a task designed to measure a participant's implicit (non-conscious) feelings towards a topic. (If you've never heard of the IAT, try it out here: tiny. cc/harvardiat) On this IAT, students were tested for negative feelings towards mathematics and art. Scores reflect the degree to which a student had more negative implicit attitudes about mathematics than art (positive score: more negative feelings about mathematics; 0: same level of negativity to both; negative score: more negative feelings about art). From the book website you can load the **Math_Gender_IAT** data set which contains data from two different labs that participated in a large-scale replication of the original study (Klein et al., 2014a, 2014b).

    a. Examine the data from the Ithaca lab. Use ESCI to make a figure of how men and women differ in their IAT scores and obtain the 95% CI for the difference. Write an APA-style results paragraph summarizing and interpreting the degree to which gender is related to implicit attitudes toward mathematics.

    b. Based on the data from the Ithaca lab, what would you predict for a second lab, which used somewhat larger samples? How similar do you expect the results to be?

    c. Examine the data from the SDSU lab. How do they compare with your prediction? Compare the two results: To what extent are they consistent with each other?

    d. Can you conclude from these results that gender causes differences in math attitudes? Explain.

Answers to Quizzes

Quiz 7.1

1) a; 2) d; 3) pooled, s_p, standard deviations; 4) $df = (N_1 + N_2 - 2)$; 5) longer; 6) transcription score in percent, interval, pen-laptop or note-taking method, 2, Pen and Laptop, nominal or categorical.

Quiz 7.2

1) standardized; 2) effect size, original units, standard deviation (or standardizer); 3) 0; 4) the pooled SD within groups (s_p), homogeneity of variance; 5) c; 6) 5/20 = 0.25, a decrease of 0.8 × 20 = 16.

Quiz 7.3

1) effect size, population, δ; 2) d; 3) less; 4) 0.40; 5) over, smaller; 6) standardizer, denominator, standard deviation, estimate.

Quiz 7.4

1) d; 2) p is the probability of obtaining the observed result, or more extreme, IF the null hypothesis is true; 3) greater than, will not; 4) larger, weaker; 5) more, less; 6) .01, >.05, .05.

Answers to In-Chapter Exercises

7.3 For a 90% CI, the critical value of t is smaller, so the CI is shorter than for 95% (actually about one-sixth shorter).

7.4 Larger σ in either or both populations is likely to give larger s_p, so the variability component increases and the CI is longer.

7.5 If N_1 is larger, $1/N_1$ is smaller and $\sqrt{\dfrac{1}{N_1} + \dfrac{1}{N_2}}$ is also smaller, so the CI is shorter. Similarly if N_2 is larger. In general, larger samples give shorter CIs, as we expect.

7.6 **Offset points** shifts some points sideways so all are visible. It also moves them very slightly up or down so they line up neatly.

7.7 Type in a data value and press Enter. You can then use Undo and Redo to watch changes in the figure and in the values reported for descriptive statistics and CIs.

7.8 Near red 9.

7.9–

7.10 There's usually little difference unless the sample sizes are considerably different and s_1 and s_2 are also distinctly different.

7.11 df changes a little and almost always becomes a non-integer.

7.12 $s_p = 5.15$ and is the pooled SD, calculated from s_1 and s_2, that's used to estimate σ, which is assumed to be the SD in both populations. For PenLaptop 1, $s_p = 6.09$, which is similar to 5.15, the value for PenLaptop 2.

7.13 The difference is 5.21 percentage points [3.43, 6.98]. We are assuming the SD is the same in the two populations. Making the assumption is reasonable because $s_1 = 4.22$ and $s_2 = 5.52$ are not very different. Similarly for PenLaptop 1.

7.16 Make your eyeballed CI on the difference a little longer than each of the separate CIs.

7.17 a. Near red 3, ES = $(M_2 - M_1) = 1.67$. Near red 5, $s_p = 2.02$, so $d = 1.67/2.02 = 0.83$.

7.18 The difference is small and the two CIs overlap almost totally, so there's no evidence of a population difference.

7.19 See Figure 7.15. $d = 0.32/4.54 = 0.07$, which suggests a very small difference.

7.20 0.83 seems big, and very different from 0.07, which seems very small, although we need the CIs.

7.21 $d = 5.71/6.09 = 0.94$, so almost one SD more transcription for laptop than pen.

7.22 $d = 0.83$ [0.05, 1.59]. Population effect size, δ, is most likely around 0.8, which is quite large, but the CI is very long, no doubt largely because the samples are small, and δ could plausibly be within about 0 to about 1.6.

7.23 The restrictions are that, to calculate the CI for δ, d must lie between -10 and 10 (which is rarely a problem) and df must not exceed 200. MoE$_{av}$ = 0.774, which is the average of upper MoE = 1.593 − 0.827 = 0.766, and lower MoE = 0.827 − 0.046 = 0.781. Upper and lower MoE are not very different, so the CI is only slightly asymmetric. In practice, asymmetry of the CI on d hardly matters.

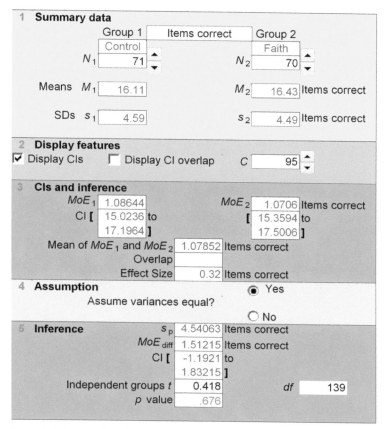

Figure 7.15. Data analysis for Aruguete 1. From **Summary two**.

7.24 Other things being equal, larger samples give more precise estimates and a shorter CI on the difference, whereas smaller samples give less precise estimates, meaning a longer CI on the difference.

7.25 The CI for δ is [−0.26, 0.40], so its center is not far from zero, and the interval is much shorter than that for Damisch 1. The Aruguete 1 result suggests the difference is at most very small.

7.26 For Damisch 1, $d = 0.83$ [0.05, 1.59]. For Aruguete 1, $d = 0.07$ [−0.26, 0.40]. The Damisch ES is large but with great uncertainty, the Aruguete ES near zero, with less uncertainty. The two CIs overlap somewhat.

7.27 $d = 0.827$ and $d_{unbiased} = 0.803$; the ratio is $0.827/0.803 = 1.030$, so d overestimates δ by 3%, when, as here, $df = 26$.

7.28 $df = 139$, and both d and $d_{unbiased} = 0.070$, so $d = d_{unbiased}$ to three decimal places, when df is so large. There's virtually no bias.

7.29 Report $d_{unbiased}$ in both cases, although the values are so similar to d that the interpretation would be the same.

7.30 The pictures emphasize the difference between the two ESs, with considerable separation of the Damisch 1 curves and close to complete overlap for Aruguete 1. However, we need to consider the two CIs. The CI for Damisch 1 is long.

7.32 a. 1.00 and 1.67; b. $d = (125 − 115)/15 = 0.67$; both z and d are numbers of SDs, the SD being the unit of measurement in each case, and d is the difference between the two z scores.

7.33 $t(149) = 5.79$, so $p < .001$. a. Assume homogeneity of variance, which is reasonable because the two sample SDs in Table 7.2 are not very different. b. Figure 7.4 reports $p = 0$, which is rounded to 3 decimal places, so is consistent with our $p < .001$. c. The data provide very strong evidence against the null hypothesis of 0, as also does the CI on the difference, which is very far from 0.

7.34 a. For College A, $M = 65.25$ and $s = 13.02$; for College B, $M = 50.67$ and $s = 12.51$; b. For A the CI is [54.4, 76.1] and for B the CI is [41.1, 60.3].

7.35 The ES = −14.58, $s_p = 12.75$ and the CI on the difference is [−27.8, −1.38]. We estimate that the College A population mean score is about 15 points higher on the HEAT than the College B mean, although the difference could plausibly be anywhere from about 1 point to about 28 points. MoE_{diff} is about 13 points, so our estimate of the population difference lacks precision; a. $t(15) = -2.35$ and $p = .03$ (the same as for $t(15) = 2.35$); b. The CI just misses 0, which is consistent with p just less than .05. The difference is statistically significant; there's a small amount of evidence against the null hypothesis of 0.

7.36 The CI on the difference is a little longer than each of the separate CIs, as we expect for independent groups.

7.37 b. When $M_2 = 12.058$, overlap is 0.500 and $p = .036$. When $M_2 = 13.141$, overlap is 0 and $p = .006$. These p values are a little smaller than the .05 and .01 expected from the rule, which suggests the rule is a bit conservative. In fact, it usually but not always is.

7.38 a. When $M_2 = 11.83$, $p = .05$, and, in the figure, the CI on the difference just touches 0, as we expect. The lower limits of that CI, and the CI for δ, are both reported as very close to 0, illustrating that the same p value applies whether we are using original units or d.

7.39 a. This common pattern illustrates the problem of relying on p values, which bounce around enormously even for close replications. Interpreting $p = .42$ and .08 as evidence that the effect "can't be real" or "didn't replicate" is a version of Red Flag 3, which highlights the danger of interpreting nonsignificance as evidence of no effect. We can conclude little from the p values. We need the ES and CI for each study. If all three gave a positive effect, together they may give evidence of a non-zero effect, perhaps strong evidence. We should combine the results using meta-analysis, and interpret, then decide whether a further study is advisable. A fourth study would be added to the meta-analysis to give an even more precise estimate of the effect.

7.40 Both dances bounce a lot, p values even more than CIs. The key point is that any single CI makes the uncertainty salient: Its length gives a reasonable idea of the amount of bouncing in the dance of the means. In striking contrast, any single p value tells us nothing about uncertainty and virtually nothing about the dance it comes from. So p tells us very little indeed.

8

The Paired Design

To compare note-taking using pen and laptop, Mueller and Oppenheimer (2014) used two independent groups of students. An alternative would be to ask a single group to use pens one day and laptops another day, so each student would provide a transcription score for both conditions. We'd then be able to compare pen and laptop *within* participants, rather than *between* participants as in the independent groups design. A single group and comparison within participants gives us the *paired design*, which is the second basic design we'll discuss for comparing two conditions. It's not always possible—think of comparing females and males—but, when it is, it can often be efficient and give relatively precise estimates. However, using a pen one day can influence performance with a laptop on another day—practice at the task, perhaps, or boredom with being in the study. We'll discuss ways to minimize this problem that can, in some cases, justify a causal conclusion, which is what we always seek.

My main example will be studies by Thomason et al. (2014) that used the paired design to evaluate a promising new approach to teaching critical thinking. Most sections in this chapter follow the pattern of the corresponding sections in Chapter 7 for independent groups. It's worth comparing back often. I close this chapter with a brief description of the two designs, and also consider the choice between the two. As you probably expect, I'll say it's a matter for judgment—which, as usual, just adds to the interest. Here's our agenda:

- The paired design, using a pretest vs. posttest example
- Confidence intervals for the paired design
- Cohen's *d* for the paired design
- NHST and *p* values for the paired design
- Interpreting the paired design
- Independent groups and the paired design: comparing and choosing

THE PAIRED DESIGN

Evaluation of a Course in Critical Thinking

Many colleges require a course in critical thinking, but such courses are not particularly effective, with a meta-analysis by Alvarez (2007) finding that average gain in critical thinking ability is only $d = 0.34$ in a semester. Courses based on *argument mapping*, however, showed about twice that gain. Argument mapping is a graphical technique for representing and critiquing an argument. Thomason et al. (2014) reported seven studies evaluating a promising approach to teaching critical thinking that combines argument mapping with a form of mastery learning (Mazur, 1997). Studies were conducted in the United States, Canada, and the United Kingdom, and each study used a single group of students. Students were tested on various well-established measures of critical thinking, both before (the Pretest) and after (the Posttest) training. Group sizes

> The *paired design* uses a single group of participants, each of whom contributes a pair of data values, one for each of the conditions being compared.

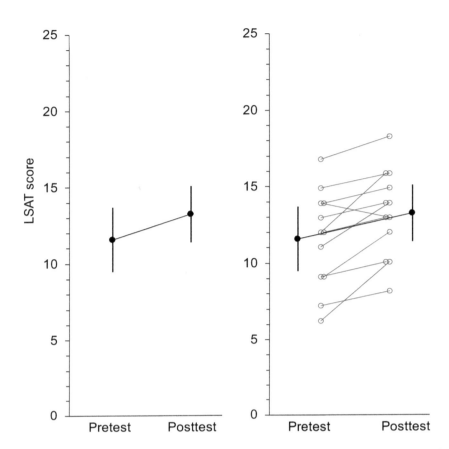

Figure 8.1. On the left, means and 95% CIs at Pretest and Posttest from the Thomason 1 paired design study of critical thinking. On the right, the same but with a pair of data points shown for each of the N = 12 students, joined by a blue line. The line joining the Pretest and Posttest means indicates a repeated measure.

ranged from 7 to 39. All the Thomason studies compared the two conditions, Pretest and Posttest, within participants, and therefore used the paired design.

Now is the moment to define a few handy terms. The IV for the independent groups design is a *between-groups variable*. The IV for the paired design is a *within-group variable*, also called a *repeated measure*. Those different IVs define a *between-groups design* and a *paired design*.

A **between-groups IV** gives a **between-groups design**, meaning that different levels of the variable are seen by independent groups of participants. For example, pen–laptop in Chapter 7.

A **within-group IV** gives a **within-group design**, meaning that all levels of the variable are seen by a single group of participants. Equivalently, a **repeated measure** gives a **repeated measure design**; for example, the **paired design**, such as pretest–posttest in this chapter.

The first Thomason study, Thomason 1, used a group of N = 12 students, whose critical thinking ability was assessed at Pretest and Posttest using the Logical Reasoning section of the Law School Aptitude Test (LSAT). Figure 8.1 presents the means and CIs for Thomason 1. The line joining the Pretest and Posttest means indicates a paired design—in other words that we have a repeated measure. The means and CIs don't look promising, with an apparently modest increase in the mean from Pretest to Posttest, and CIs that overlap substantially. However, we need to take the analysis further. What questions should spring to mind whenever you see summary statistics, or a summary figure?

 I know you don't need reminding...

I suggest:

- What data lie behind the summary statistics?
- What data lie behind what the figure shows?

On the right in Figure 8.1 we have what we need: As in Figure 7.1 (I said we'd compare back often to Chapter 7) the open dots are individual data points, and pairs of dots joined by a blue line are the Pretest and Posttest scores for one student. All but one of the lines slopes up, so 11 of the 12 students gave a higher LSAT score after the training. That looks more encouraging.

I mentioned large overlap of the two CIs on the left in Figure 8.1, which would be relevant if we had independent groups. For the paired design, however, we'll discover that overlap of those CIs is almost irrelevant for answering our research question. Now, what is that question, and what effect size do we need to answer it?

The question is simply "To what extent are Posttest scores on average greater than Pretest scores?" The effect size is the (Posttest – Pretest) mean difference, and we want the CI as well. Figure 8.2 displays these, on a difference

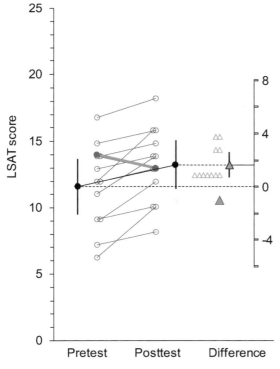

Figure 8.2. The Thomason 1 data as in Figure 8.1, with the mean difference and its 95% CI displayed on a difference axis. The line joining the Pretest and Posttest means indicates a repeated measure. The open pink triangles are the (Posttest – Pretest) differences for the $N = 12$ individual students. The data for one student are highlighted: The solid blue points joined by the heavy red line are from that student, and the large red triangle marks that student's (Posttest – Pretest) difference of –1 on the difference axis.

Table 8.1 Statistics
for the LSAT Data
from the Thomason 1
Study of Critical
Thinking

		Pretest		Posttest		Difference
N		12		12		12
Mean	M_1	11.58	M_2	13.25	M_{diff}	1.67
SD	s_1	3.32	s_2	2.90	s_{diff}	1.50
MoE	MoE_1	2.11	MoE_2	1.84	MoE_{diff}	0.95

axis. It also marks the (Posttest – Pretest) difference for each student with a pink triangle. The data for the only student whose score decreased are highlighted: The solid blue dots joined by a heavy red line and the large red triangle both show that Posttest was 1 lower than Pretest for that student. Seven open pink triangles at 1 on the difference axis show that for seven of the students the Posttest score was 1 greater than the Pretest, as indicated also by seven of the blue lines sloping up to the right by the same small amount.

The CI on the Difference

The most striking thing about Figure 8.2 is that the CI on the difference is so short. For *independent* groups that CI is a little longer than the separate CIs, as in Figure 7.2, but here it's distinctly shorter, and a short CI is great news. That's the beauty of the paired design—it often gives us a precise estimate of our effect size. Let's calculate. Table 8.1 gives the descriptive statistics.

The ES for the paired design is the mean of the differences, M_{diff}, which is always equal to $(M_2 - M_1)$.

As for independent groups, the effect size is the difference between the two means: $(M_2 - M_1) = 13.25 - 11.58 = 1.67$. However, for the paired design we focus on the (Posttest – Pretest) *differences* for each participant. The mean of those differences is M_{diff}, which is always equal to $(M_2 - M_1)$, so M_{diff} is our effect size for the paired design. Check that $M_{diff} = (M_2 - M_1)$ in the table.

Our statistical model for calculating the CI has two assumptions:

- *Random sampling.* The differences are a random sample from a population of differences. In practice this usually means that we're using a random sample of participants from the relevant population.
- *Normal population.* The population of differences is normally distributed.

For the CI I'll again start with the formula for MoE for the 95% CI on a single mean, when σ is not known:

MoE for the CI on a single mean.

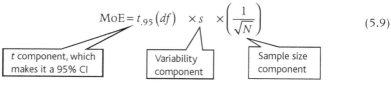

$$MoE = t_{.95}(df) \times s \times \left(\frac{1}{\sqrt{N}}\right) \tag{5.9}$$

| t component, which makes it a 95% CI | Variability component | Sample size component |

For the CI we seek on M_{diff}, we need the appropriate three components. The *t* component is $t_{.95}(df)$, where *df* for the paired design is

df for the paired design.

$$df = (N - 1) \tag{8.1}$$

So $df = (12 - 1) = 11$, and **Normal and t** tells us that $t_{.95}(11) = 2.20$.

The **variability component** is the standard deviation of the *N* differences, meaning the standard deviation of the (Posttest – Pretest) differences, with symbol s_{diff}. Table 8.1 tells us $s_{diff} = 1.50$. There's no pooling, so we don't need to assume homogeneity of variance.

The sample size component for our single group is $(1/\sqrt{N}) = (1/\sqrt{12})$ = 0.289.

Enter those components into Equation 5.9 and we find that MoE_{diff}, for the CI on the difference in the paired design, is

$$\text{MoE}_{\text{diff}} = t_{.95}(df) \times s_{\text{diff}} \times (1/\sqrt{N}) \tag{8.2}$$

> ◄ MoE for the CI on the difference in the paired design.

Use Equation 8.2 to find that $\text{MoE}_{\text{diff}} = 2.20 \times 1.50 \times 0.289 = 0.95$. This is the value reported in Table 8.1. Therefore, the difference with its CI is 1.67 [1.67 − 0.95, 1.67 + 0.95], or 1.67 [0.72, 2.62].

Our main finding is that the mean increase in LSAT score after training was 1.67 LSAT units [0.72, 2.62]. Given good understanding of the LSAT and what its scores indicate, we could interpret this result and use it to guide conclusions about the effectiveness of the innovative training procedure for improvement of students' critical thinking. Soon we'll also express the result in terms of Cohen's *d*.

Let's further consider the CI on the difference. We noted in Figure 8.2 that almost all students showed a gain from Pretest to Posttest—almost all the lines for the data pairs slope up and the corresponding open triangles are above zero on the difference axis. In addition, the triangles are much more tightly bunched than either the Pretest or Posttest scores, and, therefore, the SD of the differences ($s_{\text{diff}} = 1.50$) is smaller than both $s_1 = 3.32$ and $s_2 = 2.90$. A small SD for differences is good news, because it means the CI on the difference will be short. Indeed, $\text{MoE}_{\text{diff}} = 0.95$, which is considerably less than both $\text{MoE}_1 = 2.11$ and $\text{MoE}_2 = 1.84$.

> ◄ With the paired design, if differences are fairly consistent over participants, the CI on the mean difference is likely to be short, so precision is high.

The CI on the mean difference is shorter than either of the other CIs, which says that we're estimating the mean gain in critical thinking ability more precisely than we could estimate the mean Pretest or mean Posttest scores. The key reason for this is that the differences are fairly closely bunched—they are reasonably consistent over students, and so s_{diff} is small. We're comparing the two conditions, Pretest and Posttest, *within* rather than *between* participants. In other words, each participant is her or his own control. The choice of a paired design has given us a sensitive study.

Here's another way to think about the pattern in Figure 8.2. Note that the participants with high Pretest scores tend to have high Posttest scores as well, and those with low Pretests tend to have low Posttests as well. We say that Pretest and Posttest scores tend to be highly *correlated*. In Chapter 11 we discuss *correlation* in detail, but I'll mention here that correlation, symbol *r*, is a measure of the extent to which two variables are associated, the extent to which they vary together. Values of *r* can range from −1 through 0 to 1. High positive correlations, meaning *r* close to 1, occur when high values of one variable, for example Pretest, are generally associated with high values of the other variable, for example Posttest; and low values of Pretest with low values of Posttest. Zero correlation (*r* = 0) means no association, while negative correlation (*r* < 0) would mean that high Pretest is associated with low Posttest, and vice versa.

> ◄ *Correlation, r,* is a measure of the strength of association between two variables, such as Pretest and Posttest; *r* can take values from −1 through 0 to 1.

In Figure 8.2, the correlation between Pretest and Posttest scores is *r* = .89, which is a high positive correlation, close to the maximum of 1. Such a high correlation goes with the similarity of most of the lines joining Pretest and Posttest pairs, tight bunching of the triangles, a small s_{diff}, a short CI on the difference, and a sensitive study. In brief, when the two measures—in our example, Pretest and Posttest—are highly correlated, the paired design is especially advantageous because it gives high precision.

> ◄ With the paired design, when the two measures (for example Pretest and Posttest) are highly correlated, precision is high.

Comparing Two Designs

Here I want to consider one central aspect of the comparison of the two designs. Figure 8.3 shows the means and CIs for a study comparing two conditions, A and B, but doesn't tell us the study design. We can eyeball or sketch the difference on a difference axis, as at right, but can we eyeball the CI on the mean difference? If it's independent groups we can—simply make that CI a little longer than either of the other CIs.

▶ With the paired design, knowing the means and separate CIs is *not* sufficient to work out the CI on the mean difference. We need s_{diff} as well.

For the paired design, however, we need extra information: We need s_{diff}, a key component in Equation 8.2 that determines the length of the CI on the difference. Depending on the value of s_{diff}, the length of that CI may be just about anything, from zero up to even longer than the CIs on the separate means. Usually the CI on the difference is shorter than the other two CIs, and Figure 8.2 shows a case where it's considerably shorter—which makes us happy. Often, s_{diff} is small and the paired design is sensitive, but it may not be.

▶ For the paired design, no overlap rule is possible.

One consequence of needing extra information, beyond what Figure 8.3 tells us, is that no overlap rule is possible for the paired design. We'll see cases, such as that in Figure 8.2, in which the CIs on the two separate means overlap considerably, but the CI on the difference is short. The overlap might suggest little evidence of a difference, but the short CI should be our focus: It may tell us truly that there is strong evidence of a substantial difference. The overlap rule is very handy, but only when it applies—for independent groups. Before considering overlap of two CIs, always pause and check: If the CIs are for a repeated measure, overlap is irrelevant and perhaps misleading.

In summary, for a paired design, if we see only the means and CIs, as on the left in Figure 8.3, we can't eyeball what we really want, the CI on the difference. Most likely it's shorter than the other CIs, but we don't know how much shorter unless we have s_{diff} and can calculate.

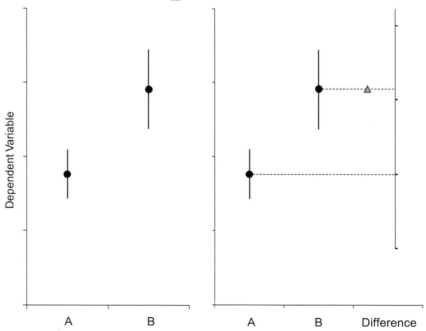

Figure 8.3. Means and 95% CIs for a fictitious study comparing conditions A and B. Given the left panel, we can eyeball the difference between the means, as marked by the pink triangle in the right panel. However, only with independent groups can we eyeball the CI on the difference.

	Pretest		Posttest		Difference	
N		16		16		
Mean	M_1	12.88	M_2	14.25	M_{diff}	
SD	s_1	3.40	s_2	4.285	s_{diff}	2.13
MoE	MoE_1	1.81	MoE_2	2.28	MoE_{diff}	

Table 8.2 Statistics for the LSAT Data from the Thomason 2 Study of Critical Thinking

A line joining the means, as in Figures 8.1 and 8.2, indicates a paired design. Including such a line is a valuable convention, much to be encouraged, but unfortunately the convention is not universally followed. Therefore, absence of such a line, as in Figure 8.3, is not a reliable indicator of independent groups. It's a deficiency of current graphical conventions that a figure like that on the left in Figure 8.3 does not indicate the design. We need to be told in the caption. If we are not told, we can't interpret—we can't tell how precisely it estimates the difference between means. Of course, it's even better to see the figure on the right, but showing also the CI on the difference.

◄ Any figure with means and CIs, such as Figure 8.3, must state the design, or it can't be interpreted.

8.1 Suppose that in Figure 8.2 the differences—the open triangles—were even more tightly bunched: Would s_{diff} be larger or smaller? What would this imply for precision and the CI on the difference? Explain. How would the correlation of Pretest and Posttest change?

8.2 Does it matter if the groups in an independent groups study are different in size? What about in a paired design?

8.3 A second study from Thomason et al. (2014) used the paired design with $N = 16$. The measure was again the LSAT. Table 8.2 shows summary data. Calculate the values in the rightmost column and find the CI on the mean difference.

ESCI for the Paired Design

esci 8.4 Fire up **Data paired** and see the Thomason 1 data as in Figure 8.4. (Scroll right and click at red 12 if necessary.) As usual, explore, read popouts and experiment. Compare values with Table 8.1 and the figure with Figure 8.2.

▨ Near red 1 note the **Differences** column, the heading **Highlight** and 4 checkboxes. Read the popouts and experiment. Explain. Compare with Figure 8.2.

▨ Near red 7 note that the correlation $r = .89$ is reported.

8.5 Compare the two columns of data shown in Figure 7.3 with the two columns in Figure 8.4. Would it make any difference if you changed the order of a few of the data values in the left column in Figure 7.3 without changing those in the right? Explain.

▨ What about in Figure 8.4: Could you change the order of a few data values just in the Pretest column? Explain.

esci 8.6 With your screen showing the data as in Figure 8.4, think how you could change a few Posttest values to decrease s_{diff}. Try out your idea.

▨ Note what happens to s_{diff}, to the pattern of lines in the figure, and to MoE_{diff} and the CI on the mean difference. Explain.

▨ Note what happens to the value of r. Explain.

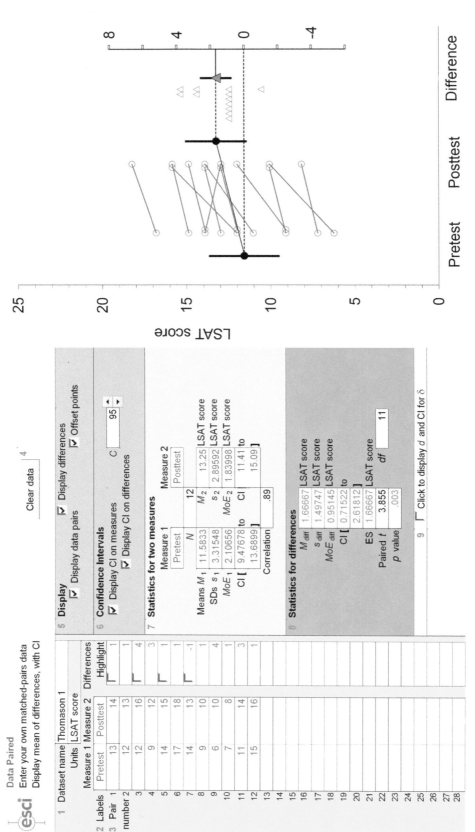

Figure 8.4. On the left the Thomason 1 data and on the right a figure similar to Figure 8.2. From **Data paired**.

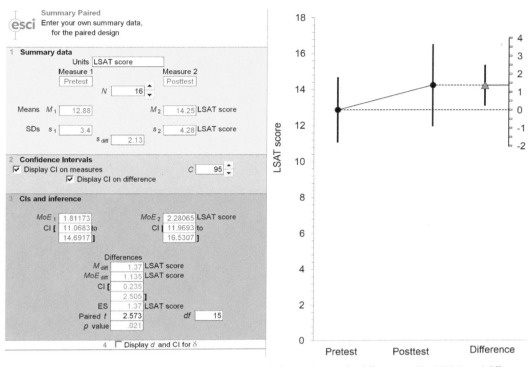

Figure 8.5. Statistics for the Thomason 2 data as in Table 8.2 and a figure showing the difference and its 95% CI on a difference axis. From **Summary paired**.

8.7 Make further changes to some Posttest values that will increase s_{diff}. Again note and explain what happens.

　　▨　What is your conclusion about s_{diff} and precision?
　　▨　What is your conclusion about correlation r?
　　▨　Put those conclusions in different words by describing when the paired design is likely to be especially advantageous.

8.8 Scroll far right and click at red 13 to load the Thomason 2 data. Check that ESCI gives the values in Table 8.2, and also your answers to Exercise 8.3.

8.9 Figure 8.5 shows **Summary paired** with summary statistics for Thomason 2, and a figure showing the difference with its CI. Compare values with those in Table 8.2.

　　▨　Note how the length of the CI on the difference compares with the other two CIs, for Thomason 2. Make the same comparison for the Thomason 1 data in Figure 8.4. Compare the effectiveness of using a paired design in the two studies.

　　▨　Open **Summary paired**. If you don't see the summary data for Thomason 2, type them in. Compare with Figure 8.5. Explore the page.

? Quiz 8.1

1. Which of the following is a paired design to find out how much Neuroaid improves IQ?
   a. One group of students drank Neuroaid and another group drank water; all students then took an IQ test.

b. One group of students took an IQ test immediately after drinking Neuroaid and, on a different day, another version of the same IQ test immediately after drinking water.

c. One group of students took an IQ test after drinking Neuroaid and their scores were compared to national norms.

d. All of the above.

2. In a paired design, two conditions are compared within / between participants, and the IV is a within-group / between-groups variable. With independent groups, two conditions are compared within / between participants, and the IV is a within-group / between-groups variable.

3. In a paired design, the effect size is _____. How is it calculated?

4. For a paired design, the variability component for the CI on the difference is _____, which is the SD of the _____ _____.

5. Paired design studies usually give more / less precise estimates than independent group studies, meaning that the CI is usually shorter / longer. A paired design is especially advantageous when s_{diff} is smaller / larger, the CI on the difference is shorter / longer, and the correlation is smaller / larger.

6. A figure shows the means and CIs for conditions A and B. The length of the CI on the effect size is _____ if the design is independent groups, and is _____ if it's a paired design.

COHEN'S *d* FOR THE PAIRED DESIGN

In Chapter 7 we discussed Cohen's *d*, the standardized effect size, and I described three ways it can be useful. It can help us:

1. understand an original-units ES;

2. compare ESs from measures in different original units that are all assessing the same characteristic or ability, such as critical thinking; and

3. compare ESs from measures that are assessing a possibly very wide range of different characteristics or abilities, such as those influenced by good sleep.

As an illustration of use 2, note that Thomason et al. (2014) used three well-established measures of critical thinking: part of the Law School Aptitude Test (LSAT), and also the California Critical Thinking Skills Test (CCTST) and the Halpern Critical Thinking Assessment (HCTA). These are all measures of critical thinking, but use quite different scales, so values in original units can't be directly compared. The researchers made extensive use of *d* to compare results from the three measures. Even within their own project they needed *d* to make sense of their findings.

The basic formula for *d* is

Basic formula for Cohen's *d*.

$$d = \frac{\text{Effect size in original units}}{\text{An appropriate standard deviation}} = \frac{\text{ES}}{\text{SD}} \tag{7.4}$$

For the paired design, M_{diff} is our effect size. We need to choose an appropriate standardizer. For pretest–posttest studies, the standard deviation of the Pretest, s_1 in Tables 8.1 and 8.2, is often a reasonable choice. However, a slightly better estimate of population standard deviation is usually an average calculated from the SDs for the two conditions—here the Pretest and Posttest SDs—using

Standardizer for paired design, s_{av}.

$$s_{av} = \sqrt{\frac{s_1^2 + s_2^2}{2}} \tag{8.3}$$

and the degrees of freedom for this standardizer is $df = (N - 1)$. Substitute in Equation 7.4 to obtain

$$d = M_{\text{diff}} / s_{\text{av}} \qquad (8.4)$$

◄ *d* for the paired design.

Consider Thomason 1, for which Table 8.1 reports $M_{\text{diff}} = 1.67$, $s_1 = 3.32$, and $s_2 = 2.90$. Equation 8.3 gives $s_{\text{av}} = \sqrt{(3.32^2 + 2.90^2)/2} = 3.11$, and Equation 8.4 gives $d = 1.67/3.11 = 0.54$. So Thomason 1 found a gain of $d = 0.54$ in LSAT score after training. We could use any or all of the approaches we discussed in Chapter 7 to interpret that value of d, including understanding of the original LSAT scores, and reference to overlapping distributions, to previous research using the LSAT in different situations, and to Cohen's rule-of-thumb value of 0.5 for a medium effect.

◄ For the paired design, the standardizer for *d* is s_{av}, which is based on the SDs for the two measures, such as pretest and posttest.

Note what we did *not* use as standardizer: s_{diff}. For the paired design we need s_{diff} to calculate the CI on the difference, but s_{diff} is not the appropriate standardizer for calculating d. I'll say more about this shortly.

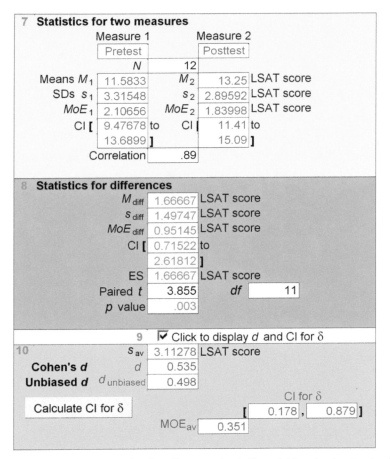

Figure 8.6. Statistics for the LSAT data from Thomason 1, as in Figure 8.4, but also showing at red 10 the panel for Cohen's *d*. From **Data paired**.

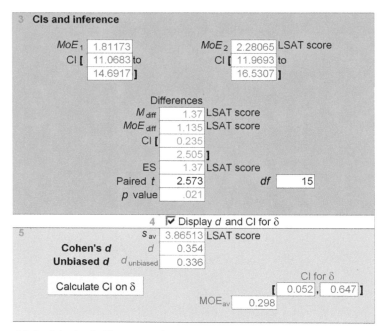

Figure 8.7. Statistics for the Thomason 2 data as in Table 8.2 and Figure 8.5, but also showing at red 5 the panel for Cohen's *d*. From **Summary paired**.

8.10 a. Use the data in Table 8.2 to calculate *d* for Thomason 2. Interpret, and compare with Thomason 1.

b. What standard deviation in the table did you *not* need to use?

8.11 The Thomason 3 study used the HCTA measure of critical thinking, and a paired design with $N = 39$. The summary statistics are: $M_1 = 67.41$, $M_2 = 71.77$, $s_1 = 7.42$, $s_2 = 5.85$, and $s_{diff} = 6.09$.

a. Do you need all those values to calculate *d*?

b. Calculate the ES, then the standardizer, then *d*.

c. Interpret, and compare with Thomason 1 and 2.

8.12 Figure 8.4 shows the Thomason 1 data. Figure 8.6 shows the same, but after clicking at red 9 to reveal at red 10 a panel showing Cohen's *d*. Find the two values required by Equation 8.4. Use that equation to calculate *d*, and compare with the value shown in the figure.

8.13 Figure 8.5 shows the Thomason 2 data as displayed by **Summary paired**. Figure 8.7 shows the same, but after clicking at red 4 to reveal at red 5 a panel showing Cohen's *d*. Find the two values required by Equation 8.4. Use that equation to calculate *d*, and compare with the value you found in Exercise 8.10, and the value shown in the figure.

Confidence Intervals on *d*

As with independent groups, for the paired design we need to assume random sampling from a normally distributed population to calculate a CI on *d*. Again the CI on *d* is a little tricky to calculate, so you need to click a button to initiate calculation. The CI is again a little asymmetric. In Figures 8.6 and 8.7 you can see the button and the values of the CI for δ, for Thomason 1 and 2.

For the paired design also we need to consider removing bias from d, unless N is large. You can see the values of d_{unbiased} in Figures 8.6 and 8.7, and can compare with d.

esci **8.14** Open **Data paired**, scroll right, and click at red 14 to load the HCTA data for Thomason 3. Click to reveal the d panel.

  a. Compare d with what you found in Exercise 8.11.
  b. Compare the values shown for d_{unbiased} and d, and comment on the amount of bias, compared with Thomason 1 and 2.
  c. Click to calculate the CI for δ. Interpret. Compare with the results from Thomason 1 and 2.

8.15 Thomason 4 used the California Critical Thinking Skills Test (CCTST) and a paired design with $N = 7$ students. The Pretest mean was 17.29 and SD was 3.04; the Posttest mean was 20.43 and SD was 4.96.

  a. Is that sufficient information to calculate an original-units effect size? An original-units CI? Explain.
  b. Is that sufficient information to calculate d? A CI on d? Explain.

esci **8.16** Type those values into **Summary paired**. Type in suitable labels, and make sure the d panel is visible.

  a. Can ESCI calculate an original-units effect size? An original-units CI? Explain.
  b. Can it calculate d? A CI on d? Explain.

8.17 Type in 3.08 as s_{diff}, the SD of the differences.

  a. What's the original-units CI?
  b. What's the CI for δ?
  c. Interpret the result of Thomason 4 along with those of the other three studies.

I should mention that ESCI uses a good approximate method for calculating a CI for δ for the paired design. However, there are restrictions, as the popouts in the d panel in **Data paired** and **Summary paired** state: The df must be at least 5 and not more than 200, the level of confidence (C) must be 95, and d_{unbiased} must lie between −2 and +2. Sorry about that. Fortunately, in practice these restrictions are rarely a problem.

Choice of Standardizer

I said that I'd discuss further our choice of standardizer for d for the paired design, and in particular why we use s_{av} and not s_{diff}. Think of d in terms of the overlap of two distributions. In our paired examples, the overlap is of the assumed population distributions of pretest and posttest scores, which Figure 8.8 illustrates for the Thomason 1 value of $d = 0.54$. The overlap is very similar to overlap in the center panel in Figure 7.10, for Cohen's medium effect.

The standardizer we need is the SD of the curves in Figure 8.8, and s_{av} is our estimate of that. For Thomason 1, $s_{\text{av}} = 3.11$ and $d = 0.54$. If instead we use s_{diff} as standardizer, we obtain $s_{\text{diff}} = 1.50$ from Table 8.1, and calculate $d = 1.67/ 1.50 = 1.11$. That's far too large to correspond to the overlap shown in Figure 8.8. My conclusion is that, for the paired design, we need s_{av} as our standardizer for d.

When reading any report of d for a study with a paired design, note what standardizer was used. Sometimes researchers wrongly use s_{diff} as standardizer, so beware suspiciously large d values reported for a paired design. As usual, unless we know how d was calculated, we can't be sure what it tells us.

◀ For the paired design, use s_{av} as standardizer for d, not s_{diff}.

◀ Beware suspiciously large d for a paired design study. Was s_{diff} used as standardizer, not s_{av}?

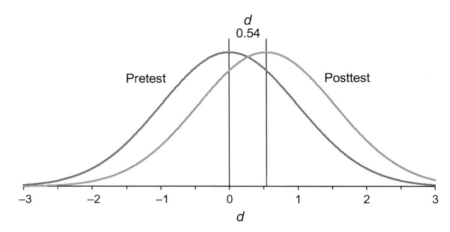

Figure 8.8. The $d = 0.54$ result of Thomason 1, illustrated as overlapping population distributions of pretest and posttest scores.

	Independent groups design	Paired design
Effect size	$(M_2 - M_1)$	M_{diff}, same as $(M_2 - M_1)$
Variability component for inference (to calculate the CI)	s_p	s_{diff}
Standardizer for d	s_p	s_{av}

Table 8.3 Effect Size, Variability Component and Standardizer for Two Designs

▶────────
The independent groups design uses s_p both for inference and as standardizer for d. By contrast, the paired design uses different quantities: s_{diff} for inference, and s_{av} as standardizer for d.

Finally in this section, consider calculation of the CI, and of d, for our two designs. We saw in Chapter 7 that, for independent groups, we assume homogeneity of variance and use s_p, the pooled SD within groups, to calculate the CI on the difference and also as standardizer for d. In contrast, for the paired design we need to use *different* quantities to calculate the CI on the difference (use s_{diff}) and as standardizer for d (use s_{av}). Table 8.3 gives a summary. It's great news that for the paired design we can use s_{diff} for inference, because small s_{diff} gives a short CI and thus a precise estimate of our effect size.

Interpretation of d

▶────────
Whatever the study design, use judgment to interpret values of d in context.

Interpretation of d is much the same, whether it comes from independent groups or a paired design. You may care to review the section *Thinking About Values of Cohen's d* in Chapter 7, while bearing in mind our examples with a paired design. Here again is the closing summary of that section. We should make our judgment of what d means in the particular situation, perhaps considering

- effect sizes in original units,
- the standardizer and reference population,
- the overlap picture for our d,
- values typical for our discipline, and
- perhaps, Cohen's or Hattie's reference values.

That's a long list, but thinking of the particular context usually prompts further questions still, such as: How difficult was it to achieve the effect? What's the cost-benefit trade-off? How big a practical difference does the effect make? What are the theoretical implications? How does the effect size compare with previous research? Consider any of those questions that are relevant, as you use your judgment to interpret *d*.

As in Chapter 7, I'll next turn from Cohen's *d* to consider NHST and *p* values.

8.18   Suppose Class W accepts a very wide range of students and has SD = 24 on a test of achievement. Suppose Class N is selective entry and has SD = 12 on the test. Over the year, Class W achieves a mean increase of 12 points, whereas Class N achieves 9.

   a.   What's *d* for the improvement in each class? Compare and interpret.

8.19   The state-wide SD on that achievement test is 15. Using this as standardizer, find *d* for the two classes. Interpret.

   a.   What standardizer would you recommend, and why?

? Quiz 8.2

1. For the paired design, using *d* may allow us to
   a. compare results from measures of various underlying characteristics.
   b. compare results from different measures of the same underlying characteristic.
   c. understand a result expressed in original units.
   d. All of the above.
2. For the paired design, the basic formula for *d* is *d* = ES/SD. The ES is _____.
3. The SD is called the standardizer. For the paired design we use _____ as standardizer.
4. If a value of *d* reported for a paired design looks suspiciously large, what error might the researchers have made?
5. Consider the variability component used to calculate the CI, and the standardizer for *d*. For independent groups, these are the same / different. For the paired design, these are the same / different.
6. For the paired design, when interpreting *d*,
   a. among other things, consider how big a practical difference the effect makes.
   b. it doesn't matter whether you use *d* or $d_{unbiased}$.
   c. the CI is likely to be long, indicating great uncertainty.
   d. to be on the safe side, also analyze the data as if the groups were independent.

NHST AND *p* VALUES FOR THE PAIRED DESIGN

My recommended approach is to use estimation, but here I'll discuss NHST, specifically the *paired t test*, which we'll use to test the null hypothesis of zero difference between Pretest and Posttest. We use the same statistical model as we used earlier in this chapter to calculate the CI on M_{diff}. As in Chapter 7, I start with Equation 6.2, which is the formula for *t* for a single group.

$$t(df) = \frac{(M - \mu_0)}{s \times \left(\frac{1}{\sqrt{N}}\right)}$$

Effect size

Variability component

Sample size component

(6.2)

The ***paired t test*** uses a *p* value to test the null hypothesis of zero difference in a study with a paired design.

t for a single group.

Once again we just need to insert the appropriate components for the paired design. Our effect size is M_{diff}. Equation 8.2 tells us that the appropriate variability component is s_{diff} and sample size component is $(1/\sqrt{N})$. Also, $df = (N-1)$. Substituting into Equation 6.2, we get

t for the paired design.

$$t(N-1) = \frac{M_{\text{diff}}}{s_{\text{diff}} \times \left(\dfrac{1}{\sqrt{N}}\right)} \tag{8.5}$$

Consider Table 8.3, specifically the two rows labeled "variability component" and "standardizer". Which row applies for the calculation of *t* for finding a *p* value? Is the answer the same for both designs?

 Thinking, discussing...

Here, as in Chapter 7, there's great similarity between the calculations for a CI and a *p* value: For both designs, the "variability component" row applies for calculating the CI, and also *t* and the *p* value.

For Thomason 1, we know from Table 8.1 and Figure 8.4 that $df = 11$,

For both designs, the *t* statistic is the mean difference (the ES) divided by the variability and sample size components. That value of *t* gives the *p* value.

$M_{\text{diff}} = 1.67$, $s_{\text{diff}} = 1.50$, and $1/\sqrt{N} = 0.289$. Substituting those values in Equation 8.5 we get $t(11) = 1.67/(1.50 \times 0.289) = 3.85$. The two tails area in **Normal and t** for $t(11) = 3.85$ is .003, which is the *p* value we seek. Note in Figure 8.4 that **Data paired** reports near red 8 the values of *df*, *t*, and *p*. Check that these match the values I've calculated above. I conclude that the *p* value for testing the null hypothesis of zero difference from Pretest to Posttest is $p = .003$. The study provided strong evidence against that null hypothesis; it found a statistically significant gain.

8.20 a. Use the statistics reported in Table 8.2 to calculate *t*, then find the *p* value for the difference between Pretest and Posttest for Thomason 2.

  b. Compare with the *p* value reported in Figure 8.5. Compare also with the CI on the mean difference in that figure. Interpret.

esci 8.21 Set up **Summary paired** with the data for Thomason 2 and display the *d* panel, as in Figure 8.7. Change M_2 and watch the CI on the mean difference and the *p* value change.

  a. Adjust M_2 so $p = .05$. What's special about the CI on the difference in the figure? What's special about the values reported for that CI? Explain.

  b. Click for the CI for δ. What's special about that CI? Explain.

  c. What's the *p* value to test the null hypothesis that δ is zero? Explain.

8.22 Table 8.4 presents data from a fictitious and unrealistically small HEAT study comparing scores for a single group of students before and after a workshop on climate change.

  a. Calculate the *M*, *s*, and CI for the Before and After scores.

  b. Calculate the differences, M_{diff}, s_{diff}, and the CI on the difference. Interpret.

  c. Calculate the *p* value to assess the null hypothesis that scores were unchanged after the workshop. What can you conclude?

  d. Compare with the CI on the difference. Explain.

Before	After
74	88
52	59
65	75
38	40
61	63
69	66
76	84
62	77

Table 8.4 Data for a Paired-Design Study Comparing HEAT Scores Before and After a Workshop

 8.23 Type the data in Table 8.4 into **Data paired**. Click to display the data points and differences. Confirm all the values you calculated.

   a. Compare the CI on the difference with the two separate CIs. Explain.

   b. Find d, $d_{unbiased}$, and the CI for δ. Interpret.

   c. Test the null hypothesis that δ is zero.

? Quiz 8.3

1. For a pretest–posttest study, you need the _____ t test, not the _____ t test.
2. When analyzing a paired design using the NHST approach, the null hypothesis is usually that _____.
3. In a paired design, how are the degrees of freedom (df) calculated?
4. In a pretest–posttest study, if all participants show zero change from pretest to posttest, what is M_{diff}? What is t? What is the result of the t test?
5. Considering the paired design, the overlap rule to compare two CIs
   a. involves the CI on the difference, not just the other two CIs.
   b. is not applicable for this design.
   c. states that CIs overlapping moderately corresponds to $p = .01$, approximately.
   d. is the same as that for independent groups.
6. For the paired design, the p value to test $\delta = 0$ is the same as / different from the p value to test the null hypothesis in original units.
7. No more prompts, but remember that it's always best for you and your friends to make your own quizzes, and to test yourselves and each other.

INTERPRETING THE PAIRED DESIGN

What conclusions can we draw from a study with the paired design? As usual we'll need judgment, but in some cases we can draw a causal conclusion, which is gold. At the start of the chapter I mentioned the complication that, for example, using a pen one day can influence performance with a laptop on another day—practice at the task, perhaps, or boredom with being in the study. More generally, the two measures from the same participant are not independent, because the first testing may have effects that persist and influence the second. These are called *carryover effects*. First I'll discuss ways to minimize these, then strategies that can in some cases achieve experimental research, justifying a causal conclusion.

A *carryover effect* in a paired design is any influence of the first measurement on the second.

The commonest way to minimize carryover effects is to *counterbalance* the order of testing. A randomly chosen half of the students would use pen first, then laptop, and the other half laptop then pen. That should balance out any carryover effect of order of testing, at least to a large extent. In this example, further counterbalancing is needed because we don't, of course, want any student to take notes of the same lecture twice. We could use videos of two different lectures, L_1 and L_2, chosen to be of similar complexity and interest. Each student would see both lectures, in counterbalanced order. We would actually use four conditions that combine our two counterbalanced features. One-quarter of the students would be randomly assigned to each of these four:

Pen–L_1 then Laptop–L_2
Pen–L_2 then Laptop–L_1
Laptop–L_1 then Pen–L_2
Laptop–L_2 then Pen–L_1

Then we would analyze as a paired design, with each participant providing a Pen and a Laptop transcription score.

> **Counterbalancing** in a paired design is the assignment of different participants to different orders of presentation, or different versions of the same condition, to reduce carryover effects.

With a pretest–posttest design we can't counterbalance order. An alternative strategy to minimize the practice carryover effect is to use two *parallel forms* of the test, and that's exactly what the Thomason team did. For example, in the studies using LSAT they chose LSAT-A and LSAT-B as tests that used different examples and questions, but probed the same abilities and were of similar difficulty. Half the students completed A at Pretest, then B at Posttest; the other half completed B first, then A.

> **Parallel forms** of a test are versions that use different questions, but measure the same characteristic and are of similar difficulty.

▶ To reduce carryover effects, consider using *counterbalancing*, two *parallel forms* of tests, and/or a control group.

In addition, we could be concerned that gains from Pretest to Posttest might reflect anything else the students experienced during that period of time—perhaps other courses they were taking, or general life experience—rather than training in critical thinking. It would be valuable to have a second group of students, a control group, who spent about the same amount of time on a conventional critical thinking course. Ideally we would assign students randomly to the control or experimental groups, measure both at Pretest and Posttest, and compare gain scores (i.e., Posttest − Pretest scores) for the two groups. That's an example of a more complex design, as we discuss in Chapters 14 and 15.

Experimental Research, Causal Conclusions

▶ A paired design with random assignment to counterbalanced orders of testing can often in practice justify a causal conclusion. We have experimental research.

Now for the second stage in this discussion of interpretation. Again recall the definition from Chapter 2:

> **Experimental** research uses random assignment of participants to groups or conditions—to the different levels of the IV that is being manipulated. It can justify a causal conclusion.

For independent groups, as we discussed in Chapter 7, random assignment to groups should give groups that on average differ in only one way, which is the IV manipulation. It's experimental research and a causal conclusion can be justified. Random assignment is the key step. For a pen–laptop study with the paired design we don't have random assignment to pen and laptop, but we can, however, assign randomly to the pen–laptop and laptop–pen orders of testing. Often in practice this counterbalancing of order does at least very largely overcome carryover effects, giving sets of scores on the DV that, on average, differ in only one way. We have experimental research and can therefore conclude that, most likely, the pen–laptop manipulation caused whatever difference we observed in the DV.

The third strategy I mentioned for overcoming carryover effects was use of a more complex design that added a control group. Participants would be randomly assigned to the independent treatment and control groups, so again we would have experimental research and could draw a causal conclusion.

As I mentioned at the end of Chapter 7, our interpretation will also depend on our assessment of the reliability and validity of the dependent variable, and all the Open Science issues: Are the comparisons planned or exploratory, has there been any selection of participants or results, and so on. Does the question "Do we have the full story?" come up in your dreams yet?

TWO DESIGNS: COMPARING AND CHOOSING

First, I'll summarize key features of the two designs, then consider making a choice.

The Independent Groups Design

The independent groups design is simple and each participant is tested only once. In addition, assuming you test everyone separately, the observations are all independent—there's no possible contamination of one observation by another. As we discussed in Chapter 7, if we compare two pre-existing groups, such as groups of students who themselves prefer to use pen or laptop, we have non-experimental research. Random assignment, in this case to separate pen and laptop groups, gives us experimental research.

The main disadvantage of independent groups is that very often there's large variability from person to person, so the difference between the means is estimated with low precision. The two conditions are compared *between* participants and so the comparison is inevitably mixed, at least to some extent, with variability from person to person. Using large groups can help, but costs more in time and effort and is not always possible.

◄ Independent groups and random assignment may justify a causal conclusion, but the effect size may be estimated with low precision.

The Paired Design

The main advantage of the paired design is that it makes the comparison of interest *within* each participant. Often the two measures—Pen and Laptop, or Pretest and Posttest—are fairly highly correlated, in which case the mean difference can be estimated with reasonable or even high precision. A small group may give an adequately precise result.

The challenge with the paired design is to come as close as possible to the ideal of two conditions that differ on only the one factor you are interested in— the IV manipulation, such as pen and laptop. As we discussed above, this requires either counterbalancing or the addition of a control group. Counterbalancing, however, is not always possible, and adding a control group takes considerable effort and also makes the study more complicated.

◄ A paired design requires additional effort to be experimental, but often the two measures are highly correlated and so the effect size may be estimated with relatively high precision.

Table 8.5
A Comparison of
Two Designs

	Independent groups design	Paired design
Variation of the IV	Between groups	Within group
Experimental research?	Easy: Use random assignment to groups	Less easy: Use random assignment to counterbalanced orders, or add a control group
Every participant is tested...	Once, which keeps things simple	Twice, which makes things a little more complicated
Group size(s)	May need to be large	Small or medium may suffice
Precision of estimation of effect size	Often low, because comparison is between participants	Can be high, because comparison is within participants
Carryover effects	Don't arise	A major concern: Try hard to minimize.

Choosing a Design

If you have the choice, a paired design may be a good choice, but only if carryover effects are not likely to be a big problem.

Designing a study can be challenging but also great fun. You can brainstorm all sorts of possibilities as you try to find the best design, the best measure, and the best way to target your research question as closely as possible. In Chapter 10 we'll take this discussion of planning further. Here I'll focus on the choice between our two designs.

Sometimes you have no choice. If you want to compare left handers and right handers, you need independent groups. If you are investigating the change from before to after some treatment, you need a paired design. Often, however, you could choose either design, as with pen vs. laptop.

Table 8.5 summarizes some important aspects of the two designs that need consideration when making a choice. If testing large samples is practical, then independent groups is appealing. If participants are scarce or if it's difficult or expensive to provide the treatment and carry out the testing, the paired design with a smaller group is likely to be best—if carryover effects can be minimized. I'll often prefer a paired design if it's practical, with careful attention to reducing carryover effects as much as possible. But, of course, you need to weigh up the pros and cons of the two designs for your questions in your particular research context.

It's time for take-home messages. Reflect, discuss, then write yours. Our main topic has been the paired design, and we've made many comparisons with independent groups. Again we've seen the importance of the CI on the difference. Recall the unfortunate ambiguity of the figure on the left in Figure 8.3. Think of the variability components for inference, and the standardizers for *d* shown in Table 8.3. When is the paired design experimental research? We closed with the fun of planning a study, often with at least two possible designs to consider.

 Quiz 8.4

1. A CI on *d* is an interval estimate of the _____ _____ in the _____, for which the symbol is ____.
2. What variability component do you use for the *t* test
   a. for the paired design?
   b. for independent groups?

3. How much does a GRE prep course improve GRE scores? To investigate, 20 students took the GRE before and after completing a prep course. The average (Posttest − Pretest) difference was 10 points. The average standard deviation (s_{av}) was 50. What is Cohen's d? Can you conclude that the prep course caused the difference? Explain.
4. What is a carryover effect?
5. To minimize carryover effects, the order of administering different levels of the IV can be varied across participants. This is known as _____.
6. Parallel forms of a test are
    a. used with independent groups to increase the precision of estimation.
    b. different versions of the test tailored for different levels of the IV.
    c. averaged to give a better estimate of an individual participant's performance.
    d. used with the paired design to reduce carryover effects.

8.24 In Exercise 8.22 you analyzed HEAT scores for a single group of students before and after a workshop on climate change.

   a. Might using the HEAT for both pretest and posttest raise a problem? What would you recommend? Explain.
   b. Can you conclude that the workshop caused any change you observe? Explain.

8.25 You wish to investigate the possible influence of caffeine on short-term memory. The two levels of your independent variable are a drink of strong regular coffee, and the same volume of decaffeinated coffee.

   a. Describe how you could conduct the study using each of the two designs.
   b. Which would you prefer and why? What precautions would you take?
   c. For the independent groups study, could you conclude that caffeine caused any difference you observe in short-term memory? Explain.
   d. For the paired study, answer the same question and explain.

8.26 Revisit your take-home messages. Revise and extend the list if you wish.

⤳ Reporting Your Work

Reporting comparisons for the paired design is pretty similar to comparing independent groups, but with a few vital additional things to remember. Typically, you need to report:

- Whether the comparison is planned or exploratory, unless this is already clear.
- Basic descriptive statistics for both sets of measurements.
- The average difference, M_{diff}, its standard deviation, and its CI.
- A standardized effect size estimate ($d_{unbiased}$ is best) with its CI. In the Method section make clear how your standardized effect size was calculated (which denominator was used).
- Essential for future meta-analysis: the standard deviation of the differences (third bullet point above) or the correlation between the two measures (discussed further in Chapter 11). Reporting both can be very helpful.
- A figure, if possible, preferably one like ESCI produces that shows the raw data, the paired nature of the data, and the estimated difference with its CI. State in the figure caption what error bars represent—95% CIs. Join the means with a line to indicate a repeated measure, as in Figures 8.1 and 8.2, and **Data paired** and **Summary paired** in ESCI.
- An interpretation of the group difference that considers not only the point estimate but also the CI. As usual, be careful to match the language you use to the research design (causal for experimental, relational for non-experimental).

◀ For the paired design, focus on the mean difference, M_{diff}; report the SD of the differences and the correlation between the two measures.

Here are examples.

The first planned analysis found that, when drinking the juice with a label stating "Generic", participants rated their enjoyment fairly high (*M* = 6.86, *s* = 2.13, scale from 1 to 10). The same participants given the same drink with the label "Organic", however, rated their enjoyment even higher (*M* = 7.82, *s* = 2.09). This difference in enjoyment was substantial, relative to the scale and previous marketing research (M_{diff} = 0.96, 95% CI [0.48, 1.44], *N* = 51, *r* = .68). In standardized terms, this is a large effect ($d_{unbiased}$ = 0.45, 95% CI [0.22, 0.69]), and the CI is consistent with at least small up to a quite large impact on enjoyment.

As expected, heart rate at rest was fairly low (*M* = 66.80 bpm, *s* = 10.8). During exploration, though, we noticed that when participants were asked to recall a memory of intense happiness their heart rate was somewhat higher (*M* = 69.50 bpm, *s* = 10.92). Thus, emotion was related to an increase in heart rate (M_{diff} = 2.70 bpm, 95% CI [0.14, 5.22], $d_{unbiased}$ = 0.24, 95% CI [0.01, 0.48], *N* = 20, *r* = .87). The CI indicates that happiness is likely related to an increase in heart rate, but the CI is quite long and the degree of increase could be anywhere from around zero up to fairly large. In addition, the analysis was exploratory. An independent replication is needed to estimate more precisely the degree to which happiness may be associated with an increased heart rate.

In a preregistered replication with a larger sample size (*N* = 48) we observed the same increase in heart rate during recall of a happy memory. Heart rate at rest was again fairly low (*M* = 63.7 bpm, *s* = 10.1). During the recall of a happy memory, heart rate was higher (*M* = 68.8 bpm, *s* = 12.8). This emotion-induced increase in heart rate was slightly larger than in the first study (M_{diff} = 5.1 bpm, 95% CI [3.0, 7.2], $d_{unbiased}$ = 0.44, 95% CI [0.24, 0.64], *r* = .82). With the larger sample size the CI is much shorter, and indicates that happiness is related to a moderate increase in heart rate.

 ## Take-Home Messages

■ The paired design uses a single group of *N* participants, each of whom is tested on both conditions being compared. Data analysis focuses on the set of *N* differences. The effect size is M_{diff}, the mean difference, which is the same as $(M_2 - M_1)$.

■ Use Equation 8.2 to calculate the CI on the mean difference, which is based on s_{diff}, the SD of the differences, and can usefully be displayed on a difference axis as in Figure 8.2. Often the two measures, such as Pretest and Posttest, are highly correlated, in which case the CI is short and gives a relatively precise estimate of the difference.

■ Cohen's *d* is an ES in original units divided by the standardizer. For the paired design, the usual standardizer is s_{av}, which is based on the SDs of the two measures, for example pretest and posttest. Always state what standardizer was used.

■ Use judgment to interpret values of *d* or $d_{unbiased}$, with the CI, in context. Where it helps, consider ESs in original units, the standardizer and reference population, previous related research, and the extent of overlap of distributions.

Polya

- If appropriate in context, consider reference values for small, medium, and large effects, for example 0.2, 0.4, 0.6 as suggested by Hattie for education, or 0.2, 0.5, 0.8 as suggested by Cohen for psychology.

- For the paired design, knowing the two means and their CIs is insufficient to eyeball the CI on the difference or the *p* value. No overlap rule is possible.

- Use Equation 8.5 to calculate *t* for the *paired t test*, which tests the null hypothesis of zero difference between the conditions.

- If either design is possible, weigh up the pros and cons in context. The paired design can often estimate effects with relatively high precision. To minimize carryover effects, consider counterbalancing, using parallel forms of measures, and, perhaps, adding a control group.

- Random assignment to counterbalanced orders of testing can give experimental research, which may justify a causal conclusion.

 ## End-of-Chapter Exercises

1) When studying new information, students often just re-read their notes or textbook. A possibly better strategy is re-reading plus practice retrieving the material. Do you recall the *Making the Most of This Book* section at the start of this book? To what extent do these two study strategies differ in promoting learning? To investigate, Kang and Pashler (2014, Experiment 1) asked 38 psychology students to study Swahili words. Each student first read the words and then studied each word four times. The style of studying varied. Each student studied half the words using only re-reading and the other half using re-reading + retrieval practice. The amount of time studying was the same for the two strategies. Students were promised $0.05/word learned as motivation to do well. Two days after studying, the students were tested for memory of all words. Table 8.6 shows summary statistics.

Table 8.6 Summary Statistics for Students' Memory for Swahili Words, With Low Reward, *N* = 38

	Re-read (%)	Re-read + Retrieval (%)	Difference
M	35	50	15
s	29	30	
s_{diff}			27.2

a. What is *df*?

b. Look up the critical value of *t*.

c. Almost there—calculate the sample size component.

d. Now calculate MoE_{diff}.

e. Calculate the 95% CI for the mean difference between the conditions.

f. Just as important as calculating the CI is interpreting it. Given that the mean difference is 15 percentage points, what does the CI tell you?

g. Type the values into **Summary paired** and check your calculations.

2) Continuing from the previous example, Kang and Pashler (2014, Experiment 1) wanted to know the extent that motivation might play a role in determining study strategy success. Within the same experiment they asked the same 38 students to learn a second set of words,

with a higher reward: $0.30/word learned. With this much higher motivation, is retrieval practice still the better study strategy? Table 8.7 shows summary statistics.

Table 8.7 Summary Statistics for Students' Memory for Swahili Words, With High Reward, $N = 38$

	Re-read (%)	Re-read + Retrieval (%)	Difference
M	36	49	13
s	32	33	
s_{diff}			24

a. Follow the same steps as in Question 1 to calculate the 95% CI on the difference.

b. Based on these results, Kang and Pashler claimed that retrieval practice is the superior study strategy regardless of motivation. Comparing the CIs you obtained, do you agree with this conclusion? Does the fact that students paid more didn't actually learn more contribute to your interpretation? Explain.

3) Anger is a powerful emotion. To what extent can feeling angry actually change your heart rate? To investigate, Lakens (2013) asked students to record their heart rate (in beats per minute) at rest before (baseline) and then while recalling a time of intense anger. This is a conceptual replication of a classic study by Ekman, Levenson, and Friesen (1983). Load the **Emotion_Heartrate** data set from the book website.

a. Use ESCI to compare heart rate during rest and anger. Write an APA-style description of this finding, incorporating the descriptive statistics (M and s for each condition), the difference and its CI, and a standardized effect size estimate (Cohen's d). Include your interpretation.

b. What if this study had been conducted as a between-participants study and had obtained the same data? Would the CI on the difference be shorter or longer? Write down your prediction and explain.

c. Test your intuitions: Use ESCI to analyze these data as an independent groups study, using the baseline data as Group 1, and anger data as Group 2. Was your prediction about the CI correct? Explain.

d. Can we conclude that feeling angry causes higher heart rate? Answer for each of the two designs considered above. In each case, explain.

4) To what extent do brand labels influence perceptions of a product? To investigate, participants were asked to participate in a taste test. All participants were actually given the *same* grape juice, but one glass was poured from a bottle labeled "Organic" and the other glass from a bottle labeled "Generic". After each tasting (in counterbalanced order), participants were asked to rate how much they enjoyed the juice on a scale from 1 (*not at all*) to 10 (*very much*). Participants were also asked to say how much they'd be willing to pay for a large container of that juice on a scale from $1 to $10. Load the **Labels_Flavor** data set from the book website. These data were collected as part of a class project by Floretta-Schiller, Berent, and Salinas (2015), whose work was inspired by a very clever study looking at the effects of fast food wrappers on children's enjoyment of food (Robinson, Borzekowski, Matheson, & Kraemer, 2007).

a. Use ESCI to compare enjoyment ratings for juice labeled organic or generic. To what extent does label influence enjoyment?

b. During debriefing, participants were probed to see if they might have suspected that the juice samples were actually the same. Five participants correctly guessed that this was the case. Would you expect the effect of label on enjoyment to be stronger or weaker with these participants excluded from the analysis? Make a prediction, then check using ESCI.

c. Should the researchers report their results with the suspicious participants included or excluded? What considerations are important in making this decision? Does it matter *when* the researchers make this decision—before seeing the data or after?

? Answers to Quizzes

Quiz 8.1

1) b; 2) within, within-group, between, between-groups; 3) M_{diff} calculated as the mean of all the N differences, or as $(M_2 - M_1)$, which gives the same value; 4) s_{diff}, the difference scores; 5) more, shorter, smaller, shorter, larger; 6) a little longer than either of the separate CIs for A and B, in most cases shorter than either of those CIs.

Quiz 8.2

1) d; 2) M_{diff}; 3) s_{av}; 4) They may have used s_{diff} rather than s_{av} as standardizer; 5) the same, different; 6) a.

Quiz 8.3

1) paired, independent groups; 2) that the population mean difference is zero; 3) $df = (N - 1)$; 4) 0, 0, do not reject the null hypothesis; 5) b; 6) the same as.

Quiz 8.4

1) Effect size, population, δ; 2) s_{diff}, s_p; 3) $d = ES/SD = 10/50 = 0.20$; no, because random assignment was not possible and carryover effects may have contributed to the difference; 4) A carryover effect is any influence of the first measurement in a paired design on the second, for example practice at taking the test; 5) counterbalancing; 6) d.

Answers to In-Chapter Exercises

8.1 Smaller, so the CI on the difference is shorter and thus the precision of estimation of the population difference is greater. Differences that are even more consistent correspond to an even higher correlation.

8.2 It doesn't matter if independent groups have different sizes, as in the PenLaptop studies, although it is usually most efficient if the two groups are of similar size. In the paired design, there is only one group and every participant is measured twice, so the number of data points is the same for the two measures, such as Pretest and Posttest.

8.3 $N = 16$, $M_{diff} = 1.37$, $MoE_{diff} = 1.14$, [0.24, 2.50].

8.4 Clicking a checkbox highlights a data pair and the corresponding difference, as for the one negative difference shown in red in Figure 8.2.

8.5 For independent groups, as in Figure 7.3, the ordering of data values for either group makes no difference, so any value can be shifted. In contrast, for the paired design as in Figure 8.4, the data values are paired, so you can't shift just values in the Pretest column. Pairs of data values could be shifted up or down, but the two values in a pair must be kept together.

8.6 Change some Posttest values to make those differences closer in size to the mean difference. That moves some open triangles in Figure 8.4 closer to the solid triangle, so s_{diff} gets smaller, the lines joining the data pairs look more similar, and MoE_{diff} and the CI on the difference become shorter. In addition, Pretest and Posttest values correspond more closely (high with high, low with low), so correlation r is greater.

8.7 As s_{diff} gets larger, the changes are in the opposite direction: The CI on the difference gets longer and so precision is lower, and r is also lower, although still positive. The general conclusion is that the paired design will be especially advantageous, by giving a high precision estimate of the mean difference, when the differences are all similar in direction and size, meaning that s_{diff} is small, r is large, and the effect of the treatment is fairly consistent over participants.

8.9 For Thomason 1, about half as long as the CIs on Pretest and Posttest means, and for Thomason 2 a little more than half as long. The paired design is effective in both cases, and a little more so in the first.

8.10 a. 0.35, a small-to-medium effect and a little less than 0.54 for Thomason 1; b. We did not need to use s_{diff}, the SD of the differences.

8.11 a. To calculate d we don't need s_{diff}; b. ES = 71.77 − 67.41 = 4.36, Equation 8.3 gives s_{av} = 6.68, d = 0.65; c. This is a medium-to-large effect, somewhat larger than found by Thomason 1 and 2.

8.12 $d = M_{diff}/s_{av} = 1.67/3.11 = 0.54$

8.13 $d = M_{diff}/s_{av} = 1.37/3.87 = 0.35$

8.14 b. d = 0.652 and $d_{unbiased}$ = 0.639; the ratio is 0.652/0.639 = 1.02, so d overestimates δ by 2%, when, as here, df = 38. Less bias here than for Thomason 1 and 2, which have smaller df; c. CI is [0.33, 0.97], so δ is most likely around 0.6 but could plausibly be anywhere from around 0.3 to 1. The values for Thomason 1 and 2 are a little smaller, but all CIs are long, so we don't have clear evidence of differences between the studies.

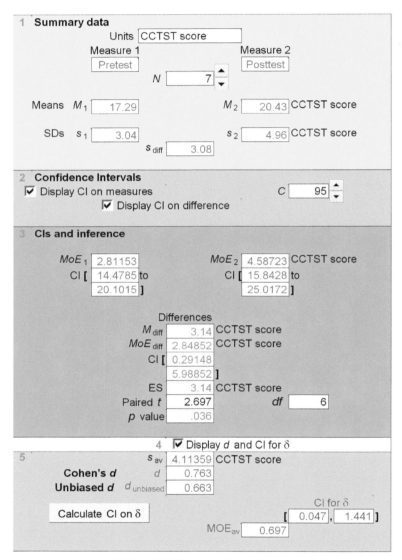

Figure 8.9. Summary CCTST data for Thomason 4. From **Summary paired**.

8.15 a. Yes, no, because the CI requires s_{diff}, the SD of the paired differences; b. Yes, no, for the same reason.

8.16 Same answers as Exercise 8.15, for the same reason.

8.17 a. Figure 8.9 shows the screen after s_{diff} entered: [0.29, 5.99], p = .04. b. CI for δ is [0.05, 1.44]; c. d = 0.763 and $d_{unbiased}$ = 0.663 suggest a medium-to-large effect, but with a very long CI, because N is only 7. The effect size is broadly comparable with those found by the other three studies.

8.18 a. Using the separate SDs gives, for W, $d = 12/24 = 0.50$ and, for N, $d = 9/12 = 0.75$, both of which are fairly large in terms of Hattie's suggestions. We don't have the CIs, which are likely to be moderately long. The difference between the two d values arises more from the different SDs than different original units ESs. For a direct comparison of classes W and N, it may be better to compare the mean increases in original units, or find some SD that's applicable to both.

8.19 For W, $d = 12/15 = 0.80$ and, for N, $d = 9/15 = 0.60$, both of which are large by Hattie's reference values, although we have no CIs. a. Using the state-wide SD probably permits the most useful comparison of the two classes, as well as comparisons with other classes in the state.

8.20 a. $t(15) = 2.57$, $p = .02$, which is consistent with the CI on the difference falling a little distance above 0; b. There is a statistically significant difference, and some evidence against the null hypothesis.

8.21 a. For $p = .05$, set $M_2 = 14.015$. The CI on the difference just touches zero on the difference axis. The CI is shown near red 3 as [0, 2.27], so 0 is the lower limit (this might be displayed as something like 3.1E-06, which is 3.1×10^{-6}, a value very close to zero, expressed in exponential notation); b. The CI for δ is [0, 0.58], also with 0 as lower limit; c. The p value is the same for original units and δ, so is .05.

8.22 a. Before: $M_1 = 62.12$, $s_1 = 12.39$, and CI [51.8, 72.5]; After: $M_2 = 69.00$, $s_2 = 15.46$, and CI [56.1, 81.9]; b. $M_{diff} = 6.88$, $s_{diff} = 6.24$, and the CI on the difference is [1.7, 12.1]; The experiment estimated the mean population improvement to be about 7 points, with the 95% CI extending from about 2 to about 12 points. The workshop did seem to lead to increased HEAT scores, although the precision of the estimate was not high. However, practice on completing the HEAT might have contributed to the higher scores on the second testing; c. $t(7) = 3.11$ and $p = .02$, so we can reject the null hypothesis of no change and conclude there was a statistically significant increase in HEAT scores from Before to After; d. The CI on the difference was a little distance from 0, corresponding to $p = .02$, indicating 0 is a relatively implausible true value.

8.23 a. The CI on the difference is around half the length of each of the separate CIs, so the paired design is sensitive and gives a relatively precise estimate of the difference; b. $d = 0.491$, $d_{unbiased} = 0.436$, and the CI for δ is [0.08, 0.88], suggesting a medium effect estimated with low precision; c. The null hypothesis that δ is zero is rejected, as $p = .02$. Before and After scores look to have a strong correlation (high with high, low with low) and indeed $r = .92$.

8.24 a. Scores on the second completion of the same test could be higher because of familiarity with the test. Using parallel forms of the HEAT could reduce such a carryover effect; b. No, because random assignment is not possible, and things other than the workshop may have influenced the increase in scores from first to second testing, for example any other experience the participants had between those times.

8.25 a, b. Using independent groups, randomly assign participants to Regular and Decaf, and make these two groups equal or about equal in size. Aim for groups as large as practical, expecting that precision of estimation of the difference would not be high. The paired design is attractive, and our preference, because it's likely to estimate the difference more precisely. Counterbalance order: A random half of the participants would receive Regular, then Decaf, and the other half the reverse order. Leave an interval of at least one day between the tests, so caffeine levels can return to normal after the Regular drink. For either design, make the testing as similar as possible on the two occasions—same time of day, and checking that participants had consumed no caffeine for, say, 12 hours before testing; c. For independent groups, if we assign participants randomly to Regular and Decaf, we have reasonable grounds for concluding that our IV manipulation (Regular vs. Decaf) caused any difference we observe in the DV—after considering sampling variability as indicated by MoE; d. For the paired study, we need to consider the extent that random assignment to the two counterbalanced orders of presentation overcomes any carryover effects. If we judge that it does so, at least largely, then we have reasonable grounds for concluding that the Regular vs. Decaf manipulation caused any observed difference.

Meta-Analysis

This is the good news chapter. In previous chapters I've said that, unfortunately, sampling variability is often large and CIs long. Jacob Cohen, the great statistical reformer, said "I suspect that the main reason they [CIs] are not reported is that they are so embarrassingly large!" (Cohen, 1994, p. 1002.)

The good news is *meta-analysis*, which can produce strong evidence where at first sight there's only weak evidence. It can turn long CIs into short ones (well, sort of), find answers in what looks like a mess, and settle heated controversies. Much of what it does can be displayed in a beautiful picture, the *forest plot*, which I'll use to explain meta-analysis and why I think it's so great. Here's our agenda:

- The forest plot, the attractive face of meta-analysis
- The simplest approach, which assumes all studies investigated the same population: *fixed effect* meta-analysis
- A more realistic approach, which assumes different studies may have investigated different populations: *random effects* meta-analysis
- *Moderator* analysis, which can give insight beyond an overall effect size
- Cohen's *d* for meta-analysis, when studies have used different original-units measures
- The seven steps in a large meta-analysis
- Meta-analyses that have changed the world

In a single phrase, think of meta-analysis as estimation extended across more than one experiment. Here's a slightly more formal definition:

> **Meta-analysis** is the quantitative integration of results from more than one study on the same or similar questions.

I'll start with a brief story. The Women, Infants, and Children welfare program in the United States provided a range of support to low-income pregnant women and mothers with young children. There were strident lobby groups who supported the program, and others who believed it should be abolished. Studies of its effectiveness gave conflicting results. By 1983 it had been running for around a decade, with an ever-growing budget. In advance of Senate hearings on its fate, a meta-analysis was commissioned to integrate results from the evaluation studies. This found a positive and usefully large overall result, and gave insight into why the program was effective. It was probably crucial to the decision to continue the program. This is an example of how decision making can be evidence-based, even in a complex and ideologically charged area of social policy.

That story comes from Morton Hunt's book *How Science Takes Stock: The Story of Meta-analysis* (1997). I highly recommend this book, which reads more like a novel than a textbook. There are simple descriptions of meta-analysis, tales of the pioneers, and numerous examples of meta-analysis finding important conclusions, despite messy and conflicting results. Two key messages are that meta-analysis needs effect size information from every study, and that NHST is irrelevant. Hunt reports that one pioneer, Gene Glass, was critical of NHST because it doesn't provide the ES information he needed. Glass stated: "Statistical significance is the least interesting thing about the results. You should describe the results in terms of measures of magnitude—not just, does a treatment affect people, but how *much* does it affect them? *That's* what we needed to know." (Hunt, pp. 29–30, emphasis in the original).

THE FOREST PLOT

In Chapter 1, I mentioned that, if we had two additional polls similar to the one we discussed, meta-analysis could combine the results of all three. Figure 9.1, same as Figure 1.4, shows the three results and uses a diamond to picture the point estimate (the center of the diamond) and 95% CI (the horizontal extent of the diamond) that are the result of the meta-analysis. The overall point estimate is a weighted average of the point estimates of the three polls. If the individual results are reasonably consistent, the overall CI will be shorter than the individual CIs, and that's the case here. So the meta-analysis provides a more precise estimate than any of the individual studies, which is good news.

Is it reasonable to combine the three? We need to judge the three to be sufficiently similar, meaning that, first, the question being asked must be the same or similar. Second, the procedures, including choice of participants, need to be reasonably similar. The studies may be close replications, but often there will be some differences, perhaps including deliberately chosen variations. We'll see later that meta-analysis can actually give additional insight when there are some limited differences among studies, so we can consider using meta-analysis even when studies are not close replications.

A *forest plot* is a CI picture that displays results from a number of studies, and a diamond that represents the result of a meta-analysis of those studies.

Meta-analysis requires that, across included studies, the questions asked and the procedures are the same or reasonably similar.

DOES A BRAIN PICTURE INCREASE CREDIBILITY?

Now for a real example. You've probably seen cross sections of the brain with brightly colored areas indicating which brain regions are most active during a particular type of cognition or emotion. Search online for fMRI (Functional Magnetic Resonance Imaging) to see such pictures and learn how they are made. They can be fascinating—are we at last able to see how thinking works? In 2008, McCabe and Castel published studies that investigated how adding a brain picture might alter judgments of the credibility of a scientific article. For one group of participants, an article was accompanied by a brain image that

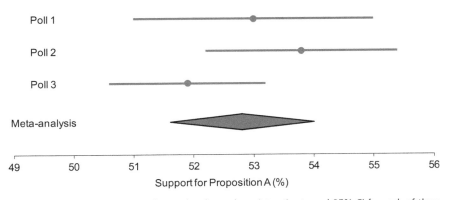

Figure 9.1. Same as Figure 1.4. A forest plot shows the point estimate and 95% CI for each of three polls, together with a diamond to represent the 95% CI that's the result of meta-analysis of the three.

was irrelevant to the article. For a second, independent group, there was no image. Participants read the article, then gave a rating of the statement "The scientific reasoning in the article made sense". The response options were 1 (strongly disagree), 2 (disagree), 3 (agree), and 4 (strongly agree). The researchers reported that mean ratings were higher with a brain picture than without, but that the difference was small. It seemed that an irrelevant brain picture may have some, but only a small influence. The authors drew appropriately cautious conclusions, but the result quickly attracted attention and there were many media reports that greatly overstated it. At least according to the popular media, it seemed that adding a brain picture made any story convincing. Search on "McCabe seeing is believing", or similar, to find media reports and blog posts. Some warned readers to watch out for brain pictures, which, they said, can trick you into believing things that aren't true.

The result intrigued some New Zealander colleagues of mine who discovered that, despite its wide recognition, the finding hadn't been replicated. They ran replication studies using the materials used by the original researchers, and found generally small ESs. I joined the team at the data analysis stage and the research was published (Michael et al., 2013). I'll discuss here a meta-analysis of two of the original studies and eight replications by our team. The studies were sufficiently similar for meta-analysis, especially considering that all the Michael studies were designed to have many features that matched the original studies.

Figure 9.2 shows meta-analysis of the two original studies, and our eight replications. The figure is complicated, so let's take it step-by-step. You may care to fire up ESCI to follow along. If so, open **ESCI intro Meta-Analysis** and go to the **Original two groups** page. You should see Figure 9.2.

At left in the figure—or on your screen—are the 10 study names. McCabe 1 and 2 refer to original results from McCabe and Castel (2008). Michael 1 to 8 refer to our replications. Then follow six columns of data: the mean rating, SD, and N for the No Brain group, which did not see a brain picture, then the same for the Brain group. To the right of the data at red 8 is a column showing the $(M_2 - M_1)$ difference between the two group means, which is our ES of interest. Next right is a column of MoE values for the individual study CIs.

The result of a meta-analysis is shown as a diamond, which is a stylized cat's-eye picture. The horizontal extent of the diamond is the 95% CI.

Further to the right is the forest plot of those individual study ESs, each with its 95% CI. At the bottom, the red diamond pictures the result of the meta-analysis. The bottom row of numbers, to the right of red 11, is the result of the meta-analysis, starting with the overall mean, which is 0.068. The CIs are shown at red 13, which is to the right of the forest plot and beyond what Figure 9.2 shows. For the result the CI is [0.012, 0.125]. The middle of the diamond marks 0.068, the point estimate, and the horizontal extent is the 95% CI, which is [0.012, 0.125]. Does that look about right for the diamond in the figure? I like this custom of using a diamond, because it identifies the result of a meta-analysis as special. In addition we can see the diamond shape as a stylized cat's eye.

9.1 If you haven't already done so, open the **Original two groups** page of **ESCI intro Meta-Analysis**. Look carefully around the screen, using the popouts to help discover what's going on. At red 1 you can type in the units or a label for the dependent variable ("Rating difference", or your choice), and names for the two groups. To complete Figure 9.2, I clicked at red 5 to see the vertical line at zero in the forest plot.

I mentioned that the result of a meta-analysis is the weighted average of all the study ESs. How should studies be weighted? If studies vary in size, should a

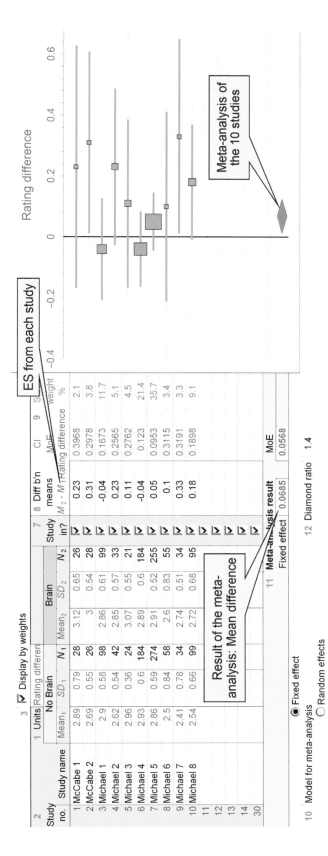

ES from each study

Result of the meta-analysis: Mean difference

Meta-analysis of the 10 studies

3 ☑ Display by weights

2 Study no.	Study name	1 Units Rating differen[ce] No Brain Mean$_1$	SD$_1$	N$_1$	Brain Mean$_2$	SD$_2$	N$_2$	7 Study in?	8 Diff b'n means $M_2 - M_1$ Rating difference	9 CI MoE	S... Weight %
1	McCabe 1	2.89	0.79	28	3.12	0.65	26	✓	0.23	0.3968	2.1
2	McCabe 2	2.69	0.55	26	3	0.54	28	✓	0.31	0.2978	3.8
3	Michael 1	2.9	0.58	98	2.86	0.61	99	✓	-0.04	0.1673	11.7
4	Michael 2	2.62	0.54	42	2.85	0.57	33	✓	0.23	0.2565	5.1
5	Michael 3	2.96	0.36	24	3.07	0.55	21	✓	0.11	0.2762	4.5
6	Michael 4	2.93	0.6	184	2.89	0.6	184	✓	-0.04	0.123	21.4
7	Michael 5	2.86	0.59	274	2.91	0.52	255	✓	0.05	0.0953	35.7
8	Michael 6	2.5	0.84	58	2.6	0.83	55	✓	0.1	0.3115	3.4
9	Michael 7	2.41	0.78	34	2.74	0.51	34	✓	0.33	0.3191	3.3
10	Michael 8	2.54	0.66	99	2.72	0.68	95	✓	0.18	0.1898	9.1
11											
12											
13											
14											
30											

11 Meta-analysis result   Fixed effect 0.0685   MoE 0.0568

10 Model for meta-analysis
● Fixed effect
○ Random effects

12 Diamond ratio   1.4

Figure 9.2. At left the summary data for 10 studies on the effect of including a brain picture on the rated credibility of an article. At right is the forest plot displaying means and 95% CIs for those studies and, at the bottom, their meta-analysis. From the **Original two groups page of ESCI intro Meta-Analysis.**

Meta-Analysis

study with larger *N* get more or less weight in the meta-analysis? If the SD varies over studies, should a study with a large SD, meaning greater variability, get more or less weight? Should a study with a longer CI get more or less weight?

 Just once for the chapter, a reminder that it's worth pausing, reflecting, discussing...

The general answer is that weights should reflect the precision of a study: Greater precision earns greater weight, so a short CI, which indicates greater precision, deserves greater weight. CI length reflects both *N* and SD, with larger *N* and smaller SD giving a shorter CI, and thus earning greater weight.

I'm not going to explain how to calculate weights—we'll leave that task to ESCI. Figure 9.2 reports values: Just to the left of the forest plot, below red 9, is a column of red study weights, which are percentages that add to 100. The largest weight is 35.7% for Michael 5, which used particularly large groups, of size 274 and 255. To see the influence of SD, compare Michael 6 and 7: Michael 7 gets almost the same weight (3.3%) despite smaller groups (each 34), because it has smaller SDs than Michael 6. The easiest way to think of weight is in terms of CI length: a shorter CI gives us better information and that deserves greater weight.

▶ ─────────
A study with a shorter CI earns greater weight— study weight is indicated by the size of the square marking the study ES.

One problem with CIs is that a longer CI tends to attract the eye, whereas we should take most notice of short CIs. Figure 9.2 follows an excellent meta-analysis convention: The forest plot uses squares of various sizes to mark the study ESs, with large squares indicating short CIs and greater weights. Large squares tend to attract the eye, which is what we want, because they are the more heavily weighted studies.

 9.2 Click a few times at red 3, to see how the forest plot changes as study ESs are displayed by weights, or not. Does anything other than the size of the squares change? If so, why?

 9.3 Click at red 3 to display by weights. Focus on a single study and predict how its weight and the forest plot would change if you changed the mean, SD, or *N* for one of the groups in that study.

▪ One at a time, test your predictions: Type in a quite different new value and watch the forest plot change, especially the weight for that study and the size of square.

▪ Type in the original value again, or use **Undo**, then test the next prediction.

The result of the meta-analysis is a rating difference of 0.068 [0.012, .125], meaning Brain was rated slightly higher on average. Let's consider that difference of 0.068. Most of the study means listed in Figure 9.2 are in the range of about 2.5 to 3. Recall that 2 indicates "disagree" and 3 indicates "agree" that the scientific reasoning in the article makes sense. The overall mean for Brain is about 2.88 (That's not in the figure—I calculated it.) and for No brain about 2.81, both of which correspond roughly to weak agreement. The meta-analysis result of 0.068 is our estimate of the effect of adding a brain picture, which on the response scale we're using is tiny. Even the upper limit of the CI was only about 0.1, a very small effect. Our conclusion is that the 10 studies together indicated, first, that brain pictures do seem to influence judgments of credibility and, second, that the influence is very small. The second conclusion—that the effect is very small—is the main finding, and what meta-analysis emphasizes. The very small size is also what any media report should highlight.

TWO MODELS FOR META-ANALYSIS: FIXED EFFECT AND RANDOM EFFECTS

Bottom left in Figure 9.2, and near red 10 on your screen, is a choice of **Model for meta-analysis**. The two possible models, or ways to calculate meta-analysis, are **Fixed effect** and **Random effects**, and the radio button for **Fixed effect** is selected. The *fixed effect model* is the simplest, and assumes that all the studies investigated the same population and, therefore, all the studies estimate the same population ES. In effect, it combines the results from all the studies as if they were one single large study. That's what Figure 9.2 reports and what I've discussed above. However, is it realistic to assume every study investigated exactly the same population? Studies inevitably differ to some extent, typically being carried out by different researchers at different times. There may also be differences in procedure, participants, and any number of other aspects. In practice, the assumption of identical populations, with every study estimating the same population ES, is rarely, if ever, justified.

Fixed effect meta-analysis assumes that all the studies investigated the same population, and all estimate the same population ES.

We can avoid the assumption by using the *random effects model*, which allows for the possibility that studies may have differed and may therefore be estimating somewhat different population ESs. Perhaps some studies had mainly humanities students and others science students, and humanities students are more easily impressed by brain pictures? Or perhaps some studies used more vivid and persuasive brain pictures?

Random effects meta-analysis allows for the possibility that the studies investigated somewhat different populations, and therefore estimate somewhat different population ESs.

To see the result of a random effects meta-analysis, click at red 10, which is at the bottom left in Figure 9.2. You should see Figure 9.3, which is the same as Figure 9.2 except that it shows a random effects rather than fixed effect meta-analysis.

 9.4 Click back and forth between the two models at red 10 and note which features change: The result of the meta-analysis? The diamond? The means and CIs of the individual studies? The weights?

As you switch between the two different ways to calculate a meta-analysis, there is no change to any of the study means or CIs. Probably the most noticeable change is in the study weights. Many of the squares marking study ESs change size, and the values in the **Study weight** column below red 9 all change. For fixed effect, the weights range from 2.1% to 35.7%, but for random effects, the weights vary much less, ranging from 3.7% to 22.0%. Random effects meta-analysis usually weights studies more evenly than fixed effect meta-analysis. It does this as part of the model's recognition that every study has a role to play, because every study may be estimating a different population ES.

Random effects meta-analysis usually weights studies more evenly than fixed effect meta-analysis.

The meta-analysis mean changes, from 0.068 to 0.094. The meta-analysis MoE changes from 0.057 to 0.079. The result is now 0.09 [0.02, 0.17]. As we switch from fixed effect to random effects the diamond shifts a little and gets distinctly longer. The diamond is longer because random effects meta-analysis is recognizing considerable variability in the study ESs, sufficient to suggest that they are indeed estimating different population ESs. The more the diamond lengthens as we switch to random effects, the greater the likely variation in the population ESs the studies are estimating—the greater the difference between humanities and science students, or between the effects of different types of brain pictures.

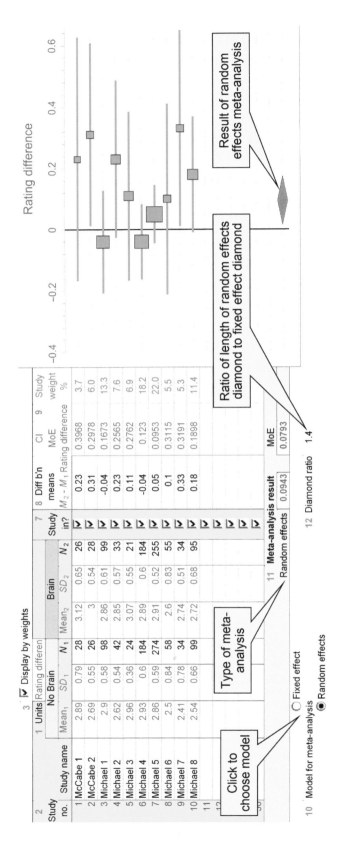

3 ☑ Display by weights

Rating difference

		1 Units	Rating differen			Brain			7	8 Diff b'n means	9 CI	9 Study weight
Study no.	Study name	No Brain							Study in?	$M_2 - M_1$ Rating difference	MoE	%
		Mean₁	SD₁	N₁	Mean₂	SD₂	N₂					
1	McCabe 1	2.89	0.79	28	3.12	0.65	26	☑	0.23	0.3968	3.7
2	McCabe 2	2.69	0.55	26	3	0.54	28	☑	0.31	0.2978	6.0
3	Michael 1	2.9	0.58	98	2.86	0.61	99	☑	-0.04	0.1673	13.3
4	Michael 2	2.62	0.54	42	2.85	0.57	33	☑	0.23	0.2565	7.6
5	Michael 3	2.96	0.36	24	3.07	0.55	21	☑	0.11	0.2762	6.9
6	Michael 4	2.93	0.6	184	2.89	0.6	184	☑	-0.04	0.123	18.2
7	Michael 5	2.86	0.59	274	2.91	0.52	255	☑	0.05	0.0953	22.0
8	Michael 6	2.5	0.84	58	2.6	0.83	55	☑	0.1	0.3115	5.5
9	Michael 7	2.41	0.78	34	2.74	0.51	34	☑	0.33	0.3191	5.3
10	Michael 8	2.54	0.66	99	2.72	0.68	95	☑	0.18	0.1898	11.4

11 Meta-analysis result
Random effects | 0.0943

MoE | 0.0793

12 Diamond ratio | 1.4

10 Model for meta-analysis
○ Fixed effect
● Random effects

Click to choose model

Type of meta-analysis

Ratio of length of random effects diamond to fixed effect diamond

Result of random effects meta-analysis

Figure 9.3. The same as Figure 9.2, but showing random effects rather than fixed effect meta-analysis.

Heterogeneity—the Variability of Effect Sizes

If all studies were estimating the same population ES, the fixed effect model would be accurate and we would describe the studies as *homogeneous*. Even so, the study ESs would bounce around, because of sampling variability. The forest plot would resemble a dance of the CIs, although with different sample sizes for different studies. On the other hand, if, as usual, the studies are estimating different population ESs, we'd expect even more variability—even more bouncing around—in the forest plot, and we say the studies are *heterogeneous*.

> Studies in a meta-analysis are *homogeneous* if they all estimate the same population ES. Otherwise they are *heterogeneous*, and estimate population ESs that are at least somewhat different.

Heterogeneity is the extent to which the *population* ESs vary. I mentioned that random effects meta-analysis allows for heterogeneity, and the length of the random effects diamond reflects the amount of heterogeneity. If population ESs differ greatly—perhaps humanities students are influenced by brain pictures way more than are science students—there's large heterogeneity and the random effects diamond is especially long. With small heterogeneity the random effects diamond is the same length as, or only a little longer than the fixed effect diamond.

Heterogeneity is the extent to which the population ESs vary.

To compare the lengths of the random effects and fixed effect diamonds, I use the *diamond ratio*, which is simply diamond length for random effects divided by diamond length for fixed effect. At the bottom in Figures 9.2 and 9.3, at red 12, the **Diamond ratio** is reported to be 1.4. It's the same as the random effects MoE divided by the fixed effect MoE, which in the brain picture meta-analysis is 0.079/0.057 = 1.4 (allowing for a small rounding error). To your eye, as you switch from fixed effect to random effects, does the diamond look to increase in length by about 40%? The diamond ratio tells us it gets 40% longer.

The *diamond ratio* is random-effects diamond length divided by fixed-effect diamond length.

The diamond ratio is an estimate of the amount of heterogeneity. If the ratio is 1 there's probably little heterogeneity, but as the ratio increases past about 1.3 and up to 2 and beyond, there is, most likely, progressively more heterogeneity. The diamond ratio is calculated from sample ESs, and is an estimate of heterogeneity, which is variation in population ESs. There's uncertainty in that estimate, so the diamond ratio is usually only a rough estimate, but it's valuable to have even a rough idea of the amount of heterogeneity.

The diamond ratio is a rough estimate of heterogeneity.

What change to the data would increase the diamond ratio? An increase in the variability of the study ESs increases the diamond ratio, which hints at larger heterogeneity of population ESs. You can experiment to see this happen.

esci 9.5 Focus on one study and think of a change in its ES that would increase variation of the study ESs. Perhaps an increase in ES of a study with a large ES, such as Michael 7? Type in a new value for one of the group means for that study to increase the ES, and note the change in the diamond ratio. Then **Undo** and experiment further.

I said just now that, in practice, different studies almost certainly estimate population ESs that differ by at least a little. The random effects model allows for such variation, and, therefore, we should routinely choose, report, and interpret random effects meta-analysis, and not fixed effect. For our 10 brain picture studies we would interpret the random effects result, which is 0.09 [0.02, 0.17]. Even if there were zero heterogeneity, which would justify the

Use random effects meta-analysis in preference to fixed effect meta-analysis.

fixed effect model, the two models give the same results, so we lose nothing by always choosing random effects.

Why, then, mention fixed effect at all? The main reason is so we can calculate the diamond ratio, our estimate of heterogeneity. If there's considerable heterogeneity, meta-analysis may offer some additional magic—the possibility of finding *moderators*, which are variables that can account for heterogeneity.

? Quiz 9.1

1. It may be reasonable to use meta-analysis to combine results from studies that are
   a. close replications.
   b. asking the same question, but using somewhat different procedures.
   c. using the same DV and procedure, but asking somewhat different questions.
   d. Any of the above.
2. Increase the SD of a study and its weight will increase / decrease; increase the N of a study and its weight will increase / decrease; increase the length of a study's CI and its weight will increase / decrease.
3. In many cases, the diamond is shorter than all the individual study _____. If so, this is good / bad news because it means precision of the result is greater / less.
4. Random effects meta-analysis allows for the possibility that the studies estimate population / sample effect sizes that are the same / different.
5. Prefer random effects / fixed effect meta-analysis to random effects / fixed effect meta-analysis.
6. When the random effects diamond is distinctly longer / shorter than the fixed effect diamond, the diamond ratio is large, which suggests that _____ is large.

MODERATOR ANALYSIS

Is heterogeneity a problem? It may be, but often it's gold. If the diamond ratio suggests we have considerable heterogeneity, we can ask: Why do the study ESs vary so much? Do our studies differ in some way that contributes to that variation? Can we identify a variable that might explain why our diamond ratio is 1.4—large enough to suggest we may have appreciable heterogeneity? Such a variable that accounts for heterogeneity is called a *moderator*, and identifying it may give great insight into why brain pictures are influential.

Consider the 10 studies. Can you think of some way they differ, some variable we could use to classify them, perhaps into two sets? I'm asking about differences in the studies themselves, not in the results they found.

> To choose a potential moderator, consider how the studies themselves differ, rather than how their results differ.

One possibility is researcher: Two studies were conducted by the McCabe team, eight by the Michael team. There's another possibility I haven't mentioned. McCabe 1 used selected science articles, but McCabe 2 used the same articles with a twist: A critique was added to each article because the researchers wondered what difference that might make to how influential a brain picture is on rated credibility. The Michael team designed studies 1 through 5 to replicate McCabe 1, and 6 through 8 to replicate McCabe 2. I'll refer to studies that used articles with no critique as the Simple studies, and the others as the Critique studies. I can say the studies differ on the Simple–Critique variable.

If adding a critique changes the effect of a brain picture, Critique studies would give different results from Simple studies. In other words, the Simple–Critique variable would cause variation in study ES. It would be a moderator because it accounts for heterogeneity—variation in population ESs, which gives variation in study ESs beyond what we'd expect because of sampling variability. The Simple–Critique variable can take only two values, so it's a *dichotomous moderator*.

> In the context of meta-analysis, a **moderator** is a variable that accounts for some heterogeneity.

Let's investigate our potential moderator, the Simple–Critique variable. ESCI can apply meta-analysis to subsets of studies, so we can compare Simple and Critique studies. Go to the **Subsets** page and you should see Figure 9.4, which shows the 10 studies, with two subsets identified by a label (**Simple** or **Critique**) in a column below red 8. The diamonds in Figure 9.4 display the results of random effects meta-analysis of all 10 studies, and of each of the subsets. The small triangle marks the difference between the two subset means on the difference axis at the bottom; the CI on this difference is also displayed.

esci 9.6   Click a few times at red 7, to see the subset analysis turned on and off. When off, random effects meta-analysis of the 10 studies is displayed, as in Figure 9.3. What changes do you see as you click the subset analysis on?

The study ESs and CIs don't change, but the subsets are identified by color—red and blue. When subset analysis is displayed, the study weights displayed are those for each subset meta-analysis, so the red weights add to 100%, as do the blue weights. The squares may change size to reflect these weights.

The difference between subset means is shown to the right of red 14, bottom center in the figure, and is 0.18 [0.04, 0.33]. In Figure 9.4, the subset diamonds and their difference (the triangle) with its CI suggest there's a clear difference between the subset means, with Critique rated an average of about 0.18 higher than Simple. That difference suggests that the Simple–Critique variable can account for some of the variability of study ESs, and, therefore, may account for some heterogeneity. Note also the diamond ratios near red 15. For all 10 studies, the ratio is 1.4, but for each subset it is 1.0, which suggests only little heterogeneity remains within each subset. Again it seems Simple–Critique can account for some heterogeneity among the set of 10, which probably results in less heterogeneity within each subset.

Overall, Figure 9.4 tells the story: The result for 10 studies is shown by the gray diamond and is 0.09 [0.02, 0.17], which suggests that brain pictures increase credibility ratings by an average of around 0.1 points. The subset diamonds and the CI on the difference axis suggest that brain pictures are more influential (average around 0.2 points) for articles with a critique, and have little or no effect for articles without a critique.

Figure 9.4 suggests that Simple–Critique is a moderator that accounts for some heterogeneity, some of the variability in effect size over studies. Identifying a moderator may lead to more sophisticated understanding—it's not just brain pictures, but brain pictures together with analytic or critical aspects of the article that prompts higher credibility ratings. Identifying a previously unsuspected variable that makes a difference can be an enormous step forward in research.

Let's step back for a moment. The McCabe team ran McCabe 2 to explore the extent that adding a critique might make a difference. However, the CIs for McCabe 1 and 2 are long and completely overlapping—they give virtually no evidence that Critique is on average any different from Simple. Even with the four additional Michael Critique studies there's considerable variation over studies,

Moderator analysis can be highly valuable by identifying a previously unsuspected variable that contributes to an effect of research interest.

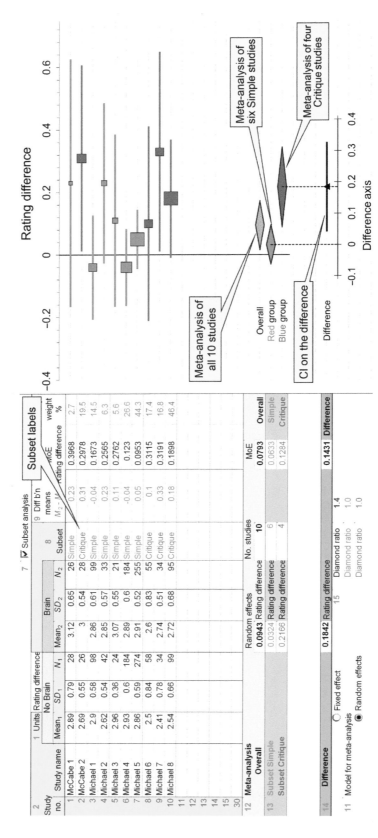

Study no.	Study name	No Brain Mean₁	SD₁	N₁	Brain Mean₂	SD₂	N₂	Subset	Diff b'n means $M_2-M...$	MoE	weight %
		1 Units Rating difference						8	9		
1	McCabe 1	2.89	0.79	28	3.12	0.65	26	Simple	0.23	0.3968	2.7
2	McCabe 2	2.69	0.55	26	3	0.54	28	Critique	0.31	0.2978	19.5
3	Michael 1	2.9	0.58	98	2.86	0.61	99	Simple	-0.04	0.1673	14.5
4	Michael 2	2.62	0.54	42	2.85	0.57	33	Simple	0.23	0.2565	6.3
5	Michael 3	2.96	0.36	24	3.07	0.55	21	Simple	0.11	0.2762	5.6
6	Michael 4	2.93	0.6	184	2.89	0.6	184	Simple	-0.04	0.123	26.6
7	Michael 5	2.86	0.59	274	2.91	0.52	255	Simple	0.05	0.0953	44.3
8	Michael 6	2.5	0.84	58	2.6	0.83	55	Critique	0.1	0.3115	17.4
9	Michael 7	2.41	0.78	34	2.74	0.51	34	Critique	0.33	0.3191	16.8
10	Michael 8	2.54	0.66	99	2.72	0.68	95	Critique	0.18	0.1898	46.4

7 ☑ Subset analysis
Subset labels

Meta-analysis

		Random effects		No. studies		MoE	
Overall		0.0943 Rating difference		10		0.0793	Overall
Subset Simple		0.0324 Rating difference		6		0.0633	Simple
Subset Critique		0.2166 Rating difference		4		0.1284	Critique

Difference		0.1842 Rating difference	15	Diamond ratio	1.4	0.1431 Difference
				Diamond ratio	1.0	
				Diamond ratio	1.0	

11 Model for meta-analysis ○ Fixed effect ● Random effects

Figure 9.4. Subsets meta-analysis of the 10 studies in Figures 9.2 and 9.3. Subsets are identified by labels in the column below red 8: **Simple** for studies without a critique, and **Critique** for those with. Simple studies appear red in the forest plot and Critique studies blue. Diamonds display results for random effects meta-analysis of all 10 studies, and of the subsets. The difference between subset means (the triangle) is displayed, with its 95% CI, on a difference axis at the bottom. From **Subsets**.

and the CI on the (Critique–Simple) difference in the forest plot is long, extending from 0.04 to 0.33. Suppose Figure 9.4 represents the current state of research on brain pictures and the Simple–Critique variable. What would you recommend?

 Pause, ponder, discuss...
Write down at least a couple of options...

You probably suggested a further study, with *N* as large as practical. Good thinking. Perhaps the best strategy would be to include both Simple and Critique in the same study, so Simple–Critique would be an IV in that study, not a moderator in a set of separate studies. Another option would be to run one or more further Critique studies, considering that we already have six Simple studies with a reasonably short meta-analysis CI (red diamond in the figure) but only four Critique studies with a much longer meta-analysis CI (blue diamond).

In fact, the Michael team did run two further Critique studies, which I didn't include in Figure 9.4. Figure 9.5 includes the additional Critique studies, Michael 9 and 10, and gives a rather different picture: The diamonds all overlap very considerably and the CI on the difference is very long compared with the difference between the subset means. The potential moderator Simple–Critique is making little or no difference. The subset diamond ratios of around 1.2 and 1.4 are similar to the overall ratio of 1.3, so there's no sign that heterogeneity within the subsets is less than heterogeneity in the whole set of 12 studies. I now have to shift from my previous conclusion, and conclude that adding a critique has little or no effect—and that's the conclusion we should take away from this discussion.

With no clear evidence that Simple–Critique is a moderator, our conclusion is based on the overall result for the full set of 12 studies, which is that the brain picture increased ratings by an average of 0.07 [0.00, 0.14] points on our four-point scale. The mean of 0.07 is tiny, and even the upper limit of 0.14 is very small. Michael et al. (2013) concluded from this meta-analysis result and other recent findings that, on average, brain pictures make little or no difference. They wrote that there is now "compelling evidence that when it comes to brains, the 'amazingly persistent meme of the overly influential image' has been wildly overstated" (p. 724). That, surely, is good news: We can continue to be fascinated by what brain images might be revealing about how the brain works, but without being unduly worried that people are being easily swayed by irrelevant material when considering a scientific article—at least not by brain images.

I have four further comments to make about moderator analysis. First, recall the distinction between planned and exploratory analysis that we discussed in Chapter 2. The distinction is just as important for moderator analysis as for any other data analysis. In our example, both teams deliberately investigated the Critique and Simple conditions with the intention to compare the two. The moderator analysis was, therefore, planned. Much more commonly, however, a meta-analysis includes studies that were not designed to be direct replications, and that differ in all sorts of ways. If possible, moderator analysis should be planned in advance, but usually in practice the meta-analyst will explore the effects of a number of potential moderators. Such exploration can suggest interesting lines of investigation for future research, but could easily be seeing faces in the clouds. As ever, it's vital to state clearly whether any moderator analysis was planned or exploratory, and to regard the result of any exploration of possible moderators as only tentative.

Second, moderators need not be dichotomous. Suppose our set of studies could be classified into three or more subsets—which perhaps used different

Moderator analysis should, where possible, be planned in advance. If exploratory, it only provides hints, possibly for further investigation.

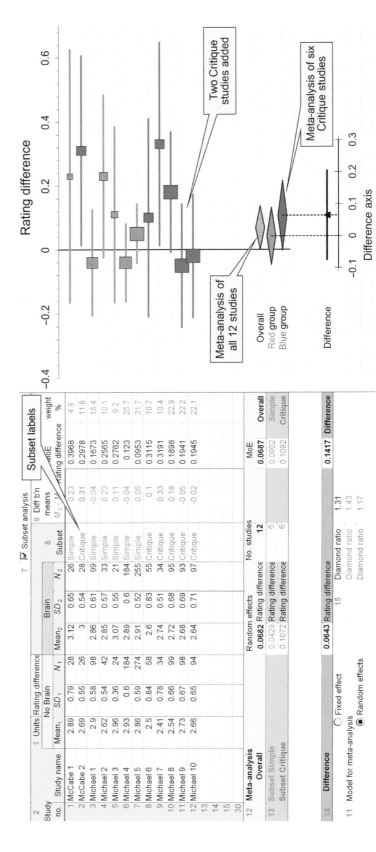

Figure 9.5. Same as Figure 9.4 but with the addition of Michael 9 and 10, two more Critique studies.

types of pictures. Then picture type could be a potential moderator, with three or more values. We could even consider a *continuous moderator*, meaning a moderator that could take any value in a range. Consider a large set of studies, some with young participants, some with old, and others using various ages in between. Mean participant age could then be a potential continuous moderator, and there are meta-analytic techniques that can assess the extent to which such a moderator can account for heterogeneity. There are other advanced techniques that can identify more than one moderator in a large set of studies.

Third, consider the initial question of whether the brain picture studies were sufficiently similar for it to be reasonable to apply meta-analysis. We may have hesitated, knowing that some included a critique and some didn't. We could proceed, however, knowing that a moderator analysis of the Simple–Critique variable might be revealing. It can be a good meta-analysis strategy to include studies that ask more or less the same question, but differ in possibly interesting ways that moderator analysis can investigate. However, as I mentioned earlier, remember to focus on differences between the studies themselves and not on the results they obtained. If the diamond ratio is large, most likely there's heterogeneity, and this may be valuable—if we can identify one or more moderators that can account for part of it.

Finally, we need to be cautious about what we conclude from a moderator analysis. Our moderator analysis was planned in advance, but, even so, we don't have an experimental study specifically designed to compare Simple and Critique, with participants randomly assigned to one or the other. Only such an experimental study could justify a conclusion that Simple–Critique most likely *caused* any difference we found, such as the difference between subsets in Figure 9.4. Rather, the studies in the two subsets of the meta-analysis may differ in some other way we haven't identified. We observed an association or correlation between Simple–Critique and rating, but that doesn't imply causation. I'll have more to say about that in Chapter 11. The point here is that any moderator analysis can support only a cautious conclusion. Even if a moderator accounts for considerable heterogeneity, we shouldn't conclude that the variable caused the ES differences we observe. Instead we might consider it a valuable suggestion, and a promising line for further research.

A moderator analysis can suggest an important relation for further investigation, but cannot establish that the moderator is *causing* changes to the ES.

9.7 Suppose you have found 40 previous studies of the effect of using visual imagery on memory for words. Overall, using visual imagery leads to higher memory scores, but the studies differ in all sorts of ways. Suggest at least one possible dichotomous moderator, one possible moderator with more than two levels, and one possible continuous moderator.

WHAT META-ANALYSIS CAN GIVE US

The first highly valuable result of a meta-analysis is the overall ES estimate, pictured by the diamond. Unless the studies are very heterogeneous, this result is likely to have greater precision than any of the individual studies. High precision, meaning a short diamond, is great news, and an excellent reason to integrate evidence over studies—and meta-analysis is the way to do that.

The second great feature of meta-analysis is its potential to identify moderators, meaning variables that can account for the variation in study ES that's common and can be large. We used meta-analysis to examine the Simple–Critique potential moderator, even though no single study had manipulated that variable. Identifying a moderator can be an enormous contribution to understanding. A strong suggestion of a variable worth further investigation can guide development of theory and also the planning of empirical research.

▶
Meta-analysis usually provides higher precision ES estimates than individual studies, and can also identify variables that are theoretically and practically important.

So that's the beauty of meta-analysis: It can give us high-precision estimates of effects, investigate questions that no single study has addressed, and identify variables that are theoretically and practically important. It's our best strategy for integrating and presenting the findings of diverse studies in a research field. It should be used often, and be highly appreciated by all researchers.

THE PROBLEM OF PUBLICATION BIAS

In Chapter 2 we discussed publication bias, which is the selection of studies to be made available according to the results they obtain. Typically, studies finding large or striking or statistically significant results are more likely to be published, and therefore more easily available for meta-analysis. We concluded that publication bias can easily cause meta-analysis to give biased and misleading results.

▶
The *file drawer effect* is the tendency for studies with a high *p* value (usually $p > .05$) to remain unpublished, and therefore not readily available for meta-analysis.

Have you noticed that so far in this chapter I've made no mention of *p* values or NHST? Meta-analysis doesn't need *p* values, and in fact meta-analysis results can be distorted because of publication bias caused by selective publication of statistically significant results. This publication bias is called the *file drawer effect*, because studies with $p > .05$ are likely to be languishing in the researcher's file drawer, or cloud storage, and not be readily available for meta-analysis.

Suppose the 12 studies in Figure 9.5 had been carried out by different researchers and published in separate journal articles. The last two studies, Michael 9 and 10, gave results close to zero. Considered individually they could easily have been rejected for journal publication as being not statistically significant and of little interest. They could be hidden in file drawers, in which case we would see only the 10 studies in Figure 9.4. We would reach the probably erroneous conclusion that the Simple–Critique variable is a substantial moderator, as well as finding a larger overall effect than the full set of 12 studies would give. Publication bias can be a major threat to the accuracy of meta-analysis, and it's a big drawback of NHST that it probably causes much publication bias.

Polya

We can investigate publication bias in our example. Figure 9.6 shows random effects meta-analysis of all 12 brain picture studies, as in Figure 9.5. (At **Original two groups** you could type in the data for Michael 9 and 10, and follow along.) I clicked at red 5 to display the zero line that marks the null hypothesis value, and at red 4 to show at left the *p* values. Check that the *p* values correspond to where the CIs fall in relation to the zero line. Only for McCabe 2 and Michael 7 do the CIs fall entirely to the right of the line and have $p < .05$, and thus qualify to be awarded "*" next to the *p* value. Below red 7 you can click to include a study, or banish it to the file drawer, so you can explore as you wish.

esci 9.8   a. Click below red 7 to remove Michael 9 and 10 and check you get the results in Figure 9.3. Remove all the studies with $p > .05$, and note the result.

b. Suppose just the studies giving a negative ES were not published. Remove them and note the result.

Removing all the $p > .05$ studies gave a much bigger estimate of the effect of a brain picture. Removing the four studies with negative ESs gave a mean effect of 0.12 [0.05, 0.19], considerably higher than 0.07 for all

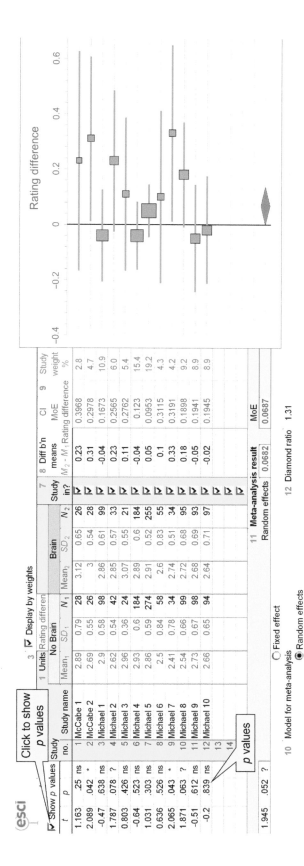

esci

Show p values

3 ☑ Display by weights

1 Units | Rating differen

p values

t	p	Study no.	Study name		No Brain			Brain			7 Study in?	8 Diff b'n means $M_2 - M_1$ Rating difference	CI MoE	9 Study weight %
					$Mean_1$	SD_1	N_1	$Mean_2$	SD_2	N_2				
1.163	.25 ns	1	McCabe 1		2.89	0.79	28	3.12	0.65	26	☑	0.23	0.3968	2.8
2.089	.042 *	2	McCabe 2		2.69	0.55	26	3	0.54	28	☑	0.31	0.2978	4.7
-0.47	.638 ns	3	Michael 1		2.9	0.58	98	2.86	0.61	99	☑	-0.04	0.1673	10.9
1.787	.078 ?	4	Michael 2		2.62	0.54	42	2.85	0.57	33	☑	0.23	0.2565	6.0
0.803	.426 ns	5	Michael 3		2.96	0.36	24	3.07	0.55	21	☑	0.11	0.2762	5.4
-0.64	.523 ns	6	Michael 4		2.93	0.6	184	2.89	0.6	184	☑	-0.04	0.123	15.4
1.031	.303 ns	7	Michael 5		2.86	0.59	274	2.91	0.52	255	☑	0.05	0.0953	19.2
0.636	.526 ns	8	Michael 6		2.5	0.84	58	2.6	0.83	55	☑	0.1	0.3115	4.3
2.065	.043 *	9	Michael 7		2.41	0.78	34	2.74	0.51	34	☑	0.33	0.3191	4.2
1.871	.063 ?	10	Michael 8		2.54	0.66	99	2.72	0.68	95	☑	0.18	0.1898	9.2
-0.51	.612 ns	11	Michael 9		2.73	0.67	98	2.68	0.69	93	☑	-0.05	0.1941	8.9
-0.2	.839 ns	12	Michael 10		2.66	0.65	94	2.64	0.71	97	☑	-0.02	0.1945	8.9
		13									☑			
		14									☑			
1.945	.052 ?													

11 Meta-analysis result | MoE
Random effects | 0.0682 | 0.0687

10 Model for meta-analysis
○ Fixed effect
● Random effects

12 Diamond ratio 1.31

Figure 9.6. Random effects meta-analysis of all 12 studies, as in Figure 9.5, with p values shown at left. From Original two groups.

12 studies. Each of our pretend publication biases increased our estimate of the effect. In other words they gave overestimates, compared with the result from all 12 studies, which is our best estimate of the effect. This is a common pattern because studies with $p > .05$ (labeled statistically nonsignificant) generally tend to have smaller estimated ESs than studies with $p < .05$ (statistically significant), and so if $p > .05$ studies tend to be unavailable, a meta-analysis of the available studies is likely to overestimate the population ES. In general, the more studies that are missing, the worse the overestimation is likely to be.

Our conclusion is that it's crucial that a meta-analysis includes all research of an acceptable quality that has been conducted on the question of interest. If we suspect studies are missing, we can't have full confidence in the meta-analysis—we simply don't have the full story.

9.9 Look back at Figure 7.14, which displays the dance of the CIs and the corresponding dance of the p values.

a. What result would a meta-analysis of all 25 studies be likely to give? (No calculations, just think.)
b. Would you expect the results of random effects and fixed effect meta-analysis to be the same? What diamond ratio would you expect? Why? Is there heterogeneity?

9.10 Imagine omitting from a meta-analysis all the studies in Figure 7.14 where the CI overlaps zero—the $p > .05$ experiments. Roughly what result would a meta-analysis of the remaining studies give? (No calculations, just eyeball.) Compare the result with the population ES we wish to estimate.

Researchers conducting meta-analysis have traditionally taken two approaches to the problem of publication bias. The first is to examine the available studies for any signs that studies may be missing. That might seem an impossible task, but in some cases it's possible, although often the results are uncertain. I won't try to explain the methods here. The second approach is simply to try very hard to find all relevant research—we try to look in researchers' file drawers. The researcher conducting the meta-analysis will search not only for journal articles, but also, for example, for papers presented at conferences, student dissertations, and reports available online. He or she will also email all researchers known to be active in the research area, requesting information about any further studies.

A much better solution would be for the results of every study of at least reasonable quality to be made available online, even if not accepted for publication in a journal. Then we could have confidence that a meta-analysis can include all relevant research and so give results that are unlikely to be distorted because of publication bias. Making results available, regardless of what they are and what the value of p is, would be a big change from past practice, but is an important Open Science goal.

We thus have a new item to add to our Open Science list: Full details of every research study carried out to a reasonable standard should be made publicly available, *whatever the results*. File drawers should be emptied out. We'll discuss this further in Chapter 10.

In the next section I'll discuss using Cohen's d for meta-analysis.

For Open Science and to avoid publication bias, the results of every study carried out to a reasonable standard should be made available, whatever the results.

9.11   Open Science applies to meta-analysis, as to any other research. What's the newly-expanded list of Open Science issues we need to have in mind? Explain why each is particularly important for meta-analysis.

?   Quiz 9.2

1. If a meta-analysis has considerable heterogeneity, then
   a. the diamond ratio will be less than 1.
   b. choosing random effects rather than fixed effect meta-analysis makes little or no difference.
   c. moderator analysis may be valuable.
   d. publication bias is probably small.
2. A moderator is a variable that accounts for variability in population _____; in other words, it accounts for some of the _____.
3. For meta-analysis, the *p* values for individual studies are
   a. used to calculate the weights.
   b. used to check the accuracy of calculations based on CIs.
   c. irrelevant.
   d. used to calculate the extent of publication bias.
4. If a moderator accounts for considerable heterogeneity, we can conclude that, most likely,
   a. it causes variation in study ESs.
   b. it was manipulated by the meta-analyst.
   c. it should be used as a DV in future research.
   d. it is associated with differences in the DV.
5. Publication bias is usually caused by preferential publication of studies that _____ _____.
6. To avoid bias, meta-analysis needs reports of all _____ _____.

COHEN'S *d* FOR META-ANALYSIS

Here's some additional magic from *d*: It allows us to apply meta-analysis to studies that used different original measures. In Chapter 7 we discussed Damisch 1, which investigated golf putting with a lucky ball. The Damisch group conducted five further investigations of superstition and luck. These used a variety of tasks and measures, and so we need to use Cohen's *d* to include them all in a meta-analysis. Reflect on this for a moment: Without a standardized effect size measure, for example Cohen's *d*, none of the meta-analysis or moderator analysis we carry out below would be possible.

> Cohen's *d* enables meta-analysis of studies that used different original-units DVs.

Calin-Jageman and Caldwell (2014) reported two studies designed to replicate Damisch 1. The first (Calin 1) followed Damisch 1 as closely as practical, although the participants were American rather than German college students. The second (Calin 2) made several changes designed to increase any effect of superstition on putting performance. The two studies also used larger sample sizes. The two Calin replications found only very small effects, in contrast to the large effects found by the Damisch group. Figure 9.7 shows meta-analysis of the $d_{unbiased}$ values from the six Damisch and two Calin studies.

9.12   Study the forest plot in Figure 9.7. Identify which studies used fairly small samples and which used much larger samples. Note the corresponding differences in study weights, sizes of square, and CI lengths. What do you make of the overall set of results?

9.13   Identify the results of the six Damisch studies, and the two Calin studies. Compare the results of those two subsets of studies. (Eyeball only, no calculations.)

esci 9.14   Open **d two groups**. You should see Figure 9.7. Look around the page to see what's going on. As usual, reading popouts can help. What data do you need to enter to carry out such a meta-analysis?

esci 9.15   Click back and forth between the two radio buttons at red 2 to select whether the meta-analysis is applied to d or $d_{unbiased}$. What changes and what doesn't change?

esci 9.16   Click the **Calculate CIs** button (top center in Figure 9.7) to recalculate all the study CIs. This may take several seconds—you can watch the CI values change as ESCI works.

esci 9.17   At red 11, click back and forth between the two models for meta-analysis. Note how the diamond changes.

a. Does the value of the diamond ratio reported at red 14 seem about right?

b. What do you conclude about heterogeneity? Does that fit with the appearance of the forest plot?

Figure 9.7 reports that random effects meta-analysis of the whole set of 8 studies found $d_{unbiased}$ = 0.54 [0.23, 0.85]. However, the most striking thing about the forest plot is what looks like a clear disjunction between the first six studies, all relatively small, which found substantial effects of around $d_{unbiased}$ of 0.6 to 0.9, and the two larger studies, which found effects of around zero.

Calin-Jageman and Caldwell (2014) followed good Open Science practice by preregistering their two replication studies, meaning that they lodged online their full research plan, including data analysis plan, in advance of starting data collection. They subsequently made the data available. You can see it all at osf.io/0zqbo. They planned to make the comparison that's shown in Figure 9.8, which uses the **d subsets** page. That page, like the **Subsets** page illustrated in Figures 9.4 and 9.5, provides meta-analyses of two subsets of studies. Figure 9.8 shows meta-analyses of the Damisch and Calin subsets, which are identified by labels in the column below red 9, and the red and blue colors.

To the right of red 14 in Figure 9.8 are the subset results: The Damisch subset comprising six studies found an average of $d_{unbiased}$ = 0.82 [0.52, 1.11], and the 2-study Calin subset found $d_{unbiased}$ = 0.05 [−0.21, 0.30]. Those subset results are illustrated by the red and blue diamonds in the forest plot. The difference between the subsets is reported to the right of red 15: −0.77 [−1.15, −0.38], illustrated in the forest plot by the triangle and CI on the difference axis at the bottom. That's a large and very clear difference between the Damisch and Calin studies.

In their discussion, Calin-Jageman and Caldwell (2014) noted that the six Damisch studies are surprisingly consistent—there looks to be less bouncing around of the six means than we might expect in a dance of the CIs—and all were reported to have p a little less than .05. It remains a puzzle why the Damisch results are all so similar, and so different from the larger Calin studies. Further investigation would be needed to understand why. Calin-Jageman and Caldwell argued that their studies, using larger sample sizes and careful

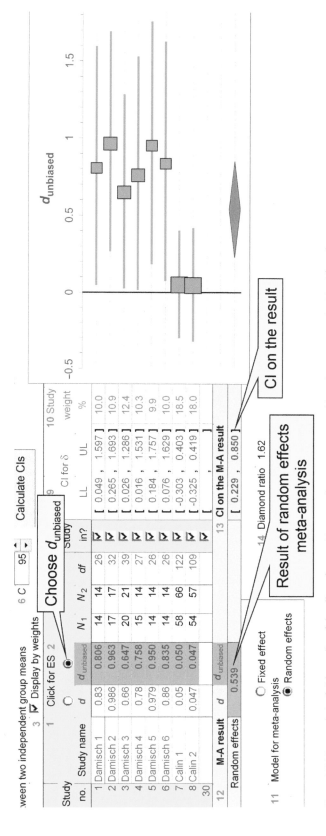

Figure 9.7. Meta-analysis of eight studies of the effect of superstition on performance, as reported by Calin-Jageman and Caldwell (2014). A random effects model was applied to $d_{unbiased}$ values from each study. From **d two groups.**

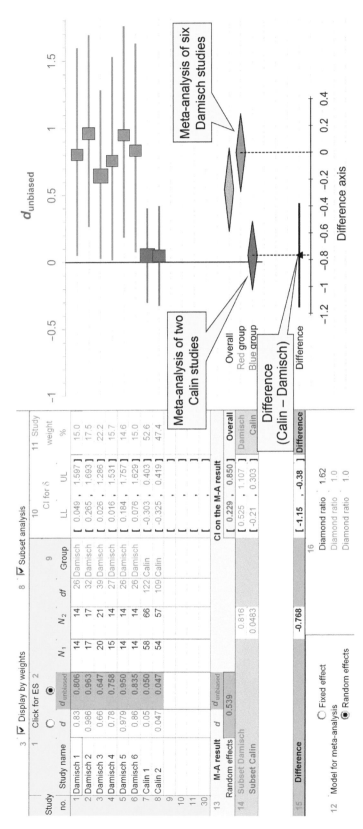

Figure 9.8. A subsets analysis of six Damisch and two Calin studies. The difference between the two subset means is shown on the difference axis at the bottom, with its CI. From **d subsets**.

procedures including preregistration, are likely to be giving trustworthy estimates of the effect of luck on performance.

As I emphasized earlier, Cohen's d was the essential tool that allowed us to bring together the eight studies. Then meta-analysis, including moderator analysis, provided the best way to analyze and understand the set of studies. It also provides the best guidance for further research on superstition and luck. Meanwhile, the later evidence throws strong doubt on the initial Damisch finding that a mention of luck is likely to give a substantial increase in performance.

Next I'll outline the seven steps for carrying out a large-scale meta-analysis.

STEPS IN A LARGE META-ANALYSIS

To carry out a meta-analysis you need a minimum of two studies, and it can often be very useful to combine just a few studies. Don't hesitate to carry out a small-scale meta-analysis whenever you have studies it would be reasonable to combine.

Carrying out a large-scale meta-analysis can be a lengthy and daunting task, but a well-done meta-analysis that integrates a whole research field can be immensely valuable. Anyone publishing such a meta-analysis should receive a prize, a promotion, and a long paid vacation!

What I'm calling a large-scale meta-analysis is also often referred to as a *systematic review*, especially in medicine. Whatever the name, we use a seven-step procedure to refine our questions, find as much of the relevant literature as possible, and use meta-analytic methods to analyze the results. Critical analysis is required at every stage. Here my example is Bisson et al. (2013), which is a systematic review on the issue of psychological therapies for post-traumatic stress disorder (PTSD). PTSD can be a chronic and terribly destructive affliction and is typically initiated by some traumatic experience, such as physical or sexual assault, or involvement in war. The 2013 report is the most recent update, after a 2007 update of the original 2005 report—it's especially valuable to have a recently updated review. I'll sketch the seven steps very briefly.

A *systematic review* seeks to include all relevant research and is almost always based on meta-analysis.

I chose Bisson et al. partly to illustrate an important practical contribution of meta-analysis. In medicine, psychology, and many other professions there's an expectation that practice should be evidence-based. *Evidence-based practice* should be the norm, meaning that professional practitioners should be able to justify their choices of therapy by referring to relevant research results. Meta-analysis is usually the best way to assemble the evidence to provide the strongest basis for evidence-based practice. Bisson et al. does that.

1. Formulate Your Problem

Bisson and colleagues decided to focus on the two types of psychotherapy currently recognized as treatments of choice for chronic PTSD: a tailored form of cognitive behavioral therapy (CBT), and eye movement desensitization and reprocessing (EMDR), which aims to help the person reprocess their memories of the traumatic event so they are less disturbing. The reviewers discussed the theoretical bases proposed for the two therapies, but the focus was on estimating therapeutic benefits rather than advancing theory. They were interested in studies that compared those therapies with other therapies, or with control treatments that did not include psychotherapy—for example, being assigned to a wait list.

They chose a number of measures, the main one being ratings by the psychologist of the severity of PTSD symptoms, before and at various times after the treatment.

2. Search the Literature and Select Studies

The reviewers formulated selection criteria for studies, including:

- PTSD must be the formal diagnosis for all participants;
- the study must be a randomized control trial (RCT), meaning that participants were randomly assigned to groups that received different treatments, for example CBT or no psychotherapy; and
- outcome data must be reported, sufficient to calculate ES differences between the groups.

They cast a very wide net: They searched many databases, bibliographies, and registers of research, and contacted numerous researchers seeking unpublished studies. They found 1,477 studies that might qualify for inclusion. Applying their criteria resulted in a pool of 70 studies involving a total of 4,761 participants.

3. Record Information About the Studies and Collect Data

The reviewers extracted a range of selected information about each of the 70 studies and included that in a database. They recorded, for example, details of the participants, the treatments, the measures, and the times the measures were taken—before the therapy, just after, and perhaps later as follow up. They also recorded means, SDs, sample sizes, and any other relevant statistical information.

4. Assess Bias

The reviewers rated each study for various types of possible bias, for example whether the clinician who rated the severity of PTSD symptoms was *blind* to (i.e., did not know) which treatment group a participant belonged to. Another example of possible bias was incomplete or selective reporting of results.

5. Design the Analyses and Analyze the Data

To plan their analyses the reviewers needed to make many decisions about how to organize the measures and data. For example, they decided to combine various similar treatments into broad groups, including tailored CBT, EMDR, other psychotherapy, and no psychotherapy. They grouped follow-up measures into short- (1–4 months), medium- (5–8 months), and long-term (9–12 months) follow up. They identified 13 comparisons they could make, for example tailored CBT vs. no psychotherapy, and tailored CBT vs. EMDR. For each comparison they planned a number of meta-analyses, each using a different measure, for example clinician rating of PTSD severity at short-term follow up, or a measure of depression immediately after treatment.

They then carried out a total of 131 meta-analyses. For some of those analyses, only a single study provided relevant data; for many only a few studies provided data, but in some cases 20–30 studies could be included. Given their focus on the effectiveness of the various therapies, rather than developing theory, they didn't carry out any moderator analyses, even though many of the meta-analyses showed heterogeneity.

6. Interpret the Findings

Many of the studies were rated as possibly biased in various ways. In addition, many used only small groups of participants, so could provide only low-precision estimates. For these reasons the reviewers judged that only very low quality evidence was available for any of the 13 comparisons. With that important qualification, they concluded that tailored CBT and EMDR were both substantially effective in treating PTSD, and there was little or no difference between those two therapies. Other psychotherapies were less effective, but more effective than no psychotherapy.

7. Present the Review

Bisson et al. (2013), a 247-page report, included an enormous amount of information about the 70 studies and details of how all of the steps of the project were carried out. The meta-analyses were presented in 131 forest plots, and the report also included a variety of tables and figures presenting summaries of the results. There were extensive critical discussions of the research field and the studies that qualified for inclusion. The reviewers discussed the implications for clinical psychological practice, and provided a plain language summary intended to be understandable by non-specialists.

Here are my main reactions to Bisson et al. (2013):

- I'm impressed and happy that experts devoted so much effort to drawing practical conclusions from 25 years of research on issues that are vitally important, especially given the vast numbers of people around the world who experience PTSD. This review provides the best current basis for evidence-based psychological practice for PTSD.
- Meta-analysis was the essential tool for integrating evidence, and forest plots gave insight into those analyses.
- I'm greatly disappointed that, despite the importance of the issues and the large number of studies conducted, the evidence was judged to be of very low quality. It's a further great strength of meta-analysis that it can often identify weaknesses in past research, and thus give valuable guidance for future research.

> Meta-analysis can identify weaknesses in past research, and thus give valuable guidance for future research.

- The review illustrates how, at every step in a large meta-analysis, choices need to be made, based on expert judgment. Choices include formulating questions, setting criteria for inclusion, grouping measures, selecting comparisons, and shaping numerous other aspects of the project.
- It also illustrates how critical discussion is needed throughout, in particular when formulating conclusions and recommendations. Conducting a large review based on meta-analysis is no mere mechanical procedure!

META-ANALYSIS CAN CHANGE THE WORLD

I'd love to tell you about a dozen or more examples of meta-analysis making fascinating and important contributions, but I'll restrict myself to five, and then I'll mention a wonderful resource based on meta-analysis.

Clumsy children lack coordination—they tend to trip over, and have difficulty manipulating objects. Clumsiness can result in a diagnosis of dyspraxia, which was the focus of Peter Wilson's PhD project (Wilson & McKenzie, 1998).

> Meta-analysis can identify important variables, and thus help shape theoretical and empirical research.

Dyspraxia was not well understood, and Wilson was keen to identify variables likely to be important in any proposed theory of the condition. The empirical literature was very messy: Many studies were small and had less than ideal designs and measures. Wilson located 50 studies that met his inclusion criteria and carried out a number of meta-analyses on various measures of children's abilities. He found a particularly large deficit for children diagnosed with dyspraxia (informally: conspicuously clumsy children) compared with control children on complex visuospatial tasks, which included, for example, visual discrimination of shapes, and building with blocks. Wilson had examined many variables and knew his analysis was exploratory and so his conclusion was tentative—it may have been cherry picked; he may have been seeing a face in the clouds. He therefore carried out his own empirical comparison of groups of children diagnosed with dyspraxia, and control children, using a battery of tests including 10 visuospatial tasks. He confirmed that children diagnosed with dyspraxia find such tasks especially difficult. This deficit had not previously been identified as a particular problem for such children, but Wilson provided strong evidence that it needs to be included as a key variable in any theory of dyspraxia. Wilson's project illustrates how meta-analysis can make a theoretical contribution by identifying important variables in a messy literature, and help shape subsequent theoretical and empirical research.

My second example is heart-rending, and a lesson in what can happen if evidence is not synthesized quantitatively. Sudden Infant Death Syndrome (SIDS), or crib death, is the death while sleeping of apparently healthy babies. When my wife and I were young parents in the late 1970s, we carefully followed what was then the best advice for reducing the risk of SIDS: Our three babies slept on their front on a sheepskin. Now, however, the best advice is that back sleeping is substantially safer. Gilbert, Salanti, Harden, and See (2005) related the history, by describing how research evidence in favor of back sleeping was building over the years, but, alas, meta-analysis was not available to integrate the evidence quantitatively. Therefore, tragically, the advice given in childcare books, including the highly popular and influential one by Doctor Spock, lagged many years behind the research. Gilbert et al. conducted meta-analyses of the research results that had been available at various time points. They found that meta-analysis of the results available in 1970 provided reasonably clear evidence that back sleeping was safer than front. The evidence strengthened during subsequent years, but still was not at the time integrated by meta-analysis. They found frequent recommendation of front sleeping as late as 1988.

Gilbert et al. estimated that, if back sleeping had been widely recommended from 1970, as many as 50,000 infant deaths could have been prevented in the developed world. Had meta-analysis been available and used in 1970, we would have achieved better understanding of SIDS and much tragedy could have been averted. I'm happy to report that our grandchildren are resolutely put down to sleep on their backs.

▶ If meta-analysis had been available and used in 1970, it might have prevented 50,000 SIDS deaths.

Third, consider the teaching of reading. Since the days when Greek slaves taught rich Romans to read, numerous methods for teaching reading have come and gone. The pendulum of popularity has swung back and forth between largely phonic methods and largely whole-word—or analytic—methods. Phonic methods pay careful attention to how letters represent sounds, whereas analytic methods emphasize complete words in a meaningful context. The two approaches are based on different theories of how we read, and how we learn to read. Much research has been conducted, and many reviews of the literature published. Since the 1960s the best of these have identified the importance of phonics. Even so, conclusions have often been equivocal and different experts have given different advice. In many English-speaking countries it seems that ideology and fashion, rather than evidence, has for many decades guided educational policy on the teaching of reading, and shaped teachers' beliefs and practices.

Then the U.S. National Reading Panel (2000) made a concerted effort to bring order to the enormous research literature. To conduct a meta-analysis on the effects of different teaching methods, they winnowed 1,072 studies down to only 38 that met their selection criteria—which included requirements as simple as having a control group and reasonable measures, and providing sufficient statistical information to calculate ESs. Based on the work of the Panel, Diane McGuinness wrote an impressive book: *Early Reading Instruction: What Science Really Tells us About How to Teach Reading* (McGuinness, 2004). She concluded that we now know how to teach reading successfully: Stories and meaning and enjoyment all matter, but early phonics is vital. The best reviews in the 1960s were right. This is an example of meta-analysis settling, in decisive fashion, a long-standing and heated controversy. The pendulum should swing no more.

> Meta-analysis supports a central role for phonics in the teaching of reading.

My final example illustrates the damage that publication bias and selective reporting can have. In the 1970s, reviews listed many well-established differences between girls and boys—in verbal ability, mathematical ability, aggressiveness, and more (Maccoby & Jacklin, 1974). Then researchers gradually realized that selective publication was distorting the picture. No doubt many "not statistically significant" studies on gender differences languished in file drawers, but there was an additional type of incomplete reporting. Many researchers studied issues other than gender and, being careful researchers, explored aspects of their data beyond their planned analyses. Often they compared scores for boys and girls, but if they found "no statistically significant difference" they were likely to omit any mention of gender from their journal articles—because they may have had no particular research interest in gender. If, however, an exploratory analysis of gender happened to find a statistically significant difference, this result (and, with luck, the means and SDs) would probably be reported. The published research on gender differences was distorted by studies in the file drawer, but also by selective reporting of gender differences found incidentally during data exploration by researchers primarily studying other issues.

> Publication bias, at least partly based on NHST, for many years distorted the conclusions drawn about gender differences.

Reviewers are now alert to these problems and make great efforts to find even unpublished results. Recent meta-analyses identify fewer and generally smaller differences, and a list of abilities on which there is little, if any, difference (Hyde, 2007).

The study of gender differences illustrates how estimation, full reporting of all studies and all analyses, and avoidance of any publication bias, are all essential if reviewers are to build an accurate picture. That's so important I want to say it again. The aim of science is to discover accurately how the world works and how people tick. Estimating the sizes of effects—the strength of gravity on Earth, the extent to which back sleeping reduces the risk of SIDS, the amount of relief from PTSD that a particular therapy is likely to provide—is core business for science. In addition, those estimates are vital information to guide how professionals, and all of us, can use science for the benefit of humanity. If estimates are systematically distorted, for example if publication bias caused by NHST means they are overestimates, then science is severely undermined. Professionals are likely to make wrong choices. Use of estimation and meta-analysis rather than NHST, and adopting the Open Science practice of reporting *all* competently conducted research, are crucial steps forward for science.

> Using estimation and meta-analysis, and following Open Science practice by reporting all well-done research, are important steps forward for science.

The Cochrane Collaboration

The world's primary resource for evidence-based healthcare is the *Cochrane Library*, an online database of more than 5,000 systematic reviews on a vast range of health and medical topics. These are developed and maintained by the Cochrane Collaboration (www.cochrane.org), a network of centers and researchers in over 120 countries. At the Cochrane home page, see "About us" for an overview. Bisson et al. (2013), which I used above to outline the seven steps of a large meta-analysis project, is a Cochrane Review.

Cochrane provides numerous resources for scholars who are preparing systematic reviews, or for anyone who is interested in meta-analysis. The Cochrane meta-analysis software, called *RevMan*, is freely available. The Cochrane Handbook covers just about any meta-analysis issue you can imagine. Check it out at handbook.cochrane.org and note how the chapter titles, from Chapters 5 to 12, correspond fairly closely with my seven steps. Much in the early chapters of the Handbook is surprisingly accessible, and some students are finding it a valuable resource for their senior and capstone projects.

I find it fascinating simply to browse the library. At the Cochrane home page, you can browse the Top 10, or click to go to the Cochrane Library and use the search function. You might enjoy clicking on 'What is Cochrane evidence and how can it help you?', then watching the video. Here are some examples of what I found:

- How does a herbal remedy compare with anti-depressant drugs? I searched for "St John's wort" and found the summary (and an interesting podcast) of a 2009 review of 29 studies involving 5,489 patients that had compared some high-grade extracts of St John's wort with anti-depressant drugs, or placebo (a pill with no active ingredient), for people with depression. The review concluded that these high-grade extracts were distinctly better than placebo, and about as effective as the drugs while having fewer side effects. This conclusion should prompt researchers to consider carefully what future research would be most informative, and clinicians to discuss possible implications for clinical practice.
- My somewhat random browsing led me to a list of interesting reports. I clicked on one with "Kangaroo mother care" (KMC) in the title—something I'd never heard of. It was a 2014 review of the effectiveness of mothers of low-birthweight infants having a lot of skin-to-skin contact with their baby, breastfeeding frequently, and leaving hospital early. The review included 18 RCTs and concluded that KMC is valuable and effective.
- I searched for "speed cameras" and found a 2012 review of 35 studies from 12 countries of the effect of fixed speed cameras on speeding and the rate of road crashes. All studies that reported crash rates found a reduction, with most reductions falling between 14% and 25%. The reviewers concluded that speed cameras make a worthwhile contribution to reducing road traffic injuries and deaths.

To go beyond the summaries and gain access to the full reviews, you need a subscription to the Cochrane Library. Many countries have national subscriptions, although in Canada and the United States only some provinces and states have subscriptions. You may need to find a library that subscribes. When you do reach a review that interests you, read the overview at the start, then scroll to the end to see all the forest plots. Enjoy the diamonds, which summarize the findings.

The Cochrane Collaboration is a great achievement and provides a wonderful resource—the Cochrane Library—which is essential if evidence-based practice of medicine and health sciences is to flourish. It's meta-analysis in action. You could use it to learn about health and help you make good choices—or to get ideas for your next research project.

The Campbell Collaboration

What about other disciplines? The *Campbell Collaboration* (www.campbellcollaboration.org) is modeled on Cochrane and has similar aims, for the fields of social welfare, crime and justice, and education. It's named after Donald T. Campbell (1916–1996), an American psychologist who argued that public policy should be evidence-based, and that policy initiatives should be regarded as experiments and evaluated as such, to guide future policy choices. The Campbell Collaboration has so far released about 100 systematic reviews, all available online.

The *Campbell Library* is an online database of systematic reviews in the fields of social welfare, crime and justice, and education.

During some quick browsing of the Campbell Library I discovered that:

- A review of 18 RCTs concluded that parental involvement with elementary children's schooling leads to a usefully large improvement in academic performance, despite median program length being only 11 weeks.
- The "Scared Straight" program takes young people who are delinquent or at risk of delinquency to visit a prison and meet inmates, with the aim of deterring future offending. A review of nine studies found evidence that such programs are counterproductive: Such visits tend to increase considerably the risk of later offending.
- A meta-analysis of 44 studies led to the conclusion that school-based anti-bullying programs can be effective. Program elements that usefully increase effectiveness were identified, and also other elements that are counterproductive.

META-ANALYTIC THINKING

Back in Chapter 1, I defined meta-analytic thinking as the consideration of any study in the context of similar studies already conducted, or to be conducted in the future. It's important because it prompts us to design any single study in the context of all related research, past and future, and to report the study in a way that helps a reviewer include the results in a future meta-analysis. It also encourages replication and, of course, meta-analysis, which together usually provide the most convincing conclusions.

I've tried to illustrate in this chapter how meta-analysis can contribute in a range of ways. Meta-analysis can:

- summarize past research to give the best basis for planning our study;
- identify from past research important variables that should be incorporated into theories and investigated empirically;
- integrate several of our own related studies, to help us see an overall picture;

- integrate our latest results with past research, to give the best basis for drawing theoretical and practical conclusions, and the best starting point for future research; and
- provide the best evidence to guide evidence-based practice.

Bearing all these roles for meta-analysis in mind is a big part of meta-analytic thinking. Do you get the feeling I'm convinced that meta-analysis is a good thing? Indeed—it's a great thing!

Finally, a few words about software for meta-analysis. Beyond what ESCI offers, *Comprehensive Meta-Analysis* (www.meta-analysis.com) is a full professional package that's widely used. I've already mentioned *RevMan*, the software from Cochrane. However, you may find *Meta-Essentials* (tiny.cc/metaessentials) most useful: It's a free, accessible Excel-based package that goes well beyond ESCI.

Have you noticed that this chapter contains no formulas? Don't worry— there will be a few in the following chapters. It's time for take-home messages. To help prompt what you might write, I'll mention the forest plot, two models for meta-analysis, heterogeneity, moderators, a standardized effect size measure, and lots of examples of how meta-analysis can help.

 Quiz 9.3

1. The Bisson et al. (2013) systematic review was from the Cochrane / Campbell Library. It reviewed RCTs that investigated the effectiveness of therapies for treating _____. It judged that the available evidence was of low / high quality.
2. You enter d, N_1, and N_2 for each study in a meta-analysis. The ES measure we choose for carrying out the meta-analysis could be _____, but we are likely to prefer _____.
3. In the 1970s, reviewers of the psychological literature identified more / fewer gender differences than they do now, partly because publication bias was probably greater / less back then.
4. Preregistration of a detailed research plan in advance of starting data collection
   a. helps avoid cherry picking.
   b. is good Open Science practice.
   c. increases our confidence in the results.
   d. All of the above.
5. Cochrane makes extensive use of NHST / meta-analysis to support the evidence-based / significance-based practice of education / medicine.
6. Using meta-analytic thinking is likely to prompt you to
   a. use NHST and p values.
   b. focus mainly on the single study you are conducting.
   c. report your study in full detail.
   d. All of the above.

9.18 a. Can you recall what approach to teaching reading was used in your elementary school? To what extent did it reflect the advice of McGuinness (2004) that early attention to phonics is vital?
   b. What approach is currently used in an elementary school near you? What attention does it pay to phonics?

9.19 Following my suggestions in the text, search Cochrane for a report on a topic that interests you. Just below the summary, click to open the abstract and try to identify all seven steps. If you can access the whole report, even better. Try to identify sections that describe what the reviewers did for each of the seven steps.

9.20 Using that report, or another of your choice, suggest a useful further experiment that picks up on any critical comment you can find about deficiencies in past research. That might, for example, be a comment that past research has used only small groups, or that many past studies have various types of biases.

9.21 Suggest a second further experiment that could advance understanding beyond what past research has given us. You might, for example, consider extending the research to a different population, or investigating a potential moderator.

9.22 In the Campbell Library, find a report that interests you.

a. If the report uses meta-analysis—not all Campbell reviews do—identify the contribution that meta-analysis makes.

b. Suggest how the findings of the report should influence practice.

9.23 Revise your take-home messages if you wish.

Reporting Your Work

Meta-analysis can be highly useful for small (minimum two) or large sets of studies. For meta-analyses intended to be comprehensive, as is usually the case for example in Cochrane research syntheses, tens or even hundreds of studies may be included. For a comprehensive meta-analysis, you would follow the seven-step plan described in this chapter and then write a report that tells the full story of every step. Here's a general breakdown of how the overall manuscript would be structured:

- The Introduction explains why the meta-analysis was conducted and what research questions will be addressed. It is great practice to preregister the meta-analysis strategy and questions in advance; if you did this, be sure to let the reader know.
- The Method section explains the nuts and bolts of how the meta-analysis was conducted: the search strategy for identifying studies, the criteria for including studies, the model used (almost always random effects), how effect sizes were calculated, what software was used, and more.
- The Results section reports the overall effect size estimate obtained, the variety observed in effect sizes, and any planned or exploratory moderator analyses.
  - Summary tables are usually used to provide information about important features of each study and the effect size each provided for the meta-analysis.
  - Forest plots are typically provided to give a visual summary of the findings.
- A critical discussion is needed of the whole process, with interpretation of the findings informed by past research.
- The References section includes a reference for each study included in the meta-analysis. These are often flagged with an asterisk (*) to distinguish them from other citations made in the manuscript.

As usual, the primary requirement is that reporting is full and detailed—you need to tell the full story.

If you are embarking on a comprehensive meta-analysis, it is wise to draw on additional resources for proper planning and reporting. For example, the *APA Manual* (APA, 2010) provides Meta-Analysis Reporting Standards (pp. 251–252) as well as a sample meta-analysis manuscript (pp. 57–59).

Although this may seem daunting, keep in mind that meta-analysis does not have to be comprehensive and complex. Meta-analysis is also a perfect tool for synthesizing results across related studies in a single manuscript, providing a quantitative synthesis of all the evidence collected. This currently isn't very common, but it should be: It's easy to do and provides a more precise estimate of the effect than any of the individual studies. For a within-paper meta-analysis, report

- whether the meta-analysis was planned prior to conducting the series of studies, or perhaps before just some of them;
- your model (almost always random effects);
- the overall estimated effect size and its CI—you can report the raw effect size, the standardized effect size, or both;

Meta-analysis can be applied to a few or to many studies. Preregister plans for all stages, including analysis, where possible.

- a forest plot—state in the figure caption what error bars and the diamond length represent (95% CIs);
- the sample sizes of the studies being integrated, unless this is already clear;
- some indication of the heterogeneity of the effect size: In this book, and ESCI, I use the diamond ratio as a simple approximate estimate of the extent of heterogeneity, but more advanced books and specialized meta-analysis software use several other measures of heterogeneity; and lastly,
- an interpretation of the overall effect size, with critical discussion informed by past research.

Here are some examples of reporting a within-paper meta-analysis:

Across the two previous studies, a random effects meta-analysis indicates an effect that is large ($d_{unbiased}$ = 0.71, 95% CI [0.27, 1.15]), especially relative to previous studies of placebo effects on motor skill. The CI is fairly long, but indicates at least a moderate effect up to a very large effect. The two studies had similar effect sizes (diamond ratio = 1.0).

We used a random effects meta-analysis to integrate results across the five studies we completed. The integrated effect size we obtained is very small ($d_{unbiased}$ = 0.09, 95% CI [-0.07, 0.24]). This CI indicates no more than a small-to-moderate placebo effect on motor skill. The five studies were consistent in this finding, with little heterogeneity of effect sizes (diamond ratio = 1.0).

Integrating our five studies with the two previous experiments on this topic, a random effects meta-analysis suggests a small placebo effect on motor skill ($d_{unbiased}$ = 0.19, 95% CI [0.01, 0.38]). The CI is moderately long, though, and is consistent with anywhere from a moderate down to a vanishingly small effect. In addition, there was substantial variation in effect size across studies (diamond ratio = 1.6), which suggests that one or more moderators may have influenced effect sizes across these studies. With a larger number of studies, moderator analysis could be considered. For now, it seems a placebo effect on motor skill may be plausible though small. Still, given that even a small improvement in motor skill can be useful in competitive sports, further investigation is warranted.

Polya

 Take-Home Messages

- Meta-analysis is a set of techniques for the quantitative integration of evidence from related studies. It usually gives more precise estimates than any of the individual studies.

- A forest plot pictures the result of each study as an ES and a CI. The study ESs are represented by squares of sizes that reflect study weights. The result of the meta-analysis is shown as a diamond, which represents the overall ES estimate and its CI.

- *Fixed effect meta-analysis* assumes that every study estimates the same population ES. *Random effects meta-analysis* allows for different studies estimating somewhat different population ESs. Routinely use random effects meta-analysis.

- *Heterogeneity* is variation in population ESs.

- The *diamond ratio* is diamond length from random effects meta-analysis divided by diamond length from fixed effect, and is a rough estimate of heterogeneity. A ratio larger than around 1.3 suggests appreciable heterogeneity.

- If there is appreciably heterogeneity, a *moderator* analysis might identify one or more variables that can account for some of the heterogeneity.

- Identifying a moderator can give insight and valuable guidance for further investigation, but does not establish that the moderator *causes* variation in ESs.

- NHST and *p* values are not needed for meta-analysis. *Publication bias*, or the *file drawer effect*, is often caused by selective publication of studies with $p < .05$, and can bias the result of a meta-analysis.

- To avoid publication bias, Open Science requires that all research of a reasonable standard should be made publicly available, whatever the results.

- Where studies have used different original-units measures, *d* may enable meta-analysis.

- Meta-analysis can be applied to two or a small number of related studies. Large-scale meta-analysis, as usually required for a substantial *systematic review*, can be a large task, comprising seven steps.

- The Cochrane Library is a large online library of systematic reviews in health and medicine that support evidence-based practice. The smaller Campbell Library plays a similar role in some social sciences.

- Meta-analytic thinking considers any study in the context of past and possible future related research, with an emphasis on replication and meta-analysis.

End-of-Chapter Exercises

1) To what extent does the wording of a question influence one's judgment? In end-of-chapter Exercise 3 in Chapter 7 we encountered the classic study of Jacowitz and Kahneman (1995), which asked participants to estimate how many babies are born each day in the United States. Participants were given either a low anchor ("more than 100 babies/day") or a high anchor ("less than 50,000 babies/day"). Those who saw the low anchor estimated many fewer births/day than those who saw the high anchor, which suggests that the wording can have a profound influence. The correct answer, as it happens, is ~11,000 births/day in 2014. To investigate the extent that these results are replicable, the Many Labs project (Klein, et al., 2014a, 2014b) repeated this classic study at many different labs around the world. You can find the summary data for 30 of these labs in the **Anchor_Estimate_MA** data set, available on the book website.

   a. Conduct a meta-analysis of the effect of anchor on estimate. Use **Original two groups** and enter the data from the 30 different sites. You can use Copy/Paste Special/Values for the first seven columns in the data file. Using a fixed effect model, what is the overall effect size estimate and its CI? Interpret.

   b. What is the diamond ratio? What does this tell you? Do you expect the CI on the overall effect size to be shorter or longer when using a random effects model?

   c. Switch to a random effects model. What is the effect size and 95% CI? Interpret.

   d. Let's explore the variation in effect size over studies. Note the **Subset** column in the data file, which indicates that some studies were conducted in the United States and others were not. Perhaps respondents from other countries may not know as much about the U.S. population and may therefore be more influenced by the anchor when having to estimate births/day in America? Test this idea by conducting the same random effects meta-analysis, but using the **Subsets** page. You can use Copy/Paste Special/Values for the first eight columns in the data file. Does location seem to be an important moderator of the anchoring effect? Why or why not?

2) To what extent does being exposed to the American flag influence political attitudes? One seminal study (Carter, Ferguson, & Hassin, 2011) explored this issue by subtly exposing participants either to images of the American flag or to control images. Next, participants were asked about their political attitudes, using a 1–7 rating scale where high scores indicate conservative attitudes. Participants exposed to the flag were found to express substantially more conservative attitudes. The Many Labs project replicated this finding at 25 different locations in the United States. The data are available in the **Flag_Priming_MA** data set.

   a. What would be more appropriate for this meta-analysis: random effects model or fixed effect model? Why?

   b. Use **Original two groups** to conduct a meta-analysis. Write a sentence interpreting the result: Based on these data, to what extent does flag exposure alter political attitudes?

   c. What is the diamond ratio? Does it seem that there is substantial variation in effect size across these different sites? Should we try subset analysis? Explain.

   d. The original study found that flag exposure produced a substantial difference in political attitudes: $(M_{Flag} - M_{No\_flag}) = 0.45$, 95% CI [0.02, 0.88]. Is this consistent with the findings from the Many Labs project? Does the fact that the CIs overlap mean that the replications succeeded in supporting the original conclusion that exposure to the American flag changes political attitudes? Discuss.

3) To what extent does gender relate to negative attitudes about mathematics? In EOC Exercise 5 in Chapter 7 we encountered the classic study of Nosek, Banaji, and Greenwald (2002) in which male and female participants completed an Implicit Association Test (IAT) that measured the extent of negative attitudes towards mathematics, compared with art. The study found that women, compared with men, tended to have more negative implicit attitudes towards mathematics. The Many Labs project (Klein, et al., 2014a, 2014b) repeated this study at locations around the world. Summary data for 30 of these labs are available in **Math_Gender_IAT_MA**. Higher scores indicate more implicit bias against mathematics.

   a. Use these summary data and **Original two groups** to conduct a meta-analysis of gender and mathematics bias. Interpret.

   b. Can this meta-analysis support a causal conclusion about gender and mathematics bias? Explain.

   c. What is the diamond ratio? What does this tell us?

   d. To explore possible variation in effect size over studies, use **Subsets** to compare results from labs in the United States with those from other labs. Interpret.

4) To what extent could feeling powerful affect your performance at motor skills? To investigate, Burgmer and Englich (2012) assigned German participants to either power or control conditions and then asked them to play golf (Experiment 1) or darts (Experiment 2). They found that participants manipulated to feel powerful performed substantially better than those in the control condition. To study this finding further, Cusack et al. (2015) conducted five replications in the United States. Across these replications they tried different ways of manipulating power, different types of tasks (golf, mirror tracing, and a cognitive task), different levels of difficulty, and different types of participant pools (undergraduates and online). Summary data from all seven studies are available in **Power_Performance_MA**.

   a. Why must you use Cohen's d (or $d_{unbiased}$) to conduct this meta-analysis?

   b. Use **d two groups** to conduct a random effects meta-analysis of this series of studies. You will need to copy the data column by column. Then be sure to click the **Calculate CIs** button to obtain CIs for d for each study. If nothing happens, be sure you have enabled macros. Interpret.

c. What is the diamond ratio? What does this tell you?

d. There were numerous differences between these studies. Use **d subsets** to explore potential moderators. Does task difficulty (normal vs. difficult) help explain the differences? Does participant pool (online vs. in-person)? What about nation (Germany vs. U.S.)?

e. Explain why your moderator analysis should be considered tentative and exploratory.

f. For thought: Based on your moderator analysis, what seems to be the most promising next study to conduct?

 ## Answers to Quizzes

Quiz 9.1

1) d; 2) decrease, increase, decrease; 3) CIs, good, greater; 4) population, different; 5) random effects, fixed effect; 6) longer, heterogeneity.

Quiz 9.2

1) c; 2) effect size, heterogeneity; 3) c; 4) d; 5) are statistically significant, have $p < .05$; 6) relevant studies that have been conducted to a reasonable standard, whatever their results.

Quiz 9.3

1) Cochrane, PTSD, low; 2) d, $d_{unbiased}$; 3) more, greater; 4) d; 5) meta-analysis, evidence-based, medicine; 6) c.

 ## Answers to In-Chapter Exercises

9.2 No.

9.3 Change either the No Brain or Brain mean for a study and see the square in the forest plot move, but no change to the weight or CI length. Increase an SD and see no change to the position of the square, but the CI get longer, the weight smaller and, perhaps, the square smaller. Increase an N and see no change to the position of the square, but the CI get shorter, the weight larger and, perhaps, the square larger. The diamond will shift and change in length, perhaps only to a tiny extent, with any of those changes to the data.

9.4 Yes; yes; no; yes. See the text.

9.5 Type in a higher Brain mean or a lower No Brain mean for a study to increase the study ES. If the study ES is already high, that increases variability of the study ESs, and, therefore, also heterogeneity and the diamond ratio.

9.6 See the text.

9.7 Whether a word is concrete (bicycle) or abstract (hope) may influence the usefulness of imagery. If some studies used concrete words, and others abstract, type of word may be a dichotomous moderator. If more than two different types of words were used by different studies, word type may be a moderator with more than two values. If different studies used different amounts of training to use imagery and if more training gives a larger— or smaller—imagery effect, then amount of training may be a continuous moderator.

9.8 a. 0.32 [0.11, 0.53]; b. See the text following the exercise.

9.9 a. The studies all come from a population with mean 10, which is the population ES. This is the same for all studies, so there is no heterogeneity. I expect meta-analysis to give a short diamond centered close to 10; b. Because there is no heterogeneity, fixed effect and random effects meta-analysis are likely to give the same result, so the diamond ratio equals 1.

9.10 Omitting the 9 studies with $p > .05$ removes studies that tend to have the lower means. Meta-analysis of the remaining 16 studies would therefore give a mean greater than 10, and thus an overestimate.

9.11 Are we seeing only a selection of all relevant research that has been conducted to a reasonable standard, because of publication bias or any other reason? Have any replications been conducted but not reported? Are all relevant studies reported in full detail, including details of all data analyses? Preregistration, if possible? We need all these because they are required if meta-analysis is to give unbiased results.

9.12 The first six have comparatively small samples, the last two distinctly larger. The first six studies agree quite closely, but disagree sharply from the last two, which themselves agree closely.

9.13 The Damisch studies all found substantial and similar effects, whereas the Calin studies both found results close to zero, with shorter CIs, meaning greater precision.

9.14 Values are needed for d, N_1, and N_2 for each study.

9.15 For each study, the CI does not change, but the square, which marks d or $d_{unbiased}$, may move, being a little further to the right for d than $d_{unbiased}$. The result of the meta-analysis, the CI on the result, and the diamond ratio all change slightly.

9.16 Calculation speed depends on the speed of your computer and the version of Excel. Excel 2003 is the fastest.

9.17 a. The diamond ratio = 1.62, which matches the change in length of the diamond as I click back and forth; b. This suggests some heterogeneity, perhaps a considerable amount, and accords with the substantial variability of study ESs in the forest plot.

9.18 a, b. I started elementary school in 1951 and can remember lots of attention to what particular letters and letter combinations "said". That's phonics. My grandchildren seem to be getting plenty of phonics along with hearing and reading whole stories. In those two cases, classroom practice seems broadly consistent with the McGuinness message.

9.19 I chose Conde-Agudelo and Díaz-Rossello (2014), which is the KMC review I mentioned. I could easily find mention in the abstract of each of the seven steps, although for Step 5 (Design the analyses and analyze the data) there was just a reference to the standard analyses used by the Cochrane Neonatal Review Group. In the full report there was considerable material on each of the seven steps, although the report used the standard Cochrane format, not a listing of seven steps.

9.20 The abstract identified the need to study whether the positive results transfer from the controlled setting of an RCT to everyday practice in a hospital. Using the jargon, the RCTs tell us the *efficacy*, but we also want to know the *effectiveness*. I would aim for a study that compared KMC adopted as standard practice in some hospitals with conventional non-KMC practice in other hospitals.

9.21 I would investigate why KMC works by studying a small group of mothers in great detail, recording many measures and tracking the babies' progress closely. I would try to identify the most important aspects of KMC for further larger-scale study.

9.22 a. I chose Winokur, Holtan, and Batchelder (2014), which reviewed research on where it is best to place a child removed from the family because of maltreatment. Should placement be with kin—family members who are not the parents—or unrelated foster parents? The reviewers included 102 studies and used 29 outcome measures. They found sufficient ES information to conduct meta-analyses using 21 of those measures, and these meta-analyses provided the main findings of the review. I'm disappointed no forest plots appear in the report; b. Placement with kin was usefully better on a range of measures, so should be preferred where possible.

10

Open Science and Planning Research

Our topic is the planning of research. I'll discuss what's called the replicability crisis, then focus on Open Science because that needs attention from the very start of planning. I'll move on to discuss pilot testing, and the formulation of sampling and analysis plans. Much of the rest of the chapter is about the vital issue of choosing N: Of course, we'd like big N, but there are costs as well as benefits, and sometimes big N is impossible. I'll take two approaches to choosing N. First, using estimation, we take the *precision for planning* approach by asking "How large an N do we need to estimate the effect we are studying with a certain precision, say within ±0.2 units of d?", where Cohen's d is the effect size measure we're using. Second, using NHST, we can take the *statistical power* approach by asking "How large an N do we need to have an 80% chance of achieving statistical significance at the .05 level when we test the null hypothesis of $\delta = 0$ in the population, if the population effect size is really, say, $\delta = 0.4$?"

Here's the agenda:

- The replicability crisis: Why many published results may be false, and what to do about it
- Open Science, and how to adopt Open Science practices
- Pilot testing, preregistration of plans, and open materials and data
- Precision for planning for the independent groups design
- Precision with *assurance*: Finding N so we can be reasonably certain our CI won't be longer than the target length we've chosen
- Precision for planning for the paired design
- Statistical power and how it can guide choice of N when planning research

THE REPLICABILITY CRISIS: WHY MANY PUBLISHED RESULTS MAY BE FALSE

In Chapter 1, I outlined a striking example of results that failed to replicate (Gorn, 1982). Here's a second example: Caruso et al. (2013) reported five studies showing "currency priming", meaning that a subtle reminder of the concept of money increases people's endorsement of free-market systems and social inequality. This was a substantial and perhaps surprising result, which was picked up by media outlets. However, Klein et al. (2014a, 2014b) published extensive replication results, which found $d = -0.02$ [−0.07, 0.03], which is a precisely estimated zero or trivially small effect.

Science progresses by identifying and correcting error. However, when few replications are carried out and probably incorrect conclusions are influential for decades (Gorn, 1982), we have a problem. An excellent explanation of the main causes of the replicability crisis was given by Ioannidis (2005) in a famous article with the stunning title "Why most published research findings are false". He identified three problems:

- *Selective publication.* Studies that do not achieve statistical significance are less likely to be published—the file drawer effect.
- *The .05 imperative.* Researchers feel enormous pressure to achieve $p < .05$ so their results have a chance of publication in a good journal, which is the key to obtaining a faculty job, tenure, and funding.
- *Lack of replication.* Once a result has reached statistical significance and been published, it is regarded as established. There is little incentive to conduct replications, and replication studies are difficult to get published. Therefore, they are rarely conducted.

In Chapter 9 I discussed the first problem, selective publication, and explained the Open Science requirement that, to avoid the problem, *all* research conducted to a reasonable standard must be made publicly available, whatever the results. Now let's consider the second and third problems.

The .05 Imperative: Questionable Research Practices and *p*-Hacking

In Chapter 2 we discussed the problem of cherry picking, of merely seeing a face in the clouds. I explained that specifying a single effect *in advance* can give us a conclusion that deserves our confidence, whereas if we inspect the data before choosing a result of interest, we are much more likely to be capitalizing on chance, of merely seeing a lump in the randomness. In other words, we should use planned analysis, and distinguish that carefully from exploratory analysis. Recently, however, researchers have started to appreciate that usually there are many more choices to make than merely choosing which result to highlight. Suppose we're comparing two independent groups. As we run and analyze the study we might make many choices, including some of these:

- If our first attempt doesn't seem to work, we make the participant's task easier and start again.
- We run 20 participants in each group, look at the data, then run 10 more. (A "run-and-check" approach: We stop the study when we like the results.)
- We note a few outliers, and exclude those aberrant results.
- The SDs differ considerably, so we use the Welch–Satterthwaite method rather than assume homogeneity of variance.
- We had used three measures of performance, but one is easier to measure and seems to give more consistent results so we drop the other two.

▶ Choices made after seeing the data are *questionable research practices*, and *p-hacking* is using these to achieve $p < .05$.

On any of those issues we could easily have made a different decision. There's a vast number of possibilities, any of which we might report as our study. Simmons, Nelson, and Simonsohn (2011) demonstrated that there are typically so many combinations that it's possible to start with random numbers, make a few judicious choices, and probably find some analysis for which $p <$ .05. As they summarize in the title of their article, "Undisclosed flexibility in data collection and analysis allows presenting anything as significant". The various choices made after seeing at least some of the data, as in my five bullet points, are *questionable research practices*. Cherry picking a single result to report is just one of many possible questionable research practices. Indulging in any of them is *p-hacking*, defined as trying multiple things until you get the desired result. Specifically, *p*-hacking is finding a way to achieve $p < .05$.

The risk of *p*-hacking emphasizes the importance of preregistration of a full research plan, including data analysis plan.

Questionable research practices arise often, and can be subtle. Any time you analyze data, you must be alert. Choose the median rather than the mean? Choose to use percentages, not the original scores? Choose to transform to Cohen's *d*? Any such decisions are questionable if made after seeing the data, because they might be influenced, perhaps unconsciously, by a desire to achieve $p < .05$ and a publishable result. To avoid such *p*-hacking, we not only need to distinguish carefully between planned and exploratory analysis but should also, wherever possible, preregister a detailed research plan, including a full data analysis plan. More on that shortly.

Lack of Replication

Now for the third problem identified by Ioannidis (2005). In many disciplines, almost all journal articles report statistically significant results, $p < .05$. Ioannidis explained how the combination of selective publication and *p*-hacking might lead to many, perhaps even the majority, of those results being false. To complete this sad picture, he argued that researchers tend to have so much faith in statistical significance indicating truth that, once a result achieves $p < .05$ and is published, it is rarely questioned, and so replication may not seem to be necessary. In addition, journals wish to publish exciting new findings, not me-too replications, so researchers have little incentive to conduct replication studies. Therefore, few replications are conducted and published false findings simply persist.

Once a result has achieved $p < .05$ and been published, it is often regarded as true. Few replications are carried out.

In summary, Ioannidis (2005) identified over-reliance on $p < .05$ as an underlying factor in all three problems he discussed. Using estimation and meta-analysis rather than *p* values should help substantially, but cannot provide the full solution. It can be just as misleading to use questionable research practices when using estimation. It's just as important to distinguish planned and exploratory analysis, and to preregister. Also, replication remains essential. Therefore, adopting estimation is a big step forward, but to overcome the three problems, we also need Open Science.

The imperative to achieve $p < .05$ underlies all three Ioannidis problems.

OPEN SCIENCE

The Center for Open Science (cos.io) was created in 2013 "to foster the openness, integrity, and reproducibility of scientific research". That's a pithy summary of the aims of Open Science. The Center's first major project is the Open Science Framework (osf.io), which is an ever-growing online environment that provides numerous facilities to help researchers use Open Science practices.

The *Open Science Framework* is an online resource to help researchers use Open Science practices.

10.1 What's the list of Open Science requirements that we've built up in previous chapters? What's the slogan?

10.2 a. Visit osf.io and click Support at the top. Click on Frequently Asked Questions (also available via FAQ if you scroll to the bottom). Click to read any of interest. Read about registration. Note that, when any document is registered, it is date-stamped. What would be most useful to register on OSF in advance of running your study?

b. At osf.io, again click Support at the top. Click on Guides to see the simple introductory resources that are available. Try one or two, to get a general idea of the OSF. You could take the plunge and sign up. It's easy and free.

10.3 a. At cos.io read the brief summaries of what the Center does. From the top menus, go to Services/Statistical Consulting and read what COS offers.

b. Find one or two services that might be helpful to you. Find one or two that you might like, but that the Center doesn't offer.

▶
Open Science is the best strategy for solving the three Ioannidis problems.

Open Science is our best prospect for escaping the replicability crisis and solving the three Ioannidis problems. It's a momentous development that requires major changes in what researchers do—especially by preregistering studies. To succeed it requires journals to revise their policies so researchers are encouraged, or even required, to adopt Open Science practices.

This is now happening. For example, *Psychological Science* has requirements for full reporting of the studies it publishes to ensure that readers are given important parts of the full story. It also "recommends the use of the 'new statistics'—effect sizes, confidence intervals, and meta-analysis—to avoid problems associated with null hypothesis significance testing (NHST)" (tiny.cc/PSsubmissionnew). There's more on that in the Preface to this book.

Open Science Badges

▶
The Center for Open Science badges acknowledge use of desirable Open Science practices.

In addition, *Psychological Science* was one of the first eight journals to offer three badges created by the Center for Open Science to acknowledge articles that use particular open practices. Here are the badges with brief descriptions. Each comes in a labeled and a simplified version:

The *Open Data* badge is earned for making the full data publicly available.

The *Open Materials* badge is earned by making publicly available sufficient information to enable replication, including details of the procedure, materials, participants, and data analysis.

The *Preregistered* badge is earned for having preregistered the design and data analysis plan for the reported research and for conducting and reporting the research according to that plan.

Not every study can be preregistered or earn badges. For example, researchers are often quick to respond to catastrophic events, such as Hurricane Katrina, not only to offer immediate assistance, but also to study people's reactions and to investigate how psychological therapies should be tailored for disaster situations. Such studies are developed on the spot and may change day by day. They can be highly valuable, despite preregistration not being possible. As another example, in some cases data cannot be made publicly available for commercial or privacy reasons.

10.4 From the home page cos.io go to Communities, read the note about Badges to Acknowledge Open Practices, then click on Learn more. State briefly in your own words why the badges were created.

Now I'll turn to four important aspect of planning: pilot testing, preregistration, open materials and data, and finally the big one—choice of *N*. These are four of the main things we need to work on to be using Open Science, and perhaps even submitting our study to *Psychological Science*.

PILOT TESTING

When you watch a good movie, it's easy to get caught up in the action and not appreciate what it took to produce the film. However, any "making of" documentary shows us that there's a tremendous amount of groundwork that takes place before filming even begins: scripts are edited and re-edited, shooting locations are scouted, lines are painstakingly rehearsed, and so much more. Then there are numerous decisions: which camera angles are best, what lighting is most effective, which scenes to cut… the list goes on. We don't see all this initial work and decision making in the final film, but it was essential to making a quality movie.

Strange to say, but research is rather like film production: In most cases, the exciting new article we read required a tremendous amount of initial planning, rehearsal, and decision making. Consider the pen–laptop article (Mueller & Oppenheimer, 2014). The authors had to decide how many students to test, what topics to have them learn about, how to measure their learning, and many other aspects of the study. To help make these decisions wisely, the researchers needed *pilot testing*. Like rehearsals prior to shooting a film, a small-scale *pilot study* tests part or all of the study being planned. Pilot studies allowed Mueller and Oppenheimer to refine all aspects of their studies before data collection commenced. This careful preliminary work led to a *research plan* for the final studies that so effectively addressed their research questions.

Sometimes previous research gives strong guidance for pilot testing, but often pilot explorations can be exciting, as you follow your hunches and, perhaps, make new discoveries. There are no restrictions—you can adjust and restart and run further participants and analyze as you wish, but the results are hardly ever for reporting, because you've been exploring. Be prepared to spend considerable time and effort on piloting, as you aim for a study you can conduct within all the practical constraints. Think hard, discuss with others, and enjoy the excitement of being creative. Pay careful attention to what your pilot participants tell you. After conducting any study you *debrief* your participants, meaning you describe the aims and how their participation is a valuable contribution. You answer their questions and ask for their perspective. Listen carefully and try to see the study through their eyes—then improve it. Finally,

Pilot testing is exploration that guides selection of all aspects of a planned study. It should lead to preregistration.

you decide that you're ready to formulate your research plan. If possible, pre-register that plan, then run your study, with good reason to hope it will answer your research questions.

Piloting is required even for a replication study. For a close replication, the goal is to mimic the original study as closely as possible, and for this you need piloting. You need to practice to make sure the protocol is being administered correctly, and that your participants experience the stimuli the same way as the participants in the original study. It's important, if possible, to contact the original researchers. With their cooperation, you can obtain the original materials and discuss any points of confusion that arise as you pilot. Let's go behind the scenes of a close replication.

Behind the Scenes: Lucky Golf Ball Replications

In Chapters 7 and 9 we met the close replication that Calin-Jageman and Caldwell (2014) conducted of Damisch 1, the lucky golf ball study. Here's some of what took place behind the scenes.

We contacted Lysann Damisch, who provided us with tremendous assistance—information on the exact putter used, where to place the golf tee, and what feedback to provide after each shot. To be really sure we were administering the study correctly, we made a videotape of our pilot procedure and sent it to her for review. This turned out to be really important—she reported that our lab assistant was too jovial when saying that the ball was lucky, which a participant could have interpreted as a lack of conviction. With this feedback, we retrained the lab assistants to match the demeanor in the original study. Protocol videos are becoming another important Open Science practice for increasing replicability—after all, if a picture is worth a thousand words, just imagine how useful a video is for conveying what, exactly, was done in the original study.

PREREGISTRATION

You wouldn't want to board an aircraft if the pilot didn't have a clear plan for getting to the destination. Open Science tells us the plan should, where possible, be preregistered before takeoff. Think of your research plan as a statement of your research questions, then the Method section of your final report, plus much of the Results section although without any data. You therefore need to consider:

Research questions—Express these in estimation terms ("To what extent?").

Participants—Who do you wish to participate and how will you recruit them? The big question is *N*—how many—which we'll discuss at length below.

Materials—Instructions to participants. Stimuli to be presented. Tasks to be completed. Measures.

Procedure—A time line of events during a testing session: instruction, practice, testing, debriefing.

Data preparation—Data coding and checking.

Exclusion rules—Should we really exclude any data as problematic? Unfortunately, participants may not follow instructions, may exhibit careless responding (such as filling in the same answer over and over), or may fail to complete the study. You don't want to include junk data—responses that probably lead to longer CIs, the opposite of what we want. It's reasonable to have exclusion rules, provided that (i) they are stated in advance, and (ii) you report fully about any exclusions you make. For example, in the pen–laptop study the researchers could have decided to exclude any participant who scored 0%

for conceptual knowledge, taking that score as evidence of a participant who didn't take the study seriously. Looking carefully at your pilot data often helps with formulating the rules, because it can reveal participant misunderstandings and the range of responses to expect. Also think carefully about any data point that's excluded: Is it offering an unexpected message you need to hear?

Data analysis—Effect sizes to be calculated and details of all analyses to be run, to provide answers to your research questions.

Studies vary enormously—tasks in the lab, a questionnaire in the shopping mall, systematic observations at the zoo, a survey posted on social media—so the above list is only a general guide. Adjust it to suit your study.

Preregistration may sound daunting, but the process is actually easy thanks to the Open Science Framework, which provides free online accounts that enable researchers to upload their materials and research plan in advance of data collection. When you are ready, a simple click of the button creates a citeable, permanent, unalterable preregistration of all your plans.

We always need to bring critical thinking to bear on any new study, but seeing a preregistration badge helps us feel confident the study was thought through in advance, rather than shaped in consultation with the data.

You might be wondering why, when I'm saying it's so important, you don't see many preregistration badges in journals. That's an excellent question. It's partly because preregistration is not always possible, but mainly because, although preregistration has long been practiced in some medical research fields, appreciation of its importance has only recently been spreading in other disciplines. I hope and expect it will become common.

One of the benefits of the Open Science push for preregistration is that it's now possible for anyone, including students, to browse the preregistered plans for completed studies and for those currently in progress. Reading these plans can be incredibly helpful, giving you a better sense of what goes into planning a study and what fascinating questions researchers are currently investigating. Here are some of my current favorites:

> Preregistration greatly reduces the risk of questionable research practices, and provides fascinating information about studies currently in progress.

- *Collaborative Replications and Education Project (CREP)* osf.io/wfc6u: This is an exciting project that encourages groups of undergraduate students, supported by their professors, to replicate published studies they choose from a list, probably as part of their statistics or methods course. Start by reading the wiki.
- *Investigating Variation in Replicability: A "Many Labs" Replication Project* osf.io/wx7ck: This was a landmark collaborative effort by numerous different labs from around the world to replicate 13 famous psychology studies. It's a treasure trove of materials, data, and ideas. Check out the videos used to ensure the replications were as similar as possible to the original studies. Click on "final manuscript" and examine Figure 1, which compares the replication and original results for all 13 effects. Caruso et al. (2013), the currency priming result I mentioned at the start of this chapter, is bottom in the figure, and shows a large discrepancy between the original result (indicated by a cross) and all the replication results (dots).
- *RRR—Strack—Chasten* osf.io/4rh87: This is a project page made by undergraduate psychology major Kelsie Chasten. For her Honors project, Kelsie applied to be part of a large, registered replication of the facial feedback hypothesis, organized by Beek, Dijkhoff, Wagenmakers, and Simons (2014, see osf.io/pkd65). Kelsie's application was accepted, so she ran participants at her

own university using the exact protocol and materials developed for the overall project. She uploaded her final data to the project page.

10.5 At osf.io, use the search function (magnifying glass, top right) to find studies you may be interested in. Often there are many files listed, but a .pdf or .docx file is most likely to be a plan or report that's interesting to read. Or click to open the project's wiki, which usually starts with an overview. Or sign up, log in, and go to Browse/New Projects at top right. Use the links at left to see popular projects and popular registrations.

OPEN MATERIALS AND DATA

To have the full story we need access to the materials and data of any study we care about. The Open Materials and Open Data badges indicate that a published study provides that information. Mueller and Oppenheimer (2014), for example, earned those two badges, and the article includes a link (osf.io/crsiz) to where anyone can access their materials and data. Calin-Jageman and Caldwell (2014), the two replications of the Damisch study, earned those two badges and, in addition, the preregistration badge (osf.io/fsadm).

> Open materials and open data assist replication, meta-analysis, and follow-up research.

Open sharing in this way has many benefits: It makes meta-analysis easier, allows anyone to check for errors of analysis and interpretation, and makes it much easier for others to replicate your work. In addition, researchers can analyze your data in different ways, perhaps to address different research questions. Of course, you must not post sensitive or identifying information about your participants, and you need to be sure your participants have consented to anonymous data sharing. When at the outset of your study you seek ethical approval, you should describe how you plan to remove identifying information and then place the materials and data on open access.

You might feel that, having made the enormous effort to collect your precious data, you want to be able to use it as part of future research, rather than release it immediately to other researchers. When there are good reasons, it can be acceptable to delay release of full data while you work further with it, but usually 12 months should be the maximum delay before it is made openly available.

What about your final full report? You'll probably want to seek journal publication, but another option is simply to place it on open access in the Open Science Framework. Recall that the first of the Ioannidis problems is selective publication, and the Open Science solution is for every study carried out to a reasonable standard to be made publicly available, whatever the results. Make sure you fulfill your responsibilities by making your report available, so your findings will be available for possible inclusion in future meta-analyses.

To summarize, here's a five-stage view of a research study:

1. *Pilot exploration*—Use pilot studies to explore as you wish. Refine your research questions, tasks, and measures. Decide the details of a study that's likely to be most informative. Formulate a detailed research plan, including your planned data analysis.

2. *Registration, planned analysis*—If possible, preregister the research plan. Run the study and carry out the planned analysis.
3. *Exploratory analysis*—If you wish, explore the data further. Watch out for exciting discoveries, although any conclusions are speculative.
4. *Full report*—Report the whole study in full detail. Make the materials and data openly available, to the extent that's possible.
5. *Seek replication*—You expected this to appear in the list, didn't you? Even if your main finding was planned—and even more so if it was exploratory—you should seek, if possible, to investigate how robust and replicable it is by either conducting a replication yourself, or seeing if you can arrange for others to replicate your work. Then meta-analysis can integrate the results. More broadly, always have meta-analysis in mind as you consider what further studies would be valuable.

? Quiz 10.1

1. What are the three problems identified by Ioannidis?
2. State whether or not each of the following is a questionable research practice:
   a. Deciding to drop some outliers from the analysis.
   b. Examining the data, then deciding to run some additional participants.
   c. Reporting full details of the data analysis.
   d. Preregistration of a research plan.
   e. Seeing the results and then deciding to use Cohen's *d*.
3. *p*-hacking is
   a. the use of questionable research practices to achieve statistical significance.
   b. the combination of *p* values from different studies, as a form of meta-analysis.
   c. appreciation that larger *p* values (values > .05) can be valuable.
   d. an important component of Open Science.
4. Researchers have been reluctant to carry out replications because
   a. there seems little point, once a finding has achieved statistical significance.
   b. journals prefer to publish new findings, not replications.
   c. journal publication is required for career advancement.
   d. All of the above.
5. *Psychological Science* recommends use of NHST / estimation, to avoid problems associated with NHST / estimation.
6. The three Open Science badges are for _____, _____, and _____.

PRECISION FOR PLANNING

Now let's turn to the central planning issue of deciding on *N*. First I'll take an estimation approach and consider what *N* we should use to get a sufficiently short CI. In other words, what *N* do we need to obtain a sufficiently precise answer to our research question? Recall that our measure of precision is the margin of error, MoE, which is half the length of the 95% CI. Consider planning a follow up to our Chapter 1 survey, which gave MoE of 2%. If we want a more precise estimate, say within ±1% instead of ±2%, we need a larger sample. We would choose 1% as our *target MoE*, meaning the MoE we'd like to achieve. Then we want to find the *N* that's likely to give us that target MoE. The rough guideline I mentioned in Chapter 1 tells us that, approximately, to halve MoE, we should multiply *N* by four.

Larger N gives smaller MoE, and thus higher precision.

Target MoE is the precision we want our study to achieve.

We need to take that relationship between N and MoE further. Large N is good because it gives higher precision—our estimate is likely to be closer to the true value. On the other hand, large N requires more time and resources and may not always be feasible. We need to weigh up costs and benefits—indeed some scientists have argued that choosing N carefully is an ethical obligation (Button et al., 2013), since we ought to be able to assure participants when recruiting them into the study that their time won't be spent in vain.

Let's take as an example the replication of Damisch 1, as we discussed in Chapter 9. Figure 10.1 shows the results from six Damisch studies, and a meta-analysis of them. The six studies had similar precision—all CIs about the same length—and the mean MoE for all six was 0.74. The figure also reports near red 12 and 13 that the meta-analysis result was 0.82 [0.53, 1.11], and MoE of 0.29 is marked. The effect size measure selected by the radio button at red 2 is $d_{unbiased}$, so MoE is expressed in the units shown on the $d_{unbiased}$ axis at the top in the figure, which I'm assuming are units of population SD. The Damisch studies all used two independent groups, with average group size of around $N = 16$.

Using the rough guideline, if our replication of Damisch used two groups each four times as large (i.e., with $N = 64$), we'd expect MoE of around half of 0.74, or 0.37. With N larger than 64, we'd expect even smaller MoE. For a more detailed view of the relationship between N and MoE, we need Figure 10.2, in which the heavy black line is a graph of N against MoE, for a study with two independent groups each of size N. MoE is plotted on the horizontal axis in units of population SD, the same units we're assuming that d, or $d_{unbiased}$, is expressed in.

We can use the slider at the bottom to position the vertical cursor labeled **Target MoE** at the MoE value that we'd like our study to achieve. Target MoE is expressed in units of population SD. The numbers on the black curve show how required N increases dramatically as we aim for shorter and shorter 95% CIs by shifting the cursor left to specify smaller and smaller values of target MoE. The values of N are based on our usual statistical model of random sampling from a normally distributed population, and assume CIs are calculated using t. In Figure 10.2 I've set the cursor to highlight, for example, a target MoE of 0.4. The cursor indicates that we need $N = 50$ to expect to achieve that MoE.

How should you choose target MoE? Good question, and I'll say more about this later. Here we'll use MoE from the Damisch studies and MoE from the meta-analysis as starting points. We could also consider the effect size we expect to find, or the ES that would be of interest to find—the smaller this is, the higher the precision we probably need to identify the effect clearly. Later I'll suggest the rough guideline that target MoE of half the expected effect size is desirable, although this may not always be practical to achieve.

One approach to selecting N would be to choose a value for target MoE, then read off from Figure 10.2 the N that's likely to give that MoE, and simply use that N in your study. It's better, however, to consider a number of values for target MoE and note the N required for each. Understanding the trade-off between target MoE and N gives a better basis for weighing the costs of running N participants against the benefits of achieving a particular level of precision. This approach of considering precision in order to choose N is called *precision*

▶
When planning research, consider what MoE a particular N is likely to give.

▶
The heavy black line in Figure 10.2 shows how required N increases dramatically as we choose smaller target MoEs.

▶
Use past research and perhaps the expected effect size to guide your choice of target MoE.

▶
Precision for planning bases choice of N on the MoE the study is likely to give. Consider N for various values of your target MoE.

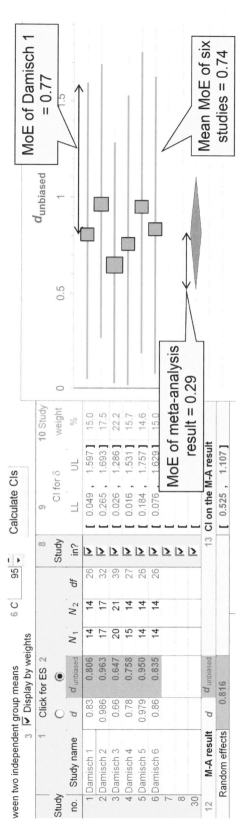

Figure 10.1. The results of six Damisch studies, as presented also in Figure 9.7, and the result of random effects meta-analysis of all six. The MoE of Damisch 1 is reported, as well as the mean MoE of the 6 studies and MoE of the result of the meta-analysis. From the **d two groups** page of ESCI intro Meta-Analysis.

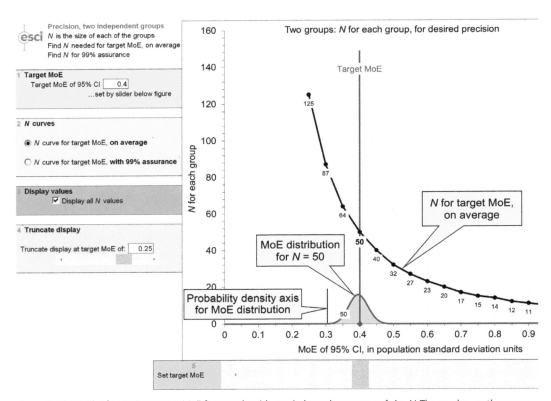

Figure 10.2. Graph of N against target MoE for a study with two independent groups of size N. The number on the cursor indicates $N = 50$ is required to achieve target MoE = 0.4, on average. From **Precision two**.

for planning. It's also called AIPE—accuracy in parameter estimation—which is another good description of this approach to planning.

10.6 Referring to Figure 10.2, what N is needed for target MoE = 0.6? For 0.3? How well do those two values of N match with our rough guideline?

10.7 a. If a study uses two independent groups of 16, what MoE do you expect for the CI on the difference between the two group means?

b. Compare your answer with MoE reported in Figure 10.1 for the six Damisch studies. Explain.

10.8 Suppose you decide your replication of the Damisch studies should have about the same precision as the meta-analysis of all six of those studies. What target MoE should you choose, and what N would you need?

10.9 a. The Calin 1 and Calin 2 replications shown in Figure 9.7 used average N of 59. What precision would you expect they found?

b. Average MoE for Calin 1 and Calin 2, as pictured in Figure 9.7, was 0.36. Is that as you expected?

esci 10.10 Fire up **ESCI intro chapters 10–16** and go to the first precision page, **Precision two**. You should see Figure 10.2. If not, move the cursor to 0.4. Your chosen target MoE is shown also at red 1.

esci 10.11 Find N for target MoE = 0.2, and 0.1. You will need to investigate the small slider at red 4.

The main curve in Figure 10.2 tells us something fundamental about how independent groups studies work. Whatever your area of research, if you have independent groups each with $N = 32$, then expect the CI on the difference between the group means to have MoE around 0.50, or half a population SD. You might even care to remember those values of $N = 32$ and MoE = 0.5, as part of your intuitions about group sizes and what they can tell us. Yes, that's moderately large N and, even so, quite a long CI, but that simply reflects the extent of sampling variability, which often is disappointingly large.

> Independent groups each with $N = 32$ give MoE = 0.5, on average.

Sorry, but now I need to discuss a small complication. Fortunately, *assurance* can help us out.

Obtaining Target MoE With Assurance

The main curve in Figure 10.2 tells us the N that will *on average* give a CI with MoE no greater than the target MoE we have chosen. However, any individual study may give MoE that's smaller or larger than target MoE.

Recall that, in the dance of the CIs, not only the sample means but also the CI lengths bounce around. Unless, that is, we know σ, the population SD, which we hardly ever do. Here I'm assuming that, as usual, we don't know σ, and therefore CIs will vary in length over replications. In Figure 10.2, the small brown curve labeled **MoE distribution** illustrates how MoE varies over repeated studies, with $N = 50$. The small vertical line to the left is the curve's probability density axis. The curve tells us MoE is most likely close to 0.4, and usually lies between 0.35 and 0.45. Rarely will MoE be as small as 0.3 or as large as 0.5.

> The *MoE distribution* illustrates how MoE varies from study to study.

That little curve is worth thinking about for a moment. If we run our study over and over, always with $N = 50$ in each group, MoE will bounce around—the CIs will vary in length. The curve tells us that, on average, MoE will be 0.4, and most often will lie between 0.35 and 0.45. Also, there's about a 50% chance we'll be unhappy because our study gives MoE larger than target MoE, larger than 0.4.

Now for the crucial step. We know that $N = 50$ will give us our target MoE of 0.4 on average, but that's not good enough. We also know that using larger N means that MoE found by our study will on average be shorter, but how much larger must N be before MoE found by our study will almost certainly be less than 0.4, our target MoE? How large an N should we use, to be pretty sure we'll obtain MoE no more than target MoE?

The answer is $N = 65$, but, to explain why, I need the concept of **assurance**. In Figure 10.3 the curve shown in Figure 10.2 still appears, but is light gray, and above it is displayed a red curve. This red upper curve is the *assurance curve*, which tells us that $N = 65$ is required for us to obtain target MoE of 0.4 with 99% assurance. Assurance is the probability, expressed as a percentage, that an individual study gives MoE no more than target MoE. Using N specified by the assurance curve, I can be 99% sure my study will obtain MoE that's no larger than target MoE. The red assurance curve tells us that, if we use $N = 65$, in the long run only 1 study in 100 will have MoE greater than our target of 0.4—assuming, as usual, that our statistical model applies.

> Increase N from 50 to 65 and, on 99% of occasions, the MoE will be less than or equal to a target MoE of 0.4.

Assurance is a bit tricky at first—maybe read the above paragraph again. Better still, close the book and say in your own words what $N = 65$ gives us. With target MoE of 0.4, why might I prefer to use $N = 65$ rather than $N = 50$?

> **Assurance** is the probability, expressed as a percentage, that a study obtains MoE no more than target MoE.

Click the lower button at red 2, which is labeled *N* **curve for target MoE, with 99% assurance**, to see the red assurance curve.

The numbers on the cursor in Figure 10.3 tell us we need to increase N from 50 to 65 to achieve 99% assurance that our study will obtain MoE no more than 0.4. The MoE distribution curve at the bottom shows variation in MoE when $N = 65$. That curve in Figure 10.3 has shifted left, so only a tiny upper tail area is to the right of the cursor—corresponding to the mere 1% chance that MoE is greater than the target MoE marked by the cursor.

10.12   Consider the MoE distribution curve in Figure 10.3.

    a. About what MoE is most likely? What range includes most MoE values?

    b. Consider the lower, gray curve in Figure 10.3. Using $N = 65$, about what MoE do we expect on average? Compare with what the MoE curve in Figure 10.3 tells us.

10.13   Suppose you want greater precision.

    a. Would you select a larger or smaller target MoE? Would you need to move the cursor in Figure 10.3 to the left or right?

    b. Would the MoE distribution curve shift left or right? Would N be larger or smaller?

10.14   Meta-analysis of the six Damisch studies had MoE = 0.29. Exercise 10.8 asked that a replication should have MoE of about 0.29, on average. You probably chose target MoE of 0.3 and found $N = 87$. What N should we use to be 99% assured that our MoE is no more than 0.3?

10.15   Recall the dance of the CIs. When, as usual, σ is not known, CI length (and therefore MoE) varies over the replications. With larger N, does MoE vary more, or less? Would the distribution of MoE values be wider or narrower?

10.16   a. For smaller target MoE, is the required N larger or smaller? Does the MoE distribution curve shift left or right?

    b. Does that distribution become wider or narrower? Explain.

    c. What happens to the width of that curve for larger target MoE?

    d. Test your predictions in ESCI.

Before moving on to the paired design, I have three comments. First, some of the exercises used the curves in Figures 10.2 and 10.3 not to plan a future study, but to look at values of MoE and N in past studies. The relation between MoE and N should be the same for a study already completed and one yet to be run. Because of sampling variability, we can't predict exactly the MoE of any individual study. Even so, we can use the curves to help plan a study, then later to check that the MoE obtained in our study is reasonable, given the N we used. A MoE that's very different from what we'd expect might signal an error in our planning, doubt about our statistical model, or that something else strange is going on that we should investigate.

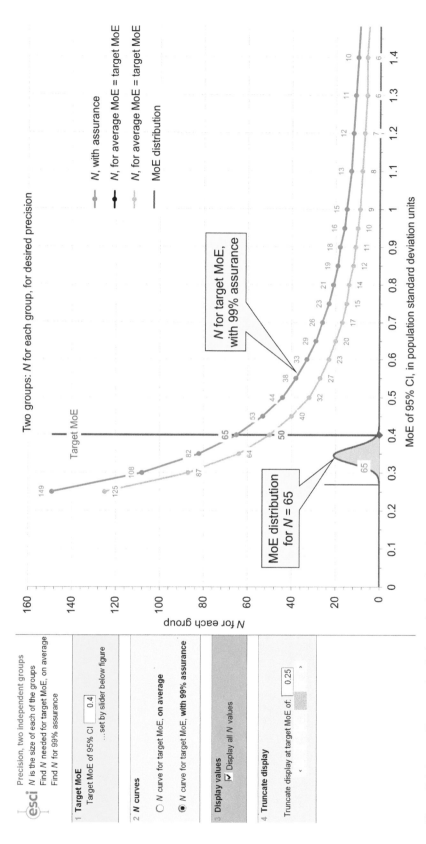

Figure 10.3. Same as Figure 10.2, but displaying also the red upper line, which is the assurance curve, a graph of *N* against target MoE, with assurance = 99%. It shows that two groups each with *N* = 65 are needed for 99% assurance that MoE will not be greater than target MoE of 0.4. The brown MoE distribution curve at the bottom has only a tiny tail area to the right of the cursor, and looks to be centered at about 0.35. The lower curve, which gives *N* for target MoE on average, is displayed gray.

▶ For precision for planning, use Cohen's *d*, assumed to be in units of population SD, σ.

▶ A replication should usually have *N* at least as large as the *N* of the original study, and probably larger.

Second, we express target MoE in population SD units. You might be thinking, however, that we hardly ever know σ, so how can we use precision for planning based on σ, the population SD? That's an excellent question. The best approach is to use Cohen's *d* (or $d_{unbiased}$) as our measure, and interpret values as numbers of population SD units, as we did in Chapter 9, and when we were discussing the Damisch and Calin studies above.

Finally, consider again our replication of Damisch 1. We've explored possibilities, but what *N* should we choose? We want our replication to stand up well alongside the original study, or, in this case, the meta-analysis of the six Damisch studies. This suggests it should be no less precise than the meta-analysis result, for which MoE = 0.29. Figure 10.3 tells us that *N* = 108 for each group would give MoE of 0.3 with 99% assurance, while *N* = 125 would give MoE of 0.25 on average. For our study to have similar precision to the meta-analysis result, we need to consider values like those. They are, of course, much larger than the group sizes of around 16 that each of the Damisch studies used.

If there are many previous studies, however, the meta-analysis may have a very short MoE and it may be unrealistic for us to use that as our target MoE. We might instead be guided in our choice of target MoE by what effect size we expect, or that the meta-analysis obtained. A little later I'll suggest that choosing target MoE to be half the expected ES can be a useful strategy. In any case, when thinking of replication we should, for a start, consider aiming for greater precision than the original study achieved, if that's feasible. Such higher precision is likely to require larger *N*.

The Paired Design

▶ For the paired design, precision is greatly influenced by the population correlation between the two measures. High correlation gives high precision, meaning a short CI.

In Chapter 8 we discussed pretest–posttest studies, as a common example of the paired design. Our main examples were the Thomason studies in which groups of students gave pretest and posttest critical thinking scores. One important conclusion was that the paired design can give high precision, meaning a short CI on the mean of the differences. It does so when the differences are consistent over participants, in which case s_{diff} is small and the correlation between the two measures—pretest and posttest scores—is high. I mentioned that correlation, *r*, takes values from −1 to 1, with values closer to 1 indicating strong positive correlation between the two variables. We'll discuss correlation in Chapter 11, but in this chapter we need it as an important aspect of the paired design. The key point is that the higher the correlation between the two measures, the shorter the CI, the higher the precision and the happier we are.

In Chapter 8, ESCI reported correlation *r* that was calculated from the paired design data. That's the sample correlation. We can also consider the correlation of the two measures in the population. I'll use the symbol ρ (Greek lower case rho, "roe") for the population correlation. Take care: Don't confuse correlation ρ with *p* as in *p* value. As you would probably guess, we often use sample *r*, calculated from data, as an estimate of the population correlation ρ. Chapter 11 has much more on that, but, now, back to the paired design.

▶ The population correlation, ρ, between the two measures in pretest–posttest studies is often in practice around .6 to .9.

In the previous section we explored how target MoE depends on *N* for independent groups. For the paired design it depends on *N* and also on the correlation. This is great news because a high correlation means a smaller *N* is needed to achieve target MoE. The complication is that, to use precision for planning, we need to know the correlation. However, before carrying out the study, how can we know what value of correlation to expect? I'll discuss later how we might choose a population correlation value to enter into our precision for planning calculations, but for now I'll just say that, in practice, pretest–posttest studies often find quite large positive correlations, between about .6 and .9.

For Figure 10.4, I chose ρ = .70 as a typical value. The cursor at target MoE = 0.4 tells us that, assuming ρ = .70, a single group as small as N = 17 gives MoE not more than 0.4, on average—that's the lower, gray curve. It also tells us we need a much larger group, with N = 28, to achieve target MoE with 99% assurance—that's the red upper curve. The small brown MoE distribution curve at the bottom shows the spread of MoE values we expect for N = 28.

 10.17 Open the **Precision paired** page and set it up as in Figure 10.4.

a. At red 1, change ρ to .60 and note how N changes. The curve may take a moment to update.

b. Change ρ to .80, and note how N changes. Try .90. What do you conclude about the influence of the correlation between pretest and posttest?

Table 10.1 reports selected summary statistics from three Thomason studies we saw in Chapter 8. The values of r in the rightmost column are the correlations of pretest and posttest scores in each study. They are estimates of population correlation ρ, which I'll assume is the same for all studies. The r values in the table vary, perhaps largely because of sampling variability.

Consider the statistics for Thomason 1. Is it reasonable that a single group of N = 12 gave MoE of 0.35, with correlation r = .89? Figure 10.5 displays the curves for ρ = .89 and target MoE = 0.35, and shows that N = 10 would, on average, obtain MoE of 0.35, and that N of 17 is required before we could be 99% assured our MoE would be no more than 0.35. It's therefore perfectly reasonable that Thomason et al. found this MoE with their N of 12.

 10.18 Enter ρ = .60 and target MoE = 0.30 to match Thomason 3 as closely as possible.

a. What N would give this MoE on average? What N is required for 99% assurance?

b. Is it reasonable that Thomason 3 found MoE = 0.32? Why?

I hope you are getting a feel for how both ρ and target MoE influence N. Small changes in target MoE, especially for values below about 0.5, give quite big changes in the required N. Similarly, even small changes in ρ make quite large changes in required N. For a given N, larger ρ gives higher precision, meaning smaller MoE. Correspondingly, larger ρ means that smaller N is needed to achieve a particular target MoE.

Now let's consider the critical thinking study we wish to run. I'll first use ρ = .70. That's a somewhat arbitrary choice, but roughly guided by the values reported in Table 10.1, especially Thomason 3, the largest study. I would like to estimate the gain in critical thinking more precisely, so I'll choose target MoE = 0.25. ESCI tells me that, with ρ = .70, we need N = 40 for average MoE = 0.25, and N = 58 for 99% assurance. We could use those values of N to guide our planning, but it would be better to explore further by trying a few different values of ρ and target MoE.

 10.19 If you aim for higher precision, with target MoE = 0.20, what N would you need?

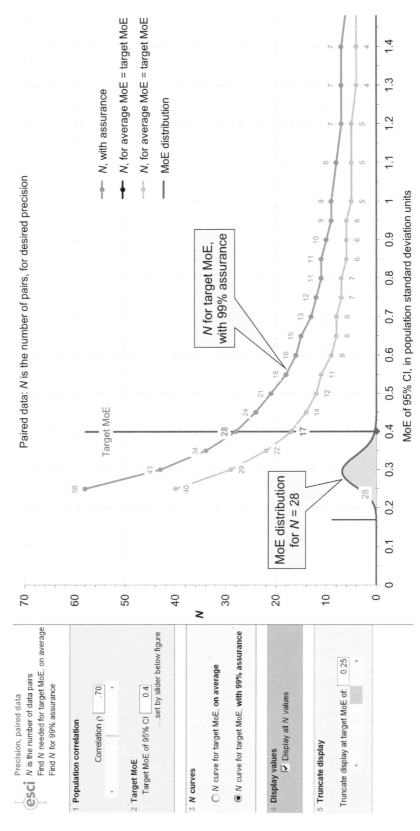

Figure 10.4 Graph of N against target MoE for the paired design. At red 1, top left, the slider has been used to set ρ = .70 as the population correlation between the two measures, such as pretest and posttest. The cursor is set at target MoE = 0.4 and shows (red upper curve) that N = 28 is required to achieve MoE not more than 0.4 with 99% assurance. The lower curve, grayed out, shows that N = 17 gives, on average, MoE not more than 0.4. From **Precision paired**.

Study	N	ES (Posttest – Pretest) $d_{unbiased}$	MoE of CI on ES	Correlation, r, of Pretest and Posttest
Thomason 1	12	0.50	0.35	.89
Thomason 2	16	0.34	0.30	.87
Thomason 3	39	0.64	0.32	.60

Table 10.1 Summary Statistics for Three Thomason Critical Thinking Studies With a Paired Design

 10.20 If you ran the study with $N = 58$, and population correlation is actually $\rho = .80$, about what MoE would you expect to get? A rough eyeballed answer is sufficient.

Further exploration with **Precision paired** could help us understand better the influence of ρ and N on the precision we might expect our replication study to achieve, and thus help us choose N for our study. We're not seeking a single "correct" N to use, but guidance as to the approximate consequences of various choices of N.

What value of ρ should we specify when using **Precision paired**? Sometimes, as above, there are previous similar studies and we can be guided by the correlations they report. Often, however, reports of research don't report those correlations. If full data are available we can calculate the correlations, but otherwise we would need to contact the researchers and ask. In any case, especially with small studies, the correlations calculated from data are not precise estimates of population correlation ρ, and so may be a poor guide to what correlation our study is likely to find. If there are no reasonably similar studies, all we can do is guess. An extreme choice would be zero, which is the population correlation for independent groups. However, paired designs with human participants in psychology and education often find correlations between about .6 and .9, so it's often reasonable to use such values when planning.

After we've completed our study we'll calculate and report the correlation r between the measures, and note how it compares with the ρ values we used during planning. That could be interesting, and may also help plan any future similar studies.

I'll now discuss a practical strategy for using precision for planning.

A Strategy for Using Precision for Planning

Cohen's d is our measure, assumed to be in units of σ, the population SD. Target MoE is expressed in the same units. Even when, as usual, we don't know σ, we can still use population SD as the unit for precision for planning. Here's an example that shows how.

Suppose we have just taken delivery of a new driving simulator and are planning a study to compare the response times of experienced and novice drivers to sudden unexpected stimuli. We may have no idea of population SD for response time. We could still use **Precision two** to tell us that two groups with $N = 32$ will on average give us MoE of 0.5 population SDs. Suppose we suspect—or previous research suggests—that there is a population difference between experienced and novice drivers of around Cohen's $d = 0.8$, which is a number of population SDs. On the left in Figure 10.6 I've shown $\delta = 0.8$

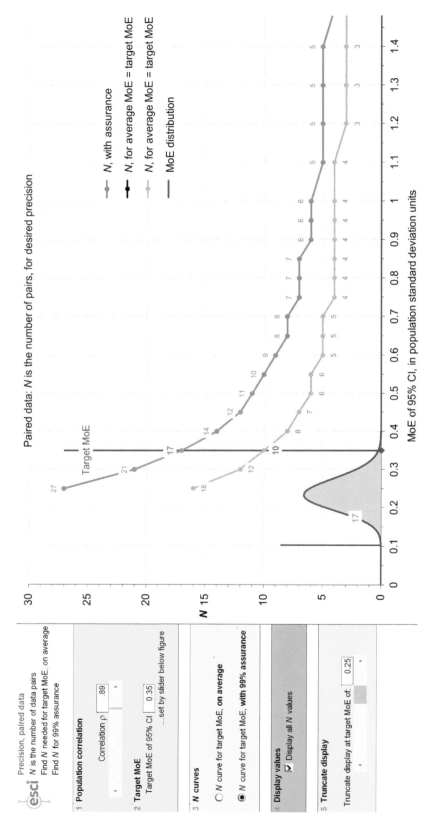

Figure 10.5. Same as Figure 10.4, but with ρ = .89, as reported near red 1 top left, and the cursor set at 0.35, both values matching those shown in Table 10.1 for Thomason 1.

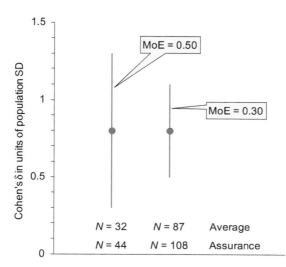

Figure 10.6. Means and 95% CIs for the difference between the means in an independent groups study. These results are expected, on average, if population effect size is δ = 0.80 and each group has N = 32 (on left), or N = 87 (on right). Any single study will give results differing from these because of sampling variability. For 99% assurance, target MoE of 0.50 requires N = 44, and target MoE of 0.30 requires N = 108, as indicated at the bottom.

with MoE of 0.5, which is roughly what we'd expect if we ran the study with two groups of N = 32 and δ is in fact 0.8. That's what we'd expect *on average* in the long run, and any single study would give d and MoE differing from these because of sampling variability. We should also note that N = 44 would be needed for 99% assurance of achieving MoE = 0.5 or less.

If we'd like greater precision we could, for example, consider target MoE = 0.30, as shown on the right in Figure 10.6. **Precision two** tells us that N = 87 is needed to achieve MoE = 0.30 on average, and N = 108 if we want 99% assurance. We can, of course, also find N for any other target MoE values we might wish to consider.

Do we need to consider, as part of planning, the likely size of the effect we're estimating? In Figure 10.6, I assumed a value, δ = 0.8, for population effect size, but precision for planning doesn't require any consideration of the effect size. When discussing N and MoE of the Thomason studies I didn't refer to the values of $d_{unbiased}$, the effect size reported in Table 10.1. Our focus is on precision, indicated by MoE. We can weigh up MoE = 0.5 or 0.3, as illustrated in Figure 10.6, and consider how useful it would be to estimate the effect size, whatever it is, within ±0.50, or ±0.30, or more generally ±(target MoE). Our focus is on the ±, the precision, the maximum likely error of estimation. That's estimation thinking, and what a precision approach to planning encourages.

Even so, it's often useful to have at least a rough idea of the effect size we might expect, especially if we'd like our study to give a CI that's some distance from zero, to give strong evidence the effect size is nonzero. If that's an aim, then a reasonable strategy is to aim for target MoE that's half the expected effect size, meaning we'd investigate target MoE = 0.4 if the expected effect size is 0.8 as in Figure 10.6. In practice, that strategy may require unrealistically large N and we may be forced to consider larger target MoE.

Consider again a replication to investigate the Damisch results in Figure 10.1. So far I've referred to MoE of the individual studies and of the meta-analysis

For precision for planning, there's no need to consider the effect size, although doing so can often be helpful: Consider target MoE of half the expected effect size.

result. Now consider the effect sizes: All studies found $d_{unbiased}$ around 0.7 to 0.9, and the meta-analysis result was 0.82, with MoE = 0.29. If the true effect is much smaller, a replication study is likely to give an estimate closer to zero, in which case MoE even as large as around 0.4 might suggest a disagreement with the Damisch results.

10.21 Suppose meta-analysis of the Damisch results estimated an effect of 0.4 instead of 0.82, again with MoE = 0.29. Would you recommend using a smaller target MoE? Explain.

In summary, to use precision for planning we need to choose

1. a design,
2. target MoE, and,
3. in the paired case only, a value for ρ.

Then ESCI can tell us the values of *N* needed to achieve target MoE on average, and with assurance. We could consider different designs as well as various values of target MoE (and perhaps ρ), to get a good understanding of our options. Then we can weigh up costs and benefits and choose a design and *N*. Making such choices must remain a matter for judgment. It can't be reduced to a formula or a few bullet points, and must, of course, take into account the practicalities of available time, resources, and participants.

Often, unfortunately, precision for planning suggests that a disappointingly large *N* is needed. If so, we might increase target MoE, or consider other designs—perhaps paired? Or we might seek other researchers interested in running similar studies, so we could combine results using meta-analysis. We might even have to conclude that we don't have the resources to conduct a useful study, and need to revise our research plans totally. In any case, precision for planning provides useful guidance in advance of conducting research.

Finally, I'll mention a great strength of precision for planning, which is that there is good continuity from the planning stage through to analysis and interpretation, and perhaps further to replications and meta-analysis. At every stage we think of estimation—of estimating the parameter of interest. Before the study we consider what precision of MoE = 0.3, for example, means in the research context. After running the study, we consider what the MoE calculated from our data (maybe around 0.2–0.4?) tells us about the uncertainty in our results. In advance, when planning, we might consider the importance of likely values of Cohen's *d* and, during interpretation, we do exactly the same for the *d* we obtained in the study. Precision for planning keeps our focus on effect sizes and estimation at every stage of research.

> *Precision for planning keeps the focus on effect sizes and estimation at every stage, from planning through to interpretation of results and beyond.*

? Quiz 10.2

1. Precision for planning requires choice of target _____, which is expressed in units of _____.

2. To aim for a CI half as long, expect required *N* to be about _____ as large.
3. Assurance of 99% means that
   a. target MoE refers to a 99% CI.
   b. the population correlation is .99.
   c. on average, 99% of studies will have MoE greater than target MoE.
   d. 99% of studies will have MoE no greater than target MoE.

4. For independent groups, precision for planning analysis indicates that $N = 32$ will give MoE of 0.50 on average. For assurance of 99%, required N will be smaller / larger. Reduce target MoE and required N will be smaller / larger.
5. For a paired design, increase ρ and required N will decrease / increase. Increase target MoE and required N will decrease / increase.
6. For a paired design, required N is strongly influenced by _____ and also by _____, which has symbol _____.

PLANNING USING STATISTICAL POWER

This second approach to choosing N is based on NHST. It asks, "What N is likely to give a sufficiently small p value that we can reject H_0, assuming there is an effect of a particular size?" We need the concept of *statistical power*, and to discuss power we need the following NHST concepts that we discussed back in Chapter 6:

▨ Type I error rate, α, often .05, which is the criterion for rejection: Reject H_0 if $p < \alpha$. Rejecting H_0 when it is true is a Type I error, a false alarm.
▨ Strict NHST, which requires statement of α in advance—which here means before any power calculation.
▨ The alternative hypothesis (H_1), which states that there is an effect. When we reject H_0, we decide in favor of H_1.
▨ Type II error, which is failing to reject H_0 when H_1 is true. We miss a true effect.
▨ Type II error rate, β, which is the probability of making a Type II error.

Recall also the courtroom analogy to NHST decision making and Table 6.1, which illustrated the four possibilities for NHST.

Statistical Power

Informally, statistical power is the chance our experiment will find an effect of a particular size, IF it exists. It's the chance our replication will find a statistically significant effect IF there really is a lucky golf ball effect of size, for example, 0.82. More formally, power is the probability we'll reject H_0, for a stated α, when H_1 is true. For power, focus on the bottom right cell in Table 6.1, which is labeled "Correctly reject H_0. We found the effect!"

> **Statistical power** is the probability that a study will find $p < \alpha$ IF an effect of a stated size exists. It's the probability of rejecting H_0 when H_1 is true.

To calculate power, H_1 must state a specific value, for example $H_1: \delta = 0.82$. I'll refer to the δ specified in H_1 as the *target effect size*, because I'm supposing the study we're planning is targeting such an effect. We're asking about the probability it will find an effect of that size, IF it exists.

◄ *Power* is the probability of rejecting H_0 IF the *target effect size*, δ, is true.

> **Target effect size** is the value of δ specified by H_1. It's the population effect size for which we calculate statistical power.

10.22 Explain in your own words the courtroom equivalent of statistical power.

10.23 a. Consider your intuitions about N. Other things being the same, would larger N give higher or lower power? Explain.

b. Consider your intuitions about target effect size: Would a larger target effect size be easier or harder to find? Would it give higher or lower power? Explain.

▶──────────
Power = $(1 - \beta)$.
──────────

The Type II error rate, β, is the probability we won't reject H_0 IF an effect of the stated size exists. Focus on the top right cell in Table 6.1. Compare with the definition of power to see that power = $(1 - \beta)$. IF there really is an effect, β tells us the glass-half-empty part of the story—the risk we won't find the effect. Power tells us the glass-half-full part by telling us the probability we'll obtain sufficiently small p to be able to reject H_0 and announce the effect.

Power depends on many aspects of a study, most notably

▨ the design, for example independent groups,
▨ chosen α, for example .05,
▨ target effect size, for example $\delta = 0.5$, and
▨ N, the size of each group.

When considering power, it's vital to keep *all* those relevant aspects of a study in mind.

Power for the Independent Groups Design

Figure 10.1 shows that meta-analysis of the six Damisch studies estimated the effect to be 0.82 [0.53, 1.11]. To plan a replication, we might want N to give sufficient power to find an effect of 0.82. Or we might focus on 0.53, the lower limit of the CI and, therefore, the smallest somewhat plausible effect, according to the Damisch results. To find values of power for a study with two independent groups we can use Figure 10.7.

Figure 10.7 gives power only for a small number of selected, illustrative values of α, target effect size δ, and N. In the upper panel, $\alpha = .05$, and in the lower, $\alpha = .01$. In each panel, an orange curve corresponds to a single value of target effect size δ, as marked. Each line shows power for N of 15, 20, 30, 40, 50, 60, 80, and 100. The upper circled point, for example, tells us that, with $\alpha = .05$, a study with two groups of size $N = 30$ would have power of .48 to find an effect of $\delta = 0.5$, which is traditionally labeled a medium-sized effect. Power = .48 means that a study with two groups of 30 has only about a coin toss chance (i.e., 50% chance) of finding statistical significance at the .05 level, if there is a medium-sized effect.

▶──────────
Power is often low in published research. Aim for high power.
──────────

Surely researchers wouldn't conduct such low-power studies? However, analyses of published research have found that in many research fields the average power to find a medium-sized effect is only around .50. Around half of such studies would, by chance, fail to find statistical significance even when there is a medium-sized effect, so are thus unlikely to be published. That's indeed wasteful. Jacob Cohen, the great statistical reformer, explained that power is vitally important, and exhorted researchers to consider power and use larger N, or find other ways to increase the power of their studies. Over the years, researchers have become more aware of power, but, even so, the power of much research to find medium-sized effects is often low. A likely reason for this unfortunate state of affairs is that researchers follow NHST custom and focus on α and Type I errors, while paying relatively little attention to β and Type II errors.

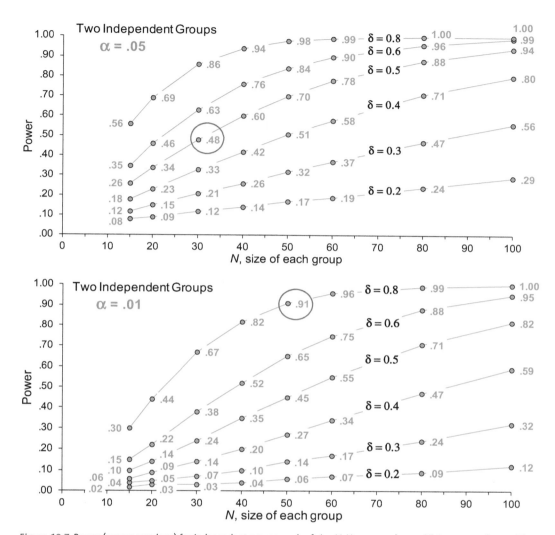

Figure 10.7. Power (orange numbers) for independent groups, each of size N. Upper panel: α = .05. Lower panel: α = .01. Each orange line corresponds to a single value of target effect size δ, as marked.

10.24 Explain what the value of .91 for the lower circled point in Figure 10.7 means.

10.25 Exercise 10.23 asked about your intuitions about how power changes if you change N.

    a. Use Figure 10.7 to check your answer—read to the right along an orange line to see the effect of increasing N.

    b. Check your answer to the question about changing target effect size— read up a column of power values to see the effect of increasing δ.

10.26 One convention is that power of .8 is adequate. Adopting this convention, find about what N you need to find a medium effect (δ = 0.5), using α = .05. Do the same using α = .01.

If power is .80, there's a 20% risk of missing an effect of the stated target size, because you don't obtain $p < \alpha$. Higher power is definitely preferable. Aim for .90 or even .95 if you can.

10.27 a. What N do you need to find a medium effect with power = .90? What N for power = .95? Use $\alpha = .05$.
   b. What about $\alpha = .01$?
   c. What about small effects ($\delta = 0.2$), for both those α values?

10.28 With two groups of $N = 20$, and $\alpha = .05$, what's the power to find an effect of $\delta = 0.40$? What about $\delta = 0.50$, and $\delta = 0.60$? What do you conclude about the influence of target effect size on power?

10.29 Consider planning a replication of Damisch.

   a. About what N would you need to have a 90% chance of statistical significance at the .01 level if there is an effect of 0.82, the mean reported by the meta-analysis in Figure 10.1?
   b. What N would you need if there is an effect of 0.53, the lower limit of the CI reported by the meta-analysis in Figure 10.1?

10.30 You read a statement that a study used two groups of $N = 50$ and had power of .70. Do you have sufficient information to interpret? Explain.

Power for independent groups depends on α, target δ, and N. All must be stated for a value of power to make sense.

I've said that, for the independent groups design, power depends on α, target δ, and N. All must be considered. I hope you are building your intuitions about how each of those influences power. Now let's move on to the paired design.

Power for the Paired Design

For the paired design, in addition to α, target δ, and N, we need to consider ρ, the population correlation between the two measures, such as pretest and posttest. As with precision for planning, to select ρ we might consider previous research or use a value around the common values of .6 to .9. Figure 10.8 reports values of power for the paired design for $\alpha = .05$ and the same values of target δ, and N that appear in Figure 10.7. Figure 10.8 provides power for just two values of ρ, namely .60 and .80. Like Figure 10.7, it's intended to be illustrative of a few common situations rather than a comprehensive tool for finding power.

Compare the values in Figure 10.8 with those in Figure 10.7, for the same α, target δ, and N. Aim to build your intuitions about how power varies with those aspects of a study, and also with ρ, the population correlation. Here are a few things you could try:

10.31 Flip back to Figure 10.7.

   a. For two groups with $N = 30$ and a medium effect, what's power?
   b. For a single group and the paired design with $N = 30$ and $\rho = .60$, what's power?
   c. What about $\rho = .80$?

10.32 In Figure 10.8, compare values for $\rho = .60$ and $\rho = .80$. What do you conclude?

10.33 Suppose you are planning a replication of the critical thinking studies reported in Table 10.1. Focus on the effect sizes found in the Thomason studies, rather than the MoE values.

   a. If there is an effect of $\delta = 0.40$, and you assume $\rho = .60$, what N might you choose?
   b. What if you assume $\rho = .80$?
   c. Explore some further cases. What might you recommend?

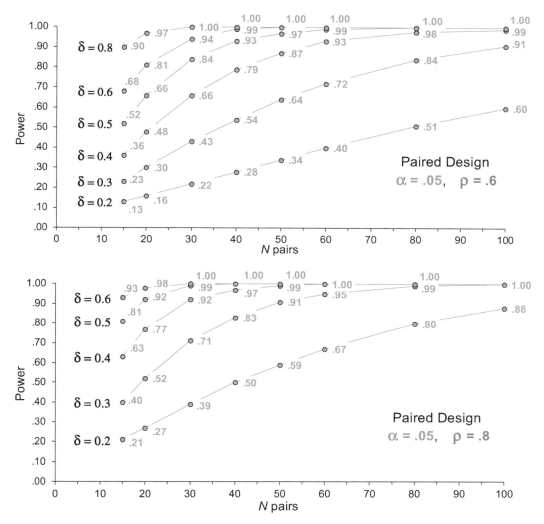

Figure 10.8. Power for the paired design, with a single group of size *N*, and α = .05. Upper panel: population correlation, ρ = .6. Lower panel: ρ = .8. Each orange line corresponds to a single value of population effect size δ, as marked. In the lower panel, no line is shown for δ = .8 because, for that effect size, power = 1.0 for all *N* of 15 or more.

A Strategy for Using Power for Planning

Do you feel you are developing intuitions about power for the two designs we've considered? I suggest that the most important intuitions are these:

- Target δ is very influential. Larger δ gives higher power, sometimes dramatically higher.
- Type I error rate α is very influential: Lower α means it's harder to reject H_0, so more misses (Type II errors) and lower power.
- Group size *N* is influential. Larger *N* gives higher power.
- For the paired design, ρ is very influential. Larger ρ gives higher power. Put another way, larger ρ requires smaller *N* for the same power.
- Once again the paired design is appealing, when it's applicable—here because it can give high power.

Target δ and α strongly influence power, as does ρ for the paired design. Changes in *N* also often give large changes in power.

Table 10.2 Effect Size and Post Hoc Power for the First Three Simulated Replications in Figure 7.14

Result	Effect size, $d_{unbiased}$	Post hoc power
1	0.37	.30
2	1.01	.97
3	0.25	.16

For power calculations, how should we choose target effect size δ? We should consider values that are of interest in the research context. We might be guided by past research, or by what we guess—or hope—is the true value. We might use Cohen's small-medium-large conventions. Usually it's best to explore a few values, to get a feel for the trade-offs among N, target δ, (and, for the paired design, ρ,) and power, all for our chosen α. Exploring those trade-offs should inform choice of N, which, as usual, is a matter for judgment. If your focus is NHST, a central part of planning should be to explore all those trade-offs to help you select your research strategy, especially your design and N.

Post Hoc Power

I need to close this section on power with a caution. Power is most valuable when used as part of planning, but it's possible to calculate power after conducting a study and, further, to use the observed value of d (or $d_{unbiased}$) as the target δ. Power calculated that way is called *post hoc power*, or *observed power*.

> **Post hoc power**, also called **observed power**, is power calculated after running the study, using the obtained effect size as target δ.

▶ Post hoc, or observed, power is useless, perhaps misleading. Never use it.

However, there's a major problem. Results of replications typically bounce around considerably. Well, post hoc power values bounce similarly. Recall Figure 7.14, which showed the dance of the CIs for 25 simulated replications of a study. Table 10.2 reports the first three replications at the top in Figure 7.14, with post hoc power for each. The values vary enormously—they can take virtually any value across the range from 0 to 1. Post hoc power tells us little or nothing beyond the effect size observed in the study. It's true that a study with the design and N of that shown in Figure 7.14 has power of .16 to find $\delta = 0.25$ and also power of .97 to find $\delta = 1.01$. However, that's uninformative and perhaps misleading, because for planning we want to know the power such a study has to find δ that, beforehand, we're interested in, or that previous research suggests is likely.

▶ Beware software that gives power without asking for a meaningful value for target δ.

In other words, post hoc power values don't tell us something fundamental about our study, but mainly merely reflect the result our study gave. My conclusion is that post hoc power is useless. Avoid post hoc power—simply never use it. I mention this because, unfortunately, some software packages report it. A software package should ask you to specify the target δ you regard as meaningful before it calculates and reports power. If it doesn't, you are probably seeing post hoc power. Interpret any such value with great care or, better, ignore it.

COMPARING POWER AND PRECISION FOR PLANNING

Good research requires good planning. I've discussed two approaches to a vital part of planning: the choice of N. There are important similarities, and also important differences. Here's a comparison:

	Precision for planning	Power for planning
The general aim	Choose N, considering costs and benefits	Same
The measure	Cohen's d (or $d_{unbiased}$), assumed to be in units of population SD	Same
The setting	Estimation of effect size	NHST, statistical significance
The focus	MoE, precision of result Small MoE is good	Power, which is the probability that $p < \alpha$, IF target δ is true— high power is good.
The specific aim	(a) Find N that gives target MoE, on average (b) Find N that gives target MoE, with assurance	Find N to give chosen power, for stated α and target δ (and ρ for paired design)
Build intuitions about how...	N varies with target MoE (and ρ for paired), on average, and with assurance	Power varies with α, target δ, and N (and ρ for paired)
One general lesson	Required N is often impractically and disappointingly large	Same

Precision or Power: Which Should We Use?

Techniques for calculating power are relatively well developed. Cohen (1988) is very helpful, and the G*Power software (tiny.cc/gpower3) is free, and can calculate power for many different measures and designs, way beyond Figures 10.7 and 10.8. Power is not often mentioned in published articles, but many researchers include a power calculation as part of applications for grant funding or ethics approval, to justify the proposed design and numbers of participants.

In contrast, precision for planning is less well developed, although techniques and software are advancing quickly. It has excellent potential and I expect it to become much more widely used, including for justifying funding and ethics applications. As I mentioned earlier, effect sizes and MoE are the focus, from planning through to interpretation of a study. This focus continues as we think of replications, and meta-analysis to integrate results over studies. When planning we need to specify target MoE, and after running the study we calculate MoE and can compare with the target, to build our understanding and contribute to the planning of further studies.

> Precision for planning is less well known than power, but it keeps the focus on estimation and has great potential.

Power, on the other hand, applies primarily at the planning stage. Later, when interpreting the study, focus shifts to p values and statistical significance. After analyzing the data we either obtain $p < \alpha$ or we don't, and can say little about the appropriateness of the earlier power calculation. Post hoc power doesn't help and may mislead. A major drawback of power is its dichotomous nature. Did you notice the dichotomous language in the power section of this chapter? In earlier chapters I've mainly spoken of effect sizes, estimates, CIs, and uncertainty, but for power I needed to talk of dichotomies, because its definition focuses on a dichotomous decision based on whether $p < \alpha$ or $p \geq \alpha$. In addition, to calculate power we need H_1 that states an exact value, so the two hypotheses, H_0 and H_1, assume a dichotomous world in which the effect is, for example, either 0 or 0.80. In most cases that's highly unrealistic, because the effect can take any of a range of values. Recall the first red flag:

> Power is defined in dichotomous terms, and requires assumption of dichotomous hypotheses, H_0 and H_1, which both state exact values.

Beware dichotomous conclusions, which may give a false sense of certainty. Prefer estimation thinking.

Red Flag 1

Any researcher who uses NHST needs to understand and consider power, but precision for planning has distinct advantages.

It's time for take-home messages. You'll recall Open Science, and pilot testing, preregistration, and badges. Then the two main sections, on precision for planning and statistical power. Looking back to my comparison of the two, just above, may help you write your take-home messages. Perhaps as you ponder a dichotomous choice between healthy apple and indulgent chocolate—or decide how much to have of your favorite.

 Quiz 10.3

1. Power is the probability of rejecting / not rejecting / accepting H_0 when the null / alternative hypothesis is true. It can take values between $-1 / 0 / .5$ and $0 / .5 / 1$.
2. If $\beta = .10$, power = _____ and the Type II error rate is _____.
3. To calculate power, we need an exact value of target _____, which is chosen and stated in advance / by convention taken to be 0.80, and is the size of effect / N we are interested in.
4. In each case, state whether power increases or decreases if everything remains the same except that you
   a. increase N.
   b. increase α.
   c. increase target δ.
   d. increase ρ in a paired design.
   e. observe a larger p value. (Hey, does this make sense?)
5. Observed power is calculated before / after running the study. For target δ the calculation uses chosen δ / obtained d. Any value of observed power is most likely useful / useless.
6. A disadvantage of power is that
   a. it considers only the null hypothesis and a single exact size of effect.
   b. it is based on dichotomous decision making.
   c. it is usually of little use after a study has been completed.
   d. All of the above.

10.34 An easy way to increase power is to select a different α. What change in α increases power? Is this a good way to increase power? Explain.

10.35 Your friend excitedly points to the screen that displays their data analysis and says that their study had power of .96. What question do you ask? Why might you be less excited?

10.36 Your ethics review board has traditionally required a power analysis as part of any application for approval of empirical studies, to justify the proposed N. You would prefer to submit a precision for planning analysis instead. Briefly explain to the board why you think they should agree to consider your proposal.

10.37 Swap lists of take-home messages with a friend, then revise your list if you wish.

Reporting Your Work

As soon as you begin thinking about a research project you can start developing a preregistration document. In fact, drafting and revising a preregistration document isn't just a good Open Science practice; it's also an excellent way of helping you develop and refine your research ideas.

The APA *Publication Manual* (APA, 2010) does not (yet) provide specific guidance on preregistration documents, but the OSF provides a very useful template for original projects plus a great preregistration checklist for direct replications (Brandt et al., 2014). These templates can be completed online (osf.io/prereg) or within your favorite word processor (osf.io/jea94). To access the first of those sites, you need to first register with OSF and login. At osf.io this is quick, easy, and free.

The OSF template for preregistering original projects includes sections for your sampling plan, measures, design, and analysis plan. Each section has prompts to help you think through key issues. For example, the design section prompts researchers conducting experiments to explain how random assignment will be conducted (an important issue!). Once you feel confident in your research plan, you simply upload the completed document to the Open Science Framework to create a permanent and citable registration of your research plan. If your goal is to publish in a journal with preregistered review (described in Chapter 16), this would be the time to submit your research plan to the journal.

Once you have completed your research, it is critical to:

- develop a research report that tells the full story of the project;
- make this report publicly available either through peer-reviewed publication or by posting the manuscript to a scientific repository like the OSF; and
- share, if possible, the materials and data in a scientific repository like the OSF.

Throughout the manuscript, be sure to mention the Open Science practices you have adopted. In particular, many journals now require specific details on sample size. Specifically, you should include a "Sampling plan" section within your method that reports:

- what sample size target you set;
- the rationale for this sample size target; and
- the "stopping rule" you used (how you determined when to end the study).

In developing and reporting a sample size target, the planning for precision approach is best, but you can supplement this with comments on statistical power.

Next are two examples of sampling plans.

> Preregister your measures, sampling plan, and analysis plan. The Open Science Framework provides excellent templates.

A Plan Based on a Target MoE

We set a sample size target of 73 to 99 participants. This was based on a target margin of error of 0.25, which was selected based on the effect sizes of 0.34 to 0.64 in previous studies (insert a reference here). In these previous studies, the pretest to posttest correlations were always >.60. For this correlation, a sample size of 73 provides, on average, the desired margin of error, and a sample size of 99 provides the desired margin of error with 99% assurance. These calculations were made using the ESCI software (Cumming, 2016). For a stopping rule, we decided to end advertising for the study once the sample size minimum was met, finishing then only the remaining appointments. Our sample size target and stopping rule were preregistered, with details available at <link to OSF preregistered plan>.

A Plan Based on Previous Sample Sizes

For this direct replication, we set a sample size goal of 64 participants per group. This was based on the original sample size of 25 participants/group and Simonsohn's recommendation (2015) to conduct replications with 2.5 times the original sample size. We expect, based on this sample target, a margin of error of roughly 0.35. In addition, this target provides power of 0.98 to detect the original effect size ($d = 0.7$). Online participant recruitment was set to close when the target sample size was obtained.

 Take-Home Messages

Open Science

- Open Science is our best strategy for countering the three Ioannidis problems of selective publication, questionable research practices and *p*-hacking, and lack of replication.

- The Center for Open Science and the Open Science Framework encourage researchers to preregister research plans, including data analysis plans, and to make all materials and data openly available, wherever possible. Badges recognize some desirable Open Science practices.

Precision for Planning

- *Target MoE*, expressed in units of population SD, is the precision we would like the planned study to achieve. Use judgment to select target MoE, in the light of past similar research if possible. Perhaps consider several values for target MoE.

- MoE varies because of sampling variability, but precision for planning tells us the *N* that will, on average, give MoE no greater than target MoE. Use **Precision two** for an independent groups study, and **Precision paired** for a paired study.

- Using *assurance* of 99%, precision for planning tells us the *N* that will give MoE no greater than target MoE on 99% of occasions. Use *N* that gives target MoE on average, and the larger *N* that gives that MoE with assurance, to guide choice of *N* for a planned study.

- For the paired design, the values of *N* are greatly influenced by ρ, the population correlation between the two measures: for a given target MoE, higher ρ requires smaller *N* (so for once, you can live with a different birthday present). Often in practice ρ is roughly .60 to .90.

Power for Planning

- Power is the probability a study will find an effect of a particular size, IF it exists.

- To calculate power, the alternative hypothesis must state an exact *target* δ, for example $H_1: \delta = 0.80$. Power is the probability that, IF the effect is exactly 0.80, the study will give $p < \alpha$ so H_0 is rejected. Power is $(1 - \beta)$.

- Power depends on the design, α, *N*, and target δ. For the paired design it also depends on ρ. Figures 10.7 and 10.8 provide illustrative values of power.

- Aim for high power, .90 or higher if possible. Explore how power varies for selected values of target δ (and ρ in the paired case) and use judgment to choose *N*.

- If using NHST, use power calculations to help plan a study. *Post hoc*, or *observed*, power is calculated using the obtained effect size and should *not* be used.

Planning, Precision, and Power

- Planning, starting with pilot testing, is important, to maximize research efficiency and reassure us that a study is likely to give worthwhile results. Planning should, where possible, lead to preregistration.

- Power is based on dichotomous NHST decision making. Precision for planning has the advantage that it emphasizes estimation, and keeps the focus on effect sizes and precision at every stage from planning through interpretation to replication and meta-analysis.

End-of-Chapter Exercises

1) Navigate to the Open Science Framework (osf.io) and use the search and browse features to find and review

   a. a preregistered analysis plan (try searching for "analysis plan").

   b. a preregistered sample size target (try searching for "sample plan" or "a priori sample").

   c. a project that includes the materials needed for replication (sign in, click Browse, select "New Projects", and explore; note four links at left).

   d. a project that includes original data.

2) Look back to end-of-chapter Exercise 4 in Chapter 7 about feelings of cleanliness and moral judgment. Schnall et al. (2008) used independent groups each with $N = 20$ and found a (Clean – Neutral) difference of $d_{unbiased} = -0.59$, 95% CI $[-1.23, 0.04]$.

   a. Approximately, what was MoE in population SD units? Consult **Precision two** and consider N. Is that MoE reasonable? Explain.

   b. You plan a replication and decide to aim for MoE of 0.3. What N would you recommend? Explain.

   c. The replication by Johnson, Cheung, and Donnellan (2014) found $d_{unbiased} = -0.01$. The MoE could not be calculated by ESCI, because $df > 200$, but it was around 0.3. Is this about what you would expect, given that Johnson et al. used $N_1 = 102$ and $N_2 = 106$? Explain.

   d. If you had decided to use two groups of $N = 150$, about what MoE would you expect? Explain.

3) In a two-groups study, target $\delta = 0.40$ and $N = 78$.

   a. With $\alpha = .05$, what's the power?

   b. If the population ES is 0.40 and only statistically significant results are published, what percentage of studies remains in the file drawer?

4) Look back at Exercise 2 above, about moral judgment, and the result that $d_{unbiased} = -0.59$, $[-1.23, 0.04]$.

   a. Suppose you plan a replication and want to have power of at least .9, using $\alpha = .05$. Choosing target $\delta = 0.6$, what N would you need?

   b. You decide to use $\alpha = .01$ instead. Now what N would you need?

   c. You find you can obtain samples with $N = 100$. Using $\delta = 0.6$, what is the power, for each of those values of α?

   d. Using $\alpha = .05$, what power did the replication by Johnson et al. have, to find $\delta = 0.3$, an effect about half as large as that found in the original study?

5) Researchers studying birds can identify individuals by fitting several colored leg bands. With bees you can apply tiny colored dots of paint to the backs of individuals. Frogs, however, are more difficult to mark. For decades, standard practice has been to clip a small amount from the end of one or more toes. The pattern of clipping identifies the individual. The method has been used successfully in many studies, but a worry remains: Might clipping

reduce a frog's chance of survival, and more so if more toes are clipped? That would not only bias the research, but perhaps threaten the species, when one aim of research is to help ensure survival of the species. Parris and McCarthy (2001), two Melbourne colleagues, reviewed the four then-available articles that reported studies of the effect of toe clipping. The articles reached conflicting conclusions, with several cases of "no statistically significant effect" being interpreted as evidence that toe clipping does not have bad consequences.

a. Which red flag springs to mind? Why?

b. Parris and McCarthy estimated the power of the studies to find a 40% decrease in survival, which would be a very large and biologically important effect. For the three studies for which they could estimate power, they estimated values from .2 to .6. Explain what these values mean.

c. Suppose the original researchers had reported an effect size (estimated percentage decrease in survival) and CI. Would you expect the CI to be short or long? Would you expect it to extend to include 0% decrease? Explain.

d. How could those studies have been improved? How could planning have helped?

e. Open Fiona Fidler's PhD thesis, at tiny.cc/fionasphd. Read the short Section 3.5 (pp. 68–71), which is a brief account of the "toe clipping wars". What main point were Parris and McCarthy trying to make? What opposition did they encounter? What is your conclusion?

6) Your friend excitedly points to her data analysis output, which states that power = .94. What do you ask? What do you explain?

7) State at least two reasons why your ethics review board requires a planning analysis, based on either power or precision, as part of every proposal for research with human participants. Explain.

8) Explain

a. at least one reason for preferring power over precision for planning.

b. at least two reasons for preferring precision over power for planning.

? Answers to Quizzes

Quiz 10.1

1) Selective publication, the $p < .05$ imperative (or questionable research practices, or p-hacking), lack of replication; 2) yes, yes, no, no, yes; 3) a; 4) d; 5) estimation, NHST; 6) open data, open materials, preregistration.

Quiz 10.2

1) MoE, population SD; 2) four times; 3) d; 4) larger, larger; 5) decrease, decrease; 6) target MoE, population correlation, ρ.

Quiz 10.3

1) rejecting, alternative, 0, 1; 2) .90, .10; 3) population effect size (δ), chosen and stated in advance, size of effect; 4) increases, increases, increases, increases, doesn't make sense; 5) after, obtained d, useless; 6) d.

Answers to In-Chapter Exercises

10.1 We need to know about all relevant studies that have been carried out to a reasonable standard, so researchers must make all such studies available. Fully detailed reporting of studies is required and, where possible, full data. Encourage replication. "Do we have the full story?"

10.2 a. Most useful is preregistration, meaning registration of a full plan for a study, including data analysis plan, in advance of running the study.

10.3 b. Useful and offered: Help using OSF, help understanding and interpreting statistical analyses, help adopting new statistical techniques. Possibly useful but not offered: Carry out statistical analyses, complete student assignments.

10.4 Badges were created to acknowledge adoption of particular Open Science practices in a journal article or other publication.

10.6 23, 87, reasonably well, because $87 \div 4$ is close to 23.

10.7 a. Around 0.72, on average; b. Mean MoE for the six Damisch studies is 0.74, which is very close to the 0.72 expected on average. Sampling variability could easily have given bigger disagreement.

10.8 0.30, close to the meta-analysis MoE of 0.29; 87 for MoE of 0.30 on average.

10.9 a, b. Around 0.35, on average, very close to the 0.36 observed.

10.11 194, 770.

10.12 a. 0.35, 0.3 to 0.4; b. The gray curve tells us that $N = 64$ gives MoE of 0.35 on average, which agrees with the center of the MoE curve, with $N = 65$, appearing at about 0.35.

10.13 a. Smaller, to the left; b. Left, larger.

10.14 108.

10.15 Less, narrower.

10.16 a. Larger, left; b. Narrower, because MoE varies less when N is larger; c. For larger target MoE, N is smaller and the curve wider. (Note that the curve in Figure 10.2 for $N = 50$ is wider than that in Figure 10.3 for $N = 65$.)

10.17 a, b. N changes dramatically. For example, for target MoE = 0.20 on average, and $\rho = .60, .80, .90$, we require, respectively, N of 80, 41, 22.

10.18 a. 37, 54; b. Yes, because 0.32 is close to 0.30.

10.19 61 (on average), 84 (assurance).

10.20 $N = 41$ for target MoE = 0.20, on average, and $N = 71$ for 0.15. Eyeball between these two and expect MoE around 0.17 for $N = 58$.

10.21 If the effect is smaller we probably want to estimate it with greater precision, meaning we should choose smaller target MoE. One reason is to help us distinguish it from zero.

10.22 Power is the probability of landing in the bottom right cell, if H_1 is true. That's the probability of deciding guilty when the accused is guilty.

10.23 a. For a given non-zero population ES, larger N is likely to give a smaller p value, and so is more likely to reject, which means power is higher; b. A larger effect should be easier to find. For a given design of study and N, a larger true effect size would be more likely to give a small p value, so more likely to reject H_0, so power would be higher.

10.24 For two independent groups of size 50, using $\alpha = .01$, the power is .91 to find an effect of size $\delta = .80$.

10.25 a, b. Power increases left to right across any line (increasing N) and up any column (increasing δ).

10.26 Using $\alpha = .05$, for $N = 60$, power is .78 and for $N = 80$, power is .88, so N of about 64 in each group gives power of .80. Using $\alpha = .01$, an N of about 96 gives power of .80.

10.27 a. About 86, about 103; b. For $\alpha = .01$, more than 100, maybe roughly 110 and 120; c. For $\delta = 0.2$, even using $\alpha = .05$, N would need to be much more than 100; for $\alpha = .01$, even larger.

10.28 .23, .34, .46; target effect size can have a very large influence on power.

10.29 a. About 50 or a little less; b. More than 100, maybe around 115.

10.30 If $\alpha = .05$ then $\delta = 0.50$ gives power of .70, but with $\alpha = .01$, then δ of around 0.65 is needed for power of .70. Other combinations of α and δ are possible. We can suggest options, but need more information for an unambiguous interpretation.

10.31 Using $\alpha = .05$: a. .48, b. .84, c. .99. Using $\alpha = .01$: a. .24, b. .62, c. .93.

10.32 Power is substantially more for $\rho = .80$ than $\rho = .60$, until the ceiling of power = 1.00 is reached. The population correlation between the measures in the paired design influences power greatly.

10.33 a. Using $\alpha = .05$, $N = 60$ gives power of .93 when $\rho = .60$; b. $N = 40$ gives power of .97 when $\rho = .80$; c. The Thomason studies suggest ρ may be around .70, between the values of .60 and .80 shown in Figure 10.8. Therefore I suggest using N around 50, which could give power of around .95, using $\alpha = .05$. I would prefer to use $\alpha = .01$, which for similar power would require higher N.

10.34 Other things remaining the same, higher α (e.g., .05 rather than .01) gives higher power, but at the expense of a higher Type I error rate, so we are hardly better off. Not a good strategy for increasing power.

10.35 You ask what δ, what target ES, was used in the power calculation. If your friend doesn't know, or says it used d obtained in the study, explain about post hoc power, and advise your friend that the high value most likely means only that they obtained a large d. Before being excited about high power, your friend should calculate power using a chosen value of δ that's of research interest in the context.

10.36 You could say that you intend to use estimation rather than NHST to analyze the data, and that a precision for planning analysis is the corresponding way to justify choice of N. You could also comment about the advantages of estimation and the disadvantages of the dichotomous decision making that a power analysis assumes.

11
Correlation

How satisfied are you with your body? Are you concerned that advertisers and the media bombard us all with images of idealized but unrealistic bodies? Are there bad consequences for some young people? Researchers investigating such questions often study the relations between variables, starting with the *correlation* between two variables. Correlation is our topic in this chapter, and Figure 11.1 is a scatterplot, a revealing picture of the correlation between Body Satisfaction (*X*) and Well-being (*Y*) for a group of 106 college students. Each point represents one student, and is positioned to reflect that person's *X* and *Y* scores.

I'll say more about the measures in a moment, but for now simply notice that there's lots of scatter, and, overall, higher *Y* scores tend to go with higher *X* scores. Our measure of that tendency is $r = .47$, where r is a units-free measure of correlation that can take any value from −1 through 0 to 1. The r of .47 here indicates a moderately strong tendency for higher values of body satisfaction to be associated with higher well-being scores.

What do you think the scatter of points might be telling us?

Do you think greater body satisfaction tends to make people feel generally good?

Can you think of any other reason for the positive correlation?

 Forgive me if once again I start the chapter with this encouragement to pause, reflect, and discuss.

Correlation helps us investigate numerous intriguing issues, and often enables meta-analysis. Correlation, in particular r, is one of the most important and widely used effect size measures in many disciplines. In addition, r leads to further highly useful statistical techniques, including regression, which we'll see in Chapter 12. So there are good reasons to know about r. Here's the agenda:

- The scatterplot, a revealing picture of correlation
- Calculating r
- The confidence interval on r
- Correlation and possible causation
- Interpreting values of r
- Using r for meta-analysis

The Body Satisfaction variable in Figure 11.1 is the mean rating of how satisfied a person is (from 1 = *very dissatisfied* to 5 = *very satisfied*) with various aspects of their body (e.g., satisfaction with one's face, one's muscle tone, one's weight...). It's a subscale of the Multidimensional Body Self-Relations Questionnaire (MBSRQ, Cash, 2000). The Well-being variable is the mean rating of strength of agreement (from 1 = *strongly disagree* to 7 = *strongly agree*) with

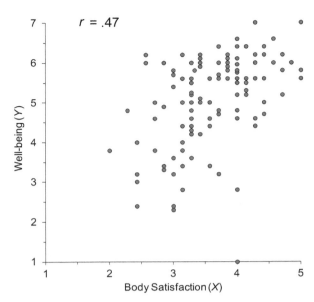

Figure 11.1. Scatterplot of Body Satisfaction (*X*) and Well-being (*Y*) scores for *N* = 106 college students.

a number of statements about a person's feeling of well-being (Diener, et al., 1985). For example, one item is "In most ways my life is close to ideal". In our data set, the two variables are correlated, *r* = .47, but with lots of scatter. One message of this chapter is that often there's considerable scatter, even when two variables show, overall, a fairly strong correlation. Note, for example, the one unhappy student, represented by the blue dot on the *X* axis, who had greater than average body satisfaction (*X* = 4), but minimum well-being (*Y* = 1).

▶
Correlation does not necessarily imply causation.

I asked what the scatter of points might be telling us. You probably immediately thought that high body satisfaction causes improved well-being: *X* causes *Y*. However, perhaps a general feeling of well-being causes us to feel generally satisfied, in particular with our body: Perhaps *Y* causes *X*? Or each could influence the other. There could easily be other variables involved as well: For example, perhaps good health tends to increase both well-being and body satisfaction. These are all speculations about *causes* between variables, but another important message of this chapter is that correlation—the association pictured in a scatterplot—may not say anything about causes. Correlation does not necessarily imply causation. Much more on that later.

▶
Correlation is driven by scatter. The focus is on spread within samples, not on means.

Before I say more about scatterplots, note a striking contrast with earlier chapters. So far in this book we have usually focused on the mean of a sample, and regarded the spread of points around that mean as a problem, a distraction. Here, however, we focus on that spread, rather than the means. We do this because correlation is driven by the scatter of data points away from their means. We're focusing on the *spread* of Well-being and Body Satisfaction scores; I haven't even reported means of those scores. Either spread or means can be important, depending on your perspective, but in this chapter and the next we're focusing on individuals and how they vary—we're focusing on difference, not sameness.

THE SCATTERPLOT, A REVEALING PICTURE OF CORRELATION

The key to correlation is the *scatterplot*, and another of the main messages of this chapter is that, for any (X, Y) relationship we care about, we need to see the scatterplot. Any single measure of correlation can capture only one aspect of such a relationship so, without the scatterplot, we may miss important things. There are other measures of correlation, but in this chapter we'll discuss the most widely used measure, Pearson's r, which can range from -1 through 0 to 1. Pearson's r measures the degree or strength of the *linear component* of an (X, Y) relationship, meaning the aspect of the relationship that can be represented by a straight line. We'll see many examples for which r does not tell the full story, and for which it's vital to see the scatterplot, perhaps in addition to calculating r. I'll come back to that idea shortly, but, first, let's consider some pictures to help build intuitions about r.

Figure 11.2 presents four scatterplots picturing different values of r. I'm following custom by labeling as X and Y the two variables, which I'm assuming have interval measurement. Each panel in the figure is a plot of $N = 50$ points, where each point is a pair of (X, Y) values. The first shows $r = .9$, which is close to the maximum of 1. The next two show lesser values of correlation, .6 and .3. On the right, X and Y are *uncorrelated* and so $r = 0$. A cloud of points as for $r = 0$, which roughly resembles a circular scatter, can be described as a shotgun blast. The cloud for $r = .3$ also looks rather like a shotgun blast. Do you think the scatter in Figure 11.1, for which $r = .47$, lies between the clouds for .6 and .3?

Figure 11.3 presents three further scatterplots. The left plot illustrates the maximum correlation, $r = 1.0$. In the center plot, Y *decreases* as X increases, so the correlation is negative: $r = -.6$. Does the plot for $-.6$ look to have roughly the same amount of scatter as the plot for .6 in Figure 11.2? That's what we'd expect. Now look back at the $r = .9$ plot in Figure 11.2. Do you feel an urge to eyeball a straight line that seems to fit, or represent the points? If so, you may be thinking of something like the plot on the right in Figure 11.3, which shows the same data with $r = .9$ as in Figure 11.2, but displays also the *regression line* of Y on X. That line tells us what Y value is most likely associated with some particular X value we might be interested in.

Regression, or more particularly *linear regression*, is our topic in Chapter 12. Correlation as we discuss it in this chapter and linear regression are closely related, so it's a useful instinct to think of a straight line that may represent, at least to some extent, the relation between X and Y. As I mentioned, it's

Pearson correlation, r, is a measure of the linear component of the relationship between two interval variables, X and Y. It takes values between -1 and 1, and is 0 if X and Y are uncorrelated.

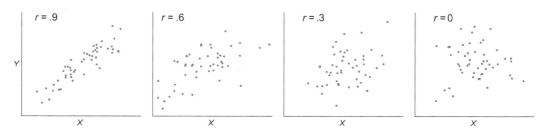

Figure 11.2. Scatterplots, each with $N = 50$, to illustrate the four indicated values of r, the Pearson correlation between X and Y.

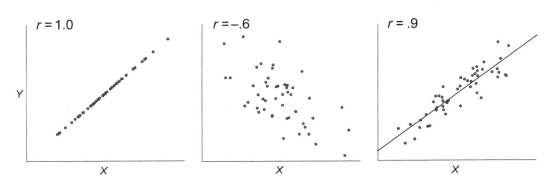

Figure 11.3. Three further scatterplots. On the left, r = 1.0, its maximum value. In the center the correlation is negative. The plot on the right is the same as that for r = .9 in Figure 11.2, but with the regression line of Y on X displayed.

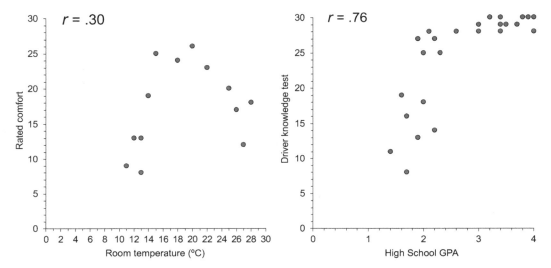

Figure 11.4. Scatterplots for two fictional data sets. On the left is an illustration of how rated room comfort (Y) might vary with room temperature (X). On the right is an illustration of how the score on an easy test—a driver knowledge test—(Y) might vary with High School GPA (X). Correlation values are shown, but in neither case does r represent the relationship well.

the strength of such a linear component in a relationship that's measured by Pearson's r. Incidentally, you may feel that the line for r = .9 in the figure should be a little steeper to fit the points well. That's a good observation, which we'll discuss in Chapter 12. For this chapter, just think informally of an eyeballed line that seems, approximately, to fit the points in a scatterplot.

Figure 11.4 shows two fictional but plausible cases in which there looks to be a relation between X and Y that's *nonlinear*—that can't be well represented by any straight line. On the left, there looks to be a *curvilinear* relation: Rated room comfort is greatest at a medium room temperature and decreases at both lower and higher temperatures. On the right, score on a driver knowledge test, required for obtaining a driver license, at first increases with High School GPA, then tops out at or near 30, the maximum possible score on the test. This pattern is typical of an easy test, and the topping out is called a *ceiling effect*: On a much harder test of driver knowledge, students with a high GPA may well do better, but the easy test denies them the opportunity. On an even harder test, students with GPA below 3 might score close to zero, and only for GPA

▶
A scatterplot may reveal that an (X, Y) relationship is *curvilinear*, or shows a *ceiling effect*.

above 3 would scores rise: That would be an example of a *floor effect*, because scores can't go below zero.

Correlation r can be calculated for any scatterplot of X and Y values, but it doesn't always make sense. On the left in Figure 11.4, $r = .30$ tells us little or nothing useful about the relationship, and may even mislead. Compare it with the $r = .30$ example in Figure 11.2. On the right, $r = .76$ does reflect the fact that, in general, Y increases as X increases, but it misses the topping out—the ceiling effect—which is probably one of the most important things to note. Yes, it's vital to see the scatterplot and to think carefully about what it tells us. The value of r may be highly informative, or irrelevant, or even misleading.

> For a full picture of an (X, Y) relationship, inspect and think about the scatterplot. The value of r may be informative, irrelevant, or misleading.

Estimating *r* From a Scatterplot

Leaving aside examples like those in Figure 11.4, it's often not difficult to make a rough estimate of r from a scatterplot. On the right in Figure 11.3, when $r = .9$ the points are quite tightly bunched to the line. In the center, with $r = -.6$ they are less tight to the imagined line, whereas on the left, for $r = 1.0$, they are on the line. For high correlations, tighter to the line means higher $|r|$, where $|r|$ is the absolute value of r, dropping the minus sign, if any. More specifically, for $|r|$ greater than around .7, degree of *tightness* to the imagined line helps when eyeballing r. Note that it's tightness that indicates r, not the slope of the line, which is easily changed just by changing the scale on the X or Y axis. Keep the Figure 11.3 examples in mind.

> For high correlation, degree of tightness to the imagined line indicates r, as in Figure 11.3.

A second eyeballing strategy is to use a cross through the means. In Figure 11.5, the second and fourth panels illustrate this idea. The vertical line is at the mean of the N values of X, and the horizontal line at the mean of the N values of Y. The second scatterplot labels the four quadrants defined by the cross: HH is high-high, meaning both X and Y are relatively high; HL is high-low, meaning X is high, Y is low, and so on. Now eyeball the numbers of points in the HH and LL quadrants, which I call the *matched* quadrants, and compare with the numbers in the LH and HL quadrants, the *mismatched* quadrants. The larger the proportion of matched quadrant points, compared with mismatched quadrant points, the larger the r. More mismatched than matched points indicates that r is negative. Actually, it's not just numbers of points that matter, but how far they are from the cross lines—we'll see that points far from the means have larger influence. However, looking at the whole pattern and noting relative numbers of points in the quadrants is often sufficient. Examine the first and third scatterplots: Eyeball the cross and estimate the r values. Look back to Figure 11.2 if that helps.

They are $r_1 = .6$ and $r_2 = .3$. Examine the second and fourth panels, which show the same scatters of points, with cross. Do the quadrants help? For high correlations I find that thinking of tightness to the line helps. For any correlation, I find that imagining the cross and thinking in terms of relative numbers of points in the quadrants helps.

> To eyeball r, consider the relative numbers of points in the quadrants defined by a cross through the X and Y means. More in HH, LL (matched quadrants) indicates r closer to 1; more in HL, LH (mismatched), r closer to -1.

Figure 11.6 shows the two examples of Figure 11.4, but with crosses through the means. Check that considering the relative numbers of points in the pairs of quadrants does lead to a rough estimate of r. Do the crosses give extra insight into the relationships? Perhaps on the right the cross makes the topping out more salient but, in general, the crosses strategy helps the eyeballing of r rather than the insightful reading of a scatterplot. One last comment: The aim of eyeballing is not numerical accuracy, but to get a rough idea of r to help appreciation of correlation and scatterplots.

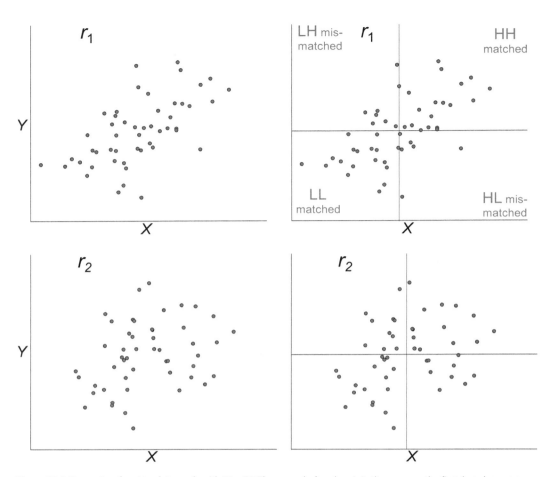

Figure 11.5. Two pairs of scatterplots, each with N = 50. The second of each pair is the same as the first, but shows a cross through the means of X and Y. Eyeball r for the first and third panels, then note how the cross can help. HH is high-high, LH is low-high, and so on. HH and LL are the matched quadrants, the other two the mismatched.

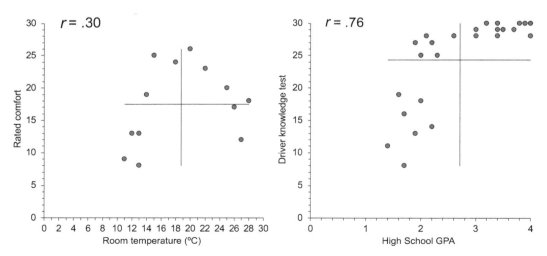

Figure 11.6. Same as Figure 11.4, but with a cross through the means of X and Y in each panel.

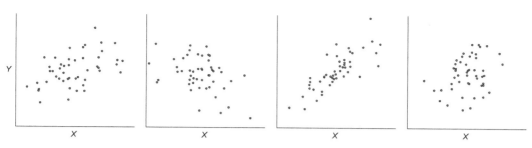

Figure 11.7. Four scatterplots, for eyeballing practice.

11.1 Eyeball *r* for each panel in Figure 11.7. In each case, compare the usefulness of tightness to the line and of quadrants.

11.2 Open the **See r** page of **ESCI intro chapters 10–16**. At red 1, choose your own *N*. At red 2, click the radio button on, and use the slider to set *r*, the correlation you wish to see. ESCI generates a data set with your chosen *N* and *r*, and displays its scatterplot.

    a. Choose, for example, *N* = 30 and *r* = .3. At red 5, click the first checkbox. Your screen should resemble Figure 11.8.

    b. Vary *N* and *r*, and see a new data set when you change a value. Explore. What does *r* = .1 look like? What about *r* = −1? *r* = .4? *r* = −.4?

11.3 At red 5 click to turn on the second checkbox, to see a cross through the means. Eyeball the relative numbers of points in the pairs of quadrants, for various values of *r*.

    a. Click to turn off the first checkbox. Practice using the cross to help with eyeballing *r*.

    b. Try negative as well as positive values. Try larger values of *N*.

11.4 a. Turn off the cross, then eyeball the cross and estimate *r*. Rough is OK.

    b. Make it a game: one person sets *r*, the other eyeballs *r* from the scatterplot. Try various values of *r*, and of *N*. Display the cross, then turn it off.

    c. Keeping *N* and *r* the same, click the button at red 4 to see new examples. Note the variation in scatterplot appearance.

11.5 Eyeball *r* for each of the four scatterplots in Figure 11.9.

All four scatterplots in Figure 11.9 have *r* = .4, illustrating how scatterplot appearance can vary, even for a single value of *r*. Eyeballing is challenging, but as I mentioned we're aiming for intuitions, not precise numbers. Refer back to Figures 11.2, 11.3, and 11.5 if that helps. Now let's use an example we met in Chapter 8 to calculate *r*.

CALCULATING *r*

Thomason 1 is a small critical thinking study with *N* = 12 and a paired pretest–posttest design. It's a great example of how correlation can be vitally important. Back in Chapter 8, Figure 8.4 showed means and CIs for pretest and posttest LSAT logical reasoning scores, and the paired differences plotted on a difference axis. The CI on the mean difference was short, compared with the other CIs, which was great news that indicated a sensitive design. As I mentioned, it was

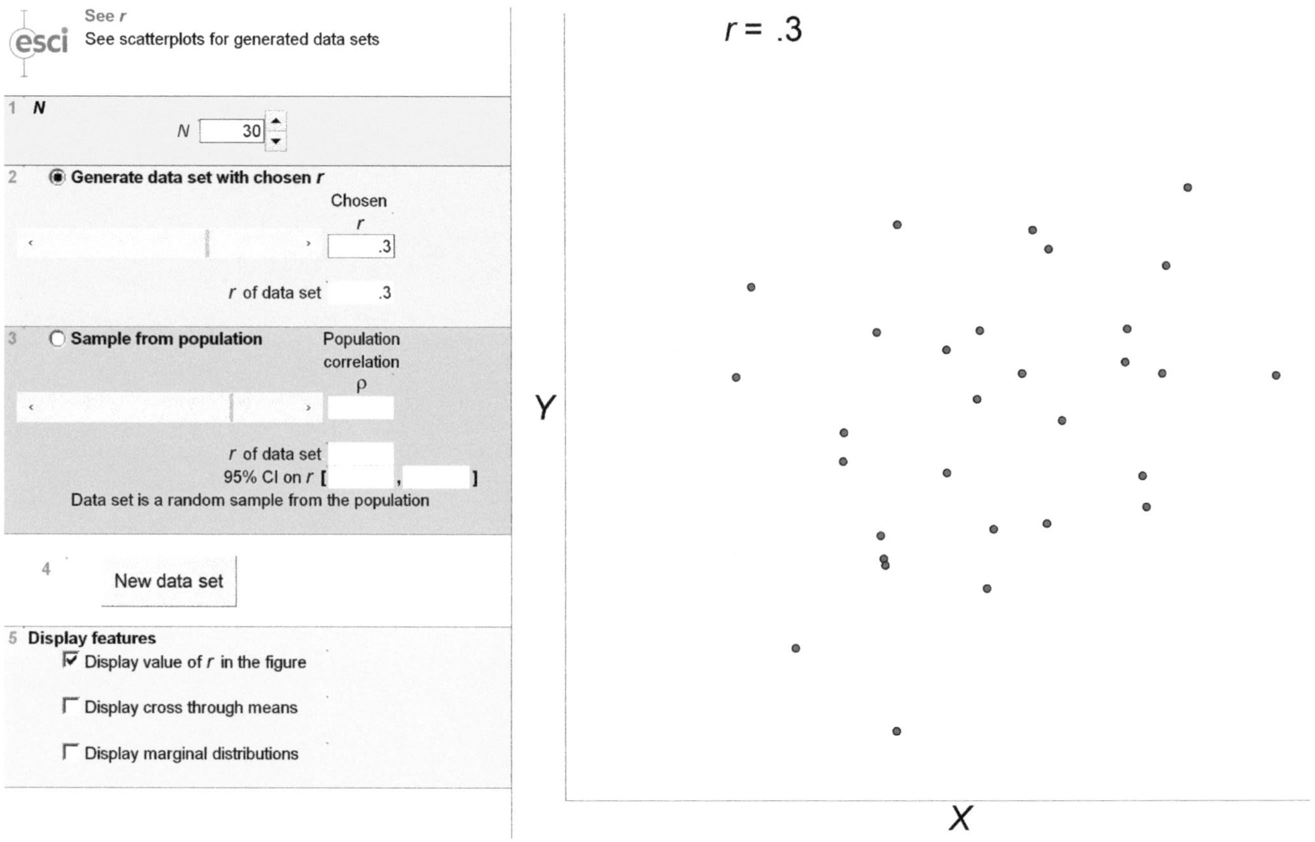

Figure 11.8. A data set generated to have our chosen $N = 30$ and $r = .3$. From **See r**.

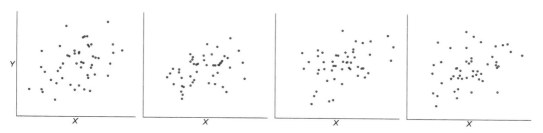

Figure 11.9. Four scatterplots, each with N = 50, for eyeballing practice.

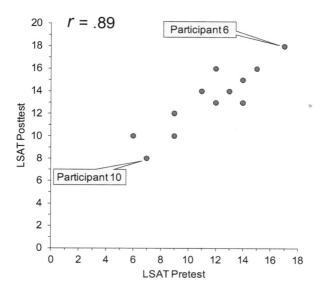

Figure 11.10. Scatterplot of the pretest and posttest data, from the paired design study Thomason 1, with N = 12. The data points for two of the participants are identified. From **Scatterplots**.

the high correlation of pretest and posttest that gave the short CI. In practice, the correlation of pretest and posttest scores is often high—at least .6 and sometimes up to .9—in which case we have a sensitive study, likely to give a relatively precise estimate. Let's calculate r for the Thomason 1 data.

Figure 11.10 is a different picture of the same data: A simple scatterplot of posttest against pretest. Participant 6, for example, scored (17, 18) on the (pretest, posttest), so did well on both, and Participant 10 scored (7, 8), two low scores. Students high on pretest were generally high on posttest, and those low on pretest were also low on posttest, so the correlation is strong and positive: r = .89.

The value of r results from the *battle of the quadrants*: The matched team (HH, LL) pushes r up toward 1, whereas the mismatched team pushes it down toward −1. The more points in a team's quadrants, and the further the points are from the means of X and Y, the stronger the team. The battle is a quantitative version of our quadrant way to eyeball r. I'll use Figure 11.11 to explain. First, note the pretest (X) and posttest (Y) scores at left, and the corresponding points in the scatterplot. The data and points for four participants are highlighted. Next, see that the X and Y values have been transformed to z scores, which appear in the columns headed Z_X and Z_Y. I used the transformation because

If the two measures (e.g., pretest and posttest) in a paired design are highly correlated, the estimate of the mean difference is likely to be precise.

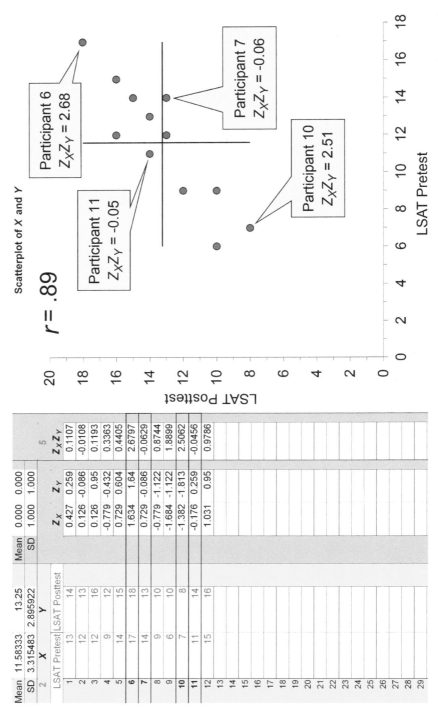

Figure 11.11. The same data as in Figure 11.10. The pretest and posttest scores are shown at left, then their transformation to z scores, then the $Z_X Z_Y$ values below red 5. In the scatterplot, one point in each of the four quadrants is identified, with its value of $Z_X Z_Y$, and the data for those four participants are highlighted at left with heavy black lines. From **Scatterplots.**

it gives a simpler formula for *r*, and links more intuitively with the battle of the quadrants. The calculation uses Equation 3.4 for *z* scores from Chapter 3, which for our *X* and *Y* gives

$$Z_X = \frac{X - M_X}{s_X} \text{ and } Z_Y = \frac{Y - M_Y}{s_Y} \qquad (11.1)$$

z scores for *X* and *Y*.

The values of M_X and s_X, the mean and SD of *X*, are shown at the top left in the figure, similarly for *Y*. For Participant 6, for example, we get

$$Z_X = \frac{(17 - 11.58)}{3.32} = 1.63$$

which is the value reported in the Z_X column for this participant. It tells us that the point for Participant 6 is around 1.6 standard deviations, or around 5 LSAT points, to the right of the vertical line of the cross in the scatterplot, which looks about right. Similarly, $Z_Y = 1.64$, and the point is indeed considerably above the horizontal line of the cross.

The next step is, for each participant, to multiply the two *z* scores to get $Z_X Z_Y$, which is that participant's contribution to *r*. The values are shown in the column below red 5 and in the scatterplot for four of the points. For the matched (HH, LL) quadrants, $Z_X Z_Y$ is positive, and for the mismatched quadrants, negative. To find *r*, we add all the $Z_X Z_Y$ values and divide by the number of degrees of freedom, $(N - 1)$:

Correlation *r* is calculated from the $Z_X Z_Y$ values, which are positive in the matched (HH, LL), and negative in the mismatched quadrants.

$$r = \frac{\sum Z_X Z_Y}{(N - 1)} \qquad (11.2)$$

Pearson correlation, *r*.

Adding the $Z_X Z_Y$ values is how the battle plays out, with the matched team contributing positive values and the mismatched team negative values. Incidentally, there's a parallel between why $(N - 1)$ appears in Equation 11.2 for *r*, and Equation 3.3 for standard deviation. (Ignore this remark if makes your eyes glaze over—you don't need to know—but 1 is subtracted because in both cases the *N* quantities added in the numerator are based on deviations from a sample mean, and calculating that mean uses one of the available *N* degrees of freedom, leaving $df = (N - 1)$ for the SD or correlation.)

11.6 Examine the $Z_X Z_Y$ values below red 5 in Figure 11.11.

   a. Identify the two that make the largest contribution to *r*.
   b. Find the corresponding points in the scatterplot. What's special about them?

esci 11.7 Open **Scatterplots**. If you don't see the data in Figure 11.11, scroll right. Click the red 16 button to transfer the Thomason 1 data back left, replacing any data there. Click at red 4 to show *z* scores, and near red 8 to choose which display features you wish to see. Your screen should resemble Figure 11.11.

esci 11.8 Type in *X* = 11 and *Y* = 11 as Participant 13. (Use **Undo** or delete to remove them.)

   a. Note the new $Z_X Z_Y$ value, and where the new point falls. Does *r* change much? Explain.
   b. Try different *X* and *Y* values for Participant 13. When does *r* change most? Explain.

The Influence of Outliers

Figure 11.12 shows the difference made by the extreme additional outlier point (3, 30), for an imagined Participant 13 who supposedly goes from tiny pretest to huge posttest scores. In practice we would have serious doubts about such values—perhaps a data-recording error, or a student who for some reason made no effort at pretest? However, the example shows that a single outlier point can dramatically change r, even swinging it from large and positive, to negative. Focus on which quadrant a point lies in, and how far it is from the means of X and Y, to understand its $Z_X Z_Y$, and, therefore, its influence on r. A point that's far from both cross lines has large (in absolute value) Z_X and Z_Y, and therefore especially large $Z_X Z_Y$. Its contribution to r can be overwhelming, as in Figure 11.12 in which a single data point changed r from .89 to −.15.

Looking for outliers is yet another reason we need to see the scatterplot. You may be thinking, however, that journal articles rarely include scatterplots, so how can we be sure that the correlation analyses we read are appropriate? That's a good question. Unless the authors tell us that the scatterplots of their data show no outliers and no signs of departure from linearity, they are asking us to take their analyses and interpretation on trust. One advantage of open data, as we discussed in Chapter 10 as part of Open Science, is that even if the scatterplot is not shown in the report, anyone can go to the data and create the scatterplot. So, if you don't see a scatterplot for any (X, Y) relationship you care about, think carefully about what it might show, and perhaps try creating it yourself.

11.9 In the column of $Z_X Z_Y$ values in Figure 11.12, find the value for the outlier point and compare with the other $Z_X Z_Y$ values. Explain why this point is so influential on r.

 11.10 You can click at red 15 to reveal a second scatterplot, which is a graph of Z_Y against Z_X. It displays the same set of points, but on axes of Z_X and Z_Y rather than X and Y. It may help clarify how any point has Z_X and Z_Y values, which multiply to give $Z_X Z_Y$.

> ### ? Quiz 11.1
>
> 1. Pearson's r indicates the degree of <u>linear</u> / nonlinear / quasi-linear / oblique relationship between two variables.
> 2. A negative correlation means that as one variable increases, the other _____.
> 3. If two variables are perfectly positively correlated, r will be ____; if the variables are perfectly negatively correlated, r will be ____; if the variables are not at all correlated, r will be ____.
> 4. When there is a strong positive relationship between two variables, a scatterplot will have most of its dots in the <u>matched</u> / mismatched / adjacent quadrants.
> 5. To calculate r, first transform the X and Y scores to _____.
> 6. When an X and a Y score are matched (both above the mean or both below the mean), then $Z_X Z_Y$ will be positive / negative and will tend to <u>increase</u> / decrease the value of r. When an X and a Y score are mismatched (one above the mean, the other below the mean), then $Z_X Z_Y$ will be positive / <u>negative</u> and will tend to increase / <u>decrease</u> the value of r.

SCATTERPLOTS THAT REVEAL

In Figure 11.4 the scatterplot of room comfort and room temperature suggested a curvilinear relation, and that of driver knowledge and High School GPA a

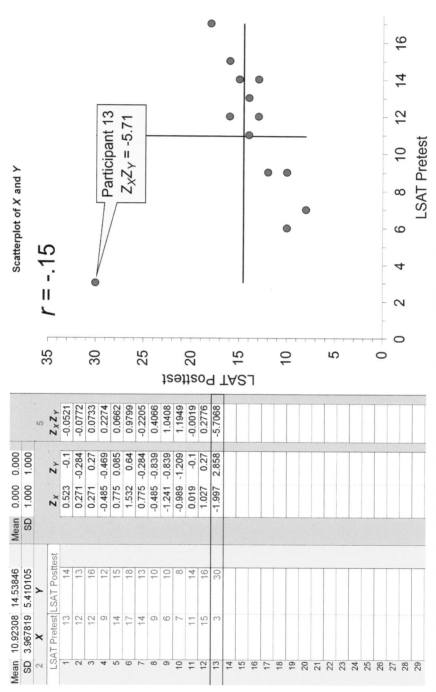

Figure 11.12. Same as Figure 11.11 except Participant 13 has been added, as an extreme outlier. Its value of $Z_X Z_Y$ outweighs all the points in the matched (HH, LL) quadrants to give negative r.

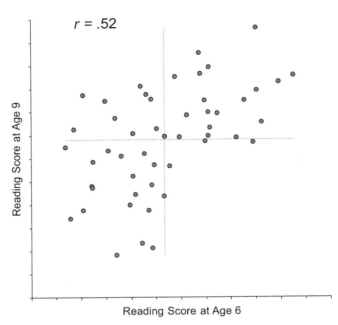

Figure 11.13. Data for *N* = 50 children showing a correlation of *r* = .52 between reading scores at ages 6 and 9. The lines mark the means. The bottom right quadrant is almost empty.

ceiling effect. These examples emphasize that we need to look carefully at the scatterplot because *r* measures only the degree of *linearity* in a relationship, and therefore often doesn't tell the whole story.

I learned that lesson many years ago, when some colleagues and I were studying children learning to read. We had reading scores for children at age 6, then again at 9. The data haven't survived, but Figure 11.13 is my reconstruction of the pattern. The correlation was about .5, but the scatterplot showed that virtually all the points fell in three quadrants, with the lower right quadrant virtually empty. A child scoring below the mean at age 6 might score above or below the mean at age 9—in the upper or lower left quadrant in the figure. However, a child scoring above the mean at age 6 was virtually guaranteed of scoring above the mean at age 9—in the HH, upper right quadrant. That's good news: If a child "gets it" (scores above the mean) by age 6, they will continue to progress. They can read. But if by age 6 they still don't quite get it (they score below the mean), then they may or may not get it by age 9. Only a few children slip considerably backward.

Our *r* of about .5 was unsurprising, but didn't tell the whole story. Our main conclusion and guide for follow-up research was given not by *r* but by the pattern in the scatterplot. It's the same lesson we've been learning all along: Always plot your data in ways that are revealing, and think carefully about what the pictures might be telling you. Don't be blinded by calculations of *r*, *p*, CIs, or anything else, but use these *along with* pictures to seek the messages within your data. In particular, if you are reading a report of research that highlights one or more correlations, then you need to see the scatterplots to have the full story.

▶ Examine the scatterplot for any (*X*, *Y*) relationship you care about.

The Effect of Range Restriction on Correlation

Range restriction is another aspect of correlation best understood by considering the scatterplot. The correlation between high school and college GPA was

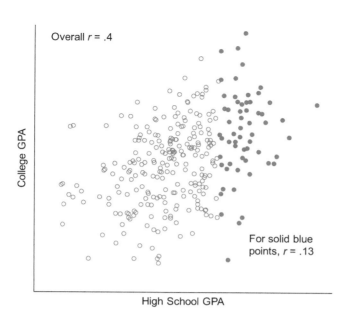

Figure 11.14. Randomly generated scatterplot with N = 300 and r = .40, which might represent college and high school GPA scores for 300 college students. Solid blue dots show students having the top 20% of high school GPA scores. For these 60 students, r = .13, the lower correlation reflecting range restriction of high school GPA.

investigated in a large meta-analysis by Richardson, Abraham, and Bond (2012), and found to average r = .40. Figure 11.14 shows what such a correlation might look like, for 300 college students. Suppose all 300 applied to enter a selective college, but the college accepted only students with a high school GPA in the top 20% of applicants—the solid blue points in Figure 11.14. For them, the correlation of high school and college GPA is r = .13. Inspecting those solid blue dots, does that look about right to you? The lower correlation reflects the restriction of the range of X, high school GPA.

In general, r can be strongly influenced by the ranges of possible X and Y values, especially for medium-sized r values, meaning values not close to 0, −1, or 1. If either range is restricted, the correlation is likely to be smaller. The more a range is restricted, the smaller the correlation is likely to be. The key lesson is that selection in either X or Y that restricts the X or Y range can yield a sample that badly underestimates the correlation in the whole population.

One problem is that graphing software often zooms the ranges on the X and Y axes to fit the data points. Always examine the range of values shown on each axis: If this doesn't cover the full range of possible values, perhaps the sample is range restricted and therefore r is misleadingly low? For example, a plot that showed high school GPA only from 3.0 to 4.0 would be suspect, and would need further investigation.

> If the range of possible X or Y values is restricted, we have **range restriction** and r is likely to be reduced.

> The X and Y axes should show the full ranges of possible X and Y values.

11.11 Suppose an elite college accepts only students with high school GPA in the top 10%. About what r would you expect for accepted students? Explain.

11.12 A survey found almost no correlation between IQ score and income, among college graduates. It concludes that a person's IQ hardly matters in the modern world. Is the conclusion justified? Explain.

11.13 In Figure 11.4, suppose you had data only for room temperature up to and including 18 °C.

a. Eyeball r.
b. Do the same if you had data only for 18 °C and above.
c. What can you conclude about range restriction?

What to Look for In a Scatterplot

I mentioned at the start that r is one of the most widely used and important effect size measures. That's true, even if much of the discussion has been about limitations and things to watch out for. Here I'll summarize by listing important things to bear in mind—or in eye—when inspecting a scatterplot.

- Pearson correlation r is a measure of the strength of the *linear* component of the (X, Y) relationship.
- Even for linear relationships, when |r| is around .3 or less, the scatterplot is close to a shotgun blast. Even for larger r there's considerable *scatter*.
- For large |r|, *tightness* to the line is helpful for eyeballing the value of r. For any r, eyeballing the balance of points in the matched and mismatched *quadrants* can help.
- Look for signs of departure from linearity, perhaps a *curvilinear* relationship, or a *ceiling* or *floor* effect.
- *Outliers* can have an enormous influence on r, which is especially sensitive to points far from the means of X and Y.
- Examine the scales on the X and Y axes for any sign of a range restriction. Also consider the sample. A *range restriction* can cause a sample to underestimate the correlation in the whole population, perhaps severely.
- Given r but no scatterplot, take care: Would the *scatterplot* reveal important aspects we're not being told?

INFERENCE: CONFIDENCE INTERVALS AND p VALUES

As a descriptive statistic, r measures the strength of the linear component of the relation between X and Y in a sample. For inference to the population, we need the CI on r, and I'll also mention p values. First comes the dance of the r values.

Dance of the r Values

Before discussing CIs on means back in Chapter 5, I used the dance of the means to illustrate the sampling variability that a CI describes. Let's do the same for correlations. I'll consider r for data sets that are random samples from a population that we assume is a very large, even infinite, collection of (X, Y) points. We assume X and Y have correlation ρ (rho) in the population—remember, don't confuse ρ with p as in p value.

With $\rho = .5$, I took 50 samples each of $N = 10$ and recorded the 50 r values. I did the same for $N = 40$ and $N = 160$. Table 11.1 reports some of my results: Because of sampling variability, the values in each column dance—this is the *dance of the r values*, or *dance of the correlations*.

We expect larger N to give less sampling variability and narrower dances, and the table shows that this happens for r. In the first column, with $N = 10$, r ranges from −.35 to .78, whereas in the last, with $N = 160$, the range is only

Values of r in repeated random samples from a population with correlation ρ will vary because of sampling variability. This is the *dance of the r values*.

N	10	40	160
	.78	.45	.59
	−.13	.28	.46
	.81	.59	.57
	.48	.31	.54
	.52	.71	.45
	.53	.39	.34
	.43	.53	.61
	.19	.50	.44
	−.35	.70	.47
	.41	.36	.52
	...	...	...
Mean of 50 *r* values	.46	.44	.51
SD of 50 *r* values	.30	.16	.06

Table 11.1 Values of *r* to Illustrate the Dance of the *r* Values

from .34 to .61. There's *much* more variation with smaller *N*. At the bottom are the means and SDs for my full sets of 50 *r* values. As we'd expect, the three means are all fairly close to ρ = .5. The SDs measure the amount of bouncing and indicate that, as expected, there's more sampling variability (a larger SD) for smaller *N*. The SD decreases markedly as *N* goes from 10 to 40 to 160.

I used the **See r** page to take samples and obtain the *r* values in Table 11.1. You can see the dance for yourself.

 11.14 At red 3, click the radio button on, to select **Sample from population**. Use the slider at red 3 to select ρ. Check the top checkbox at red 5 to display the value of *r*. Click the button at red 4 to take a random sample of *N* points. Keep clicking, and watch how *r* and the patterns of points dance.

 11.15 Try various values of *N* and ρ.

   a. For ρ = .5, compare *N* = 10 and *N* = 160. Can you see any difference in the amount of variability in *r*, meaning the width of the dance?
   b. For *N* = 40, compare ρ = 0 and ρ = .9. Any difference in the width of the dance?

THE CONFIDENCE INTERVAL ON *r*

Just as we use sample mean, *M*, to estimate population mean μ, we can use *r* for our sample as an estimate of ρ, the correlation in the population it came from. So *r* is our point estimate of ρ, and we want a CI on *r* as our interval estimate of ρ. First, we need to consider the statistical model underlying the CI calculation—in other words, the assumptions that are required. The model is that our data set of *N* pairs of (*X, Y*) values is a random sample from a very large, even infinite, population of such (*X, Y*) data pairs in which *X* and *Y* have a *bivariate normal distribution*, with correlation ρ. "Bivariate" means, as you probably guessed, that there are two variables, *X* and *Y*.

Think of a bivariate normal distribution as a smooth hill, flattish on top, with contours that are roughly elliptical in shape—in the shape of an ellipse, or oval. Panel A in Figure 11.15 illustrates the idea by showing the scatterplot for a random sample of *N* = 5,000 points from a bivariate normal distribution. The correlation is *r* = .6. Overall, both *X* and *Y* are normally distributed. In addition, if we choose a single value of *X*, the distribution of *Y* at that *X* value will be

In a *bivariate normal distribution*, *X* and *Y* are each normally distributed overall, each is normally distributed at any single value of the other, and the variance of each is homogeneous for all values of the other.

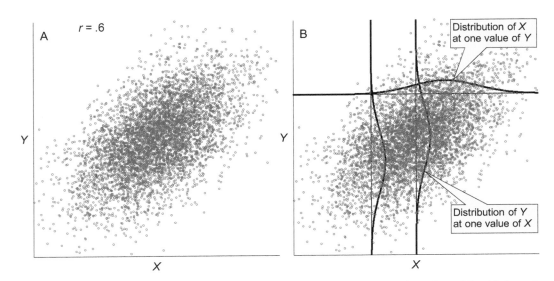

Figure 11.15. Random sample of N = 5,000 points from a bivariate normal distribution. Correlation is r = .6. Panel B shows the distributions of Y at two values of X, and the distribution of X at one value of Y.

normally distributed. Panel B illustrates such distributions of Y for two values of X. All such distributions are normal and, moreover, have the same standard deviation for every value of X. We say that the variance of Y is homogeneous for all X. The figure also shows one distribution of X values at a single value of Y. That's also normal, and also has the same standard deviation for all Y, so the variance of X is homogeneous for all Y. Scatterplots for samples from bivariate normal distributions look like those in Figures 11.2, 11.3, 11.5, 11.7, 11.8, and 11.9. The points are generally more closely clustered around the center, and become less close at positions farther from the center.

To calculate a CI on r we need to assume the data set is a random sample from a bivariate normal population. Is that a reasonable assumption? Often, but not always. It's usually close enough to reality for practical purposes, unless:

1. We have prior reason to suspect a nonlinear relationship. For example, we surely would have expected a curvilinear relationship between comfort and room temperature; or:
2. There are strong signs in the scatterplot of a nonlinear relationship, as with the two Figure 11.4 examples; or:
3. It doesn't make sense to think of our data set as a sample from a larger population. I'll say a word about this next.

If our data set is, for example, the number of points scored this season (X) and the income this year (Y) of the players in a particular basketball team, we could certainly calculate r for X and Y. However, for any kind of inference, not only for CIs on r, it needs to make sense to think of our data as a sample from a population. In this example, would it make sense to calculate a CI on the r for our team? If our interest is specifically in that team, then no, it wouldn't, because our data tell us about the whole team—the whole population we are interested in—and so we shouldn't calculate a CI. Perhaps if we were interested in basketball players in general we might think of our team as a sample, although it's hardly a random sample from that population.

If we do make the assumption of a bivariate normal population, all we need is the values of *N* and *r* and we can calculate a CI on *r* as our interval estimate of population correlation ρ. The details are complicated, so we'll simply let ESCI calculate the CI, and also the *p* value for any null hypothesis.

Figure 11.16 displays the 95% CI on *r* = .4 when *N* = 30, and near red 2 reports that the CI is [.05, .66], rounded to two decimal places. Note the CI is asymmetric, with upper MoE smaller than lower—the values are reported near red 2. The cat's-eye picture is also asymmetric—more bulge near the top, longer tail below. The null hypothesis value of $\rho_0 = 0$, as specified by the small slider near red 4, is marked by the red horizontal line. The corresponding *p* value of .028 is shown near 4. Do you agree that this *p* value looks about right? It's consistent with the lower limit of the CI being just a little above zero, so *p* is a little less than .05.

> Calculation of a CI on *r*, or a *p* value to test a null hypothesis about ρ, requires the assumption that the data are a random sample from a bivariate normal distribution. ◄

esci 11.16 Open the **One correlation** page and start with the checkboxes at red 3 and 4 *not* checked. Explore, using the spinner at red 1 to set *N* and the large vertical slider to set *r*.

a. For fixed *N*, try both positive and negative *r*.
b. Describe how the CI changes as you change *r*, with small *N*, then with large *N*. Any difference?

esci 11.17 For fixed *r*, describe how the CI changes as you change *N*. Describe how the pattern of change differs for small and large *r*.

esci 11.18 In Figure 11.1, *N* = 106 and *r* = .47. Find the CI on *r* and interpret.

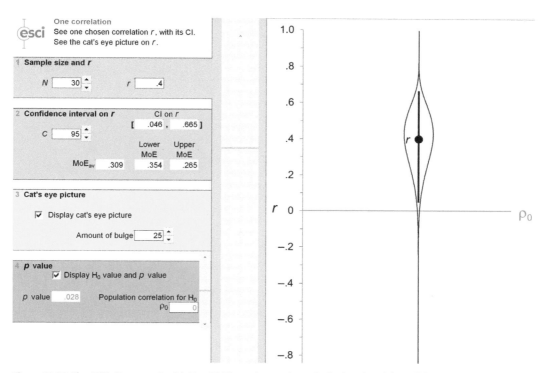

Figure 11.16. The 95% CI on *r* = .4, with *N* = 30. The cat's-eye picture is displayed, and the null hypothesis value $\rho_0 = 0$ is marked by the red line. For this null hypothesis, *p* = .028, as shown near red 4. From **One correlation**.

Correlation

 11.19 In **See r** click **Sample from population** at red 3. Set $N = 75$ and $\rho = -.7$.

    a. Take a few samples and note down the values of r.

    b. Use **One correlation** to find the CI for each, and note whether each captures ρ.

    c. If you were to take many further samples, what can you say about the CIs for those samples? What can you say about the capture of ρ?

 11.20 If you knew the CIs for all the r values in Table 11.1, how would the CI lengths compare for the three columns? For each column, what can you say about capture of $\rho = .5$?

 11.21 For a particular type of hybrid plant, a genetic model predicts a correlation of .5 between leaf length and width. You measure leaf length and width of 100 such plants and calculate $r = .36$. What do the data tell you about the model? Consider both the CI and the p value. *Hint*: For the p value, use the small slider near red 4 to set ρ_0.

 11.22 A second genetic model predicts a correlation of .25.

    a. What can you say about this second model?

    b. Considering the two models, what would you recommend?

▶
For fixed *N*, the CI on *r* gets shorter and more asymmetric as *r* moves farther from 0, especially when *r* gets close to 1 or −1.

▶
For fixed *r*, if *N* is multiplied by four, the CI on *r* becomes roughly half as long.

Figure 11.17 illustrates what you may have discovered in Exercise 11.16. With fixed N, when $r = 0$ the CI is long and symmetric. The CI gets shorter and more asymmetric as r moves farther from 0, especially as it approaches 1 or −1. Of course, no CI can extend beyond those boundaries. For values of r that are equally far above and below zero, the CIs are mirror images. The lines in the figure at 1 and −1 are "fences" that "squash" any CI that approaches, especially the MoE nearer the fence.

Figure 11.18 illustrates what you may have discovered in Exercise 11.17. With fixed r, when N is small the CI is long. Increase N and the CI gets shorter, as we'd expect. Figure 11.18 illustrates this change with N for $r = 0$, and also

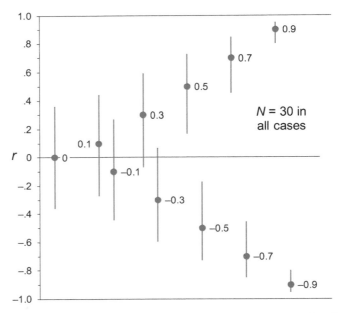

Figure 11.17. Examples of 95% CIs for various values of r, all with $N = 30$. The value of r is shown next to each point.

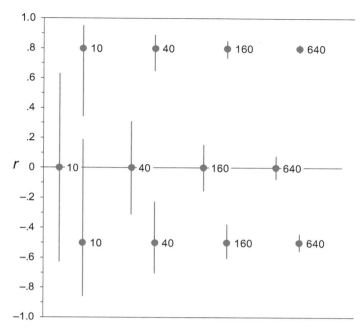

Figure 11.18. Examples of 95% CIs for various values of *N* and *r*. The value of *N* is shown next to each point. For the upper four points, *r* = .8, the middle four, *r* = 0, and the lower four, *r* = −.5.

for *r* = −.5 (lower four points) and *r* = .8 (upper four points). Recall the general guideline, which we first encountered in Chapter 1, that four times the sample size gives, approximately, a CI half as long. Does that hold for *r*? Does multiplying *N* by four give a CI on *r* that's half as long?

Yes it does, although only roughly, as you may have concluded from Figure 11.18.

11.23 Consider the SD values in Table 11.1.

    a. Note that from the first to the second column, *N* is multiplied by 4 and the SD changes from .30 to .16, which is about half.

    b. There are similar changes from the second to third column. Is that reasonable? Explain.

11.24 The length of a CI on a sample mean, *M*, depends on *N*, but it doesn't depend on *M* itself. What about a CI on *r*? Does it depend on *N*? Does it depend on *r* itself?

Now we've discussed CIs, I want to discuss planning a correlational study, then the interpretation of correlations and scatterplots. But first it's quiz time.

 Quiz 11.2

1. Before using Pearson's *r* to describe a relationship, it is essential to first look at a scatterplot of the relationship. What should you be looking for?
    a. Whether the relationship is linear; if not, *r* should probably not be used.
    b. Whether there are outliers that are having a large influence on *r*.
    c. Whether the range of either the *X* or the *Y* variable is restricted, which can produce misleading values for *r*.
    d. All of the above.

2. The larger the sample size, the longer / shorter the CI on *r*. For a fixed *N*, the closer *r* is to 0, the longer / shorter the CI.
3. A CI on *r* depends on the assumption that the data set is a(n) _____ sample from a(n) _____ distribution.
4. Jaime measures IQ in 10 students and also obtains an IQ measure for each student's mother. He finds *r* = 0.6, 95% CI [−.05, .89]. This means that the population correlation could most likely be anywhere from _____ to _____.
5. The CI Jaime obtained is quite long. To obtain a CI half as long he would need to test about _____ participants.
6. As *r* gets closer to −1 or 1, the CI becomes _____ and more _____.

Planning a Correlational Study

In Chapter 10 we discussed how to choose *N* so our planned study would give a CI with our chosen target MoE, either on average or with 99% assurance. Planning a correlational study is more complicated because, as you saw in Figures 11.17 and 11.18, for *r* the CI length depends not only on *N*, but also on *r* itself. Exercise 11.24 emphasized the same point. To use precision for planning to choose *N*, when *r* is our effect size, we would need to specify a target *r* as well as target MoE. An added complication is that, unless *r* = 0, the CI on *r* is asymmetric, so upper MoE and lower MoE are different.

Rather than attempting a detailed discussion, or making an ESCI page, I've included Figure 11.19 to give the general idea. Use this to see what CI you would obtain if *r* = .1 or .3 or .5, and you use one of the values of *N* shown in the figure. The relationship of *r*, *N*, and CI length is a bit complicated, but the

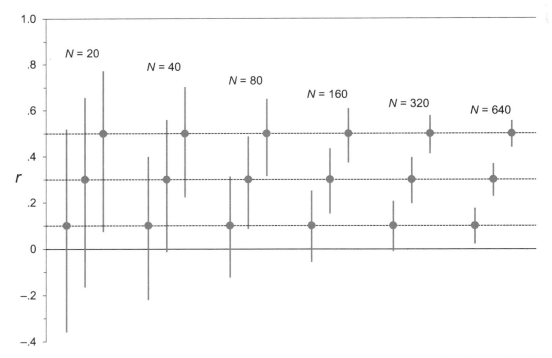

Figure 11.19. Examples of 95% CIs for *r* = .1, .3, and .5, respectively, left to right, for each of various values of *N*, as indicated at the top.

figure can help you choose N likely to give a sufficiently short CI, especially if you have some idea of the size of population correlation you are investigating.

There's one important way in which the situation with r is less complicated and less uncertain than for means. The CI depends only on r and N, and there's no additional need to estimate σ or worry about assurance. For any particular r and N, the CI is determined, and any replication with the same N that happens to give the same r will give exactly the same CI. Any sample with N = 20, for example, which has r = .1 will give exactly the leftmost CI in the figure.

Studying Figure 11.19 suggests a few approximate guidelines. For correlations between about −.5 and .5:

▨ For N up to around 40, CIs are long, with MoE usually around .3 or more.
▨ To achieve MoE of around .2 or less, in most cases N of about 100 or more is required.
▨ To achieve MoE of around .1 or less, in most cases N of about 300 or more is required.

As Figure 11.17 illustrates, for larger correlations ($|r| > .5$) CIs are shorter, especially as $|r|$ approaches 1.

11.25 a. You are investigating a correlation you suspect is around .3 to .5, but can collect data only for a sample with N = 80. About what MoE can you expect?

b. You expect r around .1 to .2, and are keen for MoE not more than 0.1. With N = 200, are you likely to achieve that? About what N are you actually likely to need?

INTERPRETING CORRELATIONS AND SCATTERPLOTS

Correlation and Causation

"Can you believe, from 1999 to 2009 the correlation was r = .95 between annual U.S. oil imports from Norway and the annual number of drivers in the U.S. who died in collisions with trains!" At www.tylervigen.com/ you can see that and many other examples of bizarre correlations. They are good for a chuckle, but also alert us to the danger of seeing causation in a correlation. As I first mentioned when discussing Figure 11.1, if X and Y correlate, there may be interesting causal links, but the scatterplot can't tell us what they are. We might even be seeing an accidental lump in randomness: Examine a large number of possibly totally unrelated variables and you'll eventually find two that correlate, simply by chance. You would most likely be seeing a face in the clouds. We can't be sure, but I suspect that r = .95 for oil imports and train collision deaths is such a blip, such a face in the clouds, with no instructive underlying causes to be found. For correlations we encounter in research, however, there are often causal links to be investigated—although there may not be.

If X and Y are uncorrelated, with r close to zero and a shotgun blast scatterplot, then *most likely* there are no interesting causal links between X and Y. However, if r and a scatterplot suggest there is some relationship between X and Y, there are several possibilities:

- Simple causation: Either X causes Y, or Y causes X.
- A more complex pattern of causation, possibly including one or more other variables.
- There are no causal links, and we're seeing a face in the clouds.

▶
Correlation does not necessarily imply causation.

Correlations can give valuable guidance as we investigate causality, but even a large r cannot immediately tell us which of the above possibilities applies. Hence the slogan "Correlation does not necessarily imply causation".

In Figure 11.4, the left scatterplot shows the curvilinear relation of Y (comfort) and X (room temperature). It's natural to assume that X causes Y, although if low comfort leads you to adjust the thermostat, Y would be influencing X. In plots of Thomason 1 posttest (Y) against pretest (X) scores, like Figures 11.10 and 11.11, we assume both X and Y are strongly influenced by a third variable, for example reasoning ability. Often we might consider various patterns of causation between X and Y, and perhaps other variables. Knowing just the correlation, however, *cannot* identify for us the pattern of causation. We need to be alert, because the slide from seeing correlation to assuming causation can be subtle and appealing, as the following example illustrates.

▶
The slide from correlation to causation may be subtle and highly plausible, although unjustified. Be alert.

"Parental divorce leads to adolescent drug use." News reports like that would, no doubt, be based on data, but would the data come from experiments, with participants randomly assigned to different conditions? Of course not—it's impossible as well as totally unethical to assign families randomly to the Divorce or the Don't divorce condition, then come back a year or two later and note their children's drug use. Without that, however, it's very difficult to draw confident conclusions about causality. The news report is almost certainly based on a correlation: Researchers noted a tendency for children of divorced parents to use drugs more than those in intact families. Many causal links may be involved, or perhaps none at all—we may only be seeing a lump in the randomness. Perhaps cause runs in the opposite direction: Children's drug use causes marital problems. Perhaps there's an indirect link, with parental education, employment status, parenting skills, and housing situation all being important influences on both divorce and adolescent drug use. Researchers have developed advanced techniques to gather and analyze data to tease out such complex patterns of causation. These usually require investigation of many variables together, then analysis of a complex data set including many correlations.

The claim made by the news report may be highly plausible. However, it implies a direct causal link, but is based on a correlation. The causal link may or may not be correct, but most likely there are several, or many, underlying causal links that will be tricky to identify and untangle. Be alert to over-interpretation of correlations, a phenomenon which can be subtle and plausible.

11.26 "Eating vegetables linked to better progress in elementary school." Discuss that news report.

a. Is it plausible? What's it probably based on?

b. What causal links might there be? How might you investigate further?

11.27 Consider a couple whose marriage is violent and dysfunctional.

a. Does an overall strong correlation between divorce and adolescent drug use mean that the couple should necessarily avoid divorce for the sake of their adolescent children?

b. Explain how an overall strong correlation need not necessarily dictate what's best in an individual case.

Town Size and Walking Speed

Here's another interesting correlation to think about. Figure 11.20 is a scatterplot of data reported by Bornstein and Bornstein (1976). The researchers unobtrusively recorded the walking speed of individuals walking in the central city square, or main downtown street, in villages, towns, and cities in six countries. They found that, remarkably, walking speed tended to be more than twice as fast in large cities as in small villages. The correlation with population (expressed on a log scale) was $r = .90$, as Figure 11.20 reports.

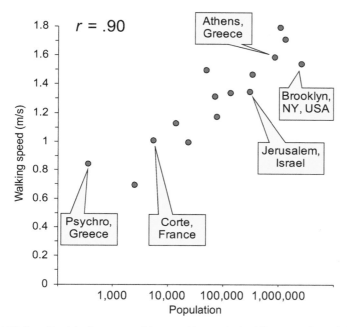

Figure 11.20. A scatterplot of average walking speed in a central public area, and population on a log scale, for towns and cities. Several of the points are identified. Data from Bornstein and Bornstein (1976).

11.28 How feasible would a close replication of the study reported in Figure 11.20 be? What would you expect it to find?

11.29 Find the CI and the p value for the r in Figure 11.20. Is it reasonable to calculate those? Explain.

11.30 Suggest causal links that might underlie the correlation in Figure 11.20. How could you investigate your suggestions?

11.31 a. Search online for "walking speed and population size" or similar. I found several fascinating discussions about the pace of life in different countries, and different-sized towns and cities. Bornstein and Bornstein (1976) was identified as the starting point, and many more recent studies were mentioned.

b. Suggest an interesting further study.

11.32 My colleague Neil Thomason recalls chatting with a farmer from rural Bolivia amid the hubbub of New York City. The man asked: "Is everyone in New York important?" He explained that back home only important people walk fast. What further investigation does that observation suggest?

Reference Values for Correlation

I've been referring to $r = .1$ or $-.1$ as a small correlation, and $r = .9$ or $-.9$ as large. In relation to the possible range from -1 to 1 that's reasonable, but, just as with Cohen's d, any interpretation of particular r values should be a knowledgeable judgment in context. That's especially important here, because correlation is used in so many different ways, in so many different contexts, that it's not possible to specify any reference values with universal applicability.

Considering psychology, Cohen did suggest $r = .1$, $.3$, and $.5$ (or, equivalently, $-.1$, $-.3$, and $-.5$) as reference values for small, medium, and large correlations, but he emphasized that judgment in context should be preferred wherever possible. Others have suggested different reference values. Hinkle, Wiersma, and Jurs (2003), for example, labeled r values above $.9$ as "very high positive", values between $.7$ and $.9$ as "high positive", between $.5$ and $.7$ as "moderate positive", between $.3$ and $.5$ as "low positive", and between $-.3$ and $.3$ as "little if any correlation" (p. 109).

> Interpret values of r in context. Correlation is used in such a variety of situations that reference values usually don't help.

Bosco et al. (2015) collected more than 140,000 values of r reported in organizational psychology research. This broad field studies people's attitudes, intentions, and performance, mostly in the context of employment. For that large set of r values, the first quartile was $.07$, the median was $.16$, and the third quartile $.32$. So researchers in this field study correlations most of whose scatterplots would fall between the two rightmost panels in Figure 11.2—they resemble shotgun blasts. Bosco et al. concluded that most research in organizational psychology focuses on correlations smaller than $r = .3$, and that $r = .2$ might often be a more realistic "medium" value. I conclude again that r, especially, needs to be interpreted in its particular context.

To interpret a value of r, consider also the CI, and any correlations reported by related past research. Also have in mind scatterplots like those in Figures 11.2 and 11.3. I'm always struck by how widely scattered the points are, even for r as large as $.6$. It's sobering to learn that many researchers are studying relationships between variables that have small values of r with scatterplots that look like shotgun blasts. Such relationships may be interesting and important—or they might not be—but, either way, it's still a shotgun blast.

Measuring Reliability and Validity

> Test-retest reliability is usually assessed by a value of r.

In Chapter 2 I introduced reliability and validity as two important features of any measure. You may recall that reliability is repeatability or consistency, and it's often assessed by using r as a measure. To estimate the test-retest reliability of a new anxiety questionnaire, for example, you might calculate r for the anxiety scores of 100 people recorded on one day, with their scores on a second day, under conditions as similar as possible to those on the first day. I'm happy to report that many well-established psychological and educational tests give test–retest reliability correlations of $.9$ or even higher. That's great news—our best measures are highly reliable.

Recall also that validity is the extent to which a measure actually measures what we want it to measure. Correlation is used in various ways to assess validity. I mentioned in Chapter 2 that we could, for example, correlate scores on the new anxiety questionnaire with scores on an already well-established measure of anxiety. A high correlation would suggest our measure of anxiety has reasonable validity. I also mentioned a test of job aptitude: The correlation between test scores and later job performance would be an estimate of the validity of the test. It's encouraging that many well-established psychological and educational tests often give validity correlations as high as .8 or .9. A good measure needs to have both good reliability and good validity. Assessing measures and developing new measures is likely to require much use of correlations.

Correlation is used in various ways to assess validity. ◄

With reliability and validity in mind, let's revisit the interpretation of r values. For reliability and validity, we might judge r values of .8 and .9 as good rather than very large, and .6 or .7 as small and inadequate rather than large. Here's an example. To study leadership, Chan (2007) obtained scores from 92 Chinese students in Hong Kong on an established rating scale for leadership, the SRBCSS, and a self-rating scale he was investigating, the RRSL. He found a correlation of $r = .38$ and reported that correlation to be statistically significant, $p < .01$, "suggesting that the Chinese RRSL has ... validity when compared with Chinese SRBCSS leadership scores" (p. 160).

A p value for r, reported without mention of a null hypothesis value, almost always refers to a null hypothesis of zero, although we should be told that explicitly. Chan's conclusion was based on the p value indicating fairly strong evidence against the population value of the correlation being zero—absolutely no correlation whatsoever. But that's *not* good evidence that the validity correlation is usefully large. A correlation of only around .4 would usually be considered poor validity. For $N = 92$, the 95% CI on $r = .38$ is [.19, .54], so the validity correlation could plausibly have been as low as .2. It would have been more informative if Chan (2007) had reported r with its CI, then interpreted the point and interval estimates in terms of what they say about validity.

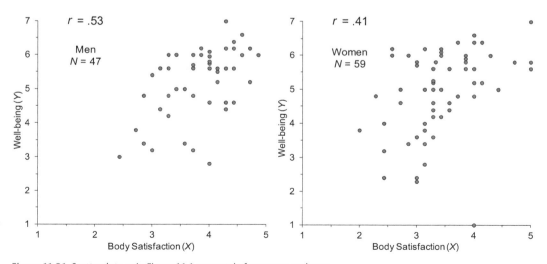

Figure 11.21. Scatterplots as in Figure 11.1, separately for women and men.

Beware any *p* value given with a value of *r*. What's the null hypothesis value, and is that, in the context, an appropriate reference point?

This example reminds us that a *p* value relates to a particular null hypothesis value. To interpret *p* we need to know that value, and consider its appropriateness as a reference point, in the context. Small *p* might lead us to reject the null hypothesis, but, for correlation, zero may be an inappropriate reference point, especially when assessing reliability or validity. Considering *r* and its CI is likely to lead to a better justified conclusion.

THE CI ON THE DIFFERENCE BETWEEN TWO INDEPENDENT CORRELATIONS

Now for some more inference. To compare two independent correlations we need the CI on the difference. By "independent" I mean the two correlations come from separate groups—for example the correlations for women and for men. The sample of 106 students whose data are shown in Figure 11.1 comprised 59 women and 47 men. Figure 11.21 shows the separate scatterplots, and that $r = .41$ for women and $r = .53$ for men. Is that surprising? Isn't body satisfaction considered more central to well-being by women? Before we get too excited by what may be an unexpected difference, we need to see the CI on that difference.

The CI on *r* is usually long, unless *N* is very large. The CI on the difference between two independent *r* values is usually especially long.

The CI on a difference between *r* values is tricky to calculate, but I use a good approximate method described by Zou (2007). Figure 11.22 displays $r_1 = .41$ for women, and $r_2 = .53$ for men, each with its CI. The difference between those correlations and the CI on the difference are displayed at right. The difference is shown at red 6 on the left to be $(r_2 - r_1) = 0.12$ [−0.19, 0.42] to two decimal places. As usual, I was surprised how long the CIs are, even with groups as large as 59 and 47. The CI on the difference tells us there's considerable uncertainty, because the population difference between the correlations for women and men could plausibly be as low as around −0.2 or as high as around 0.4. So there's no evidence of a population difference.

11.33 In Figure 11.22, at red 7 on the left, the *p* value is reported. What's the null hypothesis? Interpret and compare with the CI.

11.34 a. At **Two correlations**, set the *N* values at red 1 and 2 and use the two large sliders to set the correlations for our example. Click at red 6 for the difference axis and red 7 for the *p* value. Your screen should resemble Figure 11.22.

b. Suppose the two groups had been four times the size (236 women, 188 men) and obtained the same r_1 and r_2 values. Find the CI on the difference and interpret.

11.35 Using the original group sizes and r_1 value, how large would r_2 need to be for the *p* value to be less than .05? How does that strike you?

CORRELATION *r* FOR META-ANALYSIS

Is genius born or made? Could any of us be Michael Jordan, or Mozart, if we worked sufficiently hard to develop the requisite skills? Meta-analysis of correlations can help answer such questions. The issue here is the extent that practice and effort may be sufficient for achieving the highest levels of expertise. Ericsson, Krampe, and Tesch-Romer (1993) argued that years of effort is what matters most: "Many characteristics once believed to reflect innate talent are actually the result of intense practice extended for a minimum of 10 years" (p. 363). This view

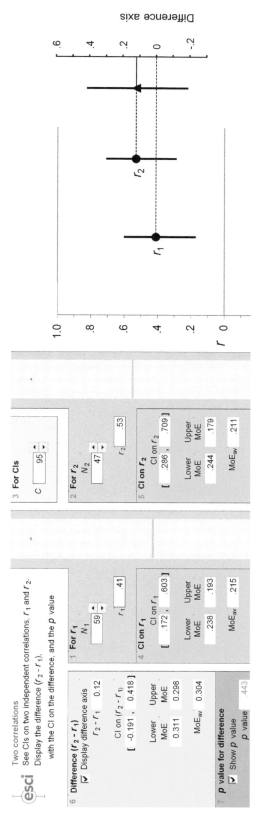

Figure 11.22. The difference between two correlations from Figure 11.21: $r_1 = .41$ with $N = 59$ for women, and $r_2 = .53$ with $N = 47$ for men. The difference is depicted by the triangle at right on the difference axis, with its CI. The limits of the CI on $(r_2 - r_1)$ are shown at left, near red 6. From **Two correlations**.

▶
r can be a useful
effect size measure
for meta-analysis.

was enormously popularized by Malcolm Gladwell (2008), who argued in his book *Outliers* that 10,000 hours of focused practice is the key to achieving expertise.

However, this view is now being challenged, with one important contribution being a large meta-analysis of correlations between amount of intense practice and level of achievement: Macnamara et al. (2014) combined 157 correlations reported in a wide range of fields, from sports to music and education, and found $r = .35$ [.30, .39].

Figure 11.23 shows some of the data from Macnamara et al. (2014). As usual, to carry out meta-analysis we need to judge that all the studies are examining the same or sufficiently similar questions. The figure shows the random effects meta-analysis of the 16 main correlations for music. You can see at red 7 that the overall result is $r = .41$ [.28, .53], which is consistent with the main conclusion of the larger meta-analysis. The example shows that *r* can be useful for meta-analysis. Indeed correlation *r* and Cohen's *d* are probably the most widely used effect size measures for meta-analysis.

The researchers' conclusion was that, in many fields, the correlation between amount of practice and achievement is only modest, a result that conflicts with the established position of Ericsson and others. Search online for "10,000 hours and expertise", or "10,000 hours", and you should easily find articles describing the Ericsson–Gladwell position. You should also find recent articles with titles like "Scientists debunk the myth…" of 10,000 hours. No-one doubts that long effort and persistent focused practice is needed to achieve expertise, but the question is the extent of the contribution of other factors, notably innate talent. Thanks partly to meta-analysis of correlations, it seems that once again we can believe that genius is to some extent born, and not only made.

It's time for take-home messages. To write yours, you could think back to the pictures we've encountered. Scatterplots of course, but also quadrants and the battle, shotgun blasts, confidence intervals of course, and finally a forest plot. I couldn't think of any good picture of causation—maybe an arrow?—but causation probably springs to mind anyway.

? Quiz 11.3

1. For a particular *N*, the CI for $r = .6$ is longer / shorter than the CI for $r = .3$. For a particular *r*, larger *N* gives a CI that is longer / shorter.
2. Correlation does not necessarily imply _____.
3. Messerli (2012) reported that countries in which people eat lots of chocolate also tend to win lots of Nobel prizes ($r = .79$, 95% CI [.55, .91], $N = 22$). Does this mean eating chocolate will cause you to win a Nobel prize? Suggest some other explanations for this association.
4. For *r*, Cohen's reference values are _____, _____, and _____ for small, medium, and large, but interpretation of *r* should depend on the _____.
5. The CI on the difference between two independent correlations is
   a. not helpful unless sample sizes are very large.
   b. sure to include zero.
   c. shorter than either of the CIs on the two separate correlations.
   d. longer than either of the CIs on the two separate correlations.
6. Considering meta-analysis,
   a. it's a disadvantage that the CI on *r* is almost always asymmetric.
   b. values of *r* need to be transformed to values of Cohen's *d*.
   c. it's advisable to use the fixed effect model when using *r*.
   d. None of the above.

2 ☑ Display by weight

1 Effect size, r, for each study

11 Study weight %

Study no.	Study name	r	N	Study in?	LL , UL Correlation r	Study weight %
1	Violin, viola	.67	109	▷	[.551 , .762]	8.0
2	Strings	.51	55	▷	[.283 , .683]	6.8
3	Piano	.4	19	▷	[-.066 , .723]	4.0
4	Piano	.46	30	▷	[.12 , .704]	5.2
5	Piano	.47	19	▷	[.02 , .762]	4.0
6	Piano	.228	52	▷	[-.048 , .471]	6.6
7	Piano	-.224	24	▷	[-.575 , .197]	4.6
8	Piano	.104	52	▷	[-.174 , .366]	6.6
9	Piano	.322	16	▷	[-.207 , .705]	3.5
10	All	.231	97	▷	[.033 , .411]	7.8
11	Piano	.67	57	▷	[.496 , .792]	6.8
12	Piano	.41	107	▷	[.239 , .557]	8.0
13	Band	.34	178	▷	[.203 , .464]	8.6
14	Music majors	.31	64	▷	[.069 , .516]	7.1
15	Music majors	.54	19	▷	[.114 , .798]	4.0
16	All	.583	135	▷	[.459 , .685]	8.3
17					[,]	
30					[,]	

7 Meta-analysis result

Random effects .406 [.28 , .532]

8 Model for meta-analysis
○ Fixed effect
● Random effects

9 Diamond ratio 2.03

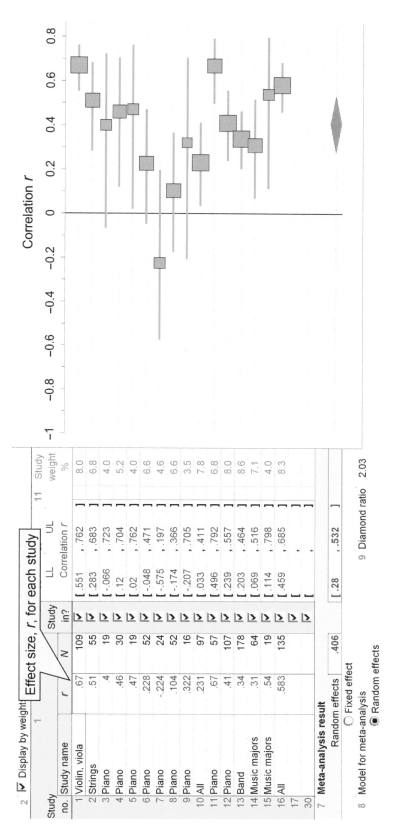

Correlation r

Figure 11.23. Random effects meta-analysis of the 16 main correlations of amount of practice with level of achievement, for music, from Macnamara et al. (2014). For each study the instrument or type of music training is shown under **Study name**, and *r* and *N* have been entered below red 1. From **Single r** in **ESCI intro Meta-Analysis**.

11.36 Open the **Single r** page of **ESCI intro Meta-Analysis** and you should see the data shown in Figure 11.23.

  a. At red 8, click between fixed effect and random effects meta-analysis, and note the diamond ratio.

  b. What can you say about heterogeneity? Is your response consistent with the appearance of the forest plot? Explain.

11.37 Which CIs in the forest plot are most asymmetric? Is that what you expect?

 11.38 Click at red 4 to display *p* values for the individual studies and the result.

  a. What null hypothesis do the *p* values relate to? What could you conclude?

  b. Compare your conclusion with the conclusion of Macnamara et al. (2014).

  c. Which approach to data analysis, the one using *p* you have just looked at or that of Macnamara et al., should we prefer and why?

11.39 Revise your take-home messages if you wish.

 ## Reporting Your Work

Correlation may not imply causation, but identifying and interpreting associations between variables still serves as one of the most important tools available for scientific research. When reporting correlations, you should usually include:

- whether examining the correlation is planned or exploratory, unless this is already clear—be sure your research plan is more thought out than just "examine all possible correlations" or you'll likely be seeing faces in the clouds;
- basic descriptive statistics for both variables being correlated;
- a scatterplot if possible;
- the value of *r* and its CI. Remember that calculating a CI requires assuming the data are a sample from a bivariate normal population. If that seems problematic, make a comment and consider not reporting a CI;
- the sample size for calculating *r* (which, due to missing data, may not be the same as the sample size collected);
- if desired, the *p* value—be sure to state the null hypothesis, which is usually but not always that $\rho = 0$;
- an interpretation of the correlation that considers not only the point estimate but also the CI—consider what the full range of the CI means in terms of correlation strength, interpreted in the context, including any relevant past research; if range restriction is evident make your interpretation suitably tentative.

Typically, you will be reporting correlations for non-experimental research, where no variables have been manipulated. In this case, an essential guideline for reporting is to avoid causal language. That is, avoid phrases like "the effect of *X* on *Y*" or "*X* produced a change in *Y*". Instead, use language suggesting association without causation. For example:

- The relationship between *X* and *Y* was examined.
- Participants with high *X* also tended to have high *Y*.
- This shows that *X* is weakly related to *Y*.
- There was a strong association between *X* and *Y*.

Finally, report *r* values without a zero before the decimal point (e.g., *r* = .36). That's due to the persnickety APA style rule you've read about in previous chapters that there is no leading zero for statistics that cannot exceed 1 (APA, 2010, p. 113) in absolute value.
Here are some text-only examples:

The correlation between well-being and self-esteem was $r = .35$, 95% CI [.16, .53], $N = 95$. Relative to other correlates of well-being that have been reported, this is a fairly strong

▶ For correlations, report *r*, its CI, and sample size. Be sure to include a scatterplot and to discuss how well assumptions for correlation are met.

relationship. The CI, however, is somewhat long and consistent with anywhere from a weak positive to a very strong positive relationship.

The correlation between well-being and gratitude was $r = .35$, 95% CI [−.11, .69], $N = 20$. The CI is quite long. These data are only sufficient to rule out a strong negative relationship between these variables.

The correlation between well-being and GPA was $r = .02$, 95% CI [−.18, .22], $N = 95$. The CI suggests at most a weak positive or negative relationship between these variables.

It is popular in journal articles to report large numbers of correlations using a correlation matrix. This is a very efficient way of reporting correlations, but be sure to include confidence intervals. As you can see in Table 11.2, in a correlation matrix each variable is represented along both rows and columns. Each cell reports the r value between its row and column variables. The diagonal cells are not reported because these are cells where the row and column variables are the same. (What would the correlation be between a variable and itself? Think about it or use ESCI to try for yourself.) Note that a correlation matrix is symmetric above and below the diagonal, so usually only one or the other is filled in. Although that may sound complicated when written out, in practice correlation matrices are easy to use. For example, in the matrix of three variables below, what is the correlation between well-being and negative affect? Between negative and positive affect? If this is making sense, your answers should be −.34 and −.10.

Table 11.2 Correlation Matrix for Different Components of Happiness

	Well-being	Positive Affect	Negative Affect
Well-being	—		
Positive Affect	.37 [.25, .47]	—	
Negative Affect	−.34 [−.44, −.22]	−.10 [−.22, .02]	—

Although you know that seeing a scatterplot is essential to interpreting the relationship between two variables, you'll notice that many journal articles report r values without accompanying scatterplots. This is a convention left over from a time when preparing figures was time consuming and expensive. Nowadays, figures are cheaper and there is a stronger emphasis on showing the data. Therefore, try to include scatterplots for key correlations whenever possible. Some statistical software even allows the creation of scatterplot matrices, in which each correlation value in a correlation matrix is represented by its scatterplot. This is an extremely powerful way to summarize lots of relationships at once. Follow this link: tiny. cc/spmatrix to an example of a scatterplot matrix. There are four variables, so six scatterplots, which are shown in the lower triangle of the matrix. The r values themselves are shown in the upper triangle.

 Take-Home Messages

■ Pearson correlation, r, is a measure of the strength of the linear component of the relation between two interval variables, X and Y. It can take values between −1 and 1.

■ The scatterplot of X and Y is a picture of the N data points. The cross through the X and Y means can be helpful for eyeballing: r reflects the balance between points in the matched (HH, LL) quadrants and in the mismatched (LH, HL) quadrants.

■ The value of r is the sum of the $Z_X Z_Y$ values for the points, divided by $(N − 1)$. It's the outcome of a battle between the matched and mismatched quadrants.

■ Seeing the scatterplot is essential for understanding aspects of the relation between X and Y beyond the linear component measured by r. Watch for range restrictions, floor or ceiling effects, and curvilinear relationships.

Polya

- To calculate the CI on r, the CI on the difference between two independent correlations, or a p value, we must assume a bivariate normal population of (X, Y) values, with population correlation ρ. CIs are usually asymmetric and CI length depends on both N and r.
- The p value can be calculated using any ρ value as null hypothesis, but often $\rho_0 = 0$ is used without sufficient thought as to whether it's appropriate in the context.
- Correlation does not necessarily imply causality. An r value may be merely a face in the clouds, or there may be complex causal links amongst X, Y, and perhaps other variables.
- Values of r need to be interpreted in context. The Cohen reference values of .1, .3, and .5, and any other reference values, are only applicable in some contexts.
- Correlation is often used to assess the reliability and validity of measures, but beware p values and prefer CIs. Good measures can have values of $r = .8$ or higher.
- It can be useful to combine values of r by meta-analysis.

 End-of-Chapter Exercises

1) For each of the scatterplots in Figure 11.24, eyeball an r value.

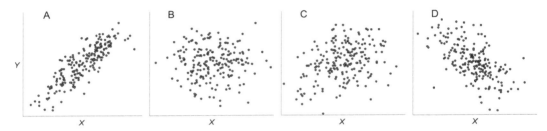

Figure 11.24. Four scatterplots for eyeballing practice.

2) To what extent does initial performance in a class relate to performance on a final exam? Table 11.3 lists first exam and final exam scores for nine students enrolled in an introductory psychology course. Exam scores are percentages, where 0 = no answers correct and 100 = all answers correct. You can load this data set (**Exam_Scores**) from the book website.

Table 11.3 Initial and Final Exam Scores for Nine Students

StudentID	Exam 1, X	Final Exam, Y	Z_x	Z_y	$Z_x Z_y$
1177	85.0	72.0			
1288	96.8	92.0			
1327	100.0	96.0			
1911	100.0	95.0			
1862	84.3	91.0			
1578	83.0	88.0			
1022	96.8	77.0			
1915	89.5	86.0			
1116	54.0	75.0			
Mean	87.71	85.78			
SD	14.35	8.97			

$$\text{Total} \sum Z_X Z_Y$$

$$(N-1)$$

$$r = \frac{\sum Z_X Z_Y}{(N-1)}$$

a. Enter the first and final exam scores into ESCI to generate a scatterplot. Just looking at the scatterplot, what r value do you eyeball?

b. Are there any cautions with using r to describe this data set? Does the relationship seem strongly nonlinear, is there restriction of range or a ceiling effect, or are there extreme outliers? Remember that to assess restriction of range it's best to set the scales of X and Y to show the full possible range of 0–100. You could edit the two axes to show that range.

c. Fill the blanks in Table 11.3 to calculate r, using a calculator or spreadsheet. Fill the Z_X and Z_Y columns, then multiply each student's pair of z scores to fill the $Z_X Z_Y$ column. Then complete the calculations to fill the bottom right cells and find r.

d. Using ESCI, you should find the same value of Pearson's r between Exam 1 and Final Exam scores.

3) Below are correlations reported in recent journal articles. For each, use the **One correlation** page of ESCI to calculate the 95% CI for ρ (rho). Then interpret. Assume that the authors verified that the relationships are reasonably linear and otherwise appropriate for description using r.

a. To what extent does income inequality relate to academic dishonesty? To investigate, Neville (2012) measured income inequality for each U.S. state, then measured search traffic for each state related to academic dishonesty (e.g. "buy term papers", "free college papers"). He found that states with higher income inequality also tend to have higher levels of search traffic related to academic dishonesty: $r = .45$, $N = 50$.

b. To what extent is early success in school related to income later in life? Ritchie et al. (2013) obtained annual income data for a large sample of British adults, then correlated these with reading scores from age 7. (For most participants, this was about 40 years prior to the income measurement.) Early reading scores were correlated with income, $r = .21$, $N = 1000$.

c. The full study of Ritchie et al. (2013) was much larger, with more than 14,000 participants. Would the CI for the full study be shorter or longer than you just calculated using $N = 1000$? Would it be greatly or only slightly different in length?

d. To what extent is your weight related to your ideas about diet and exercise? McFerran et al. (2013) conducted an online study in which participants were asked to report their Body Mass Index (BMI). Participants also rated the degree to which they believed exercise is more important than diet for controlling weight. The belief in exercise to control weight was correlated with BMI: $r = .25$, $N = 84$.

4) For each of the findings in Exercise 3, give at least two different causal explanations that could underlie the observed correlation.

5) For each of the findings in Exercise 3, use Figure 11.19 to select a sample size you consider reasonable for replicating the original study. Choosing N is a matter of judgment, but consider where a likely CI might fall in relation to 0. Also consider the CI on the original value or r that you found when answering Question 3 and remember that ρ could easily be anywhere within that interval, or even a little beyond it.

6) Is there really such a thing as beauty sleep? To investigate, researchers decided to examine the extent to which sleep relates to attractiveness. Each of 70 college students self-reported the amount of sleep they had the night before. In addition, a photograph was taken of each participant and rated for attractiveness on a scale from 1 to 10 by two judges of the opposite gender. The average rating score was used. You can load this data set (**Sleep_Beauty**) from the book website.

a. What is r and the 95% CI for the relationship between sleep and attractiveness?

b. Like you, the researchers obtained a negative correlation. They concluded that those who sleep more are somewhat *less* attractive. You can see, however, that these researchers have made at least one serious error. Explain.

7) Clinton conducted a survey of college students to determine the extent to which well-being is related to campus involvement (**Campus_Involvement** data set on the book website). Participants completed a measure of subjective well-being (scale from 1 to 5) and a measure of campus involvement (scale from 1 to 5). Participants also reported gender (male or female) and commuter status (0 = resident, 1 = commuter).

a. What is the relationship between well-being and campus involvement for commuters? For residents? To what extent is this relationship different for these two groups of students? Interpret.

b. What is the relationship between well-being and campus involvement for men? For women? To what extent is this relationship different for these two groups of students? Interpret.

8) To what extent is analytic thinking incompatible with religious faith? Gervais & Norenzayan (2012) asked participants to complete a test of analytic thinking and a scale of religious belief. Scores on the analytic thinking task were negatively related to religious belief, $r = -.22$, $N = 179$. Later, Sanchez, Sundermeier, Gray, and Calin-Jageman (2016) conducted a close replication of this study using an online sample. They found $r = -.07$, $N = 454$. Use the **Single r** page of **ESCI intro Meta-Analysis** to integrate these two findings. Interpret, considering the result and its CI, and also the diamond ratio. What can you conclude?

❓ Answers to Quizzes

Quiz 11.1

1) linear; 2) decreases; 3) 1, −1, 0; 4) matched; 5) z scores; 6) positive, increase, negative, decrease.

Quiz 11.2

1) d; 2) shorter, longer; 3) random, bivariate normal; 4) very weakly negative to very strongly positive; 5) about four times as many participants: 4 × 10 = 40; 6) shorter, asymmetric.

Quiz 11.3

1) shorter, shorter; 2) causation; 3) No; wealth could be a common factor, enabling both larger chocolate consumption and larger expenditure on science education and research. Indeed Ortega (2013) pointed out that an indicator of wealth (GDP, or gross domestic product) is strongly correlated with both chocolate consumption and amount of Nobel prize success; 4) .1, .3, .5, context; 5) d; 6) d.

Answers to In-Chapter Exercises

11.1 .5, −.4, .8, .3. I prefer quadrants, except for .8, for which tightness to the line is useful.

11.2 b. .1: shotgun blast; −1: points exactly on a line sloping down to the right; Figure 11.9 illustrates $r = .4$; −.4: mirror image of $r = .4$.

11.5 They are all $r = .4$.

11.6 a. Participants 6 and 10, as marked in scatterplot; b. They are the farthest from the center of the cross, and from the two mean lines.

11.8 a. $Z_x Z_y = 0.1238$; r decreases to .88, only a small change because the extra point fits with the previous general pattern; b. r changes most when $Z_x Z_y$ is large and negative, because that influences the battle most; points at top left or bottom right give that large negative contribution.

11.9 It's large and negative, so has an enormous influence in the battle of the quadrants, because other values tend to be small and mainly positive.

11.11 The range of X is even more restricted, so it is likely that r is even smaller than .13.

11.12 By selecting only college graduates, the range of IQ scores is probably restricted, meaning the correlation between IQ scores and income would be reduced. In the whole population, that correlation may be large, meaning IQ would matter for income.

11.13 a. Up to and including 18 °C: I eyeballed .8 (calculated $r = .83$); b. For 18 °C and above, I eyeballed −.8 (calculated $r = -.85$); c. The effect of range restriction on r depends greatly on the relationship, especially if nonlinear.

11.15 a. For $\rho = .5$, in fact for any fixed ρ, larger N gives less variation in r, meaning a narrower dance.
b. For $N = 40$, in fact for any fixed N, the widest variation is for $\rho = 0$ and the dance becomes narrower for ρ approaching 1 or −1.

11.16 a. For a given N and r, the CI for $-r$ is the mirror image of the CI for r.
b. For any given N, the CI is long and symmetric when $r = 0$, and becomes shorter and more asymmetric as r becomes closer to 1 or −1. For larger N, the CI is generally shorter, but the pattern of change with r is similar. See Figure 11.17.

11.17 The CI gets shorter as N increases, whatever the r. See Figure 11.18.

11.18 [.31, .61], so the population correlation is most likely around .4 to .5 but may plausibly be as low as around .3 or as high as around .6. The long CI signals considerable uncertainty.

11.19 a, b, c. The r values and CIs bounce around. In the long run, 95% of the CIs should include $\rho = -.7$.

11.20 In each column the CIs would bounce around. For $N = 10$ the intervals would be generally longest, and most variable in length. For $N = 160$, shortest and least variable. $N = 40$ would be intermediate. Long run capture rate should be 95% in all columns.

11.21 CI is [.18, .52]. Set $\rho_0 = .5$ and note that $p = .09$. Because $p > .05$, we can't reject that model. Correspondingly, the CI includes .5, but tells us that a wide range of values of ρ, roughly from .2 to .5, are plausibly consistent with the data.

11.22 a. CI is still [.18, .52]. Set $\rho_0 = .25$ and see $p = .23$. Because $p > .05$, we cannot reject the second model either, and .25 is within the CI; b. We need a more precise estimate of ρ to allow us to assess the two models better, so should collect a larger sample of data.

11.23 b. The SD values apply to the sampling distributions of r values, so they are standard errors. (Recall that SE is the standard deviation of a sampling distribution, e.g., the mean heap.) For means, SE = (population SD)/$\sqrt{N}$, which fits with the SD values in the table approximately halving as N is multiplied by 4. The pattern is reasonable, and the guideline seems to apply, at least roughly, for correlations as well as means.

11.24 The CI on r depends on N but also on r itself, as Figure 11.17 illustrates.

11.25 a. About 0.2; b. No, $N = 200$ gives MoE of roughly 0.15. Need N of over 300 (actually, more than 320) for MoE no more than 0.1.

11.26 a. The claim is almost certainly based on a correlation of reported vegetable consumption with school progress. It may be plausible, but quite likely reflects a number of causal relations; b. Perhaps a stable family, good parental education, and parental employment are all associated with both eating more vegetables and doing well at school. It may be possible to assign families randomly to low or high vegetable consumption conditions, then monitor school progress, but quite likely we couldn't run that study long enough to reveal any changes in performance. More complex methods would be needed to tease out multiple causal links.

11.27 a. No, for such a couple, divorce might bring calm to their children's lives and less pressure to use drugs; b. Any individual case is likely to have many aspects to consider, and an overall correlation is only one. Especially for a couple on the brink of divorce, the overall correlation may be of little relevance or even likely to mislead.

11.28 Very feasible; you could take further samples of towns and cities, and measure walking speeds. The results could easily be similar.

11.29 [.72, .97], $p < .001$ using $\rho_0 = 0$. It's reasonable to calculate those because it's reasonable to regard the 15 towns and cities studied as a random sample from the bivariate normal distribution of all towns and cities. The scatterplot in Figure 11.20 shows no strong signs of departure from what would be expected from such a distribution.

11.30 Perhaps people's general sense of urgency (the "pace of life") is greater in cities and prompts faster walking. To investigate, we could seek measures—perhaps of people's attitudes—that assessed the pace of life as directly as possible, and correlate those measures with log population.

11.31 b. We could ask people about their life goals, their immediate concerns, and their sense of urgency, and look for correlations with population size of town or city.

11.32 I would start by trying to understand what "important" might mean to the farmer. Wealthy? Powerful? Educated? From a Bolivian city rather than a village? Then think of correlations that might be informative to investigate.

11.33 Null hypothesis is no difference between the population correlations. The p of .44 means we can't reject the null hypothesis at the .05 level, which is consistent with the CI easily including 0 and the conclusion of no evidence of a population difference.

11.34 b. Difference is 0.12 [−0.03, 0.27], shorter but still a fairly long CI. Still no evidence of a difference. The p value is .12, so again we can't reject the null hypothesis.

11.35　$r_2 = .681$ for $p = .05$. That's a large difference between .41 for women and .68 for men, before obtaining even the weak evidence of $p = .05$ of a population difference.

11.36　a. Diamond ratio = 2.0, which is large and matches how the diamond appears to change between the two models of meta-analysis; b. There is considerable heterogeneity, which is consistent with very large bouncing of the CIs in the forest plot, including a number of CIs that do not overlap at all.

11.37　The CIs closest to 1 are most asymmetric, as we expect.

11.38　a. The popouts explain that p refers to $\rho_0 = 0$. Nine of 16 studies have $p < .05$, and the overall result is $p < .001$, so we confidently reject the null hypothesis that $\rho_0 = 0$ and conclude there's a statistically significant positive correlation of amount of practice with achievement; b. Macnamara et al. estimated the correlation quite precisely and interpreted the value as indicating a correlation considerably smaller than the theory of Ericsson predicts; c. The estimation approach is more informative, and was used by Macnamara et al. to arrive at a conclusion that corresponds closely with the research question they were investigating.

12
Regression

In Chapter 11 we saw that correlation is a measure of the relationship between X and Y. Like correlation, *regression* is based on a data set of (X, Y) pairs, but it's different from correlation in that it gives an estimate of Y for a value of X that we choose. So correlation is a number that summarizes, overall, how X and Y relate, whereas regression takes a chosen single value of X and provides an estimate of Y for that X. Recall that Figure 11.1 was a scatterplot of Well-being (the Y variable) and Body Satisfaction (the X variable), for 106 college students. Figure 11.21 showed the separate scatterplots for women and men. Suppose Daniel scores $X = 3.0$ for Body Satisfaction: What Well-being score would we expect for him, assuming he comes from the same population of college students? We can use regression to estimate Y (Daniel's Well-being score) for $X = 3.0$. There are two steps:

1. Calculate from the data the *regression line for Y on X*.
2. Use that line to calculate an estimate of Y for $X = 3.0$.

Regression focuses on what X can tell us about Y. Almost always, X can tell us part of the story of Y, but not all of it. Informally, the full story of Y divides into two parts:

$$\text{The story of } Y = \text{What } X \text{ can tell us about } Y + \text{The remainder} \quad (12.1)$$

First part, uses regression   Second part, what's left over

◀ The informal story of Y.

Regression is thus different from correlation, but the two are intimately linked. We'll see that X makes its contribution to the Y story (the first part) via the regression line, but it's r that determines how large this contribution is. If the correlation is large, X and the regression line give considerable information about Y; if small, they tell only a small proportion of the Y story.

I said that correlation is an effect size measure that has long been routinely reported and interpreted by researchers, which is excellent. For regression the news is even better, because researchers not only report and interpret regression effect sizes, but quite often report regression CIs as well—meaning they are already largely using the new statistics.

Here's the agenda for this chapter:

- The regression line for Y on X: minimizing the standard deviation of residuals
- Regression, correlation, and the slope of the regression line
- The proportion of variance accounted for: r^2
- Regression reversed: the regression of X on Y
- Assumptions underlying simple linear regression
- Confidence intervals and the uncertainty of estimation of Y
- A possibly strange natural phenomenon: regression to the mean

THE REGRESSION LINE FOR *Y* ON *X*

We use the **regression line** of *Y on X* to calculate an estimate for the *predicted* variable *Y* from a value of *predictor* variable *X*.

Figure 12.1 shows the scatterplot of Well-being (*Y*) and Body Satisfaction (*X*), for *N* = 47 men, as in Figure 11.21. First, some regression jargon. The line in Figure 12.1 is the *regression line*. For correlation, as we discussed in Chapter 11, the two variables *X* and *Y* are interchangeable, meaning we can swap the labels *X* and *Y* and still calculate the same *r*. With regression, however, the two variables have different roles: *X* is the *predictor* variable and *Y* the *predicted* variable, also known as the *criterion* variable. Those terms reflect the frequent use of regression for prediction—we often regard the regression estimate of *Y*, for a particular value of *X*, as a prediction for *Y*. We speak of "the regression of *Y* on *X*" or "the regression of *Y* against *X*". (Later we'll consider the reverse, the regression of *X* on *Y*, for estimating *X* given a particular value of *Y*.)

> For the regression of *Y* on *X*, *X* is the **predictor variable** and *Y* the **predicted variable**, also known as the **criterion variable**.

In Figure 12.1, the regression line of *Y* on *X* tells us that, if *X* = 3.0 for Daniel, then our best point estimate of Daniel's Well-being score is $\hat{Y} = 4.44$. We use $\hat{Y}$, which we say as "*Y*-hat", for the *regression estimate*—the estimated value of *Y* calculated from the regression line. Later we'll find that there's large uncertainty in that estimate, which is hardly surprising given only a medium number of data points (*N* = 47) and the considerable scatter that gives a correlation of only medium size (*r* = .53).

> The **regression estimate** is $\hat{Y}$, which is the value of *Y* calculated from the regression line for a particular value of *X*.

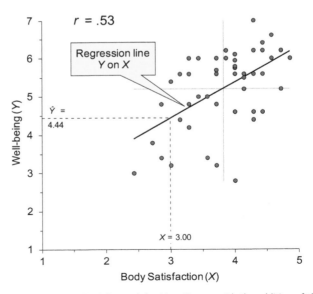

Figure 12.1. Same as Figure 11.21, left panel, for *N* = 47 men, with the addition of the regression line of *Y* on *X*. If Body Satisfaction is *X* = 3.0, the Well-being score calculated from the regression line is $\hat{Y}$ = 4.44 as the dashed lines indicate. The cross of horizontal and vertical lines marks (M_x, M_y), the point at the two means.

I'm talking about estimating Y for a particular value of X. That doesn't mean I'm making any assumption about X causing Y. Just as with correlation, there might be any pattern of causation between X, Y, and other variables, or no causation at all. With regression, as with correlation, we are working with the relationship between X and Y in some data set. There may well be interesting causation to investigate, but perhaps not.

> Using regression to estimate Y from X makes no assumption about possible causal links between X, Y, and other variables.

As you can see in Figure 12.1, the regression line goes through the point (M_x, M_y), the means of X and Y, which is marked in the figure by the cross of horizontal and vertical lines. The regression line is designed to give the best estimate of Y for any particular value of X. How is its slope (sometimes called its gradient) determined? I'll take two approaches to answering that central question. The first considers estimation error and how we can minimize it.

Minimizing the Standard Deviation of the Residuals

We want the best regression estimates we can get, meaning we want to minimize estimation error. By *estimation error*, I mean $(Y - \hat{Y})$, which is the vertical distance between a data point and the line, as marked by the red vertical lines in Figure 12.2. The Y refers to the data point—one of the dots in Figure 12.2—and the $\hat{Y}$ refers to the other end of its vertical line, which lies on the regression line. There are N data points and therefore N of the $(Y - \hat{Y})$ values, which are also called *residuals*, the idea being that, while the $\hat{Y}$ estimates calculated from the line tell us the first part of the story of Y—the first part in informal Equation 12.1—the second part is told by the $(Y - \hat{Y})$ values and is the remaining, or residual, part of the story. We'll come back to this idea.

> $(Y - \hat{Y})$ is an *estimation error*, or *residual*, where Y is an observed value for some value of X, and $\hat{Y}$ is the estimated value given by the regression line for that value of X.

A *residual* is $(Y - \hat{Y})$, the difference between the value of Y for a data point (X, Y), and $\hat{Y}$, the regression estimate for that value of X.

The regression line is selected to minimize estimation error. More precisely, it's selected so that the standard deviation of the residuals is minimized. Imagine rotating

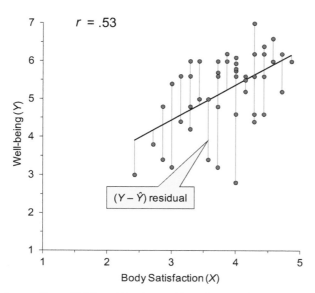

Figure 12.2. Same as Figure 12.1, but with red vertical lines, from the data points to the regression line, to mark the $(Y - \hat{Y})$ residuals.

the regression line in Figure 12.2 about the point (M_x, M_y) and noting the changes to all the residuals. Rotate it a little clockwise or counterclockwise and some of the red vertical lines become a little longer, others a little shorter. Almost certainly, the standard deviation of the residuals changes. In fact, the regression line in the figure is positioned so that the SD is as small as possible. Rotate the line either way and the SD increases—we'll see that happen in ESCI in a moment. Therefore, the regression line will, on average, give us better estimates than lines with larger or smaller slopes.

The SD of the residuals is written as $s_{Y.X}$, which is a measure of the variation of the data points from the line. The equation is

SD of residuals.

$$s_{Y.X} = \sqrt{\frac{\sum \left(Y - \hat{Y}\right)^2}{(N-2)}} \quad \underset{\boxed{df}}{\overset{\boxed{SS(\text{residuals})}}{}} \tag{12.2}$$

where the summation is over all N data points. The numerator under the square root is called the *sum of squares of residuals*, or SS(residuals). The denominator is the degrees of freedom, which is $(N-2)$. (Optional extra remark: The minus 2 reflects the fact that two degrees of freedom are used up by estimating both the intercept and the slope of the regression line, which are the determining features of the line, as we'll see in a moment.) I'll talk about minimizing the SD of residuals, on the left side in Equation 12.2. However, that's equivalent to minimizing the SS(residuals), the sum of squares of residuals, on the right side, which is what many textbooks discuss. In summary, the slope of the regression line is chosen to give us the best regression estimates based on our data set, and it does this by minimizing $s_{Y.X}$, the SD of residuals. Let's see how the minimization works.

I'll now shift to the small Thomason 1 data set, to keep things simple. Figure 12.3 shows the scatterplot for that data set, as in Figure 11.10, with the regression line and the red $(Y - \hat{Y})$ residuals displayed. At red 12 below the scatterplot is the equation of the regression line for Y on X:

Regression line,
Y on X.

$$\hat{Y} = a + b \times X \tag{12.3}$$

$$\underset{\boxed{\text{Intercept}} \quad \boxed{\text{Slope}}}{}$$

 12.1 Fire up the **Scatterplots** page of **ESCI intro chapters 10–16**. If necessary, scroll right and click at red 16 to load the Thomason 1 data set. At the top, click at red 9 to reveal a panel with regression information. Click at red 10 to display the regression line, and at red 13 to mark the residuals with vertical red lines. Your screen should resemble Figure 12.3.

As you may know, the *intercept* is the value of $\hat{Y}$ when $X = 0$, and, therefore, is where the line, extended if necessary, intersects the Y axis. For the Thomason 1 data set, the estimates from the data—which are calculated by fitting the line so it goes through the means and minimizes $s_{Y.X}$, the SD of residuals—are $a = 4.22$ and $b = 0.78$. (As usual, I'm rounding the values displayed by ESCI.) That b value is the *slope* of the regression line. As you can see in Figure 12.3, the regression equation for predicting the posttest score (Y), given a pretest score (X), is:

Regression line for
Thomason 1.

$$\hat{Y} = 4.22 + 0.78 \times X \tag{12.4}$$

Now consider what we want to minimize—the SD of the residuals, which for the regression line is reported near red 13 to be $s_{Y.X} = 1.37$. Let's investigate the minimization.

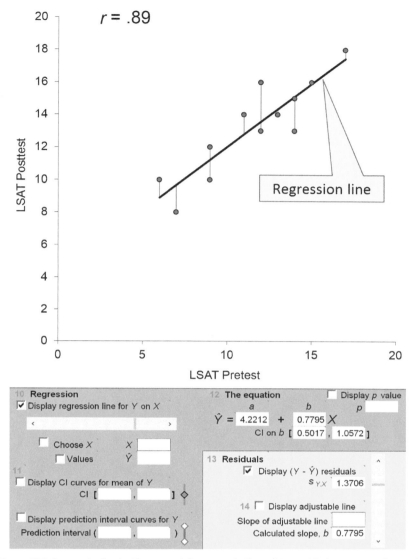

Figure 12.3. Scatterplot for the Thomason 1 data set, as in Figure 11.10, with the regression line and red (Y − Ŷ) residuals displayed. For the data set, N = 12 and r = .89. From **Scatterplots**.

esci 12.2 Click at red 14 to display a red adjustable line in place of the black regression line. Use the slider to change the slope of the red line, while still seeing the residuals marked by the fine vertical lines.

    a. Over what range can you adjust the slope of the adjustable line?

    b. Watch $s_{Y.X}$ near red 13. How does it change as you rotate the adjustable line?

    c. What happens when the slope of the adjustable line is, as close as possible, equal to b, whose value in the equation is displayed also below red 14?

I hope you found that the minimum value of $s_{Y.X}$ was 1.37, and that this occurred when the slope of the adjustable line was equal (or very close to equal) to b = 0.78, at which moment the line changed from red to black. Rotating the line

The regression line of Y on X minimizes $s_{Y.X}$, the SD of residuals.

either way increased s_{YX}. Does the regression line look, roughly, as though it fits the pattern of points? Now for the second approach to thinking about the slope.

Regression Line Slope, and Correlation

I'll discuss some thought experiments about predicting the GPA of a student I'll call Robert. As in Chapter 4, I'll use the international GPA scale that ranges from 1 to 7. If I gave you no information about Robert, what would be your best guess of his GPA?

 Thinking, thinking. Discussing, discussing.

It would be the mean GPA of all students, the mean usually being the best choice of a single value to represent a population. For your college, the mean may be, say, 4.5. Now suppose I told you that Robert is 176 cm tall. I also reported GPA and height data for a sample of 40 students, not including Robert, as pictured in Panel A of Figure 12.4. The correlation happens to be $r = 0$, so telling you Robert's height gives you no information about his GPA. Therefore, the college mean of 4.5 is still your best GPA prediction. If you didn't know that college mean of 4.5, you could use M_Y, the mean of Y for the sample, which is 4.4. That mean is marked by the heavy horizontal line, M_Y in the figure. In Panel A, because $r = 0$, whatever the value of X (a student's height) the horizontal line at a GPA of $M_Y = 4.4$ is the best point estimate based on the data. In other words, the regression line is that horizontal line, $\hat{Y} = M_Y = 4.4$, and its slope is zero. For any value of X, our regression estimate is $\hat{Y} = 4.4$, but we expect great uncertainty in that estimate because there's so much scatter in the data points, and $r = 0$. What I'm saying is that, if $r = 0$, height gives no information about GPA, so we can't do better than use $M_Y = 4.4$ as our estimate of Robert's GPA—but don't expect it to be a good estimate.

▶ ——————————
The slope of the $r = 1$ line is (s_Y/s_X), the ratio of the two SDs.
——————————

Next you decide to investigate the Nifty test (no, I hadn't heard of it before either) as a possible predictor variable. You test 20 students on the Nifty, and later record their GPA at the end of the year. Panel B presents the data, and shows that, remarkably, the correlation is $r = 1.0$. The line in Panel B goes through all the points and is the regression line that we'd use to estimate GPA. Its slope is (s_Y/s_X), where, as you may recall, s_Y and s_X are the standard deviations of Y and X respectively. That slope is the ratio of the two standard deviations, and so its units are (GPA units)/(Nifty scale units) or, in general, (units of Y)/(units of X). It's worth remembering that the slope of the $r = 1$ regression line is (s_Y/s_X). We'll be seeing it again.

Knowing a student's Nifty score gives excellent information about that student's GPA—sufficient information for us to make a fully accurate estimate of that student's GPA. Therefore, in this case with $r = 1$ all the points lie on the regression line. If Robert, not in our sample of 20, scores $X = 90$ on the Nifty, Panel B illustrates that the GPA estimate given by the line is $\hat{Y} = 5.9$. Assuming Robert is from the same population as our sample, we estimate his GPA will be 5.9.

Recall Equation 12.1, our informal expression for the story of Y. By "story of Y" I'm actually referring to the variability of Y about its mean, so, still informally, I can write:

▶ ——————————
The informal story of Y.
——————————

$$\text{The story of } Y =$$

(What X tells us about *the variability of* Y) + The residuals   (12.5)

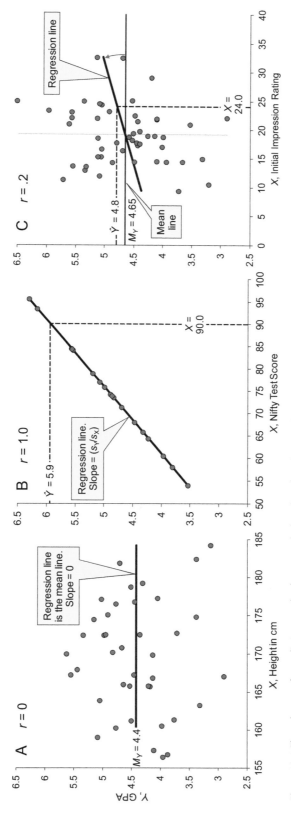

Figure 12.4. Three data sets for predicting a student's GPA, Y, which is plotted on the vertical axis in every panel. Panel A is the scatterplot of GPA and X, which is height, for a sample of $N = 40$ students, with $r = 0$. Panel B pictures GPA and X, which is Nifty test score, for a sample of $N = 20$ students, with $r = 1.0$. Panel C pictures GPA and X, which is initial impression rating, for a sample of $N = 50$ students, with $r = .2$.

Consider the two extreme cases, $r = 0$ and $r = 1$, that we discussed above.

- If $r = 0$, as in Panel A of Figure 12.4, we use M_Y as the estimate, for any X. The horizontal mean line is the regression line, with slope zero.
- Also when $r = 0$, knowing X gives no information about Y, and so the first term on the right in Equation 12.5 is zero and the second term, the residuals, must be giving us the full story of Y. Typically, as in Panel A, the residuals are large.
- If $r = 1$, as in Panel B, the line on which all points fall is the regression line, with slope (s_Y/s_X).
- Also when $r = 1$, knowing X gives complete information about Y, and so the first term on the right in Equation 12.5 tells the full story. The residuals are all zero, and they tell no part of the story of Y.

Panels A and B illustrate the two extreme cases for the slope of the regression line. What would you guess is the slope when $0 < r < 1$, and so X gives some but not full information about Y? That's worth pondering: Consider Panels A and B of Figure 12.4, and r close to 0, and r close to 1.

 Take a break, discuss. Draw some sketches?

▶ _____
As r increases from 0 to 1, X gives progressively better information about Y, and the slope of the regression line increases from 0 toward (s_Y/s_X); the line rotates counterclockwise from horizontal.

If your intuition suggests compromise between the two extreme cases, give yourself a pat on the back. For $r = 0$, knowing X gives us no information about Y, then for progressively larger r, knowing X gives us progressively more information about Y, until $r = 1$ and we have complete information about Y. Correspondingly, the regression line rotates smoothly between the horizontal mean line and a line with slope (s_Y/s_X), as r changes from 0 to 1. (There's a similar smooth change for negative correlations.) The smooth change in slope as r changes is a key point, so I'll say it again: The regression line slope is somewhere between the zero slope of the horizontal mean line and the slope of the line through the points when $r = 1$, with correlation r determining where it lies between those two extremes.

Panel C of Figure 12.4 illustrates a case in which $r = .2$. I'm supposing that we rate our initial impression of a student, and assess how useful an estimate of GPA those ratings might provide. In a sample of $N = 50$ students, the correlation of those ratings with GPA at the end of the year was $r = .2$. The horizontal mean line at M_Y is shown and the regression line has rotated a small amount from horizontal.

▶ _____
To obtain the regression line of Y on X, rotate from the horizontal mean line, M_Y, until the slope is r times (s_Y/s_X).

The slope is actually $r \times (s_Y/s_X)$, so it's r that tells us how far to rotate from horizontal. When $r = 1$, the slope is $1 \times (s_Y/s_X)$, the slope in Panel B.

The dashed lines in Panel C show that, if the impression rating for Robert, who's not in the sample of 50, is $X = 24.0$, our GPA regression estimate for him would be $\hat{Y} = 4.8$. Because r is small, there's much scatter in the figure and so the residuals are large, and, therefore, we expect considerable uncertainty in that estimate.

We've now taken two approaches to specifying the regression line:

1. The line that minimizes $s_{Y.X}$, the SD of the estimation errors.
2. The line with a slope that's a compromise, based on r, between horizontal and the line for $r = 1$. Its slope is $r \times (s_Y/s_X)$.

The remarkable thing is that these two approaches give the *same* line. Our two approaches finish in the same place. We can now state the formula for the regression line, and be happy that this is the line that minimizes estimation error.

The regression line passes through (M_X, M_Y), as illustrated in Figure 12.1, and has slope of $r \times (s_Y/s_X)$. That information plus some algebra gives us formulas for the intercept, a, and slope, b, in Equation 12.3, the equation of the regression line. The formulas are:

$$b = r \times \left(\frac{s_Y}{s_X} \right) \qquad (12.6)$$

Correlation

Slope of line for $r = 1$

◄ Slope, regression of Y on X.

$$a = M_Y - b \times M_X \qquad (12.7)$$

◄ Intercept, regression of Y on X.

Substituting for a and b in Equation 12.3 gives an alternative form of the equation of the regression line of Y on X:

$$\hat{Y} = \left[M_Y - r\left(\frac{s_Y}{s_X} \right) M_X \right] + \left[r\left(\frac{s_Y}{s_X} \right) \right] X \qquad (12.8)$$

Intercept, a

Slope, b

◄ Regression line, Y on X.

That equation gives the regression line of Y on X, as displayed in Figures 12.1 to 12.4. To use the equation to calculate the regression line, we need just the following summary information from a data set of N pairs of (X, Y) values: M_X, M_Y, s_X, s_Y, and r.

? Quiz 12.1

1. In regression, the variable being predicted is $X/Y/\hat{Y}$, the variable being used to make the prediction is $X/Y/\hat{Y}$ and the prediction we make is $X/Y/\hat{Y}$.
2. In the regression equation, b is the _____ and a is the _____.
3. What is a residual? How is a residual calculated?
4. Which of the following r values would be the *most* useful for using with regression? Which would be the *least* useful?
   a. $r = 0$
   b. $r = .3$
   c. $r = -.6$
   d. $r = .05$
5. The _____ of the regression line of Y on X is $r \times \left(\dfrac{s_Y}{s_X} \right)$.
6. The regression line is chosen to minimize
   a. the slope.
   b. the intercept.
   c. the correlation.
   d. the sum of squares of residuals.

The Linear Component of a Relationship

In Chapter 11 we saw that r measures just the linear component of the relationship between two variables, X and Y, and that we need to see the scatterplot to be sure we have the full story. We can calculate a value of r whatever the scatterplot, but Figure 11.4 illustrated two cases in which r could easily mislead. The regression we're discussing is called *linear regression* because it,

▶
Simple regression uses a single predictor (*X*), and *multiple regression* more than one predictor (*X*₁, *X*₂, ...), to predict *Y*. Use and interpret multiple regression with great caution.

too, expresses the linear component of the relationship, by means of a straight line. Once again this may not be the full story and thoughtful inspection of the scatterplot is always necessary. Further, it's called *simple linear regression* because there's just one predictor, *X*.

Beyond that is *multiple linear regression*, which estimates *Y* from two or more predictors, X_1, X_2, ... That's beyond the scope of this book, but sufficiently important to be worth a brief mention. If, for example, you use number of years of education (*X*) to predict annual income (*Y*), you are using simple regression as we discuss in this chapter. If, however, you use not only years of education (X_1), but also, say, age (X_2) and a measure of socioeconomic status (X_3) to predict income, you would be using multiple regression. Multiple regression often, although not always, gives a better prediction of *Y*. It also provides estimates of the relative contributions of the various predictors (X_1, X_2, ...) to the prediction of *Y*. It can be highly valuable to have, for example, an indication that years of education makes a larger (or maybe smaller?) contribution than socioeconomic status to expected income. I need to warn you, however, that multiple regression is often misused and can be very tricky to interpret. One major issue is that the estimated contribution of, say, X_1 depends on the full set of predictors (X_1, X_2, ...). Drop one of those predictors—or add another—and the relative contributions of *all* the predictors to the prediction of *Y* may change drastically. I won't try to explain in detail, but the take-home message—all you need to keep at the back of your mind—is that multiple regression can be highly useful, but using it properly requires a fair bit of knowledge. Be very cautious about any conclusion you read that's based on multiple regression.

Now back to simple regression. Recall that one or two outliers can be very influential on the mean and standard deviation, and one or two points that don't fit the general pattern can make a big difference to *r*, as Figure 11.12 illustrates. One or two such points can also make a big difference to the regression line. Figure 12.5 illustrates this by displaying the Thomason 1 data set, and the same with the addition of a point at (18, 7) for a student who did very well on the pretest, but terribly on the posttest. That single aberrant point drops *r* from .89 to .40 and reduces the slope of the regression line from 0.78 to 0.36. The scatterplot on the right might lead us to doubt the usefulness of linear regression for these data, or we might consider calculating regression twice, once for the full data set, and once without the aberrant point. As always, examine the data carefully and make a reality check for anything statistical that you calculate.

You may be thinking that journal articles rarely include scatterplots, so how can we be sure that the correlation and regression analyses we read are appropriate? That's a good question. Unless the authors tell us that the scatterplots show no signs of departure from linearity, they are asking us to take their analyses and interpretation on trust. We should always, however, keep in mind possible limitations. For correlation and regression, always remember that it's the linear component being assessed. Keep a sharp lookout for any indication of outliers.

12.3 Consider a data set with $N = 12$, $M_X = 11.58$, $M_Y = 13.25$, $s_X = 3.32$, $s_Y = 2.90$, and $r = .89$.

   a. Use Equation 12.8 to calculate the regression equation of *Y* on *X*.

   b. What *Y* would you estimate for *X* = 9? Would you expect small or large uncertainty in that estimate? Why?

   c. What *Y* would you estimate for *X* = 0? Might there be some problem with that?

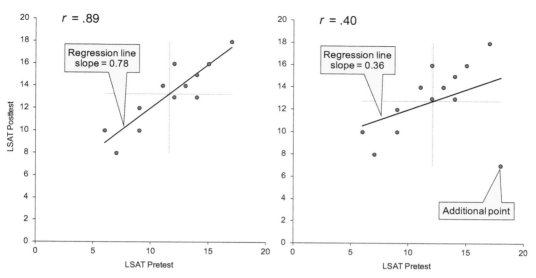

Figure 12.5. Scatterplot at left is for the Thomason 1 data set, as in Figure 12.3. Scatterplot on the right is the same, but with the addition of an outlier data point at (18, 7).

esci 12.4 Open **Scatterplots** and, if necessary, scroll right and click at red 16 to load the Thomason 1 data set.

    a. Reveal the regression panel and click the three checkboxes at red 10 to display the regression line and mark an X value and the corresponding $\hat{Y}$.

    b. Use the slider to set $X = 9$, as closely as possible. What is $\hat{Y}$? Explain what that $\hat{Y}$ value tells us.

esci 12.5 Examine the descriptive statistics reported at red 3 and compare with the values I stated for Exercise 12.3.

    a. Compare your calculated regression equation with that shown at red 12.

    b. Compare your calculated $\hat{Y}$ for $X = 9$ with your answer to Exercise 12.4.

esci 12.6 Below red 2 find the two students who scored $X = 9$ on the pretest.

    a. What posttest scores did they obtain?

    b. Compare with our $\hat{Y}$ estimated value for $X = 9$. Is there a problem? Explain.

esci 12.7 You discover that the results for one student were omitted from the data set. That student scored $X = 12$ on the pretest and $Y = 7$ on the posttest. Enter those additional data values below red 2 and watch what changes. Use **Undo** and **Redo** to note the changes as the additional point is removed and added.

    a. What happens to r? Explain.

    b. Does the slope of the regression line change much? Does the regression line seem to represent the points reasonably? Explain.

    c. Compare the changes given by addition of (12, 7) with the changes illustrated in Figure 12.5 for the addition of the point (18, 7). Which point is more influential? Explain and draw a general conclusion.

Regression Using *z* Scores

A scatterplot of (X, Y) data pairs is usually displayed using the original units of X and Y. Figures 12.1 to 12.5 all show such scatterplots of data in original units. Alternatively, as we saw in Chapter 11, a scatterplot may display the corresponding standardized scores, Z_X and Z_Y. Figure 12.6 shows both scatterplots for the Thomason 1 data set: original units on the left, as in Figure 12.3, and z scores on the right. The z scores are calculated so that the mean is zero and the SD is 1, for both Z_X and Z_Y. Therefore, in the scatterplot of z scores the regression line passes through $(0, 0)$, the means point. The slope of the line for $r = 1$ is (s_y/s_x), which here is $(1/1) = 1$, so that line would slope at 45° upward to the right. The slope of the regression line is r times that, or $r \times 1 = r$. The equation of the *standardized regression line* of Z_Y on Z_X is therefore:

▶

Regression line, Z_Y on Z_X.

$$Z_{\hat{Y}} = r \times Z_X \qquad (12.9)$$

Slope

▶

The *standardized regression line* of Z_Y on Z_X has intercept zero, and slope r.

This equation (12.9) is the conversion of Equation 12.3 to standardized scores. It has no term for the intercept, because the line passes through $(0, 0)$ and so the intercept is zero.

I need to mention a customary symbol that's very poorly chosen, as if designed to make life confusing for all of us. In the regression world, the slope of the standardized regression line expressed by Equation 12.9 is almost always given the symbol β. It's a highly valuable convention to use Greek letters for population parameters, but here β refers to a slope estimate calculated from a data set, using standardized scores, so β is a sample statistic, not a population

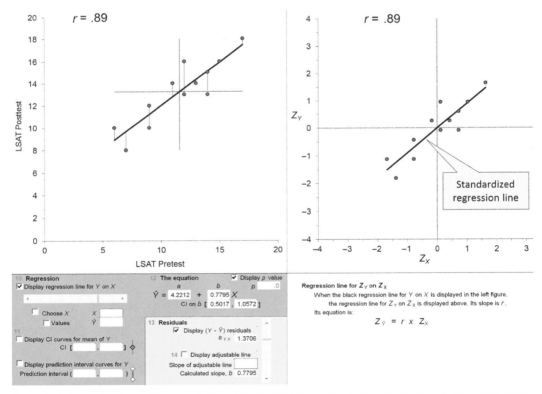

Figure 12.6. Scatterplots for the Thomason 1 data set. On the left is the scatterplot in original units, as in Figure 12.3, and on the right the same data transformed to z scores. In each figure, the regression line and cross through the means are displayed. From **Scatterplots**.

parameter. We could use it as our point estimate of the standardized regression slope in the population, but we would need to find some other symbol, perhaps $\beta_{\text{population}}$, for that population parameter.

It's crazy to use a Greek letter for a sample statistic, but in this case, unfortunately, it's the norm. If you see reference to β in the context of simple linear regression, think of Equation 12.9 and remember that $\beta = r$. A regression slope is sometimes referred to as a *regression weight*, so β is often referred to as the *standardized regression weight*. Despite it being a Greek letter, we have to remember that it's a sample statistic, not a population parameter. Sorry about that.

> The slope of the standardized regression line of Z_y on Z_x is referred to as β, called the *standardized regression weight*.

 12.8 Observe the Thomason 1 data set in **Scatterplots** and click at red 15 to reveal the second scatterplot. Display the regression line and cross through the means. Compare with Figure 12.6.

   a. Type in the additional data point (18, 7). Again use **Undo** and **Redo**, and note changes in both scatterplots.

   b. What is β for the original 12 points? For 13 points? Explain.

12.9 Suppose that for this month in your city the daily maximum temperature is approximately normally distributed with mean 20 °C and standard deviation 4 °C. The correlation of maximum temperature from one day to the next is $r = .6$.

   a. Suppose the maximum today is 14 °C, and we wish to estimate tomorrow's maximum. What would you choose as X and Y?

   b. Find Z_x, and use Equation 12.9 to calculate $Z_{\hat{y}}$. What is your prediction of tomorrow's maximum?

   c. If $r = 0$, what's your prediction for tomorrow's maximum?

   d. For r larger than .6, would tomorrow's prediction be closer to today's maximum, or further away? Explain.

12.10 The height of adult women is approximately normally distributed with mean 162 cm and SD 6 cm.

   a. Susan is $X = 174$ cm tall. Find Z_x.

   b. Suppose $r = .5$ for the heights of a woman (X) and her adult daughter (Y). Use Equation 12.9 to find $Z_{\hat{y}}$ for Susan's daughter. Find her estimated height, $\hat{Y}$.

   c. Find the estimated height of Susan's granddaughter, when adult. And her great-granddaughter.

12.11 Now let Y be the height of Susan's mother.

   a. Find $Z_{\hat{y}}$ and $\hat{Y}$.

   b. Explain what that $\hat{Y}$ is, and how it relates to the starting information that Susan is $X = 174$ cm tall.

The pattern of height of a woman, and estimated heights of her mother, daughter, granddaughter, and so on, is worth pondering and discussing. It was discussed extensively around a century ago when these statistical ideas were being developed, although then it was mainly about fathers and sons. Some people thought the regression analysis seems to imply that, after a few generations, all the descendants of Susan would have about the same height—the population mean. That's tricky to think about, and was often described as a paradox. How does it strike you? We'll discuss it further a little later.

THE PROPORTION OF VARIANCE ACCOUNTED FOR: r^2

I now want to discuss a useful interpretation of r^2, the square of the correlation. Consider Figure 12.7, in which I'm imagining we wish to estimate Y, Maria's height. Panel A reports data for $N = 30$ pairs of women who are identical twins, with $r = .80$. If Maria (not in that sample) has an identical twin, then the high correlation means that knowing the twin's height, X, gives us good information about Maria's height. The regression line is rotated most of the way toward (s_Y/s_X), the slope of the $r = 1$ line, and residuals are generally not large.

By contrast, Panel C reports heights for $N = 30$ pairs of women who are best friends, with $r = .20$. If we are told X, the height of Maria's (female) best friend, the low correlation means that the regression line gives an estimate,

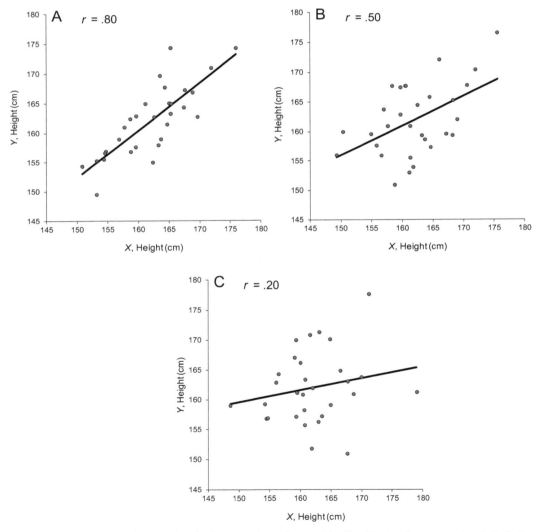

Figure 12.7. Scatterplots for fictitious data for three samples, each comprising $N = 30$ pairs of women, and each displaying the regression line for Y on X. Panel A displays women's heights for pairs of identical twins, with $r = .80$. Panel B displays heights for pairs of sisters, with $r = .50$. Panel C displays heights for pairs of women who are best friends, with $r = .20$.

$\hat{Y}$, of Maria's height that's likely to be poor. The regression line is rotated only a small amount from horizontal and residuals are generally large. Panel B displays data for $N = 30$ pairs of sisters, with $r = .50$, so the regression slope is intermediate between those of Panels A and C.

Our informal idea, in Equations 12.1 and 12.5, is that the regression line provides $\hat{Y}$ estimates calculated from X that tell part of the story about Y, the remainder lying with the residuals. In Panel A, correlation is high, the regression line tells much of the story of Y, and residuals are small. In Panel C, correlation is low, the line tells only a small portion of the Y story, and residuals are large.

Slightly more formally, our story becomes:

Variance of $Y =$

Variance of $\hat{Y}$ estimates + Variance of $(Y - \hat{Y})$ residuals   (12.10)

Why use variance? You don't need to know, but if you're curious: As I mentioned in Chapter 4, variance has the valuable statistical property that variances add—as in Equation 12.10—when the different sources of variability are independent. Now to formulas. If these are becoming eye-glazing, think back to the informal account above.

Equation 12.2 gave the basic formula for $s_{Y.X}$, the SD of the residuals:

$$s_{Y.X} = \sqrt{\frac{\sum \left(Y - \hat{Y}\right)^2}{(N-2)}} \qquad (12.2)$$

Here's a second equation for $s_{Y.X}$ that gives the same results as Equation 12.2, although I won't try to explain why it's true:

$$s_{Y.X} = s_Y \times \sqrt{1 - r^2} \qquad (12.11)$$

which is an equation involving two standard deviations. Square it to give an equation about variances:

$$s_{Y.X}^2 = s_Y^2 \times (1 - r^2) \qquad (12.12)$$

which can be rearranged to give:

$$s_Y^2 = \left[r^2 \times s_Y^2\right] + s_{Y.X}^2 \qquad (12.13)$$

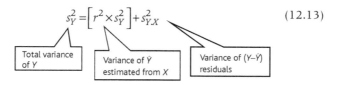

Total variance of Y | Variance of $\hat{Y}$ estimated from X | Variance of $(Y - \hat{Y})$ residuals

Equation 12.13 is just a formalization of informal Equation 12.10. It tells us that the total variance of Y in our data set is the sum of two components: the variance of $\hat{Y}$ values estimated from X, and the variance of the $(Y - \hat{Y})$ residuals. The first component is referred to as the variance of Y that's *attributable to X*, or *accounted for by X*. Equation 12.13 also tells us that, in terms of variance, r^2 is the proportion of the Y story that's told by the regression line; the remaining $(1 - r^2)$ is with the residuals.

As usual, we're not making any assumptions about causation—we're not, for example, claiming that X *causes* the regression component of the variance of Y.

If |r| is zero or small, where |r| is the absolute value of r, does X account for much of the variance of Y? If |r| is large, does X account for much of the variance of Y?

Enter small or large values of r into Equation 12.13... Reflect, discuss...

If $r = 0$, the $\left[r^2 \times s_Y^2\right]$ term in the equation is zero and the variance of the residuals equals the total variance of Y, as in Figure 12.4, Panel A. The regression line is horizontal and doesn't help, and residuals are generally large. At the other extreme, if $r = 1$, the $\left[r^2 \times s_Y^2\right]$ term is s_Y^2, and so $s_{Y.X}^2 = 0$, meaning there's no variance in the residuals. As in Panel B, the estimates are perfectly accurate, and all residuals are zero.

As r increases from 0 to 1, the regression line rotates from horizontal toward (s_y/s_x), the slope of the $r = 1$ line. Also, the $\left[r^2 \times s_Y^2\right]$ term increases, meaning that the regression line can use X to account for more and more of the variance in Y, and the variance of the residuals decreases. In a nutshell, r^2 is the proportion of s_Y^2, the total variance of Y, that can be attributed to X, or accounted for by X.

In Panel B of Figure 12.7, $r = .5$ for the heights of sisters. Therefore, a woman's height (X) accounts for $r^2 = .5^2 = .25$, or 25% of the variance in her sister's height (Y).

> r^2 is the proportion of s_Y^2, the variance of Y, that is accounted for by X.

12.12 a. What percentage of the variance of a woman's height is attributable to the height of her identical twin, based on the r value from Figure 12.7? What percentage is variance of the residuals? Considering Panel A of Figure 12.7, does that seem reasonable?

b. Answer the same questions for a woman's best friend and Panel C.

I conclude that, when X and Y are strongly correlated, a regression line allows us to make better estimates of Y based on X, and the residuals are smaller. Large (in absolute magnitude) correlations are indeed useful.

REGRESSION REVERSED: THE REGRESSION OF *X* ON *Y*

It's customary to arrange things so X is the predictor and Y the predicted variable, and to consider the regression of Y on X. I did say, however, that I'd mention regression the other way round: the regression of X on Y. This refers, of course, to estimating a value of X for a particular value of Y, so the roles of predictor and predicted variable are swapped. Let's consider the Thomason 3 data set.

For that data set, Figure 12.8 displays the scatterplot for $N = 39$ students who gave HCTA scores before and after training in critical thinking. The correlation is $r = .60$, and in each panel a regression line and the cross through the means are displayed. I'm not going to give formulas, but think of a regression line as a compromise between a mean line and the $r = 1$ line, with r determining the degree of compromise. The familiar regression line of Y on X is displayed on the left. It's the heavy line that's rotated counterclockwise from the horizontal mean line through M_y, with the amount of rotation determined by $r = .60$.

Now consider the right panel and estimation of X for a given value of Y. If $r = 0$, knowing Y gives us no information about X, so our best prediction is $M_{x'}$ which is the vertical mean line at about 67. For $r > 0$, the regression line will be

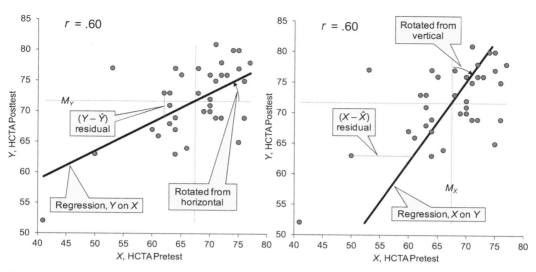

Figure 12.8. Scatterplot for the Thomason 3 data set for $N = 39$ students who gave HCTA scores at pretest (X) and posttest (Y). In each panel, a regression line and the cross through the means are displayed. The left panel illustrates the regression line of Y on X, which is rotated counterclockwise from the horizontal mean line at M_Y. An example $(Y - \hat{Y})$ residual is displayed red. The panel at right illustrates how the regression line of X on Y is rotated clockwise from the vertical mean line at M_X. An example $(X - \hat{X})$ residual is displayed red.

rotated clockwise, and the larger the *r*, the more the rotation from the vertical. The result is the heavy line labeled as "Regression, *X* on *Y*".

It may seem weird to have two different lines for a single data set, as in Figure 12.8. Both lines give estimates with minimum SD of the residuals, but residuals are defined differently in the two cases, so the two lines are almost always different. For the regression line of *Y* on *X*, the $(Y - \hat{Y})$ residuals are the focus; these are the vertical distances of the data points from the line, as in Figures 12.2 and 12.3. One of these is displayed red in the left panel of Figure 12.8. The *Y* on *X* regression line minimizes $s_{Y.X}$, the SD of the vertical, *Y* residuals.

By contrast, for the regression line of *X* on *Y*, the $(X - \hat{X})$ residuals are the focus, and these are the horizontal distances of the data points from the *X* on *Y* regression line. One of these is displayed red in the right panel. The *X* on *Y* regression line minimizes $s_{X.Y}$, the SD of those horizontal, *X* residuals.

> The regression line of *X* on *Y* minimizes $s_{X.Y}$, the SD of the *X* residuals.

12.13 **a.** When do the two regression lines have similar slopes?
 b. When are the two regression lines the same? What is their slope?
 c. When are the two regression lines most different in slope? Explain.

? Quiz 12.2

1. Before using regression it is important to see the scatterplot. What should you be asking as you inspect it?
 a. Is the relationship linear, because otherwise linear regression should not be used?
 b. Are there outliers, which can have a very strong influence on the regression equation?
 c. Both a and b.
2. Regression is easy with standardized scores (*z* scores). Given a Z_X, you can calculate the prediction $Z_{\hat{Y}}$ by simply _____.
3. By regression convention, β is the _____ of the standardized regression line; it is equal to _____.

4. Which of the following is true about r^2?
   a. r^2 is calculated simply by multiplying r by itself ($r \times r$).
   b. r^2 reflects the strength of the correlation, and can vary from 0 to 1.
   c. r^2 represents the proportion of variance of Y accounted for by knowing X.
   d. All of the above.
5. If X and Y are correlated, $r = -.4$, then X accounts for ____% of the variance of Y. If the correlation is $r = .1$, X accounts for only ____% of the variance of Y. If X accounts for 64% of the variance of Y, then $r = $ ____ or ____.
6. The regression line for predicting Y from X minimizes the SD of the $(Y - \hat{Y}) / (X - \hat{X})$ residuals, whereas the regression line for predicting X from Y minimizes the SD of the $(Y - \hat{Y}) / (X - \hat{X})$ residuals.

ASSUMPTIONS UNDERLYING REGRESSION PREDICTIONS

> For a $\hat{Y}$ estimate to make sense as a prediction, we need to assume random sampling of Y values at any particular value of X.

For the simple linear regression we're discussing, we're assuming both X and Y have interval scaling. In addition, for $\hat{Y}$ estimates to be usable as predictions for new cases, we need to assume random sampling of Y values at any particular value of X. For an example, recall the imaginary Hot Earth Awareness Test, the HEAT. Suppose we're interested in the increase in HEAT scores for students in successive years at your college. Figure 12.9 is a scatterplot of a random sample with $N = 20$ at each year level. Because Y is randomly sampled at each X value, we are justified in using the regression line of Y on X, as shown in the figure, for making predictions. It's not a problem that the X values—1, 2, 3, and 4—were chosen for convenience and are not a random sample.

In addition, we should make predictions only for cases from the same population as the data set. Informally, we're assuming that the relationship observed in the data set holds also for that particular case. For our example, we could use the regression line to make predictions for students at your college,

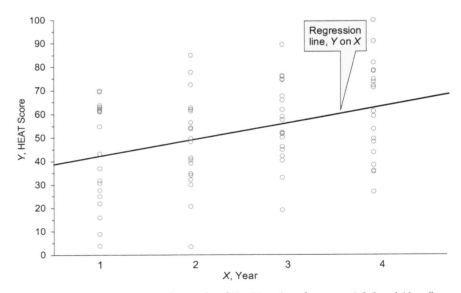

Figure 12.9. Fictitious HEAT scores for samples of $N = 20$ students from years 1, 2, 3, and 4 in college. The predictor variable, X, is year, and the predicted, Y, is HEAT score. The regression line is calculated for the data set of 80 points.

but not for other students—unless we made the additional assumption that students at your college are similar to some wider population of students, at least in relation to HEAT scores.

> Any prediction from a regression line requires the assumption that the particular case comes from the same population as the data set.

What if X for the individual case lies outside the range of X in the data set? That suggests that the individual case doesn't comes from the same population—in other words, the assumption that the relationship in the data set applies to the individual case is likely to be suspect, or even silly. A regression line doesn't necessarily apply beyond the range of X values in the original data. It's easy to find crazy examples of regression estimates beyond the original range of X that make no sense. For example, if your friend proudly reports that, over the last two months he has lost 1 kg, you can helpfully say "Great, at that rate in about ten years you'll weigh nothing!"

> Be especially cautious about any estimate for X beyond the range of X in the data set.

To discourage possibly unjustified extrapolation—trying to extend the relationship beyond the ranges of the data—ESCI doesn't display the regression line or calculate a $\hat{Y}$ value for X beyond its range in the data set. When using regression, just as any other time we're working with data, it's essential to keep thinking about the meaning of what we're doing. Does it make sense?

Now I'll summarize this brief section on assumptions.

Regression prediction. For a $\hat{Y}$ estimate to make sense as a prediction for a new case, we need to assume:

1. random sampling of Y values at any particular value of X;
2. that the new case comes from the same population as the data. In particular, X for the new case should lie within or close to the range of X in the data; we should be very cautious if it lies much beyond that range.

INFERENCE, AND MEASURING THE UNCERTAINTY OF PREDICTION

At last some CIs, in fact two of them. In this section I'll discuss, first, a CI on the regression slope, b, and second, CI curves for the whole regression line. Then I'll discuss a prediction interval for individual values of Y. There will be cool pictures, with curvy lines.

A Confidence Interval on b, the Regression Slope

We use b, the slope of the regression line, to estimate the population slope, which I'll call $b_{population}$. (I'd like to call it β, but unfortunately β has another meaning.) Now I want a CI on b. Figure 12.3 shows at red 12 that the regression equation for Thomason 1 is $\hat{Y} = 4.22 + 0.78 \times X$. Therefore $b = 0.78$ is our estimate of the population slope, which tells us that one extra LSAT point at pretest (that's X) is likely to be associated, on average, with an increase of around 0.8 points on the LSAT at posttest (which is Y).

Just below the equation is the CI on b, which is [0.50, 1.06], our interval estimate of $b_{population}$. We can interpret that CI as we do any other CI: Most likely the slope of the regression line in the population lies in the interval, with values around 0.78 the most likely. Also, our interval is one from a dance, and may be red—it may miss the true value, although probably not by much. The CI is so far from zero that the p value for testing the null hypothesis that $b_{population} = 0$ would be tiny. Figure 12.6 reports the regression analysis and shows near red 12 that indeed $p = 0$, to three decimal places. If you wished to report a p value, you would report $p < .001$.

> The CI on b, the slope of the regression line in the data set, is the interval estimate for $b_{population}$, the regression slope in the population.

For a given b, what would you expect to happen to the CI if N were much larger? Much smaller?

I hope you agree those are very easy questions. As usual, other things being the same, larger N gives us shorter CIs, and thus a more precise estimate of $b_{population}$.

Now for a real example. Zaval et al. (2015) asked a sample of 244 U.S. online respondents about environmental issues, especially climate change, and their willingness to take action for the sake of future generations. Respondents rated agreement with statements like "I feel a sense of responsibility to future generations" and "It is important to me to leave a positive legacy." Responses were combined to give a "Legacy Motivation" scale, range 1 to 6, where higher values indicate a greater concern about what legacy one leaves to future generations. Respondents were later offered $10, and asked to nominate some proportion to donate to an environmental cause; they would keep the remainder for themselves. To what extent did people who were more concerned about future generations choose to donate more? The regression of amount donated (Y) against Legacy Motivation score (X) had slope of $b = \$0.73$ per Legacy Motivation scale unit [0.35, 1.12]. That value of b means an increase of one point on the Legacy Motivation scale, which ranges from 1 to 6, gives, on average, an increased donation of 73 cents from the $10, with CI from 35 to 112 cents. Yes, they donated more, but that doesn't look like a large effect. Zaval et al. used that result to guide further research, including investigation of ways to increase legacy motivation.

 12.14 In Scatterplots, scroll right and click at red 19 to load the BodyWellFM data, the full data set for $N = 106$ women and men as in Figure 11.1. (Note that the axes extend beyond the scale ranges of the two measures, which are 1–5 and 1–7. If you know about Excel you can click near the edge of the figure to select it, then edit the scale ranges for the X and Y axes.) Click at red 9 then 10 to display the regression line for Well-being (Y) on Body Satisfaction (X).

a. What is the regression equation? State b and explain what it tells us.
b. State and interpret the CI on b.
c. Click near red 12 to show the p value. Explain and interpret.
d. Click near red 7 to show the p value for testing the null hypothesis that the population correlation is zero. How do the two p values compare? Does this seem reasonable?
e. Is it reasonable to apply regression to this data set? What assumptions are we making, for what calculations?

Exercise 12.14 referred to the p values for b near red 12, and r near red 7. The first assesses the null hypothesis that $b_{population}$, the regression slope in the population, is zero. The second assesses the null hypothesis that ρ, the population correlation, is zero. The two p values are calculated using different formulas, but should be the same, or very close to the same. This makes sense because zero correlation, as in Panel A of Figure 12.4, corresponds to a horizontal regression line, meaning the slope is zero. Regression slope is zero if, and only if, correlation is zero. Assessing the two null hypotheses should give the same answer, in particular the same p value.

Confidence Intervals for the Mean of Y, at every X

Our second CI is not a couple of values in square brackets, but two curves in the scatterplot. In Figure 12.10, the scatterplots are as in Figure 12.7, but

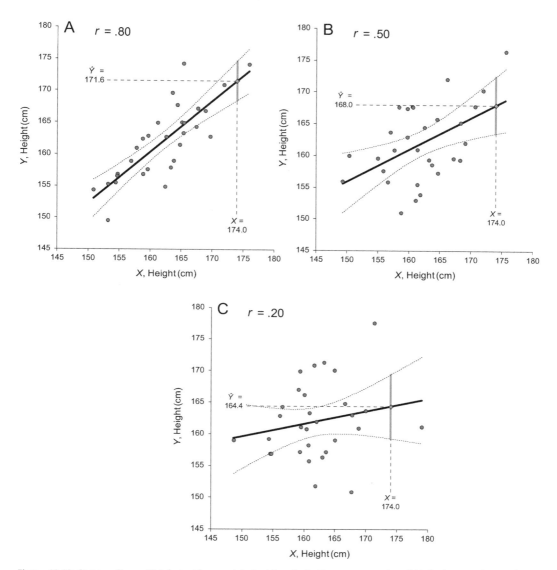

Figure 12.10. Same as Figure 12.7, but with curved dashed lines indicating, at every value of X, the lower and upper limits of the CI for the population mean of Y. The $\hat{Y}$ value, as given by the regression line for $X = 174$, is marked in each scatterplot, and the heavy red vertical line is the CI on this $\hat{Y}$ value. This CI is the vertical extent between the dashed curves and is the CI for the population mean of Y at $X = 174$ cm.

with the addition of dashed curves above and below the regression line. These curves are sometimes called "the CI on the regression line", but that's vague wording. Let's focus on a particular value, $X = 174$, as marked in the scatterplots. Recall Figure 12.9, which illustrates a sample extending vertically above an X value, the sample coming from a population of Y values at that X. That's also the case in Figure 12.10. We assume that vertically above $X = 174$ on the graph (technically, above a very short interval close to 174) there's an arbitrarily large population of Y values. There are such populations across the full range of X values.

The figure marks the $\hat{Y}$ values given by the regression lines in the three panels, all for $X = 174$ cm. In each panel, the heavy red vertical line between the two dashed curves is the CI on the $\hat{Y}$ value, meaning the CI for the mean of the Y population at that X value. In Panel A, for example, the regression line gives $\hat{Y} = 171.6$ cm. The population is the heights (Y values) of an assumed very large number of women who have an identical twin with height very close to $X = 174$ cm. Our estimate of the mean of that population is our estimate of Maria's height—given that her identical twin is 174 cm tall. When I used **Scatterplots** to make Panel A, I clicked at red 11 to display the dashed CI curves, and saw that the CI on $\hat{Y}$, at $X = 174$, is [168.5, 174.7]. So we estimate Maria's height as 171.6 cm [168.5, 174.7].

> The curved CI lines mark the lower and upper limits of the CI for the mean of the Y population at each X value.

Why are the CI lines curved? Think of a dance of the regression lines. Imagine taking repeated samples of size $N = 30$ pairs of identical twin women. Display the regression line for each. Sampling variability would cause those lines to bounce around: up and down a bit, and also rotated either way a bit. The dashed CI lines give us a rough idea of the extent of bouncing around. Because the bouncing includes rotation, the dashed CI lines need to be further apart for more extreme values of X. Putting it another way, CIs will be longer at X values further away from M_X.

Across the three panels in Figure 12.10, the regression line slopes decrease from A to C, because r decreases from .8 to .2. Now consider the dashed CI lines. Does it make sense that they are wider apart and more strongly curved in C than A? Given the greater scatter of points corresponding to $r = .2$ in Panel C, it's reasonable that the dance of the regression lines would show more energetic bouncing—larger jumps up and down, larger rotations—than for $r = .8$ in Panel A. So the CI lines need to be further apart and more curved in C than A.

12.15 If Maria's best woman friend is 174 cm tall, Panel C estimates Maria's height as $\hat{Y} = 164.4$ cm [159.3, 169.5].

a. Explain what that CI refers to.
b. Compare that CI with [168.5, 174.7], the CI stated above for Panel A. Explain the difference.

12.16 a. What proportion of the variance in a woman's height (Y) is accounted for by the variance in her identical twin's height? What proportion by her best woman friend's height?
b. What are the corresponding proportions for variance of the residuals?
c. What aspects of the display in Panels A and C reflect all those proportions?

Prediction Intervals for Individual Values of Y

We've been estimating the *mean* of Y for a particular X. If Maria's identical twin is 174 cm tall, Panel A estimates Maria's height as $\hat{Y} = 171.6$ cm [168.5, 174.7]. The CI tells us that the *mean* of the population of women with a 174 cm tall identical twin is, most likely, between about 168 and 175 cm. However, individual women have heights that are scattered below and above that mean. To get some idea of how widely scattered, we need the *prediction interval* for the height of an individual woman in that population.

> The prediction interval for individual values of Y at a particular X value reflects both uncertainty in the estimate of mean Y, and the spread of individual Y values.

This is our final uncertainty topic—considering the prediction of individual values of Y at a particular X. We need a prediction interval, not a CI, because CIs estimate population parameters such as means, but here we focus on individual values, not a parameter. In other words, we are interested in individual Y values at $X = 174$ cm, not the mean of all such Y values, as we considered in the previous subsection. We can expect the prediction interval for an individual Y value at $X = 174$ cm to be long because it must reflect:

1. uncertainty in the population mean of Y at this X, as quantified by the CI we discussed in the previous subsection, plus also
2. the spread of individual values, as indicated by the SD of that population.

Figure 12.11 is the same as Figure 12.10, but with the addition of two more dashed lines in each panel, to mark the lower and upper limits of the prediction interval for individual values of Y, at each X value.

Figure 12.11 shows that the prediction intervals are indeed long. In each panel the prediction interval for individual values of Y, when $X = 174$ cm, is marked by the fine green vertical line between the two open diamonds. For

◄ Prediction intervals for an individual case are often long, even when CIs on b and $\hat{Y}$ are short. Individual cases may be widely spread.

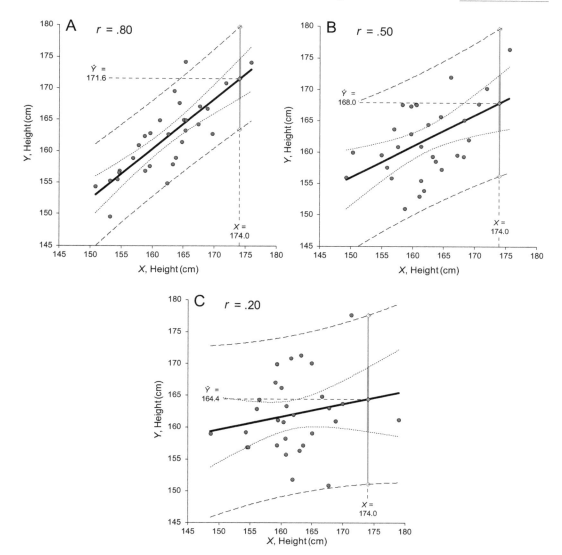

Figure 12.11. Same as Figure 12.10, but with display also of longer-dashed lines indicating, at every value of X, the lower and upper limits of the prediction interval for individual values of Y. The fine green vertical line between the two open green diamonds is the prediction interval on $\hat{Y}$ at the chosen value of X.

Panel A, the prediction interval is (163.5, 179.7). Despite the large correlation, $r = .8$, the heights of individual women who have an identical twin of height $X = 174$ cm are widely spread. We shouldn't be surprised if Maria herself is, perhaps, 165 cm, or even 181 cm tall. That's a sobering but important lesson: When considering regression, keep in mind that individual cases are likely to be widely spread, even if we get nice short CIs for slopes and means.

Do long prediction intervals mean that regression predictions are useless? In Panel A, eyeball the prediction intervals for $X = 152$ cm and $X = 174$ cm. Each is long, but they are very different, with only modest overlap. They could, therefore, give us useful predictions for individuals, even though the long intervals remind us that individual values are widely spread. However, doing the same for Panel C gives prediction intervals that are largely overlapping, so, for small r, and, therefore, a regression line not far from horizontal, prediction intervals for individual Y values may be of limited practical value.

Here's a thought experiment: Suppose Figure 12.11 was based on three samples of $N = 1,000$, rather than $N = 30$, and that r was, once again, .8, .5, and .2 for the three panels. Consider the CI curves for mean Y, as also displayed in Figure 12.10. How do you think those pairs of curves may be different with the much larger samples? Now consider the prediction interval curves. How do you think they may be different from those in Figure 12.11?

Thinking, thinking, discussing...

Think about CIs for a population parameter, and the spread of individual values in a population, which is relevant for prediction intervals. I'll discuss this thought experiment shortly.

12.17 In Exercise 12.15, I stated that Panel C estimates Maria's height as $\hat{Y} = 164.4$ cm [159.3, 169.5]. The prediction interval is (151.1, 177.7). Interpret those two intervals and explain the difference.

12.18 In **Scatterplots**, load the Thomason 3 data and turn on the regression line and the CI curves for the mean of Y, the HCTA posttest.

a. Display a chosen X value and the corresponding $\hat{Y}$ value. Select $X = 72$. Note $\hat{Y}$ and its CI, for this X value. Interpret.

b. Display the prediction interval curves. Note the prediction interval for $X = 72$ and interpret.

Back to that thought experiment. With $N = 1,000$ the CI for mean Y at some X would be much shorter, and so the CI curves much closer to the regression line than in Figures 12.10 and 12.11. The prediction interval is shortened a little by that shortening of the CI—that's component 1 I described above. However, the second component is the spread of individual values in the population of Y values at the particular X and this is not influenced by the size of the sample we take. Therefore, prediction intervals are only a little shorter with $N = 1,000$, and the longer-dashed prediction interval curves only a little closer to the regression line.

ASSUMPTIONS UNDERLYING REGRESSION CIS AND PREDICTION INTERVALS

In an earlier section I said that regression predictions require the assumption of random sampling of Y values at any particular value of X. For regression CIs we need more. We need to assume, in addition, that Y is normally distributed in the population and that the variance of Y is homogeneous for all X. To illustrate, I'll use Figure 12.12, which is the same as Figure 12.9 but displays also the population of Y (HEAT scores) at each X. We need to assume those populations are normally distributed, and that all have the same standard deviation, meaning that we need homogeneity of variance of Y for all X. I generated the data in the two figures by sampling randomly from the populations shown, which all do have the same standard deviation, so the assumptions needed for regression CIs are met.

Note that, for regression CIs, we need to make assumptions only for the predicted variable, Y. Just as for regression prediction, the X values can be chosen for convenience and need not be a sample. Contrast with the requirement for bivariate normality when we calculate CIs on *correlation r*, as we discussed in Chapter 11. For regression CIs, however, it's not a problem if X and Y *do* come from a bivariate normal population, because that gives us what we need: Y that's sampled from a normal population and variance of Y that's homogeneous for all X.

To consider whether the assumptions needed for regression CIs are justified, consider the nature of Y: Is it reasonable to assume it's sampled from a normally distributed population? We also need homogeneity of variance of Y for all X, but this can be difficult to assess. It's common to make that assumption unless there are strong reasons against, or strong indications in the data that the standard deviation of Y changes across the range of X.

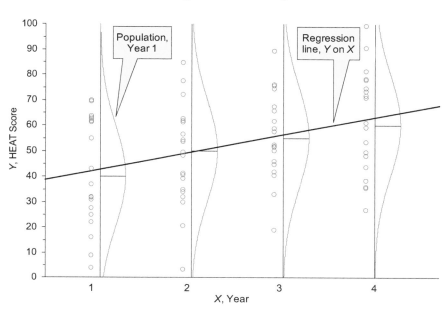

Figure 12.12. Same as Figure 12.9, but showing also the population of Y (HEAT scores) at each year, assumed to be normally distributed. The short horizontal lines mark population means.

I've said those assumptions are needed for "regression CIs", but I should be more specific. They are needed for the CI on b, the CI for the mean of Y at a particular X, as in Figure 12.10, and also for the prediction interval for individual values of Y at a particular X, as in Figure 12.11. For the latter two intervals we also need the assumption that the case with the particular X value, for which we calculate the interval, is from the same population as the data.

Now I'll summarize both the previous section on assumptions and this section.

Regression prediction, from previous section. For a $\hat{Y}$ estimate to make sense as a prediction for a new case, we need to assume:

1. random sampling of Y values at any particular value of X;
2. that the new case comes from the same population as the data. In particular, X for the new case should lie within or close to the range of X in the data—we should be very cautious if it lies much beyond that range.

CI on regression slope, b. To calculate such a CI, we need Assumption 1 above and also need to assume:

3. that the population of Y values at any particular value of X is normally distributed;
4. homogeneity of variance of Y across all values of X.

CI for the mean of Y at a particular X. To calculate such a CI, as in Figure 12.10, we need:

▨ all of Assumptions 1, 2, 3, and 4 above.

Prediction interval for individual values of Y. To calculate such an interval for a particular value of X, as in Figure 12.11, we again need:

▨ all of Assumptions 1, 2, 3, and 4 above.

THREE INTERVALS: WHICH SHOULD I USE?

At this point you are entitled to feel that there's lots going on that's different, but sufficiently similar to be confusing. I hope it helps if I use an example to summarize. It's vital to know the range of options you have, and to be able to choose which you need. Let's go back to Daniel, who scored $X = 3.0$ for Body Satisfaction. We have four main options. If you wish to follow along, go to **Scatterplots**, scroll right and click at red 21 to load the BodyWellM data set for the $N = 47$ males as in Figure 12.1.

1. *Find the regression equation and use it to make a $\hat{Y}$ estimate.* I'm interested in the research question of how X and Y relate, so I want the regression equation for Y on X. I'm willing to assume random sampling of Y, so I clicked at red 9 and saw

Regression line,
Y on X.

$$\hat{Y} = 1.66 + 0.93 \times X \qquad (12.14)$$

The regression slope in the sample is $b = 0.93$, meaning that, on average, 1 unit increase in Body Satisfaction corresponds to a 0.93 unit increase in Well-being. (Not necessarily causal!)

What's our estimate of Daniel's Well-being (Y) score? I'll assume Daniel is from the same student population as the data. I could use Equation 12.14 to calculate $\hat{Y}$ for Daniel's $X = 3.0$, but instead I clicked three checkboxes at red 10 and used the slider to set $X = 3.0$ and find $\hat{Y} = 4.44$ as our point estimate for Daniel.

2. *Find the confidence interval on b.* My research interest is in X and Y *in the population*, so the regression line is a good start, but as well as the point estimate, $b = 0.93$, of the population slope, I want the interval estimate. This is shown near red 12 as [0.48, 1.38], a long interval because our sample isn't large. This CI relies on the reasonable assumption that we have random sampling of Y from a normally distributed population with homogeneous variance across all X. We estimate $b_{population} = 0.93$ [0.48, 1.38].

3. *Find the confidence interval for mean Y at a particular X.* For $X = 3.0$, we found $\hat{Y} = 4.44$, our point estimate of mean Y of the population of all students who have $X = 3.0$. I clicked at red 11 and saw two dotted curves and a vertical red CI, as in Figure 12.10. The CI is [3.99, 4.89], which is our interval estimate of mean Y when $X = 3.0$. To conclude, our estimate of Daniel's Well-being score is $\hat{Y} = 4.44$ [3.99, 4.89].

4. *Find the prediction interval for individual values of Y at a particular X.* That CI might mislead us into thinking we have a fairly precise idea of Daniel's Well-being score. A quick glance at the large scatter in Figure 12.1 should remind us that individual points are widely spread. For a more realistic idea of Daniel's Y score we need the prediction interval for Y, when $X = 3.0$. I clicked lower below red 11 and saw that interval to be (2.60, 6.28). I also saw the curved, dashed lines and vertical green interval between diamonds, as in Figure 12.11. The long prediction interval reflects both the uncertainty in estimating mean Y at $X = 3.0$ (the CI we found in 3 above) and the large vertical spread of individual values of Y for students with $X = 3.0$. The Y score of our particular subject, Daniel, is most likely around 4 or 5, but could be anywhere in the prediction interval (2.60, 6.28), or even a small distance beyond.

So, which should you choose? That depends on what you want. To study the relationship of X and Y, you probably want the regression equation and CI on b (use 1 and 2 above). If you want to know about all students with $X = 3.0$, use 3. If you want the best guidance for one particular student, for example Daniel, use 4.

REGRESSION TO THE MEAN: A POSSIBLY STRANGE NATURAL PHENOMENON

Whenever a correlation is not 1 or −1, *regression to the mean* occurs. It's a natural and inevitable phenomenon, so it's worth discussing, although it can seem strange. Consider our estimates of Maria's height. In Panel A of Figure 12.10, correlation is .8, the regression line is steep, and $X = 174$ cm gives an estimate of $\hat{Y} = 171.6$ cm for Maria. In Panel C, correlation is .2, the regression line is not far from horizontal, and $X = 174$ cm gives an estimate of $\hat{Y} = 164.4$ cm.

The regression equation and CI on b tell about the relation of X and Y in the population. $\hat{Y}$ and its CI tell about all cases having a stated X value. The prediction interval tells about individual Y values for a stated X value.

Whenever the correlation of X and Y is not 1 or −1, a $\hat{Y}$ estimate is closer to the mean than the X value it was estimated from. This is *regression to the mean*.

▶
Small *r* indicates regression line near horizontal and much regression to the mean. Large *r* indicates steep regression line and little regression to the mean.

Both $\hat{Y}$ estimates have shifted, or *regressed*, closer to the mean than X, and the larger the correlation, the steeper the regression line and the smaller the shift toward the mean.

Figure 12.13 shows this in a different way, the curved red arrows indicating how the $\hat{Y}$ values are closer to the mean of 162 cm than the X values from which they were calculated. For $r = .8$, the shift is small—from 174 down to 171.6 cm, but for $r = .2$ the shift is larger. The red arrow on the left shows a third case: If $r = .5$, $X = 156$ cm gives $\hat{Y} = 159$ cm, which is also shifted closer to the mean, and by an intermediate amount.

Here's an example we might consider strange: Recall Exercises 12.10 and 12.11 about Susan and her female relatives. Here I'll discuss the pattern without using formulas. The correlation is positive (and not 1) for the heights of Susan and her daughter. (Studies of women's and daughters' heights typically report correlations near .5, the value I stated earlier, but the pattern I'm discussing doesn't depend on any particular value of *r*). Susan is 174 cm tall, well above the mean, so we expect her daughter's height to regress downward toward the mean. We expect her granddaughter's height when adult to regress even further down toward the mean, and so on for further generations. Might this suggest that, after a few generations, every woman is pretty much of average height? That's why this phenomenon has sometimes been considered a paradox.

Now consider going backward in time, rather than forward. The correlation for the heights of Susan and her mother is also positive (and not 1). Therefore, we expect Susan's mother's height to regress down toward the mean, her grandmother's height even further down, and so on. All those statements going forward and backward in time are actually true in the world. Regression to the mean may seem strange, but it captures something important about how correlation works in practice.

Note that causation plays no part in this discussion, which depends only on *r*. We used regression in Figure 12.10 to estimate Maria's height without

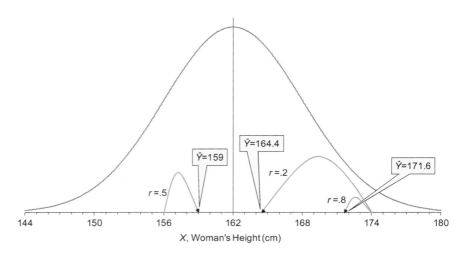

Figure 12.13. Normal distribution of women's heights, with mean 162 cm and standard deviation 6 cm. The three curved red arrows illustrate regression predictions of height ($\hat{Y}$ values) for three different situations. The shortest arrow illustrates $X = 174$ cm and $r = .8$; the longest illustrates the same X and $r = .2$; and the arrow on the left illustrates $X = 156$ and $r = .5$. The red arrows highlight the extent to which the $\hat{Y}$ estimate regresses toward the mean in each case: Larger *r* gives less regression—as we'd expect.

any mention of causation—only the correlations mattered. For a particular r, we'll see the same pattern of regression to the mean, whatever X and Y are measuring and regardless of any causation or lack of causation.

Regression to the Mean and the Variability of Y

The key issue is that we've been discussing point estimates of the *mean* of Y, which don't tell us anything about the *variability* of Y. Consider an extreme case: Suppose the correlation between the heights of women who are neighbors is $r = 0$. If I tell you the height of Maria's woman neighbor, what's your estimate of Maria's height? Yes, 162 cm, the mean, and the regression line is horizontal. What's the extent of regression to the mean? It's 100%. However, we expect the standard deviation of the heights of women neighbors (including Maria) to be the same as that of all women, 6 cm. A large amount of regression to the mean doesn't reduce the amount of variability of Y. Our particular Maria could be short or tall. Even if our best height estimate for Susan's great-great-great-granddaughter is almost totally regressed to the mean, that doesn't imply any reduction in the standard deviation for that younger generation of women. Same for her great-great-great-grandmother. There is no paradox.

> A $\hat{Y}$ estimate is regressed toward the mean (unless $|r| = 1$), but this does not imply any decrease in the variability of Y.

In other words, regression estimates the mean, but individual cases are likely to show great variability. That's why the prediction interval for individual values of Y is long, as in Figure 12.11. Our estimate for Susan's daughter is 168 cm, but a particular daughter may be shorter or taller than 168 cm, perhaps even taller than Susan. My family provides two examples: I'm 192 cm tall, well above average. Regression would lead me to expect sons who are shorter than me. However, both my sons are distinctly taller than me. Unlikely, but in our case true. And, in case you are wondering, my wife is not a giant!

Regression to the mean may be tricky to think about, but it happens in the world all the time. Let's consider some examples.

Everyday Regression to the Mean

Suppose you are very pleased with your basketball (or golf, or favorite computer game) score today, one of the best you have achieved. What's your prediction for next time you play? Your scores for two successive times you play are probably positively correlated, but there's almost certainly some variability in how you perform, in which case r is less than 1. Therefore, if today's score is high, your next score will, on average, be regressed toward the mean, and therefore lower than today's. If you score a personal best one day, but do less well the next day, you don't need to search for any complex reasons, because the decrease may have been caused by nothing more than the boring old natural phenomenon of regression to the mean. Conversely, after a really bad day, be encouraged that next time you are likely to do better, merely because of regression to the mean. But no guarantees.

> Regression to the mean occurs often in the world, whenever two variables are less than perfectly correlated and one is used to make an estimate for the other.

When any variables X and Y are correlated less than perfectly, meaning r is not 1 or -1, then, given a value of X, the mean Y we expect is less extreme, less distant from the mean, somewhat regressed toward the mean, compared with that given value of X. The higher the correlation, the less the regression to the mean, but only if $|r| = 1$ is there no regression.

When learning to fly, one of the greatest challenges is achieving a smooth landing, and student pilots typically spend many hours making practice landings. An instructor who had studied psychology and knew about positive reinforcement and punishment decided that, to help her students improve, she would systematically give a few words of praise whenever a student achieved a particularly smooth landing, and a few harsh words after any very bumpy landing. She kept careful records and was disappointed to find that, after a good landing and praise, a student would, on average, make a less good landing. However, after receiving harsh words for a poor landing, a student was likely to make a better landing. She concluded that praise didn't work, but punishment—her harsh words—did. Were her conclusions justified? Does psychology have it wrong about praise and positive reinforcement?

That story is worth considering and discussing, especially if you have studied what psychology says about positive reinforcement. I'll come back to it shortly, but take a break and call a friend to discuss the story. Is it plausible?

12.19 A large basketball club fields many teams. Each week they give a special mention to the three players scoring the most points that week. The committee observes that only rarely does a player receive a special mention for two weeks in a row. They fear that receiving a special mention somehow puts players off their game, so the scheme is discontinued. Was that decision justified? Explain.

12.20 I dare not tell my friends, but I believe that a headache will go away if I wear a pink hat, face north, and wiggle my toes for one minute. I tried it secretly for my most recent five headaches, and every time my headache was distinctly less severe an hour later. Can I expect my headache treatment to make me famous? Explain.

Back to the flying instructor. We hope that the student's landings gradually improve, but, from landing to landing, there's almost certainly considerable variation in quality. In other words, there's less than a perfect correlation from one landing to the next. Therefore, a pattern, on average, of less good landings after particularly smooth landings, can be explained by regression to the mean. Seeing improvement, on average, after particularly rocky landings can be explained the same way. In other words, because of variation in the quality of successive landings, the correlation is less than perfect and so regression to the mean occurs. We'd therefore expect the observed pattern, even if the praise and admonishment had no effect.

There's an additional interesting twist to this story. Consider what the instructor experiences. Regression to the mean leads to the instructor being punished (student likely to land less well) for giving praise, but rewarded (a better landing) for giving punishment—the harsh words. It's an unfortunate fact that we go through life tending to be punished after we give reward, but rewarded after we give admonishment. How sad! Perhaps, to compensate, we should all try hard to limit our criticisms of other people, and find reasons for giving positive comments?

Here's a final point about regression to the mean. It always occurs, unless $|r| = 1$, but to know the direction of regression of the $\hat{Y}$ estimate we need to know whether the X value is below or above the mean. If you tell me your basketball score and I have no idea whether it's below or above your typical or mean score, I can't say whether your score tomorrow is likely to be higher or lower. Only if you tell me that it's a particularly poor or good score—for you—can I say that tomorrow you are likely to do better, or worse, respectively, because of regression to the mean. Of course that's an average estimate, and on a particular tomorrow your score could jump either way.

Always keep in mind regression to the mean as a possible explanation—it happens in all sorts of common situations and sometimes has surprising consequences. Think of the everyday meaning of the word "regression". Does our topic in this final section of the chapter suggest why the statistical technique we've been discussing was given that name?

It's almost time, at last, for take-home messages. To help you write yours, you might think back to some of the pictures we've discussed: a scatterplot with a regression line, the short vertical lines that are the residuals, three scatterplots and regression lines for estimating Maria's height, dashed CI curves, and even more widely spaced curves for prediction intervals. Reflect again on Susan and her relatives, and on the comments you might make to a student pilot practicing landings.

? Quiz 12.3

1. When making a prediction about a new case,
   a. the new case must be from the same population sampled to generate the regression equation.
   b. it must make sense to assume random sampling of Y at any level of X.
   c. we should be especially cautious of making predictions for any X value outside the range of the sample used to generate the regression equation.
   d. All of the above.
2. Consider the assumption that X and Y have a bivariate normal distribution in the population. For each purpose below, state whether that assumption is or is not necessary.
   a. To calculate r
   b. To calculate the CI on r
   c. To calculate prediction $\hat{Y}$ for a particular value of X
   d. To calculate the CI on b
   e. To calculate the prediction interval for Y at a particular value of X
3. Ange is using regression to use GRE scores to predict graduate school success. For each purpose listed below, which of the following intervals should she use?
   (i) CI on b, (ii) CI for mean of Y at X, (iii) prediction interval for individual values of Y at a specific X.
   a. Ange wants to describe the typical level of success expected for students who score 160 on the GRE.
   b. Ange is helping to evaluate a particular applicant who has scored 169 on the GRE; she wants to express the likely range of possibilities for this applicant.
   c. Ange wants to express the degree to which GRE scores are related to graduate school success.
4. For the different intervals above, which will change the least as larger sample sizes are collected? Why?
5. If the absolute value of the correlation of two variables is less than ____, the estimate of the predicted variable will be closer to / further from the mean than the value of the predictor variable used to make the estimate. This phenomenon is called _____
_____.

6. The couple next door sometimes have loud arguments, which I find disturbing. Whenever they have an especially loud exchange I concentrate hard and try to send them a mental message of calm. It seems to work—usually, within half an hour they are much quieter. Does this show I have wonderful powers of the mind? Explain.

12.21 An advertisement encourages people to enroll for further training by declaring that every extra year of education increases annual income by an average of $7,000.

   a. Assuming that figure comes from a regression analysis, explain what it's telling us.
   b. What assumptions are implicit in the encouragement of the ad? Are they reasonable?

12.22 I told you about my belief that wearing a pink hat, and so forth, fixes any headache I have.

   a. Suppose I always follow that ritual whenever I have a headache. Is my belief in the effectiveness of the ritual likely to weaken or strengthen over time? Explain.
   b. You might regard my belief in that ritual as superstition. (Of course, I don't.) Describe some other superstition that might be perpetuated in the same way.
   c. Tell me about a belief of yours that's perpetuated in the same way. You don't need to answer this publicly.

12.23 You have developed a computer game to help teach spelling. A group of children who scored more than one standard deviation below their age norm on a spelling test played your game for two sessions. They took the test again a week later and obtained a distinctly higher average score.

   a. Should you be encouraged? Explain.
   b. Suggest a better design of study to assess your game.

12.24 If you wish, revise your take-home messages.

Reporting Your Work

Regression provides a chance to quantitatively explore the relationship between two variables. Reporting it is similar to reporting correlation, but focuses on the regression equation. Your research report should typically include these elements:

- Whether the regression analysis is planned or exploratory, unless this is already clear
- Basic descriptive statistics for both the X and Y variables
- A scatterplot with the regression line
- The regression equation, including the CI for the slope
- If desired, the p value for the slope, usually against the null hypothesis that $b_{population} = 0$
- If desired, the standardized slope, β, and its CI; For regression with only one predictor variable, this is the same as r and its CI, so you do not need to report both
- Discussion of the regression equation that focuses on the slope and its CI; specifically, consider how the slope informs thinking about how changes in the X variable relate to changes in the Y variable—but be careful to avoid causal language
- A discussion of the degree to which the assumptions for regression are met; when assumptions are violated, be sure your interpretation is suitably tentative

▶
Reporting regression is similar to reporting correlation but focuses on the regression equation.

As planned, we used linear regression analysis to predict well-being scores from body satisfaction scores (b = 0.82, 95% CI [0.51, 1.12], a = 2.10). This CI is fairly long but

indicates that each unit of additional body satisfaction is
associated with a half up to a full unit of additional well-
being (1-7 scale). Relative to other predictors of well-being
this is a strong relationship. One caution in this analysis is
the restricted range of the body satisfaction scores, as all
participants scored at least 2 on this 1-5 scale.

Often regression analysis is reported simply to provide a quantitative sense of how the
X and Y variables are related. Clearly, though, an additional benefit of regression analysis is
the ability to make predictions about general trends or even specific individuals.

- If you are making predictions only about general trends in the Y variable (what mean Y is
likely for various values of X), then include the CI for the mean of Y for each value of X of
interest (and include these curves in the scatterplot).
- If you are making predictions about specific individuals, then include Y prediction intervals
(and include the prediction interval lines in the scatterplot).

For example:

Based on this regression analysis, participants with a body
image score of 2 would be predicted to have an average well-
being of 3.74, 95% CI [3.21, 4.26]. This indicates that the
average well-being in this group is likely to be moderate.

Based on this regression analysis, a participant with a body
image score of 2 would be predicted to have a well-being score
of 3.74, 95% PI (1.62, 5.85). This is a very long prediction
interval, but it indicates that a participant at this low-
end score for body satisfaction is very unlikely to be at the
highest levels for well-being.

Take-Home Messages

- Like correlation, the regression line is an expression of the linear component of the
relationship of X and Y, but neither may provide the full story of that relationship. In
neither case is there necessarily any causation.

- The regression line for Y on X minimizes the SD of the $(Y - \hat{Y})$ residuals. It passes through
the means point (M_X, M_Y) and has slope $b = r \times (s_Y/s_X)$, which is r times the slope of the
$r = 1$ line.

- The standardized regression line of Z_Y on Z_X passes through (0, 0) and has slope r.

- The proportion of s_Y^2, the total variance of Y, that can be accounted for by X is r^2; the
remaining proportion is $(1 - r^2)$, which is $s_{Y \cdot X}^2$, the variance of the residuals.

- To use a $\hat{Y}$ estimate for a new case with a particular value of X, we need to assume Y is
randomly sampled and that the new case comes from the same population as the data
set. Calculating any CI, or a prediction interval, requires in addition the assumptions that
Y comes from a normal population and that the variance of Y is homogeneous for all X.

- The CI on b, the sample regression slope, is the interval estimate for $b_{population}$, the population
regression slope.

- Curved CI lines mark the lower and upper limits of the CI for the mean of the Y population at
each X value.

- The prediction interval for individual values of Y at a particular X value is usually long,
because it reflects both uncertainty in the estimate of mean Y at that value of X, and the
spread of individual Y values.

- Unless two variables are perfectly correlated, an estimate for the predicted variable shows
regression to the mean, a natural phenomenon occurring frequently in the world.

End-of-Chapter Exercises

1) It probably comes as no surprise to learn that friendly people tend to have more close friends than unfriendly people. To what extent can you predict how many friends someone has just from knowing how friendly they are? To investigate, 64 psychology majors completed a questionnaire measuring their friendliness and their number of close friends. The two variables were moderately correlated, $r = .34$, 95% CI [.10, .54]. Table 12.1 shows descriptive statistics.

Table 12.1 Summary Statistics for Friendliness and Numbers of Close Friends for $N = 64$ Students

Friendliness (scale from 1–5), X		Number of close friends (open ended), Y	
M	s	M	s
3.58	0.43	8.33	6.27

a. Think about those values. Does it seem reasonable to assume Y is normally distributed in the population?

b. Before using this information for regression, it would be best to see a scatterplot. What would you be looking for to confirm that regression is appropriate?

c. We'd like to use friendliness to predict number of close friends. What is the slope in the regression equation?

d. What is the intercept in the regression equation?

e. Using the regression equation, how many friends do you predict for someone who is fairly unfriendly ($X = 2$)?

f. Using the regression equation, how many friends do you predict for someone who is very friendly ($X = 5$)?

g. No mathematics, just think: How many friends do you predict for someone of exactly average friendliness ($X = 3.6$)? Why? Use the regression equation to check your intuition.

h. If you find out that your participant of average friendliness actually has 10 friends, what is the residual of prediction?

i. Calculate the regression equation going the other way: using number of close friends to predict friendliness.

j. What if someone reported having 300 close friends? What would their predicted level of friendliness be? Recall that friendliness was measured on a scale from 1 to 5. What's gone wrong using regression?

k. The sample data came from undergraduate psychology majors in the United States. Would it be reasonable to use this data set to make predictions about European psychology majors? About U.S. high school students? About Facebook users?

2) Maybe you're thinking about buying a house after college? Regression can help you hunt for a bargain. Use the book website to download the **Home_Prices** data set. This file contains real-estate listings from 1997 to 2003 in a city in California. Let's explore the extent to which the size of the home (in square meters) predicts the sale price.

a. Use ESCI to create a scatterplot of the relationship between home size (X) and asking price (Y). Does this data set seem suitable for use with regression?

b. To what extent is home size and asking price related in this sample? What is the 95% CI for the relationship between home size and asking price in the population of houses?

c. What is the regression equation for predicting asking price from home size?

d. Use ESCI to show the residuals for home prices—notice that some houses are listed at prices that fall above the regression line and others at prices that fall below. If you are hunting for a bargain, which type of house would you want to look at? Why? What is the house with the largest negative residual?

e. Does a large residual mean that the seller has made a mistake and should adjust the asking price? Why or why not?

f. If a house has a size of 185.8 m², what is the predicted asking price?

g. How well can we predict the mean asking price for houses of 185 m²? Use ESCI to obtain the 95% CI for the mean of Y when $X = 185$.

h. How well would our predictions hold up with a new data set? To investigate, 10 further cases, not included in the regression analysis, were taken from the same population. These are listed in Table 12.2, which is partially completed. For each house, use ESCI to predict price from house size. Record the prediction ($\hat{Y}$), the 95% prediction interval (PI), and calculate the residual ($Y - \hat{Y}$). In the second column from the right, record whether or not the PI includes the asking price. For the first two houses, check you get the same values as shown. Fill in values for the last four houses. In how many of the 10 cases does the PI include Y, the asking price? Calculations to the nearest $1,000 are fine.

Table 12.2 A Further Sample of 10 Houses In a Californian City

Case	Size, X (m²)	$\hat{Y}$ ($1,000)	95% PI ($1,000)		Asking Price, Y ($1,000)	Within PI? (Y/N)	Residual ($1,000)
1	133.8	297	−56	650	149	Y	−148
2	158.0	362	9	716	549	Y	187
3	142.7	321	−32	674	435	Y	114
4	121.7	264	-89	617	299	Y	35
5	203.2	485	132	838	625	Y	140
6	195.1	463	110	817	399	Y	−64
7	140.4				187		
8	197.9				1,290		
9	130.1				265		
10	113.8				199		

i. For a given X, our 95% PIs are really long. Yet we can predict the *mean* of Y for a given X with a very short 95% CI (as in g above). Why the difference? Would an even larger sample size help shorten the PIs substantially? Explain.

j. The data for this regression analysis were collected from 1997 to 2003. In 2015, a realtor is asked to help sell a house in the same city that is 99.1 m². What is the predicted price for this house using the regression equation you have from the 1997–2003 data set? Would it be reasonable to use this prediction in setting a price for this house? Why or why not? Do regression equations have expiration dates? Should they?

3) Happiness may not be important just for the person feeling it; happiness may also promote kind, altruistic behavior. Brethel-Haurwitz et al. (2014) examined this idea by collecting data on U.S. states. A Gallup poll in 2010 was used to measure each state's well-being index, a measure of mean happiness for the state's residents on a scale from 0 to 100. Next, a kidney donation database for 1999–2010 was used to figure out each state's rate (number of donations per 1,000,000 people) of non-directed kidney donations—that's giving one kidney to a stranger, an extremely generous and altruistic thing to do! You can download the data from the book website (**Altruism_Happiness**).

a. Use ESCI to create a scatterplot of the relationship between a state's 2010 well-being index (X) and rate of kidney donations (Y). Any comments on the scatterplot? Does this data set seem suitable for use with regression?

b. To what extent is a state's well-being index and rate of kidney donation related in this sample? What is the 95% CI for the relationship in the population? What does "population" refer to?

c. What is the regression equation for predicting rate of kidney donation from well-being index?

d. In Table 12.3 record the predictions for four states, in the column labeled $\hat{Y}$ (2010).

Table 12.3 Well-Being Means for Four States, for 2010 and 2013

State	Well_Being_2010	$\hat{Y}$ (2010)	Well_Being_2013	$\hat{Y}$ (2013)
WY	69.2		65.6	
HI	71		68.4	
ND	68		70.4	
NV	64.2		66.6	

e. The table includes updated well-being means, for 2013. Use those to make predictions, and record these in the column labeled $\hat{Y}$ (2013). Compare with the predictions based on the 2010 well-being data. Discuss which we should use.

f. To make predictions using the 2013 well-being means you used the regression equation generated using the 2010 well-being data. Discuss the extent that's reasonable.

g. From 2008 to 2013 Gallup measured state-wide well-being based on six indicators: life evaluations, emotional health, work environment, physical health, healthy behavior, and access to services. In 2014, however, Gallup changed the way it measures state-wide well-being; it now bases scores on five somewhat different indicators: purpose, social life, financial satisfaction, community, and physical health. Can the regression equation you developed be used with 2014 well-being data? Discuss.

Answers to Quizzes

Quiz 12.1

1) Y, X, $\hat{Y}$; 2) slope, intercept; 3) A residual is an error in prediction, calculated as $(Y - \hat{Y})$, which is the difference between the actual and predicted value of Y; 4) most useful is c., $r = -.6$; least useful is a., $r = 0$. The best predictions come from the strongest relationship, but the direction of the relationship does not matter for making good predictions; 5) slope; 6) d.

Quiz 12.2

1) c; 2) multiplying Z_X by r (so $Z_Y = r \times Z_X$); 3) slope, r; 4) d; 5) 16, 1, .8, −.8; 6) $(Y - \hat{Y})$, $(X - \bar{X})$.

Quiz 12.3

1) d; 2) No, yes, no, no, no (for c–e, less restrictive assumptions are required); 3) a. needs (ii), b. needs (iii), c. needs (i); 4) The prediction interval for individual Y at a particular X will change least because this depends not only on uncertainty in the estimate of mean Y at that value of X, but also on the spread of individual Y values at that level of X, which doesn't change for different N; 5) 1, closer to, regression to the mean; 6) I may have such powers (I suspect you do too), but this observation doesn't give good supporting evidence. Most likely, the noise level is lower 30 minutes after a very loud exchange simply because of variation over time and regression to the mean.

 ## Answers to In-Chapter Exercises

12.2   a. From 0 (horizontal) to 0.87; b. It's large for slope 0 or 0.87 and smaller in between; c. When the slope is 0.78, the same (or almost the same) as the calculated value of b, then $s_{Y.X} = 1.37$, its minimum value, and the line and values change from red to black.

12.3   a. $\hat{Y} = 4.22 + 0.78 \times X$; b. 11.24, small, because r is large and therefore the points are not scattered widely; c. For $X = 0$, $\hat{Y} = 4.22$, but $X = 0$ is way outside the range of X for which we have data, and the relationship of X and Y might not be the same so far beyond that range. A pretest score of 0 might suggest an absent or delinquent student, so $\hat{Y} = 0$ might be a better guess, but that's a guess—not a regression estimate.

12.4   b. $\hat{Y} = 11.24$ is our best point estimate of Y when $X = 9$, based on the regression line.

12.5   a, b. All the same.

12.6   a. 12, 10; b. Those points do not lie on the regression line, and therefore their Y values do not equal $\hat{Y} = 11.24$, which is no problem.

12.7   a. The point reduces r from .89 to .74 because it's an outlier; b. Slope changes from 0.78 to 0.76. The line drops, because of the low outlier, but rotates only a little because the new point is close to the mean of X. The line represents the points less well with the outlier added; c. The point (18, 7) is much more influential than (12, 7), making a much larger change to r, because it's more extreme, especially by being extreme on X as well as Y. Points that are outliers on both X and Y have much more influence on r and b.

12.8   a. In both scatterplots, r and the regression slope change greatly. In the left figure the means cross moves, but not in the right figure; b. $\beta = r$ and is .89 for the original points and .40 with the additional point. Both regression slopes change accordingly.

12.9   a. Today's temperature, X, and tomorrow's, Y; b. $Z_X = (14 - 20)/4 = -1.5$. $Z_{\hat{Y}} = .6 \times (-1.5) = -0.90$, so prediction is $\hat{Y} = 20 + (-0.90) \times 4 = 16.4\,°C$, c. If $r = 0$, predict 20 °C, the mean; d. Closer because regression line is steeper.

12.10 a. 2; b. $Z_{\hat{Y}} = .5 \times 2 = 1$. $\hat{Y} = 168$ cm; c. For $X = 168$ for the daughter, $\hat{Y} = 165$ cm for the granddaughter. $\hat{Y} = 163.5$ cm for the great-granddaughter.

12.11 a. $Z_{\hat{Y}} = .5 \times 2 = 1$; b. $\hat{Y} = 168$ cm is the best estimate of a mother's height, given her daughter (Susan) is $X = 174$ cm tall.

12.12 a. 64%, so 36% of variance in Y is the variance of the residuals, which no doubt fits with Panel A, although variance is hard to eyeball; b. For Panel C, 4% and 96%, again perhaps reasonable.

12.13 a. When r is close to 1 or −1; b. When $r = 1$ or −1, the two regression lines are the same, with slope (s_Y/s_X) or $-(s_Y/s_X)$; c. They are most different when $r = 0$, in which case the Y on X line is horizontal at M_Y, the mean of Y, and the X on Y line is vertical at M_X.

12.14 a. $\hat{Y} = 2.10 + 0.82X$; $b = 0.82$ is the regression slope in the data, meaning the slope of the regression line of Y on X; b. The CI on b is [0.52, 1.12], so the slope in the population could plausibly be anywhere in that fairly long interval; c. At red 12, ESCI shows $p = 0$ (which we'd report as $p < .001$) for the null hypothesis of zero regression slope in the population; d. At red 7, $p = 0$. The two p values are the same, as we'd expect, because if $r = 0$ the slope of the regression line is also 0; e. To calculate the regression line we're assuming random sampling of Y (Well-being), which is probably reasonable. To calculate the CI on b, and the p value at red 12, we need to assume also that Y is normally distributed in the population, with variance that is homogeneous for all X. To calculate the p value at red 7, for correlation, we need the stronger assumption that the data are from a bivariate normal population. All those assumptions are probably reasonable.

12.15 a. The CI tells us that the mean height of all women who have a best woman friend who is 174 cm tall lies, most likely, in that interval; b. The CI for Panel A tells us the same, but for all women who have an identical twin who is 174 cm tall. It's much shorter because the correlation is much higher, so we have much better information about Maria's likely height.

12.16 a. 64%, 4%, and these values reflect the very different slopes of the two regression lines; b. 36%, 96%; c. The differing Y residuals in the two scatterplots—the differing amounts of scatter of the points around the regression line in A and C.

12.17 The CI estimates the mean height of all women with a best woman friend who's 174 cm tall, whereas the much longer prediction interval reflects that uncertainty and in addition the variation in height of all those individual women. It tells us about the spread in the distribution of heights of all women with a best woman friend who's 174 cm tall.

12.18 a. $\hat{Y}$ = 73.9 [72.1, 75.8], so 73.9 is the best point estimate of population mean posttest HCTA when the pretest is 72, and that CI is the interval estimate for that mean; b. The prediction interval is (64.2, 83.7) and tells us about the full distribution of individual posttest scores when pretest = 72.

12.19 Performance week to week no doubt shows some variability, so the correlation is less than 1, and therefore regression to the mean must occur: an extreme performance this week is likely to be followed by a less extreme performance next week. There is no need to invoke any extra reason, such as a player being put off their game. It may be worth bringing the awards back.

12.20 Headache usually varies over time, so regression to the mean could explain why a headache now is, on average, followed by lesser headache in an hour. My ritual could easily be having no effect, unless my belief is strong enough to produce a placebo effect. Alas, I can't expect my headache treatment to make me famous.

12.21 a. The $7,000 is no doubt b for the regression line of annual income on years of education, probably based on data for a large sample of people. It implies that, on average, income increases by that amount for an additional year of education; b. The ad assumes causality of income by education, whereas no doubt there are many other variables involved. For example, intelligence, family background, and personal motivation may be, to some extent, causal for both years of education, and income.

12.22 a. By regression to the mean, quite often my headache reduces and so my belief in the ritual could be strengthened; b. Other superstitions that could be reinforced in the same way need to predict an event likely to happen because of regression to the mean. The superstition must relate to an extreme value on X leading to a less extreme value on Y, where X and Y are correlated. A belief that it rains more at weekends does not qualify, but a belief that shouting at the clouds on a very wet day causes the following day to be less wet does qualify.

12.23 a. Children selected for scoring poorly are likely to do less poorly, on average, at a second testing, by regression to the mean—so your game may have no effect; b. A better study would randomly allocate your poor spellers either to a group who work with your game, or another group who have some comparison activity, perhaps working with a textbook.

13

Frequencies, Proportions, and Risk

So far in this book we've mainly used effect size measures that rely on interval scaling—including means, Cohen's *d*, and correlations. In this chapter we take a step back to require only nominal scaling and focus on the *proportion*, which is a highly useful ES measure based on frequencies, or simple counts. We'll consider research questions for which a proportion provides the answer and, as we've done so many times with other ES measures, we'll focus on the CI as well as the point estimate. Then we'll discuss research questions where we need the difference between two proportions and the CI on that difference. My first example investigates the possibility of telepathy, which is communication with another person using a psychic power, through "the power of the mind".

Do some people have psychic powers, powers that science doesn't know about? Can some people bend spoons at a distance, or use telepathy to communicate with others? Some claimed psychics give highly convincing demonstrations, which persuade many people that their psychic powers are real. However, stage magicians can also impress us with demonstrations of what look like psychic phenomena. Many people believe psychic powers exist, while many others are convinced that they don't.

Some scientists investigate possible psychic powers, under the label of *parapsychology*. Some studies of telepathy are especially relevant here because they can be analyzed simply by calculating the proportion of trials that were correct. The *proportion* is a simple effect size measure that's calculated from frequencies.

The agenda for this chapter is:

- Psychic powers and research in parapsychology
- Frequencies, nominal scaling, and proportions
- The CI on a proportion
- The difference between two proportions, and the CI on this difference
- Frequency tables analyzed using proportions, and via an alternative approach: the chi-square statistic
- Another application of proportions: risk, and the difference between risks

RESEARCH ON POSSIBLE PSYCHIC POWERS

Mentalists are stage magicians with a particular interest in using their skills to demonstrate what look like psychic phenomena. Many are both convincing and entertaining. Some magicians challenge psychics to demonstrate their claimed powers under conditions allowing scientific scrutiny. For a famous example, search online for "James Randi"—who has long had on offer a cash prize, now $1,000,000, for anyone who can demonstrate psychic powers under agreed scientific conditions. So far, he has not had to pay up. For an entertaining take on psychic powers, see the Woody Allen movie *Magic in the Moonlight*. You can find the plot on the Internet, but it may be more fun to watch the movie.

Even impressive demonstrations by mentalists using their magic skills don't prove that psychic powers don't exist, but they set a challenge for scientists working in parapsychology: Experimental procedures must be sufficiently watertight to rule out the possibility that mentalist techniques, rather than psychic powers, can explain any positive results.

Before discussing frequencies, proportions, and then, at last, the example, I want to mention a useful slogan for any scientist: "Extraordinary claims require extraordinary evidence". The claim that telepathy exists (minds can communicate at a distance, as if by magic —really?) is extraordinary. We should therefore be looking for extraordinarily strong evidence before we are convinced that telepathy has been demonstrated. Researchers in this field thus have twin challenges: First, to design studies so that even expert mentalists agree that any positive results can't be explained by stage magic techniques; and, second, to find very strong evidence. Even more than usual we'll want replication, and cumulation of evidence over studies. Open Science requirements are especially relevant: We simply must have the full story.

> Extraordinary claims require extraordinary evidence.

PROPORTIONS

It's almost time to meet proportions, but first I need to say a little about frequencies, which we met back in Chapters 2 and 3.

Frequencies

> *Frequencies* are counts of the number of data points in an interval or category.

Frequencies are simply counts of the number of data points in some interval or category. In Chapter 3, Figure 3.3 Panels C and D and Figure 3.4 show frequency histograms. In all those examples, the variable has interval scaling. Recall from Chapter 2 that interval scaling means the variable "has distance": We assume each unit on the scale is equivalent, as for time or weight. In those histograms, a frequency is the number of data points within a bin. For example, in Figure 3.3 D, six data points lie in the bin from 12 to 16 transcription percentage.

However, frequencies can also be used when our variable has ordinal, or even only nominal scaling. Figure 13.1 displays fictitious frequency data for a 7-point rating scale. The response categories are ordered, so we have ordinal scaling. The full set of frequencies gives us a good overview of the data.

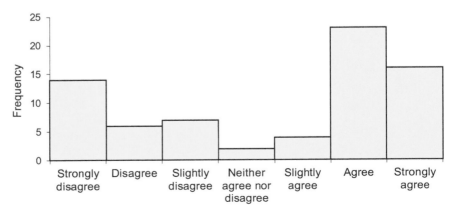

Figure 13.1. Frequency histogram for responses to a 7-point rating scale, assumed to have ordinal scaling. Fictitious data.

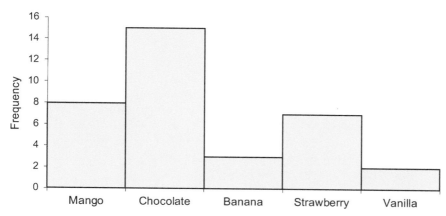

Figure 13.2. Frequency histogram for preferences for various flavors of ice cream, assumed to have only nominal scaling. Fictitious data.

Figure 13.2 displays fictitious frequency data for a group of people's preferences for flavors of ice cream. Again the figure showing the full set of frequencies gives us a good overview. We probably don't have any good way to order the flavors, so our measurement scale is nominal—also referred to as categorical. All we can do is count the number of cases in each category. Those frequencies give us the full story, and the only summary descriptive statistic of note is the mode, which, as we saw in Chapter 3, is simply the category having the largest frequency—chocolate in our example.

Frequencies are needed for nominal scaling, and can be used with ordinal or interval scaling.

Proportions for Frequencies

A *proportion* is simply a chosen frequency, say X, divided by N, the total number of cases. I'll use upper-case P for proportion, to minimize confusion with p as in p value, so the basic formula for a proportion is

$$P = X/N \qquad (13.1)$$

Proportion, P

If I get 17 of the 20 items on a test correct, my proportion correct is, of course, $P = 17/20 = .85$. The minimum value of X is 0, and the maximum is N, so proportion, P, can range from 0 to 1.

I have defined proportion as the ratio of two frequencies, but it's also possible to calculate a proportion for quantities measured on an interval scale, like time, rather than for frequencies. We might, for example, record the total time asleep and express that as a proportion of the time spent in bed. That's perfectly legitimate, although in this chapter I'll discuss only proportions defined as the ratio of two frequencies, because my main interest is in how we can best analyze nominal data, and frequencies used with nominal data.

Proportions are especially useful for analyzing frequency data.

Now, at last, the example. It comes from Bem and Honorton (1994), which was published, after searching peer review, by *Psychological Bulletin*. Its acceptance for publication in what is psychology's top review journal prompted much discussion and controversy.

The Ganzfeld Experiment

The most common recent procedure for investigating possible telepathy involves one person—the sender—in an isolated, soundproof room who seeks to send information by telepathy to a second person—the receiver—who is in a different

In a ganzfeld experiment, a sender attempts telepathy to a receiver.

isolated, soundproof room. A computer chooses randomly from a database a picture or short video clip to present to the sender, who concentrates hard on that picture, or repeated video clip, typically for 30 minutes. The receiver is reclining comfortably, with half ping-pong balls over the eyes, in a diffuse reddish light, hearing white noise over headphones. The receiver is thus in a *ganzfeld* (German for "entire field")—receiving minimal perceptual stimulation. The receiver speaks aloud, reporting whatever thoughts happen to occur. Later the receiver is shown four pictures, or video clips, one of which was the target seen by the sender. The receiver chooses from the four, and records a hit if the target is chosen. By chance, if there is no telepathy, the proportion of hits should be around .25.

Polya

There are anecdotal claims that telepathy may be associated with meditation, hypnosis, or dreams. The ganzfeld is intended to encourage a meditative state, free of distraction, which may be conducive to telepathy. To read more about the procedure, search online for "Ganzfeld experiment".

Daryl Bem was an experienced mentalist, as well as research psychologist, who, a decade earlier, had been one of several outside experts invited to scrutinize the laboratory and experimental procedures of parapsychology researcher Charles Honorton. Bem not only judged them adequate, but joined the research effort and became a coauthor with Honorton. Bem and Honorton (1994) first reviewed early ganzfeld studies and described how the experimental procedure had been improved to reduce the chance that results could be influenced by various possible biases, or leakages of information from sender to receiver. For example, the randomization procedure was carried out automatically by computer, and all stimuli were presented under computer control. Bem and Honorton then presented data from studies conducted with the improved procedure.

Table 13.1 presents basic data from 10 studies reported by Bem and Honorton (1994). Three pilot studies helped refine the procedures, then four studies used novice receivers. Study 5 used 20 students of music, drama, or dance as receivers, in response to suggestions that creative people might be more likely to show telepathy. Studies 6 and 7 used receivers who had participated in an earlier study. The proportion of hits expected by chance is .25 and Table 13.1 shows that all but Study 1 found proportions higher than .25. The bottom row in the table is the result of a simple meta-analysis of the 10 studies, which in this case is based on simply adding the frequencies for all studies. It shows that the overall proportion of hits was .32. This proportion, .32, is our point estimate of performance in the population of receivers from which the samples of participants were drawn. To go further, we need to consider CIs.

THE CONFIDENCE INTERVAL ON A PROPORTION

To calculate a CI on $P = X/N$, assume the N events are independent and each has the same probability of being a hit.

When working with means, our first step beyond the mean was to find the CI. We'll do the same here, by finding the CI on a proportion. Let's say that our proportion, $P = X/N$, refers to X hits in N items or events. To calculate a CI on

Study	Participants	Number of trials	Number of hits	Proportion of hits	95% CI
Pilot 1	Novice	22	8	.36	[.2, .57]
Pilot 2	Novice	9	3	.33	[.12, .65]
Pilot 3	Novice	35	10	.29	[.16, .45]
Study 1	Novice	50	12	.24	[.14, .37]
Study 2	Novice	50	18	.36	[.24, .5]
Study 3	Novice	50	15	.3	[.19, .44]
Study 4	Novice	36	12	.33	[.2, .5]
Study 5	Julliard	20	10	.5	[.3, .7]
Study 6	Experienced	7	3	.43	[.16, .75]
Study 7	Experienced	50	15	.3	[.19, .44]
All novice	Novice	252	78	.31	[.26, .37]
All experienced	Experienced	57	18	.32	[.21, .44]
All		329	106	.32	[.27, .37]

Table 13.1 Results of 10 Ganzfeld Studies From Bem and Honorton (1994)

P, we need to assume that the N items or events are independent and that each has the same probability of being a hit. With these assumptions, we can obtain an excellent approximation to the CI, which is shown in Figure 13.3. For this figure I entered the result of Pilot 1 in **One proportion**, by using the spinners at red 1 to set $X = 8$ and $N = 22$. At red 1 you can see that the proportion is $P = .364$ and at red 3 that the 95% CI is [.197, .57], which is the CI that appears, rounded, for Pilot 1 in the final column of Table 13.1.

I'm not going to explain how that CI was calculated, because the method is a little complicated. Many books give formulas for an approximate method based on the normal distribution, but that approximation is poor for small frequencies. The method used by ESCI is the one recommended by statisticians, which works even for very small frequencies ($P = 1/3$, for example) and for $P = 0$ or 1. To read about this preferred method, and a comparison with the conventional normal distribution method, see Chapter 6 of a useful book about CIs with the lovely title of *Statistics with Confidence* (Altman, Machin, Bryant, & Gardner, 2000).

 13.1 Open the **One proportion** page of **ESCI intro chapters 10–16**. Explore. Compare with Figure 13.3. Check a few of the other CIs reported in Table 13.1.

 13.2 With a fixed N, perhaps $N = 20$, see how the CI changes as you change X from 0 to 20. Summarize.

13.3 Explain what the three values shown at red 3 just below the CI tell us. Do the values correspond reasonably with the CI that ESCI displays in the figure?

 13.4 Set $X = 14$ and $N = 22$.

    a. Compare the proportion and CI with that for $X = 8$ and $N = 22$ as shown in Figure 13.3. Explain.

    b. Compare also the three lower values shown at red 3 for the two cases ($X = 8$ and 14). Explain.

 13.5 a. With a fixed P, perhaps $P = .2$, see how the CI changes for $P = 1/5$, 8/40, and 32/160. Summarize. *Note.* To set N or X, use the spinner or type in a number, but make sure that X is no larger than N.

    b. Do that again by using small, medium, and large values of X and N, all with some other fixed value of P. Summarize.

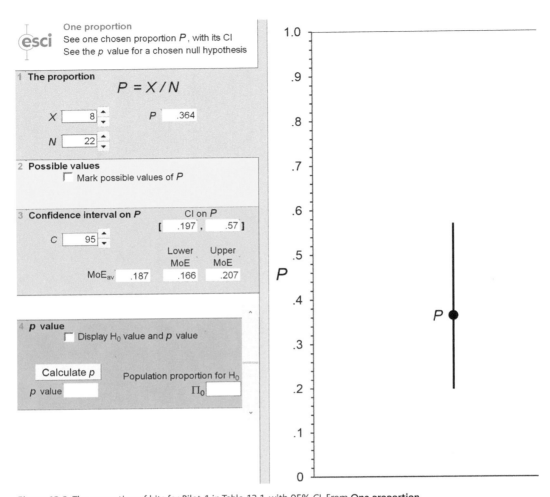

Figure 13.3. The proportion of hits for Pilot 1 in Table 13.1, with 95% CI. From **One proportion**.

esci 13.6 Click at red 2 and see some lines. Vary X and N and explain what the lines tell us.

esci 13.7 Describe the CI when $X = 0$. Vary N. Explain.

13.8 If we know only that $P = .85$, can we calculate the CI? Explain.

esci 13.9 Recall the approximate guideline that a CI is about half as long when N is multiplied by 4. For a fixed P, does that guideline hold for proportions?

13.10 Noting the result reported in the bottom row of Table 13.1, interpret the overall result of the 10 studies.

To calculate a p value for a proportion, assume the N events are independent and each has the same probability of being a hit.

The p Value for a Proportion

For the telepathy experiments, the sample ES is P, which is an estimate of the proportion in the population. I'll refer to that population proportion as Π (Greek upper case pi), in accord with the convention of using the corresponding Greek letter for the population parameter. If no telepathy occurred and the receivers guessed, we expect the proportion of hits to be .25, so $\Pi = .25$, and we would

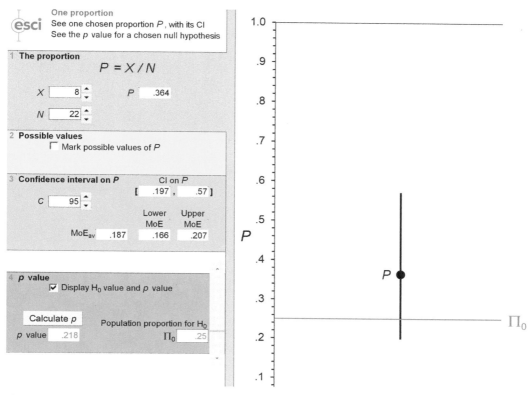

Figure 13.4. The same as Figure 13.3, but showing also the *p* value for a null hypothesis value of $\Pi_0 = .25$ marked by the red line.

choose $\Pi_0 = .25$ as our null hypothesis value for calculating a *p* value. Figure 13.4 shows that ESCI can do this for us. As for a CI, we need to have frequencies, and to make the assumption about independent events each with the same probability of being a hit.

esci 13.11 Click at red 4 to turn on the *p* value, and use the small slider to set the null hypothesis value, which is marked by a red horizontal line in the figure. Note the *p* value. Considering the CI in the figure, is the *p* value as you expect? Explain.

esci 13.12 For a few of the other studies reported in Table 13.1, consider the CI and make your estimate of the *p* value, then compare with the *p* value that ESCI reports.

esci 13.13 Find the *p* value for the combination of all 10 studies. Interpret, and compare with your earlier interpretation of the CI.

? Quiz 13.1

1. Frequencies are
   a. especially useful with ordinal or interval scaling.
   b. especially useful for calculation of the median.
   c. counts that allow determination of the mode.
   d. numbers that range from 0 to 1.

2. A basic guideline in science is that extraordinary _____ require extraordinary _____.
3. A proportion needs to be expressed in terms of _____ if we are to calculate a CI.
4. To calculate a CI on proportion $P = X/N$, we need to assume that _____
   _____ and that _____
   _____.
5. The CI on proportion $P = X/N$ is typically symmetric / asymmetric, and becomes shorter / longer as N increases.
6. To calculate a p value for a proportion P, the null hypothesis value has symbol _____, which refers to the proportion in the sample / population IF the null hypothesis is true / false.

Percentages and Proportions

Multiply any proportion by 100 to get the corresponding percentage, so my test performance of 17 of 20 items correct was .85 or 85% correct. Similarly, divide any percentage by 100 to express as a proportion. However, percentages can be tricky, so we need to take care.

A percentage may refer to frequencies (17 correct out of 20 items), or to interval or ratio measurements, such as time asleep as a percentage of the time spent in bed. However, I'm focusing on frequencies, proportions based on frequencies, and the CI on such proportions. Therefore, if we have a percentage and want to find the CI, two conditions must be met:

1. The percentage must be based on frequencies, so there's an equivalent $P = X/N$.
2. We must be willing to assume the N items or events are independent, and that each has the same probability of being a hit.

If both conditions are met we can use ESCI to find the CI on P. I might feel that some of the 20 items on the test I completed were harder than others, so they don't all have the same probability of being answered correctly. However, if I'm willing to assume the probability doesn't vary much across the items, I can calculate a CI, at least approximately.

Consider for a moment the example I mentioned earlier of the proportion of time in bed that was sleep. That might, for example, be 7 hours out of a total 8 in bed, or 420 minutes out of 480 in bed. Those times have ratio scaling, but we could regard the numbers as frequencies, and calculate the proportion $P = 7/8 = .875$, or percentage (87.5%), of time asleep. However, we can't use the methods of this chapter to find a CI or a p value for that proportion. The 8 hours or 480 minutes are not all separate, independent items or events, but are, of course, linked in a single sequence. They are not independent because whether you are asleep this minute is sure to be highly correlated with whether or not you were asleep in the minute just before. So Condition 2 above does not hold. In summary, you can say that you were asleep for a proportion $P = 7/8$ of the night, but that's not a proportion that we can analyze using the methods of this chapter.

Going back to my test performance, $P = 17/20 = .85$, and ESCI tells me the CI is [.64, .95]. I could interpret those three proportions (the point estimate and the two limits of the CI), or convert to percentages and say that I scored 85% [64, 95] on the test. That's a long CI, from 64% to 95%, which suggests the test of 20 items is not giving a very precise estimate of my ability. Testing me on a larger number of items should give a more precise estimate.

The first caution when working with percentages is, therefore, that we can calculate a CI only if we can convert to frequencies—and we're prepared to make the assumptions of Condition 2 above.

Percentages require caution. Only if they can be expressed in terms of frequencies can we calculate a CI or *p* value.

While discussing percentages I'd like to mention a second caution, even if this isn't strictly a proportion issue. Suppose last year 20% of people were late paying their dues, and that, after the new payment system came in this year, 30% of people were late. One report said "10% increase in late payments" (30 is 10 more than 20), another said "50% increase" (30 is 50% more than 20), and a third said "late payment rate up by 10 percentage points" (an increase of 10, from 20 to 30). They are all more or less correct, so percentages give lots of scope for confusion—or being deliberately misleading. The most common problem is that "10% increase" leaves us in doubt between a change from 20% to 30%, and a change from 20% to 22%, which would indeed be an increase of 10% of the original number of late payers.

When reporting a change, referring to "an increase of 10 percentage points" is safest, but it's better still to mention both the before and after percentages, so we can be sure. If you hear about a change reported using percentages, take care to bring to mind the different possibilities, and seek clarification if necessary.

There are other traps with percentages—sometimes it's not clear what the percentage is *of*—but I'll leave percentages now and return to proportions. The key point to remember is that proportions expressed in terms of frequencies are what we need for inference—to calculate a CI or a *p* value.

esci 13.14 A test comprises 60 true/false items. Laura scores 80% correct.

a. Calculate a CI for her performance. What assumptions do you need to make? Interpret.

b. Express the CI in terms of proportions, and of percentages. Do you have a preference? Explain.

c. To calculate a *p* value for her result, what null hypothesis value would you choose?

d. Find the *p* value and interpret.

THE DIFFERENCE BETWEEN TWO INDEPENDENT PROPORTIONS

In Study 5, Bem and Honorton used Julliard students of music, drama, or dance to investigate whether such creative participants might be more likely than novices to show telepathy. Table 13.1 reports the proportions and CIs for Study 5 and for all studies using novices. Our research question asks about the difference between those two proportions, and so our ES is that difference and, as usual, we'll want the CI on the difference. The two proportions are independent because they come from different studies that used different participants. ESCI can give us a CI on the difference between two such independent proportions, as Figure 13.5 illustrates. I entered the hit proportions for novices (P_1) and Julliard students (P_2) at red 1 and 2 in **Two proportions**. The difference and its CI are reported at red 6 at left to be 0.19 [−0.02, 0.4], and are displayed on a difference axis at right. Note that proportions and the CIs on proportions always lie between 0 and 1, but that *differences* between proportions can be negative, and we can have CIs on differences that include both positive and negative values, as here.

We can calculate the CI on the difference between two proportions if they are independent.

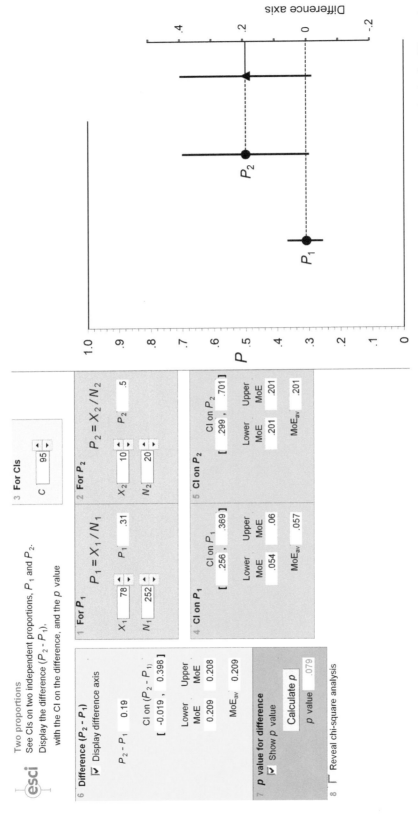

Figure 13.5. The difference between proportions of hits for novice participants (P_1), and Julliard students (P_2), with 95% CI. Values are reported at red 6 at left. The p value for the difference is shown at red 7 at left. From **Two proportions**.

The *p* value for the difference is shown at red 7 at left to be $p = .08$, which corresponds with the CI on the difference just including 0, as the figure illustrates. The CI on the difference is long, mainly because there were only 20 Julliard students, so their CI was long, extending from around .3 to around .7. The long CI on the difference, from around 0 to around .4, means we have very little, if any, evidence of a possible population difference in hit proportions between Julliard students and other novices.

13.15 Use the frequencies reported near the bottom in Table 13.1 to compare the hit proportions of novice and experienced participants. Interpret.

Bem and Honorton (1994) reported more data and analyses than I've described here, and concluded that they were presenting strong evidence for telepathy. The journal published a critique by Ray Hyman (1994), who disagreed with their conclusions, and a reply by Bem (1994). Does the original article provide the extraordinary evidence required to support the extraordinary claim of telepathy? I noted earlier that Bem and Honorton made great efforts to improve on procedures used in earlier telepathy research, as they attempted to minimize the scope for any bias or conventional communication channel to account for any positive finding. However, they were working some two decades before Open Science ideas were recognized as important, especially preregistration. I invite you to consider, and discuss with your friends, what conclusion you feel is justified, and what further research might be useful. You might discuss what "extraordinary evidence" would look like: Evidence produced by especially well-conducted research? Results providing extremely strong evidence against the null hypothesis of guessing? Both?

THE RELATION BETWEEN TWO VARIABLES: FREQUENCY TABLES

A common research question asks about the relation between two *classification variables*, and a common data set obtained to try to answer such a question is a 2 × 2 table of frequencies as in Table 13.2. Our approach to analyzing such a table and answering the question will be to calculate proportions and the difference between two proportions. My example is a landmark randomized control trial of diet. People living in Mediterranean countries have rather low rates of heart disease and some cancers. Is this because of genetics, or lifestyle, or diet, or what? The Lyon Diet Heart Study, reported by de Lorgeril et al. (1998) investigated diet. The researchers randomly allocated 605 patients who had survived one heart attack to a diet similar to one recommended by the American Heart Association (the Control diet), or a Mediterranean (Med) diet, for four years. The Med diet included more cereals, vegetables, and fish, and less dairy and meat. The researchers monitored how well the patients kept to their allocated diet, and recorded numerous variables, including blood levels of various nutrients, and many aspects of participants' health. The two classification variables in Table 13.2 A are Control or Med diet (the column variable), and Cancer or No cancer during the four years (the row variable). The research question asks about the relation between those variables—more specifically, to what extent was the proportion of people with cancer different for the two diets?

Using proportions can often be a good strategy for examining the relation between two classification variables.

Table 13.2
Frequencies for
Any Cancer, and
for Cardiac Death,
From de Lorgeril
et al. (1998)

A	Control	Med	Total
Cancer	17	7	24
No cancer	286	295	581
Total	303	302	605

B	Control	Med	Total
Cardiac death	19	6	25
No cardiac death	284	296	580
Total	303	302	605

Note. Control = conventional prudent diet. Med = Mediterranean diet.

Table 13.2 reports the frequencies for any cancer diagnosis, and for cardiac death—death from another heart attack—during the four years. Panel A shows there were 17/303 cancers in the Control group, and 7/302 in the Med group. I entered those frequencies into **Two proportions** and found the Control and Med proportions were .056 and .023, respectively. The research question here is "What difference does the Med diet make to the risk of getting cancer?" Our best answer is provided by the difference between those proportions—which come from separate groups of participants, and are thus independent. The difference between .023 and .056 was −0.033 [−0.067, −0.001]. The groups were large, but even so the CI on the difference indicates considerable uncertainty. Most likely the Med diet reduced the risk of cancer, but the reduction could be anywhere from tiny to considerable.

You may have wondered why I focused on the proportions of people with cancer, rather than the proportions without. That's a good thought. I could just as easily have analyzed the complementary proportions, those for people with no cancer.

esci 13.16 a. Enter the proportions of people in each group with no cancer into **Two proportions** and find the difference with its CI.
   b. Compare with the difference and CI we found above. Interpret.

esci 13.17 What is the research question for Panel B of Table 13.2? Analyze the frequencies and interpret.

One striking aspect of the example is that the Control diet was similar to a diet recommended by the American Heart Association. It would hardly be news if Med were better than a junk food diet, but finding it substantially better than the chosen, already good Control diet is valuable news, even if the study can't tell us how relevant its findings are for people who have not had heart attacks.

Are you already putting aside the soda and chocolate and reaching for an oatmeal cookie and an apple?

Whenever you see a table of frequencies as in Table 13.2, think of proportions. ESCI can give you CIs on those proportions. Further, if your two proportions are independent, **Two proportions** can give you the CI on the difference. Very often that difference is the ES of research interest, so the difference and its CI is what you need to best answer your research question.

Here's another example to illustrate the usefulness of proportions. Imagine you have a bed partner. In the dead of night you hear your partner breathing, then the breathing stops for some time, and does so repeatedly. That's sleep apnea, which can be incredibly scary for the person who is awake. Research has linked sleep apnea with heart disease, depression, and other bad outcomes. Search for "sleep apnea" to learn more. Many people have it, but do not know: It's an important issue that deserves more attention and research.

My example investigated a possible link between attention deficit and hyperactivity disorder (ADHD) in children and a syndrome known as

	ADHD before surgery?		
	No	Yes	Total
Change from before to after surgery? Yes	0	11	11
No	55	11	66
Total	55	22	77

Table 13.3
Frequencies of Children Whose Diagnosis of ADHD Changed From Before to After Surgery, From Chervin et al. (2006)

sleep-disordered breathing (SDB). SDB includes sleep apnea, snoring, and other breathing problems during sleep. Chervin et al. (2006) studied children who were about to have their tonsils removed to improve SDB. The researchers assessed the children's sleep, and their cognitive and behavioral functioning, before the tonsillectomy and one year later. In the group of 77 children, 22 were diagnosed with ADHD before the operation, but only 11 were given this diagnosis at follow up, one year later.

Those figures might suggest that we should simply find the difference between the proportions of children with ADHD at the two time points: What's the decrease from 22/77 to 11/77? However, those two proportions refer to the same group of 77 children, so are not independent. We need to reorganize the frequencies to obtain independence, then we can calculate the CI on the difference between two independent proportions. Table 13.3 shows how: Consider two groups of children, the 55 who did not at first have ADHD and the 22 who did. The groups are separate, so proportions from the two groups are independent. Our research question asks about the change in ADHD diagnosis from before to after the operation, so we need to focus on that change. In each group, find the proportion of children whose ADHD diagnosis changed: P_1 = 0/55 = 0 for those without ADHD initially, and P_2 = 11/22 = .5 for those with an initial ADHD diagnosis.

I suspect that's a bit tricky to follow, but I hope the table helps. Note that the four *main cells* in the table, not including the totals, contain frequencies that add to 77, the overall group size. In the top left cell, 0 with ADHD after but not before; top right, 11 with ADHD before but not after; bottom left, 55 with no ADHD before or after; and bottom right, 11 with ADHD both before and after. Each child is counted in exactly one of those four main cells. That's what we need for the proportions to be independent. Look back at Table 13.2, Panel A. The four main cells have frequencies that add to 605, the overall total. Each person in the study is counted in one and only one of those four cells. Therefore, the two proportions we calculate are independent because they refer to separate groups of people. Confirm that the same is true of Panel B. It's always worth checking: We need a frequency table in which each person (or event, or whatever the frequencies are counting) is counted in one and only one of the main cells in the table. Once we have such a frequency table we can calculate two independent proportions, and find the CI on the difference.

Using the frequencies in Table 13.3, the **Two proportions** page tells me that the difference is $(P_2 - P_1)$ = 11/22 − 0/55 = .5 − 0 = 0.5, with 95% CI of [0.3, 0.69]. Note that all the changes in diagnoses were in the group initially diagnosed to have ADHD. This confirms what we can see clearly from the frequencies themselves, that there was a very large and clear difference between the 50% reduction in ADHD diagnoses in the group who had ADHD at the start,

Frequency data may need rearranging to give two proportions that are independent.

and the zero change in those who did not. This is a remarkable finding: Half the children with ADHD no longer received that diagnosis a year after the surgery.

You might be thinking that the reduction in ADHD diagnoses was obvious and large, so why did we bother with CIs at all? Yes, the difference of 0.5 is large, but it is the CI of [0.3, 0.69], which is far from zero, that tells us that we have strong evidence of a substantial effect. Even with a large effect we need the CI to tell us about strength of evidence.

Some of the symptoms of ADHD, including attention difficulties, are also symptoms of lack of sleep. Perhaps some children diagnosed as having ADHD mainly have a sleep problem caused by SDB? Further, if tonsillectomy fixes the sleep problem, perhaps the ADHD is fixed also? The results of Chervin et al. (2006) hint at that intriguing possibility, and a meta-analysis by Sedky et al. (2014) supported the idea.

Children with ADHD are often prescribed stimulant or other drugs. If, at least for some children, the primary problem is SDB, it would seem best to investigate a child's sleep before taking the drastic step of prescribing drugs, which may manage symptoms but not fix the problem. Proportions are very simple measures, based on simple counts, but they can contribute to research on fascinating questions with the potential for enormous human benefit. Next I'll introduce an alternative approach to frequency tables.

? Quiz 13.2

1. Ten years ago, 6% of a trucking corporation's drivers were women; now 9% are. The change is best expressed as
   a. a 3% increase.
   b. a 50% increase.
   c. an increase of 3 percentage points.
   d. Any of the above.
2. To calculate the CI on a percentage, it is necessary to
   a. divide by 100.
   b. express as a ratio of two frequencies.
   c. ensure that it refers to independent events, each with the same probability of being a hit.
   d. All of the above.
3. To calculate a CI on the difference between two proportions, each must be based on frequencies / percentages / means and the two must be equal / independent / correlated.
4. When calculating a p value for the difference between two proportions, the null hypothesis is usually that _____.
5. Considering a 2 × 2 table of frequencies, the effect size of research interest is usually
   a. the difference between two independent proportions.
   b. the overall proportion.
   c. the correlation between two proportions.
   d. the extent of independence of the four main cells.
6. If proportions calculated from frequencies in a 2 × 2 table are not independent, it may be possible to rearrange / condense / expand the table so proportions are correlated / identical / independent and the frequencies in the four main cells add to 1 / 100 / overall N, in which case we can calculate a CI / a p value / both a CI and p value.

CHI-SQUARE, AN ALTERNATIVE APPROACH TO EXAMINING THE RELATION IN FREQUENCY TABLES

This is an optional extra section that describes an alternative approach to investigating the relation between two classification variables when we have a frequency table. The approach is based on the χ^2 statistic. That's Greek

	Novice		Julliard		Total
	Observed frequencies Obs	*Expected frequencies Exp*	Observed frequencies Obs	*Expected frequencies Exp*	
Hit	78	*88 × 252/272 = 81.53*	10	*88 × 20/272 = 6.47*	88
Miss	174	*184 × 252/272 = 170.47*	10	*184 × 20/272 = 13.53*	184
Total	252	252	20	20	272

Table 13.4 Frequency Table of Hits and Misses for Novice and Julliard Participants, From Table 13.1

lower-case chi ("ky", rhymes with sky), squared. Using chi-square is the most common way to calculate a p value for testing a null hypothesis for a frequency table. To explain, I'll use Table 13.4, which presents data for Novice and Julliard participants from Table 13.1, as shown also in Figure 13.5. The 2 × 2 table presents all four combinations of the column variable (Novice or Julliard) and row variable (Hit or Miss). The data are shown in the columns labeled *Observed frequencies*.

The null hypothesis is that there is no association in the population between the column and row variables. In other words, knowing whether a person is a novice or from Julliard gives us no information about whether they made a hit or a miss. This is just another way of saying that the proportion of Hits is the same for Novice and Julliard, which is exactly the null hypothesis we considered when using proportions to analyze these data. Yes, a chi-square analysis tests the same null hypothesis as the proportions analysis, but with chi-square the tradition is to express it as "no association between the column and row classification variables".

> The chi-square statistic, χ^2, is used to test the null hypothesis of no association in the population between the column and row classification variables in a frequency table.

Just a bit more jargon: In Table 13.4, the *column totals* are 252 and 20, and *row totals* are 88 and 184. The *grand total* is 272. As before, the four *main cells* are the data cells that contain 78, 174, 10, and 10. Now, there are three steps to using chi-square to find the p value:

1. *Find the expected frequencies* if the null hypothesis is true. We assume the grand total, and column and row totals are all fixed, and need to calculate the *expected frequencies* for the four main cells. These are what we'd expect if the null hypothesis is true. For each main cell, the formula is:

   Expected frequency = Row total × column total/Grand total   (13.2)

   The table shows the calculations for the four main cells. For the top left cell (Novice, Hit), for example, the row total is 88 and column total is 252, so the expected frequency is 88 × 252/272 = 81.53.

2. *Calculate chi-square* from the observed and expected frequencies.

   For each main cell calculate

   Contribution to χ^2 = (Obs − Exp)^2/Exp   (13.3)

where "Obs" means observed frequency, and "Exp" means expected frequency. For the top left cell this is (78 − 81.53)^2 / 81.53 = 0.153. The contribution is a measure of how far Obs departs from Exp, or how far the data differ from what we'd expect if the null hypothesis is true. You could check that the contributions from the other cells are 0.073, 1.925, and 0.921.

Chi-square is simply the sum of those contributions for the four main cells:

$$\chi^2 = 0.153 + 0.073 + 1.925 + 0.921 = 3.072 \qquad (13.4)$$

▶ χ^2 is a measure of difference between observed and expected frequencies. Large χ^2 means large difference, small p value, and strong evidence against the null hypothesis.

3. *Find the p value* corresponding to the calculated value of chi-square. We'll use the fact that, for a 2 × 2 table, there is just one degree of freedom, so $df = 1$. Large values of χ^2 mean Obs differs more from Exp, which means the data depart from what we'd expect if the null hypothesis is true. Therefore, large χ^2 means stronger evidence against the null hypothesis, which indicates smaller p. We'll use ESCI to give us p.

Figure 13.6 is the same as Figure 13.5 except that I clicked at red 8 to reveal the chi-square analysis. The X and N values entered at red 1 and 2 to define the two proportions are copied down as the bold frequencies in the table at red 9. I typed in labels for the columns and rows. Check that the observed and expected frequencies match Table 13.4. At red 10 you can see $\chi^2 = 3.072$ and $df = 1$, as we expect, and $p = .08$. This p value is almost the same as $p = .079$ given by the proportions analysis and shown above near red 7. These p values correspond to the CI on the difference in the figure overlapping just a little with zero on the difference axis. We conclude that we have no, or at most very weak, evidence of an association between the column and row variables. The NHST conclusion is that, at the .05 level, we cannot reject the null hypothesis of no association between the two variables.

Assumptions for Chi-Square

The main assumption required for a chi-square analysis is the same as for a proportions analysis: The four main cells must contain counts of separate, independent people or things, and each person or thing must be counted in exactly one of the four main cells. The sum of these four frequencies must equal the grand total.

▶ Chi-square analysis requires that all expected frequencies should be at least about 5.

In addition, the chi-square analysis relies on approximations, which are less accurate when the expected frequencies are small. The guideline is that no *expected* frequency should be less than about 5. In our example, the smallest expected frequency is 6.47 for Julliard, Hit, so the chi-square approximation is acceptable. The proportions analysis also relies on approximations, but generally is close to accurate, and small frequencies are not a problem. Note that chi-square cannot be calculated if $X_1 = X_2 = 0$, or $X_1 = N_1$ and $X_2 = N_2$.

The Phi Coefficient, an Effect Size Measure

The null hypothesis states there is no association between column and row classification variables. The corresponding effect size is, therefore, a measure of the strength of any such association. If there is an association, the observed frequencies would differ from the expected, and the stronger the association, the larger the difference. Chi-square is a measure of the difference between observed and expected frequencies, but it's not an effect size measure because it reflects also the total sample size, the grand total. Chi-square is what we need to obtain a p value, but an adjustment is needed to derive a measure of effect size.

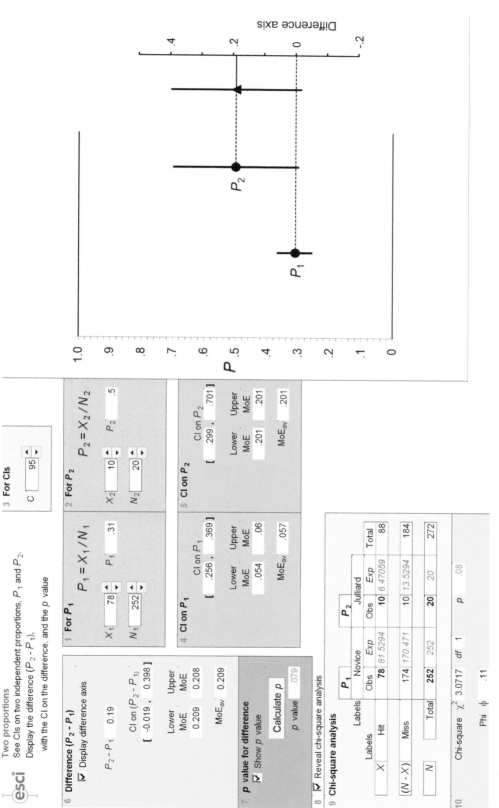

Figure 13.6. Same as Figure 13.5, but with chi-square analysis revealed, bottom left.

The effect size measure is the *phi coefficient*, ϕ, (Greek lower case phi, "fie", rhymes with sky) given by this formula:

▶

Phi coefficient, ϕ.

$$\phi = \sqrt{\frac{\chi^2}{N}}$$
(13.5)

▶

The *phi coefficient*, ϕ, is a measure of strength of association in a 2 × 2 table. It's a type of correlation.

where N is the grand total. For our example, $\phi = \sqrt{3.072/272} = .11$, which is the value shown at red 10 in Figure 13.6. Think of phi as a type of correlation that can take values from 0 to 1, so .11 is a small correlation, a small degree of association between the two classification variables. Cohen's reference values for phi are the same as for correlation r: .1, .3, and .5 for small, medium, and large, respectively. As usual, we should interpret phi in the context, with Cohen's values a last resort.

13.18 Table 13.5 shows data from Panel A of Table 13.2.
 a. I've calculated the expected frequency for the first main cell. Calculate the remaining three.
 b. Are the assumptions required for chi-square analysis met? Explain.
 c. Calculate the contribution to χ^2 for each of the four cells, then find χ^2.
 d. Explain in words what the value of χ^2 reflects.
 e. Calculate the phi coefficient, ϕ, and explain what it tells us.

esci 13.19 Enter the observed frequencies in Table 13.5 into **Two proportions**. Reveal the chi-square analysis. Check your calculated values of expected frequencies, χ^2 and ϕ.

 a. State the null hypothesis in two different ways.
 b. Note the *p* value. Interpret.
 c. Compare with the *p* value given by the proportions analysis. Compare *p* with the CIs in the figure.

esci 13.20 In your completed Table 13.5, use the *expected* frequencies to calculate the proportion of Control participants expected to have cancer, and the same for Med participants. Compare the two proportions and explain.

13.21 A frequency must be an integer, so how can an expected frequency be a decimal like 12.02?

Proportions or Chi-Square?

Researchers most commonly use chi-square, rather than proportions, to analyze frequency tables, probably because their focus has been on NHST. The phi coefficient is only rarely reported alongside a chi-square analysis, although

Table 13.5 Observed and Expected Frequencies for Any Cancer From de Lorgeril et al. (1998)

	Control		Med		Total
	Obs	Exp	Obs	Exp	
Cancer	17	24 × 303/605 = 12.02	7		24
No cancer	286		295		581
Total	303	303	302	302	605

it would certainly be best practice always to report phi with any chi-square analysis. A proportions analysis has several advantages:

1. *Focus on effect size and estimation.* The starting point of a proportions analysis is two proportions and the difference between them. A figure showing these, with their CIs, as in Figure 13.5, is informative about effect sizes and precision, and thus supports estimation thinking. A *p* value can be calculated if required.

2. *Familiarity of effect size measure.* Proportion and difference between two proportions may be more familiar, more easily represented visually in figures, and more readily interpreted than the phi coefficient.

3. *Fewer restrictions.* Both approaches require frequencies of separate, independent people or objects. Chi-square requires in addition that expected frequencies not be too small. A proportions analysis can be used with very small frequencies and is thus applicable in a wider variety of situations.

> A proportions analysis keeps the focus on effect sizes and estimation, and can be used with small expected frequencies.

Why then do I include this section on chi-square? Because you are likely to see chi-square analyses reported in journal articles, and need to know what they tell us. See the box *Reporting Your Work* for more on chi-square.

Now for a quite different use of proportions.

RISK, AND THE DIFFERENCE BETWEEN RISKS

One of the most important uses of proportions is to estimate *risk*, which is simply a probability. Risk usually refers to bad outcomes, but can be applied to any outcome. It may sound a bit odd, but it's quite acceptable to talk of the risk of winning the lottery.

> *Risk* is the probability that a particular outcome will occur.

Being able to weigh up risks, and use them to help make decisions, is a vital part of modern life and of statistical thinking. One crucial issue turns out to be the way that risks are presented. Here's an example from the work of Gerd Gigerenzer—of which more shortly.

In 1995, news media in Britain reported evidence that taking third-generation contraceptive pills increases the risk of a dangerous type of blood clot by 100%. This news led to panic, and many women stopped taking the new pills. Unwanted pregnancies increased and there were an estimated additional 13,000 abortions in the following year. The increase in risk of the blood clots was actually from about 1 in 7,000 to about 2 in 7,000 women. Yes, that's a 100% increase, but had the result been expressed in terms of 1 or 2 in 7,000, perhaps women would have reacted differently. The harm of the extra abortions probably greatly outweighed the harm of the small numbers of extra blood clots expected if women had continued with the new pills. However, a headline announcing a 100% increase in risk no doubt sells more newspapers than fiddly figures about so many in 7,000.

Consider Panel B of Table 13.2, and how we might present the results. For Exercise 13.17 you probably found that the proportions of cardiac deaths in the four year period was .063 and .020 for Control and Med, respectively. Let's round those to .06 and .02. Here are three ways we might report the Control result:

▨ The probability of dying of a further heart attack is about .06.

▨ The probability of dying of a further heart attack is about 6%.

▨ On average, about 6 in 100 people will die of a further heart attack.

13.22 a. Express the Med result in those three ways.

b. Express the difference between the two results in several different ways. Which do you think would be must understandable to lay people?

 It's late in the chapter for my traditional reminder, but this is a particularly good spot to pause, reflect, and discuss. Perhaps while chomping another apple.

Thinking about the difference, you may have identified three questions:

1. Should we think of proportions (.06), percentages (6%), or frequencies (6 in 100)?

2. Should we focus on the difference (.06 − .02 = .04, for example) or the ratio (.02 is one-third of .06)?

3. Should we report just the difference or ratio, or also provide the two separate results?

The story about third-generation pills suggests that it's best to express the risks in terms of frequencies, and to provide both risks, instead of—or perhaps as well as—the difference or ratio. Taking this approach, we'd say that the Med diet reduces the risk of cardiac death from about 6 in 100 to about 2 in 100. You could also say that the risk was reduced by two-thirds, or by 4 percentage points, or by a factor of 3, but I suspect that saying any of those hardly adds anything and may be confusing. Does that seem to you like a good strategy?

Gerd Gigerenzer and other researchers have studied various ways to present risks and risk differences. They report evidence that it's usually best to express risks, and differences in risk, in terms of *natural frequencies*, which are simply integers expressing a risk in terms of so many per hundred, or thousand, or other convenient number. Saying that risk increases from 1 to 2 in 7,000 gives a clear message the risk is small, although not to be ignored. It also says doubling the risk gives a risk that's still small. Reporting a comparison of two risks as a percentage difference (an increase of 100%), or a risk ratio (the risk is doubled), tends to exaggerate the difference, and also the risk itself, as it did for the third-generation pill example. There's evidence that people, including doctors and other health professionals, often severely misunderstand risk reported in that way. In contrast, reporting risks and comparisons of risks in terms of natural frequencies generally gives more accurate understanding.

▶ It's usually best to express risks in terms of **natural frequencies**.

▶ When comparing two risks, report both risks and not only the difference or ratio.

Search for "Harding Center for Health Literacy" (Gigerenzer is the director) for videos, podcasts, and articles about risk and how best to present it. There are many fascinating stories. Gigerenzer's book *Risk Savvy* (2014) is entertaining, with many examples and good advice about easy ways to understand risk better. Using natural frequencies is usually the best strategy. If you see risk or risk differences presented in other ways, mentally transform them to natural frequencies, and see whether that helps.

There's a further twist to this tale. Sedrakyan and Shih (2007) investigated how risks are expressed in medical journals. They found that about 1 in 2 of the review articles they analyzed did not use natural frequencies to express any of the risks they reported. That's bad news and a familiar lesson once again: Even with the best journals, we need to think carefully about what we read, which may not be presented in the most readily understood way.

A Risk Example: Breast Cancer

I searched online for "Breast cancer risk assessment tool" and found the risk calculator provided by the U.S. National Cancer Institute. You might find a similar calculator for your country, if you're not American. Using the U.S. tool, I answered the questions for a 35-year-old white woman with no history of breast cancer and no first degree relative (mother, sister, or daughter) having had breast cancer. To all the other questions I answered "unknown". The tool said that the risk such a woman would develop breast cancer in the next five years is 0.2%, and in her lifetime is 6.9%.

It's nearly time for take-home messages. It's a short chapter, so I'll leave you to recall the various aspects of frequencies and proportions that we've discussed. Perhaps while you enjoy your favorite salad—with a Mediterranean dressing, of course.

13.23 Use an online tool for breast cancer risk to obtain estimated risks for the next five years, and for lifetime, for a woman of your choice.

 a. Express the two risks in two other ways.
 b. Try explaining those risks to a friend who hasn't read this chapter. Ask them to explain the risks in their own words. What works best? Why?

13.24 Use the calculator again, giving the same answers except saying that the woman has one first degree relative who has had breast cancer.

 a. What two risks do you get?
 b. Express these two risks in whatever way you think best.
 c. Express the increase in risk given by the family history of breast cancer as you choose, perhaps in more than one way.
 d. Try explaining the risk increase to your friend. What works best, and why?

13.25 Read the advice at the website about using the tool and interpreting its results, and the limitations on what the tool can do. Would you suggest any revisions?

13.26 For any particular case and time period, the tool gives a single value of risk.

 a. What would that value be based on?
 b. Is giving a single value reasonable? What might be an alternative?
 c. Do you think that would be better or worse? Why?

? Quiz 13.3

1. For a chi-square analysis of a 2 × 2 frequency table, the usual null hypothesis is that _____ _____. This is <u>equivalent to / rather different from</u> the null hypothesis when analyzing the table in terms of the difference between two proportions.
2. The larger the value of chi-square, the <u>greater / smaller</u> the differences between the observed and expected frequencies, the <u>smaller / larger</u> the *p* value, and the <u>stronger / weaker</u> the evidence against the null hypothesis.
3. Chi-square analysis requires that every <u>observed / expected</u> frequency should be at least about <u>1 / 5 / 10</u>.
4. For a chi-square analysis of a 2 × 2 table, the effect size measure is <u>φ / r / ρ / χ</u>, which can take values from <u>−1 / 0 / 1 / 2</u> to <u>−1 / 0 / 1/ 2</u> and is a type of <u>correlation / regression / variance</u>.
5. A .15 risk may alternatively be expressed as (i) a probability of _____, or (ii) a probability of _____%, or (iii) 15 in _____. Usually, the best strategy is to express risk as <u>(i) / (ii) / (iii)</u>.
6. The change from a risk of .10 to a risk of .15 is usually best expressed as
   a. an increase of .05.
   b. an increase of 50%.
   c. an increase of 5%.
   d. an increase from 2 in 20 to 3 in 20.

13.27 Read over your take-home messages, swap with a friend, then revise if you wish.

✂ Reporting Your Work

Proportions cannot exceed 1, so like *p* values and Pearson's *r* they are reported in APA style without a leading zero (APA, 2010, p. 113).

Proportions are probably the most convenient way to summarize nominal variables, especially those related to the demographic characteristics of your participants:

```
Most of the 100 participants were science majors (P = .60),
but some were humanities majors (P = .30) and a few were
social-science majors (P = .10).
```

When it is clear that there are only two possible levels for a nominal variable you need report only one level:

```
Of the 120 participants who reported their gender, the
proportion of female participants was P = .45.
```

If you are making inferences about a proportion, include:

▪ whether the estimate is planned or exploratory, unless this is already clear;
▪ the sample size that forms the denominator of the proportion, unless this is already clear;
▪ the proportion and its CI;
▪ an interpretation that considers the full range of the CI; and
▪ if desired, the *p* value for comparing to the proportion to a specified null hypothesis value.

For example:

```
For the 22 attempts at communication, the proportion of
hits for Pilot 1 was P = .36 [.2, .57]. This is above
chance performance of .25, but the CI is fairly long and
does not exclude the possibility of merely random responding
(p = .20).
```

See Table 13.1 for an efficient way to summarize lots of individual proportions and their associated CIs in APA format. Remember that even for proportions some CIs are red, and that the more estimates you make the more likely you are to have at least some misleading CIs.

If you are making inferences about the differences between two independent proportions, you should typically report:

- whether the comparison is planned or exploratory, unless this is already clear;
- the sample sizes for the denominators of each proportion, unless this is already clear;
- the proportion for each group or condition;
- the difference between the proportions and the CI on the difference; and,
- if desired, you can also report the chi-square analysis. This should include the value of chi-square, its degrees of freedom, the p value, and (typically) ϕ. Because ϕ values cannot exceed 1, do not use a leading 0 when reporting a value.

◄ When comparing independent proportions, focus on the difference and the CI on the difference.

Here is an example from the de Lorgeril et al. (1998) study discussed in the text.

Of the 303 participants in the control diet condition, the proportion who were diagnosed with cancer by the end of the study was $P_{Control}$ = .056. Of the 302 participants who ate the Mediterranean diet, the proportion who were diagnosed with cancer at the end of this study was P_{Med} = .023. Our planned comparison of these cancer rates indicates that the Mediterranean diet reduced the proportion of cancer diagnoses: $(P_{Med} - P_{Control})$ = -.033, 95% CI [-.067, -.001], χ^2 = 4.30, p = .04, ϕ = .08. This CI is fairly long and suggests the benefits of the diet could be anywhere from very large down to quite small. Given the ease with which the diet can be adopted, however, we judge the result to be meaningful and potentially life saving.

It can also be helpful to use tables to present the frequencies underlying comparisons between proportions. Tables 13.2 through 13.5 are models you can use that follow APA formatting.

Take-Home Messages

Frequencies

- Frequencies are counts of data points in a category, or falling within a range of values. Frequencies can be used with interval or ordinal scaling, but are necessary for nominal variables—also called categorical variables.

Proportions

- Research questions about proportions or a difference between independent proportions, can be answered by proportions and differences estimated using frequency data, with their CIs.

- Proportion, P, is the ratio X/N, where N is the total number of events or people, X of which are hits—meaning they fall in the category of interest; P lies between 0 and 1.

- Proportions can be transformed to percentages, and vice versa, but percentages can be tricky, especially when two percentages are compared.

- To calculate a CI or a p value for a proportion, using the methods of this chapter, P needs to be based on frequencies, and the N events or people must be independent and all have the same probability of being a hit.

- The CI on a proportion lies fully between 0 and 1. It is generally asymmetric, with its longer arm closer to .5.

■ The relation between two classification variables can be investigated by using the difference between two proportions, and its CI, based on the appropriate 2 × 2 frequency table. For the two proportions to be independent, each event or person must be counted in one and only one of the four main cells in the table.

Chi-Square

■ Chi-square, χ^2, tests the null hypothesis of no association between the column and row classification variables in a 2 × 2 frequency table. It's a measure of the difference between observed frequencies and the frequencies expected if the null hypothesis is true. Large χ^2 means small p and strong evidence against the null hypothesis.

■ Like a proportions analysis, a chi-square analysis requires independence of the events or persons counted in the frequency table. Chi-square analysis also requires that the minimum expected frequency is about 5.

■ The phi coefficient, ϕ, which lies between 0 and 1, is a type of correlation and also a measure of strength of association.

Risk

■ A proportion is often useful to estimate a risk, which is the probability that a particular event, usually a bad event, will occur.

■ Risks and differences between risks are usually best understood if expressed in terms of natural frequencies, such as 8 in 100, or 3 in 1,000.

 End-of-Chapter Exercises

1) How long is the CI on a proportion ($P = X/N$), and how does CI length vary with N? For the following cases, write down your guesses (discuss with a friend?) for the CI, then use **One proportion** or **Two proportions** to find the answer.

   a. 15 heads in 20 tosses of a coin. Think of this in terms of frequencies and also as a proportion $P = 15/20 = .75$. Express the CI both ways. It may help to click at red 2 in **One proportion** for lines that indicate P for each discrete number of heads.

   b. 1 head in 20 tosses.

   c. 8 heads in 20 tosses.

   d. 40 heads in 100 tosses.

   e. 400 heads in 1,000 tosses.

2) How different do two proportions need to be before the two CIs don't overlap? In each case write down your guess, then check.

   a. Tim hits 8 baskets out of 20. How many out of 20 does Meg need to hit to beat Tim, with the two CIs not overlapping? What is Meg's proportion of hits?

   b. Same question, but Tim and Meg each have 80 shots. Tim hits 32.

   c. What do the CIs for Tim in a and b say about the guideline that N four times larger gives a CI about half as long. Does it apply to these proportions?

3) Rozin et al. (2014) were interested in the psychology of belonging to a prestigious group. They asked about the extent to which people in the group but near the border might be likely to emphasize their membership of the group, whereas people near the center would feel sufficiently confident about group membership not to mention it so often. The researchers

were at the University of Pennsylvania, which they described as a "marginal" Ivy League school. One of their studies compared students from that university with students from Harvard, which is at the center of the prestigious Ivy League group of universities. Students were asked to write "7 things you think of when you describe your university to other people". None of the 30 Harvard students mentioned "Ivy League" in their responses, but 9 of the 33 Penn students did.

a. Express the researchers' aim as a question about proportions. Make a table of frequencies, analyze these, and answer the research question.

b. What null hypothesis would a chi-square analysis test? Carry out that analysis and interpret. Is it appropriate to carry out that analysis? What is ϕ? Interpret.

c. In another of their studies, Rozin and colleagues found that small U.S. international airports use the word "international" to describe themselves on their websites more often than major airports do. Explain how this study addresses the same issue as the Ivy League study.

d. Can you suggest an alternative explanation for the Rozin et al. results?

e. Think of another prestigious group for which you could investigate the center vs. border question, and describe a study you could run.

f. Physics is at the center of science, but some people regard psychology as near the border. Suggest a study to investigate the extent that psychology might use the label "science" more often than physics does. Explain how you would analyze your study.

4) We tend to think that our political beliefs are held for deep-seated and logical reasons, but many experiments have shown that political opinions can be strongly influenced by seemingly trivial factors. One classic study by Rugg (1941) asked participants their opinion about speeches against democracy. A randomly chosen half of the participants were asked if such speeches should be allowed. The other half were asked if such speeches should be forbidden. Amazingly, this seemingly trivial change in wording seemed to radically alter the responses. This classic study was replicated at 36 sites as part of the Many Labs project (Klein et al., 2014a, 2014b). In Table 13.6, the left panel contains results from one site (Czech Republic) and the right panel contains results from all sites combined. The Permit column is the numbers who were willing to tolerate speeches against democracy (a "Yes" to the Allow question or a "No" to the Forbid question) and the Ban column is the numbers who were unwilling to tolerate such speeches (a "No" to the Allow question or a "Yes" to the Forbid question).

Table 13.6 Attitudes About Speeches Against Democracy by Wording of Question

Czech Republic	Permit	Ban	Total	All Studies	Permit	Ban	Total
"Allow" Phrasing	33	11	44	"Allow" Phrasing	2381	793	3174
"Forbid" Phrasing	34	6	40	"Forbid" Phrasing	2941	229	3170
Total	67	17	84	Total	5322	1022	6344

a. Will we be able to draw causal conclusions from this study? Explain.

b. For the overall data, what proportion is willing to tolerate speeches against democracy when asked if such speeches should be allowed? What proportion when asked if such speeches should be banned? Are those proportions independent? Explain.

c. Use **Two proportions** to obtain the CI for the difference between those proportions. Interpret.

    d. For the sample from the Czech Republic, calculate the proportion permitting for both question forms and then calculate the difference and the CI on the difference. Interpret.

    e. For the sample from the Czech Republic, find the p value for the difference between the two proportions, and also for the chi-square value. Using the NHST approach, how would the data from the Czech Republic be interpreted? Does this seem like a wise conclusion given what you know about the overall analysis? Does interpretation of the CI from the Czech Republic lead to a better conclusion?

5) My colleague Mark Burgman uses in his teaching an example of a trial of a proposed tree harvesting plan that assessed breeding success in a particular species of owl. The foresters wanted to demonstrate that their harvesting plan would not harm the owls. They studied owl breeding in an area of forest from which trees had been harvested in accord with the plan, and compared with a similar but untouched area of forest. This species of owl usually raises one fledgling each year, occasionally more than one. To simplify, let's assume a pair of owls raises either 0 or 1 fledgling in a year. There were 3 breeding pairs in the harvested area and another 3 in the comparison area, and the foresters recorded the number of pairs in each area that raised a fledgling. The foresters used the NHST approach and interpreted lack of statistical significance as evidence that harvesting did not reduce owl breeding success.

    a. Think back to Chapter 10 on precision and power. What strikes you about the study?

    b. The foresters assumed that any difference had been caused by the harvesting. Is that assumption justified? Explain.

    c. Suppose 3/3 pairs raised fledglings in the untouched area. Find the CI on the difference between proportions of pairs that raised a fledgling for $X = 0$ pairs in the harvested area. Do the same for $X = 1$ or 2 pairs raising fledglings in the harvested area.

    d. In which of those cases was the difference statistically significant at the .05 level? How great could the difference have been with the foresters' conclusion still being that harvesting did not reduce owl breeding?

    e. Suppose breeding success could be tracked for 20 pairs in each area, and that 20/20 pairs raised fledglings in the untouched area. Suppose $X/20$ pairs raised fledglings in the harvested area. What is the smallest value of X that would lead to a conclusion that harvesting did not reduce breeding?

    f. What conclusions do you draw from this example? Alas, it really happened, with 3 pairs in each area, and the study was presented as evidence that the proposed harvesting plan would not harm the owls.

6) Choose some condition you find interesting, such as dyslexia, eating disorder, autism, disturbed sleep, or having a road crash. Search for "risk of...", "prevalence of...", "how common is … in males and females?", or similar. Find information about the percentages of people, or of males and females separately, who have the condition.

    a. How are the risks or percentages presented? Discuss the effectiveness of presentation.

    b. Find cases where a range is suggested, such as "a 20% to 30% chance", or "3 to 4 times more likely". Why would such a range be given? Discuss.

? Answers to Quizzes

Quiz 13.1

1) c; 2) claims, evidence; 3) frequencies; 4) the N items or events are independent, each has the same probability of being a hit; 5) asymmetric, shorter; 6) Π_0, population, true.

Quiz 13.2

1) c; 2) d; 3) frequencies, independent; 4) the two proportions do not differ in the population; 5) a; 6) rearrange, independent, overall N, both a CI and a p value.

Quiz 13.3

1) there is no association in the population between the column and row variables, equivalent to; 2) greater, smaller, stronger; 3) expected, 5; 4) ϕ, 0, 1, correlation; 5) .15, 15, 100, (iii); 6) d.

 # Answers to In-Chapter Exercises

13.2   The CI always lies fully between 0 and 1, and is asymmetric, with the longer arm toward .5. It is longest (and is almost always symmetric) for $P = .5$ and becomes shorter and more asymmetric as P approaches 0 or 1.

13.3   The lower and upper MoE values are the lengths of the lower and upper arms of the CI, respectively, and MoE_{av} is the average of our two arms and the measure of precision.

13.4   a. The proportions are complementary, because they add to 1. The two CIs are mirror images. They are the same length and the two arms are the same length, but swapped; b. In other words, lower MoE of 8/22 equals upper MoE of 14/22, and MoE_{av} is the same, which illustrates that the two CIs give us essentially the same information, because they both refer to an 8–14 split of 22 events.

13.5   a. The CI is at first very long and very asymmetric, then gets progressively shorter and less asymmetric; b. For a different fixed value of P the pattern is similar, but the CIs are longer and less asymmetric for a value of P closer to .5, and shorter and more asymmetric for a value of P closer to 0 or 1.

13.6   Gray horizontal lines mark the possible values of P, for a given N. For small N, there are few lines, widely spaced. As N increases there are more lines, closer together.

13.7   When $X = 0$, P must also be 0. The CI has only an upper arm, which becomes shorter or longer as N increases or decreases, as we expect.

13.8   No, we need to know the frequency X and total N, because the length of the CI on $P = .85$ will vary greatly, depending on X and N.

13.9   For a fixed P, larger N gives a shorter CI, but the guideline holds only very roughly and only in some cases, no doubt because CIs are constrained to lie between 0 and 1.

13.10   The population proportion is estimated to be .32 [.27, .37], so the true value is, most plausibly, in that range. If telepathy does not exist and receivers were guessing, we expect .25. This lies only a little outside the CI, so is rather implausible, but the strength of evidence that .25 is not the true value is not extraordinary.

13.11   The p value of .22 is consistent with the 95% CI extending a little distance past the null hypothesis value, as in the figure.

13.12   In every case, the p value corresponds with where the CI falls in relation to the null hypothesis value.

13.13   Use the spinners to set $X = 106$ and $N = 329$, and the small slider to set $\Pi_0 = .25$, and see $p = .002$. This is quite strong evidence that the true value is greater than .25, but I would not regard it as extraordinary evidence.

13.14   a, b. 80% is 48/60 and the CI is [.68, .88] in terms of proportions and [68, 88] in terms of percentages. I'm assuming the questions are independent and all have the same probability of being answered correctly. Her true score, reflecting her true ability on the test, most likely lies around 80%, and plausibly anywhere in the range of the CI. We need to use a proportion to calculate the CI, but percentages are more commonly used for test results in education, so I would discuss the result using percentages; c. Guessing corresponds to $\Pi_0 = .5$, so that's the null hypothesis value; d. The CI is very far from .5, and $p < .001$, so we have very strong evidence that her performance was better than expected by chance.

13.15   Assuming the two sets of studies are independent, the CI on $18/57 - 78/252 = 0.006$ [−0.12, 0.15] so any population difference is zero or extremely small. There is no sign that experienced receivers do better. The experienced participants had participated as novices in one of the earlier studies and so, strictly, the two sets of studies were not fully independent. In practice they were probably sufficiently separate to be regarded as close to independent.

13.16   a, b. The difference is $295/302 - 286/303 = 0.033$ [0.001, 0.067], which is the mirror image of the CI on the difference between the proportions for cancer, so we come to the same conclusion as before.

13.17   What difference does the Med diet make to the risk of dying from another heart attack? The difference is $6/302 - 19/303 = -0.043$ [−0.078, −0.011]. (You may have reversed the subtraction and obtained the same result, but with the sign reversed.) The difference in favor of Med is slightly larger than for cancer, and more clearly different from zero because the CI is a little further from zero for cardiac death.

13.18   a. Control, No cancer = 290.98; Med, Cancer = 11.98; Med, No cancer = 290.02; b. Yes, because all expected frequencies are more than 5; c. $\chi^2 = 2.063 + 0.085 + 2.070 + 0.086 = 4.304$; d. χ^2 is a measure of the difference between the observed and expected frequencies, which is influenced by the strength of association and the grand total; e. $\phi = .08$ is a type of correlation, or the strength of association between the (Control, Med) and the (Cancer, No cancer) classification variables; .08 suggests a small or very small association.

13.19   a. The null hypothesis is either that (i) there is zero association in the population between the column and row classification variables, or that (ii) the two population proportions are equal; b. For chi-square, $p = .038$, so there is some evidence against the null hypothesis; at the .05 level we can reject the null hypothesis and conclude there is some association; c. For proportions, $p = .042$, so the p for chi-square is very close to accurate. The CI on the difference in the figure has its upper limit very close to zero, consistent with p close to .05. (For a better figure for this example, if you know Excel you could format the vertical axis so its scale runs from $-.2$ to $.3$, rather than from $-.2$ to 1.2.)

13.20 $12.02/303 = .040$, $11.98/302 = .040$. The expected frequencies assume the null hypothesis is true, which is equivalent to assuming those two proportions are the same, as found here.

13.21   If I toss a fair coin 3 times, I expect on average to get 1.5 heads, even though no trial can give a fractional number of heads. An expected frequency is a long-term average, if the null hypothesis is true.

13.22   a. .02, 2%, and about 2 in 100 people, or 1 in 50 people; b. The Med diet reduces the risk from about .06 to .02, from about 6% to 2%, from about 6 to 2 people in 100, on average. For Med, the risk is one-third as great as for Control. I suspect people would understand best a reduction from 6 to 2 in 100, or 3 to 1 in 50, although I would also note that the Med risk is only one-third as great.

13.23   a. I found risks of .002 for the next 5 years and .069 lifetime risk, or about 1 woman in 500 and 1 in 14; b. My non-statistical friends say they strongly prefer 1 in 500 and 1 in 14, although there was discussion about whether 7 in 100 might be easier to understand than 1 in 14.

13.24   a, b. I found .5% and 16.8%, which are probabilities of .005 and .168; in natural frequencies, about 5 in 1,000 and 17 in 100, or about 1 in 200 and 1 in 6; c. Having a first-degree relative who has had breast cancer increases the risks from about 2 to 5 in 1,000 for the next 5 years, and from about 7 to 17 in 100 for the lifetime; d. Again, my friends strongly preferred natural frequencies, and they also noted the ratio—having a close relative affected gives an increase of a factor of about 2.5 in risk.

13.25   The aims and limitations seem to me well described in accessible language. I would be interested to discover whether presenting all risks in natural frequencies would, in the context of the calculator, be more easily understood by general users. That's an issue worth studying empirically.

13.26   a–c. The website has a link to an "About the Tool" page that explains the tool and the background to each question, and includes references to the research on which risk estimates are based. The risk estimates could be accompanied by a CI, whose length would probably vary widely for different cases, depending on the precision of the research on which particular estimates were based. Providing such CIs would give more complete evidence-based guidance to users, but would make understanding its results more complicated. It's another empirical question worth investigation, but I suspect that for most users the simplicity of a single value is better.

14

Extended Designs: One Independent Variable

In this chapter we consider designs that extend beyond the simple comparison of two conditions. Beyond pen and laptop, you could compare both with a third option, perhaps having full printed notes of the lecture. Considering critical thinking, you could assess not just pretest and posttest scores, but also scores a month and a year later—it's a vital issue how long any gains endure. Such studies add one or more further conditions and, therefore, are taking a step beyond the two basic designs we discussed in Chapters 7 and 8. They have extended designs, but with still just one IV (independent variable). In Chapter 15 we'll take a further step beyond, and consider extended designs that have more than one IV.

Extended designs often save time and money, because they let us ask multiple questions in a single study. They can also answer questions that simpler studies just can't address. Even so, they are not much harder to understand, because the basic way to analyze them is to focus on selected differences and their CIs, as we've done many times before. Keep in mind that all the extended designs we'll discuss in this and the next chapter are extensions of the independent groups and paired designs we discussed in Chapters 7 and 8.

There's a danger: Extended designs usually offer so many potential comparisons that, after running the study, it's tempting to explore the data and choose the big effects. However, this could easily be cherry picking, merely seeing faces in the clouds. With extended designs it's especially important to use good Open Science practice: First, where possible preregister your research plan, including a detailed plan for data analysis; second, follow that plan as you run the study and analyze the data; and finally, distinguish very clearly in your research report between the planned data analysis and any subsequent exploratory data analysis.

Here's the agenda:

- More than two independent groups: the *one-way independent groups design*
- The key to analysis: comparisons and contrasts of means, with their CIs
- Good Open Science practice: preregistration, planned analysis, and exploratory analysis
- One group, but more conditions to compare: the *one-way repeated measure design*
- An alternative approach: the *analysis of variance (ANOVA)*

THE ONE-WAY INDEPENDENT GROUPS DESIGN

This design is an extension of two independent groups that's made by simply adding one or more extra groups. Adding a full-printed-notes group to our pen–laptop study would give a *one-way independent groups design*. "One-way" means

The *one-way independent groups design* has a single IV with more than two levels, and a group for each level of the IV.

there's one IV: the type of notes. This has three levels: pen, laptop, and printed. There are three independent groups, one for each level. As for two independent groups, each participant experiences just one level of the IV. If the IV has four or more levels, we would need four or more independent groups of participants.

> The *one-way independent groups design* has a single IV with three or more levels. Each level is experienced by an independent group of participants.

This design is sometimes called the completely randomized design, but that's a vague and unhelpful name.

My example investigates sex, violence, and TV ads.

VIOLENCE, SEX, AND ADVERTISING EFFECTIVENESS

"If it bleeds, it leads." Many in the news business believe that violence and/or sex attracts viewers and sells newspapers. Advertisers might therefore be keen to have their ads appear during shows with, say, violent content. However, Bushman and colleagues have made the provocative suggestion that viewers might become particularly absorbed by such content and therefore pay *less* attention to the ads. If so, television networks would have a financial reason to reduce violence in their programs, a change that would delight many parents and educators.

Bushman (2005) reported an investigation of people's memory for ads that were presented during different types of television show. He wanted to estimate to what extent violent content, compared with neutral content, might lead to reduced memory for ads, and perhaps reduced purchasing intentions for advertised products. He investigated the same questions for shows with sexual content. He chose a three-group design as an efficient way to investigate both types of content. A sample of 252 typical TV viewers were randomly assigned to watch one of three types of show. Some watched a Neutral show (e.g., America's Funniest Animals), some a show with Violent content (e.g., Cops), and others a show with Sexual content (e.g., Sex in the City). The viewers watched different shows, but all saw the same 12 ads inserted into the shows. The ads were genuine advertisements, but for little-known products, so most viewers had never seen the ads before. To enhance realism, viewers watched the shows in easy chairs, with snacks and soda available.

After the viewing came a surprise memory test for the ads. I'll discuss the data for memory recognition: Participants saw a list of 12 products, with four brand names for each type of product, just one of which had appeared in an ad. For each set of four brands, participants had to choose which one they felt they recognized from the ads they had just seen, so the maximum score was 12.

Bushman posed two research questions: relative to Neutral,

▶ In the one-way independent groups design, examine *comparisons* that correspond with the research questions.

▪ to what extent would Violent change memory performance, and
▪ to what extent would Sexual change memory performance?

Examining those questions illustrates our main analysis strategy: We keep it simple by focusing on selected *comparisons*, which are differences that correspond with the research questions.

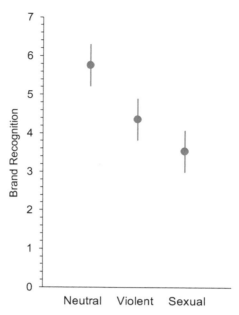

Figure 14.1. Means and 95% CIs for number of brands recognized, out of 12, for three independent groups, from Bushman (2005).

A *comparison* is the difference between two means.

Figure 14.1 reports group means for brand recognition, with CIs. After viewing a Neutral show, an average of only around half the brands in the ads recently viewed were recognized. Considering Bushman's two questions, the mean for Violent was 24% lower than Neutral, and the mean for Sexual 39% lower than Neutral. These two comparisons suggest that, compared with a Neutral show, violent and sexual content reduced memory substantially.

Our general strategy is important enough to deserve bullet points. To analyze a one-way independent groups design:

- select those *few* comparisons that correspond with our main research questions;
- focus on those selected comparisons and use CIs to guide interpretation of each.

We have two possible approaches for assessing a comparison:

1. *Interpret the CI on a difference.* Note the CI on the comparison—the CI on the difference between the two means being compared—and interpret the difference and its CI. This is our preferred approach. In a moment we'll calculate that CI, but, if we have just the separate means with their CIs as in Figure 14.1, we can eyeball what we want because the CI on a comparison is a little longer than either of the CIs on the separate means.

2. *Compare two independent CIs.* Alternatively, because the means in Figure 14.1 are independent, we can apply the overlap rule from Chapter 7 to the two means in a comparison.

   2.1 If two independent CIs just touch end-to-end, or have a gap, we have moderate evidence of a population difference in the means. (And $p < .01$, approximately.)

   2.2 If they overlap a little, no more than half of MoE, we have a small amount of evidence of a difference. (And $p < .05$, approximately.)

> For independent groups, we can use the overlap rule to eyeball any comparison.

The CIs for Neutral and Violent, for example, have a gap, so we have strong evidence of a population difference. For the comparison of Neutral and Sexual, the CIs have an even larger gap, so we have even stronger evidence of a population difference. Now let's calculate.

Calculating Comparisons of Two Means

A comparison is simply the difference between two means, $(M_2 - M_1)$, for example. We want, first, the CI on each group mean, as in Figure 14.1, and then the CI on any selected comparison, for example Neutral and Violent.

Back in Chapter 7, to calculate MoE for the CI on the difference between independent means, we pooled s_1 and s_2 to calculate s_p, the pooled SD, which is our best estimate of σ. We used this formula:

> Pooled SD for two independent groups.

$$s_p = \sqrt{\frac{(n_1 - 1)s_1^2 + (n_2 - 1)s_2^2}{n_1 + n_2 - 2}} \qquad (7.2)$$

Using this formula relied on the assumption of homogeneity of variance for the independent groups. For two groups, I used N_1 and N_2 for the group sizes, but here I'm using n_1, n_2, ..., in accord with the convention that, for extended designs, the size of Group i is referred to as n_i, and N is used for the *grand total*, which is $n_1 + n_2 + n_3 + \ldots$.

Now we have three groups. An advantage of the one-way independent groups design is that we should be able to get an even better estimate of σ, the population SD, by pooling over *all* the groups. This requires us to assume homogeneity of variance across all the groups. I'll say more about assumptions shortly, but researchers are often willing to make the assumption. Assuming homogeneity of variance for our three groups, an extension of Equation 7.2 gives an estimate of σ that's pooled over all three:

> Pooled SD for three independent groups.

$$s_p = \sqrt{\frac{(n_1 - 1)s_1^2 + (n_2 - 1)s_2^2 + (n_3 - 1)s_3^2}{n_1 + n_2 + n_3 - 3}} \qquad (14.1)$$

As you'd expect, s_3 is the SD of the third group. The degrees of freedom of that estimate, s_p, is the denominator in Equation 14.1:

$$df = (n_1 - 1) + (n_2 - 1) + (n_3 - 1) = n_1 + n_2 + n_3 - 3 = (N - 3) \qquad (14.2)$$

Including the third group increases the *df*, which is why the pooled estimate is more precise. For more than three groups, simply extend the formulas to include n_4 and s_4, n_5 and s_5, ..., as needed to include all the groups. We can use this relatively precise estimate, s_p, to calculate the CIs on individual means and on the differences corresponding to our selected comparisons.

Violence, Sex, and Advertising Effectiveness

Calculating MoE for the CI on the mean of a single group, for example the first group, requires a small adaptation of Equation 5.9, which was our basic formula for MoE for a single mean:

$$\text{MoE} = t_{.95}(df) \times s_p \times (1/\sqrt{n_1}) \qquad (14.3)$$

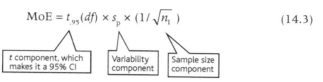

MoE for the CI on a single mean.

where s_p is given by Equation 14.1 and df by Equation 14.2. For any other mean, simply replace n_1 with the relevant group size, n_2 or n_3, for example.

To calculate MoE for the CI on a comparison, which is the difference between two means—say, the means for the first and second groups—we need a small adaptation of Equation 7.3, which was our basic formula for MoE for the difference between independent means:

$$\text{MoE}_{\text{diff}} = t_{.95}(df) \times s_p \times \sqrt{\frac{1}{n_1} + \frac{1}{n_2}} \qquad (14.4)$$

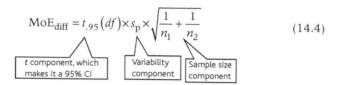

MoE for the CI on a comparison, one-way independent groups design.

where, once again, s_p is given by Equation 14.1 and df by Equation 14.2. For other comparisons, simply replace n_1 and n_2 with the sizes of the two groups in the comparison.

Table 14.1 presents summary descriptive statistics for brand recognition from Bushman (2005). We need to know only n, M, and s for each group to be able to apply the formulas above to calculate MoE for the individual means, as in Figure 14.1, and for any comparison.

14.1 For our example, calculate the pooled SD, df, and MoE and the CI for the Neutral mean. Compare with Figure 14.1.

14.2 Calculate the comparison of Neutral and Violent, including its CI.

I opened the **Ind groups comparisons** page of **ESCI intro chapters 10–16** and saw Figure 14.2, which presents the data in Table 14.1. The ESCI figure matches Figure 14.1, the summary statistics are shown at red 3 and the values calculated for the individual CIs at red 4. The grand total is the total number of participants and is shown near red 3 as $N = 252$. This ESCI page will calculate CIs and comparisons when given either summary statistics, as in Table 14.1, or the full data. At red 2, radio buttons let you select what you wish to enter. In Figure 14.2, the left button is selected, meaning that I entered the summary statistics at red 3, rather than the full data at red 5—the full data area is grayed out.

		Group 1 Neutral	Group 2 Violent	Group 3 Sexual
Size	n	84	84	84
Mean	M	5.76	4.36	3.54
SD	s	2.47	2.57	2.57

Table 14.1 Summary Descriptive Statistics for Brand Recognition, From Bushman (2005)

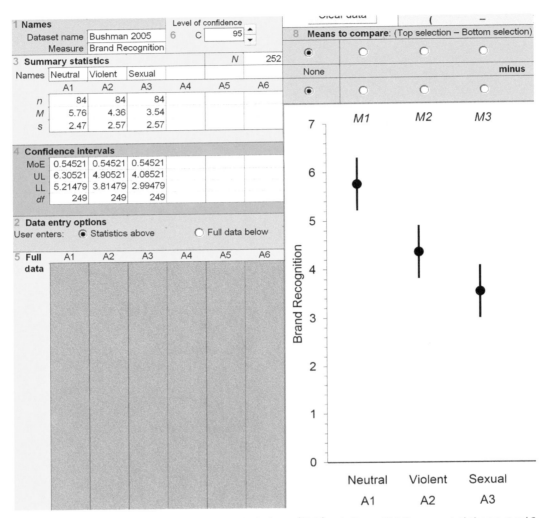

Figure 14.2. Means and 95% CIs for the three groups in Bushman (2005), as in Figure 14.1. Summary statistics are at red 3 and are the same as those in Table 14.1. Values for the individual CIs are at red 4. From **Ind groups comparisons**.

This ESCI page displays data for up to six groups, which can be given brief names at red 3, and are also identified by the conventional labels A1, A2, …, A6. The corresponding means are labeled M1, M2, …, M6 on this page. In the table of values at red 3, below A1 are n, M, and s values for the first group, and similarly for other groups. (The formulas in the text above use the standard symbols n_1, M_1, and s_1, but subscripts on the ESCI screen can get tiny and confusing, so I use M1 instead of M_1.)

The next step is to examine comparisons. In ESCI that's a simple matter of clicking two radio buttons, one in each of the rows at red 8. I clicked above M1 in the top row and M2 in the lower row, and saw Figure 14.3, which displays the (M1 – M2) or (Neutral—Violent) comparison. The comparison and its CI are pictured at right on a floating difference axis. The values are reported above, at red 9, and show that the comparison is 1.40 [0.63, 2.17]. I clicked the checkbox at top right to see that $p < .001$.

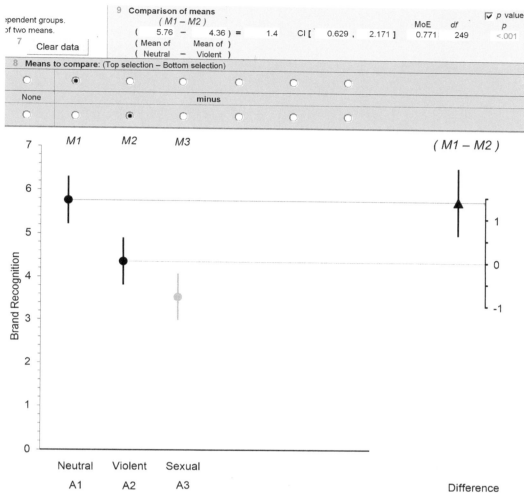

Figure 14.3. Data as in Figure 14.2, with the (*M1 – M2*) comparison selected at red 8 for display on the difference axis. Values of the comparison and its CI, and the *p* value, are shown at red 9.

14.3 Fire up **Ind groups comparisons.** If you don't see the Bushman 2005 data, as in Table 14.1 and Figure 14.2, you will need to type them in. If necessary, first click at red 7 to clear data, and red 2 to select **Statistics above.** If necessary, type labels at red 1, then brief group names at red 3, then the summary statistics.

14.4 Check your answer to Exercise 14.1 with the values that ESCI reports, as in Figure 14.2.

14.5 Click twice near red 8 to display the comparison of Neutral and Violent, compare with Figure 14.3, and check your answer to Exercise 14.2.

   a. Explain what the triangle and its CI displayed on the difference axis is telling us.

   b. If necessary, click at top right to display the *p* value. Explain what the *p* value is telling us. Compare with the CI on the difference axis.

   c. Compare with the discussion above using the overlap rule for that comparison.

14.6 Display the comparison of Neutral and Sexual.

   a. Interpret the CI and *p* value.

   b. Compare with the discussion above using the overlap rule for that comparison.

 14.7 Explore what the ESCI page offers. Read the popouts. Find how to display the $(M2 - M1)$ comparison, rather than $(M1 - M2)$, and explain how the two compare.

 14.8 a. Think of a possible change to one or more values of *n* at red 3, predict what difference it would make to the figure, then make the change to test your prediction.

   b. Do the same for values of *s*.

   c. Make testing such predictions a game.

We selected the comparisons of Neutral and Violent, and Neutral and Sexual as corresponding to the research questions, so interpretation of these comparisons provides the basis for the study's main conclusion that violent and sexual content lead to considerably reduced memory for brands presented in ads.

It's often a good strategy to use multiple measures to obtain a fuller picture, and Bushman did this by using additional measures of memory. He also investigated consumer behavior by asking participants to choose which brands they would be most likely to buy, and which discount coupons they would prefer to have. The patterns of means were similar for all the measures, suggesting that violent and sexual content not only reduces memory for ads, but may also influence purchasing behavior. Advertisers and TV networks may be wise to take note.

> *Converging evidence* can strengthen a conclusion.

Finding that different measures give similar results may also allow us to draw a more confident conclusion. Additional measures to some extent provide *converging evidence* to support the conclusion. A single measure, or single comparison, may suggest an interesting conclusion, but with uncertainty. Rather than worrying too much about exactly how confident we can be in that conclusion, we could look for further relevant lines of evidence. Is there some other measure, or comparison that could help answer our research question? If so, that might greatly strengthen the conclusion, especially if the two measures are rather different—for example, brand recognition memory and purchasing behavior. Bushman's range of measures provided a fuller picture and also reinforced his main conclusion that some types of content can influence viewers' response to ads substantially.

ASSUMPTIONS FOR THE ONE-WAY INDEPENDENT GROUPS DESIGN

Having analyzed our first example, let's step back and consider assumptions. The basic assumptions we are making in this chapter are that

- the data for each group are sampled from a population that's normally distributed, and
- each sample is a random sample from its population.
  For the one-way independent groups design we also assume that

the samples are independent.

In addition, the analysis above assumes that

variance is homogeneous across all groups. In other words, the population underlying each sample has the same standard deviation, σ.

The assumption of homogeneity of variance across all groups is often, but not always, reasonable. Examining the standard deviations of the individual groups provides some guidance. As a rough rule, we would like the largest SD to be not more than about twice the smallest SD if we are to rely on the assumption. For the Bushman example, the standard deviations for the three groups are shown as the values of *s* at red 3 in Figure 14.2. The three happen to be very similar, and, therefore, it's reasonable to assume homogeneity of variance.

> If the largest and smallest SDs differ by no more than a factor of about two, it's probably reasonable to assume homogeneity of variance and use s_p.

If we are not willing to make the assumption, one option is to calculate each comparison using the standard deviations of only the groups being compared. To do this we could copy the summary statistics for those two groups to the **Summary two** sheet, which we discussed in Chapter 7, and choose whether or not to assume homogeneity of variance for just those two groups.

? Quiz 14.1

1. The one-way independent groups design has <u>one IV / two IVs / two or more IVs</u>. The number of groups is equal to <u>the number of IVs / the number of levels of the IV / N</u>.
2. A comparison is the <u>sum of / difference between / SD of</u> two group <u>means / sample sizes / SDs</u>.
3. Planned analysis should specify comparisons that
   a. appear largest, on examination of the data.
   b. have SDs that are closest to homogeneous.
   c. correspond most closely with the research questions.
   d. cover all possible pairs of groups in the study.
4. The assumption of <u>homogeneity / heterogeneity</u> of <u>means / variance</u> permits us to pool over groups and thus calculate a more precise estimate of the <u>mean / SD</u> of the <u>sample / population</u>.
5. A figure that displays the means and CIs for several independent groups allows us to
   a. use the overlap rule to assess, approximately, any comparison.
   b. do very little, without further targeted calculations.
   c. use the overlap rule to assess, approximately, the overall effect size.
   d. identify which comparisons had been planned and preregistered.
6. With several independent groups, if the largest group SD is no more than about twice the smallest group SD, it's probably reasonable to assume _____.

AN EXAMPLE WITH FULL DATA: STUDENT MOTIVATION

How do you think you would react to feedback that gave encouragement and reassurance, or, instead, encouragement and challenge? Carol Dweck and her colleagues have investigated many such questions about how people respond to different types of feedback—I mentioned some of that research in the *Making the Most of This Book* section at the start of the book. My next example comes from Dweck's research group and illustrates data analysis that starts with the full data, rather than only summary statistics. Rattan et al. (2012) asked their college student participants to imagine they were undertaking a mathematics course and had just received a low score (65%) on the first test of the year. Participants were assigned randomly into three groups, which received different feedback along with the low score. The Comfort group received positive encouragement and also reassurance, the Challenge group received positive encouragement and also challenge, and the Control group received just the positive encouragement. Participants then responded to a range of questions about how they felt about the course and their professor. I'll discuss data for their ratings of their own motivation toward mathematics, made after they had received the feedback.

14.9   a. State what you think may be the two main research questions.
       b. State the two comparisons that correspond to these.

esci   14.10 To load the data, scroll right in **Ind groups comparisons** and click at red 10 to transfer left the Rattan data set. Any previous data are cleared and the radio button on the right at red 2 automatically selected to indicate that full data are available at red 5 for analysis. Your screen should resemble Figure 14.4. The Challenge group is labeled "Challng" because names must be short.

       a. Could you change the values at red 3? At red 5? Read the popouts and explain.
       b. Is it reasonable to assume homogeneity of variance? Explain.
       c. Examine the two comparisons you chose, and interpret.

esci   14.11 Have a further play at this page. You could, for example:

       a. at red 5, change some of the data. Does the figure change as you expect?
       b. type in some invented data for extra groups, perhaps A4 and A5. Give them short names at red 3. Does the figure change as you expect?
       c. click in the two rows at red 8 to select a comparison to examine.
       d. click at red 7 to clear the data. To enter data from your own study with a one-way independent groups design, at red 5 type the data in, or use Paste Special/Values to copy data from the clipboard.

FROM COMPARISONS TO CONTRASTS

> A *subset contrast* is the difference between the means of two subsets of group means.

Suppose Rattan et al. (2012) were primarily interested in the effect of reassurance feedback, and wished to compare Comfort with both other groups together, perhaps by comparing the Comfort mean with the combined mean of the Challenge and Control means. To do this we need to move from comparisons to *contrasts* of means. A contrast is a combination of means and may be complicated—it may, for example, summarize the linear trend over many means. However, I'll focus on the simplest and most widely used type of contrast, a *subset contrast*. Subset contrasts often provide the best approach to analyzing the one-way independent groups design. A *subset* of means is simply a selection of one or more group means, and a subset contrast is:

> Subset contrast.

$$\text{Subset contrast} = (\text{Mean of one subset of means}) - (\text{Mean of another subset of means}) \quad (14.5)$$

Here's a simple example: One subset is the single Comfort mean, and the other contains the Challenge and Control means. To see this contrast with its

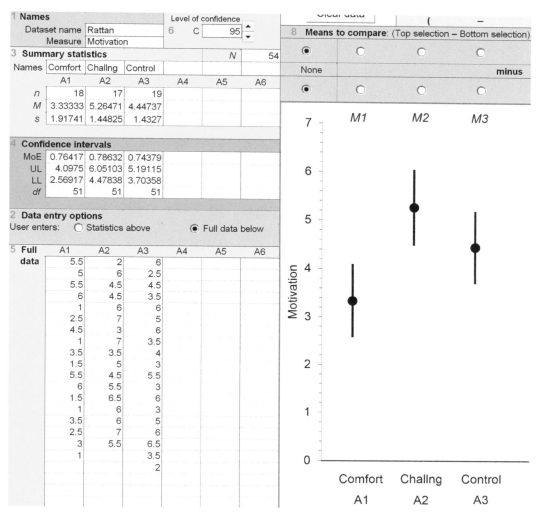

Figure 14.4. Full data at red 5, from Rattan et al. (2012), and means and 95% CIs for ratings of motivation towards mathematics, after receiving one of three types of feedback. The Challenge group is labeled "Challng". From **Ind groups comparisons**. The data are courtesy of Aneeta Rattan.

CI I moved to the next page in ESCI, **Ind groups contrasts**. I scrolled right and clicked at red 10 to load the Rattan data. Figure 14.5 illustrates what I did: At red 8, in the green area I clicked the checkboxes above *M2* and *M3* to define one subset, which is identified as green. In the blue area I clicked above *M1* to define the other subset, which is blue. The figure displays, towards the right, the subset means as squares, which are green and blue, and their difference as the triangle, which is thus the contrast we want. This contrast with its CI is displayed on the difference axis.

The values for the subset means and their CIs are shown at red 8 to the right of the checkboxes. More importantly, at red 9 we can see that the contrast is 1.52 [0.59, 2.46], meaning that feedback that includes reassurance (Comfort group) prompts ratings of motivation towards mathematics that are an average of about 1.5 units lower than ratings after the feedback given in the other two

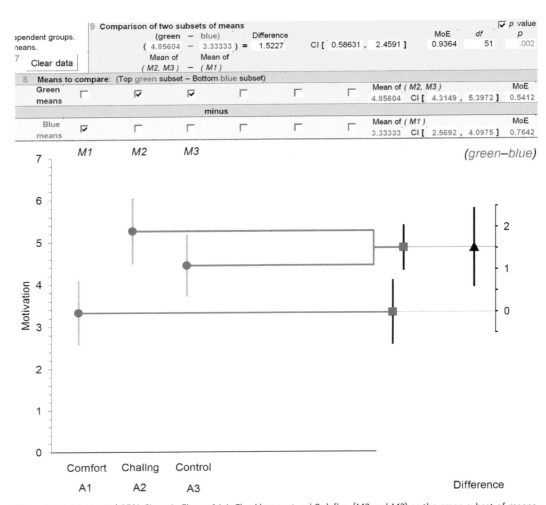

Figure 14.5. Means and 95% CIs as in Figure 14.4. Checkboxes at red 8 define (*M2* and *M3*) as the green subset of means, and *M1* as the blue subset. Means of the subsets are displayed as squares, with CIs. The difference between the two subset means is the contrast and is displayed as the triangle, and shown with its CI on the difference axis. From **Ind groups contrasts**.

groups. That's a very substantial difference on the 7-point motivation rating scale. The CI is long but indicates that it's reasonable to expect at least a modest boost in motivation (a minimum of around 0.6 units on the 7-point scale) in the population.

esci 14.12 **Set up Ind groups contrasts so you can see the Rattan means as in Figure 14.5.** Read the popouts and experiment with the two rows of checkboxes at red 8, then explain what a subset contrast is and how it is displayed.

Rattan et al. (2012) reported data for additional measures, and also three further studies, which showed how type of feedback and also teachers' attitudes can strongly influence students' motivation and expectations. Their general finding is important: Students are generally more motivated by challenge than comfort.

Now for an example with six groups—of mice.

Type of mouse	Normal	Alz-prone	Alz-prone	Normal	Alz-prone	Alz-prone
Feeding	Free	Free	Diet	Free	Free	Diet
Age (months)	10	10	10	17	17	17
Group label	NFree10	AFree10	ADiet10	NFree17	AFree17	ADiet17
	A1	A2	A3	A4	A5	A6
Mean	M1	M2	M3	M4	M5	M6

Table 14.2 Groups Used by Halagappa et al. (2007)

Note. Alz-prone = Alzheimer-prone; Diet = 40% less food than normal.

CAN EATING LESS DELAY ALZHEIMER'S?

Could eating much less delay Alzheimer's? If so, that would be great news. Halagappa et al. (2007) investigated the possibility by using a mouse model, meaning they used Alzheimer-prone mice, which were genetically predisposed to develop neural degeneration typical of Alzheimer's. The researchers used six independent groups of mice, three tested in mouse middle age when 10 months old, and three in mouse old age when 17 months. At each age there was a control group of normal mice that ate freely (the NFree10 and NFree17 groups), a group of Alzheimer-prone mice that also ate freely (the AFree10 and AFree17 groups), and another Alzheimer-prone group restricted to 40% less food than normal (the ADiet10 and ADiet17 groups). Table 14.2 lists the factors that define the groups, the group labels, and their means, *M1*, *M2*, ... (as we'll see them displayed in ESCI). I'll discuss one measure of mouse cognition: the percent time spent near the target of a water maze, with higher values indicating better learning and memory.

Let's consider some major research questions, and contrasts that match them. One basic question concerns age: Overall, how did the middle-aged groups compare with the old groups? A second question asks how, within the four Alzheimer-prone groups, food restricted groups (ADiet10 and ADiet17) compared with freely eating groups (AFree10 and AFree17).

14.13 a. State which subsets of means you would choose for the middle-aged vs. old contrast.

b. State which subsets you would choose for the second contrast.

14.14 Close **ESCI intro chapters 10–16** (don't Save) and reopen it. At the **Ind groups contrasts** page you should see summary cognition data for Halagappa, as in Figure 14.6. If not, you will need to type in at red 3 the labels and values from red 3 in Figure 14.6. Is it reasonable to assume homogeneity of variance? Explain.

14.15 At red 8, click checkboxes to define the two subsets of means needed for the middle-aged vs. old contrast. Identify the value and CI for this contrast. Interpret.

14.16 Clear all checkboxes at red 8. (It's easy to get confused when setting up contrasts. Note that no mean can be included in both subsets. It's usually easiest to start by clearing all checkboxes.) Click checkboxes to display the second contrast: ADiet vs. AFree, for Alzheimer-prone groups. Identify the value and CI for this contrast. Interpret.

For the age of testing contrast, at red 8 (top in Figure 14.6) I clicked checkboxes to specify *M1*, *M2*, and *M3* as the green subset of middle-aged groups, and *M4*, *M5*, and *M6* as the blue subset of old groups. Figure 14.7 shows how ESCI

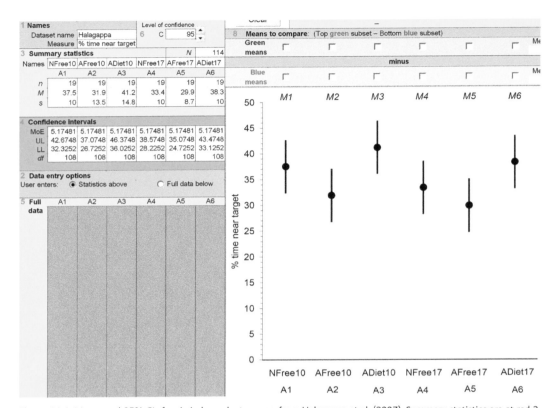

Figure 14.6. Means and 95% CIs for six independent groups, from Halagappa et al. (2007). Summary statistics are at red 3, top left. From **Ind groups contrasts**.

displays that contrast. The *M1*, *M2*, and *M3* means are green and their mean is displayed as the green square at right. The *M4*, *M5*, and *M6* means are blue and their mean is the blue square. The triangle marks the contrast, and at red 9 its value is reported as 3.0 [−1.2, 7.2] percentage points. The small mean (only 3 percentage points) and extent of the CI suggests there is little or no evidence of an overall age difference.

esci 14.17 For Exercise 14.15 you might have chosen *M1*, *M2*, and *M3* as the blue subset, and *M4*, *M5*, and *M6* as the green. Set up that contrast and compare with Figure 14.7. Explain.

The main research question concerns the extent that the restricted diet might slow cognitive decline in Alzheimer-prone mice. In other words, to what extent do ADiet groups perform better than AFree groups? First, consider that comparison at 10 months. We could go back to **Ind groups comparisons**, but a comparison is also a subset contrast with just one mean in each subset, so we can use **Ind groups contrasts** to examine a comparison.

esci 14.18 a. Clear all checkboxes at red 8. Click to select *M3* (ADiet10) as the green and *M2* (AFree10) as the blue subset. What's the difference and what does this tell us?

b. Clear checkboxes and select two means to examine the ADiet vs. AFree comparison at 17 months. What's the difference and your interpretation?

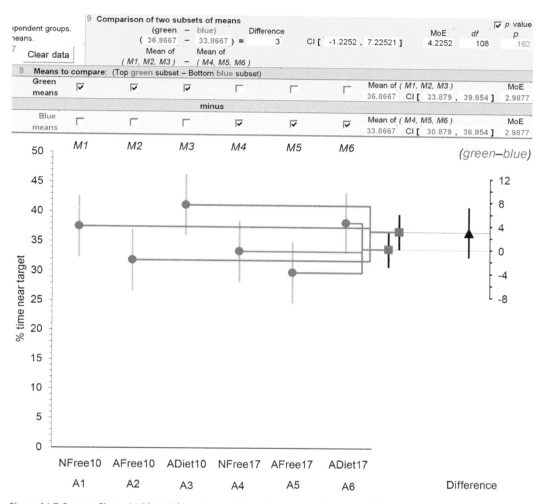

Figure 14.7. Same as Figure 14.6 but with a contrast displayed to compare the three middle-aged groups (means *M1, M2,* and *M3,* indicated by checkboxes near red 8 as the green subset) with the three old groups (*M4, M5,* and *M6,* as the blue subset). The squares mark the subset means, and the triangle, with CI, marks the contrast on the difference axis. Values of the contrast and its CI are at red 9, at top.

esci 14.19 a. Combine those two comparisons to see a contrast of the two ADiet groups with the two AFree groups. What's the difference and your interpretation?

b. Compare with your answer to Exercise 14.16.

esci 14.20 Compare MoE for the contrast with MoE for the two separate comparisons. Explain.

The contrast you examined in Exercise 14.19 most fully addresses the main research question and is shown in Figure 14.8. The contrast is reported near red 9 to be 8.8 percentage points [3.7, 14.0], with ADiet showing greater learning and memory than AFree. It provides strong evidence that the restricted diet improved cognitive performance in the Alzheimer-prone mice, although we would need to know more about the swimming maze task to judge how large or important the observed mean improvement of around 9 percentage points is.

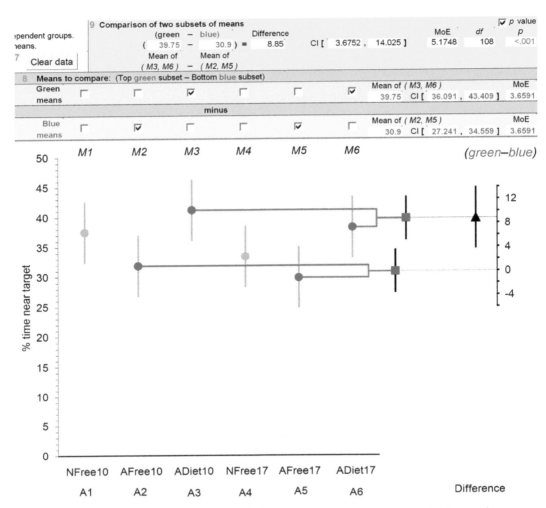

9 Comparison of two subsets of means								☑ p value
	(green − blue)		Difference			MoE	df	p
	(39.75 − 30.9) =		8.85	CI [3.6752 , 14.025]		5.1748	108	<.001
	Mean of Mean of							
	(M3, M6) − (M2, M5)							

8 **Means to compare:** (Top green subset − Bottom blue subset)

Green means	☐	☐	☑	☐	☐	☑	Mean of (M3, M6) 39.75 CI [36.091 , 43.409]	MoE 3.6591

minus

Blue means	☐	☑	☐	☐	☑	☐	Mean of (M2, M5) 30.9 CI [27.241 , 34.559]	MoE 3.6591

Figure 14.8. Same as Figure 14.7, but with a contrast displayed to compare the mean of the two ADiet groups (M6 and M3, the green subset) with the mean of the two AFree groups (M5 and M2, the blue subset). The squares mark the ADiet and AFree means, with 95% CIs, and the triangle, with CI, marks the difference between those means on the difference axis.

Halagappa et al. (2007) reported other analyses and data that supported a conclusion that a restricted diet overcame the Alzheimer's cognitive decline. Of course, mice are not humans, but good animal models can give insight, and also help guide research with humans. Results like those of Halagappa et al. suggest that calorie-restriction diets and, perhaps, intermittent fasting as in the 5:2 diet (Mosley & Spencer, 2013), may have health benefits. Evidence that practically achievable changes to diet can delay Alzheimer's in humans would be exciting news indeed.

The one-way independent groups design is simple and flexible. The **Ind groups comparisons** and **Ind groups contrasts** pages are designed to allow you to see and interpret comparisons and subset contrasts of your choice. The key to analysis is to choose comparisons and contrasts that most closely relate to your research questions.

Examine comparisons and contrasts that relate most closely to the research questions.

Now for more on the distinction between planned and exploratory analysis, which has particular relevance for analyses based on comparisons and contrasts.

PLANNED AND EXPLORATORY ANALYSIS

Planned Analysis

In Chapter 2, Figure 2.2 showed 10 means with CIs. The key point was that if we choose which of the 10 to focus on—probably the largest or most striking—only after seeing the data, then we could very easily be responding to a lump in the randomness, seeing a face in the clouds. That's why we should preregister a planned analysis that states which effects match our research questions. Figure 14.6 shows six means with CIs, so once again our planned analysis needs to be specified in advance. However, the issue is even larger here because we are interested in comparisons and there are 15 of them we could analyze. Other than comparisons, would you believe that, with six means, there's an amazing 286 subset contrasts? So there's massive scope for exploration and an enormous risk of faces in the clouds if we merely look around in the data for anything that might be interesting.

The risk of cherry picking, of capitalizing on chance, increases rapidly as the number of means or conditions increases: With 3 means there are 6 comparisons and subset contrasts, but with 6 means there are 15 comparisons + 286 contrasts = 301 altogether. So, for the extended designs we are discussing in this and the following chapter, planned analysis is essential if we are to have confidence in any conclusion, and even more so as the number of means or conditions increases.

The risk of merely seeing faces in the clouds increases rapidly with the number of means or conditions in a study.

The key is to focus on the few comparisons and contrasts that relate most directly to our research questions, but what counts as "few"? How many effects should we include in our planned analysis? It's a great strength of extended designs that they can address more than a single research question, but if we specify too many contrasts in our plan we might hardly reduce the risk of cherry picking. I'll refer to a contrast specified in advance as a *planned contrast*, which could be a comparisons or a subset contrast. In choosing how many planned contrasts to specify, there are two aspects to consider.

> A *planned contrast* is a comparison or subset contrast that is specified in advance, preferably as part of a preregistered data analysis plan.

First, we need to consider the number of conditions or groups. If a study has, for example, a one-way independent groups design with k groups, then there are $df = (k - 1)$ degrees of freedom for the possible differences among group means. This implies that the group means could potentially answer a maximum of $(k - 1)$ separate questions, and so, perhaps, we should examine a maximum of $(k-1)$ planned contrasts. If we consider more than $(k-1)$, there must be some redundancy among the questions we are asking.

> Planned contrasts can ask a maximum of *df* separate questions.

For example, in our mouse study we compared *M3* and *M2*, then *M6* and *M5*, then the contrast that combined those two comparisons. Because the contrast combines the two comparisons, it cannot answer a question that's independent of, or separate from, the questions answered by the two comparisons. If we did choose to include all three questions in a planned analysis, we should note that our conclusions about the three are not independent. We may feel that looking at all three gives us a full picture, but, for our planned analysis to be as informative as possible, it's usually best to choose contrasts that are reasonably separate. My conclusion is that we should keep in mind the maximum of *df* separate questions we can ask, where $df = (k-1)$ for the one-way independent groups design, and we should choose contrasts with minimal redundancy.

> Choose planned contrasts that match the research questions and make most sense.

The most important consideration is that the contrasts we examine make sense, and help us understand what the data tell us about our research questions. Usually our study is designed to ask a small number of questions, no more than *df*, and, therefore, choosing the best-matching contrast for each question is likely to give no more than *df* planned contrasts. However, I'm happy to examine a slightly larger number if that makes sense in the context—just be aware that we can't answer more than *df* truly separate questions.

The second consideration is the risk that one or more of the planned contrasts merely reflects a lump in the randomness. This risk increases as we examine more contrasts. The more CIs we examine, the greater the risk that at least one is red. This should lead us to be more cautious with our conclusions if there are more than, say, two or three planned contrasts. The more contrasts there are in our planned analysis, the more cautious we should be, and the stronger the evidence we should require before drawing a confident conclusion.

In summary, for planned analysis:

1. Specify a limited number of contrasts in advance. These should correspond with the research questions and, preferably, be reasonably separate. The maximum number of genuinely separate questions that can be answered is *df*.
2. For more than two or three contrasts, interpret with some caution, and more cautiously as the number of contrasts increases.

Exploratory Analysis

> As the number of available contrasts increases, risk increases that exploration sees faces in the clouds.

Following planned analysis, it's often valuable to explore—you may find the first hint of some exciting and completely unexpected effect. For exploratory analysis, the most important consideration is not the number of contrasts we examine, but the number of contrasts available for examination—the number we potentially could examine. If that number is large—for six means it's 301—and we focus on results that look impressive, we are at great risk of focusing on CIs that are red. Lumps in the randomness often include CIs that are red, and exploration is especially likely to focus on such CIs and therefore mislead us. We might be making a stunning discovery, or seeing faces in the clouds. That's the risk of data exploration, and why exploratory analysis can give only tentative, speculative conclusions.

Number of groups or conditions	Number of comparisons	Number of subset contrasts	Total
2	1	0	1
3	3	3	6
4	6	19	25
5	10	80	90
6	15	286	301

Table 14.3 Numbers of Effects for Different Numbers of Groups or Conditions

We should be especially cautious, and seek greater strength of evidence, as the number of groups or conditions increases—meaning there are many more effects we could examine. Table 14.3 shows how the number increases very rapidly with number of groups or conditions. The precise numbers don't matter, but the message is important: Even with only three or four conditions there are many effects we *could* examine, and the number increases rapidly with more conditions.

In summary, for exploratory analysis:

1. Examine any contrasts that look interesting and draw tentative conclusions.
2. Seek greater strength of evidence, and draw conclusions that are increasingly speculative and tentative, as the number of contrasts available for potential examination increases.

With designs like those in this chapter and the next, exploratory analysis is often referred to as examination of *post hoc contrasts*, meaning contrasts chosen after seeing the data. Many researchers working within an NHST framework calculate for post hoc contrasts a criterion, smaller than the conventional .05, for a *p* value to indicate statistical significance. As the number of contrasts available for examination increases, an even smaller *p* value is required. That's a reasonable approach, but it assumes dichotomous decision making, which I'm keen to minimize. I'm also hesitant about giving much importance to precisely calculated *p* values, when Red Flag 5, the dance of the *p* values, reminds us that any *p* value may be very different on replication. I therefore prefer the less formal and more widely applicable approach to exploratory analysis that I've described above.

Post hoc contrasts are chosen after seeing the data. They are part of data exploration.

Planned and Exploratory Analysis: Closing Comments

I have three closing comments. First, looking back at our discussion of the three example studies, were the comparisons and contrasts we examined planned or exploratory? Considering the research questions those studies were designed to address, I expect that the researchers would regard them as planned, and would have chosen in advance at least most of the effects we examined. Of course, good Open Science practice would now be to have preregistered the planned analysis.

Second, for each of the examples in this chapter we analyzed only a single measure, but in each case the researchers had used other measures and reported additional analyses, and these supported their conclusions. As I mentioned earlier when discussing the Bushman example, it's a good strategy to seek converging evidence to strengthen a conclusion. In general, we should not agonize too much about the exact size of a single estimated effect, or exactly how strong the evidence is, because a replication would give a different estimate

Seek converging evidence. It's often better to have two or more separate indications of an effect than a single, even if stronger, indication.

and different strength of evidence. Instead, we should, where possible, seek converging evidence, usually from additional measures or analyses. It's often more persuasive and instructive to have two or three indications of an effect than a single, even if stronger, indication. Also, the closer those indications are to being fully independent, the better.

Third, I hardly need say it again, but whenever multiple measures or multiple analyses are mentioned we need to remind ourselves that everything must be reported in full detail. There must be no selection of the measure or analysis that happens to give results we like—all must be considered and reported, preferably in accord with the preregistered analysis plan. Do phrases like "if possible, preregistered" haunt your dreams yet?

In conclusion, the main points are these:

- At every stage, distinguish clearly between planned and exploratory analysis. Planned analysis must be specified in advance, preferably as part of a preregistered research plan.
- We can have reasonable confidence in interpreting planned contrasts—the point estimates and CIs—as the answers to our research questions. These are our main findings.
- Be aware of the great risk of cherry picking. Any conclusions based on exploration are only tentative, and more so when there were larger numbers of effects we could have examined.
- Where possible, seek converging evidence to support major conclusions.

14.21 If for his 2005 ad-memory study Bushman had stated in advance three planned comparisons, what cautions would you advise?

14.22 In the Halagappa mouse study, consider the contrast of NFree10 and NFree17 vs. AFree10 and AFree17.

    a. What question does that contrast ask?

    b. Use ESCI to examine the contrast. Report it and interpret.

14.23 a. In the Halagappa study, which is the highest mean? The lowest? Examine and interpret the comparison of the two.

    b. Would it matter whether that comparison had been selected in advance, or chosen after inspecting the data? Explain.

? Quiz 14.2

1. A subset comparison / contrast is the difference between the means / differences of two subsets of group means / SDs.
2. Preregistration of the planned analysis is especially important for extended designs with many means because, in this case
   a. exploratory analysis is especially likely to discover valuable unexpected findings.
   b. there are many more comparisons to consider than subset contrasts.
   c. the risk of cherry picking, seeing faces in the clouds, is especially large.
   d. All of the above.
3. In a one-way independent groups design with k groups, the df is _____ and the maximum number of separate research questions that can be addressed is _____.
4. Aim to choose a set of planned contrasts so that
   a. the number of contrasts is not too large.
   b. they make good sense in the research context.
   c. they address the main research questions.
   d. All of the above.

5. Planned / exploratory analysis may discover unexpected but important results, but it could easily be cherry picking / preregistered and so any conclusion should be tentative / confident.
6. Following planned analysis, then exploratory analysis, it may be valuable to
   a. look for further variables or analyses that could provide converging evidence.
   b. re-analyze the most interesting exploratory results as planned contrasts.
   c. retrospectively preregister the most interesting of the exploratory results.
   d. carry out additional analyses as planned contrasts that address additional research questions.

THE ONE-WAY REPEATED MEASURE DESIGN

If we start with a paired design, then add one or more additional levels to the independent variable, we get the *one-way repeated measure design*. As well as Pretest and Posttest, for example, we might collect critical thinking scores for the same group at Follow Up a month or a year later. The IV of testing time would then have three, rather than two levels. If you were a participant, you'd complete a critical thinking test three times.

◄ The *one-way repeated measure design* has a single independent variable with more than two levels, and one group that experiences every level of the IV.

Recalling definitions from Chapter 8, we can say that the one-way independent groups design we discussed earlier is a between-groups design and its IV is a between-groups variable, because different levels of the IV are seen by different groups. By contrast, the one-way repeated measure design I've just introduced is a within-group design and its IV is a within-group variable, also called a repeated measure, because there's a single group of participants who experience all the levels of the IV. Phew—recite those sentences a few times and I suspect you'll be totally clear about between groups and within group—or perhaps making a couple of pictures is a better strategy. Either way, within vs. between was a vital distinction during our discussions in Chapters 7 and 8, and it's a vital distinction again here.

My example of the one-way repeated measure design is a critical thinking study reported by Donohue et al. (2002) in which a group of 20 students provided Pretest scores on the California Critical Thinking Skills Test (Facione & Facione, 1992) at the start of a one-semester college freshman critical thinking course. They also provided Posttest scores at the end of the semester, then Follow Up scores around nine months later. Figure 14.9 displays the mean and CI at the three testing times. Like the Thomason studies we discussed in Chapter 8, the course was based on argument mapping. The mean improvement from Pretest to Posttest was an impressive $d_{unbiased} = 0.95$, using the published standard deviation of the test as standardizer. The figure shows that the mean improvement was fully maintained nine months later, which is another impressive result.

Figure 14.9 includes a line joining the means to indicate a repeated measure. As I mentioned in Chapter 8, using a line to signal a repeated measure is a useful convention, which I recommend using where possible, although unfortunately it's not universally followed. Why do we need to know? Recall the paired design in Chapter 8: One of the conclusions was that seeing only the two separate means (e.g., Pretest and Posttest) with their CIs is not sufficient information for us to eyeball or calculate the difference with its CI. That CI is calculated from the standard deviation of the (Posttest – Pretest) *differences*, so we need to know that SD as well. Similarly for the one-way repeated measure design: The separate CIs shown in Figure 14.9 *cannot* be used to assess any of the contrasts or comparisons of the three means, which are our primary research focus. From now on, read "contrasts" to mean "comparisons or subset contrasts".

◄ When possible, use a line joining the means to indicate a repeated measure, as in Figure 14.9.

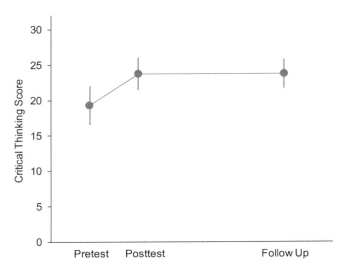

Figure 14.9. Mean and 95% CI for critical thinking scores at three times, for a single group of $N = 20$ freshman. Data from Donohue et al. (2002).

Just as there can be no overlap rules for the two separate CIs in a paired design, we can't use the CIs on the separate means in Figure 14.9 to calculate CIs on any contrasts of those means. We need additional information, which in practice means the full data. Figure 14.10 presents, as smaller colored dots, the full data underlying the means and CIs in Figure 14.9. The colored lines joining the data points are necessary to indicate the repeated measure for each individual student.

Analyzing the Repeated Measure Design

The main features of the data analysis strategy for the within-group design are the same as for the independent groups design. Once again we simplify things by focusing on contrasts of means:

▦ Select in advance a small number of contrasts that most closely correspond to the research questions. If the IV has k levels, $df = (k-1)$ and so the study can address a maximum of $(k-1)$ separate questions. Preregister your planned contrasts if possible.

▦ Calculate the mean and CI for each planned contrast, present them in figures, and report and interpret them as the main findings.

▦ Explore further contrasts if you wish, but note that any findings are only speculative.

The earlier discussion about distinguishing clearly between planned and exploratory analysis is just as relevant here. It's important to preregister the data analysis plan where possible, and to be sensitive to the number of planned contrasts examined, and, for exploratory analysis, the number that could be examined.

Carrying out calculations for the one-way repeated measure design is beyond the scope of this book and ESCI, but I will discuss some important aspects. First, consider the effect of having a repeated measure. Focus, for example, on the comparison of Posttest and Follow Up in Figure 14.10. If I enter

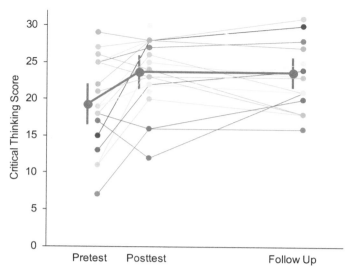

Figure 14.10. Same as Figure 14.9, but also displaying data for the 20 individual students. The Pretest, Posttest, and Follow Up data points for any single student are joined by a thin colored line.

those 20 pairs of data points into ESCI's **Data paired** page, the estimate of the difference between the Posttest and Follow Up means is 0 [−1.6, 1.6] points on the test. The correlation between the Posttest and Follow Up scores is $r = .72$, which accords with my statement in Chapter 10 that pretest–posttest designs often in practice have correlations around .6 to .9.

If I ignore the pairing of the scores, meaning I ignore the correlation and assume two independent groups, I can enter the same data into **Data two**. That page estimates the difference as 0 [−3.0, 3.0], a CI that's almost twice as long and thus a much less precise estimate. Scores at the different levels of a repeated measure often, although not always, show substantial positive correlations. When they do, the correlations explain why repeated measure designs often give relatively precise estimates of contrasts—they are often sensitive designs.

> Repeated measure designs often give relatively precise estimates of comparisons and contrasts.

The reason for positive correlations with repeated measures is that any contrast is being made *within* each participant, so the typically large variability from participant to participant is removed from the contrast. Compare with independent group designs, in which any contrast must be made *between* different participants.

Consider what ESCI pages for the one-way repeated measure design would look like. Both comparisons and contrasts pages would be very similar to those for the one-way independent groups design, except for these aspects:

- There would be no option for entering only summary statistics, because these don't provide sufficient information to calculate CIs on contrasts. Full data would be required.
- The means would be joined by a line to signal the repeated measure, as in Figure 14.9.
- The CIs on the selected comparison or contrast would usually be shorter than the separate CIs on the means. (For independent groups they are virtually always longer.)
- The correlation would be reported for any selected comparison.

Assumptions for Repeated Measure Analysis

The assumptions required for repeated measure analysis are similar to those for independent groups, but with one slightly complicated addition. Here they are:

- The data at each level of the IV are a random sample from a population that's normally distributed.
- Variance is homogeneous across the different levels of the repeated measure. In other words, the population at each level of the IV has the same standard deviation, σ.

The slightly complicated additional assumption is satisfied if:

▶ To analyze the repeated measure design, make the assumption that the correlations are homogeneous.

- The population correlation is the same for every pair of levels of the IV. In other words, the correlation of the Pretest and Posttest populations is the same as that of the Pretest and Follow Up, and the Posttest and Follow Up populations. Think of this as a kind of "homogeneity of correlation" requirement.

For our example, the spread of the data points looks roughly similar at all three levels of the IV in Figure 14.10, suggesting it's reasonable to assume homogeneity of variance. Considering the last assumption, we could calculate the correlation for each pair of levels of the IV, but with N as small as 20 the sample correlations can vary greatly because of sampling variability, so it would take extremely different correlations calculated for the different pairs of levels to persuade me not to make the final assumption.

Making all the assumptions, what comparisons or contrasts would we choose? Earlier I reported the comparison of Posttest and Follow Up, but Donohue et al. (2002) elected to focus on two planned comparisons: Pretest and Posttest, and Pretest and Follow Up. Reporting and interpreting those provided the main basis for their discussion and conclusions.

Choosing a Design

Should we choose independent groups or a repeated measure? In Chapter 8 we compared the two independent groups and paired designs. Very similar considerations apply here:

- Sometimes you have no choice. For example, our critical thinking study required repeated testing, which means a repeated measure design.
- Often you could choose either. For example, comparing Pen, Laptop, and Printed Notes could work with either design.
- Advantages of the independent groups design are that it's simple, each person is tested only once, and, assuming you test everyone separately, the observations are all independent, as they need to be.
- The main disadvantage of independent groups is that usually there's large variability from person to person, so contrasts are estimated with low precision. You may need large groups to get reasonable precision.
- The main advantage of a repeated measure is that, as we discussed earlier, it makes contrasts *within* each participant and so usually gives relatively precise estimates. A smaller group may suffice.

■ A disadvantage of a repeated measure is that each participant sees all levels of the IV, so needs to be tested multiple times. Therefore, carryover effects can be a problem and causal conclusions can't be drawn, unless, as we discussed in Chapter 8, we have a suitable randomization strategy to counterbalance order or compare with an appropriate control group.

> Repeated measure designs are usually more sensitive, but carryover effects require attention.

Most textbooks describe the two one-way designs we've been discussing under the heading "analysis of variance", so I'd better say something about that next.

14.24 In a memory study I present four types of stimuli, namely letters, digits, symbols, and pictures, to a single group of children.

    a. What's the IV, and how many levels does it have?
    b. What type of IV is it? Give two answers.
    c. What's the design?
    d. In this study, what does homogeneity of variance refer to?
    e. What does homogeneity of correlation refer to?

14.25 What different design could I have used for that study? Compare the two designs and make a recommendation.

ANALYSIS OF VARIANCE

I've described the analysis of both one-way designs in terms of planned and exploratory contrasts. This approach is the simplest to understand and picture, most strongly tied to an estimation approach, and usually most closely matching what researchers wish to know. It has also been long advocated by leading scholars, including Rosenthal and Rosnow (1985) and Steiger (2004). In addition, many textbooks explain and recommend planned contrasts—with good reason. Despite all that, the most common approach to analyzing and reporting our one-way designs, and more complex designs, takes a different approach, called *analysis of variance* (ANOVA). Contrasts have many advantages, and can address the great majority, if not all, the questions that ANOVA can address, so it's hard to know why ANOVA continues to dominate. But it does. I encourage you to work with contrasts where you can and, as usual, to make figures with CIs and then use these as the basis for interpretation. But I need to say something about ANOVA so you can understand older journal articles, and reports from researchers who still use this approach.

> Contrasts have many advantages over ANOVA.

ANOVA for the One-Way Independent Groups Design

ANOVA focuses on testing hypotheses. For the one-way independent groups design the null hypothesis is that all group population means are the same:

$$H_0: \mu_{A1} = \mu_{A2} = \mu_{A3} = \dots \tag{14.6}$$

where the labels A1, A2, ..., refer to the different levels of the IV, which is also referred to as *Factor A*. (In the next chapter we'll have a second IV, called, would you believe, Factor B.) Another way of expressing that null hypothesis is that the *main effect of A* is zero, where "main effect" refers to all the A group population means.

> ANOVA uses the *F* statistic to test the null hypothesis that the population group means are equal.

> Large *F* means low *p*, and *p* < .05 means the ***main effect*** is statistically significant.

> Following a statistically significant main effect, post hoc contrasts may be examined. Planned contrasts are usually preferable.

ANOVA proceeds by calculating from the data a test statistic, *F*, then finding the corresponding *p* value and using that to test the null hypothesis. If *F* is sufficiently large, *p* will be sufficiently small, for example < .05, to reject the null hypothesis and state that we have a *statistically significant A main effect*. This means that somewhere among the A group means there is, most likely, some difference, but it tells us nothing about where that difference might be. It also gives us no size estimates of any difference or differences.

Finding a statistically significant main effect is often followed by post hoc contrasts. These are chosen after seeing the means and are, therefore, exploratory. They are typically calculated using some method that adjusts downward the *p* value criterion for declaring a contrast statistically significant to allow for the number of contrasts that could have been examined. This procedure thus has two levels of protection: A post hoc contrast is declared statistically significant only after (i) there is a statistically significant main effect, and (ii) the contrast itself achieves the more exacting *p* value criterion—perhaps .02 rather than .05. As a result, this overall procedure is usually conservative, and only contrasts that are particularly large are likely to achieve statistical significance. As we discussed earlier, selecting planned contrasts in advance, where possible, is preferable to using ANOVA.

Now consider planning the next study. A post hoc contrast that looked interesting in the first study can be chosen as a planned contrast for the next study—just as any interesting result from exploratory analysis can be stated as one or more planned contrasts to be investigated in future studies.

The assumptions required for ANOVA are the same as required for contrasts analysis. In particular, we need to assume homogeneity of variance.

The *F* statistic is a ratio, which weighs the variability for some effect against some reference variability. For independent groups, *F* weighs the variability of the group means against the variability of the data within a group, pooled over all groups:

$$\text{Informally, } F = \frac{variability\,of\,group\,means}{variability\,of\,data\,within\,a\,group,\,pooled\,over\,all\,groups} \quad (14.7)$$

A difference, or differences, between any of the group means will increase *F*, which means the *p* value is lower and the main effect more likely to achieve statistical significance.

In a journal article, you may read something like "the main effect of type of feedback was statistically significant, $F(2, 38) = 4.41$, $p = .02$." The *F* statistic requires two *df* values, which are reported in the parentheses. The first, 2, refers to the numerator in Equation 14.7 and is one less than the number of groups, so here there were three groups. The second, 38, refers to the denominator in the equation. As usual, think of the *p* value in terms of strength of evidence—how strongly we should doubt the null hypothesis.

Along with a value of *F* for a main effect you may see reported an effect size estimate. The most common ANOVA effect size measures are η^2 (lower case Greek eta, like "eat-uh", squared), partial η^2, and ω^2 (lower case Greek omega, squared). These are all estimates of the proportion of variance attributable to the main effect—the proportion of overall variance accounted for by the extent the group means vary. Larger values reflect larger differences among group means and, because they are proportions, values must lie between 0 and 1. Values are often small, such as .04 or .09, but sometimes can be .5 or .7

or even larger. You may read something like "$F(2, 38) = 4.41$, $p = .02$, partial $\eta^2 = .13$." It's hard to build intuitions about these effect size measures, or to give them convincing interpretation in a particular context. The mean and CI for a contrast are easier to include in a figure and, almost certainly, easier to interpret in context.

ANOVA for the One-Way Repeated Measure Design

Most of the discussion above applies here also. For the repeated measure design, the null hypothesis is, for example,

$$H_0: \mu_{\text{Pretest}} = \mu_{\text{Posttest}} = \cdots \qquad (14.8)$$

for all the levels of the IV. As always, F is a ratio of effect variability to some reference variability. Here the numerator is the variability of the means at the different levels of the IV (Pretest, Posttest, …). The denominator is more complex, but for a good reason. Because we have a repeated measure and comparisons are made within participants, the person-to-person variability can be removed from the denominator, which is thus considerably smaller. Therefore, F is larger and the p value smaller and the A main effect more likely to achieve statistical significance. That's another way of saying the design is sensitive.

The assumptions are the same as for contrasts analysis, including homogeneity of variance and what I called homogeneity of correlation. The same ANOVA effect size measures may be reported. However, I once again recommend where possible an analysis strategy based on planned contrasts, then, optionally, exploration of additional contrasts.

It's take-home messages time. To write yours, bring to mind ads during violent television shows, challenging feedback, calorie-restricted diets, and training in critical thinking. If that doesn't help much, think of comparisons and contrasts, planned and exploratory analysis, and independent groups and a repeated measure. Also think of the Open Science themes, especially pre-registration of an analysis plan. You'll recognize that, following Rattan et al. (2012), I'm trying to give you challenging things to think about here, while, of course, also trying to be encouraging.

 Quiz 14.3

1. In the one-way repeated measure design, there is (or are) one IV / two IVs / two or more IVs and one group / two groups / two or more groups. Each participant sees one level / all levels of an IV.
2. Compared with a one-way independent groups design, the one-way repeated measure design is likely to
   a. require more participants.
   b. give longer CIs on effects of interest.
   c. have fewer carryover effects.
   d. None of the above.
3. In a figure displaying means and CIs for a repeated measure design, a line joining the CIs / means / differences signals the nature of the IV / DV.
4. Analysis of the one-way repeated measure design requires assumption of homogeneity of
   a. variance.
   b. correlation.
   c. both variance and correlation.
   d. neither variance nor correlation.

5. ANOVA uses the _r_ / _F_ / η^2 statistic to test the null hypothesis that the population group means are <u>the same</u> / different. When that statistic is sufficiently large, the _p_ value is sufficiently large / <u>small</u>, and the null hypothesis is <u>rejected</u> / not rejected.

6. Following a statistically significant ANOVA main effect, post hoc _____ may be examined, although _____ _____ are usually preferable to ANOVA.

14.26 a. In the Halagappa mouse study, what null hypothesis would ANOVA test?

b. If ANOVA gave $F(5, 108) = 3.82, p = .003$, what would you conclude? Interpret.

c. Could you follow with post hoc contrasts? Compare with a planned contrasts strategy.

14.27 a. In the Donohue critical thinking study, what null hypothesis would ANOVA test?

b. If ANOVA gave large _F_ and $p < .05$, what would you conclude? Interpret.

c. What post hoc contrasts might you examine? Compare with a planned contrasts strategy.

14.28 Wait, discuss, and reflect, then revisit your take-home messages if you wish.

Reporting Your Work

▶
Break complex designs into simple contrasts. For each contrast, focus on the group difference and its CI.

Study designs can become quite complex, but the basic strategy for analyzing and reporting your research remains straightforward: Focus on a limited number of contrasts to estimate effect sizes of interest, then interpret those estimates and their CIs. Preferably the contrasts analyzed will have been planned and preregistered. Although your analysis may be quite focused, be sure to tell the full story—provide details and basic descriptive statistics for _all_ groups and conditions, even if they are not essential for your main conclusions.

For each contrast your report will typically include:

- whether the contrast is planned or exploratory, unless this is already clear;
- basic descriptive statistics for the groups being compared;
- the group difference, $(M_2 - M_1)$ and its CI;
- a standardized effect size estimate ($d_{unbiased}$ is best), preferably with its CI. ESCI does not provide these in the complex design pages, but you can enter data from a specific contrast into the **Data two** or **Data paired** pages to obtain standardized effect size estimates and CIs. In the Method section make clear how your standardized effect size was calculated (which denominator was used);
- a figure if possible, preferably one like ESCI produces that emphasizes the estimated group difference and its CI. Use lines connecting the means for repeated measures designs but not for independent groups designs. State in the figure caption what error bars represent—95% CIs;
- if desired, ANOVA results, which should include _F_, its degrees of freedom, and its associated _p_ value; and
- an interpretation of the group difference that considers not only the point estimate but also the CI.

Here is an example using data from Bushman (2005):

Participants who watched a TV show with neutral content recognized nearly half of the 12 brands advertised during the show ($M = 5.76$, $s = 2.47$). Fewer brands were recognized by participants who watched a show with violent content ($M = 4.36$, $s = 2.57$), and even fewer by those who watched a show with sexual content ($M = 3.54$, $s = 2.57$).

The planned contrast between the violent and neutral conditions indicates violence produces a mild impairment of brand recognition: $(M_{Violent} - M_{Neutral}) = -1.40$, 95% CI [-2.17, -0.63], $d_{unbiased} = -0.55$, 95% CI [-0.86, -0.25]. The CI is fairly long, but consistent with at least a quarter-point reduction in recognition. Given the money involved in advertising, we judge even a small difference in recognition to be of practical importance.

The planned contrast between the sexual and neutral conditions revealed that sexual content produces a large impairment in brand recognition: $(M_{Sexual} - M_{Neutral}) = -2.22$, 95% CI [-2.99, -1.45], $d_{unbiased} = -0.88$, 95% CI [-1.20, -0.56]. The CI is consistent with a decline in advertising effectiveness that is anywhere from substantial up to very large.

We also explored the extent that violent and sexual content may lead to different brand recognition: $(M_{Sexual} - M_{Violent}) = -0.82$, 95% CI [-1.59, -0.05], $d_{unbiased} = -0.32$, 95% CI [-0.62, -0.01]. The CI is long and extends up to effectively no difference in recognition. But this comparison is suggestive and may warrant additional research to investigate the extent that sexual content is even more distracting than violent content, for brand recognition.

Take-Home Messages

General Analysis Strategy

■ A *comparison* is the difference between two means. A *subset contrast* is the difference between the means of two subsets of means. Examining comparisons and contrasts, with their CIs, is the basic analysis strategy. A figure helps. (From here on, "contrasts" includes comparisons.)

■ Distinguish carefully between planned and exploratory analysis. Where possible, preregister a data analysis plan, including specification of planned contrasts.

■ Choose a small number of planned contrasts that make sense and most closely match the research questions. The maximum number of separate questions that contrasts can answer is *df*, which is one less than the number of levels of the IV.

■ Optionally, follow planned analysis with exploration, but beware cherry picking: Any findings may be lumps in the randomness and are only speculative. The larger the number of potential contrasts, the more tentative is any conclusion.

One-Way Independent Groups Design

■ The *one-way independent groups design* has a single IV with more than two levels, and a group for each level.

■ Assuming homogeneity of variance across all groups permits CIs on contrasts to be calculated using a pooled estimate of σ, the assumed common population SD.

One-Way Repeated Measure Design

■ The *one-way repeated measure design* has a single IV with more than two levels, and one group that experiences every level of that IV.

■ Assume homogeneity of variance across all levels of the IV, and also homogeneity of correlation.

■ Contrasts are made within participants, so the repeated measure design is likely to give more precise estimates than an independent groups design, although carryover effects may be a problem.

Analysis of Variance

- ■ ANOVA tests the null hypothesis that the population means for all levels of the IV are equal. A sufficiently large F means a small p value, rejection of the null hypothesis, and the conclusion that there is a statistically significant main effect of the IV.

- ■ Finding a statistically significant main effect may be followed by examination of any post hoc contrasts of interest.

- ■ An analysis strategy based on contrasts has strong advantages over ANOVA.

 End-of-Chapter Exercises

1) To what extent does study strategy influence learning? To investigate, psychology students were randomly assigned to three groups and asked to learn biology facts using one of three different strategies: a) Self-Explain (explaining for each fact what new knowledge is gained and how it relates to what is already known), b) Elab Interrogation (elaborative interrogation: stating for each fact why it makes sense), or c) Repetition Control (stating each fact over and over). After studying, students took a 25-point fill-the-blank test (O'Reilly, Symons, & MacLatchy-Gaudet, 1998). Table 14.4 shows the results.

Table 14.4 Summary Statistics of Test Scores (out of 25) for Students Assigned Different Study Strategies

	Self-Explain	Elab Interrogation	Repetition Control
N	18	18	19
M	17.06	12.44	12.34
s	5.42	5.89	5.13

a. Will we be able to draw causal comparisons from this study? Explain.

b. Does it seem reasonable to assume homogeneity of variance? What other assumptions would need to be considered before examining contrasts between the groups?

c. Calculate s_p using Equation 14.1. It may be helpful to use a spreadsheet.

d. Calculate df for comparisons in this study using Equation 14.2. Use **Normal and t** to find the corresponding $t_{.95}(df)$.

e. To what extent is self-explaining a better strategy than repetition? First, calculate the 95% MoE for this comparison using Equation 14.4, then find the 95% CI for the difference between the self-explanation and repetition control groups. Then interpret.

f. To what extent is elaborative interrogation a better strategy than repetition? Will you need to re-calculate the MoE? Explain. Find the CI and interpret.

g. Check your work using ESCI. The summary data in Table 14.4 are also available on the book website (**Study_Strategies**). In **Ind groups comparison**, clear data if necessary, select **Statistics above** at red 2, then use copy and paste (as usual, use Paste Special/ Values) for the summary data at red 3. Type in names at red 1 and red 3. Select at red 8 to choose a comparison to analyze. Does your work agree with what you find in ESCI? Hopefully!

h. We could also compare elaborative interrogation with self-explaining. And we could compare the two strategies together against basic repetition—a subset contrast. However, what issue do we need to be aware of if we conduct more and more comparisons?

i. As you analyzed the first and second comparisons, did you wonder whether they had been planned? What would be the best analysis strategy, and when would it be decided?

j.   Bonus: Before the experiment began, students were asked to rate their previous knowledge about the circulatory system on a scale from 5 to 20. Summary results for Previous Knowledge are available in the same data file (**Study_Strategies**). Using NHST the researchers found no statistically significant differences in prior knowledge between the groups and thus concluded that "groups did not differ in their perceived prior knowledge" (p. 439, O'Reilly et al., 1998). What red flag does this raise? Use ESCI to analyze two comparisons of prior knowledge between the three groups. Then interpret: Is there good evidence that prior knowledge was very similar at the start of the study? How might this influence your interpretation of the test results you just analyzed?

2) Continuing from the previous question on study strategy, students in this study were also asked to rate the ease of using their assigned study strategy on a scale from 1 to 5. Table 14.5 shows the results (also in the **Study_Strategies** data set).

Table 14.5 Summary Statistics of Perceived Difficulty of Different Study Strategies

	Self-Explain	Elab Interrogation	Repetition Control
N	18	18	19
M	2.94	0.87	2.58
s	1.16	1.94	0.84

a.   Does it seem reasonable to assume homogeneity of variance? Explain. What other assumptions would it be good to check?

b.   Calculate s_p using Equation 14.1.

c.   Calculate df for comparisons in this study using Equation 14.2. What is the corresponding $t_{.95}(df)$ value?

d.   To what extent is self-explaining perceived to be an easier strategy compared with repetition? Calculate the 95% MoE for this comparison, then the 95% CI, and then interpret. You can check your work with **Ind groups comparisons**.

e.   To what extent is elaborative interrogation perceived to be an easier strategy than repetition?

f.   The researchers who conducted this study were surprised that elaborative interrogation was not very effective for learning. Do these results shed any light on why that might be?

3) To what extent is a religious upbringing related to prosocial behavior in childhood? To investigate, a large international sample of children was asked to play a game in which they were given 10 stickers but then asked if they would give some of these stickers away to another child who had not been able to be tested that day. The number of stickers donated was considered a measure of altruistic sharing. In addition, the parents of each child reported the family's religion. Table 14.6 shows summary data, which are also available on the book website (**Religion_Sharing**).

Table 14.6 Summary Statistics of Sharing Stickers for Families of Different Religious Orientation

	Non-religious	Christian	Muslim
N	323	280	510
M	4.09	3.33	3.20
s	2.52	2.46	2.24

a.   Will we be able to draw causal comparisons from this study? Explain.

b.   One of the researcher's primary research questions is the extent to which different types of religious upbringing relate to differences in children's sharing. Use **Ind groups comparisons** to compare children of Christian and Muslim parents, then interpret.

c.   A second research question posed by the researchers is the extent to which non-religious vs. religious upbringing relates to differences in sharing. Use **Ind groups contrasts** to compare children of non-religious parents with those of religious parents (Christian or Muslim), then interpret.

d.   The results are consistent with the idea that religious upbringing decreases sharing. What are some alternative explanations?

4)   To what extent might choosing organic foods make us morally smug? To investigate, Eskine (2013) asked participants to rate images of organic food, neutral (control) food, or comfort food. Next, under the guise of a different study, all participants completed a moral judgment scale in which they read different controversial scenarios and rated how morally wrong they judged them to be (scale of 1–7). Table 14.7 shows summary data, which are also available in the **Organic_Moral** data set on the book website.

Table 14.7 Summary Statistics of Moral Judgments (1–7 Scale) After Different Food Exposures

	Organic	Control	Comfort
N	21	21	21
M	5.58	5.08	4.89
s	0.59	0.62	0.57

a.   To what extent did organic food exposure alter moral judgments relative to the control group?

b.   To what extent did comfort food exposure alter moral judgments relative to the control group?

5)   After the results of Eskine (2013) were published, Moery & Calin-Jageman (2016) conducted a series of close replications. We obtained original materials from Eskine, piloted the procedure, and preregistered our sampling and analysis plan. The OSF page osf.io/atkn7 has all the details. The data from one of these close replications are available on the book website (**Organic_Moral**).

a.   Based on the effect observed in the original study between organic and control, what sample size would you plan for a close replication?

b.   In this close replication, to what extent did exposure to organic food alter moral judgment? How does this compare with the original finding?

c.   In the replication, to what extent did exposure to comfort food alter moral judgment? How does this compare with the original finding?

d.   Overall, how does this replication attempt relate to the original finding? Does it undermine the original finding, support it, or leave the results ambiguous? Explain, and suggest what the next steps should be.

Answers to Quizzes

Quiz 14.1

1) one IV, the number of levels of the IV; 2) difference between, means; 3) c; 4) homogeneity, variance, SD, population; 5) a; 6) homogeneity of variance.

Quiz 14.2

1) contrast, means, means; 2) c; 3) $(k - 1)$, $(k - 1)$; 4) d; 5) exploratory, cherry picking, tentative; 6) a.

Quiz 14.3

1) one IV, one group, all levels; 2) d; 3) means, IV; 4) c; 5) F, the same, small, rejected; 6) contrasts, planned contrasts.

 ## Answers to In-Chapter Exercises

14.1   2.54, 249, 0.55, [5.21, 6.31]. CI looks compatible with Figure 14.1.

14.2   The (Neutral − Violent) comparison = 1.40 [0.63, 2.17].

14.4   Pooled SD not shown by ESCI, but others match.

14.5   a. Triangle marks the difference between Neutral and Violent means and the CI indicates the precision of estimation of that comparison; b. $p < .001$ indicates very strong evidence that comparison is greater than zero, which matches the CI being distant from zero; c. This accords with the overlap rule indicating strong evidence of a difference between Neutral and Violent means because of the distinct gap between the two CIs.

14.6   a. The (Neutral − Sexual) comparison = 2.22 [1.45, 2.99], which is a very substantial decrease in brand recognition, from 5.76 to 3.54, when a show has sexual content. $p < .001$ indicates very strong evidence the comparison is greater than zero. Again, the very small p value corresponds to the CI being distant from zero; b. Result is consistent with the large gap between the two separate CIs.

14.7 $(M1 − M2)$ = 1.40 [0.63, 2.17]. For $(M2 − M1)$ click $M2$ in the top row at red 8 and $M1$ in the bottom, and find the same values but negative: −1.40 [−2.17, −0.63].

14.8   a. Larger n decreases CI length for that mean, smaller increases it. CI for comparison is always a little longer than the longer of the two separate CIs; b. Any larger s increases CI length for all means and comparisons, because of pooling; smaller decreases it. (Big change to any s might mean the assumption of homogeneity is not justified.)

14.9   a, b. Perhaps Comfort vs. Control, which is $(M1 − M3)$, and Challenge vs. Control, $(M2 − M3)$.

14.10   a. The right radio button at red 2 is selected because full data not summary statistics were loaded, so values at red 5 but not red 3 can be changed; b. It's reasonable to assume homogeneity of variance because the values of s for the 3 groups, at red 3, don't differ much; c. $(M1 − M3)$ = −1.11 [−2.18, −0.05], quite a large difference on the 7-point rating scale, but the CI is so long that there's only a little evidence the difference is non-zero. $(M2 − M3)$ = 0.82 [−0.26, 1.90], a moderate difference in rating but the CI is so long there's no evidence the difference is non-zero.

14.12   Click one or more checkboxes in the green row at red 8 to see selected means shown green and their mean shown as a green square at right. Same for blue. No mean can be in both subsets. The subset contrast is the difference between the green and blue squares, and is shown as a triangle on the difference axis, with its CI.

14.13   a. Middle-aged vs. old: $(M1, M2, M3)$, $(M4, M5, M6)$; b. Diet vs. free for Alzheimer-prone mice: $(M3, M6)$, $(M2, M5)$.

14.14   Yes, largest and smallest s (near red 3) don't differ by more than a factor of 2.

14.15   3.00 [−1.22, 7.23], small mean, only 3 percentage points, long CI, no evidence of any age difference.

14.16   8.85 [3.68, 14.02], considerable effect, very strong evidence ADiet showed greater learning than AFree.

14.17   −3.00 [−7.23, 1.22], same but sign changed.

14.18   a. 9.30 [1.98, 16.62]. In middle-aged Alzheimer mice, restricted diet considerably improves performance, although CI is long, around 2 to 17; b. Comparison of ADiet17 and AFree17 is 8.40 [1.08, 15.72]. Same result and interpretation for old as for middle-aged.

14.19 a, b. Same as 14.16.

14.20 5.18 for the contrast, but 7.32 for each comparison; MoE the same for each comparison because both based on pooled SD and *n* the same for all groups. Contrast MoE shorter because based on two groups in each subset and therefore larger total *n*.

14.21 3 groups so *df* = 2, so only 2 separate questions can be answered, and 3 comparisons must have some redundancy—not all separate.

14.22 a. Difference between normal and Alzheimer mice with no diet restriction, averaged over ages; b. 4.55 [−0.62, 9.72], merely hinting that Alzheimer mice may show a deficit, but the CI is quite long so no clear conclusion.

14.23 a. ADiet10, AFree17, difference = 11.30 [3.98, 18.62], a large difference. CI is quite long but shows strong evidence the comparison is non-zero; b. If planned we could be reasonably confident in that conclusion, although it doesn't seem to correspond to a likely research question. If chosen after seeing the data it's exploratory and we should probably disregard it.

14.24 a, b. The IV is stimulus type, with 4 levels, and is a within-group or repeated measure IV; c. The design is one-way repeated measure; d. Homogeneity of variance refers to equality of population variance at every level of the IV; e. Homogeneity of correlation refers to equality of population correlation between all pairs of levels of the IV.

14.25 One-way independent groups, which is probably less sensitive and would require many more children, although each would need to be tested on only one stimulus type. For the repeated measure design, carryover effects, for example practice or fatigue, may be large, so it would be important to counterbalance order of presentation, and also ensure that the testing sessions were not too long for the children. On balance, repeated measure is probably better.

14.26 a. That population means for all six groups are the same; b. Reject that null hypothesis and conclude there was very strong evidence of some difference or differences among the group means; c. Yes, but using post hoc contrasts is a less sensitive strategy. Any contrast would have to be larger to be convincing than if that same contrast had been stated in advance as a planned contrast. Using planned contrasts is a better strategy, where possible.

14.27 a. That population means at Pretest, Posttest, and Follow Up are all the same; b. Reject that null hypothesis and conclude there was a small amount of evidence of some difference or differences among those means; c. You might choose to examine the post hoc subset contrast—chosen after seeing the data—of Pretest vs. (Mean of Posttest and Follow Up). Using some post hoc technique, that contrast would have to be larger to achieve statistical significance than if it had been specified in advance as a planned contrast. As usual, a planned contrast approach is probably better than ANOVA.

15

Extended Designs: Two Independent Variables

In this chapter we'll add a second independent variable. We could, for example, study pen and laptop in different disciplines, by investigating, say, the extent that note-taking in engineering works differently from note-taking in philosophy. Discipline would be the second IV and we would have a *two-way* design. We could use four independent groups, one for each combination of note taking method (Pen or Laptop) with discipline (Engineering or Philosophy). That would be a *two-way independent groups design*.

A two-way design is efficient, because it allows us to ask more questions in a single experiment—questions about each of the IVs. But there's more: We can also ask about a possible *interaction* between the two IVs. If the effect of Pen vs. Laptop is different in different disciplines—perhaps pen is better in philosophy but laptop in engineering—then we say the two IVs *interact*. People are so complex and endlessly fascinating it's not surprising that researchers who study people very often encounter interacting variables. For example, if you rate different styles of music as more enjoyable depending on whether you are at a party or in church, then, for you, music style *interacts* with the setting. If I ask "What music do you like?" you can't give a full answer without mentioning parties and church, and perhaps other settings as well. There are two IVs—type of music, and setting—and they interact. Two-way designs are an important addition to the researcher's toolkit. They are used very often and the main focus is often the interaction.

Beyond independent groups, we can also consider repeated measure IVs. As usual, when they are appropriate they usually give sensitive designs and relatively precise estimates. We could also add a third IV, or a fourth or more, and get truly complicated designs capable of asking lots of questions. But simple is often good, and simpler designs can often tell a clearer and more convincing story. Our main focus will be on 2 × 2 examples, meaning there are two IVs each with two levels. That's often a good size and complexity of design to aim for.

Here's the agenda:

- Adding a second IV to make the simplest factorial design: the *two-way independent groups design*
- Main effects and interactions, with their CIs
- Two-way factorial designs with one or two repeated measure IVs
- IVs with more than two levels
- A general strategy for analyzing one-way designs and two-way factorial designs

THE TWO-WAY INDEPENDENT GROUPS DESIGN

The *two-way independent groups design* is our first with more than a single IV. We'll consider the simplest case, which has two between-groups IVs, each having two

The *two-way independent groups design* has two IVs, and a group for every combination of levels of the two IVs.

levels. The Pen–Laptop study compared two groups of students, one using Pen and the other Laptop. To add a second IV, with Engineering and Philosophy as its two levels, we would need four independent groups: Pen & Engineering, Pen & Philosophy, Laptop & Engineering, and Laptop & Philosophy. Any student in our study fits with just one of those four combinations. To make the groups we would obtain as close as possible to a random sample of engineering majors and randomly assign half of them to the Pen & Engineering group and the other half to the Laptop & Engineering group. We'd do the same for a sample of philosophy majors to make the other two groups.

> The **two-way independent groups design** has two IVs. Every combination of the levels of the two IVs is experienced by an independent group of participants.

▶ A **factorial design** includes all combinations of the levels of all IVs.

Now a little more jargon. We refer to any design that includes all combinations of the levels of two or more IVs as a *factorial design*. All the designs we'll consider in this chapter are factorial designs. Our first example has two IVs each with two levels, and is therefore a 2 × 2 factorial design. The original Pen–Laptop study had one IV, referred to as "A", with two levels: A1 (Pen) and A2 (Laptop). We now have a second IV, which I'll label "B", also with two levels: B1 (Engineering) and B2 (Philosophy). One of our four groups combines Pen (A1) and Engineering (B1), so is the A1B1 group, and so on for the other groups.

I'd like to know the findings of this example factorial design, but unfortunately it's fictional. So I'll choose a different 2 × 2 factorial design example, which addresses another interesting question by bringing together two major research topics and investigating the extent that sleep deprivation might influence false memory.

AN EXAMPLE: SLEEP DEPRIVATION AND FALSE MEMORY

Suppose you witness a robbery in which a thief steals a purse and puts it in his pants pocket. Later you read a description of the event that includes a statement that he put it in his jacket pocket. That misinformation may prompt you to be convinced that you originally saw the thief put it in his jacket rather than his pants. Even the wording of a later question can distort memory for the original event. Such distorted or *false memory* is a troubling phenomenon with major consequences for the value of eyewitness testimony in court, the investigation of possible child abuse, and many other aspects of life. For example, eyewitness misidentifications are thought to be the leading cause of wrongful criminal convictions in the United States. Search for "false memory" or "false memory syndrome" for description and examples.

Frenda et al. (2014) used four groups of students and a 2 × 2 two-way independent groups design to investigate how sleep deprivation might influence false memory. Students came to the lab in the evening and either slept normally or were kept awake all night. They saw pictures that described a robbery—the critical event—either in the evening, or in the morning. Then in the morning all students read a description that included misinformation. A little later they completed several memory tasks that referred to the original event. A false memory score assessed the extent to which the misinformation distorted a participant's memory for the event. The researchers designed the study to compare the extent of false memory when a person lacks sleep when

		Between-groups independent variable (A)	
		Evening (A1)	Morning (A2)
Between-groups independent variable (B)	Sleep (B1)	Evening Sleep Group A1B1	Morning Sleep Group A2B1
	Nosleep (B2)	Evening Nosleep Group A1B2	Morning Nosleep Group A2B2

Table 15.1 The Four Independent Groups in Frenda et al. (2014)

they *witness* a critical event (in the morning, after no sleep), compared with lacking sleep when they *recall* the event (witnessed the previous evening).

Table 15.1 describes the variables and groups. Seeing pictures that described the critical event in the evening or the morning was independent variable "A" with levels A1 (Evening) and A2 (Morning). Sleeping normally or not sleeping at all was independent variable "B" with levels B1 (Sleep) and B2 (Nosleep). Students were assigned randomly to the four groups described in the table. For example, the Evening Sleep group (A1B1) saw pictures of the critical event in the evening, then had normal sleep, whereas the Morning Nosleep group (A2B2) had no sleep overnight, then saw the pictures of the critical event only in the morning. Note that "Morning Sleep", for example, doesn't mean that the students slept in the morning, but that they slept overnight and then in the morning saw pictures of the critical event.

Our main strategy for analyzing factorial designs is the same as we used with the simpler designs in the previous chapter: Choose contrasts that correspond best to the research questions. Here we might consider this line of thinking:

1. Seeing the event in the evening meant it had to be remembered all night, so memory for the event might be weaker in the morning and, therefore, more susceptible to the misinformation. If so, Evening would show more false memory than Morning. Overall, what's the effect of evening or morning presentation of the event? Compare the mean of the two Evening groups with the mean of the two Morning groups.

That question asks about the overall effect of Evening vs. Morning, after averaging over Sleep/Nosleep, the other IV. That overall effect is the *main effect* of the Evening/Morning IV, which we calculate as:

(mean of the two Morning group means – mean of the two Evening group means)

I can also write that as:

(overall Morning mean – overall Evening mean)

More briefly, I'll refer to that Evening/Morning main effect as the (Morning – Evening) difference, but remember that it's the means we are subtracting.

The *main effect* of an IV is its overall effect, based on means at each of its levels after averaging over all other IVs.

2. Sleep deprivation degrades cognitive processing and therefore might enhance false memory. Overall, what's the effect of sleeping or not? Compare the mean of the two Nosleep groups with the mean of the two Sleep groups. This is (Nosleep – Sleep), the main effect of the Sleep/Nosleep IV.

3. Perhaps sleep deprivation might be more disruptive for Evening, where the event must be remembered overnight, than for Morning? Consider the difference that sleeping or not might have on the Evening groups, and compare with the difference that sleeping or not might have on the Morning groups. In other words, examine the difference of these differences.

▶ In a 2 × 2 design, the difference of the differences is the 2 × 2 interaction.

This third question asks about the *interaction* of the two IVs: To what extent is the effect of the Sleep/Nosleep IV different at the two levels of the Evening/Morning IV? The difference of the differences is how we quantify that interaction in a 2 × 2 design.

> The *interaction* of two IVs is the extent to which the effect of one IV is different at different levels of the other IV.

In the 2 × 2 design we're discussing, the interaction is a *2 × 2 interaction*, because it refers to a 2 × 2 table of means, as in Table 15.1. Later we'll see 3 × 2 and other more complex interactions, which refer to larger tables of means.

It's easier to think about particular contrasts while seeing a set of means, but I deliberately suggested those questions before referring to the results, to emphasize that we should consider our questions and planned contrasts in advance. Now for the data.

Main Effects

Figure 15.1 shows the mean false memory score and 95% CI, for each group. High scores indicate more false memories, with a maximum of 6. The groups and means are labeled as in Table 15.1. The Sleep/Nosleep difference looks to be different—in fact going in the opposite direction—for Evening and Morning,

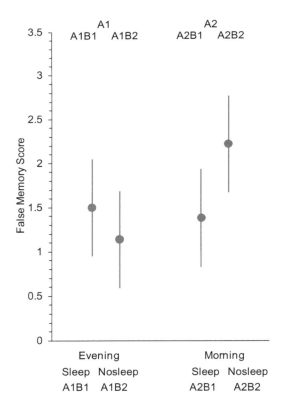

Figure 15.1. Mean false memory scores (maximum 6) and 95% CIs for four independent groups, from Frenda et al. (2014). The study had a factorial design with independent variable "A" having levels A1 (Evening) and A2 (Morning), and independent variable "B" having levels B1 (Sleep) and B2 (Nosleep). Labels are as in Table 15.1. The data are courtesy Steven Frenda.

which suggests an interaction. We'll come to that in a moment, but let's start by considering the first question, which asked about the main effect of evening or morning presentation of the critical event. We need to compare the mean of the two Evening groups with the mean of the two Morning groups. For the Evening groups, see the two means on the left in Figure 15.1. To my eyeball, the mean of those two means is about 1.3, so this is my eyeballed estimate of the overall Evening mean. The mean of the two means on the right looks to me about 1.8, which is my eyeballed estimate of the overall Morning mean. So the (Morning – Evening) difference is about $1.8 - 1.3 = 0.5$ and this is my rough estimate of the main effect of the A independent variable.

I should also note that the main effect of our IV has one degree of freedom. In general, the main effect of an IV with k levels has

$$df = (k - 1) \tag{15.1}$$

> The main effect of an IV with k levels has $df = (k - 1)$.

In our example, both IVs have two levels, so $k = 2$ and $df = 1$ for each main effect.

Figure 15.2 shows how the **Ind groups 2 × 2** page in ESCI displays the main effect of Evening/Morning. It displays the same four means and CIs, and labels, as in Figure 15.1. To see the main effect display, at red 8 in the **Main effects** panel (upper middle in the figure) I checked **A: Evening/Morning**. That automatically selected at red 7 the two A2 (Morning) means as the green subset and the two A1 (Evening) means as the blue subset. As in the **Ind groups contrasts** page, the green and blue squares mark the means of those two subsets. The main effect is the difference between those means, and is marked by the triangle on the difference axis. The values are shown at red 10 at the top: The main effect is $1.80 - 1.32 = 0.48$ $[-0.07, 1.03]$. My eyeballed value of 0.5 from Figure 15.1 was close. The main effect of Evening/Morning is a difference of around 0.5 out of 6 on the false memory scale, but the long CI extends from around 0 to 1, so there's considerable uncertainty in the estimate and little or no evidence of a positive difference. If anything, Morning shows more false memory than Evening, contrary to my initial speculation when stating Question 1.

esci 15.1 Open the **Ind groups 2 × 2** page of **ESCI intro chapters 10–16**. You should see summary statistics for the Frenda data, as in Figure 15.3. If not, clear any data, make sure the upper radio button at red 2 is selected, then at red 1 and red 3 type in the summary statistics and labels from Figure 15.3. You need enter only n, M, and s for each group. Compare your displayed means and CIs with Figures 15.1 and 15.2. Note how the means entered near red 3 correspond with the means displayed in the figure.

esci 15.2 Click at red 8 to show the Evening/Morning main effect and compare with Figure 15.2. Note the p value near red 10, top right, and compare with the CI on the main effect.

esci 15.3 Consider the Sleep/Nosleep main effect.

    a. Which group means are combined into subsets?
    b. Eyeball the overall mean for Sleep, and the same for Nosleep. What is your eyeball estimate of the Sleep/Nosleep main effect?
    c. Click at red 8 to display that main effect and check your eyeballing.

esci 15.4 Use that main effect and CI to answer our second research question, which asked about the effect of sleep deprivation.

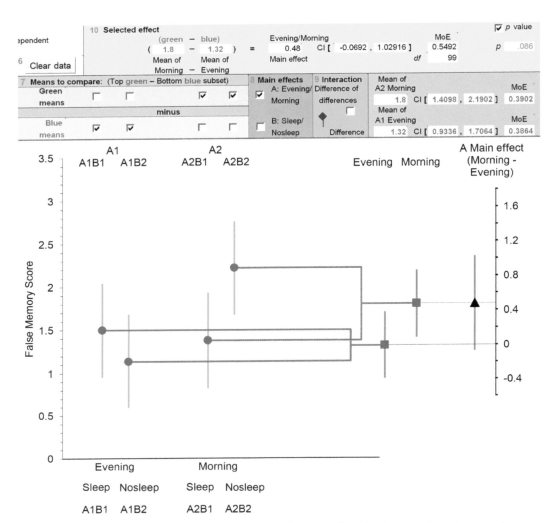

Figure 15.2. Means and 95% CIs as in Figure 15.1, with display of the main effect of A, the Evening/Morning IV, as selected by the checkbox at red 8. The squares mark the means for Evening (blue square) and Morning (green square), and the (Morning − Evening) difference is marked by the triangle on the difference axis. The value of the difference, its CI, and the p value are shown near red 10 in the upper panel. From **Ind groups 2 × 2**.

The Interaction

Our third research question asked about the interaction—the difference of the differences. We wish to compare the effect of sleep disruption for Evening and Morning. Let's eyeball, step by step:

1. Sleep disruption for Morning is the (Nosleep – Sleep) difference for the two Morning groups, or the (A2B2 – A2B1) difference between the two group means on the right in Figure 15.1. That looks to be about 0.8.
2. Sleep disruption for Evening is the (Nosleep – Sleep) difference for the two Evening groups, or (A1B2 – A1B1), the difference between the two means on the left in Figure 15.1. That looks like about −0.4.
3. The 2 × 2 interaction is the difference between those two differences, which is (Morning difference – Evening difference), or about 0.8 – (−0.4) = 1.2.

1 **Names**			5 C	
Dataset name	Frenda		95	
Measure	False Memory Score			

3 **Summary statistics**			Between-groups IV		
			A1	**A2**	
		Names	Evening	Morning	
			A1B1	A2B1	
		n	26	25	
	B1	M	1.5	1.38	
Name Sleep		s	1.38	1.5	
		MoE	0.54643	0.55725	
		UL	2.04643	1.93725	
		LL	0.95357	0.82275	
		df	99	99	
			A1B2	A2B2	
		n	26	26	
	B2	M	1.14	2.22	
Name Nosleep		s	0.96	1.68	
		MoE	0.54643	0.54643	
		UL	1.68643	2.76643	
		LL	0.59357	1.67357	
		df	99	99	

Between-groups independent variable (IV)

Figure 15.3. Summary statistics and labels for the Frenda data. From **Ind groups 2 × 2**.

You may have chosen to carry out the subtractions the other way round, in which case you should have found the same answer but with a minus sign. Either way is fine, but be consistent all through and take care to interpret correctly at the end.

Now click at red 9 to see how ESCI displays the interaction, as the difference of the two differences. Figure 15.4 shows what I saw. The two differences we are interested in are marked by the purple vertical lines ending in diamonds. Think of the diamonds as arrow heads indicating the sign of the difference: The difference on the right, for Morning, is positive (0.84) and the arrow points up; the difference on the left is negative (−0.36) and the arrow points down. The slanted dotted lines highlight how the two differences compare. The horizontal dotted lines show that the triangle marks the difference of the differences, with its CI, on the difference axis. As usual, all the values are shown near red 10 at the top.

 15.5 Click at red 9 to see the interaction. Compare with Figure 15.4.

a. Identify the values of the two differences reported near red 10, and explain how these differences are calculated from the group means.

b. Explain how the two differences are displayed in the figure, and together give the value marked by the triangle on the difference axis.

c. Compare with our three steps of eyeballing.

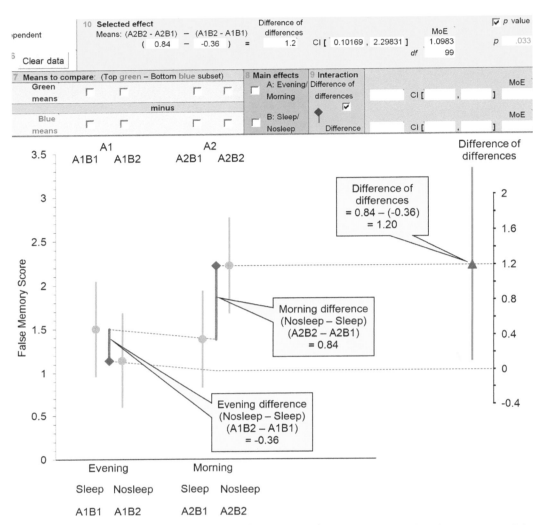

Figure 15.4. Means and 95% CIs as in Figure 15.2. The (Nosleep – Sleep) differences between the right two means and the left two means are marked by the purple lines ending in diamonds, and the values of the differences are reported near red 10 at the top. The slanted dotted lines make a comparison of the two differences. The difference between the differences is marked by the triangle on the difference axis, with its CI.

The difference of the differences, which is our measure of the 2 × 2 interaction, is reported near red 10 to be 1.20 [0.10, 2.30]. It combines the two Sleep/Nosleep differences that, as we noted earlier, go in opposite directions for Evening and Morning. The CI is long, but the effect size, 1.2 units out of 6, is quite large, and there's weak evidence that the true value is greater than zero. This suggests that sleep deprivation seemed to give increased false memory when the critical event was first presented in the morning, compared with the evening. In other words, sleep deprivation was, perhaps, relatively more disrupting for the initial entering of the critical event into memory (Morning condition) than when memory for the event had to be maintained overnight (Evening condition) before being retrieved in the morning. Interpreting that interaction was the main conclusion of the study, and the main contribution to understanding the nature of false memory and how it occurs: More false memory is likely when a person lacks sleep when they *witness* the critical event, compared with lacking sleep while *recalling* the event and being questioned about it.

It can be tricky to express an interaction in words and work out what it's telling us. The key is to refer back to the means in the figure, and focus on the differences, such as those indicated by the purple vertical lines with diamonds in Figure 15.4. Describe those differences in your own words, eyeball and note down their values, then do the same for the difference of differences, which is the interaction we want to understand.

Finally, I should note that the 2 × 2 interaction in a 2 × 2 design has one degree of freedom.

A Second Approach to the Interaction

Question 3 asked how (Nosleep – Sleep) might differ at Morning and Evening. Instead, we could ask how (Morning – Evening) might be different in the Sleep and Nosleep conditions. Fortunately, that turns out to be the same—there's only a single interaction in a 2 × 2 design, but there are two different ways to look at it.

 15.6 a. Identify on your screen, or in Figure 15.4, the two relevant means, and eyeball the (Morning – Evening) difference for the Nosleep condition.
   b. Do the same for the Sleep condition.
   c. Find the difference of your two eyeballed differences.
   d. Explain what that tells us, and compare with the interaction we discussed just above.

I suspect you found that the two routes led to the same result. There are four means and just one 2 × 2 interaction, with *df* = 1, but we can get to the interaction in two ways, depending on which pairs of means we consider first. The two routes to the interaction suggest alternative descriptions. Above I concluded that sleep deprivation (i.e., Sleep/Nosleep) seems to give increased false memory when the critical event is first presented in the morning, compared with the Evening condition. Taking the second approach, I'd say that later presentation of the critical event (i.e. Morning rather than Evening) gives increased false memory to a greater extent when sleep deprived than after normal sleep. You could try making sense of that last statement by matching it up with your eyeballed estimates of the (Morning – Evening) difference in the Sleep and Nosleep conditions.

? Quiz 15.1

1. The 2 × 2 two-way independent groups design has two DVs / IVs, each of which has 1 / 2 / 4 levels, and the design has a total of 1 / 2 / 4 groups.
2. A factorial design includes all combinations of the means / levels / differences of all DVs / IVs.
3. The main effect of independent variable A is
   a. its effect at the main level of independent variable B.
   b. the difference between the effect of A at the two levels of B.
   c. the mean of its main level.
   d. the overall effect of A, averaged over the two levels of B.

4. In a 2 × 2 independent groups design, independent variable A has $df =$ _____, independent variable B has $df =$ _____, and the interaction has $df =$ _____.
5. In a 2 × 2 independent groups design, the interaction is
   a. the difference between the two main effects.
   b. the extent that the effect of independent variable A is different at the two levels of independent variable B.
   c. the average of the A difference and the B difference.
   d. a nuisance, usually of no interest to the researcher.
6. Our general approach to analyzing the data from a study with an extended design is to choose _____ that correspond with the research questions, and for each one to calculate the _____ and its _____ as the basis for interpretation.

ASSUMPTIONS FOR THE TWO-WAY INDEPENDENT GROUPS DESIGN

Throughout the book, a basic assumption of our statistical model is usually that

■ the data for each group are a random sample from a population that's normally distributed.

In the previous chapter, for the one-way independent groups design, our model also assumed that

■ the samples are independent, and
■ variance is homogeneous across all groups. In other words, the population underlying each sample has the same standard deviation, σ.

> If the largest and smallest SDs differ by no more than a factor of about two, it's probably reasonable to assume homogeneity of variance and use s_p.

Analysis of the two-way independent groups design requires all those assumptions, and the **Ind groups 2 × 2** page makes them. The assumption of homogeneity of variance across all groups is often, but not always, reasonable. Examining the standard deviations of the individual groups provides some guidance. As a rough rule, we would like the largest SD to be not more than about twice the smallest SD if we are to rely on the assumption. For the Frenda example, the standard deviations for the four groups are shown as the values of s at red 3 in Figure 15.3. The four values are fairly similar, and so it's reasonable to assume homogeneity of variance.

PATTERNS OF MEANS FOR A 2 × 2 FACTORIAL DESIGN

Figures showing means are often revealing, and are especially useful for designs with more than one IV, and for understanding interactions. I'll take a simple case, and discuss how we can eyeball the main effects and interaction from a figure of means for a 2 × 2 factorial design.

> Where necessary, slightly offset means in a figure so that all CIs are easily visible, as in Figure 15.5.

I'll discuss a fictitious study of enjoyment ratings for different types of music in different settings. Suppose we have four independent groups who each rate their enjoyment of a single type of music (Rock or Classical) in a single setting (Party or Church). Figure 15.5 shows a possible pattern of the four group mean enjoyment ratings. The two Party means are offset horizontally by a small amount, so the two CIs can be clearly seen; similarly for the two Church means. That's good practice when designing figures, to avoid any risk

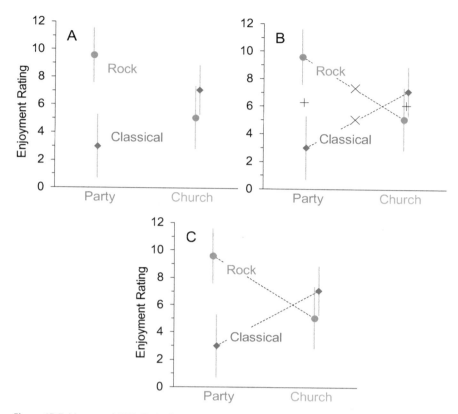

Figure 15.5. Means and 95% CIs for fictitious results of a 2 × 2 two-way independent groups study. In Panel B, + marks the means of Party and Church and × marks the means of Rock and Classical.

of CIs overlaying one another. Compare the display of means in Panel A with the way ESCI displays four group means, as in Figures 15.2 and 15.4. The only difference is that ESCI displaces the means a little further horizontally, so there's more space for clear labeling.

Main Effects

First, focus on Panel A and consider main effects. For the Party/Church main effect, we need the Party mean, which is simply the mean of the two means on the left. I eyeball those means to be about 3 (for Party, Classical) and 9.5 (Party, Rock), so the Party mean is about 6. I eyeball the Church mean also to be about 6. The Party/Church main effect is (Church − Party), which on my eyeballing is about 0.

15.7 Eyeball from Figure 15.5A the Rock and Classical means, and estimate the Rock/Classical main effect.

In Panel B, the two red Rock means are joined by a dotted line, as are the two blue Classical means. I include those lines to help our eyeballing, but they are different from the lines joining means in the previous chapter, where solid lines indicated a repeated measure. Here the lines are dotted, and all groups are independent, so there's no repeated measure. In Panel B, the Party and Church means are marked with a + symbol, and the Rock and Classical means with a × symbol. Check that these match your eyeballing. Comparing the two + symbols gives the Party/Church main effect, and the two × symbols the Rock/ Classical main effect.

The means in Panel A thus give us all we need to eyeball the two main effects. If it helps, first imagine Panel B and the + and × symbols, as an intermediate step.

The Interaction

For the 2 × 2 interaction of the Party/Church and Rock/Classical IVs, we need the difference of the differences. In Panel A, compare Rock and Classical for the two settings. For Party, the Rock mean is much larger than the Classical mean, but for Church it's somewhat lower, so there's a considerable difference between those two differences, which means a large interaction. Not surprisingly! The considerable difference of the differences corresponds to the crossing of the dotted lines, which is pictured most clearly in Panel C.

To estimate a value for the interaction, we can eyeball (Classical – Rock) at Church as around 7 – 5 = 2, and that difference at Party as around 3 – 9 = –6, so the interaction is around 2 – (–6) = 8, which is a very large distance on the enjoyment rating scale.

Figure 15.6 displays the same means again in Panel A, and two further possible patterns of means in Panels B and C.

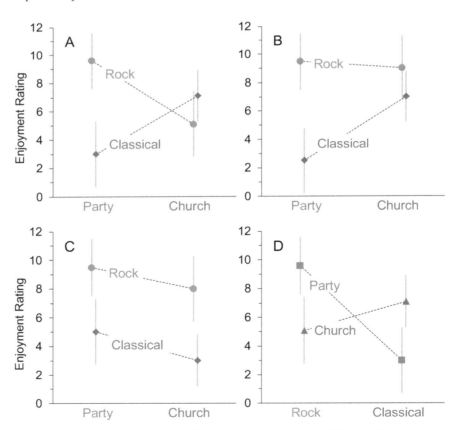

Figure 15.6. Patterns of means for the fictitious example shown in Figure 15.5. Panel A is the same as Panel C of Figure 15.5. Panels B and C show further possible patterns. Panel D is a different representation of the means in Panel A.

15.8 In Panel B of Figure 15.6, eyeball and describe the two main effects. Also describe the interaction.

15.9 Do the same for Panel C.

15.10 a. In Panel D, note the different labels. Compare the four means with those in Panel A.

b. Describe the two main effects and compare with our earlier discussion of Figure 15.5.

c. Describe the interaction, and compare with our discussion of the interaction in that figure.

I said that the considerable 2 × 2 interaction in Panel C of Figure 15.5 corresponds to the crossing of the dotted lines. In Figure 15.6, Panel B illustrates a smaller but still sizeable interaction, and the dotted lines don't cross but they have very different slopes. In Panel C, by contrast, there's little or no interaction and the lines are close to parallel. The general rule is that lines close to parallel signal little or no interaction, and lines far from parallel signal an interaction, whether or not the lines cross.

In Panel D, the IVs have been swapped, with Rock/Classical on the horizontal axis, rather than Party/Church. Panels A and D picture the same means, just arranged differently. The simple choice of which IV to mark on the horizontal axis can give a different picture, so might give a reader quite a different impression of the results. Because the four means are the same, if you eyeball the main effects and interaction in Panel D, you should reach the same conclusions as for Panel A.

As ever, think carefully about what any figure shows, and bring to mind other ways the same data could be represented. Transforming in your mind's eye between Panel A and Panel D is a bit tricky, but it's important when you see a figure like Panel A to remember that there is an alternative. A bit of practice and you'll be able to see Panel A and sketch what Panel D would look like, even if creating it in your mind's eye is a challenge.

> Lines with quite different slopes indicate an interaction, as in Panels A, B, and D of Figure 15.6. ◀

15.11 a. Sketch the alternative version of Panel B of Figure 15.6.

b. Describe the main effects and interaction. Compare with your answer to Exercise 15.8.

In Figures 15.5 and 15.6, the CIs are in gray because here we're focusing on patterns of means. In practice, of course, we need to consider CIs as well when we discuss or interpret any mean, main effect, or interaction.

In those two figures, the dotted lines help us see the 2 × 2 interaction, and their comparative slopes suggest whether the interaction is around zero, small, or large. Look back to Figure 15.1 and imagine a dotted line joining the Evening and Morning means for Sleep, and another joining Evening and Morning for Nosleep. Your mind's eye should be seeing something like Figure 15.7. The very different slopes indicate a large interaction, agreeing with Figure 15.4, which displayed the interaction as the difference of differences.

Moderation

Here's one more way to think about an interaction. Panel A of Figure 15.6 shows the main effect of the Rock/Classical IV, which is the overall effect of type of music on average enjoyment ratings. The second IV is Party/Church, which we can think of as altering or *moderating* the effect of Rock/Classical on

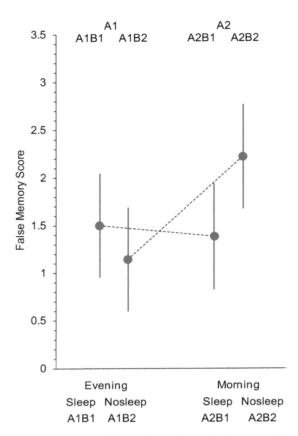

Figure 15.7. Same as Figure 15.1, but with dotted lines joining the Evening and Morning means for the Sleep condition, and the same for Nosleep. The very different slopes of the lines indicate a large interaction.

enjoyment. Yes, setting alters, or *moderates* the effect that type of music has on enjoyment. Whatever wording we use, it's the interaction that tells us about such moderation.

A moderator is simply a variable that alters the effect of another variable.

> A *moderating variable*, or *moderator*, is an IV that alters the effect of another IV on the DV.

That's a bit tricky, so it's probably worth reading all that again, while referring back to the figure and the earlier wording we used when discussing the interaction of setting and type of music.

It's vital to note that I'm not merely saying that the second IV also has an effect on the DV. *Moderation* refers to the influence the second IV has on *the effect of the first IV on the DV*. That's the interaction. If there's no interaction, there's no moderation.

Moderation refers to the influence the second IV has on the effect of the first IV on the DV.

Here's another example of a moderator: Greater affluence is generally associated with people eating more meat. Level of affluence is our first IV and the DV is amount of meat consumed. However, for vegetarians that relation does not hold at all. Of course! The moderator is a dichotomous IV, Vegetarian/Nonvegetarian, and it's a very strong moderator of the effect of affluence on the amount of meat eaten. The two IVs interact strongly: For non-vegetarians, there may be a large effect of affluence on meat consumption, but, for vegetarians, there's no effect at all—meat consumption is zero, no matter how great the affluence. Strong interaction goes together with strong moderation.

Which variable is the moderator? Any time there's an interaction, we can regard *either* variable as the moderator—just as we can think about the interaction in either of two different ways. We could choose setting (Party/Church) as the first IV and note its overall effect on enjoyment. Then type of music (Rock/Classical), strongly moderates that effect of setting on enjoyment. Whenever we have an interaction, we can say that either variable moderates the effect of the other. Choose whichever way to state the moderation—and whichever way to look at the interaction—makes most sense in the particular case.

Given an interaction of two IVs, we can say that either IV moderates the effect of the other on the DV.

In Chapter 9 we discussed moderators in the context of meta-analysis. There is a parallel with moderators as we're discussing here, but if this is confusing, simply skip this paragraph. In meta-analysis, a moderator is a variable that accounts for heterogeneity, meaning effect size differences over studies. So a moderator is a variable that may account for differences in the effect of primary interest, which is the effect size displayed in the forest plot. Therefore, with meta-analysis, as in this chapter, a moderator is a variable associated with changes in some effect that is of primary research interest.

Can we say that a moderator *causes* the change in the effect of the first IV? As usual, that depends on our design. If we have random assignment of participants to groups or conditions, most likely we can draw a causal conclusion. If not, we can't. With moderators in meta-analysis no random assignment is possible, so we are noting an association and can't justify any causal conclusion. Similarly, observing a 2 × 2 interaction in a study that lacks random assignment means that we have moderation but no grounds for a causal conclusion. I said above that moderation refers to the second IV altering the effect of the first IV. That sounds like the moderator causing the change in the effect. Being more careful, I should have said that moderation refers to an association between the moderator and a difference in the primary effect. However, that's probably harder to understand when the idea is new.

Moderation doesn't necessarily imply causality.

Why did I include this section on moderators? First, because moderation and interaction are often talked about interchangeably, so you need to know that the two are closely related. Second, a common research strategy is to study some interesting main effect, for example that affluence is associated with eating more meat. Then the next step is to investigate that relationship further, especially by considering how other variables may change it. To what extent does that primary relationship of affluence and meat consumption perhaps differ in different cultures? In past centuries rather than now? In rural communities rather than urban? Among vegetarians! Those are all questions about possible moderators of the primary effect. After investigating interesting effects using the one-IV techniques of Chapters 7, 8, and 14, you can consider possible moderators of those effects, which means you need the two-IV techniques of this chapter and you need to consider interactions.

After studying some effect, it can be a good research strategy to investigate possible moderators of that effect.

Whenever you read about some interesting effect and are wondering about what study comes next, your first thought should be a replication. After that, it's often most useful to consider studies that examine possible moderators of the effect. To what extent is the effect moderated by gender—perhaps it occurs more strongly with women than men? By level of stress—perhaps much less strong when a person is highly stressed? By age—perhaps the effect is very different in children? What about underwater, or while riding a bicycle? Brainstorming about possible moderators can be great fun, as well as scientifically productive.

15.12 a. Consider the pen–laptop study. What is the primary effect?

b. Suggest a possible moderator of that effect and briefly say why.

15.13 a. Consider the Thomason studies of critical thinking. What is the primary effect?

b. Suggest a possible moderator of that effect and briefly say why.

CHOOSING CONTRASTS

In Chapter 14, I discussed the following data analysis strategy:

▶───────────
For two-way designs, use planned and exploratory data analysis.

1. *Planned analysis.* Specify a few chosen effects in advance. Analyze these and present the results with confidence.
2. *Exploratory analysis.* Following planned analysis, you may, if you wish, examine any effect; however, any conclusion is merely speculative.
3. When reporting research, distinguish clearly between the results of planned analysis and speculations based on exploration.

I recommend exactly the same strategy for the designs we discuss in this chapter.

For the 2 × 2 two-way independent groups design, as we've been discussing, there are four group means and therefore a total of $df = 3$ for any effects based on those means. We have been discussing two main effects, each with $df = 1$, and a 2 × 2 interaction, also with $df = 1$, for a total of three degrees of freedom. Often those two main effects and the interaction are the effects that correspond most closely with the research questions, and, therefore, we'll nominate those as the three planned effects to "use up" our three degrees of freedom. That's what I did for the Frenda study. A big advantage is that the three are independent, meaning that they answer three quite separate questions.

However, there are other options. We could examine any comparisons or contrasts of the four group means, either as planned or exploratory analysis. Suppose in the Frenda study you were especially interested in the effect of sleep deprivation, not as a main effect, but specifically for evening and, separately, for morning presentation of the critical event. You might specify:

1. A comparison of the Nosleep and Sleep means, for Evening.

▶───────────
A *simple main effect* is the effect of one IV at a single level of another IV.

That comparison is referred to as a *simple main effect*, because it examines the effect of one IV (Sleep/Nosleep) at a single level of the other IV (the Evening level of the Evening/Morning IV).

2. A comparison of the Nosleep and Sleep means, for Morning.

That's another simple main effect. To examine it, I clicked twice at red 7 in **Ind groups 2 × 2** to compare just those two group means. Figure 15.8 shows what I saw. The comparison we want is shown as the triangle on the difference axis, and the values are reported above, at red 10. Of course, you could display in a similar way the first simple main effect, which I specified just above.

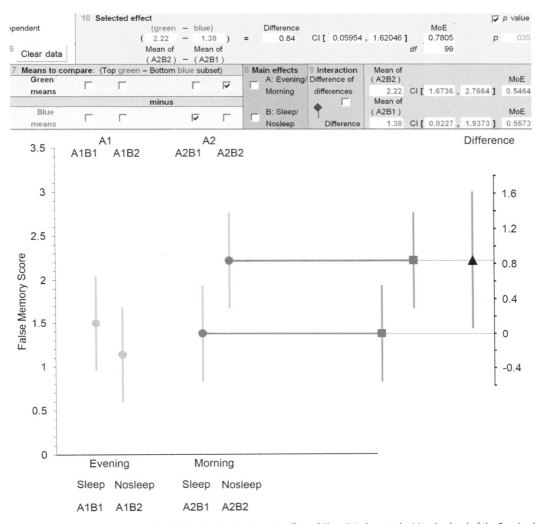

Figure 15.8. Same as Figure 15.2, but displaying the simple main effect of Sleep/Nosleep at the Morning level of the Evening/ Morning IV.

3. The interaction, which we can think of as a comparison of those two simple main effects.

The three effects listed above—two simple main effects and the interaction— are not separate, because, as Point 3 notes, the interaction is the difference between the two simple main effects. If that's puzzling, identify those two simple main effects and the interaction in Figure 15.7. Maybe draw and label your own picture of means, and try to explain to a friend. Interactions can be tricky to think about, but pictures should help.

If you felt those three effects—two simple main effects and the interaction—matched your research questions, you could nominate the three as your planned analysis, even though they are not independent. If, however, you nominated also one or two main effects, you would be asking more questions than there are degrees of freedom (total $df = 3$) and the questions would overlap even more. As usual, after collecting the data and carrying out the planned analysis, you could elect to explore further by examining any effects that seem interesting—but any conclusion would be only speculative.

So far I've emphasized the wide choice of contrasts you have, even with a 2 × 2 design. Shortly we'll consider larger designs and these, of course, offer even more choice. When choosing contrasts, the most important guideline is that the planned contrasts should reflect as closely as possible your research questions, which should have been chosen and stated early in the planning stage. However, I should highlight two sets of contrasts for 2 × 2 designs, because these probably cover the majority of studies with a 2 × 2 factorial design, whether the two IVs are both between-groups, both within-group, or one of each.

Main effects and interaction. This is probably the most common choice and was our first approach for the Frenda study. The contrasts are:

1. Main effect of A. The main effect of the Evening/Morning IV.
2. Main effect of B. The main effect of the Sleep/Nosleep IV.
3. Interaction of A and B. The difference of the differences. To what extent is the effect of the Sleep/Nosleep IV different at the two levels of the Evening/ Morning IV? Equivalently, to what extent is the effect of the Evening/ Morning IV different at the two levels of the Sleep/Nosleep IV?

Interaction and selected simple main effects. As I mentioned earlier, often the main reason for choosing a 2 × 2 design is that the interaction is of particular interest. One of our approaches to the Frenda study focused on the interaction. The contrasts could be:

1. The interaction of A and B—focus on the extent the (Nosleep – Sleep) difference may differ between Morning and Evening
2. A selected simple main effect that throws light on the interaction—perhaps the (Nosleep – Sleep) difference at Morning
3. A second simple main effect that does the same—the (Nosleep – Sleep) difference at Evening

Even for the more complex designs that we'll discuss later in this chapter, keep in mind those two common approaches to selecting planned contrasts, especially if you ever feel there are too many options and it's hard to choose! It's time to step beyond the 2 × 2 independent groups design.

BEYOND THE TWO-WAY INDEPENDENT GROUPS DESIGN

We've been discussing the simplest factorial design, which has two between-groups IVs, each with just two levels. There are three ways to expand to more complex factorial designs:

■ Change one or two of the IVs from between-groups to within-group IVs. (Recall that a within-group IV is also referred to as a repeated measure.) Perhaps ask the same people about their enjoyment of Rock and Classical music, so Rock/Classical is now a repeated measure.

- Increase the number of levels of one or more of the IVs to more than two. Perhaps consider Jazz as well as Rock and Classical, so there are now three levels of the IV of music type.
- Add further IVs to give three-way, four-way, or even larger designs. Perhaps add participant age as a third IV, and collect music enjoyment ratings for different types of music, in different settings, from people in a number of different age groups. That's a three-way design, which may be bordering on being too complicated to fully grasp, even for experienced researchers.

I'll discuss examples to illustrate various possibilities, although I won't be carrying out much data analysis because that's beyond the scope of this book and beyond what ESCI can do. Consult the workbooks available at the book's website (tiny.cc/itns) for data analysis possibilities offered by other software. For all factorial designs, our analysis strategy remains the same: For the planned analysis, specify effects that correspond to the research questions, then, following data collection and planned analysis, optionally conduct exploratory analysis. Often the effects of most interest will be effects with one degree of freedom, like those we have examined in the previous chapter and earlier in this chapter. In other words, it's often of most interest to focus on selected comparisons, contrasts, and 2 × 2 interactions that are the difference of differences. Any such effect has $df = 1$, and so we can find the mean and CI, and use these to interpret the effect.

> ◀ For any factorial design, carry out planned analysis, followed optionally by exploration.

2 × 2 DESIGNS WITH A REPEATED MEASURE

Mindfulness and the Brain: An Example RCT

If we change one of the between-groups IVs to a repeated measure, we get the simplest *randomized control trial* (RCT) design, which is a two-way factorial design with one repeated measure. This design is also referred to as a *mixed design*, because it includes at least one between-groups IV and one repeated measure.

> ◀ A *randomized control trial* (RCT) has a two-way factorial design with one repeated measure.

A *mixed design* includes at least one between-groups IV and one repeated measure.

My example is a well-known study of mindfulness meditation by Hölzel et al. (2011). People who wanted to reduce stress, and were not experienced meditators, were assigned to a Meditation ($N = 16$) or a Control ($N = 17$) group. The Meditation group participated in eight weeks of intensive training and practice of mindfulness meditation. The researchers used a questionnaire to assess a range of emotional and cognitive variables both before (Pretest) and after (Posttest) the eight-week period. All assessment was conducted while the participants were not meditating. The study is notable for including brain imaging to assess possible changes in participants' brains from Pretest to Posttest. The researchers measured *gray matter concentration*, which increases in brain regions that experience higher and more frequent activation. The researchers expected that the hippocampus may be especially responsive to meditation because it has been implicated in the regulation of emotion, arousal, and general responsiveness. They therefore included in their planned analysis the assessment of any changes to gray matter concentration in the hippocampus.

Figure 15.9 reports means and 95% CIs for gray matter concentration in the hippocampus at Pretest and Posttest for the two groups. Control/Meditation is, of course, a between-groups IV whereas Pretest/Posttest is a repeated measure, as indicated by the solid lines in the figure.

Here are a couple of questions to think about and discuss, perhaps while you relax to whatever type of music earns your highest enjoyment ratings.

1. Which effects would you nominate for your planned analysis of these data? Or, rather, which would you have nominated at the start of the study, before collecting data or seeing Figure 15.9?
2. Which effects in Figure 15.9 can you assess by using the displayed CIs? Which require some other CI?

 Pause here, as you enjoy the music and consider those questions. Perhaps meditate for a while.

▶────────────
In an RCT, the interaction is likely to be of most interest.
────────────

Without looking at the results in Figure 15.9, it's safe to say that the main interest is in the possible effect of the meditation training, estimated by the (Posttest − Pretest) change. However, participants in the control group may also have shown change, simply because of the passage of time or because they were part of the study and undertook the Pretest and Posttest. We therefore want to compare the (Posttest − Pretest) change in the Meditation group with that change in the Control group. That's the interaction, which is, therefore, the first effect we nominate for planned analysis:

▨ The 2 × 2 interaction of Pretest/Posttest and Control/Meditation. It's probably most natural to think of this as the difference of the two (Posttest − Pretest) differences: To what extent—if at all—did the Meditation group show a greater increase in hippocampal gray matter concentration than the Control group?

In addition, we might choose the two simple main effects of Pretest/Posttest:

▨ The (Posttest − Pretest) difference for the Meditation group, which estimates change attributable to the meditation training and practice, and any other

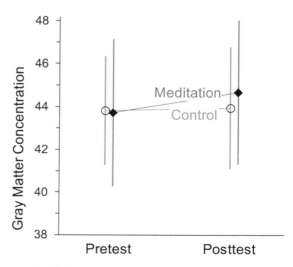

Figure 15.9. Means and 95% CIs for gray matter concentration in the hippocampus, for the RCT of mindfulness meditation reported by Hölzel et al. (2011). Solid lines indicate that Pretest/Posttest is a repeated measure. Data courtesy of Britta Hölzel.

possible causes, including the passage of time and the experience of being in the study and undertaking the Pretest and Posttest.

- The (Posttest – Pretest) difference for the Control group, which estimates change attributable to any of those possible causes other than the meditation.

Those three contrasts are not independent, so when making the interpretation keep in mind that they are not asking three separate questions. In addition to the interaction, instead of those two *simple* main effects you might have selected the two main effects. Or perhaps you chose the two simple main effects of Control/Meditation, meaning the (Meditation – Control) difference at Pretest, and the same difference at Posttest. In any case it's probably best to specify at most three effects for planned analysis, because in a 2 × 2 study we have *df* = 3 for effects based on the group means.

My second question asked about using the CIs displayed in Figure 15.9 to assess effects. All the CIs in the figure are much longer than any difference between means, so we might at first think that the study cannot have estimated any effect with useful precision, which would be very disappointing. However, there's hope—because we have a repeated measure. Remember from Chapter 8 that with a repeated measure we can't assess the difference by noting the overlap of the two CIs—the overlap rule is relevant only for independent means. This is good news, because with a repeated measure the CI on the difference may be usefully short.

Consider, for example, the (Meditation – Control) difference at Posttest. That comparison involves two means that are independent because they refer to the separate Meditation and Control groups. We can therefore eyeball the difference between the means as about 1, and note that the CI on that difference would be a little longer than either of the separate CIs, indicating very low precision for estimating that difference. The overlap rule tells us that, because

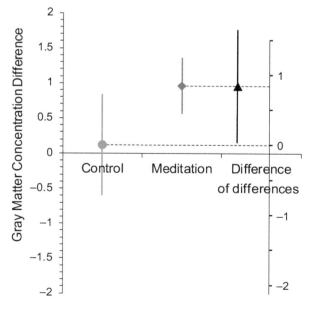

Figure 15.10. Means and 95% CIs for the (Posttest – Pretest) difference in gray matter concentration in the hippocampus, for the Control and Meditation groups. The difference of those differences, which is the interaction, is displayed with its CI on the axis on the right. Data courtesy of Britta Hölzel.

the two CIs overlap almost entirely, there's no evidence of any population difference between the means.

What about the (Posttest – Pretest) difference for Meditation? Those two means are not independent, because Pretest/Posttest is a repeated measure. Therefore the long CIs displayed in the figure are not relevant for assessing that difference. As in Chapter 8 for the paired design, the overlap rule doesn't apply and we need further information, beyond what Figure 15.9 presents, to calculate the CI we need. In the Meditation group, the correlation of Pretest and Posttest scores is very high, $r = .99$, and so the CI on the (Posttest – Pretest) difference for Meditation is pleasingly short. That difference is 0.96 [0.56, 1.36]. In the Control group, the correlation is also high, $r = .97$, and the (Posttest – Pretest) difference is 0.12 [−0.61, 0.84]. Those two differences and their CIs are displayed in Figure 15.10. The especially high correlation for Meditation gave an especially short CI, with MoE of only 0.40.

The interaction of Control/Meditation and Pretest/Posttest is the effect of greatest interest. It's the difference of those two differences, which is 0.84 [0.03, 1.65]. That difference of differences is displayed with its CI on the axis on the right in the figure. The study thus estimates that gray matter concentration in the hippocampus increased by around 0.8 units more, after eight weeks of mindfulness meditation, than for the control participants. With knowledge of the gray matter measure and the research context we'd be able to comment about how large and important a change of around 0.8 might be, and perhaps how likely it is to endure. The CI was long, as Figure 15.10 illustrates, with the lower limit around zero, so the study provided just a little evidence the population increase was greater than zero. (The p value was .04.)

Hölzel et al. (2011) used ANOVA to analyze the data, and for the interaction reported $F(1, 29) = 4.92$, $p = .04$. The two approaches reported the same p value and therefore agreed in finding a little evidence of a non-zero interaction. If you read such an ANOVA report with $p = .04$ for an interaction, you could bring to mind a figure like Figure 15.10, with the CI on the difference of differences extending approximately to zero.

▶ In an RCT, the interaction and differences of most interest *cannot* be assessed in a figure of means and CIs like Figure 15.9. A figure of differences, like Figure 15.10, is needed.

15.14 a. Consider Figure 15.9. Identify an effect that can be assessed in that figure and explain why.
b. Identify an effect that can't be assessed using the information in that figure, and explain why.

15.15 Consider the main effect of Pretest/Posttest. Can it be assessed in that figure? Explain.

15.16 Consider Figure 15.10.

a. Explain what the first mean displayed, labeled "Control" represents and how it relates to what's displayed in Figure 15.9.
b. Do the same for the second mean displayed, labeled "Meditation".
c. Explain what the triangle represents. How does its CI relate to the two CIs at left in the figure?

Assumptions and calculations for an RCT. In Chapter 14, we first considered independent groups, and saw means and CIs for various contrasts. Then for the one-way repeated measure design we considered contrasts and their CIs, although the calculations involved the repeated measure and were, therefore, a little more complicated. We also needed the additional assumption that correlation is homogeneous. I noted that ESCI does not have a page for the repeated measure design, although such a page would look similar to the **Ind groups comparisons** or **Ind groups contrasts** pages, but would require entry of the full data.

For two-way factorial designs the pattern is similar. With two between-groups IVs, **Ind groups 2 × 2** calculates and displays contrasts and the interaction (the difference of differences), with CIs. With one or more repeated measures, calculations involving a repeated measure are more complicated and need additional assumptions like the homogeneity of correlation. Again, ESCI does not have a page for designs with a repeated measure, for example the RCT. However, here are two exercises that illustrate how you can use ESCI to carry out the analysis we saw above for the Hölzel 2 × 2 RCT.

15.17 Table 15.2 provides summary gray matter concentration data from the Hölzel study. For the Control data, enter the Pretest and Posttest means and SDs into the **Summary paired** page of **ESCI intro chapters 3–8**. Don't forget that for paired data like these you also need to enter the SD of the differences, s_{diff}.

   a. Find the (Posttest – Pretest) difference and its CI, and compare with what I stated above in the text.

   b. Do the same for the Meditation data.

15.18 We would like to compare (Posttest – Pretest) for Control with the same for Meditation.

   a. Is this a between-groups or a within-group comparison? Do you have appropriate information in the table to calculate the comparison and its CI?

   b. Use an appropriate ESCI page to calculate that comparison and its CI. Again compare with the values I stated above in the text.

Those two exercises illustrated how you could analyze a 2 × 2 RCT study, given appropriate summary data as in Table 15.2. The steps were:

1. Compare Pretest and Posttest for Control, using **Summary paired**.
2. Compare Pretest and Posttest for Meditation, using **Summary paired** again.
3. Compare the (Posttest – Pretest) differences for Control with the same for Meditation, using **Summary two**.

If you had the full data you could, of course, use the same three steps, but using **Data paired** twice, then **Data two**. If in doubt, a good general approach is to sketch a picture of means and CIs, focus on whichever effect corresponds to your research question, then find a way to calculate the comparison and CI you need.

Conclusions from this RCT. Reflect for a moment on the RCT for mindfulness meditation that we've been discussing. What lessons about design and data analysis should we take from this example? Also, considering the main result

	Control (n = 17)			Meditation (n = 16)		
	Pretest	Posttest	(Posttest – Pretest)	Pretest	Posttest	(Posttest – Pretest)
M	43.81	43.93	0.12	43.71	44.67	0.96
s	4.91	5.51		6.43	6.30	
s_{diff}			1.41			0.76

Table 15.2 Summary Gray Matter Concentration Data, From Hölzel et al. (2011)

about brain changes resulting from meditation, what questions do you have? What further research would you like to see?

> For two-way designs, examine effects having one degree of freedom, where these match the research questions.

Considering the design and data analysis, the first lesson is that our general strategy of examining effects having one degree of freedom applies here also. These effects include comparisons, simple main effects, and interactions (difference of differences). Prefer such contrasts, assuming of course that they address the research questions.

> A repeated measure gives increased precision when its correlation is high.

The Hölzel study also illustrates dramatically the lesson we've learned many times: A paired design—in fact any design with a repeated measure—can give increased precision, and greatly increased precision if the correlation of the levels of the repeated measure (e.g., Pretest and Posttest) is high. MoE for the CIs in Figure 15.9 ranges from 2.5 to 3.4, whereas MoE is much smaller for the CIs in Figure 15.10, with MoE for the interaction being 0.8. Seeing Figure 15.9 for the first time, you might be greatly discouraged by the long CIs, but then you'd remember that Pretest/Posttest is a repeated measure and that the differences and interaction of most interest can't be assessed in that figure. You'd be much encouraged to see Figure 15.10, which displays shorter CIs on the differences and the crucial interaction.

The evidence of brain changes in Figure 15.10 is not strong, but Hölzel et al. (2011) reported other measures and analyses as well. In other words, they used a strategy of finding converging approaches to support their main conclusion, which was that training and practice in mindfulness meditation not only leads to improvements in psychological well-being—indicated by their analysis of the questionnaire data—but also to measurable changes in the brain. Further, they speculated that the brain changes are likely to be, at least to some extent, enduring. We would now like one or more replications of these findings, and also investigation of how long and how fully the brain changes endure.

The Hölzel et al. (2011) findings provide further evidence that brain and behavior are tightly integrated, and that even the adult brain is plastic and can change in response to changed behavior. That's a dramatically different view of the brain than was generally accepted as recently as a decade or two ago. It's enormously exciting to think that what we work at, what we learn, and how we conduct our lives can change our brains, which may in turn influence what we can do in the future. As I mentioned in the *Making the Most of This Book* section, perhaps working at retrieval of tricky ideas does change your brain and make you smarter. It's worth persisting!

? Quiz 15.2

1. To analyze an independent groups design, we usually assume _____ of variance across all _____.
2. That assumption is probably reasonable if
   a. considering the group SDs, the largest SD is no more than about twice the smallest.
   b. considering all pairs of groups, all the correlations are heterogeneous.
   c. the group means are all related in a linear fashion.
   d. the DV has interval scaling.
3. In a 2 × 2 factorial design, there is little or no interaction if the dotted lines joining means
   a. differ in slope but don't cross.
   b. differ greatly in slope and cross.
   c. are close to parallel.
   d. meet, or almost meet, at a point.

4. A simple main / subsidiary effect is the correlation / effect of one IV at a single level / mean of another IV.

5. In a 2 × 2 RCT, the figure showing the 4 means and CIs allows us to assess comparisons that involve only the between-groups / within-group IV, but not comparisons that involve the between-groups / within-group IV.

6. In an RCT, the interaction is likely to be estimated with greater precision if the correlation / difference of the DV at different levels of the repeated measure is lower / higher.

The Seductive Allure of Neuroscience: Two Repeated Measures

After all that discussion of gray matter in the brain, consider this question: Is the explanation of an interesting psychological phenomenon more convincing if it includes reference to neuroscience, even if the neuroscience information is irrelevant to the explanation? Weisberg et al. (2008) reported investigation of that question in an article with the arresting title: *The seductive allure of neuroscience explanations*. One of their studies was a two-way design with two repeated measures, so once again we have two IVs, but this time they are both repeated measures. Once again we have a 2 × 2 factorial design, but this time only one group of participants. A single group of $N = 22$ students from a mid-level cognitive neuroscience course read brief descriptions of psychological phenomena, each of which was followed by an explanation. The explanation was Good or Bad, and was presented either Without or With neuroscience information—which, when provided, was irrelevant to the quality of the explanation. The IVs were thus Good/Bad explanations, presented Without/With neuroscience. Students rated how satisfactory they found each explanation, on a 7-point scale from −3 (very unsatisfying) to 3 (very satisfying). All students read and rated items with all four types of explanation, reflecting the fact that the two IVs were both repeated measures.

15.19 Before looking ahead at the results, recommend which effects should be nominated for the planned analysis.

Figure 15.11 shows the means and CIs for the four conditions. It would be logical to display solid lines joining the means to signal the two repeated measures, but adding four solid lines to the figure gives a visual mess, and I won't even include it to illustrate. It's a highly valuable convention to use solid lines to signal a repeated measure, but I can't recall ever having seen a figure in which the convention has been used for more than a single repeated measure. As usual, when seeing a figure with means and CIs it's vital to know the status of every IV: between-groups or repeated measure. For two repeated measures, as in Figure 15.11, solid lines joining means for both IVs are impractical, so the figure caption must tell us. Instead I've added two dotted lines to help us see the interaction.

> With more than one repeated measure IV, don't join means in a figure with solid lines, but explain in the caption.

15.20 a. In Figure 15.11, make eyeball estimates of the two main effects and the interaction.
    b. Is there any effect that can be assessed using the information in the figure? Explain.
    c. Consider the CIs on the main effects and the interaction. How would you expect them to compare in length with the CIs in the figure? Why?

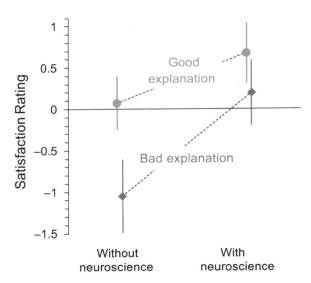

Figure 15.11. Means and 95% CIs for ratings, on a scale from −3 to 3, of satisfaction with explanations of psychological phenomena. One group of N = 22 students participated. The two repeated measure IVs were Good/Bad explanations, and Without/With neuroscience information. Data from Weisberg et al. (2008).

I suspect you concluded that there's no comparison of means that we can assess using the information in the figure. Because both IVs are repeated measures, we need to have the full data to be able to calculate CIs for any difference, including the main effects, simple main effects, and interaction.

Weisberg et al. (2008) applied ANOVA and reported:

Main effect of Good/Bad explanations, $F(1, 21) = 50.9$, $p < .001$.
Main effect of Without/With neuroscience, $F(1, 21) = 47.1$, $p < .001$.
Interaction, $F(1, 21) = 8.7$, $p = .008$.

► Use *p* values reported for ANOVA to help eyeball the CIs on effects of interest, and thus assist interpretation.

In Exercise 15.20 you eyeballed point estimates of the main effects and interaction. The very small *p* values from the ANOVA tell us that the CIs on those point estimates would all be somewhat distant from zero—we have very strong evidence that all those effects are non-zero.

15.21 Using your eyeball estimates of the main effects and interaction, and the discussion above, interpret the set of results.

15.22 Describe the interaction in terms of one IV moderating the effect of the other.

15.23 a. Discuss the appropriateness of using this design to investigate the questions addressed by Weisberg et al.

b. Compare with at least one alternative design, and make your recommendation.

Now we step beyond 2 × 2 designs.

EXTENDING BEYOND 2 × 2 DESIGNS

Study Techniques: An Example of a 3 × 2 Design

As a first step beyond 2 × 2 designs, I'll discuss a 3 × 2 example. One of the authors of *Make It Stick* (Brown et al., 2014), Mark McDaniel, and colleagues reported an investigation (McDaniel et al., 2009) of a study technique that emphasized retrieval: the 3R (read-recite-review) technique. In one of their studies they assigned students to three independent groups ($n = 24$ for each), which used 3R, or note-taking (Note), or rereading (Reread) strategies to study text passages that presented new information. In all conditions, students were allowed to spend as much time as they wished using the assigned technique to study each text. Students were later asked to recall as much as they could of the content of the passages, the measure being the number out of a possible 30 idea units in each passage that the student could recall. For half the passages, recall was a few minutes after presentation (Immediate), and for the other half recall was one week later (Delayed). Every student undertook both Immediate and Delayed recall. Therefore, the 3R/Note/Reread IV was between-groups, and the Immediate/Delayed IV was a repeated measure. The design was thus 3 × 2, with one repeated measure. Incidentally, why not call it a 2 × 3 design? There is a custom that between-groups IVs are listed first, followed by any repeated measures. However, the custom is not always followed, so be sure to make very clear the status (between-groups or repeated measure) of every IV. ESCI does not have a page for this design, but such a page would be an extension of **Ind groups 2 × 2** that permitted one between-groups IV to have three levels, and recognized the other IV as a repeated measure.

Our analysis, first planned then perhaps exploratory, will focus on effects with one degree of freedom. These may include contrasts, main effects, simple main effects, and 2 × 2 interactions—such an interaction being a difference of differences.

Before looking ahead to see the results, we need to think about the aims of the study, identify the main research questions, and state the corresponding effects that we'd specify for the planned analysis—preregistered of course.

Note-taking and rereading are commonly used study strategies, so we can regard them as control or reference conditions. Our primary interest is probably in how 3R compares, so my first step is to combine Note and Reread. The + symbols in the figure mark the means of the Note and Reread means. I'll refer to that combination as NoteReread, and I'll focus first on the (3R − NoteReread) difference. I'll examine that difference for Immediate, and for Delayed, and then I'll examine the difference between those two differences, which is the interaction of NoteReread/3R and Immediate/Delayed. All those effects have one degree of freedom, and so, given the full data, it would be possible to calculate a point estimate and CI for each. Those estimates and CIs would be the results of our planned analysis and the main basis for our conclusions from the study.

Combining means over levels, such as Note and Read to form NoteRead, is often a useful strategy for obtaining effects with one degree of freedom that are of research interest, and also readily interpretable. Subset contrasts, as we discussed in Chapter 14, are a simple example of such combination of means over levels.

For an IV with more than two levels, consider combining some levels to get effects of interest with one degree of freedom.

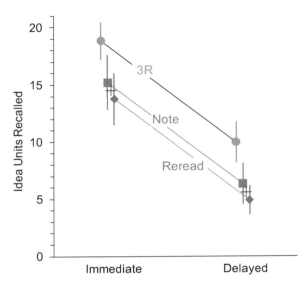

Figure 15.12. Means and 95% CIs for number of idea units recalled from a text passage, maximum 30. Three groups each of $n = 24$ students participated, one group for each of the 3R, note-taking (Note), and rereading (Reread) study strategies. Recall was Immediate, or Delayed by one week, and Immediate/Delayed was a repeated measure. The + symbols indicate the means of the Note and Reread means. Data from McDaniel et al. (2009), and courtesy Mark McDaniel.

Now examine Figure 15.12, which displays means and CIs. Identify our planned contrasts. Also identify which effects we could assess using the CIs displayed, and others for which we would need further information and other CIs.

 That's worth spending some time on. Find someone for a chat about it...

15.24 a. Make an eyeball estimate from Figure 15.12 of the (3R – NoteReread) difference at Immediate. Do the same for Delayed.
   b. MoE for the CI on those differences is roughly 2. Interpret those differences and make conclusions about 3R compared with the other commonly used study techniques.

15.25 a. Compare those two differences. Is there any sign of an interaction? Interpret.
   b. What do the lines in the figure say about that interaction?

You might have chosen other effects, either in advance for planned analysis, or later as exploration. For example, if you wish to compare the two commonly used techniques, you could examine the (Note – Reread) differences. If you feel that only the Delayed condition is important for student learning, you might examine some simple main effects at Delayed, perhaps (3R – Note) and (3R – Reread).

McDaniel et al. (2009) conducted a 3 × 2 ANOVA and reported:

▦ For the 3R/Note/Reread main effect, $F(2, 69) = 10.80, p < .001$.
▦ For the Immediate/Delayed main effect, $F(1, 69) = 328.70, p < .001$.
▦ For the interaction of those two IVs, $F < 1$, which means p is large (actually $p > .3$ here).

The 3R/Note/Reread main effect has three levels, so $df = 2$ for the differences among the three means. The very small p for that main effect allowed the researchers to reject the null hypothesis that all three population means are the same, and provides strong evidence for one or more differences among the three means. The researchers examined post hoc contrasts and found statistically significant differences between 3R and Note, and 3R and Reread, but not between Note and Reread. Bring to mind the overlap rule for independent CIs, and consider how well those post hoc contrast conclusions correspond with the patterns of CIs for both Immediate and Delayed conditions. Do you agree that we could have drawn the same conclusions by applying the rule to what the figure displays?

The interaction examined by the ANOVA is the 3 × 2 interaction of 3R/Note/Reread and Immediate/Delayed. This interaction, which has $df = 2$, refers to the extent that the (Delayed – Immediate) difference might vary across the three study techniques. Equivalently, it refers to the extent that the pattern of the three study technique means is different at Immediate and Delayed. The three lines in the figure are very close to parallel, which indicates no such variation, and, therefore, that there is very little or no interaction. This is consistent with our earlier discussion of interaction, and the large p value—which indicates no evidence against the null hypothesis of no interaction in the population.

15.26 **a.** Make an eyeball estimate of the (Delayed – Immediate) difference, combined over the three study techniques.

b. Guess what MoE for the CI on that difference might be. Compare with the p value reported for the Immediate/Delayed main effect.

All our analyses are based on means and differences, but it's worth thinking about the values shown in Figure 15.12 in different ways as well. In fact it's always worth thinking about alternative ways to read figures, and express results. In this case, think of the advantage of 3R over NoteReread as a percentage. At Immediate, the 3R mean is about 30% greater than the NoteReread mean marked by the + symbol. That sounds like a worthwhile improvement in learning. However, we are more interested in Delayed, because the whole point of studying is to remember as well as understand. One week later, at Delayed, 3R has a 78% advantage over NoteReread! That, surely, is a dramatic difference, well worth bearing in mind when next you are studying. It was results like this that prompted McDaniel and his coauthors to write *Make It Stick* and to emphasize that challenging retrieval is an effective study technique.

Partial Fasting and Obesity: An Example of a 3 × 5 Design

In Chapter 14, I discussed evidence from Halagappa et al. (2007) suggesting that restricting calorie intake—reducing the total amount eaten in a day—might delay cognitive decline with aging, at least in mice and possibly also in humans. My last example here comes from Chaix et al. (2014), an article that's become famous, which investigated the effect that time-restricted eating might have on health and fitness. There was no limitation on the amount eaten, only on the period that food was available each day. The article reported a large set of studies of mice, and analyses of numerous measures under numerous conditions. The results are most easily grasped from the graphical abstract, which

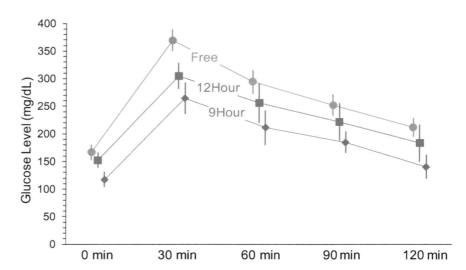

Figure 15.13. Means and 95% CIs for blood glucose level for three groups of mice (each $n = 8$) given junk food and permitted to eat freely (Free) or with food available for only 12 hr (12Hour) or 9 hr (9Hour) each day. Results are reported for five time points following a big dose of glucose, with time as a repeated measure. Data from Chaix et al. (2014).

you can see at tiny.cc/fastingfood, in which the main findings are summarized using humorous cartoons.

The main aim was to investigate the effect of restricted eating time on the health and fitness of mice fed the equivalent of a junk food diet. Mice in the Free condition could eat freely at any time, those in the 9Hour condition could eat as much as they wished but only during a 9-hr period each day, and those in the 12Hour condition only for a 12-hr period. The Free mice not surprisingly became obese and developed signs of diabetes and other illnesses. Remarkably, however, mice in the time-restricted eating conditions did not become obese and remained comparatively healthy—despite their junk food diet and no restriction on the amount they could eat, only on when they could eat.

One study examined glucose tolerance. Mice were given a big dose of glucose—the equivalent of a big sugar hit—then glucose levels in the blood were monitored over the following two hours. A blood glucose level that goes high and is slow to decrease suggests diabetes. The main planned comparisons would be the difference in overall blood glucose level during the two hours between Free and 9Hour, and between Free and 12Hour. Figure 15.13 shows the results.

15.27 Can we use information in the figure to assess the (Free – 9Hour) difference at a particular time point? The (Free – 12Hour) difference? Explain.

15.28 a. Make your eyeball estimate of the overall mean for Free, averaging over all time points.

b. Do the same for 9Hour and 12Hour.

c. Use those three estimated means to estimate the (Free − 9Hour) difference and the (Free − 12Hour) difference.

d. MoE for the CIs on those differences is roughly around 25. Interpret the two differences, which are our two main planned comparisons, and draw conclusions.

15.29 ANOVA of these data would examine two main effects and their interaction.

a. Name and describe the main effects and state how many levels each has.

b. About what p values would you expect to find for each main effect?

15.30 Describe the interaction in two ways. About what p value would you expect for the interaction?

15.31 A researcher wishes to estimate how much higher blood glucose is in Free mice than 9Hour mice at time 0, before the big glucose dose could have any effect.

a. Make an eyeball estimate of that difference and interpret.

b. Do the same for 30 min, when blood glucose is around its maximum.

c. Compare those two differences, and explain what that comparison tells us.

This example is a great illustration of the importance of simply looking at a figure and thinking, which may give us clear answers to our main research questions, perhaps even without any need for formal analysis. In response to Exercises 15.27 and 15.28 you probably stated that, because we have three independent groups, the CIs in the figure permit us to assess the main comparisons we're interested in. More broadly, the three curves marked by the solid lines are very similar in shape, and the vertical separation between the curves is quite large compared with MoE of the CIs, and, therefore, we have clear evidence that blood glucose concentration follows a very similar time-course for each group, but with Free being always distinctly higher than 9Hour, and 12Hour always lying between. That may be all we need to justify the main conclusion that, following a big glucose dose, blood glucose reaches much higher levels in Free mice then mice with 9-hr time restricted eating. This pattern suggests diabetes in the Free mice, and it seems that time-restricted eating avoids or greatly reduces such signs of diabetes—despite even the 9Hour mice eating any amount of junk food during the nine eating hours each day!

> Always examine figures carefully and think what messages may be gleaned from such inspection.

In some of their studies, the researchers maintained the restricted eating time for five days each week, and allowed unrestricted eating at weekends. They found that often the benefits of restricted eating largely persisted, despite the weekend "holidays" from the restrictions.

These and many other converging results led Chaix et al. (2014) to conclude that restricting eating time, rather than the amount eaten, may be highly effective in reducing or avoiding obesity, diabetes, and other illnesses, despite a less than ideal diet. That's a remarkable conclusion, definitely worth further research. Watch out for human studies, which may give further support for the health value of, for example, the popular 5:2 diet, in which food intake is greatly reduced on two days each week. Or perhaps, of eating only between, say, noon and 7 p.m. on at least several days every week.

ANALYZING ONE-WAY AND FACTORIAL DESIGNS: A SUMMARY

Here's an outline of my recommended approach, both for the one-way designs we discussed in Chapter 14 and the factorial designs in this chapter:

1. Focus on selected effects with one degree of freedom, including comparisons, contrasts, simple main effects, and 2×2 interactions. Consider combining levels to get effects of interest that have one degree of freedom.

2. In advance of running the study, specify the small number of effects that correspond to the main research questions. It's usually best if these effects are reasonably separate. If there are k means, no more than $df = (k-1)$ separate questions can be asked, so it's usually best if the number of effects specified for planned analysis is no more than about df. Preregister your research plan if you can.

3. Note the assumptions required for analysis, including homogeneity of variance and, with one or more repeated measures, more complex assumptions including homogeneity of correlation.

4. After running the study, calculate means and CIs for all conditions and display in a figure. Make very clear whether each IV is between-groups or a repeated measure. If there's one repeated measure, signal this with a solid line that joins the means for the different levels of that IV. Examine the figure. Lines joining means in the figure that cross or are far from parallel suggest a sizeable interaction.

5. Where possible, calculate the mean and CI for each of the effects selected for planned analysis. Interpret and draw conclusions.

6. Examine the figure some more, and consider alternative ways the results might be presented. If you wish, explore the data by examining any further effects that may be of interest. The results are only speculative, and more speculative as the number of possible effects that could be examined increases.

An alternative, more traditional and widely used approach is ANOVA, which focuses on testing a null hypothesis for each main effect and interaction. For a main effect, the null hypothesis states that the population means are the same for all levels of the IV. For an interaction of IV1 and IV2, the null hypothesis states that the pattern of means across all levels of IV1 is the same at each level of IV2. Equivalently, the pattern of means across all levels of IV2 is the same at each level of IV1. For each main effect and interaction, ANOVA provides a value of the F statistic and the corresponding p value, and may also provide an effect size, such as η^2, which is the proportion of total variance attributable to the main effect or interaction. Large values of F mean small p values. As usual, the smaller the p, the stronger the evidence against the null hypothesis.

A main effect involving k means has $df = (k-1)$. If a main effect or interaction with $df = 2$ or more is declared statistically significant, because p is sufficiently small, post hoc tests may be used to examine any contrasts of the means involved.

PLANNING MORE COMPLEX DESIGNS

In Chapter 10 we discussed the selection of N for studies with an independent groups or paired design. They are the two simple cases for which ESCI can provide guidance about N for a target MoE that you choose. Similar tools for more complex designs are not yet available, but will be highly valuable when they do appear, because then we can use the precision for planning approach for complex as well as simple designs.

Meanwhile, here are some general comments about planning a study with a more complex design.

- The biggest lesson is one that we've learned many times: If possible and practical, and if carryover effects can be overcome, generally prefer a repeated measure.
- For a chosen comparison of two means in a complex design, the **Precision two** or **Precision paired** pages can give approximate guidance about choice of n for the group or groups involved in the comparison.
- For an interaction in a 2 × 2 independent groups design, we expect the CI on the interaction to be longer than the CIs on the relevant simple main effects, as in Figure 15.10. A particular target MoE for the interaction will need larger n than the same target MoE for one of the simple main effects, perhaps n around twice as large.
- For more complex designs we need better software that supports precision for planning. Developing such software will be a wonderful contribution.

We're almost at take-home messages. When writing yours, it may help to look back at the messages at the end of Chapter 14. Are you thinking of skipping breakfast tomorrow, or perhaps several days next week?

? Quiz 15.3

1. A two-way design with just one group of participants has 1 IV / 2 IVs / 4 IVs, each of which is a between-groups / within-group IV.
2. A solid line joining means in a figure indicates an IV that is between-groups / a repeated measure, which is likely to give increased / decreased precision for effects involving its means.
3. Where possible, it's usually best to focus on effects for which $df =$ _____. These may include simple _____ effects and 1 × 1 / 2 × 2 / 3 × 2 interactions.
4. For an IV with more than 2 levels, consider
   a. running a different study instead.
   b. averaging over some levels to obtain contrasts with $df = 1$.
   c. using comparisons of means that have df greater than 1.
   d. None of the above.
5. With k means, no more than _____ separate questions can be asked, so planned analysis should specify no more than about _____ contrasts.
6. When ANOVA of a two-way study finds an interaction to have $p = .004$,
   a. the main effects are likely to be large.
   b. we have strong evidence that the effect of one IV is different at different levels of the other IV.
   c. most likely, the effect of one IV is quite similar at all levels of the other IV.
   d. the two IVs are likely to show the same, or close to the same, patterns of means.

15.32 The Halagappa et al. (2007) study we discussed in Chapter 14 used six independent groups: NFree10, AFree10, ADiet10, NFree17, AFree17, ADiet17.

a. Rather than a one-way design with six levels of a single between-groups IV, explain how it could be regarded as a 3 × 2 two-way design with two between-groups IVs. Identify the two IVs and the levels of each.
b. For this 3 × 2 design, what effects would you choose for planned analysis? Explain.
c. Describe one 2 × 2 interaction that may be of research interest and explain why.

15.33 Revisit your take-home messages if you wish.

Reporting Your Work

Estimating interactions provides a new level of sophistication to your research. It can be challenging at first to write a clear interpretation of an interaction. Fortunately, though, the basic pattern for reporting is familiar and straightforward. Focus on the specific main effects, interactions, or simple main effects that are relevant to answering your research questions. Ideally, you will have planned and preregistered a *limited* set of specific analyses (usually no more than degrees of freedom). For each, your research report should typically include:

- whether the analysis is planned or exploratory, unless this is already clear;
- basic descriptive statistics for each condition or cell (typically the mean, standard deviation, and sample size);
- the means of the groups being compared, the estimated effect, and its CI;
- a standardized effect size estimate ($d_{unbiased}$ is best), preferably with its CI. In the Method section make clear how your standardized effect size was calculated (which denominator was used). ESCI doesn't provide standardized effect sizes for complex designs, but you can obtain them for main effects and simple effects using the **Data two** or **Data paired** pages. See the final end-of-chapter exercise for steps to use ESCI to obtain a standardized effect size estimate and CI for an interaction in a randomized control trial;
- a figure if possible. Choose and edit your figure to best represent the effects of interest. Avoid clutter, but if possible use lines connecting the means for repeated measures designs. State in the figure caption what error bars represent—95% CIs;
- if desired, ANOVA results, which should include *F*, its degrees of freedom, and its associated *p* value for each main effect, interaction, or simple main effect of interest; and
- an interpretation of the estimated effect that considers not only the point estimate but also the CI. For interactions, try to express as clearly as possible what the difference in effects actually means (see examples below).

▶ For interactions, report the difference of the differences and its CI. Interpret the full range of the CI and try to clearly express the practical meaning of the interaction.

Although you will focus on key analyses to answer your research questions, your research report must still provide the full story: For *every* measure provide the mean, standard deviation, and sample size for *every* condition. You will almost certainly need tables and figures to effectively report complex designs.

Here is an example using data from Frenda et al. (2014):

Out of six possible points, false memory scores were somewhat higher in the morning (*M* = 1.80) than in the evening (*M* = 1.32). Thus, our planned and preregistered analysis of the main effect of time of day indicated a small increase in false memory in the morning: ($M_{Morning}$ − $M_{Evening}$) = 0.48, 95% CI[-0.07, 1.03]. This CI is fairly long, and indicates that false memories could be anywhere from no more likely up to much more likely in the morning condition.

Next, we conducted a planned and preregistered analysis of the main effect of sleep deprivation. False memory scores were similar in sleep deprived ($M = 1.68$) and non-deprived conditions ($M = 1.44$). The main effect of sleep deprivation, then, was small, ($M_{\text{Nosleep}} - M_{\text{Sleep}}$) $= 0.24$, 95% CI$[-0.31, 0.79]$. The CI, however, indicates considerable uncertainty about the degree to which sleep deprivation, on its own, might influence false memories.

Finally, we planned and preregistered an examination of the interaction between sleep deprivation and time of day to estimate the degree to which time of day might moderate the effects of sleep deprivation. In the evening condition, false memory scores were similar but slightly lower for the sleep deprived group: ($M_{\text{NoSleep}} - M_{\text{Sleep}}$) $= -0.36$. In the morning condition, however, sleep-deprived participants had substantially higher false memory scores relative to those who had slept: ($M_{\text{NoSleep}} - M_{\text{Sleep}}$) $= 0.84$. Thus, there was a large difference in how sleep deprivation influenced false memory for the different times of day: ($M_{\text{MorningDifference}} - M_{\text{EveningDifference}}$) $= 1.2$, 95% CI $[0.10, 2.30]$. This CI is long and consistent with a range of effect sizes from quite small up to very large. It seems likely from this interaction, however, that time of day moderates the effects of sleep deprivation on false memory, with a substantial impairment evident primarily in the morning condition. Additional research will be needed to estimate the degree of moderation more precisely.

Take-Home Messages

■ A *factorial design* includes every combination of the levels of all IVs. The simplest is the 2 × 2 two-way independent groups design, which has two between-groups IVs and four groups.

■ A two-way factorial design may have one or two within-group IVs, also called repeated measures. A *randomized control trial* (RCT) has one repeated measure. Always make clear whether each IV is between-groups or a repeated measure, for example in figure captions.

■ The *main effect* of an IV is its overall effect, after averaging over all other IVs, and has $df = (k - 1)$ if the IV has k levels. A *simple main effect* is the effect of an IV at a single level of another IV.

■ A 2 × 2 *interaction* is the difference of two differences, and has $df = 1$. More generally, an interaction is the extent to which the pattern of means across the levels of an IV differs at the different levels of a second IV. Lines that cross, or are far from parallel, indicate sizeable interactions.

■ A *moderator* is a second IV that is associated with a change in the effect of the first IV. In the presence of a 2 × 2 interaction, either IV can be said to be *moderating* the effect of the other IV on the DV.

■ If possible, focus on effects with $df = 1$, including contrasts, main effects, simple main effects, and 2 × 2 interactions.

■ In a figure, slightly offset the means so all CIs are easily visible. With one repeated measure, join the means at its different levels with solid lines.

■ In a figure of means and CIs, the difference between two independent means can be assessed, but any effect involving a repeated measure requires full data for its CI to be calculated.

■ Where possible, preregister a planned analysis of a limited number of contrasts. Optionally follow planned analysis with exploratory analysis.

■ Assumptions usually required include homogeneity of variance across groups. With one or more repeated measures, further assumptions are needed, for example homogeneity of correlation.

■ ANOVA tests null hypotheses for each main effect and interaction. For any effect, large F gives small p, which may permit rejection of the null hypothesis. An effect found statistically significant may be explored further with post hoc tests of any contrasts of the means involved in the effect.

End-of-Chapter Exercises

1) For each of the following, identify the design, identify the types of IVs (between participants or within participants), state if the conclusions drawn relate to main effects or interactions, and state if causal conclusions can be drawn.

   a. Male and female participants were recruited from a first-year college class (Park, Young, Troisi, & Pinkus, 2011). Participants first viewed images related to romance or intelligence. Next, participants rated their interest in different majors related to science and mathematics on a scale from 1 (not interested) to 7 (very interested). For females, interest in science and mathematics majors was less after viewing images related to romance; for men interest was similar regardless of images viewed.

   b. Participants learned a list of words on land or underwater during a SCUBA dive (Godden & Baddeley, 1975). Later, memory was tested on land or underwater. Memory was best when the learning and recall locations were matched.

   c. Alcohol-dependent participants were randomly assigned to treatment with either placebo or acamprosate, a drug thought to help reduce cravings for alcohol (Paille et al., 1995). Daily drinking was self-reported before treatment began and again six months into treatment. In the placebo-treated group self-reported drinking was largely unchanged, but in the acamprosate group there was a substantial decline.

   d. Children in pre-school, kindergarten, or first grade were recruited who had either an older sibling or a younger sibling (Ruffman, Perner, Naito, Parkin, & Clements, 1998). Each child completed a set of false-belief tasks meant to measure that child's theory of mind. It was found that theory of mind became more sophisticated with age, and that those with older siblings consistently outperformed those with younger siblings.

2) To what extent is maintaining gender norms important to our sense of identity? In one intriguing study, McCarty & Kelly (2015) noted that, on their college campus, doors were often held open for women but rarely for men. They wondered to what extent this practice might influence self-esteem, and if the influence would be different for women (for whom this behavior is consistent with gender norms) than for men (for whom this behavior may violate gender norms). To investigate, the researchers stationed a male confederate outside a busy academic building. When a male or female approached the building on their own, the confederate walked with them to the entrance and either held the door open or not. Next, a second confederate stationed inside the building approached the prospective participant and asked them to complete a brief survey which measured (among other things) self-esteem on a scale from 1 to 10. Results are in the Table 15.3.

Table 15.3 Self-Esteem by Gender and Door-Holding Condition, From McCarty & Kelly (2015)

		Men	Women
Door not held	n	39	39
	M	8.35	8.59
	s	1.05	1.19
Door held	n	28	37
	M	7.42	8.77
	s	1.34	1.02

   a. What type of design is this?

   b. Will we be able to draw causal conclusions from this study? Explain.

c. Given the research questions, what effects do you think the researchers planned to assess?

d. For men, to what extent does door holding impact self-esteem? Use **Ind groups 2 × 2** to create a figure and obtain a CI for this research question. Interpret.

e. For women, to what extent does door holding impact self-esteem? Obtain a CI for this research question. Interpret.

f. To what extent does door-holding and gender interact to determine self-esteem? Obtain a CI for this research question. Interpret.

g. Not all the participants who entered the academic building agreed to take the survey. What potential concerns does this raise for this study and what information would you want to know to help evaluate this concern?

3) Video games can be violent and they can also be challenging. To what extent might these factors cause aggressive behavior? To explore, Hilgard (2015) asked male participants to play one of four versions of a video game for 15 minutes. The game was customized so that it could vary in violence (shooting zombies or helping aliens) and difficulty (targets controlled by tough AI or dumb AI). After the game, players were provoked by being given an insulting evaluation by a confederate. Participants then got to decide how long the confederate should hold their hand in painfully cold ice water (between 0 and 80 seconds), and this was taken as a measure of aggressive behavior. You can find the materials and analysis plan for this study on the Open Science Framework: osf.io/cwenz You can retrieve a simplified version of the data set from the book website (**Videogame_ Aggression**).

a. What type of design is this?

b. Will we be able to draw causal conclusions from this study? Explain.

c. What effects would you plan to analyze for this study? Why?

d. Overall, to what extent does video game violence alter aggressive behavior? (What is the main effect of violence?) Use **Ind groups 2 × 2** to create a figure and obtain a CI for this research question. Interpret.

e. Difficult games require lots of cognitive resources, and some have suggested that this can lead to a temporary lack of self-control that facilitates aggressive behavior. Overall, to what extent does game difficulty alter aggressive behavior? (What is the main effect of difficulty?) Obtain a CI for this research question. Interpret.

f. To what extent do video game violence and difficulty interact to determine aggression? Obtain a CI for this research question. Interpret, and be sure to try to put into words what this interaction means.

g. There has been considerable debate over links between video games and aggression. Some meta-analyses have supported a small effect of video game exposure on aggressive behavior, but critics have argued these results could be skewed by publication bias. Several individual studies have found little to no effect of video game exposure on aggressive behavior, but critics on the other side have pointed out that some of these were too small to give precise estimates of effect sizes. How did Hilgard design this study to contribute to resolving these issues?

4) Self-explaining is a learning strategy where students write or say their own explanations of the material they are studying. Self-explaining has generally been found to be more effective than standard studying, but it may also take more time. This raises the question of whether it's the study strategy or the extra time that benefits learning. To help explore this issue,

grade school children took a pretest of mathematics conceptual knowledge, studied mathematics problems, and then took a similar posttest (McEldoon, Durkin, & Rittle-Johnson, 2013). Participants were randomly assigned to one of three study conditions: normal study (the control group), self-explaining, or normal study + additional practice. You can find the data from this study on the book website (**Self-Explain_Time**). The scores in this file represent percent correct for each test taken.

a. What type of design is this?

b. Will we be able to draw causal conclusions? Explain.

c. To what extent did participants in the normal study group improve their math skills? Use the **Data paired** page to obtain the mean difference and its CI. Note that this analysis calculates a difference column representing each participant's change from pretest to posttest. Check that your differences match the column of differences provided in the data file; we'll use these differences again shortly.

d. To what extent did participants in the self-explain group improve their math skills? Again note the difference scores for each participant.

e. As an additional planned contrast of research interest, consider to what extent gains in the self-explain group differ from gains in the control group. Analyze the *difference scores* in the **Ind groups comparison** page. You will obtain the average difference of the difference scores and its CI. Interpret. What does this CI estimate: a main effect or an interaction?

f. Bonus: To what extent did gains in the normal+practice group differ from gains in the self-explain group? Again use the **Data paired** page to estimate gains in the normal+practice group, then compare these difference scores with the self-explain difference scores using the **Ind groups comparison** page. Does this study provide strong evidence that self-explaining provides benefits above and beyond time-on-task?

? Answers to Quizzes

Quiz 15.1

1) IVs, 2, 4; 2) levels, IVs; 3) d; 4) 1, 1, 1; 5) b; 6) contrasts, mean, CI.

Quiz 15.2

1) homogeneity, groups; 2) a; 3) c; 4) main, effect, level; 5) between-groups, within-group; 6) correlation, higher.

Quiz 15.3

1) 2 IVs, within-group; 2) a repeated measure, increased; 3) 1, main, 2×2; 4) b; 5) $(k - 1)$, $(k - 1)$; 6) b.

📝 Answers to In-Chapter Exercises

15.1 The CIs on the means in the figure have MoE values as shown near red 3.

15.2 $p = .086$, which corresponds with the CI on the main effect, displayed on the difference axis, extending a small distance past zero.

15.3 a. Evening and Morning means are combined for each of Sleep and Nosleep; b. About 1.4 for Sleep and 1.7 for Nosleep; c. Estimate (Nosleep − Sleep) difference as around 0.3 (actually 0.24).

15.4 Main effect is 0.24 [−0.31, 0.79], so the effect is comparatively small and the CI long.

15.5   a. 0.84 is the (Nosleep − Sleep) difference for Morning, and −0.36 the same for Evening; b. These differences are pictured as purple lines ending in diamonds, combined as illustrated by the slanted dotted lines to give their difference of 1.20, which is marked by the triangle on the difference axis; c. Together, a. and b. give us the three steps.

15.6   a. Eyeball, but then find near red 3 the values of means, so for Nosleep, the (Morning − Evening) difference is 2.22 − 1.14 = 1.08; b. For Sleep, difference is 1.38 − 1.50 = −0.12; c. The interaction is the difference of those two differences, which is 1.08 − (−0.12) = 1.20 as before; d. Here the interaction is the extent to which Morning and Evening differ for Nosleep, compared with Sleep. Before we considered the extent that Nosleep and Sleep differ for Evening, compared with Morning. Same answer.

15.7   Rock 7, Classical 5, main effect (Classical − Rock) = −2 eyeballed.

15.8   Main effects: (Classical − Rock) around 5 − 9 = −4, so Rock overall rated 4 points above Classical, and (Church − Party) around 8 − 6 = 2, so Church overall rated 2 points above Party. For interaction, eyeball (Classical − Rock) at Church is around 7 − 9 = −2, and at Party is around 2 − 9 = −7, so the interaction is around −2 − (−7) = 5, which is large but not as large as in Panel A.

15.9   (Classical − Rock) around 4 − 9 = −5, so Rock 5 above Classical, and (Church − Party) around 6 − 7 = −1, so Church is 1 point below Party. For the interaction, lines are close to parallel, so there is close to zero interaction.

15.10   a–c. Same 4 means, same main effects, same interaction.

15.11   a. See Figure 15.14; b. Same main effects and interaction as before.

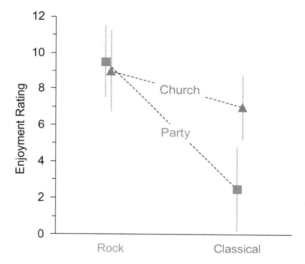

Figure 15.14. Same four means and 95% CIs as in Panel B of Figure 15.6, but with Rock/Classical, rather than Party/Church, on the horizontal axis.

15.12   a. The effect of Pen/Laptop, the first IV, on transcription %; b. A moderator may be type of test (Factual/ Conceptual), with laptop transcription perhaps better if factual knowledge is to be tested, but worse if understanding of concepts is required.

15.13   a. The effect of training in argument mapping, the first IV, on critical thinking score; b. A moderator may be level of visual thinking ability, with students who find visual thinking difficult perhaps not being helped as much by argument maps.

15.14   a. (Meditation − Control) at Pretest or at Posttest can be assessed because Meditation and Control are independent groups, so those two means are independent; b. Any effects involving a Pretest and a Posttest mean cannot be assessed from the figure, because Pretest/Posttest is a repeated measure, so those two means are not independent.

15.15   We can eyeball from the figure the overall means for Pretest and Posttest, averaged over Control and Meditation, and also the main effect, which is the difference between those two overall means. But we can't eyeball the CI on the difference, so we can't assess the main effect from the figure.

15.16   a. Mean labeled "Control" is the difference between the Posttest and Pretest means for Control displayed as two open circles in Figure 15.9; b. "Meditation" is the same for the two filled diamonds; c. The triangle is the (Meditation − Control) difference between the two means just to its left, and is the difference of the differences, which is the interaction of Pretest/Posttest and Control/Meditation.

15.17   a. For Control, enter M and s for Pretest and Posttest, and s_{diff}, and find the difference is 0.12 [−0.61, 0.84], as in the text; b. Similarly for Meditation.

15.18 a. Between-groups, and we do have the information we need. Use **Summary two** and enter the mean of the differences for Control and Meditation, and the two s_{diff} values, because they are the SDs of the two groups of differences; b. The interaction is 0.84 [0.03, 1.65], as in the text.

15.19 Main effect of Without/With. Interaction of Without/With and Good/Bad. Perhaps also the main effect of Good/Bad to check that students do find Good explanations better.

15.20 a. Main effects: Good is about $0.4 - (-0.4) = 0.8$ higher than Bad. With is about $0.5 - (-0.5) = 1.0$ higher than Without. Interaction: (With − Without) for Good is about $0.7 - 0.1 = 0.6$, and for Bad is about $0.2 - (-1.0) = 1.2$, so difference $= 0.6 - 1.2 = -0.6$; b. No effects can be assessed because both IVs are repeated measures, so there are no independent means; c. Each IV probably has a moderate or high correlation between scores at its two levels, so CIs on effects are very likely to be shorter than the CIs on means, although this is not guaranteed. The CI on the interaction is a little longer than CIs on simple main effects, but is still likely to be shorter than the CIs on means, although again this is not guaranteed.

15.21 Overall, explanations With neuroscience were rated about 1.0 scale units higher than those Without, which is a large difference on the 7-point scale. Good explanations were rated 0.8 higher than Bad, so the two main effects are similar in size. Having neuroscience increased the rating of Bad explanations by about 0.6 scale units more than that of Good explanations, which is quite a large difference—just over half a unit on the rating scale. Even for neuroscience students, seeing neuroscience information that was irrelevant to the soundness of the explanation led them to rate an explanation as more satisfying, and more so when the explanation was unsound (the Bad condition) than Good. "Seductive allure" indeed.

15.22 Neuroscience moderated the effect of Good/Bad, because that effect was smaller for With than Without neuroscience. Or, Good/Bad moderated the effect of Neuroscience, because the effect of With/Without neuroscience was smaller for Good than Bad.

15.23 a. All students saw all four conditions, so the comparisons of interest were all made within participants and were thus likely to be estimated with high precision. The danger was carryover effects arising from a student reading and rating a series of items from different conditions. Possible carryover effects were judged unlikely to influence ratings greatly. If anything they might reduce differences, making the substantial differences found all the more striking; b. A study could be designed with either or both IVs as between-groups IVs, to avoid any risk of carryover effects, but the likely lower precision suggests that the original design was probably better.

15.24 a. 4.5, 4.5; b. MoE of about 2 means the differences are both around 4.5 [2.5, 6.5], which is a large number of idea units out of a maximum of 30, so we conclude 3R is considerably better than the other techniques, which don't differ much.

15.25 a, b. Differences are very similar, no sign of an interaction, as also indicated by the three solid lines being very close to parallel. The 3R advantage is about the same at immediate testing and one week later, whichever study technique was used.

15.26 a. Overall, Immediate is around $16 - 7 = 9$ higher than Delayed. b. Immediate/Delayed is a repeated measure, so MoE is likely to be fairly short, maybe around 1 to 2, but we don't know unless we can calculate from the full data. In any case, the difference of 9 is very much greater, so the p value will be tiny, as was reported.

15.27 Yes and yes, because those differences refer to means of independent groups.

15.28 a, b. Around 260 for Free, 180 for 9Hour, and 220 for 12Hour; c. So (Free − 9Hour) is around 80 and (Free − 12Hour) around 40; d. These look to be very substantial differences in glucose level, each estimated within roughly ±25 of the population values. Time restriction made a substantial difference, more so when eating was restricted to 9 than 12 hours.

15.29 a. Main effect of the between-groups IV: Free/12Hour/9Hour, with three levels. Main effect of the repeated measure: 0/30/60/90/120 minutes after the glucose dose, with five levels; b. For Free/12Hour/9Hour, the differences are so large compared with MoE of the CIs that p for the main effect would be tiny. For the repeated measure there are very large differences over time. We don't know MoE but can be confident the CIs would be short, so p for the main effect would be tiny.

15.30 The interaction is the extent to which the pattern of (i) Free/12Hour/9Hour group means differs at the different time points, or (ii) 0/30/60/90/120-min means differs for the different groups. The lines in the figure are all not far from parallel, suggesting little or no interaction and large p.

15.31 a. At time zero, Free is about 50 more than 9Hour, a substantially higher level; b. By 30 minutes Free is around 100, or a little more, higher than 9Hour, an even larger difference; c. So Free starts off looking diabetic, then the glucose dose causes an even larger increase than for 9Hour, which is a further sign of diabetes.

15.32 a. Regard NFree/AFree/ADiet as one between-groups IV, with 3 levels, and 10/17, or MiddleAged/Old, as a second between-groups IV, with 2 levels. There are six combinations of levels, each with a group; b. For planned analysis, choose the two effects we analyzed in Chapter 14: The main effect of 10/17 to assess the overall effect of age, and the contrast of the two ADiet groups with the two AFree groups, all those four groups being of Alzheimer-prone mice, to examine the effect of calorie restriction in such mice; c. The 2×2 interaction of 10/17 and ADiet/AFree in Alzheimer-prone mice is probably of greatest research interest. It examines the extent to which the effect of calorie restriction in such mice might differ in middle and old ages. The four means are highlighted in Figure 14.8 and to my eyeball that interaction is near zero.

16

Future Directions

If you have made it this far, then well done indeed! My aim in this chapter is to recap and develop a little further our basic plan for conducting research, to outline some current developments in Open Science, then to look ahead to a few of the challenges that lie beyond the simple situations and analyses we've encountered so far in this book. The main conclusion is that all the fundamentals that we've discussed, including experimental research, Open Science, and the estimation approach, are likely to be what's needed, whatever the research questions, however complex the situation.

As illustrations of future challenges, I'll discuss populations that are far from normally distributed, archival data available in a database, studies with thousands of variables rather than one or two and, finally, the current hot topic of big data.

Here's the agenda:

- A 10-step plan for doing good research
- Advances in Open Science, including preregistered review and crowd-sourced research
- Dealing with non-normal data: Robust statistical methods
- Archival data, sometimes collected over decades
- Dealing with thousands of variables: Pictures of the brain
- Big data: Millions or billions of pieces of information

A STEP-BY-STEP RESEARCH PLAN

Here's a development of the Chapter 1 plan that includes expanded attention to Open Science issues. We're now up to 10 steps.

1. Use knowledge of past research, good ideas, and pilot testing to refine your research questions and develop the measures and procedures that seem best for answering these questions. Continue piloting, exploring, and refining as you wish. Use estimation thinking throughout.
2. State the research questions. Express them as "how much" or "to what extent" questions, and identify the effect size measure that's most appropriate for answering each question. Often the measure we want is a difference. Consider reliability and validity.
3. Design a study that uses the chosen measure(s) and is likely to give good point and interval estimates to answer your questions.
4. If possible, preregister a detailed plan for the study, including a detailed data analysis plan.
5. Follow the plan to run the study, make one or more figures, examine the data, and follow the data analysis plan to calculate point and interval estimates. Display confidence intervals in the figures.

6. Interpret the point and interval estimates, using your judgment in the research context.

7. If you wish, explore the data further, to possibly suggest speculative conclusions that might guide future research.

8. Report the study, whatever the results. Even if not accepted by a journal, upload the report to a research archive, such as OSF. Make sure to state that there was no selective reporting of just some of the results, and give full details of every aspect of the study. Explain any departures from the preregistered plan.

9. If possible, make all the materials and the data openly available. If appropriate, include a video showing the running of the study, to make accurate replication easier.

10. Adopt meta-analytic thinking throughout. Consider conducting your own replication.

As before, this list is not meant to be a comprehensive guide to conducting good research, but it expresses the important steps. It's a demanding list, and includes steps that in the past have usually not been followed. However, adopting Open Science means that it's important to follow all those steps to the maximum extent we can. I keep mentioning Open Science, but how important is it really?

HOW IMPORTANT IS OPEN SCIENCE?

The three Ioannidis problems and the replicability crisis tell us that some proportion of published research can't be trusted, but how severe is the problem? Replication projects are beginning to answer this question. We have met some of these, but here I'll give a brief overview of two.

Estimating the Replicability of Past Research

▶ Many Labs 1 conducted many replications of 16 effects and in some cases found considerable disagreement with the original studies.

Many Labs 1 investigated to what extent a small sample of published results can be trusted. In Chapter 10, I suggested you visit osf.io/wx7ck and click on "final manuscript" to see the report of that project. Figure 1 of the report summarizes a huge effort to run many replications of studies that had identified 16 interesting effects. Broadly speaking, in seven cases the replications found results similar to the original, in four cases effects at least twice as large, in three cases distinctly smaller effects, and in two cases effects very close to zero.

▶ The Reproducibility Project: Psychology conducted close replications of 100 studies and in roughly 60% found effects smaller or much smaller than the original studies had found.

A second example is The Reproducibility Project: Psychology, which replicated 100 notable studies in social and cognitive psychology (Open Science Collaboration, 2015). Each was replicated by one lab, with careful efforts to make the replication as similar as possible to the original, but, in most cases, with much larger samples. The replication studies obtained effects that were, on average, just half the size of the effects obtained in the original studies—that's a striking and disturbing difference. Broadly speaking, around 40% of replications (about 25% in social and 50% in cognitive psychology) found results roughly similar to the original results, whereas 60% found somewhat smaller, or very much smaller effects.

The 100 original studies were all published in high-quality journals after scrutiny by peer reviewers, and in virtually all cases reported clear and statistically significant effects. They met all standards that were until recently regarded as adequate. However, the studies had not been preregistered and we can't tell the extent to which there may have been selection of what was reported. The published results may, to some extent, have been cherry picked. Indeed, a recent study (Franco, Malhotra, & Simonovits, 2015) of a sample of psychology papers found that 40% failed to report all study conditions and 70% failed to report all dependent measures. These omissions were not random: The reported findings had much bigger effect sizes than the unreported ones. That's classic cherry picking! In contrast, the replication projects just discussed followed the new standards of Open Science. All were preregistered and reported in full detail, so we can be confident we have the full story and that the results were not cherry picked.

It may be, then, that a disturbingly large proportion of published results would not hold up well on replication. In particular, published effect sizes are likely in many cases to be overestimates of population effects. Open Science is indeed necessary, and, in fact, very much needed.

> Replication projects suggest that a considerable proportion of published effects, in psychology at least, are overestimates, perhaps severe overestimates, of true effects.

16.1 Visit cos.io and click on the "See some examples" link under Metascience—which means the science of doing science. You will probably see brief summaries of Many Labs 1, 2, 3, and perhaps more. Read about each and try to see how they fit together.

16.2 At cos.io, again click on the "See some examples" link under Metascience. If you can see Reproducibility Project: Psychology (RP:P), read the summary then click "Learn more". Alternatively, at osf.io, search for "Estimating the Reproducibility of Psychological Science", then click on the Wiki for the project with that name. Either way, under Contents click on "*Science article*" to see the summary article published in top journal *Science*. Read as much as you find interesting.

    a. Scroll down to see Figure 3, which is a scatterplot of the replication effect sizes against the original effect sizes. Each dot marks the value of an original ES and the replication ES of that same effect. Dots below the diagonal line are cases where the replication ES was lower than the original ES; most dots are below the line.

    b. What does the project say about the published research literature in social and cognitive psychology? Is it encouraging or disappointing?

ADVANCES IN OPEN SCIENCE

Open Science is a current frontier of research excitement—it's probably the most important advance for many years in how to do good science. Some important Open Science practices are rapidly becoming the norm, including open materials and data, and even preregistration of research and analysis plans.

Many researchers find preregistration, in particular, a big challenge and a dramatic change from past practice. However, here's a tiny, but remarkable, sign of its acceptance: In December 2015, D. Stephen Lindsay, editor of *Psychological Science*, declared in an editorial: "Personally, I aim never again to submit for publication a study that was not preregistered." (Lindsay, 2015, p. 1828). And he says he is now "requiring my students to do it as well" (Lindsay, tiny.cc/Lindsayprereg).

Open Science is not yet fully evolved—there are additional frontiers being explored that may soon become widespread. I'll describe two that seem especially promising.

Preregistered Review

Many journal editors are promoting Open Science practices by issuing new guidelines for conducting and reporting research, and by offering the Center for Open Science badges we met in Chapter 10. The novel policy of *preregistered review* is particularly interesting.

Journals have traditionally used peer review to scrutinize reports of completed research, so they have decided what to accept for publication only after seeing the final data, analysis, and interpretation. Preregistration opens up the possibility that peer reviewing could be applied to the preregistered research plan, *before* data collection commences. The replication studies in the Reproducibility Project: Psychology were all peer-reviewed in this way—their research plans were scrutinized and possibly revised before being preregistered, and before the studies themselves commenced.

Some journals are now experimenting with preregistered review, meaning that they review the full research plan before it is preregistered. If the research question is judged sufficiently interesting and the study design sufficiently rigorous for answering the question, then the journal commits to publishing the final report, whatever the results, subject only to checking that the plan has been accurately followed and that the report is fully detailed.

> *Preregistered review* is peer reviewing of the full research plan before it is preregistered and before data collection commences.

▶ Preregistered review allows plans to be refined at the start, helps avoid publication bias, and emphasizes choice of worthwhile research questions over the cherry picking of results.

Reflect on that for a moment: The journal is agreeing to publish a report of research before knowing the results! That's a stunning change from past practice in which journals would publish only research that found new or surprising results. However, recall the Open Science principle that all research conducted to a reasonable standard must be made publicly available—to avoid selective publication, which has done so much damage. It's great that some journals are using preregistered review to make publication decisions. You may also enjoy submitting to a journal using preregistered review because it helps you gain the input and advice of expert reviewers before running the study, a much more efficient way to do good work. Moreover, if your plan is accepted and you preregister it, perhaps after revision in response to reviewers' advice, then you'll have a great incentive to follow through with the study—your work will be published, whatever the results.

▶ The *TOP Guidelines* are example policies that journals can adopt to encourage, or require, Open Science practices.

Beyond preregistered review, journal editors are considering a wide range of Open Science issues. Following discussions by many editors, Nosek et al. (2015) published in *Science* the *Transparency and Openness Promotion (TOP) Guidelines*. These describe policies that journal editors can adopt to encourage, or require, various Open Science practices for research they publish. More than 700 journals have already signed to indicate support, and possible adoption of some version of these policies.

Another initiative (see opennessinitiative.org) encourages researchers, in their role as reviewers for journals, to decline to give a full review of any manuscript that does not follow Open Science practices—or does not at least explain why these were not possible in the particular case. Open Science is advancing fast.

Replication and Crowd-Sourced Research

Replication is at the heart of Open Science, and I've mentioned two large replication projects. In addition, funding bodies are beginning to fund systematic replications, which is a clear change from past practice in which only research likely to give a breakthrough would be funded.

One exciting aspect of these replication efforts is that many use *crowd-sourcing* to find research teams interested in participating. A researcher who wishes to initiate a replication project issues a call for expressions of interest, perhaps from research teams anywhere around the world. Anyone expressing interest then discusses with the originator and all other teams exactly how the project will proceed. They invite the researchers who conducted the original study being replicated to participate by providing any additional materials or information needed for the replications to be as close as possible to the original study. The research plan will be refined, then scrutinized by others in the project and perhaps independent reviewers, then revised again. All materials and successive versions of the research plan will be uploaded to OSF. Agreement to publish may be sought from a journal offering preregistered review. When all is ready, the research and analysis plan is preregistered and data collection commences, perhaps by several teams in different countries. Excitement mounts as data come in and the teams post their results to OSF for all to see. Finally, everything is written up, including a meta-analysis to integrate all the results, including the result of the original study. All materials, analyses, and the full data are made available on OSF.

Crowd-sourced projects offer fantastic opportunities for student groups, including undergraduate students, to participate. In many such projects students are indeed playing a valuable role. For example, I mentioned in Chapter 10 the CREP project, which you can read about at osf.io/wfc6u. You've also seen a number of other examples in the end-of-chapter exercises. Look out for opportunities to join a project in an area you find interesting. You could browse osf. io for ideas and invitations to participate.

Crowd-sourced projects invite participation by interested research groups, often including student groups.

16.3 Go to cos.io/top, which describes the TOP Guidelines, and look around.

    a. How many journal signatories are there, and what have they undertaken to do?

    b. Near the top, click on "Summary worksheet of the TOP Guidelines". Choose a row, perhaps "Data transparency" or "Preregistration of analysis plans", and read the summary policies in the four columns. What changes as you shift from left to right?

    c. Suggest an example project for which one of the Level 3 policies would be difficult or impossible.

    d. Scroll down to the list of links at the bottom of the page and click on "The Preregistration Challenge" (or go to cos.io/prereg). How much money could you win? What do you need to do to get the money?

16.4 Visit osf.io and search for "Many Lab". Read about Many Lab, which is a site to support replication projects. Scroll and you will probably discover Many Labs 2 and 3 and 4 and perhaps more. Read as your interest leads. A good strategy can be to click on the Wiki of anything of interest, for further description.

16.5 At osf.io find at least one opportunity to join a crowd-sourced replication effort. CREP or Many Lab may be a useful starting point.

16.6 In Chapter 13, an end-of-chapter exercise discussed the finding by Rozin et al. (2014) that members near the periphery of a group are more likely to mention group membership than are members near the center. They presented data for three different groups: universities, international airports, and Ivy League universities. They also reported that they had investigated the periphery–center idea for various uses of the word "science". Why did they tell us that? Should it change the message we take from the article?

16.7 Find an experienced researcher and ask them about the 10-step plan. Suppose they say that it looks fine in theory, but in practice it's too demanding of time and effort, and, anyway, some steps are not that important. What evidence could you present to justify using the full plan whenever possible?

The research world is indeed changing as Open Science advances. It's a wonderful time to be learning about research and perhaps planning your first studies. What you choose to do is helping shape how science will be done. Reflect and enjoy!

Now for a few examples of the research challenges you might meet, beyond what we've discussed in this book. Just remember that in every case Open Science is relevant and that, usually, an estimation approach is best. My first example considers non-normal data. Just take this quiz first...

? Quiz 16.1

1. The 10-step research plan emphasizes
   a. preregistration of a detailed research plan.
   b. choice of an effect size measure that corresponds with each research question.
   c. consideration of replication and meta-analysis.
   d. All of the above.
2. In what order should you do the following? Conduct a study, preregister a study, pilot testing, plan a study.
3. The Open Science Framework (OSF) is
   a. a set of online facilities to help researchers practice Open Science.
   b. a large collection of journals that have agreed to encourage Open Science.
   c. a growing body of researchers who have taken the Open Science oath.
   d. a format and template to help you write up your research reports.
4. The main Open Science slogan is the question: _____?
5. Preregistered review scrutinizes research before / during / after data collection, and may decide to publish research dependent on / regardless of what results are obtained.
6. Crowd-sourced replication research may invite participation by teams of established researchers / students / both established researchers and students and is likely to focus on close / more distant replication.

DEALING WITH NON-NORMAL DATA

So far we've assumed that our samples are from normally distributed populations. Fortunately, the central limit theorem, which we explored in Chapter 4, tells us that the mean heap is close to normal, even for many non-normal populations. This means that our conventional statistical techniques are likely to give reasonable results, at least for moderately non-normal populations, and especially when N is not too small.

However, researchers quite often encounter data that seem to come from populations that depart greatly from normality. Perhaps they are highly skewed or there are extreme outliers. In such cases conventional statistical techniques often don't give reasonable results, meaning, for example, that conventional 95% CIs would not include μ on 95% of occasions. *Robust* statistical techniques are often an excellent choice in such situations. "Robust" means resistant, at least to some extent, to departures from one or more assumptions. At present, robust techniques are not widely used, but they deserve to be better known and used more often.

◀ *Robust* statistical techniques are resistant to departures from some assumptions.

We've already encountered one robust technique: the Welch–Satterthwaite method for calculating a CI on the difference between two independent means. To use it, click **No** at red 8 in **Data two** or red 4 in **Summary two** of **ESCI intro chapters 3–8**. It's robust to departures from homogeneity of variance, and so doesn't need that assumption.

Here I'll describe a robust technique that's highly useful for non-normal data: CIs based on *trimmed means*, for the difference between two independent groups. This technique is robust against many departures from normality, but it still requires other assumptions, notably random sampling from the population.

Trimmed Means for Two Independent Groups

Consider the data set with $N = 18$ shown on the left in Figure 16.1. There are two extreme high outliers, which, as we discovered in Chapter 3, have great influence by increasing substantially both the conventional mean, $M = 1.33$, and standard deviation, $s = 0.59$. Why, then, don't we simply remove the two obviously extreme points? The trouble is that there's no good way to choose which, if any, points really are aberrant. The robust approach I'll describe is a principled way to permit outliers to have some influence, without letting them dominate.

The first step is to *trim* a proportion of the points from both ends of the data set. Experts advise that usually the best choice is 20% trimming, meaning the lowest 20%, and highest 20% of data points are trimmed. Then the *trimmed mean*, M_t, is simply the mean of the remaining central 60% of points. The number of points to trim from each end is 20% of N, rounded down to the nearest integer. In the example we trim $0.20 \times 18 = 3.6$, rounded down to 3, points from each end. Figure 16.1, on the right, shows the trimmed points as crosses. The points not trimmed are shown as filled red dots, and the trimmed mean, M_t, is simply the mean of those points. Its value of $M_t = 1.20$ is lower than M because the two high outliers are among the points trimmed.

◀ The 20% *trimmed mean*, M_t, is the mean of the points remaining after the top 20% and bottom 20% of points are trimmed.

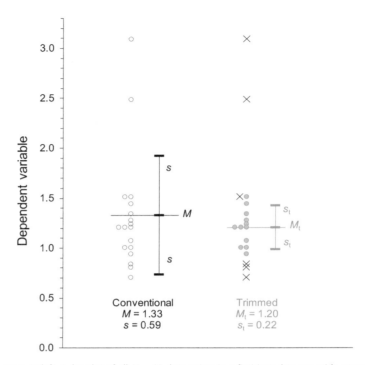

Figure 16.1. At left: a dot plot of all $N = 18$ data points in a fictitious data set, with conventional mean, M, and standard deviation, s, reported. The upper and lower black crossbars are distance s above and below M. At right: 20% trimming, the top three and bottom three data points are trimmed (and displayed as crosses) and the trimmed mean, M_t, for the remaining 12 red points, and corresponding standard deviation, s_t, are reported. The upper and lower red crossbars are distance s_t above and below M_t.

▶
The standard deviation for the trimmed analysis, s_t, is calculated using all data points, but trimmed points have much reduced influence.

The standard deviation for the trimmed analysis is $s_t = 0.22$, which is calculated using a formula that recognizes the trimming but allows all 18 points to have an influence. The crossbars in the figure mark distances s and s_t above and below M and M_t, and illustrate that s_t is much less than half the size of s. The small s_t reflects the much reduced influence of outliers on this measure of variability within a data set.

An illustration of the use of trimming is the scoring of international diving and figure skating. A panel of, for example, seven or nine judges each awards a score. The lowest and highest are dropped and the competitor awarded the mean of the remaining scores, which is thus a trimmed mean.

The next step is to use the trimmed mean and corresponding standard deviation to calculate a 95% CI. The trimmed mean is our point estimate of the population trimmed mean, and the CI our interval estimate of that same parameter.

Figure 16.2 shows in the left figure the blue dot plots of data for independent samples of 21-year-old males and females who were asked to state their number of sexual partners. I excerpted the data from the British National Survey of

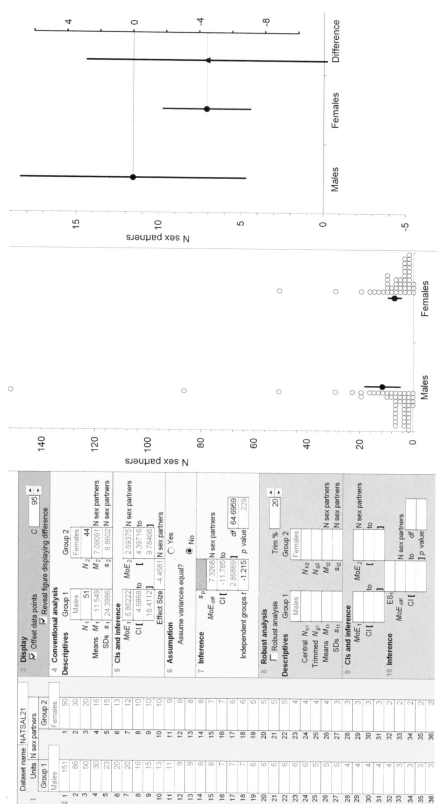

Figure 16.2. Conventional analysis of data from NATSAL (2005), comprising reported number of sexual partners by British samples of 21-year-old males and females, without assuming homogeneity of variance. Panels at red 4, 5, and 7 report values. From the **Robust two** page of **ESCI intro chapters 10–16**.

Sexual Attitudes and Lifestyles (NATSAL, 2005). The figure reports conventional analysis, but at red 6 **No** is selected, so homogeneity of variance is not assumed and Welch–Satterthwaite is used to calculate the 95% CI on the difference. As usual, the difference between the group means is shown on a difference axis in the figure on the right. The results are the same as those given by the **Data two** page, as we used in Chapter 7, but the figure is from **Robust two**.

I then clicked the checkbox at red 8 to get the robust analysis based on trimmed means, which is shown in Figure 16.3. The conventional analysis is grayed out, and robust analysis with 20% trimming is shown at red 8, 9, and 10. In the left figure, trimmed points are displayed as crosses and remaining data points as filled red circles, and the large red dots mark M_t for each group. The 95% CIs have been calculated using M_t and s_t for each group, and the figure on the right displays the difference between the two trimmed means, with its CI.

16.8 Suppose in Figure 16.1 that the two very high points came from Einstein and Darwin—two scientists who were in many ways extreme outliers. How would you feel about trimming?

16.9 a. For Group 1, compare the mean in Figure 16.2 and trimmed mean in Figure 16.3. Do they differ much? Explain.

b. Do the same for the Group 1 standard deviations.

c. Do the same for Group 2, means and standard deviations.

d. Compare the values for males and females.

16.10 Compare the difference and its CI in the two figures. What conclusions would you make in the two cases? Explain.

esci 16.11 If you haven't already, fire up **Robust two** and see the analysis of the NATSAL21 data set. If you don't see that, scroll right and click at red 13 to load the data. Click at red 8 for robust analysis.

a. Use the spinner at red 8 to adjust the amount of trim. Describe how points in the dot plots change and explain what that indicates.

b. What is the trimmed mean with 0% trimming? With 50% trimming, or as close to 50% as you can get?

esci 16.12 Scroll right and click at red 15 to load the PenLaptop 2 data set. Again compare conventional and robust approaches.

With 0% trimming, so all data points are included, the robust analysis gives exactly the same results as conventional Welch–Satterthwaite, as shown in Figure 16.2. Yes, the robust analysis does not require assumption of homogeneity of variance.

Just as the mean and median are two different ways to summarize the general location of a data set, the conventional and robust analyses are alternative ways to summarize the data and estimate a population parameter. Using mean or median is not a question of right and wrong, but of judging which is more appropriate in a particular situation. Similarly, we need to judge whether a robust analysis that estimates the population trimmed mean is more justifiable in the research situation, especially considering skew and outliers. For the NATSAL21 data set, the extreme outliers, especially for males, suggest we should prefer robust. Note that it's not an alternative

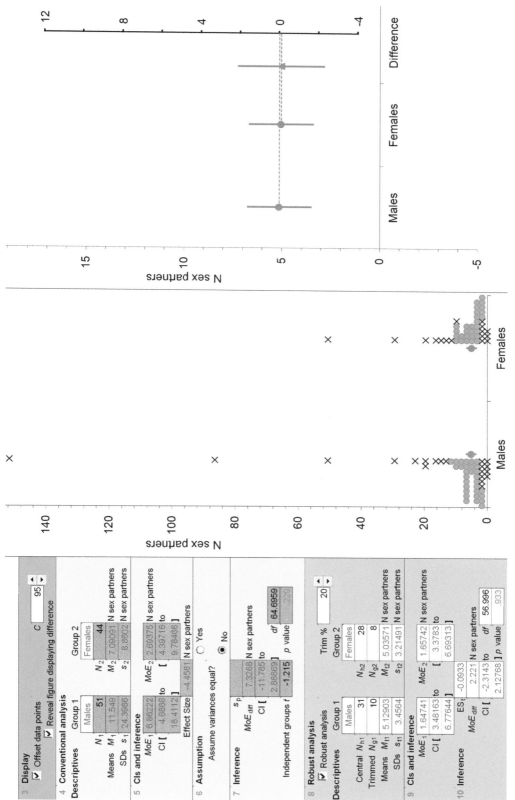

Figure 16.3. Same as Figure 16.2 but displaying robust analysis. The conventional analysis is grayed out, and robust analysis with 20% trimming from each end of each set of group data is shown at red 8, 9, and 10. In the left figure, trimmed points are displayed as crosses and retained data points as filled red circles.

way to estimate the population mean, but a good way to estimate a different parameter, the population trimmed mean. For a highly skewed population distribution, the trimmed mean may well give more insight about the sample and population. Choosing the most appropriate parameter to estimate requires careful thought in the research context. Here we'd probably prefer the trimmed mean.

Open Science Requirements

▶ If choosing robust after seeing the data, report both conventional and robust analyses.

A preregistered data analysis plan should state what analysis will be used. However, it has been common practice to examine the data before choosing between conventional and robust approaches. That's appropriate when we're exploring, but, from the perspective of planned analysis and preregistration, choices made after seeing the data are questionable research practices, which could be influenced, perhaps unconsciously, by a desire to achieve $p < .05$, or a short CI. If, as usual in the past, the research plan was not preregistered and a robust analysis seems appropriate, good practice is to report both conventional and robust analyses.

If you preregistered with no mention of robust analysis, but, after seeing the data, that approach seems strongly indicated, then you can consider a departure from your plan, in which case it's essential to report both analyses and full details of your reasoning.

In this section I've described a good way to deal with non-normal data. A general lesson is that, if you are concerned about any statistical assumption you need to make, then you should seek expert advice. There may be some robust technique that's appropriate for your situation.

ARCHIVAL DATA

▶ Archival data are data in an existing database. They can be used to address additional questions.

Not every research question requires collection of new data. It can be very efficient to find *archival data*, meaning data in an existing database, and use it to answer research questions beyond those considered by the researchers who originally collected the data. Moreover, the Open Science demand for open data wherever possible means that more and more data will be available for use by other researchers. However, there are challenges with using archival data. A major one is that it's hard to specify a planned analysis—which must be fully independent of the data—when the data are already available. Yet we know that without planned analysis we are left only with exploratory analysis, which runs the risk of capitalizing on chance, of merely seeing faces in the clouds.

▶ Longitudinal research can be highly valuable, but is challenging to set up and maintain.

My example is the Australian Temperament Project (ATP), which has been collecting data for more than 30 years. It's therefore also an example of *longitudinal research*, which is essential for studying how people develop over decades. However, longitudinal research is challenging to set up and maintain. For a start, it's very hard to retain participants, because people move overseas, decide they no longer wish to participate, or simply can't be contacted. In addition, most research careers and funding are based on achievement and publication in the short term, and so there are few projects around the world that have been collecting data for decades—and their databases are, correspondingly, precious.

The Australian Temperament Project

The project began in 1983 with a sample of 2,443 families with young infants from across the state of Victoria in Australia. In the following 30 years, there have been 15 waves of data collection, always from the parents, and often also from teachers and other professionals. From about 11 years old, the children themselves have provided information. Mailed questionnaires have been supplemented by observations and interviews with selected subsamples. A remarkable feature has been the project's retention rate: After 30 years more than two-thirds of the original families are still involved. Many of the original infants are now raising their own children and so the project is continuing as a study of three generations.

Temperament refers to personality, especially behavioral aspects that are apparent in infancy. The central focus of the ATP has been on how temperament develops, and further issues of interest include educational progress, mental health, relationships, risky behaviors, and social competence. One major finding has been that temperament usually persists strongly, and the seeds of later anxieties or problematic behavior can often be seen in difficult early temperament traits. Another conclusion is that early identification of children at risk, then early intervention, can be effective in reducing later problems. There's more about the project at tiny.cc/atpwebsite, and Vassallo and Sanson (2013, tiny.cc/atp30) is an excellent summary. You might be interested in Chapters 5 and 6 on alcohol use and driving behavior—compare with your own country, if not Australia.

Longitudinal Analyses and Archival Data

At the start of a longitudinal project, sample selection is critical because the same sample will be providing data throughout the project and so it's especially important that the sample is representative of the population. The ATP took advice from the Australian Bureau of Statistics to choose a sample representative of all Victorian infants and families. Conclusions from the project will thus apply broadly, at least across Victoria and, most likely, across all of Australia. The extent to which a conclusion applies in other countries is a matter for judgment and further research, and depends to some extent on similarity of relevant aspects of Australian and the other country's culture.

In a large longitudinal project, many important questions require analyses of *time series* data, meaning data collected at a large number of time points. In Chapter 15, the Chaix et al. (2014) study on mouse fitness and obesity had five time points over 2 h, but the ATP has time series data extending over decades, which allow researchers to address questions about long-term change. Specialized statistical techniques are needed, often similar to the techniques used to analyze time series data in economics (e.g., GDP growth or the inflation rate over many years) or meteorology (e.g., average temperatures over many years).

Time series data can extend over many years, and be used to address questions of long-term change. Specialized analysis techniques may be needed.

Over time, the database of a large and well-run longitudinal project becomes more and more valuable, both because its time series extend for longer, and, usually, because additional researchers apply further analyses to selected archival data to address further questions. In addition, some studies collect new data to be integrated and compared with selected archival data.

Open Science Issues

All the statistical and Open Science issues we've discussed are relevant for the analysis of archival data.

Preregistration, and Planned and Exploratory Analysis. Suppose you plan to analyze archival ATP data to investigate the relationship between infant temperament and the commission of driving offenses 20+ years later. You could explore the data, by making scatterplots and tables of frequencies, and calculating various correlations and regressions. However, that would be exploration, and any relationships you discover could be lumps in the randomness. There's only one database, so, once you've explored, you have lost the chance to conduct a planned analysis. Is there a better way?

One good approach is to choose a sample of the ATP participants. Explore their data, seeking an analysis strategy that's most informative about your research questions, and preregister that as your data analysis plan. Then, for the first time, access the remainder of the database—which you haven't previously examined—apply your planned analysis, obtain no doubt fascinating answers to your questions, and report your study in full detail.

This strategy means you need to be very careful about examining the whole database, because that amounts to exploration, and you lose the opportunity for planned analysis. The general principle of distinguishing carefully between exploratory and planned analysis is just as important in the archival context as elsewhere.

Open materials, open data. You may have no problem earning the open materials badge by making full details of your procedures and data analysis available. Open data is, however, more problematic. The ATP research leaders tell me that they are keen to establish collaborations with other researchers, but that they cannot release any original data, even after individual identifying information is removed. The project commenced long before open data became recognized as important, and the project's ethical approval requires that the data be kept confidential. One reason the project has achieved an impressively high retention rate over 30+ years is that participants have been repeatedly assured that their data will be kept completely confidential. Note that the database includes sensitive information, such as police records and DNA samples. If the project were being initiated today, the researchers would aim to make as much of the data openly available as possible, of course without any individually identifying information.

I conclude that analysis of archival data, and longitudinal research, can both be highly valuable and rewarding, even if challenging. The full range of Open Science considerations apply, but it may take careful consideration to decide how best to respond to each Open Science concern.

> Given a large existing database, explore a sample to develop an analysis strategy, then apply this as a planned analysis to the rest of the database.

> Open Science issues apply when analyzing archival data and in longitudinal research, but thought is needed to find the best way to respond to each issue.

16.13 a. Suppose a large longitudinal project on the development of gifted and talented children made its database open to all. You read a news report that analysis of that database shows that people who were musically talented as children are more likely to divorce later in life. What might you conclude? What questions would you ask about the analysis underlying the claim?

b. Are there any dangers in making a large data set openly available? What policy on data accessibility would you recommend?

? Quiz 16.2

1. Robust statistical analysis requires more / fewer assumptions than conventional analysis, for example by requiring / not requiring the population to be normally distributed.
2. The trimmed mean of a sample is more / less influenced by outliers than the conventional mean and is our point estimate of the conventional mean / trimmed mean of the population.

3. If, after seeing your data, you observe that it is markedly non-normal and then decide to carry out a robust analysis, you should
   a. report the robust analysis as exploratory analysis, which offers only tentative findings.
   b. quickly register an analysis plan including robust analysis.
   c. report both conventional and robust analyses, with no mention of exploratory analysis.
   d. not in fact carry out a robust analysis, and simply report only the conventional analysis.
4. In longitudinal research, why is choosing the sample critical?
5. When using an existing large archival data set, a good strategy is to
   a. use past research to plan the exploratory analysis to be applied to the whole data set.
   b. explore half the data set, then explore the other half, and check how similar the results are.
   c. explore a subset, then preregister an analysis plan to be applied to the remainder of the data set.
   d. explore the full data set, then choose an analysis plan to apply to a large subset.
6. Open Science is likely to lead to more / less research data being available to all, and to greater / reduced opportunity for students and others to use archival data to answer their own research questions.

DEALING WITH NUMEROUS DEPENDENT VARIABLES

Beyond studies with one or two measures are those using techniques that give thousands or even millions of measures, for example various techniques for studying the brain. In Chapter 9, one of the meta-analysis examples involved brain pictures. Search online for "fMRI" (functional magnetic resonance imaging) or "fMRI images" to see images of brain cross-sections with colors indicating regions of heightened neural activity. Development of wonderful brain imaging techniques, especially fMRI, has led to exciting research that investigates how brain activity relates to many types of cognition, and also to emotions, political attitudes, responses to advertising, and numerous other things. Brain imaging is a hot research area for good reason, but in 2009 it was challenged by a dead fish. More on that in a moment, but first a few words about fMRI.

Increased neural activity in the brain prompts increased local blood flow, which can be detected via changes in a magnetic field around the participant. Complex equipment and software gives an image on the screen of a selected slice through the brain, with colored regions. There are many steps of physiological reasoning and assumptions between neural activity in some brain region and the color of the corresponding small area on the fMRI screen. Of most relevance for us is the statistical reasoning used to decide which areas should be colored.

fMRI analysis is usually based on 100,000 or more *voxels*, each a tiny volume in the brain, perhaps 1 mm across. Neural activity is measured for each voxel, so we have values for thousands of dependent variables, one for each voxel, and each is usually measured repeatedly in a series of trials. Complex statistical procedures are used to analyze the overall pattern of activity. Usually, patterns are compared for two conditions—perhaps the participant looks at an emotional or a neutral picture. When a small cluster of adjacent voxels shows markedly higher activity for the emotional than the neutral picture, the corresponding area in the brain image is colored. You might think that the brighter the color, the greater the neural activity, so activity level is the effect size. However, fMRI analysis has usually focused on p values, not effect sizes. Brightness of color indicates how small p is in those regions—how strong the evidence is that activity level is greater for the emotional than the neutral picture. The analysis gives many thousands of p values, and areas with a cluster of very small p values are colored. The smaller the p, the brighter the color. Are you thinking that having so many p values might raise a problem?

16.14 Recall the dance of the p values. Imagine fMRI replications—perhaps we record the colored fMRI image for the same stimuli and participant a number of times, with a one-minute break between recordings. Then we replay the images at, say, one every second. How might the colored areas in successive images appear? What would you conclude?

Recall our discussion in Chapter 14 of exploratory analysis and multiple comparisons: When there are many possible comparisons, exploratory analysis is at particular risk of finding false positive results—of identifying only lumps in the randomness, faces in the clouds. fMRI researchers recognized the problem by using a very low p value criterion, often $p < .001$, for a region to be colored.

Now comes the dead fish: Bennett et al. (2009, tiny.cc/salmonposter) placed a dead salmon in their fMRI machine and compared patterns when a picture or no picture was shown to the fish. Of course there's no neural activity in a dead fish, so any patterns given by the machine might reflect, for example, bone and muscle, but can't be reflecting neural activity. Moreover, the fMRI patterns with and without the picture placed in front of the fish could differ only randomly, so any region earning color would have to be a false positive.

Using a $p < .001$ criterion the researchers identified a small region in the fish that met the criterion for heightened neural activity and was brightly colored. However, they suspected that the number of comparisons was so large that using a $p < .001$ criterion was insufficient protection from false positive results. Using knowledge of the number of voxels—in other words, the number of DVs—they calculated what stricter criterion would be appropriate for the number of possible comparisons in their study. They found that when they used this stricter criterion, this even smaller p value, all color disappeared. The best place to read about the dead salmon is at Ignobel (2012, tiny.cc/deadsalmon). Since 2009, most fMRI reports have used the more appropriate, stricter criterion.

▶ The dead salmon reminds us that when there are many DVs, or many possible comparisons, exploring is dangerous, and invites false positive findings.

I tell the dead salmon story to illustrate how, even for the most complex and high-tech situation, our basic statistical and Open Science ideas—for example the multiple comparisons problem—are still highly relevant. Expect those ideas to be relevant whenever there is a large number of DVs, for example in other new and complex fields such as genetic analysis. Remember the basics and never be blinded by media hype, complex equipment, or bright colors on a computer screen. In other words, this is not primarily a story about a dead fish, or even about brain images, but about how to deal with large numbers of DVs and potential comparisons.

The Open Science solution is, as usual, to specify in advance a limited number of planned comparisons. If you explore when there are very many DVs, there's an enormous risk of capitalizing on chance, of obtaining false positives.

It's best to avoid this risk, but sometimes that's impractical, as for the above type of fMRI study, in which case you need to set an extremely strict criterion—perhaps an extremely small p value—for any effect that you wish to identify as possibly of interest. The dead fish tells us this, loud and clear. Then you'll be especially keen to run a replication and use planned analysis to investigate further any tentative findings suggested by data exploration in the first study.

BIG DATA

Beyond studies with $N = 20$, or even 200, are studies with much larger N. When N is enormous, how long are CIs likely to be? Of course—they are likely to be extremely short, so we hardly need to worry about estimation error, and can focus on the sizes of effects and their practical meaning.

Before getting to an example, here's a question: Can knowing about statistics make you rich and famous? Well, perhaps: In 2009, Hal Varian, then Google's chief economist, famously stated (tiny.cc/Varianstats) that

> The sexy job in the next ten years will be statisticians. The ability to take data—to be able to understand it, to process it, ... to visualize it, to communicate it—that's going to be a hugely important skill in the next decades, not only at the professional level but even ... for elementary school kids, for high school kids, for college kids. Because now we really do have essentially free and ubiquitous data.

"Free and ubiquitous data"—also referred to as *big data*—presents a dramatic contrast with earlier chapters in which the challenge was always to find N large enough to give reasonably precise estimates, and to find similar studies so meta-analysis can give more precise answers to our research questions. It's a different world when we consider the vast databases of emails and other messages, purchases and payments, information about online searches, links between people, and information about people themselves. Such databases are held by governments, Google, LinkedIn, Facebook, Amazon, and many other companies. These databases are collecting big data and they are expanding by the hour.

Brain Points for Better Learning

Can big data be useful for researchers? If so, to what extent do our ideas of estimation and Open Science have relevance? My example is a computer game. Consider what you might say to a child who has just finished a painting. Perhaps "That's lovely, you are great at art!" or "That's lovely, I can see you've been trying really hard!" Which comes naturally to you? As a child, which did you hear more often? As I first mentioned in the *Making the Most of This Book* section, Carol Dweck and her colleagues have published many studies finding that mention of effort leads to better persistence and progress. The key issue is the extent to which the child (and parent and teacher) have a *fixed* mindset—the belief that "I'm just no good at mathematics"—or a *growth* mindset, which holds that there are no fixed limits, and that effort and application can lead to learning. Praising effort is effective because it encourages a child to have a growth mindset, to believe they can do better, and to persist. My example applies that idea to an educational computer game.

O'Rourke et al. (2014, tiny.cc/brainpoints) prepared two versions of Refraction, a game to help elementary school students learn fractions. The two versions were as similar as possible, but the control version awarded points for each level completed, whereas the experimental version aimed to develop a growth mindset as well as teach fractions. It awarded *brain points* for effort and use of strategy, as well as for improved understanding of fractions. The versions were made available through the BrainPOP website (www.brainpop.com), which was being used by around 20% of elementary schools in the United States. Any child choosing to use Refraction was assigned randomly on first login to work with either the control or experimental version. The system collected detailed data about every child's performance.

During just 10 days, the researchers obtained data from more than 7,000 children with each version of the game. They found that children working with the experimental version played longer and completed more levels than those using the control version, and were also more likely to use the strategies rewarded by the brain points system. Many of the effect sizes were small, around $d = 0.1$, but that's hardly surprising considering that children used the game for only around 3 minutes on average. Another notable result was that the experimental version was better at retaining lower-performing children. These are important findings—it's rare for anything in education to make a difference after only a few minutes. They suggest how educational games can be designed to be more effective and engaging, while also encouraging students towards a growth mindset—the belief that persistence and effort can lead to successful learning.

The study estimated effect sizes. Yes, the CIs were extremely short, but what about p values? Ponder that question for a moment.

▶
Big data offers many exciting research opportunities. CIs are likely to be extremely short, and p values tiny. But careful thought is needed to interpret effect sizes.

With such large N, even small effect sizes had tiny p values. The researchers reported several cases of $p < .0001$, but the exact p values had several more zeroes. In other words, with very large N, any non-zero effect size is, for practical purposes, estimated with no error, and is almost certainly different from zero in the population. CIs and p values become virtually irrelevant, and our attention can be focused on the effect sizes themselves, which is great news. Even so, critical thought remains as important as ever. The effect sizes may be estimated very precisely, but what do they mean? Are they large enough to matter? Are they really answering our research questions?

Being able to run such online studies offers enormous potential for educational research. The Refraction study not only showed how learning can be improved, but allowed the researchers to study the performance of children at a range of skill levels, and also to investigate a higher-level educational aim, the development of a growth mindset. Developing and piloting the game, setting up the study, and analyzing the data were, no doubt, large tasks, but collecting the data required little more than waiting 10 days—to obtain data for more than 14,000 children! If you want even more, just wait a few more days.

Innovative online and big-data methods have huge potential to revolutionize research in many fields. They can often sidestep some of the problems of traditional research, especially that of obtaining sufficiently large N. It may be easy to carry out pilot tests, even with quite large N, before finalizing materials and design, preregistration, then running a study with extremely large N. However, careful and critical thought remains essential. What do you want for your birthday? Perhaps a large online study?

16.15 a. Choose a study or a research field that you know about. In that context suggest an online study with big *N* that might be feasible.

   b. Compare your suggested study with a conventional small-*N* version.

Now, for one last time, please reach for the coffee or chocolate and write down your take-home messages. I suggest writing a list for this chapter, and another for the whole book. Maybe sleep on those lists before turning ahead and looking at mine. Are you dreaming about the dances yet? For this chapter, think of a 10-step plan, Open Science (of course), non-normal data, archival data, many DVs, and big data. For the whole book, I elected to write seven major messages, but you can write as many or as few as you like.

Now for the new-statistics way of wishing you well:

"May all your confidence intervals be short!"

 ## Quiz 16.3

1. The main point of the dead salmon study was to emphasize that
   a. fMRI is sufficiently sensitive to identify neural activity even in a dead fish.
   b. analyzing an enormous number of results and focusing on extreme ones is likely to mislead.
   c. effect size measures of critical brain processes cannot be analyzed using NHST.
   d. $p < .001$ is typically a reasonable criterion for defining statistical significance.
2. In the context of fMRI, what is a voxel?
3. Brain regions discussed in reports of fMRI research should preferably be identified in advance / by exploration of the data, especially considering that a small / large / very large number of DVs is being recorded.
4. While discussing "free and ubiquitous data", Varian wished to emphasize that
   a. even children now need to be able to understand and deal with data.
   b. only a few highly trained statisticians will be needed.
   c. the study of statistics will steadily become less necessary.
   d. most statisticians are rich and famous.
5. Dweck argues that a _____ mindset is more / less preferable than a fixed mindset, is best promoted by challenge / comfort, and is likely to lead to less / more persistence by the student.
6. Working with big data, precision of estimation is likely to be very low / low / high / very high, the CIs very short / short / long / very long, and p values very small / small / not so small.

16.16 Do other things for a while, then come back and revise your two sets of take-home messages.

Reporting Your Work

You've made it this far! Chapter 1 started with some basic principles for reporting your work. Here's a recap of these principles supplemented with some of the most important specific points covered in the intervening chapters.

Tell the full story

Give a complete account of your research process and the data you collected. Don't selectively report results.

▪ Always make clear which analyses were planned and which are exploratory.
▪ Specify how you planned a sample size (or if you didn't) and how you decided when to end data collection.

When reporting your work, *tell the full story* is still the guiding rule. When reading the work of others, make sure you are getting the full story.

▓ Specify any data points that were excluded, transformed, or trimmed. Make clear when these decisions were made (hopefully in advance of seeing the data) and why.

▓ Report all Open Science practices you have adopted, especially if you preregistered your analysis or sampling plans. Give the link to the preregistered plan.

▓ Don't omit measures or conditions from your research report, even if they end up not being essential to answering your research questions.

▓ Let your reader know that the report is complete.

▓ Seek to make your research report publically available, either in a peer-reviewed journal or an online repository.

Provide sufficient detail

Include all the details necessary for someone else to replicate your work. Include all the data necessary for someone else to incorporate your results into a meta-analysis. Share your data online, if possible.

▓ Share your materials in an online repository if possible. State the link.

▓ Share your data in an online repository if possible. Again, state the link.

▓ Provide basic descriptive statistics for all measures collected: a measure of location, a measure of spread, and sample size. The mean and standard deviation are often the best choice for measures of spread and location, but use your judgment. For nominal measures, frequencies and proportions are usually the most effective way to summarize the data.

▓ For comparisons between groups or conditions, report each group mean, standard deviation, and sample size. If the comparison is of a repeated measure, it is essential for future meta-analysis to report the correlation between measures and/or the standard deviation of the differences.

▓ Provide standardized effect sizes and CIs when possible. For comparisons between two groups, $d_{unbiased}$ is best, but other standardized effect sizes are available for other research designs.

▓ For correlations, be sure that the sample size for each correlation is clear, as these can be different for each correlation due to missing data.

▓ Focus any research report on point and interval estimates. It is ok, though, to supplement this with NHST information.

Show the data

Whenever possible, provide figures that show your key findings. Prefer figures that show all the data rather than just summary statistics.

▓ Select figures that emphasize the effect size and CI important for evaluating your research questions.

▓ Use lines to connect means across repeated measures designs but avoid these for independent group designs.

▓ State in the figure caption what error bars represent—95% CIs.

▓ Use a reasonable scale on your graphs. One good default is to use a scale that shows the entire possible range of the measure being depicted. If you have multiple graphs reporting the same variable, try to use the same scale for all of them so that your reader can easily make comparisons across figures.

▓ Edit your figures carefully and avoid visual clutter.

Interpret the point estimate and CI

Focus your conclusions and interpretation on the point estimate *and* confidence interval.

▓ Start with quantitative questions (e.g., "To what extent does X correlate with Y?") and make quantitative interpretations (e.g., "X is only very weakly correlated with Y.").

▓ Give an interpretation that respects the full range of the CI, considering what the lower limit, point estimate, and upper limit might mean.

▓ Although some rough guidelines are available for evaluating effect sizes, use your judgment and make your interpretations within the context of previous research.

- Match your conclusions to the research design. Only draw causal conclusions for experimental research. Use language that matches the design.
- Seek replication and use meta-analysis whenever appropriate.

Use APA style

Finally, let's recap some of the specific APA style rules (APA, 2010) that are of special relevance for reporting results:

- Roman letters serving as statistical symbols are italicized (e.g., *M*) but Greek letters serving as statistical symbols are not italicized (e.g., μ).
- Statistics that cannot exceed 1 in absolute value are reported without a leading 0. These include *p*, *r*, proportions, and φ.
- APA style is a *pre*-publication format. If your manuscript is going directly to readers, you should adapt accordingly.
- Report statistics using a reasonable number of decimal places (see Chapter 3). For each measure, be consistent in the number of decimal places used to report its mean, CI, and standard deviation.
- If you *do* report NHST analyses, report *p* values with an exact ($p = .03$) rather than relative ($p < .05$) value. Give two decimal places, or three for values less than .02. However, state $p < .001$ rather than stating exact very small values.

  Remember that this is not a complete guide—you'll probably also need to consult the APA *Manual* frequently as you write your initial manuscripts. Hopefully, though, you are on the way to becoming a good writer and reader of research reports. I can't wait to see what you can accomplish!

 # Take-Home Messages for Chapter 16

The 10-Step Plan and Open Science

- The step-by-step research plan based on estimation has now expanded to 10 steps, with extra attention to preregistration and other Open Science practices.

- Replication projects suggest that a disturbingly large proportion of published research may overestimate the sizes of effects, perhaps considerably. Open Science is vitally important.

- Some journals are offering preregistered review, which provides researchers with expert advice before data collection commences and guarantees publication, whatever results are obtained.

- Replications are increasingly being encouraged and funded, often as crowd-sourced research, which in many cases allows students to play a central role.

Some Further Research Challenges

- With clearly non-normal data, or when other statistical assumptions might not be met, consider robust techniques. CIs based on trimmed means are good interval estimates for population trimmed means, without needing to assume normality or homogeneity of variance.

- Analysis of archival data presents challenges, but can be highly valuable. Explore a subset, then preregister an analysis plan to be applied to the remainder of the database. Longitudinal research is also challenging, but necessary for many important questions.

- With very large numbers of DVs, for example from fMRI brain images, be very wary of the dangers of exploration and cherry picking. Our basic ideas of estimation, planned and exploratory data analysis, and replication still apply.

- The advent of big data offers many research possibilities. Very large *N* usually means that CIs and *p* values are not important, because estimates are for practical purposes accurate. However, critical thought about effects and their meaning is still necessary.

- Open Science issues are relevant in all research situations, whatever the design, measures, and statistical techniques. Careful thought may be needed to decide how best to meet Open Science goals.

Take-Home Messages for the Whole Book

■ It's an exciting time to be learning about research and statistics. Open Science promises better research outcomes—it has recently burst on to the scene and is changing things for all researchers. Enjoy being at the forefront.

■ Adopt estimation thinking and, where possible, formulate research questions in estimation terms ("To what extent...?"). Design studies that give point and interval effect size estimates, and use these for interpretation. A short CI means a precise estimate, which is what we want.

■ Results vary with replication, often to a surprising extent. The dance of the means and dance of the CIs can be surprisingly wide—lots of bouncing around. CIs may be disappointingly long, but they give accurate information about uncertainty in data.

■ Recognize the five red flags that express cautions about *p* values and NHST. The dance of the *p* values is very wide indeed. Usually prefer estimation.

■ Building a cumulative quantitative discipline requires replication, and meta-analysis to combine evidence over studies and increase the precision of effect size estimates. Think of any study in the context of replication and meta-analysis.

■ The key Open Science question is "Do we have the full story?" Wherever possible, adopt Open Science practices: preregister studies, report research in full detail, and make materials and data openly available.

■ Careful critical thought is always needed. Keep practicalities and real-world meaning in mind. Be prepared to use your judgment. Enjoy the fascination of research.

 End-of-Chapter Exercises

1) Follow the directions in Exercise 16.3 to see information about the TOP Guidelines. Follow the link to the *Science* article on transparency and openness (Nosek et al., 2015). Read the first few paragraphs, and note the reference to "null results"—results that don't achieve statistical significance.

   a. Explain the null result problem being referred to. Which red flag is relevant?

   b. What is the solution being advocated in the article?

2) Go to opensourcemalaria.org and, at that home page, click "Read More", then browse the FAQ.

   a. Describe the aim of the project, and the main ways that it is different from most medical research. Could you join the project?

   b. In the answer to the first question in the FAQ, click on "set of six laws". Which do you think are the most important laws, and why?

   c. What is your reaction to the project and how it is set up?

3) In **Robust two**, scroll right and click at red 14 to load the Dana data set reported by Wilcox (2009, p. 195).

   a. Explore conventional and robust approaches. Discuss.

   b. A possible strategy is to start with zero trimming, then use the spinner near red 8 to increase trimming until the data points that are clear outliers have been trimmed. Is this a wise strategy? Explain.

4) Download the ATP report by Vassallo and Sanson (2013, tiny.cc/atp30). Browse as you wish.

   a. Read Chapters 5 and 6, especially the sections on alcohol use and driving. How do you think the results compare with those in your country, if not Australia?

    b. Suppose you become fascinated by the possible relationships between different types of risky behavior, especially drinking alcohol and unsafe driving. Suppose you then arrange collaboration with ATP researchers and have access to the full database. Explain the steps you would take to run a study on the relation between drinking and driving.

5) You read a fascinating article that includes several brain pictures, which show small brain areas in a range of bright colors. State two questions you should ask and explain what information in the article you want to see for each of them.

6) The step-by-step research plans stated in Chapter 1, and at the start of this chapter, are written as guidelines for a researcher.

    a. Consider instead the perspective of the reader of a journal article. Which of the 10 steps in the plan at the start of this chapter should be identifiable in the article?

    b. Could any be omitted? Explain.

7) In the Preface to this book we mentioned the tutorial article (Cumming, 2014, available from tiny.cc/tnswhyhow) published by *Psychological Science* when it introduced new Open Science requirements and strongly encouraged use of the new statistics. Download the article.

    a. Read as your interest takes you. Do you recognize many of the figures? (Note that we now prefer to picture a CI without the little cross bars at the ends, so a CI is simply a line with a dot for the point estimate, as in this book.)

    b. Read the 25 guidelines stated in Table 1 on p. 8. Are there any that you don't recognize from this book? (In the first and last guidelines, replace "research integrity" with "Open Science", which is the term that's now in wide use and what we prefer.)

? Answers to Quizzes

Quiz 16.1

1) d; 2) pilot testing, plan a study, preregister a study, conduct a study; 3) a; 4) Do we have the full story? 5) before, regardless of; 6) both established researchers and students, close.

Quiz 16.2

1) fewer, not requiring; 2) less, trimmed mean; 3) a; 4) That sample will be used for the duration of the study, so we need it to be representative of the population; 5) c; 6) more, greater.

Quiz 16.3

1) b; 2) A tiny region in the brain, typically about 1 mm across; 3) in advance, very large; 4) a; 5) growth, more, challenge, more; 6) very high, very short, very small.

Answers to In-Chapter Exercises

16.1 Many Labs 2 was like 1 but larger, studying more effects. Many Labs 3 ran studies at various times during a semester to investigate, with undergraduate participants, the extent to which results varied with time of semester.

16.2 a, b. It is disappointing that replication in so many cases finds smaller, or much smaller, effects, which suggests that selection or questionable research practices contributed to at least some of the original studies. However, it is hard to estimate how serious the problem is because for each effect there is only a single original study and one replication, both with CIs indicating uncertainty, and some being medium to long.

16.3 a. When I visited, 714 journals and 62 organizations had signed to indicate support. The journals had also promised to undertake, within one year, a review of their policies to see to what extent they could adopt the TOP guidelines; b. In the TOP summary as you move from Level 0 to Level 3 the requirements become more exacting; c. Some studies cannot be preregistered because they are responsive to unpredicted events, such as Hurricane Katrina. Some data cannot be made open because of privacy or commercial issues; d. The Preregistration Challenge offers 1,000 researchers $1,000 each for planning and preregistering a study, then running it and reporting it fully. OSF offers an easy fill-the-blanks procedure for preregistration.

16.6 Open Science requires full disclosure, including details of variables and analyses not fully described in the report. If the researchers had examined many more groups and presented results only for a selected three, they may have been cherry picking, which would undermine our confidence in the results. Only one other group (science) had been investigated, so we are reassured.

16.7 Almost certainly it is the Open Science requirements that the researcher will question, especially preregistration and replication. Many Labs 1 and the Reproducibility Project: Psychology are just some of the sources of evidence we've met that justify the Open Science requirements.

16.8 Outliers may be irrelevant and a nuisance, or may be telling us something of crucial importance. Trim thoughtfully and consider what outliers may be saying.

16.9 a, b. For males, $M = 11.5$ is much greater than $M_t = 5.1$ and $s = 24.4$ is very much greater than $s_t = 3.5$, because of the influence of high outliers; c. For females, the data are less skewed and, in particular, do not have the two extreme high outliers of the male sample. For females, $M = 7.1$ is greater than $M_t = 5.0$, and $s = 8.9$ is much greater than $s_t = 3.2$; d. Looking at those values differently, the male mean (11.5) is considerably larger than the female (7.1), but the trimmed means are almost the same (5.1 and 5.0). The two s_t values (3.5 and 3.1) are also very similar. The trimmed analysis tells us that, overall, male and female responses were quite similar, except for two extreme male responses. Conventional analysis hides that fact.

16.10 Conventional difference (Females–Males) = −4.5, robust difference = −0.1, consistent with Exercise 16.9. The CI on the difference for conventional means has MoE = 7.3 and for trimmed means has MoE = 2.2. Therefore the difference between the population trimmed means is estimated much more precisely than for the conventional means, which is another big advantage of robust analysis for this data set.

16.11 a. With a higher trim percentage, more points are trimmed and displayed as crosses, and omitted from calculation of M_t; b. With 0% trimming, robust mean and SD are the same as conventional. With 50% trimming, when N is even all points are removed, and when N is odd, only one point remains, which is at the median.

16.12 The small amount of skew in both groups means that M_t is a little lower than M for both. However the (Laptop–Pen) difference is similar for conventional (5.2) and robust (5.6) analyses, and the two CIs on the difference have almost the same MoE (1.6 in each case). There is little reason to carry out the robust analysis.

16.13 a. Before drawing any conclusion we would need more details of the analysis. If the result arose during exploration it's only speculation and probably should not have been published. We'd ask especially whether the analysis had been planned before seeing the data; b. It's a danger that openly available data can be analyzed by anyone, whether or not competent and scrupulous. The project would not want its good name associated with poor and possibly misleading analyses. One possibility is to make the data available only to qualified researchers, although that is not the Open Science ideal. As usual, any dramatic claim in the media must be scrutinized very carefully, even if based on a large and reputable database.

16.14 On replication the p value for each voxel is likely to be quite different, so colored areas could change considerably. I would expect to see colored blobs changing somewhat in position, size, and shape. Dancing amoebas?

16.15 a. Think of some large existing database you could access, for example open data on OSF, or some online system used by many people, like BrainPOP. Then you need to choose research questions that such a system could answer; b. Look forward to enjoying very short CIs!

Appendix:
The ESCI Software

ESCI ("ESS-key") is *Exploratory Software for Confidence Intervals*. There are three sections to this appendix:

- Guidance for downloading and using ESCI.
- A summary of what each ESCI page offers, in the three ESCI files that accompany this book. The filenames of those files start with "ESCI intro".
- A guide for where in ESCI to look, if you have a particular data analysis requirement. For example, you may have data in original units from a paired design, or a 2 × 2 table of frequencies.

DOWNLOADING ESCI

ESCI runs under Microsoft Excel, and a licensed copy of Excel is required to run ESCI. The three ESCI files that accompany this book can be downloaded freely from the book website at www.routledge.com/cw/cumming (Note that ESCI for my earlier book, Cumming 2012, is different. That earlier version of ESCI can be downloaded from www.thenewstatistics.com).

> Make sure you save any ESCI file on your local hard disk before you open and run it.

Make sure you save any ESCI file on your own local hard disk before you open and run it. At the book website you can find any news about updates to ESCI, and any errors that have been discovered in the book or software. The custom is that every file name includes the date of last modification, so, for example, **ESCI intro chapters 3–8 Oct 1 2016** would be the October 1, 2016 version. You can thus easily check that you are using the latest version. At the **Intro** page of any file, scroll down to see the license conditions for ESCI.

LOADING AND RUNNING ESCI

ESCI files are regular Excel workbooks, and should open immediately in Excel.

Macros

Many ESCI pages use small programs called "VBA macros" to carry out operations triggered by your clicking of a button, or other actions. Therefore, those operations will not work unless macros are enabled, so make sure you enable macros before you start using ESCI. You should be able to nominate ESCI files as trusted, so you don't need to enable macros every time you load an ESCI file.

> Make sure macros are enabled before you start using ESCI.

Popout Comments

When you hover the mouse near any little red triangle you should see a **popout comment**. If you don't, you need to adjust your Excel settings to specify that comments should be visible.

Entering Your Own Data

To clear data, use the **Clear data** button, or select the cells with data and press the Delete key. Then type in your own data, using Enter (on Mac, return) or the down arrow key after each value. Or, usually better, copy a column of data values from some other file, then click to select the top empty data cell in ESCI and use **Paste Special/Values**, or **Paste Values**—different versions of Excel offer slightly different options.

Screen Resolution and Display Size

ESCI is designed so the display conveniently fits the screen for **screen resolution** of about 1680 × 1050 or similar. It may help to use full screen display.

You may choose to change your screen resolution, but, if you do this, some aspects of the display may not appear so neat, for example the neat stacking of means in the mean heap. Alternatively, on any page you can adjust the zoom by changing it from the usual 100% or 120% but, if zoom is changed too far, labels and values may not fit so well in their cells.

Protection

Pages are protected, to reduce the chance of making inadvertent changes, but protection can be removed—no password is needed. Remove protection if you wish, but take care, and be sure not to save the workbook or, if you wish to save, give it a different name.

Using Figures Outside Excel

An ESCI figure can be transferred to a Word document. Click a little in from the edge of the figure, to select it: You'll see the border of the figure highlighted. Copy, then paste. **Paste Special/Picture (Enhanced metafile)** works well. Allowing copy and paste of figures requires that figures are not protected. Therefore they can be accidentally changed. If that happens, try **Undo**. Otherwise, exit from Excel—don't Save—and restart ESCI.

An alternative is to use (in Windows) the Prnt Scrn key to transfer an image of the whole screen to the clipboard. Paste this into a Paint program (or similar), use the rectangle select tool to select an area of the image, then copy and paste this into your Word document. **Paste Special/Picture (Windows metafile)** works well.

Editing of Figures

Figures can be changed as desired, using any Excel editing facilities: Change axis labels, change scaling on an axis, change chart format.... It's usually best to edit a figure as you wish, before copying it from ESCI to your Word document.

To deselect a figure, after edit or copy, press the Esc key once or twice.

Number Formats

In most cases ESCI reports numbers to an appropriate number of decimal places. A p value, for example, may be reported as .0 or as .000, either of which actually means it's zero when rounded to three decimal places. Exact values for p should not be reported if less than .001, so report such a value as $p < .001$. Don't report $p = 0$.

In some cases ESCI uses a general format for numbers, to accommodate a very wide range of possible values. In such cases, extremely small or large values may be reported in scientific format: 0.0000045 may appear as 4.5E-06, meaning 4.5×10^{-6}. Similarly, 26,800,000 may appear as 2.7E+07, meaning 2.7×10^7.

ESCI Formulas and Calculations

Most formulas and arrays of data are visible if you scroll right or down, so if you like you can see how ESCI does its work. Some formulas need to be placed behind the figures. Similarly, you can examine the VBA code if you wish.

STRATEGY FOR GETTING STARTED WITH A NEW ESCI PAGE

- Look for a suitable video at the book website; many of these demonstrate how to use one or more ESCI pages.
- At the ESCI page you are interested in, scan the display, read the labels, and hover the mouse over any little red triangle to see a popout comment.
- A new page may look confusing, but one way to start is to follow the bold red numbers 1, 2, …, in sequence, reading the popouts as you go. Note that when, in the ESCI exercises, I say something like "click near red 4", I may be referring to clicking anywhere in the colored area that has red 4 in the top left.
- Experiment. See what happens when you click buttons, spinners, radio buttons, check boxes, or sliders. You won't break anything, usually you can retreat, and if all else fails you can exit from Excel (don't Save) and start again. Discuss what you see with a friend.
- Discover how ESCI works, yes, but focus your thinking on the statistical ideas—they are the most interesting things, and what really matters.
- In Chapter 3, just before the start of the first ESCI exercises, see the further hints about using ESCI for statistical learning.

Finally, here's what may be the most useful strategy of all:

- As you play around, keep thinking how you could use ESCI to explain the statistical ideas to someone else. Then have a go at doing that.

THE ESCI FILES AND THEIR PAGES

The ESCI files available on the book website at www.routledge.com/cw/cumming are:
ESCI intro chapters 3–8
ESCI intro Meta-Analysis
ESCI intro chapters 10–16

ESCI intro chapters 3–8

The pages within this file are as named in bold below. I use the same format for the pages of the other files, which follow. In ESCI, to go to different pages, use the tabs at the bottom of the Excel screen.

Intro—Introductory page. Overview. License information.

Describe—See *Chapter 3*. See a data set displayed in three ways, including a frequency histogram and a dot plot. Calculate and see basic descriptive statistics.

Normal—See *Chapters 3* and *4*. See the normal distribution. Find tail areas, and critical values of z.

Normal and t—See *Chapter 5*. See the normal and t distributions. Find tail areas, and critical values of z and t.

CIjumping—See *Chapters 4* and *5*. See a population, samples, sample means, and CIs. Explore the mean heap, dance of the means, central limit theorem, and dance of the CIs.

CI and p—See *Chapter 6*. See sample mean, M, null hypothesis value, μ_0, and the 95% CI. Explore how position of the 95% CI is related to the p value.

Data two—See *Chapter 7*. Type or use **Paste Special/Values** to enter your own data, for the independent groups design. See one or two figures, with CIs, and d and $d_{unbiased}$.

Summary two—See *Chapter 7*. Enter summary data for your own independent groups. Obtain calculated values of CIs, and d and $d_{unbiased}$, and see CI figures.

d picture—See *Chapters 7* and *8*. See how two populations relate for a chosen value of Cohen's d.

Data paired—See *Chapter 8*. Enter your own data, for the paired design. See a figure with a difference axis, with CIs, and d and $d_{unbiased}$.

Summary paired—See *Chapter 8*. Enter summary data for your own paired design. Obtain calculated values of CIs, and d and $d_{unbiased}$, and see a CI figure.

ESCI intro Meta-Analysis

Intro—Introductory page. Overview. License information.

Original two groups—See *Chapter 9*. Meta-analysis of the difference between independent means, in original units, for up to 30 studies.

Subsets—See *Chapter 9*. Meta-analysis of the difference between independent means, in original units, for up to 30 studies, plus analysis of two subsets of studies.

d two groups—*See Chapter 9*. Meta-analysis for independent groups, using d or $d_{unbiased}$, for up to 30 studies.

d subsets—See *Chapter 9*. Meta-analysis for independent groups, using d or $d_{unbiased}$, for up to 30 studies, plus analysis of two subsets of studies.

Single r—See *Chapter 11*. Meta-analysis of Pearson's correlation, r, for up to 30 studies.

ESCI intro chapters 10–16

Intro—Introductory page. Overview. License information.

Precision two—See *Chapter 10*. See precision curves for independent groups. Find N for target MoE on average, and with assurance.

Precision paired—See *Chapter 10*. See precision curves for paired data. Find N for target MoE on average, and with assurance.

See r—See *Chapter 11*. See scatterplots with a chosen value of r, or for random samples from a population with chosen Pearson's ρ.

Scatterplots—See *Chapters 11* and *12*. See a scatterplot and correlation, r, for your own data set of two variables, X and Y. See also the scatterplot of z scores. Calculate and see regression in original and standardized units.

One correlation—See *Chapter 11*. See a figure showing a correlation, r, with its CI. See a cat's-eye picture on the CI.

Two correlations—See *Chapter 11*. See a figure showing two independent *r* values, with their CIs. See the CI on the difference.

One proportion—See *Chapter 13*. See a figure showing a proportion, *P*, with its CI. See the *p* value for testing a chosen null hypothesis.

Two proportions—See *Chapter 13*. See a figure showing two independent proportions, with their CIs. See the CI on the difference, and the *p* value. See chi-square analysis of a 2 × 2 table of frequencies.

Ind groups comparisons—See *Chapter 14*. Enter either summary statistics or full data for up to six independent groups. See means and CIs, and investigate any comparison of two means.

Ind groups contrasts—See *Chapter 14*. Enter either summary statistics or full data for up to six independent groups. See means and CIs, and investigate any contrast of two subset means.

Ind groups 2 × 2—See *Chapter 15*. Enter either summary statistics or full data for a 2 × 2 two-way factorial design with two between-groups independent variables. See means and CIs, and the interaction.

Robust two—See *Chapter 16*. Enter data for two independent groups. See means and difference between the means, with CIs, for conventional and robust analyses.

ESCI FOR ANALYZING YOUR OWN DATA

Contents List for This Section

To use ESCI to analyze your own data, first choose from the numbered list of seven subsections below, considering your DV and the analysis task you have in mind. The subsection itself should guide you to the ESCI page most likely to provide what you need.

For further information about any ESCI page mentioned in this section, see the section immediately above.

Types of Dependent Variable

1. A variable, *X*, in original units
2. Cohen's *d*
3. Pearson's correlation, *r*
4. Frequencies

Types of Analysis Task

5. Areas and critical values for *z* or *t*
6. Meta-analysis
7. Precision for planning

1. A VARIABLE, *X*, IN ORIGINAL UNITS

Single Group Design, Full Data

At the **Describe** page of **ESCI intro chapters 3–8**, enter your data. See descriptive statistics, a frequency histogram, and a dot plot. See *Chapter 3*.

At the **Data two** page of **ESCI intro chapters 3–8**, enter your data as Group 1 and leave Group 2 blank. See summary statistics, the CI on the mean, and a figure. See *Chapter 5*.

Single Group Design, Summary Data

At the **Summary two** page of **ESCI intro chapters 3–8**, enter your data as Group 1 and leave Group 2 blank. See the CI on the mean, and a figure. See *Chapter 5*.

Independent Groups Design, Full Data

At the **Data two** page of **ESCI intro chapters 3–8**, enter your data. See summary statistics, the CIs on the means and the difference, and a figure. Click at red 10 for a second figure, and at red 11 and 12 to see d and $d_{unbiased}$, and the CI for δ. See *Chapter 7*.

At the **Robust two** page of **ESCI intro chapters 10–16**, enter your data. See either conventional or robust analyses, with figures showing CIs. See *Chapter 16*.

Independent Groups Design, Summary Data

At the **Summary two** page of **ESCI intro chapters 3–8**, enter your data. See the CIs on the means and the difference, and a figure. Click at red 6 for a second figure, and at red 7 and 8 to see d and $d_{unbiased}$, and the CI for δ. See *Chapter 7*.

Paired Design, Full Data

At the **Data paired** page of **ESCI intro chapters 3–8**, enter your data. See summary statistics, the CIs on the means and the difference, and a figure. Click at red 9 and 10 to see d and $d_{unbiased}$, and the CI for δ. See *Chapter 8*.

Paired Design, Summary Data

At the **Summary paired** page of **ESCI intro chapters 3–8**, enter your data. See the CIs on the means and the difference, and a figure. Click at red 4 and 5 to see d and $d_{unbiased}$, and the CI for δ. See *Chapter 8*.

More Than Two Independent Groups, One IV, Full Data

At the **Ind groups comparisons** page of **ESCI intro chapters 10–16**, click at red 2 to select **Full data below**. Enter your data. See summary statistics and a figure with CIs. Select a comparison of two means and see the comparison and its CI. See *Chapter 14*.

At the **Ind groups contrasts** page of **ESCI intro chapters 10–16**, click at red 2 to select **Full data below**. Enter your data. See summary statistics and a figure with CIs. Select two subsets of means and see the contrast of those subsets and its CI. See *Chapter 14*.

More Than Two Independent Groups, One IV, Summary Data

Use the same two pages as above for full data, but click at red 2 to select **Statistics above**. Select a comparison or contrast and see the results and CI. See *Chapter 14*.

Independent Groups, 2 × 2 Factorial Design, Full Data

At the **Ind groups 2 × 2** page of **ESCI intro chapters 10–16**, click at red 2 to select **Full data at right**. Enter your data and see summary statistics. Select a subsets contrast, main effect, or interaction, and see the calculated result and figure with CIs. See *Chapter 15*.

Independent Groups, 2 × 2 Factorial Design, Summary Data

At the **Ind groups 2 × 2** page of **ESCI intro chapters 10–16**, click at red 2 to select **Statistics above**. Then proceed as for full data above. See *Chapter 15*.

2. COHEN'S *d*

To appreciate what your *d* implies for the overlap of two population normal distributions, use the **d picture** page of **ESCI intro chapters 3–8**. See *Chapter 7*.

To calculate *d* and $d_{unbiased}$, and the CI for δ, for your data, see the appropriate subsection above for *X*, for independent groups or the paired design. See *Chapters 7 or 8*.

If you have a value of *d* for independent groups, you can enter that *d* and N_1 and N_2 into the **d two groups** page of **ESCI intro Meta-Analysis** to calculate the corresponding $d_{unbiased}$ and the CI for δ. See *Chapters 7 and 9*.

3. PEARSON'S CORRELATION, *r*

Two Variables, *X* and *Y*, in Original Units, Full Data

At the **Scatterplots** page of **ESCI intro chapters 10–16**, enter your paired (*X*, *Y*) data. See summary statistics and the scatterplot. Click at red 15 for a second scatterplot, of standardized scores. Click at red 9 for regression calculations and display. See *Chapters 11 and 12*.

One or Two Values of Correlation, *r*

At the **One correlation** page of **ESCI intro chapters 10–16**, enter *r* and *N* to see the CI on *r* and the *p* value for testing a selected H_0. See *Chapter 11*.

At the **Two correlations** page of **ESCI intro chapters 10–16**, enter r_1, r_2, N_1, and N_2 to see the CIs on r_1, r_2, and the difference, and the *p* value for the difference. See *Chapter 11*.

4. FREQUENCIES

One Proportion

At the **One proportion** page of **ESCI intro chapters 10–16**, enter integers *X* and *N* for proportion $P = X/N$. See the CI on *P* and the *p* value for testing a selected H_0. See *Chapter 13*.

Two Proportions or a 2 × 2 Frequency Table

At the **Two proportions** page of **ESCI intro chapters 10–16**, enter X_1, N_1, X_2, and N_2 for independent proportions P_1 and P_2. See CIs and the *p* value for the difference. Click at red 8 for the chi-square analysis and φ. See *Chapter 13*.

5. AREAS AND CRITICAL VALUES FOR *z* OR *t*

To use ESCI to find critical values for *z* or *t*, use the **Normal** or **Normal and t** page of **ESCI intro chapters 3–8**.

6. META-ANALYSIS

Independent Groups Design, Data in Original Units

At the **Original two groups** page of **ESCI intro Meta-Analysis**, enter means, SDs, and sample sizes for two groups for each study, to see the forest plot and meta-analysis. See *Chapter 9*.

At the **Subsets** page, enter the same information, and labels to identify two subsets of studies, to see meta-analyses of the subsets and a comparison of the two. See *Chapter 9*.

Independent Groups Design, Cohen's *d*

At the **d two groups** page, enter *d* and the two sample sizes for each study, to see $d_{unbiased}$, and the forest plot and meta-analysis. See *Chapter 9*.

At the **d subsets** page, enter the same information, and labels to identify two subsets of studies, to see meta-analyses of the subsets and a comparison of the two. See *Chapter 9*.

Pearson's Correlation, *r*

At the **Single r** page, enter *r* and *N* for each study to see the forest plot and meta-analysis. See *Chapter 11*.

7. PRECISION FOR PLANNING

Independent Groups Design

Use the **Precision two** page of **ESCI intro chapters 10–16** to find *N* for target MoE on average, and with assurance. See *Chapter 10*.

Paired Design

Use the **Precision paired** page of **ESCI intro chapters 10–16** to find *N* for target MoE on average, and with assurance. See *Chapter 10*.

Answers to End-of-Chapter Exercises

CHAPTER 1. ASKING AND ANSWERING RESEARCH QUESTIONS

1) Pain study:
   a. The point estimate is 34%, the interval estimate is the 95% CI and is the interval from 19% to 49%, and MoE is 34 − 19 = 15% or 49 − 34 = 15%.
   b. We are 95% confident the population decrease in pain rating is in [19, 49], and any value in that interval is plausible as the population average decrease, whereas any value outside it is relatively implausible. Interpretation: I suspect a 34% reduction is enough to be clinically valuable; perhaps any reduction in the range from 19% to 49% could be clinically useful.
   c. The CI seems very long, and I would like to have a more precise estimate of the benefit of relaxation. I'm concerned that there may be other studies or other results that haven't been reported, and also that we don't have full details of how the study was conducted.

2) The main difference is that the point estimate of 13% is considerably lower. I suspect a decrease of 13% may not be of much clinical importance, although someone with more knowledge of the context may disagree. The CI is even a little longer, so I'm even keener to have a more precise estimate.

3) Pain study replication:
   a. Use a sample size four times as large as in the original study. Otherwise the replication would be as similar to the original as possible.
   b. The results might be 30% [23, 37]—a similar point estimate and MoE of 7, about half of 15.
   c. The meta-analysis might give 31% [26, 36]. The point estimate lies between those of the two studies. The CI is shorter than those from the two studies, as we expect from a meta-analysis. The interpretation is as before, but now we have a more precise estimate. A replication giving similar results reassures us an original result was not an aberration.
   d. Replication and meta-analysis usually give us precise, or much more precise, estimates, which is great.

CHAPTER 2. RESEARCH FUNDAMENTALS: DON'T FOOL YOURSELF

1) Random sampling of university students: Options a and e represent random sampling because both give every member of the population the same chance to be selected. Options b, c, and d are not random sampling—each involves some level of random behavior, but not the key step of random selection of participants from the whole population.

2) Scales of measurement:
   a. Nominal—political orientation is simply categorized and the labels have no numerical, or even ordered, meaning.
   b. Ordinal or Interval—a rating scale like this can be interpreted as either ordinal or interval, depending on whether it seems reasonable to assume that the participants perceived the scale as having equal spacing between the labels on successive numbers (interval) or not

(ordinal). This is *not* nominal measurement because scores can be at least ordered, and not a ratio scale because there is not a true 0 representing a complete lack of liberalness.

   c. Ratio—participants can have a score of 0 which reflects a true absence of agreement with the set of opinions.

   d. This can be interpreted as ordinal or interval.

   e. Ordinal.

3) Educational DVDs and word knowledge:

   a. This is a non-experimental study because there was no random assignment or manipulation of different levels of DVD ownership.

   b. As usual for non-experimental research, there are lots of possible explanations for the finding because the groups could differ in lots of ways beyond DVD ownership. For example, wealthier families might both own lots of DVDs and also provide their children with more support for word learning.

   c. Ratio, because there is a true 0: no DVDs owned.

   d. Reliability, assessing the extent that the measurement is repeatable.

   e. It is a bit difficult to specify the intended population, but the researchers would probably like to draw conclusions about all children in general, or at least about all children in the country where the research is conducted. Given that the intended population is large and poorly defined, it seems very unlikely that random sampling was used.

   f. How far to generalize depends on your judgment of the degree to which the sample would resemble or differ from other groups. It's a judgment call. One perspective might be to emphasize commonality across the human race and to assume that what works for one group of children would likely work for others. Cross-cultural psychologists, though, would probably point out that we tend to underestimate how profoundly culture influences behavior, and might wisely counsel us to be cautious about drawing conclusions far from the original research context.

4) Money exposure and egalitarian attitudes:

   a. Experimental.

   b. Open Science requires reporting the full story. There may have been good reasons for omitting the four other studies, but it appears the decision of what to report was based on the results obtained, with only the studies favoring the researchers' hypothesis being reported. This seriously distorts our evaluation of the evidence. A meta-analysis of only the published studies is likely to show a clear and consistent effect of money exposure on egalitarian attitudes. Analysis of the whole set of studies, however, is likely to show a much smaller and/or uncertain effect.

   c. The authors most likely originally intended to analyze the scale average, so analyzing each item on its own would be an exploratory analysis. There is nothing wrong with exploration, but research reports need to make clear which analyses were exploratory and must treat conclusions from exploratory analysis as very tentative.

CHAPTER 3. PICTURING AND DESCRIBING DATA

1) ACT Scores: Table 3.5 adds calculated values to Table 3.3. Note that the data have been sorted by ACT score to make it easier to identify the median (in bold) and IQR.

   a. $M = 24.1$, Median = 24, Mode = 24.

   b. $s = 4.61$, Range = 17 to 31. For IQR, the Excel function PERCENTILE gives 20.5 and 27.5 for the 25th and 75th percentiles, respectively. An alternative approach is to take the median of the lower 6 scores, which is 20.5, and median of the upper 6, which is 27.5. Either way, IQR is from 20.5 to 27.5. Other methods may give slightly different values.

Table 3.5 Completed Version of Table 3.3, With ACT Scores for Exercise 1

Student	ACT	$(X_i - M)$	$(X_i - M)^2$
8	17	−7.09	50.28
7	18	−6.09	37.10
5	20	−4.09	16.74
9	21	−3.09	9.55
2	24	−0.09	0.01
11	**24**	−0.09	0.01
1	26	1.91	3.64
6	27	2.91	8.46
3	28	3.91	15.28
10	29	4.91	24.10
4	31	6.91	47.74
Total	265.00		212.91
Denominator	11		10
M	24.09		
s^2			21.29
s			4.61

2) Student Survey:

   a. Positive affect is relatively normally distributed—there is a single, strong peak and the distribution is fairly symmetrical. The mean score of 3.43 is a little above the midpoint of the 1–5 scale, indicating that students on average feel moderate levels of positive affect. There is wide spread, with $s = 0.71$ and scores ranging across almost the full range.

   b. There is strong positive skew, with most students aged 18–22, but a long upper tail of ages ranging up to nearly 60. The mean (21.8 years) is most affected by the outliers, and the median (20 years) is probably a more useful indicator of location. The skew causes the mean to be larger than the median. The college has mostly younger students, but also some older returning and non-traditional students. Removing outliers would misrepresent the sample, by omitting those older students. They should be removed only if there is reason to examine the subgroup of younger students, perhaps aged up to about 32.

   c. There is considerable positive skew. Most students report relatively little exercise, but the right tail pulls the mean (54.7) way above the median (22). The extreme outlier of 1,810 corresponds to engaging in strenuous exercise 201 times per week, which is hardly credible. Most likely, the student didn't understand the question, made an error, or gave a non-serious answer, so there is good reason to delete this outlier, which would decrease the SD. If it is deleted, s decreases from 135 to 64.7. As always, if you delete an outlier, report how, when, and why the decision was made to remove it.

   d. Raven IQ Scores are relatively normally distributed. The mean is .377, median is .375, and standard deviation is .199. In contrast, GPA is very strongly negatively skewed, with scores stacked up near 4.0, the top of the GPA scale. A long tail extends down to very low values of GPA. The mean is 3.34, median is 3.40, and SD is 0.51. Different variables can have different distributions, even for the same sample. However, we expect IQ and GPA to be related, so it's perhaps surprising that their two distributions are so different. The GPA distribution, with most of the scores concentrated in the 3.5–4.0 range, suggests that the testing is not sufficiently challenging to distinguish among students in the upper parts of the distribution. You may have heard of grade inflation occurring in the last one or two decades. Search online for "college grade inflation", or similar, and you should easily find statistics describing a dramatic increase in the proportion of A grades in recent years, and interesting discussion about likely causes and consequences.

e. No! It doesn't make sense to calculate a mean for data on a nominal scale. It's often convenient to represent nominal data with numerical codes, but it's important to remember that these codes have no numerical meaning, and thus calculation of most descriptive statistics doesn't make sense. Nominal data can be summarized with frequencies (175 females and 68 males) and relative frequencies (72.0% females and 28.0% males).

3) Scores in context:

a. With $X = .875$, $M = .377$, $s = .199$ we calculate $z = 2.50$. This student is tied for top score in the sample.

b. With $X = 3.9$, $M = 3.34$, $s = 0.508$, we calculate $z = 1.10$. This participant stands out more on the IQ measure ($z = 2.50$) than on GPA ($z = 1.10$).

c. For positive affect: $X = 2.0$, $M = 3.43$, $s = 0.71$ and we calculate $z = -2.01$. For negative affect: $X = 2.0$, $M = 2.32$, $s = 0.75$ and we calculate $z = -0.43$. The positive affect score is more unusual than the negative affect score, within this sample.

d. For age, $X = 59$, $M = 21.8$, $s = 5.56$ and we calculate $z = 6.69$, which is an extreme outlier! For exercise, $X = 1,810$, $M = 54.8$, $s = 135.3$ and we calculate $z = 12.97$, which is a very extreme outlier!

4) Religious belief:

a. I predicted an approximately flat distribution, with similar frequencies of strong, moderate, and non-believers.

b. The distribution is clearly bimodal: Most respondents answered 100 (strongly believe in God) or 0 (strongly disbelieve in God), and relatively few participants gave scores between the extremes. My prediction was quite wrong. This is a good illustration of multiple peaks (two in this case) indicating distinct groups of participants.

c. With such a strongly bimodal distribution, none of the three measures of location does a great job of representing the distribution. Both the mean (48.2) and median (50) represent an intermediate level of belief that is actually rare; reporting only one mode would be misleading. The best non-graphical strategy would be to describe the distribution in words and report the location of each mode: one at 0 level of belief, the other at 100.

CHAPTER 4. THE NORMAL DISTRIBUTION AND SAMPLING

1) z scores: a. $z = 0$; b. $z = 2$; c. $z = -1$; d. $z = 3$.

2) Percent better: a. 50%; b. 2.28%; c. 84.1%; d. 0.1%.

3) Gabriela and Sylvia:

a. Sylvia's sample will have the smaller SE because she has collected a larger sample.

b. Combining the two samples will yield a smaller SE.

c. For Gabriela, SE = 1; For Sylvia, SE = 0.83; Combined, SE = 0.64.

d. What sample size is sufficient is a judgment call, which we'll discuss further in Chapter 10. For now we can note that the combined data set provides SE = 0.64, meaning that many repeated samples would give sample mean satisfaction scores that would bounce around (i.e., form a mean heap) with standard deviation of 0.64. Given that satisfaction has a theoretical range from 1 to 20, this suggests that any one sample mean will provide a moderately precise estimate, reasonably close to the population mean. This analysis suggests we have sufficient data, although collecting more would of course most likely give us a better estimate.

4) Nursing home and random sampling: c and d represent random sampling because both give each member of the population an equal chance to be in the study, and members of the sample are selected independently.

5) Skew:

a. Home prices tend to be positively skewed (longer tail to the right), because there is a lower boundary of zero, but in effect no maximum—typically a few houses have extremely high prices. These form the long upper tail of the distribution.

b. Scores on an easy test tend to be negatively skewed (longer tail to the left). If the test is very easy, most scores will be piled up near the maximum, but there can still be a tail to the left representing a few students who scored poorly.

c. Age at time of death tends to be negatively skewed (longer tail to the left). Death can strike at any time (☹), leading to a long lower tail; however, many people (in wealthy countries) die at around 70–85 years old, and no one lives forever, so the distribution is truncated at the upper end. Search for "distribution of age at death", or similar, to quickly find graphs showing strong negative skew.

d. Number of children in a family tends to be positively skewed (longer tail to the right) because 0 is a firm minimum, and then scores extend upward from there, with many families having, say, 1–4 children and a small number of families having many children.

6) Anything that limits, filters, selects, or caps scores on the high or low end can lead to skew. Selection is not the only thing that can produce skew, but any time your participants have been subjected to some type of selection process you should be alert to the possibility of skew in the variables used to make the selection (and in any related variables). Also, if the mean and median differ by more than a small amount, most likely there is skew, with the mean being "pulled" in the direction of the longer tail.

CHAPTER 5. CONFIDENCE INTERVALS AND EFFECT SIZES

1) ACT with $N = 9$:

a. Using $\sigma = 5$ we obtain: $M = 23.1$, 95% CI [19.8, 26.4], MoE = 3.3.

b. Yes, the CI contains 22, the true mean. Of course, the sample size is small and the CI is quite long, so it was not a precise estimate of the population mean.

c. Using $s = 5.44$ we obtain: $M = 23.1$, 95% CI [18.9, 27.3], MoE = 4.18. This CI is longer than the CI based on σ. Using s, the t critical value is larger than the z critical value used with σ, which makes the CI based on s longer, and more so for small N. This assumes the observed s is close to the true σ.

d. The more data collected, the shorter the CI will become. To cut the CI length in half requires N approximately 4 times as large.

e. **Data two** is designed to analyze and present data from two independent groups, as we'll discuss in Chapter 7. Here we're using it to analyze and present data for a single group.

2) Large sample of ACT scores:

a. With N this large, we expect a short CI.

b. Figure 5.12 shows the data and statistics. I've named the data set **ACT Large**. Near red 6 and 7: $M = 24.2$, 95% CI [23.6, 24.7], MoE = 0.55, so the entire range of uncertainty is barely over 1 point for an exam where scores range from 1 to 36. This seems precise!

c. Although quite precise, this sample does *not* provide an accurate estimate of mean ACT in the population—the true value of 22 is 1.6 points lower than the lower limit of the CI. Some CIs are red! Or perhaps there is bias in the data? A CI indicates uncertainty arising from sampling variability, but CIs cannot compensate for other factors that could distort or bias sample values. Our statistical model requires random sampling, as the best way to ensure the sample is representative of the population. Convenience samples may yield systematic differences from the population—for example, students with low ACT scores might have elected not to answer the ACT question. Also, self-report can introduce systematic bias—some respondents may report an exaggerated ACT score.

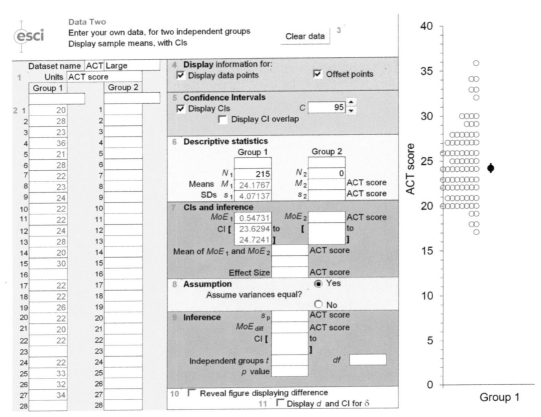

Figure 5.12. ACT scores ($N = 215$) are shown near red 2 at left. The figure shows individual data points (open circles), mean, and 95% CI. (Because of limited space in the figure, only about the first third of the data points are displayed as open circles. See the popouts near red 4.) Values of a number of statistics are shown near red 6 and 7. From **Data two**.

3) More variables from the student survey:

   a. For GPA: $M = 3.34$, 95% CI [3.29, 3.41], MoE = 0.06. This indicates that the average GPA at this school is fairly high, likely around a 3.3, which is a B+.

   b. For subjective well-being: $M = 4.94$, 95% CI [4.78, 5.10], MoE = 0.16. Given that this variable was measured on a scale from 1 to 7, it seems the average at this school is to be fairly happy, nearly a full point above the midpoint of the scale. This CI plus inspection of a stacked dot plot both seem to support the contention by Diener and Diener that most people are happy.

   c. For wealth: $M = 2.90$, 95% CI[2.78, 3.02], MoE = 0.12. Note that this item asked participants to rate on a 1–5 scale how wealthy they feel relative to others at their school, with a score of 3 indicating "average". It's interesting, then, that students on average feel about average in terms of wealth. This doesn't have to be the case! For example, when asked to self-assess different academic skills, there is a tendency for most people to see themselves as above average.

4) Student survey replication:

   a. We should expect most measures to give means within the original CI, but not necessarily all. An original 95% CI has about an 83% chance of capturing the mean of a close replication (see Figure 5.10 and Table 5.1).

b. For GPA: $M = 3.31$, 95% CI [3.21, 3.40], so the mean is within the CI from the first study; for subjective well-being: $M = 4.66$ [4.46, 4.87], so the mean is a little below the lower bound of the CI from the original study. For wealth: $M = 2.94$ 95% [2.79, 3.10], and so the mean is within the CI from the original study. Overall, two out of three of the variables we measured have replication values within the original CI, and one does not.

c. Yes, the two sets of results are quite similar, and sampling variation can easily account for the small differences. However, differences between the estimates in the two sets of results might also reflect real differences. For example, happiness might have changed between the first and second study. Any departure from a close replication could also cause differences, for example any change to the sampling procedure, or to the wording or ordering of the survey questions.

5) Anxiety in city dwellers:

a. No! Avoid any such probability statement about a CI.

b. No! A CI is an inferential statistic that estimates a population parameter, with length indicating precision of the estimate. It's not a descriptive statistic that indicates spread in the population or sample. For that, use a standard deviation.

c. Yes, a reasonable statement, noting where the CI falls in the full 1–5 range of the scale.

d. Probably too extreme. Shorter would be better, but the CI gives a moderately precise estimate.

6) Political attitudes in business majors:

a. The CI will indeed shorten, but M will almost certainly change, so the interval won't remain centered on exactly 8.

b. M will most likely remain in the original CI, especially considering that's long, so this statement is most likely correct.

c. There is a tiny chance that M will shift so far as to lie outside the original CI.

d. No!

CHAPTER 6. p VALUES, NULL HYPOTHESIS SIGNIFICANCE TESTING, AND CONFIDENCE INTERVALS

1) b, d, e, and h are statistically significant and would lead to rejecting the null hypothesis. Note that for e, the negative z value would occur if IQ scores after Neuroaid are *lower* than national norms.

2) b.

3) Online chemistry course study:

a. z because you know σ, the population SD, provided you think it reasonable to use this SD for your student population.

b. $z = \dfrac{M - \mu_0}{\sigma / \sqrt{N}} = \dfrac{82 - 80}{12 / \sqrt{36}} = \dfrac{2}{12/6} = \dfrac{2}{2} = 1$

c. $p = .317$, which we would report as $p = .32$.

d. This p value is not lower than .05, so we would *not* reject the null hypothesis. We do not have evidence that the online chemistry class leads to better or worse learning.

e. $SE = 12 / \sqrt{36} = 12/6 = 2$

MoE $= 1.96 \times 2 = 3.92$

Difference $(M_2 - M_1) = 2$ points, 95% CI [−1.92, 5.92]

The confidence interval shows the full range of plausible estimates for how the online course compares to the national average. It emphasizes thinking about the degree to which the class could be beneficial rather than a simple Yes/No statement about its having any benefit. The CI is quite long, indicating that the study estimated the effect of online delivery with relatively low precision.

f. No, a non-significant finding does *not* mean the null hypothesis is true (see Red Flag 3: Beware Accepting the Null Hypothesis). The CI, which is [−1.92, 5.92], makes this clearer, as we can see that plausible differences range from online students doing slightly worse, through no difference, up to online students doing moderately better.

g. For the participants in the online chemistry course ($N = 36$), the average final exam score ($M = 82$, $s = 12$) was 2 points higher than the national norm, 95% CI [−1.9, 5.9], so the effect of online delivery could plausibly be anywhere in that interval. This was not a statistically significant difference ($z = 1$, $p = 0.32$).

4) Lauren's study:

a. If the null is true, α is the risk of making a Type I error. In this case, Lauren has followed the convention of using .05, which means a 5% risk IF the null is true.

b. If the null is not true, the risk of Type II error is determined by α (significance level), sample size, the variability of the dependent variable (i.e., σ, the population SD), and the size of the effect (smaller effects, higher chance of Type II error). Of these, Lauren can most easily control sample size: the bigger the sample size, the less likely she is to make a Type II error, everything else being the same, IF the null is not true.

c. Lauren can reduce the risk of Type I error by selecting a lower α (e.g. $\alpha = .01$), but this increases the risks of Type II error should the null actually be false.

d. The *best* way to reduce the risk of Type II error is to use a larger sample size. It's also possible to use a higher α, but this has the drawback of increasing the risk of Type I error, IF the null is actually true.

5) Sleep and learning:

a. t because you do not know σ, the population SD.

b. $t = \dfrac{M - \mu_0}{s / \sqrt{N}} = \dfrac{3.9 - 0}{12.2 / \sqrt{11}} = 1.06$

c. For $t = 1.06$ with $df = 10$: $p = .31$.

d. No, with a significance level (α) of .05, $p > \alpha$ so this is not a statistically significant result and using NHST we would decide not to reject the null hypothesis.

e. This interpretation seems to be based partly on accepting the null. Red Flag 3: A statistically non-significant difference does not mean that the null hypothesis (no learning) is true. In other words, "no significant improvement" does not imply zero improvement.

f. After sleep deprivation, average improvement is 3.9, 95% CI [−4.3, 12.1], so the results are consistent with a wide range of effects of sleep deprivation on learning—from causing skill deterioration (negative scores), to blocking learning (no change in scores), to substantial learning (positive scores). The effect was not estimated with high precision.

g. Answers above to c, d, and f include the major information to include.

CHAPTER 7. THE INDEPENDENT GROUPS DESIGN

1) Presentation style and predicted learning:

a. The two groups have similar standard deviations, so it's reasonable to assume homogeneity of variance.

b. For independent groups, $df = (N_1 + N_2 - 2) = 40$

c. $t_{.95}(40) = 2.02$

d. $s_p = 22.02$

e. sample size component = 0.3086

f. $MoE_{diff} = 13.74$

g. The difference is −23 percentage points, 95% CI [−36.7, −9.3].

h. In this sample, a halting lecture style decreased students' predicted learning substantially, from 48% to 25%, approximately half. The CI ranges from approximately 9 to 37 percentage points, which corresponds to a range from about one whole letter grade (10 percentage points) to almost four letter grades! The CI indicates that any value in that range is plausible for the decrease in the population.

2) Presentation style and actual learning:

a. $df = 40$; $t_{.95}(40) = 2.02$; $s_p = 24.08$; sample size component = 0.3086; $MoE_{diff} = 15.02$. The difference is −4 percentage points, 95% CI [−19.0, 11.0].

b. In this sample, actual learning is similar in the two groups, with those given a halting lecture scoring only 4 percentage points worse than those given a fluent lecture. However, the CI is long, and is consistent with a wide range of impacts for halting lectures, from severely impaired (−19) up to strongly enhanced (11). Clearly, students' pessimistic learning predictions in the halting condition were not fully confirmed, but these data don't provide much clarity on the degree to which halting lectures impact actual learning.

3) Anchors and estimation:

a. The figure shows tremendous spread of estimated scores in both conditions, but most high-anchor participants gave estimates that are well above the mean for the low-anchor group.

b. The high-anchor group has a higher SD, but the values seem similar enough (within a factor of 2) to assume equal population variances.

c. Anchors had a strong influence on estimation. Low-anchor participants estimated fewer births/day ($M_1 = 2799$, $s_1 = 757$, $N_1 = 37$) than those given the high anchor ($M_2 = 3804$, $s_2 = 995$, $N_2 = 34$). The high anchor increased estimates by a mean of 1,005 births/day, 95% CI [589, 1422], $d_{unbiased} = 1.13$ [0.64, 1.64]. The confidence intervals are quite long, but suggest that plausible differences in the population are also moderate to very large.

d. For estimates of the population of Chicago, the low anchor was 200,000 and the high 5,000,000. Rounded to the nearest 1,000, the low-anchor participants gave much lower estimates ($M_1 = 577,000$, $s_1 = 492,000$, $N_1 = 45$), than those given the high anchor ($M_2 = 2,989,000$, $s_2 = 1,211,000$, $N_2 = 35$). The two SDs differ sufficiently for us to prefer to avoid the homogeneity assumption. The high anchor increased estimates by a mean 2,411,000, 95% CI [1,972,000, 2,849,000], using the Welch method, which is a very large and clear difference. Note that we don't calculate $d_{unbiased}$ because we are not assuming homogeneity of variance. For estimates of the height of Mount Everest, the low anchor was 2,000 feet (1 foot = 0.3048 m) and the high 45,500 ft. The low-anchor participants gave very much lower estimates ($M_1 = 6,777$ ft, $s_1 = 7,215$, $N_1 = 40$) than those given the high anchor ($M_2 = 36,427$ ft, $s_2 = 7,451$, $N_2 = 43$). The SDs are similar, so we make the assumption of homogeneity of variance. The high anchor increased estimates by a mean 29,650 ft, 95% CI [26,442, 32,857], $d_{unbiased} = 4.00$ [3.28, 4.79], which is an extremely large and clear difference.

4) Cleanliness and moral judgment:

a. The figure shows those in the neutral group ($M_1 = 5.81$, $s_1 = 1.47$, $N_1 = 20$) made judgments that were more harsh than those in the clean group ($M_2 = 4.98$, $s_2 = 1.26$, $N_2 = 20$). The (Clean − Neutral) difference was −0.83, 95% CI [−1.70, 0.05], $d_{unbiased} = -0.59$, 95% CI [−1.23, 0.04]. This is a large difference in the sample of nearly a full point on a scale from 0–9. However, the CI is long and consistent with a large decrease, no change, or even a tiny increase in harshness of judgment.

b. The data are consistent with a wide range of possibilities. It is plausible, based on these data, to conclude that cleanliness may strongly reduce the harshness of moral judgments, but the data are also consistent with a weak effect, no effect, or even a tiny effect in the opposite direction.

c. Given the long CI in the original study, you would probably be quite uncertain about what point estimate to expect. However, the larger sample sizes mean we can expect a shorter CI in the replication.

d. In the replication, those in the neutral condition (M_1 = 6.48, s_1 = 1.13, N_1 = 102) gave judgements very similar to those in the clean condition (M_2 = 6.47, s_2 = 1.12, N_2 = 106). The difference, which was in the same direction as in the original study, but tiny, was −0.01, 95% CI [−0.32, 0.29], $d_{unbiased}$ = −0.01. Moreover, the CI is fairly short, and suggests that the effect in the population is within a third of a point of zero.

e. This replication is consistent with the original study, in that its point estimate of −0.01 is within the CI of the original study. The shorter CI of the replication throws doubt on a large part of the long CI of the original, and suggests that the effect is at most fairly small.

f. It can be difficult to intuitively integrate findings that appear to differ. We often want to believe one study or the other. Meta-analysis can integrate evidence from the two, as we'll discuss in Chapter 9. It would probably find that the effect is around zero to small.

5) Mathematics attitudes:

a. At the Ithaca lab, there was a wide variety of IAT scores, ranging from a considerably stronger implicit bias against mathematics than art, through to the reverse. Men showed less implicit bias against mathematics (M_1 = 0.28, s_1 = 0.56, N_1 = 17) than women did (M_2 = 0.56, s_2 = 0.46, N_2 = 71). The difference was moderately large, and was 0.28, 95% CI [0.03, 0.54], $d_{unbiased}$ = 0.59, 95% CI [0.06, 1.13]. The CI is fairly long because the sample sizes were small, leaving considerable uncertainty about the size of the gender difference in implicit attitudes towards mathematics—the data are consistent with a difference anywhere from large down to around zero.

b. You were probably uncertain about your prediction for the replication, because of the long CI for the Ithaca data, although with larger sample sizes the CI from the second lab should be shorter.

c. The data from the SDSU lab show a similar pattern. Men showed less implicit bias against mathematics (M_1 = 0.22, s_1 = 0.49, N_1 = 38) than women (M_2 = 0.47, s_2 = 0.55, N_2 = 117). Again, this difference was fairly large, and was 0.24, 95% CI [0.05, 0.44], $d_{unbiased}$ = 0.45 95% CI [0.09, 0.82], again with a fairly long CI. Although both studies leave uncertainty about the size of the gender difference, they both found female college students have more negative implicit attitudes to mathematics than do males, by around an average 0.25 units on the IAT scale. Meta-analysis of the two studies would probably also find an average difference of around 0.25, with a shorter CI.

d. These were non-experimental studies (gender was not manipulated!), so can only show a relationship between gender and implicit bias. We cannot make causal conclusions from non-experimental research.

CHAPTER 8. THE PAIRED DESIGN

1) Re-reading, with and without retrieval practice:

a. $df = (N - 1) = 37$

b. $t_{.95}(37) = 2.026$

c. sample size component = 0.1622

d. MoE_{diff} = 8.94

e. M_{diff} = 15.0, 95% CI [6.1, 23.9]

f. The CI suggests that retrieval practice improves learning by around 15 percentage points. Considering that 10 percentage points corresponds to about one letter grade, plausible differences range from moderate (about half a letter-grade) to very large (more than 2 letter grades).

2) Re-reading, with and without retrieval practice, with strong motivation (i.e., high reward):

    a. df, $t_{.95}$, and the sample size component are the same as in (1), but $s_{diff} = 24$ is smaller, and this yields MoE_{diff} of 7.89. Therefore $M_{diff} = 13.0$, 95% CI [5.1, 20.9], which is very similar to the result of (1) and again suggests that retrieval practice produces somewhere between moderate and very large gains in learning.

    b. The similarity of the effect and CI for the two levels of motivation suggests that the effect of retrieval practice is similar, regardless of motivation. This conclusion is based on the *difference* between re-reading and re-reading+retrieval for the two levels of motivation, not on the overall level of learning in either condition. Two additional points need consideration. First, both CIs are long, so precision is low and there could easily be a non-zero effect of strength of motivation. Second, did the different payments really induce different levels of motivation? This needs investigation, especially considering evidence (e.g., Deci, Koestner, & Ryan, 1999) that financial incentives don't always lead to better learning.

3) Emotion and heart rate:

    a. Sample size was $N = 68$. Average heart rate at baseline, in beats per minute (BPM), was low to moderate ($M_1 = 64.6$ BPM, $s_1 = 10.3$) and during recall of an angry emotion it was higher ($M_2 = 72.1$ BPM, $s_2 = 12.1$), an increase of 7.5 BPM, 95% CI [5.4, 9.6]; $d_{unbiased} = 0.66$, 95% CI [0.45, 0.88]. The CI on the difference is fairly short, and we can conclude that heart rate increases considerably during recall of memories of anger. Note, however, that the order of taking baseline and anger heart rate measures was not counterbalanced, so a carryover effect is possible.

    b. We usually expect a lower precision estimate from independent groups, so can predict a longer CI on the difference.

    c. When analyzed as a between subjects study we obtain: $(M_2 - M_1) = M_{diff} = 7.5$, 95% CI [3.7, 11.3]. This is the same effect size, but a CI almost twice as long. As you probably predicted, independent groups would give a considerably less precise estimate of the degree to which angry memories influence heart rate.

    d. For the paired design, there was no mention of random assignment to counterbalanced orders of the rest and anger testing conditions, so we cannot make a causal conclusion. For independent groups, if we have random assignment of participants to groups, we could conclude that, most likely, the anger recall caused the heart rate increase.

4) Labels and product perceptions:

    a. Sample size was $N = 51$. Average enjoyment rating with the generic label was moderately high on the 1–10 scale ($M_1 = 6.86$, $s_1 = 2.13$), and even higher with the organic label ($M_2 = 7.82$, $s_2 = 2.09$). The mean difference associated with the mere change in label was fairly large, almost one point, and was $M_{diff} = 0.97$, 95% CI [0.48, 1.44]; $d_{unbiased} = 0.45$, 95% CI [0.22, 0.69].

    b. With the suspicious participants removed, $N = 46$, and $M_{diff} = 1.07$, 95% CI [0.54, 1.59]; $d_{unbiased} = 0.53$, 95% CI [0.26, 0.81]. This is a slightly larger effect, because the suspicious participants rated the juice very similarly with both labels, consistent with their suspicion that the labels were a ruse. Their data therefore pulled the mean difference towards 0.

    c. Including or excluding such participants is a judgment call. On one hand, the suspicious participants saw through the experiment, so may not provide a good measure of how labels influence perceptions for most people. On the other hand, in real life some consumers probably do succeed in ignoring brand labels, so perhaps these participants really should be included. The biggest consideration in weighing this issue is to make the decision *before* seeing the data, so that the choice is not influenced by which estimate you prefer. Pre-specifying such exclusion criteria can be difficult; Chapter 10 has more on this issue. You could choose to report two analyses: The first as you planned in advance, perhaps including all participants, and the second an exploratory analysis that excludes the suspicious participants.

CHAPTER 9. META-ANALYSIS

1) Anchoring effect: Babies born per day in the U.S.:

   a. $(M_2 - M_1) = 1,123$, 95% CI [1,068, 1,178]. (This CI is shown to the right of the forest plot.) Wording has a big influence on judgment, and switching from a low to a high anchor increases estimated births/day by more than 1,000. This is actually about a 40% increase from the low- to the high-anchor condition.

   b. 1.88, which suggests considerable heterogeneity. Switching to a random effects model will almost double the length of the CI.

   c. $(M_2 - M_1) = 1,245$, 95% CI [1,142, 1,348]. Even though the CI is now longer, it is still clear that anchoring has a very substantial influence on judgment.

   d. Using subset analysis with a random effects model, $(M_2 - M_1) = 1,203$, 95% CI [1,083, 1,324] for studies conducted in the United States and 1,317, 95% CI [1,147, 1,487] for those outside the U.S. So studies conducted outside the U.S.A. had a slightly larger mean influence of anchor, the difference being 114, 95% CI [−95, 322], but the CI leaves considerable uncertainty about this difference, which could plausibly be modestly smaller, the same, or somewhat bigger than for labs in the U.S. Also note that the diamond ratio was 1.99 for the U.S. and 1.36 for other labs, suggesting that considerable heterogeneity remains within the two subsets. Location of a lab in or beyond the U.S. does not seem to be an important moderator of the anchor effect.

2) Flag exposure and political attitudes:

   a. In general, the random effects model is preferred because it more realistically assumes that the effect size could vary across labs, conditions, and studies.

   b. Note that ESCI reports $(M_{No\_flag} - M_{Flag})$, given the way the data set is arranged. Reverse the sign, and random effects meta-analysis found $(M_{Flag} - M_{No\_flag})$ was = 0.004, 95% CI [−0.05, 0.06], in units of the 1–7 rating scale. This result suggests that exposure to the American flag has at most a very tiny effect on political attitudes.

   c. The diamond ratio is 1.0, meaning that the fixed effect model gives the same CI. There is little variation of study ESs, and likely to be little or no heterogeneity of population ESs. Therefore subset analysis is unlikely be informative.

   d. The replication results definitely do not provide support for the claim that flag exposure substantially influences political attitudes. The CI from the original study *does* overlap with the CI for the replication effect, but only because the CI from the original study is extremely long, meaning that the original study was uninformative. The very short CI very close to zero that Many Labs obtained throws great doubt on the original finding.

3) Gender and implicit bias against mathematics:

   a. $(M_{Female} - M_{Male}) = 0.27$, 95% CI [0.23, 0.30] units on the IAT scale, using a random effects model, indicating that females have moderately higher bias against mathematics than do males.

   b. A causal conclusion cannot be drawn because this is a non-experimental study. There could be lots of group differences beyond gender that could potentially explain this observation (e.g. simple level of exposure to or training in mathematics).

   c. 1.29, which suggests a modest amount of variation in effect size among these studies.

   d. Subset analysis indicates that the link between gender and math bias may be very modestly larger outside the United States (0.29, 95% CI [0.23, 0.35]) than within it (0.26, 95% CI [0.21, 0.30]). However, the CI on the difference is comparatively long (0.03, 95% CI

[−0.04, 0.11]) and so the difference could plausibly be anywhere from very small negative to small positive. Note also that the diamond ratio is 1.41 for U.S. labs and 1.13 for other labs, which are values similar to 1.29 for the whole data set. The U.S./Non-U.S. variable does not seem to be a useful moderator.

4) Power and performance:

a. We need d or $d_{unbiased}$ because the studies used different DVs—the raw scores were for performance at golf, darts, mirror tracing, and word production.

b. Across all seven studies, $d_{unbiased} = 0.20$, 95% CI [0.03, 0.36], which suggests that the effect of power on performance could be anywhere from tiny to around small-medium.

c. The diamond ratio is 1.19, which suggests that there may be some, but not very substantial variation in effect size over studies.

d. Task difficulty does not seem a promising moderator: The difference between the overall effect sizes for the normal and difficult tasks is very small, 0.01, 95% CI [−0.40, 0.42], and the diamond ratios are larger for the subsets than the whole set of studies. The CI for the difference is very long because there are so few studies, so we can say very little about the possible effect of difficulty. Participant pool seems a bit more promising, as online studies give a smaller overall effect size, the difference being −0.34, 95% CI [−0.63, −0.05], although the CI is again long. Country may be more promising, with studies conducted in the U.S. providing substantially weaker effect sizes, the difference being −0.60, 95% CI [−1.06, −0.13]. Again, the CI is long, but the results are consistent with power possibly having a much bigger effect on performance in Germany than in the U.S.

e. Moderator analysis is non-experimental and exploratory, and therefore we should consider conclusions from moderator analysis as highly tentative and should, if we wish, seek ways to investigate any proposed moderator, if possible as a manipulated IV within a future study.

f. This is a matter for judgment, and would depend on what potential moderator you most suspect might account for the substantial differences in effect size observed across the 7 experiments. If your hunch is with culture, it would be good to conduct one or more studies with both German and U.S. students. If you are interested in the possible effect of online administration, you could compare online and in-the-lab presentation within the one study. The results suggest that moderator effects may be small, so you should consider using large groups: In Chapter 10 there's more on how to choose N. Remember also that any moderator analysis is exploratory—we may be seeing faces in the clouds rather than a real difference in effect size.

CHAPTER 10. OPEN SCIENCE AND PLANNING RESEARCH

1) Exploring the Open Science Framework:

a. Analysis plan. Lots of examples to explore, but here's the analysis plan for a very interesting project: osf.io/2senq Click "wiki" to read the whole plan, and click the link at the top to explore the whole project. As you'll see, the project investigates the extent to which Open Science Badges work—the extent that rewarding the sharing of materials and data makes it more likely that these will actually be shared. So that's an Open Science project about the effectiveness of a new Open Science practice!

b. Sample plan. Again, lots of examples to explore, but here's an interesting one (McCarthy, 2014) that explains very clearly how a target sample size was selected for a replication project: osf.io/g3kt6 Note that this link points to a registration of the project made on Dec 22, 2013, before data collection commenced. You'll see a link at the top of the page to take you to the project's overall homepage (osf.io/zqwa2), where you'll see updated information that includes the final results.

c. Open materials. Of the many you could explore, here's a very interesting one, osf.io/ ct89g, the OSF page for the 3rd iteration of the Many Labs project. This project explores the extent that experimental results with psychology participant pools might vary over the course of a semester. You'll find all the materials needed to replicate 10 famous psychology experiments.

d. Open data. Try exploring this page (osf.io/ezcuj) which contains all the materials and data for the Reproducibility Project: Psychology (Open Science Collaboration, 2015).

2) Cleanliness and moral judgment:

a. About half the length of the CI, or about 0.6. **Precision two** tells us that two groups of $N = 20$ give MoE of 0.65 on average and $N = 23$ give 0.60 on average, so obtaining around 0.6 with $N = 20$ is perfectly reasonable.

b. $N = 87$ for MoE = 0.3 on average, and $N = 108$ for that MoE with 99% assurance. Use at least 100 if possible.

c. With those N values around 100, MoE of about 0.3 is perfectly reasonable.

d. Using eyeball interpolation with the **Precision two** curves, $N = 150$ gives MoE of about 0.23 on average and about 0.25 with assurance, so we expect MoE of around 0.23 and not more than 0.25.

3) Two-groups study:

a. .70

b. 30%.

4) Moral judgment, and statistical power calculations:

a. Using Figure 10.7, $N = 60$.

b. Interpolating, about $N = 85$.

c. Power = .99 and .95 for $\alpha = .05$ and .01, respectively.

d. A little more than .56, because the sample sizes were a little more than 100.

5) Frogs and toe clipping:

a. Beware accepting the null hypothesis. Lack of statistical significance does not justify a conclusion of no effect.

b. If toe clipping actually caused a 40% decline in survival, the study had only a .2 (or up to .6) chance of finding a statistically significant effect. If there were a smaller, but still important, decline, the probability of detecting it would be even lower.

c. There was much uncertainty, so a long CI. If toe clipping caused a 40% decline and power = .2, the chance of obtaining statistical significance is .2, and therefore the chance of not obtaining it, meaning that the CI extends to zero decrease, is $(1 - .2) = .8$.

d. Use larger N and, possibly, improved design or procedure. Planning would have alerted the researchers in advance to the insensitivity of their studies, allowing them to use larger N, or improve the studies in some other way.

e. First, that the studies they reviewed had low power, even for large effects, so finding non-statistically significant results was not surprising and certainly not evidence of zero decline. They also re-analyzed the data and combined results to find very strong evidence that toe clipping causes considerable decline in survival rate, and even stronger decline when increasing numbers of toes are clipped. These conclusions were justified and important. Opponents interpreted the Parris and McCarthy article as opposing toe clipping for reason of animal rights, whereas the researchers presented evidence that toe clipping was detrimental both to research and to the frog populations. Fidler reported the difficulty that Parris and McCarthy had in getting their analysis published, at least partly because several articles finding no statistically significant difference were believed to justify a conclusion that toe clipping causes no problem. If you understand the red flag and its importance you are ahead of a number of the contributors to the toe clipping wars! Incidentally, Fiona Fidler's PhD thesis is a great read.

6) You inquire whether the software had asked her to specify a target δ. If not, the software is probably reporting post hoc power, which, you explain, tells us little or nothing beyond the effect size found by the study, and should be ignored.

7) To be ethically acceptable, a study must be scientifically worthwhile, so N must be sufficient for the study to be likely to give usefully precise estimates, or have usefully high power. Second, participants' likely inconvenience or discomfort should be minimized, and so no more participants should be used than can be justified by a planning analysis.

8) Precision vs. power for planning:

   a. Power is widely understood by researchers, at least to some extent, even if not widely used. There is good, easily available software for calculating power.

   b. Precision for planning works in an estimation framework, which is more informative than NHST and de-emphasizes dichotomous thinking. There need be less concern about red flags. Second, it keeps the focus on effect size estimates and precision, consistently all the way from planning a study, through interpretation, to consideration of replications and meta-analysis.

CHAPTER 11. CORRELATION

1) .9, 0, .33, −.6. An eyeballed value within ±.1 is great, and within ±.2 is good, except that for the first you obviously should not suggest a value of 1 or more!

2) First to final exam scores:

   a. The scatterplot suggests a positive relationship, but with scatter. Guesstimates from roughly .4 to .7 would be reasonable for r. It can be harder to eyeball r with small data sets.

   b. There don't seem to be any strong cautions needed. The relationship does not seem strongly nonlinear. There's one very low score on exam 1, but this doesn't seem to be an invalid score or a strong outlier. Perhaps other students had low scores on exam 1 but then dropped the course. There may be some sign of a ceiling at 100. We should keep these possibilities in mind when interpreting r.

   c. Table 11.4 is the filled-in version.

   d. ESCI reports $r = .57$.

Table 11.4 Completed Table for Initial and Final Exam Scores for 10 Students

StudentID	Exam 1, X	Final Exam, Y	z_X	z_Y	$z_X z_Y$
1177	85.0	72.0	−0.19	−1.54	0.29
1288	96.8	92.0	0.63	0.69	0.44
1327	100.0	96.0	0.86	1.14	0.98
1911	100.0	95.0	0.86	1.03	0.88
1862	84.3	91.0	−0.24	0.58	−0.14
1578	83.0	88.0	−0.33	0.25	−0.08
1022	96.8	77.0	0.63	−0.98	−0.62
1915	89.5	86.0	0.12	0.02	0.00
1116	54.0	75.0	−2.35	−1.20	2.82
Mean	87.71	85.78			
SD	14.35	8.97			

Total $\sum z_X z_Y$ 4.57

$(N - 1)$ 8

$r = \dfrac{\sum z_X z_Y}{(N - 1)}$ .57

3) Correlations from journals:

   a. $r = .45$, 95% CI [.20, .65], $N = 50$, which indicates that income inequality and academic dishonesty could have a weak to moderate positive relationship over U.S. states.

   b. $r = .21$, 95% CI [.15, .27], $N = 1,000$, which indicates that there is likely a weak positive relationship between early reading ability and adult income.

   c. With more than 14,000 participants, the CI would be very much shorter than you just calculated for $N = 1,000$.

   d. $r = .25$, 95% CI [.04, .44], $N = 84$, which indicates considerable uncertainty about the relationship between BMI and belief in exercise to control weight; the relationship in the population could be moderate but could also be vanishingly weak.

4) There are usually lots of possible explanations for a correlation, so your suggestions may differ from mine. A good alternative explanation should explain why the two variables are correlated. It may be reasonable to note that "the sample size was too small" or "the measurements may not have been valid", but an alternative explanation proposes a causal pathway for the observed correlation.

   a. Obvious possibility: Income inequality motivates dishonest behavior. However, perhaps population density might be a third variable that plays a role—densely populated states may have more income inequality and also more people able to generate search traffic about cheating. Or, perhaps, elite colleges with high pressure to cheat are primarily located in wealthy states that have higher levels of income inequality. When thinking of such possibilities, also think of what data would throw light on each.

   b. Obvious possibility: Early reading skills cause higher adult earning. The temporal order of the measurements rules out the reverse—high adult income can't be causing good early reading skills! There are many other possibilities. For example, high parental socioeconomic status could encourage good early reading skills and also provide financial and social support that helps to get a high-paying job in adulthood. Even in developmental studies, correlation does not necessarily mean causation.

   c. Larger N gives a shorter CI, but need not change any of the discussion about possible explanations.

   d. Obvious possibility: An erroneous belief that weight control is all about exercise rather than diet leads to poor weight control and thus higher BMI. As usual, there are many other possibilities. Not to bang on this drum too much, but low socioeconomic status could prompt poor dietary knowledge as well as high BMI. Perhaps high BMI leads to the notion that weight control is all about exercise, as those with a high BMI may have already tried controlling weight through diet and failed. While speculating about this correlation is interesting, it's important to note that the small sample size leaves considerable uncertainty about the strength of the relationship, which may be so weak as to be inconsequential. The original paper provides additional data.

5) Figure 11.19 can help guide choice of N, but, as always, you also need to consider practicalities in your research context, including the ease or difficulty of recruiting N participants and actually running a study of that size. As we discussed in Chapter 10, you should aim for sufficiently large N for your study to be usefully informative, but not more arduous and expensive than necessary. In each case, consider (i) that your replication is likely to find r somewhere within the original CI, or only a little outside it, (ii) the CI length that Figure 11.19 indicates for any r and N you are considering, and (iii) your desired precision, for example you may prefer to find evidence that the population correlation is nonzero and so you'd like a CI some distance from zero. All too often, these considerations suggest N that's larger than practical, in which case you'll need to compromise, or seek further similar results you can combine using meta-analysis.

a. Given $r = .45$, 95% CI [.20, .65], replication N of around 80 would seem reasonable. There are only 50 U.S. states, so a replication would need to use data from other countries, or perhaps smaller units, such as counties, within the United States.

b. Given an original finding of $r = .21$, 95% CI [.15, .27], replication N should be at least 320, preferably more.

c. With such very large data sets, CI length is pleasingly short. If the replication will draw on a different population, we should consider whether there are any important differences between the two populations.

d. For an original finding of $r = .25$, 95% CI [.04, .44], replication N of more than 640 would probably be necessary. If the population correlation is around the upper end of that CI, a smaller replication N would suffice, but of course we don't know that ρ value.

6) Beauty sleep:

a. $r = -.31$, 95% CI [−.51, −.08].

b. The scatterplot suggests a nonlinear, inverted-U shaped relationship, with attractiveness being highest with moderate sleep, and declining with either more or less sleep. Pearson's r cannot adequately describe such a relationship and may mislead. These are fake data; nonlinear relationships don't always show up as clearly in real data. As usual, it's essential to examine the scatterplot before using r to summarize a relationship. In addition, if the author's conclusion hinted at causation—amount of sleep causes attractiveness—then that's a further problem with their interpretation.

7) Well-being and campus involvement:

a. For commuters, $r = .68$, 95% CI [.50, .80], $N = 53$. For residents, $r = .16$, 95% CI [−.11, .40], $N = 59$. It seems that the correlation between campus involvement and happiness is actually stronger for commuters than for residents. The difference between the two values of r is 0.52, 95% CI [.22, .81]. The student group who collected these data expected the opposite, and we're still unclear why there seems to be a much strong relation between campus involvement and well-being among commuters than residents. Note that the mean and SD for the two variables are not very different for the two groups, which makes the observed difference in correlation even more puzzling. As usual, be prepared at any time during research to be surprised, and to think of what further study might be revealing.

b. For women, $r = .31$, 95% CI [.08, .50], $N = 75$. For men, $r = .39$, 95% CI [.07, .64], $N = 36$. The relationship is similar for women and men, with a difference of .08, 95% CI [−.29, .41]. This CI is fairly long, and includes the possibility that the relationship is moderately stronger in women, not at all different, and quite a bit stronger in men. More data would be needed to estimate any difference between the female and male correlations more precisely.

8) Using a random effects model to integrate the findings of Gervais et al. (2012) with Sanchez et al. (2016) we obtain $r = -.13$, 95% CI [−.28, .01], total $N = 633$, for the relationship between analytic thinking and religious belief. This suggests that the true relationship could be anywhere from moderately negative to around zero. The CI is long, indicating considerable uncertainty. Also, the diamond ratio is 1.89, a quite large value that suggests considerable heterogeneity. The two studies may disagree, and further studies are needed to give insight and a more precise estimate.

CHAPTER 12. REGRESSION

1) Friendliness and number of close friends:

a. Number of friends (Y) can't be less than 0. With mean of 8.33 and SD as large as 6.27, we must have positive skew—a small number of people have large numbers of friends—which suggests that Y in the population is not normally distributed. However, we'll hope that it's not too far from normal, and will make the assumption so we can use regression.

b. You should examine the scatterplot for any signs the relationship is nonlinear, and also look for outliers and restriction of range. The scatterplot would also probably show the positive skew in Y.

c. $b = 4.96$

d. $a = -9.42$

e. $\hat{Y} = 0.50$ friends

f. $\hat{Y} = 15.37$ friends

g. $\hat{Y} = 8.3$. For someone of average friendliness, you would predict the average number of friends. The regression line always goes through the point (M_x, M_y).

h. Residual $= (Y - \hat{Y}) = 10 - 8.3 = 1.7$

i. $\hat{X} = 0.023 + 3.39 \times Y$

j. If $Y = 300$, the prediction would be $\hat{X} = 10.38$, which doesn't make sense given that friendliness was measured on a scale from 1–5. The problem is that we've used a number of close friends ($Y = 300$) that is far outside the range used to generate the regression equation. The mean number of close friends was 8.3, with $SD = 6.3$, and so someone who says they have 300 close friends is an extreme outlier ($Z_y = 47$) relative to the original data set.

k. Applying regression beyond the original population is a matter of judgment—it depends on whether there are substantive differences between the new and the original populations in the way the two variables relate to each other. This can be especially tenuous across cultures. You can always use the regression equation to calculate a prediction, but the predictions may be completely inaccurate in a new context.

2) Home size and asking price:

a. The scatterplot shows a strong positive relationship between home size and asking price. The relationship seems linear. There are some outliers, but none seem to be drastically influencing the relationship. This data set seems suitable to use for linear regression.

b. $r = 0.78$, 95% CI [.73, .82].

c. $\hat{Y} = -\$66,024 + 2713X$

d. If we consider just price per square meter, bargains are the houses that fall below the regression line. (In practice we'd also consider many other factors, including condition and location.) Eyeballing from the scatterplot, the biggest bargain seems to be a house of about 310 m² at about $160,000. (Going back to the original data set, it is listing 149069, a 4-bedroom, 2-bathroom foreclosed home of 312.9 m² being sold for $155,900.) Click near red 10 and use the slider to set the cursor as close as possible to passing through the low point that has the largest negative residual. You should find that a house of this size is predicted to sell for roughly about $780,000. Thus, the $(Y - \hat{Y})$ residual is, roughly, $160,000 - $780,000 = -$620,000$.

e. Not necessarily. Many other factors help determine the sale price. This house is actually a foreclosure, so may be in terrible condition. To include other factors in making our predictions we could use multiple regression, a more advanced technique that's beyond the scope of this book.

f. I set $X = 185.7$ as the closest available value in ESCI and found $\hat{Y} = \$438,000$, to the closest $1,000.

g. Click at red 11 and see that, for $X = 185.7$ m², the mean of Y is predicted to be $438,000, 95% CI [$417,000, $459,000], all to the closest $1,000.

h. Table 12.4 lists the predictions, the $\hat{Y}$ and the PI, and the residual for each house, all to the closest $1,000. If your values approximately match these within about $1,000, that's fine. The second column from the right indicates that the asking price (Y) was within the PI in 9 of the 10 cases. In the long run, if all assumptions of our statistical model are met, we expect that for 95% of cases the asking price will be within the PI. Note that some of

Table 12.4 Completed Version of Table 12.2

Case	Size, X (m²)	Ŷ ($1,000)	95% PI ($1,000)		Asking Price, Y ($1,000)	Within PI? (Y/N)	Residual ($1,000)
1	133.8	297	−56	650	149	Y	−148
2	158.0	362	9	716	549	Y	187
3	142.7	321	−32	674	435	Y	114
4	121.7	264	−89	617	299	Y	35
5	203.2	485	132	838	625	Y	140
6	195.1	463	110	817	399	Y	−64
7	140.4	315	−38	668	187	Y	−128
8	197.9	471	118	824	1,290	N	819
9	130.1	287	−66	640	265	Y	−22
10	113.8	243	−111	596	199	Y	−44

the PI limits are negative, which indicates that our statistical model does not fit reality perfectly, because in practice house prices are rarely if ever negative.

i. The prediction interval depends not only on our uncertainty about the regression relationship, but also on the variation in the variable being predicted. The larger the sample, the less uncertainty about the magnitude of the relationship between the predictor and predicted variables, but the natural variation in the predicted variable does not change. In contrast, the 95% CI for mean Y at a particular X depends primarily on sample size.

j. Using the 1993–2003 data, $\hat{Y} = \$203,000$ when $X = 99.1$ m². However, we shouldn't take this prediction seriously, as much has probably changed since the data set was collected, including inflation, changes to the housing market, and wider changes in the economy. A quick check in 2015 found that most houses of this size were actually selling for around $300,000. It's a matter of judgment to decide when new cases are different enough that a regression equation should be abandoned or updated. This example shows that the difference may be in time, rather than the more obvious difference if we consider houses in a different city.

3) Happiness and kidney donations:

a. The scatterplot shows a reasonably strong linear relationship with no major outliers, and no strong signs of nonlinearity. There may be some restriction of range, as all states are within a 10 point range on the 100-point well-being index. However, we would not expect state averages to vary over anything like the range that individual people vary over, which is what the 100-point scale is designed to represent. We can proceed with the regression analysis, but take care to only make predictions within the range of the original data. One interesting point might be considered an outlier: Utah has well-being of 67.9, somewhat above average, but a donation rate of 29.4, almost double the overall mean for all states of 15.3, and clearly above all other states and the regression line. That point is worth further investigation.

b. $r = .52$, 95% CI [.28, .70]. The population is a notional larger set of states, from which the 50 U.S. states are our sample. We would probably hesitate to generalize the correlation and regression results for this data set to other countries, given that organ donation, in particular, may be seen differently in different countries and cultures.

c. $\hat{Y} = -43.8 + 0.893X$

d. See Table 12.5.

e. For these four states, well-being means have changed considerably from 2010 to 2013, although we would need to know the CI on the difference before we would make too much of the apparent change. The different means give, of course, somewhat different predictions of donation rate. If there have been real changes in well-being, the predictions based on the more recent data are probably more useful now.

Table 12.5 Completed Version of Table 12.3

State	Well_Being_2010	Ŷ (2010)	Well_Being_2013	Ŷ (2013)
WY	69.2	18.0	65.6	14.8
HI	71	19.6	68.4	17.3
ND	68	16.9	70.4	19.0
NV	64.2	13.5	66.6	15.7

f. The best assessment of the relationship between well-being and donation rate would be based on well-being and donation rate data that refer to the same period. The donation data are from 1999–2010, and therefore the 2010 well-being data are likely to give a more valid regression equation. Unless we can find more recent donation data, using that regression equation with 2013 well-being data may be a reasonable way to make predictions now.

g. A change in the way a variable is measured can make a regression equation invalid—as usual, this depends on your judgment of the extent to which the change is substantive. In this case, it seems that Gallup has changed the measurement of its well-being index pretty dramatically, and we should be very cautious about using a regression equation developed from the old formulation to make predictions from the new index.

CHAPTER 13. FREQUENCIES, PROPORTIONS, AND RISK

1) Proportions and CIs:

a. $P = .75$, [.53, .89]. Counting the gray lines tells us that the CI extends approximately from 11 to 18 out of 20.

b. $P = .05$, [.01, .24]. From 0 to 5 out of 20, approximately.

c. $P = .40$, [.22, .61]. From 4 to 12 out of 20, approximately.

d. $P = .40$, [.31, .50]. Multiply the CI limits by 100 to find the CI extends from 31 to 50 out of 100, approximately.

e. $P = .40$, [.37, .43]. From 370 to 430 out of 1,000, approximately.

2) Comparing two proportions:

a. 17, which is $P = .85$.

b. 50, which is $P = .62$.

c. For Tim, $P = .40$, and the CI is [.22, .61] for $N = 20$, and [.30, .51] for $N = 80$. Lengths are .39 and .21, so the second is about half as long as the first, as the rule states.

3) Belonging to a group

a. What is the difference between the proportion of Penn students and Harvard students mentioning Ivy League? Table 13.8 shows the frequencies. The difference was 9/33 – 0/30 = 0.27 [0.11, 0.44] so Penn students are clearly more likely to mention Ivy League, by a substantial amount.

Table 13.8 Frequencies of Students Who Did or Did Not Mention Ive League (Rozin et al., 2014)

		Harvard	Penn	Total
Mention Ivy League?	Yes	0	9	9
	No	30	24	54
Total		30	33	63

b. That the two classification variables (Mention/No mention, and Harvard/Penn) are not associated in the population. $\chi^2 = 9.55$, $p = .002$, so reject the null hypothesis and conclude there is strong evidence of an association, in agreement with the proportions analysis. Two expected frequencies are about 4.7 and 4.3, which are sufficiently small to suggest the chi-square approximation may not be very good. The p value for the difference between the two proportions is .004, different from .002, which also suggests that the chi-square approximation is not wonderful in this case—although the two p values send the same message of strong evidence against the null. The phi coefficient is $\phi = .39$, perhaps a medium association.

c. Being classified as international is, presumably, prestigious for an airport. A major airport, such as John F. Kennedy in New York, is widely known as international so is central to the international category. In contrast, a smaller airport such as John Wayne, just south of Los Angeles, is international, but near the border of that category. Investigating how often they refer to themselves as international addresses the researchers' question.

d. At least in the Ivy League and international airport examples, the mention of Ivy League or international may be prompted simply because the listener or reader is less likely to have the information, so mentioning it is informative, rather than an assertion of group membership. Rozin et al. (2014) came close to responding to that possibility in their discussion of further examples and possible theoretical models.

e. In another of their studies, Rozin et al. (2014) compared leading U.S. universities with smaller local colleges with no or few PhD programs, but which are still officially recognized as universities. They found that the latter institutions, close to the border of the prestigious category "university", were considerably more likely to use the term "university" when making a self-reference on their websites.

f. You could examine the proportions of research journals in the two disciplines that include the word "science" in their title, or perhaps the proportions of university departments that include "science" in their title. Find the CI on the difference between the psychology and physics proportions, and interpret.

4) Question wording:

a. Yes, this is experimental research in which participants were randomly assigned to one of the two wording conditions.

b. $P_{\text{Allow}} = .75$, 95% CI [.74, .77], $P_{\text{Forbid}} = .93$, 95%CI [.92, .94]. They are independent because they refer to separate groups of participants—the groups given the differently worded questions.

c. $(P_{\text{Forbid}} - P_{\text{Allow}}) = 0.18$, 95%CI [0.16, 0.20]. This indicates that those given the Forbid question were 18 percentage points more likely to permit speeches against democracy. The very short CI indicates that this is likely quite close to the true difference in proportions.

d. $P_{\text{Allow}} = .75$, 95% CI [.61, .85], $P_{\text{Forbid}} = .85$, 95%CI [.71, .93], $(P_{\text{Forbid}} - P_{\text{Allow}}) = 0.10$, 95%CI [−0.08, 0.27]. This indicates that those given the Forbid question were 10 percentage points more likely to permit speeches against democracy, but that there is considerable uncertainty about this difference. Specifically, the CI is consistent with anywhere from a slight decrease in tolerance up to a large increase in tolerance, and this includes the possibility of no change at all. The CI also includes the 18 percentage point increase observed for the overall data set, so we don't have evidence that the Czech data disagree with the overall data.

e. $p = .26$; $\chi^2(1) = 1.30$, $p = .26$. Using NHST we would fail to reject the null, and conclude that the evidence does not sufficiently warrant the conclusion that wording influences attitude. Given the overall results, we have very strong evidence that wording does in fact influence the attitude reported. The data from this site do trend in the right direction, and interpretation of the CI would focus on the fact that the CI leaves considerable uncertainty but does include the possibility of a wording effect. The NHST approach has the danger of being interpreted in a categorical manner (supports/does not support).

5) Breeding success of owls:

a. $N = 3$ in each area is tiny, so any difference in breeding success between the two areas can be estimated only with very low precision. Alternatively, thinking of power, even a large difference is likely not to give a statistically significant result.

b. The IV is Harvested or Not harvested, but there is no mention that the levels of that IV were randomly allocated—ideally each to not just one, but to a considerable number of patches of forest. We are told that the harvested and untouched areas were similar, but there is no guarantee that they were the same in all ways relevant to owl breeding, except for harvesting, and so any claim that harvesting caused an observed difference would be dubious. On the other hand, if we had strong evidence of little or no difference (lots of data and a short CI very close to 0), we would have grounds for concluding that, most likely, harvesting together with any other differences between the areas had little or no influence on owl breeding success.

c. For $X = 0$, the difference is 1.0 [0.21, 1.0] so the CI does not include 0 and there is some evidence of a difference. For $X = 1$, the difference is 0.67 [−0.06, 0.94] and for $X = 2$ the difference is 0.33 [−0.29, 0.79]. In both cases the CI is long and includes 0.

d. Only for $X = 0$ is the null hypothesis of no difference rejected. Even with 3 in the untouched area and 1 in the harvested area there is no statistically significant difference, so the foresters running the study would claim there was no decrease in owl breeding.

e. For $X = 15$, 16, and 17, the p value is, respectively, .025, .05, and .10, so $X = 15$ in the harvested area is only borderline statistically significant.

f. Even a decrease from 20 in the untouched area to $X = 15$ in the harvested area (a 25% decrease) might lead to a conclusion of no reduction in breeding. With the crazily small samples of 3, even a 67% reduction was taken as supporting that conclusion. It's unfortunate that anyone wishing to find no effect, in particular polluters and those wanting to do other potentially damaging things to the environment, or human health, are encouraged by traditional NHST practices to run small, insensitive studies, likely to lead to a conclusion of "no statistically significant damage" even when substantial damage is being caused. The red flag about not accepting the null hypothesis is highly important!

6) I searched for "road crash risk for males and females" and easily found a factsheet from the U.S. Centers for Disease Control and Prevention with a wide range of terrible messages. It seemed well-written for a general audience, and used a variety of what seemed to me effective ways to express and highlight risks.

a. Here are a few quotes: "In 2011, about 2,650 teens in the United States aged 16–19 were killed… in motor-vehicle crashes. That means that seven teens ages 16 to 19 died every day from motor vehicle injuries." "Teen drivers ages 16 to 19 are nearly three times more likely than drivers aged 20 and older to be in a fatal crash." "The motor vehicle death rate for male drivers and passengers ages 16 to 19 was almost two times that of their female counterparts."

b. No ranges ("a 20% to 30% chance") were given to indicate uncertainty in the estimates, but I suspect they would just have complicated the stark messages. For making a decision about whether to undergo a particular cancer treatment, the value of the risk and the uncertainty of the estimate may be important, but for road crashes the message is scarily high risk, rather than any nuance about whether the risk is, for example, "nearly 3 times more likely" or only 2 times.

CHAPTER 14. EXTENDED DESIGNS: ONE INDEPENDENT VARIABLE

1) Study strategy and learning:

   a. Yes. This is experimental research with manipulation of study strategy, and random assignment to groups. We can draw conclusions about the causal effect of study strategy on learning, although we also need to assume that our statistical model applies, the manipulation worked as intended, and the measure of learning is valid. Our statistical model includes random sampling, which is probably unrealistic, so we would need to rely on judgment to generalize the conclusion to other students, for example with different majors or in another college. Would the students in the study be reasonably representative of those different populations?

   b. Yes, s is similar across the three groups. We also need to judge that the distribution of learning scores in each group is not very different from normal.

   c. $s_p = 5.48$

   d. $df = 52$; $t_{.95}(52) = 2.007$

   e. 95% MoE = 3.62. $(M_{\text{self-explain}} - M_{\text{control}}) = 4.72$, 95% CI [1.10, 8.34]. This indicates a clear benefit for self-explaining, but with considerable uncertainty as to how much it helps. The CI is consistent with anywhere from a smallish gain (1 question out of 25) to a very large gain (8 questions out of 25).

   f. MoE = 3.62, as before, because in both cases MoE is based on same df and same s_p. The difference is $(M_{\text{elab int}} - M_{\text{control}}) = 0.10$. 95% CI [−3.52, 3.72]. This indicates no clear benefit for this strategy, but with considerable uncertainty: There could be any effect from elaborative interrogation somewhat impairing learning, having no effect, to somewhat fostering learning.

   g. You should find the same answers in ESCI within rounding error.

   h. The more comparisons and contrasts we make, the greater the risk of capitalizing on chance and finding a "difference" that is merely sampling variability, a lump in the randomness.

   i. Ideally a small number of planned contrasts would have been stated as part of a preregistered data analysis plan. The first two you analyzed could easily have been chosen as corresponding closely with the main research questions, and stated in advance as planned contrasts. Any further contrasts would then be exploratory, and giving only tentative conclusions.

   j. The red flag is leaping from statistical non-significance to accepting the null hypothesis. Just because the differences found were not large enough to reach statistical significance does not mean the group means were all equal at the start of the study. Random assignment and sampling variability can easily give group means that differ somewhat. For perceived Previous Knowledge, comparing the self-explain with the control group shows $(M_{\text{self-explain}} - M_{\text{control}}) = 0.10$, 95% CI [−1.81, 2.01]. You could calculate that $d = 0.04$, although ESCI does not report d for comparisons. This indicates prior knowledge was probably fairly similar between groups, but could have been different by a moderate amount. Comparing the elaborative interrogation and control groups shows $(M_{\text{elab int}} - M_{\text{control}}) = -1.07$, 95% CI [−2.98, 0.84], and $d = -0.37$. (Again, I calculated that d separately). This hints that the elaborative interrogation group may have had somewhat lower perceived prior knowledge, although the CI is long. These comparisons are relevant because we would like to conclude that differences in learning after studying are caused by the study strategy alone, not by a combination of study strategy and prior knowledge. For the elaborative interrogation group, possibly lower prior knowledge could be part of why this group ended up showing little learning benefit from the strategy. One good strategy to consider would be to use learning gain scores for each participant, so the data point for each would be that participant's (posttest − pretest) score. More generally, as usual, we need replication!

2) Study strategy and perceived ease of use:

a. The ratio of the largest to smallest SD (1.94/0.84) is a little greater than 2, which suggests this assumption is a bit tenuous. We might consider comparing these groups without pooling variance using Data two and switching to not assuming homogeneity of variance. We should also check that scores for each group are relatively normally distributed.

b. $s_p = 1.38$

c. $df = 52$. $t_{.95}(52) = 2.007$

d. 95% MoE = 0.91. $(M_{\text{self-explain}} - M_{\text{control}}) = 0.36$, 95% CI [−0.55, 1.27]. This hints that participants may found self-explaining a little easier than those in the control condition, but there is considerable uncertainty: It would be plausible for self-explaining to be somewhat harder, no different, all the way up to considerably easier. Remember that this is a 5-point scale, so the CI is quite long relative to the scale.

e. 95% MoE = 0.91. $(M_{\text{elab int}} - M_{\text{control}}) = -1.71$. 95% CI [−2.62, −0.80], which indicates that elaborative interrogation is considered substantially harder than repetition, anywhere from nearly 1 to more than 2 points on the 5 point scale.

f. Possibly—it seems that participants found the elaborative interrogation strategy to be difficult to apply. This could be a reason why these students didn't get much benefit from this strategy.

3) Religious upbringing and altruism/sharing:

a. No, there cannot be random assignment and so this is non-experimental research and we cannot draw causal conclusions. We should be careful to use only language suggesting association and not suggesting cause.

b. Comparing children raised in Christian vs. Muslim countries for stickers shared we obtain: $(M_{\text{Christian}} - M_{\text{Muslim}}) = 0.13$, 95% CI [−0.22, 0.48]. The CI is fairly short and suggests there is little, if any, difference in altruism/sharing between children raised in these different faiths.

c. Comparing children raised in Non-religious vs. Religious (Christian or Muslim) families for stickers shared we obtain: $(M_{\text{Non-religious}} - M_{\text{Religious}}) = 0.83$, 95% CI [0.51, 1.14]. This indicate that, out of 10 stickers, it is plausible that children raised in non-religious households share around 0.5 to 1 sticker more than children raised in religious households.

d. These groups probably differ in lots of ways beyond religion—they could differ in socio-economic status, city/rural setting, parental age, parental education, literacy level, and so much more. Any of these additional group differences could relate to the difference in sticker sharing, especially given that the actual difference is fairly modest.

4) Organic food and moral reasoning—original study:

a. Comparing moral reasoning scores for the group exposed to organic food and the control group, we find $(M_{\text{organic}} - M_{\text{control}}) = 0.50$, 95% CI [0.13, 0.87]. I also calculated that $d = 0.82$. The CI suggests an increase in the harshness of moral judgments with organic food exposure of around half a point on the 1–7 scale, although the change could be anywhere from very small to quite large.

b. Comparing moral reasoning scores for the group exposed to comfort food and the control group, we find $(M_{\text{comfort}} - M_{\text{control}}) = -0.19$, 95% CI [−0.56, 0.18]. I calculated that $d = -0.32$. The CI leaves considerable uncertainty—comfort food exposure may decrease moral judgments a little, but the data are also consistent with no effect or a small increase.

5) Organic food and moral reasoning—replication study:

a. The original study found d of 0.82 for the difference in moral reasoning between the organic and control groups. We would like MoE of less than half that size, and perhaps even less, in case the original study overestimated the population effect size. A possible target MoE, then, might be 0.3, in which case **Precision two** tells us we'd need $N = 108$ in each group to have 99% assurance of an MoE of 0.3 or less. That was impractical, so we noted that target MoE of 0.5 with assurance requires $N = 44$. In practice we could achieve groups approaching that size.

b. Comparing the group exposed to organic food and the control group, we find $(M_{organic} - M_{control}) = 0.19$, 95% CI [−0.21, 0.59]. This does not indicate a strong effect of organic food on moral reasoning, but the CI is quite long, and includes 0.50, the original estimate of the effect.

c. Comparing the comfort and control groups, we find $(M_{comfort} - M_{control}) = -0.05$, 95% CI [−0.45, 0.35], suggesting a small or zero effect, but with the CI again moderately long and extending to a moderate change in either direction. It also includes −0.19, the original estimate of the effect.

d. Overall, these results are somewhat ambiguous. The strong effect reported in the original study was not observed, yet the CIs from the replication study included the point estimates found in the original study. So this replication study does not contradict the original findings, but it would probably cause us to lower our estimate for how big an effect organic food exposure might have on moral reasoning. At this stage, it would be best to a) conduct additional replications, and b) use meta-analysis to integrate results together to produce overall estimates incorporating all the available data. Moery took both of these steps; you can find out what happened by checking osf.io/atkn7 for the Open Science Page for the project.

CHAPTER 15. EXTENDED DESIGNS: TWO INDEPENDENT VARIABLES

1) Research designs

a. This is a 2 × 2 independent groups design. The IVs (gender and type of image) are both between-groups variables. Causal conclusions can be drawn related to type of image, assuming the two types of images were randomly assigned to different participants. However, causal conclusions may not be drawn related to gender nor the interaction of gender and image, because gender is not a manipulated variable. The main research finding is an interaction.

b. This is a 2 × 2 independent groups design. The IVs (learning location, recall location) are both between-groups variables. Causal conclusions can be drawn for both variables, assuming participants were randomly assigned to the four conditions. The main research finding is an interaction.

c. This is a 2 × 2 mixed design, also referred to as an RCT. Treatment is a between-groups variable, time of measurement is a within-group variable. Causal conclusions can be drawn. The main research finding is an interaction.

d. This is a 3 × 2 independent groups design. The IVs (grade level, sibling) are both between-groups variables. Causal conclusions are not justified because neither variable was created with random assignment. The research findings are both main effects.

2) Door holding and self-esteem:

a. This is a 2 × 2 independent groups design.

b. Causal conclusions cannot be drawn for the gender variable nor for the interaction involving gender because participants could not be randomly assigned to levels of this variable. Assuming participants were randomly assigned to the door held or not held conditions, a causal conclusion could be drawn about the main effect of this IV.

c. The researchers specifically predicted that door-holding would have a negative impact on men's self-esteem, but not on women's. This is a predicted interaction, so this was one of their planned analyses. They also planned to analyze the effect of door holding for men only and for women only. These additional effects are not fully independent of the interaction, but when there is evidence for an interaction these simple effects analyses can help make sense of it.

d. Men who had the door held for them reported lower self-esteem than men who did not, $(M_{Doorheld} - M_{Notheld}) = -0.93$, 95% CI [−1.49, −0.37]. Given the scale of measurement is from 1 to 10, this indicates that door-holding could lower male self-esteem by a moderate to substantial amount.

e. Women who had the door held for them reported slightly higher self-esteem than women who did not, $(M_{Doorheld} - M_{Notheld}) = 0.18$, 95% CI [−0.34, 0.70]. The CI indicates considerable uncertainty about the effect of door-holding on women's self-esteem, with a small decline, no difference, up to a moderate increase all being plausible.

f. $M_{FemaleDifference - MaleDifference} = 1.11$, 95% CI [0.35, 1.87]. There is considerable uncertainty here, but the CI indicates anywhere from a small to large difference in how door-holding impacts male and female self-esteem.

g. Three concerns would be 1) if a large proportion declined to participate, meaning the data are not particularly representative, 2) if declining to participate was not equal across the groups, introducing a potential confound, and/or 3) if the types of students who declined to participate were systematically different from those who did, a threat to generalizability. We'd like to know more about all of these issues, though the last one is not easy to investigate because we have no further information about participants who declined to participate. The researchers reported that 73% of potential participants did agree to be part of the study, but did not indicate if the proportion varied across groups.

3) Video games and aggression:

a. This is a 2 × 2 independent groups design.

b. Causal conclusions can be drawn because participants were randomly assigned to groups.

c. There are several options here. Hilgard chose to look at the main effect of violence, the main effect of challenge, and for a possible interaction between the two.

d. The SDs in all groups were large, around 22 to 26 s and therefore, despite the fairly large groups (around 56), the CIs were long. The main effect of violence was $(M_{Violent} - M_{Nonviolent}) = 2.3$ s, 95% CI [−4.2, 8.8]. Acute exposure to video game violence produced at most only a very small increase in aggression, and the CI indicates the effect could plausibly be anywhere from around 4 s shorter to 9 s longer in the ice water.

e. $(M_{Challenging} - M_{Easy}) = 2.9$ s, 95% CI [−3.6, 9.4]. The main effect of difficulty was a small increase in aggression, and the CI indicates the effect is likely to be anywhere from around 4 s shorter to 9 s longer in the ice water.

f. For violent games, making the game more difficult produced a small decrease in aggression (−4.4 s). For non-violent games, making the game more difficult produce a moderate increase in aggression (+10.2 s). The interaction, which is the difference of those two differences, is $M_{ViolentDifference - NonViolentDifference} = -14.5$ s, 95% CI [−27.5, −1.6]. This suggests that difficulty may have a different effect in violent vs. non-violent games, although there is considerable uncertainty, and the interaction could be anywhere from quite large to very small—considering that aggression was measured on a scale from 0 to 80 s.

g. To help prevent publication bias, Hilgard publically preregistered his design and posted his completed thesis online. To help ensure negative results would be informative, Hilgard used a relatively large sample size, which was planned based on considerations of previous effect sizes observed.

4) Self-explaining vs. Time on task:

a. This is a 3 × 2 mixed design. The first variable is study strategy; it has 3 levels (control, self-explain, normal+additional practice); it is a between-groups variable. The second variable is test; it has 2 levels (pretest, posttest); it is a within-group variable.

b. Yes. Participants were randomly assigned to study condition, so this is an experiment that can support causal conclusions.

c. M_{diff} = 6.27%, 95% CI [−1.44, 13.98]. On average, children in the control group, who studied normally, improved by over half a letter grade (1 letter grade corresponds to 10% improvement), but with the small sample size this leaves considerable uncertainty about the mean amount of learning in the population. The data are consistent with a very small decrease in scores, no change in scores, all the way up to more than a letter-grade improvement.

d. M_{diff} = 17.14%, 95% CI [8.53, 25.76]. On average, children who used self-explaining improved by nearly two letter grades. The CI is again long, but only consistent with large to very large improvements in mathematics skill (possibly up to 2.5 letter grades!).

e. Note that the two standard deviations are similar, so it's reasonable to assume homogeneity of variance. $M_{Self-ExplainDifference - NormalDifference}$ = 10.87%, 95% CI [−0.57, 22.31]. This indicates that improvements in the self-explain group were on average considerably higher than in the control group. The CI is very long—the advantage for self-explaining could be around zero up to very large (2 whole letter grades!). There is only weak evidence that self-explain strategy does lead to greater improvements in mathematics skills than normal studying. This effect is an interaction of type of studying (normal or self-explain) and time of testing (pretest or posttest).

f. $M_{Self-ExplainDifference - AdditionalPracticeDifference}$ = 11.77%, 95% CI [3.20, 20.33]. This indicates that the gains found in the self-explain group are also on average larger than in the additional practice group. The CI is again long, so the data are consistent with self-explaining being very modestly better up to very much better. This is a notable finding, as the additional practice group did improve (M_{diff} = 5.38%, 95% CI [1.03, 9.72]), but the self-explain group improved by even more. For this measure of conceptual understanding, then, self-explaining seems to provide benefits above and beyond extra time on task. The original study, however, included other measures of learning, and not all showed such a clear advantage. Note in this example how we have used a number of planned contrasts, each with one degree of freedom, to find our best estimation answers to the research questions central to the study.

CHAPTER 16. FUTURE DIRECTIONS

1) Reproducibility Project: Psychology:

a. The problem is selected publication of results that reach statistical significance, also known as the file drawer problem. The red flag is "beware accepting the null hypothesis", because selective publication may suggest that lack of statistical significance implies no effect.

b. The aim is to assist journals to encourage or require authors to use Open Science practices. Specifically, note the bottom right hand cell of the summary table (p. 1424) that refers to "peer review before observing the study outcomes", meaning that an article describing a good study is accepted for publication whatever results it obtains. This, together with pre-registration and full reporting, should overcome the file drawer problem.

2) Open Source Malaria (OSM):

a. OSM is taking a novel approach to finding a cure for malaria. All aspects of the project are open to all, and anyone can join, providing they agree to make all their work and data open to all. This is in stark contrast with most medical research, in which discoveries are often kept confidential, at least until patents are secured, and full data are often not made open.

b. All are important to the project, but perhaps numbers 1, 2, and 6 are particularly important, and defining of the project.

c. My reaction when I heard of this project was delight that researchers had found a practical way to pursue research that may have immense benefit for humanity but was unlikely to attract large commercial support, by following Open Science principles so fully.

3) Robust analysis of the Dana data set:

a. High outliers in both groups mean that M_t is lower than M, and by about the same amount in the two groups. All robust CIs are less than half the length of conventional CIs, so the robust analysis gives more precise estimates. This, together with the strong skew in both groups, suggests that the robust analysis is probably more useful.

b. This is an exploration strategy, in which the analysis chosen depends on the data. Planned is much preferable. Also, it's often not clear which points should be regarded as clear outliers.

4) The Australian Temperament Project:

a. An important consideration is the minimum legal drinking age—in Australia it's 18. See "Legal drinking age" in Wikipedia.

b. It's difficult to plan a study fully independently from the data, because you have already read some ATP results. You could explore a subset of the database to help you plan. Decide on questions and an analysis strategy, preregister, then apply that to the full database. You might follow with exploration.

5) Brain pictures. Were the brain areas examined nominated in advance, or selected by data exploration? Planned analysis is much preferable. Second, is any effect size information provided, or are you seeing areas of low p values? If, as usual, p values are pictured, you should also ask the dead fish question: Was an arbitrary criterion like $p < .001$ used to select highlighted areas, or an appropriate more stringent criterion?

6) The 10-step research plan

a. Steps 2 to 6, and 8, must all be reported, with full details in the article, or in an online supplement. Data exploration (Step 7) is usually worth doing, but may not reveal anything worth reporting as speculation. The materials and data should be provided (Step 9), usually online, or there should be explanation of why they cannot be released.

b. Pilot testing (Step 1) need not be reported, although often it's mentioned to help justify aspects of the study. Step 10 need not be mentioned, although comments about possible replication and meta-analysis might be included.

7) The *Psychological Science* tutorial article:

a. Most of the figures should be familiar.

b. We've discussed all 25, although Guidelines 10 and 11 are rather stronger than most of the NHST statements in this book. If you recognized all, or even close to all, you have done wonderfully well and deserve an enormous pat on the back. The article and guidelines were published for accomplished and successful researchers, not only for students, so if you grasp the main issues your understanding is, at least in some ways, right up there. Well done!

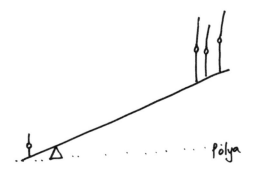

Pólya

Glossary

This is not a complete glossary of statistical terms. It focuses on selected terms that are important in this book, and includes expressions of my invention. Use the Subject Index to find where in the book a term is explained or pictured. For symbols and abbreviations, see the summary pages at the very start of the book.

Alternative hypothesis (H_1) A statement about a population parameter that is alternative to the null hypothesis in NHST. It often states that there is a non-zero effect of a stated exact size, for example H_1: $\mu = 50$.

Analysis of variance (ANOVA) NHST approach to the analysis of more complex designs, which is based on F tests.

Archival data Data in an existing database.

Assurance When using precision for planning, **assurance** is the probability, expressed as a percentage, that our obtained MoE is no more than target MoE. We generally use assurance = 99%.

Bars Short for **error bars**.

Between-groups design Design, such as the independent groups design, in which the IV is a between-groups variable.

Between-groups variable A variable whose different levels are seen by independent groups of participants.

Big data Very large data sets, which in some cases are "Free and ubiquitous data".

Bimodal distribution A distribution with two overall peaks.

Bin An interval on the X axis, as used in a frequency histogram.

Bivariate normal distribution X and Y have this distribution if they are each normally distributed overall, each is normally distributed at any single value of the other, and the variance of each is homogeneous for all values of the other.

Campbell Collaboration A worldwide collaboration of researchers that supports evidence-based practice in a range of social sciences.

Campbell Library Online database of more than 100 systematic reviews in the fields of social welfare, crime and justice, and education.

Capitalizing on chance Cherry picking. Focusing on effects identified in exploratory analysis that may merely reflect sampling variability.

Carryover effect In a paired design, any influence of the first measurement on the second.

Cat's-eye picture My name for the two curves, as in Figures 5.1 and 5.9, that depict how plausibility or likelihood varies across and beyond a CI.

Ceiling effect Crowding of data points in a scatterplot caused by an upper limit to the values a variable can take. A ceiling effect can reduce correlation r.

Center for Open Science (COS, cos.io) Center that promotes Open Science practices and encourages replication.

Central limit theorem A piece of magic: A theorem in statistics that states that the sampling distribution of a variable that's the sum, or mean, of many independent influences almost always has, approximately, a normal distribution.

Central tendency Location.

Chasing noise Cherry picking. Capitalizing on chance.

Cherry picking Exploratory analysis that identifies results that may easily be mere sampling variability, lumps in the randomness, faces in the clouds. Capitalizing on chance. Chasing noise.

Clinical significance Often used in the sense of "clinical importance".

Close replication A replication that uses a new sample, but otherwise is as similar as possible to the original study. Also called an **exact** or **literal replication**.

Cochrane A worldwide collaboration of healthcare professionals and policy makers that supports evidence-based practice in healthcare. Also referred to as the **Cochrane Collaboration**.

Cochrane Library An online database of thousands of systematic reviews that supports evidence-based practice in healthcare.

Cohen's d A standardized ES expressed in units of some appropriate SD. It can often be considered a kind of z score.

Comparison The difference between two means.

Conceptual replication More distant replication of a study.

Condition A value that can be taken by the independent variable. **Conditions** are also called **levels** or **treatments**.

Confidence interval (CI) An interval estimate calculated from sample data that indicates the precision of a point estimate.

Confidence level (C) Same as **level of confidence**. Most often 95, as for a 95% CI.

Confound An unwanted difference between groups, which is likely to limit the conclusions we can draw from a study.

Control condition The condition that provides a baseline or starting point for a comparison.

Control group A group that experiences the **control condition**.

Construct The underlying characteristic we wish to study, for example anxiety, well-being, or self-confidence.

Continuous variable A variable that can take any of the unlimited number of values in some range.

Contrast A linear combination of the means of different groups or conditions.

Convenience sample A practically achievable—rather than random—sample from a population.

Correlation (r) *See* **Pearson's correlation**.

Counterbalancing Random assignment of participants in a study with a paired design to different testing orders, or other conditions, to reduce any carryover effects.

Criterion variable *See* **Predict<u>or</u> variable**.

Curve SE The SE of a sampling distribution. In ESCI it refers to the theoretical sampling distribution of the mean. *See* Figure 4.8.

Dance of the confidence intervals My name for a sequence of CIs, from successive samples, falling down the screen in ESCI as in Figures 5.4 and 5.6.

Dance of the means My name for a sequence of sample means falling down the screen in ESCI, as in Figure 4.6.

Dance of the p values My name for the sequence of bouncing-around *p* values for successive studies, as in Figure 7.14.

Dance of the r values My name for the sequence of *r* values given by repeated sampling, as in Table 11.1.

Data analysis plan Detailed plan of intended data analysis, ideally to be preregistered before data collection commences.

Degrees of freedom (*df*) Number of separate, independent pieces of information we have that relate to the question at hand.

Dependent variable The variable that's measured in a study and provides the data to be analyzed.

Descriptive statistic A summary number, such as the mean, that tells us about a set of data.

Deviation The distance of a data point from the mean.

Diamond ratio The random effects diamond length divided by the fixed effect diamond length. An estimate of heterogeneity. Values greater than 1 suggest greater heterogeneity.

Dichotomous thinking Thinking that focuses on two mutually exclusive alternatives, notably the NHST decisions to reject or not reject a null hypothesis.

Difference axis My name for an axis in a figure that has its zero aligned with one sample mean so it can display the difference between two sample means, and the CI on that difference, as in Figures 7.2 and 8.2.

Discrete variable A variable that can take only distinct or separated values.

Distribution The way the data points in a data set are distributed along the *X* axis.

Don't fool yourself (DFY) A warning statement. See Chapter 2.

Dot plot Figure in which every data point is represented as a dot that marks its value on the *X* axis, as in Figure 3.3A.

Effect Anything that's of research interest.

Effect size (ES) The amount of anything that might be of interest. The size of an effect.

Effect size measure A measure used to express an ES.

Empirical sampling distribution The distribution of a number of values of a sample statistic. For example, the **mean heap**.

Equal-intervals assumption The assumption that one unit on the measurement scale is the same at all points on the scale. This assumption is required for interval measurement.

Error bars (also *bars*) Two line segments that mark an interval either side of a mean or other point estimate in a figure, preferably representing a 95% CI.

Error of estimation Same as **estimation error.**

ES estimate (also *sample ES*) ES calculated from data and used as an estimate of the population ES.

Estimation An approach to statistical inference that uses sample data to calculate point and interval estimates of population parameters.

Estimation error (or *error of estimation*) Difference, for example $(M - \mu)$, between a point estimate calculated from sample data, and the population parameter it estimates. *See also* **residual**.

Estimation language Language that focuses on ESs, and on "How much?" questions, rather than dichotomous "Is there an effect?" questions.

Estimation thinking Thinking that focuses on the sizes of effects. Contrast with **dichotomous thinking**.

Exact replication Close replication of a study.

Experimental research Research that uses random assignment of participants to groups or conditions—to the different levels of the IV that is being manipulated. It can justify a causal conclusion.

Exploratory analysis Data analysis that was not specified in advance. It can discover unexpected and valuable findings, but these are only speculations, possibly for further investigation. **Exploratory analysis** can easily be cherry picking, merely seeing faces in the clouds. Also called **post hoc analysis**.

Evidence-based practice Practice, in medicine, statistics, or another profession, that is based on research evidence.

Faces in the clouds Spurious apparent patterns in sampling variability, lumps in the randomness. Interpreting such patterns is cherry picking.

Factorial design Design that includes all combinations of the levels of all IVs.

False negative A Type II error, a miss. Non-rejection of the null hypothesis, IF it is false.

False positive A Type I error. Rejection of the null hypothesis, IF it is true.

File drawer effect Tendency for results that are not statistically significant to remain unpublished, thus potentially biasing the availability of studies for meta-analysis.

First quartile The 25th percentile.

Fixed effect model Simplest model of meta-analysis, which assumes each included study estimates a single fixed population parameter, for example μ or δ.

Floor effect Crowding of data points in a scatterplot caused by a lower limit to the values a variable can take. A floor effect can reduce correlation r.

Forest plot A CI figure that shows point and interval estimates for individual studies, and displays the meta-analysis result as a diamond, as in Figure 1.4 and Chapter 9.

Frequency The number of cases or data points in a category or bin.

Frequency histogram Figure showing the number of data points in each of a number of bins along the X axis, as in Figures 3.3C and D.

Grand total (N) The sum of sizes of all groups.

Heterogeneity The extent to which population ESs vary among the studies included in a meta-analysis.

Heterogeneous The studies in a meta-analysis are **heterogeneous** if they estimate different population ESs.

Homogeneity of variance Assumption that population variance is the same for each of the groups in an independent groups design.

Homogeneous The studies in a meta-analysis are **homogeneous** if they all estimate the same population ES, meaning that the fixed effect model is applicable.

Independent groups design A design comprising two independent groups of participants, of sizes N_1 and N_2, possibly different.

Independent groups t test NHST that uses a p value to test the null hypothesis of zero difference in a study with an independent groups design.

Independent variable (IV) The variable whose values are chosen or manipulated by the researcher. The IV can take a number of **levels**.

Inference See statistical inference.

Inferential statistic A statistic, such as a CI, that's calculated from sample data and tells us about the underlying population.

Interaction The extent to which the effect of one IV is different at different levels of another IV. An interaction is often attributable to a **moderator**.

Intercept (a) In regression, the value of $\hat{Y}$ when $X = 0$. The Y value where the line, extended if necessary, intersects the Y axis.

Interquartile range (IQR) Interval from the first to the third quartile.

Interval estimate A CI, which is a range of plausible values for a population parameter.

Interval measurement Same as **interval level of measurement** and **interval scaling**. The third of the four NOIR levels, which requires the equal-intervals assumption. It has distance but no true zero. The mean and SD can be calculated, but not ratios or percentages. Examples: longitude, birth year.

Inverse probability fallacy Incorrect belief that the p value is the probability the null hypothesis is true.

Law of large numbers A law of statistics, which states that, when random samples are sufficiently large, they match the population closely.

"Law" of small numbers A widespread misconception that even small samples match the population closely.

Left skew Asymmetry of a distribution, with the left tail longer and larger than the right. Also called **negative skew**.

Level A value that can be taken by the independent variable. **Levels** are also called **conditions** or **treatments**.

Level of confidence (C, also **confidence level**) The 95 in "95% CI", where 95% CIs are those that, in the long run, will include the population parameter for 95% of replications.

Level of measurement One of the NOIR levels of measurement. *See* **nominal**, **ordinal**, **interval**, **ratio**.

Likelihood The cat's-eye picture of a CI shows how **plausibility** or **likelihood** varies across and beyond the CI, as in Figures 5.1 and 5.9.

Likert scale A scale comprising items that ask for ratings, often with 7 points, of a respondent's strength of agreement or disagreement with a number of statements.

Limit Either end of a CI.

Linear regression See **regression.**

Literal replication Close replication of a study.

Location The region of the *X* axis where, generally, a data set is found.

Longitudinal research Research that collects data over an extended period of time.

Lower limit (LL) Lower end of a CI.

Lumps in the randomness Spurious apparent patterns in sampling variability, faces in the clouds. Interpreting such patterns is cherry picking.

Main effect The overall effect of an IV, based on means at each of its levels after averaging over any other IVs.

Margin of error (MoE) The length of one arm of a CI. The maximum likely estimation error.

Mean Average.

Mean heap My name for the empirical sampling distribution of the sample mean. In ESCI it's a pile of green dots that represent sample means. See Figure 4.7.

Measure The DV, often represented by *X*.

Measurement A process of assigning numbers or other labels to express the values that a variable takes.

Measurement error Difference between an observed data value and what is, in some sense, the true underlying value.

Median The *X* value below and above which half the data points in a data set lie. The 50th percentile.

Meta-analysis A set of techniques for the quantitative integration of results from two or more studies on the same or similar issues.

Meta-analytic thinking Estimation thinking that keeps meta-analysis in mind, and considers any result in the context of past and potential future results on the same issue.

Mixed design A design that includes at least one between-groups IV and one repeated measure.

Mode The most frequent data value.

Moderating variable Same as **moderator.**

Moderator (also **moderating variable**) An IV that alters the effect of another IV on the DV. A moderator often gives rise to an **interaction.** In the context of meta-analysis, a **moderator** is a variable that influences the ES being studied in the meta-analysis.

Moderator analysis Analysis within meta-analysis that seeks to identify moderator variables that can account for some of the ES variability between studies.

Modified replication More distant replication of a study.

More distant replication A replication that's somewhat different from the original study. It's also called a **modified** or **conceptual** replication.

Multiple regression Regression with a single predicted, or criterion, variable and more than one predictor variable.

Natural frequencies A risk expressed in **natural frequencies** is stated as so many cases per hundred, or thousand, or other convenient number.

Negative skew Asymmetry of a distribution, with the left hand tail longer and larger than the right. Also called **left skew**.

New statistics See **the new statistics**.

NOIR Nominal, ordinal, interval, ratio. The four levels of measurement, from least detailed to most detailed.

Nominal measurement Same as *nominal* (or *categorical*) *level of measurement* and *nominal* (or *categorical*) *scaling*. The lowest of the 4 NOIR levels, which uses labels to distinguish categories but doesn't have order. Frequencies can be found, but not, for example, the median or mean. Example: ice cream flavors.

Non-experimental research Research that uses pre-existing groups, not formed by random assignment or manipulation of the IV. It cannot justify a causal conclusion.

Normal distribution Continuous symmetric bell-shaped distribution with two parameters, μ and σ, as in Figure 3.5.

Null hypothesis (H_0) A statement about a population parameter, often H_0: $\mu = 0$, that is tested by NHST.

Null hypothesis significance testing (NHST) An approach to statistical inference that uses a *p* value to either reject, or not reject, a null hypothesis.

Observed power See **post hoc power**.

One-sided alternative hypothesis An H_1 that includes values that differ in only one direction from the null hypothesis value. For example, H_1: $\mu > 50$. Also called a **directional alternative hypothesis**.

One-tailed p value The *p* value calculated by including only values more extreme than the obtained result in the direction specified by the one-sided, or directional, alternative hypothesis, H_1.

One-way independent groups design Design with a single IV and more than two independent groups.

One-way repeated measure design Design with a single IV with more than two levels, and one group that experiences every level of the IV.

Open data Making full data openly available from an enduring website.

Open materials Making the full materials used in a study openly available from an enduring website.

Open Science A set of evolving strategies designed to make science more open, replicable, and trustworthy.

Open Science Framework (OSF, osf.io) An online resource provided by the Center for Open Science to help researchers use Open Science practices.

Operationalization A practical way to measure a construct. For example, the State-Trait Anxiety Inventory (STAI) score operationalizes anxiety.

Ordinal measurement Same as **ordinal level of measurement** and **ordinal scaling**. The second of the four NOIR levels, which has order but not the equal-intervals assumption. The median and percentiles can be calculated, but not the mean or SD. Example: ranking of performance as 1st, 2nd, 3rd, ...

Original units Units, such as milliseconds (ms), centimeters (cm), or dollars ($), in which a data value or ES was first measured.

Outlier A data point that is extreme, relative to others in a data set.

Overlap rule If independent 95% CIs just touch, there is moderate evidence of a difference (and p is about .01); if they overlap moderately, there is a small amount of evidence of a difference (and p is about .05).

Paired design A design comprising one group of N participants, each of whom supplies a pair of data values, one on each of two measures; for example pretest and posttest.

Paired t test NHST that uses a p value to test the null hypothesis of zero difference in a study with a paired design.

Parallel forms Two versions of a test that use different questions, but measure the same characteristic and are of similar difficulty.

Pearson's correlation, r Measure of the linear component of the relationship between two variables, usually X and Y.

Percentile The value of X below which the stated percentage of data points lie.

p-hacking The use of questionable research practices to achieve $p < .05$.

Phi coefficient (ϕ) Measure of strength of association in a 2×2 frequency table, which is a type of correlation.

Pilot testing Small exploration studies that guide selection of all aspects of a planned study. Where possible, it should lead to preregistration.

Planned analysis Data analysis that is specified in advance, preferably as a preregistered data analysis plan. It provides the best basis for conclusions.

Planned contrast A comparison or subset contrast that is specified in advance, preferably as part of a preregistered data analysis plan.

Plausibility The cat's-eye picture of a CI shows how **plausibility** or **likelihood** varies across and beyond the CI, as in Figures 5.1 and 5.9.

Point estimate A single value that is our best estimate of a population parameter.

Pooled SD SD calculated from the standard deviations of two or more independent groups as a combined estimate of the population SD, which is assumed the same for all groups.

Population A set of values, usually assumed large or infinite, about which we wish to draw conclusions.

Population ES ES in the population, usually unknown and to be estimated.

Population parameter A value, for example μ or σ, of a characteristic of a population. It's usually fixed but unknown.

Positive skew Asymmetry of a distribution, with the right-hand tail longer and larger than the left. Also called **right skew**.

Post hoc analysis See exploratory analysis.

Post hoc contrast Contrast chosen after seeing the data, which is part of data exploration.

Post hoc power (also **observed power**) Power calculated after completing the study, using as target δ the effect size d obtained in the study. It can easily mislead, so never use it.

Power See **Statistical power**.

Practical significance Often used in the sense of "practical importance".

Precision Largest likely estimation error, measured by MoE of a 95% CI.

Precision for planning Planning by choosing N so a study is likely to obtain MoE no longer than some chosen target MoE.

Predicted variable Regression provides an estimate for the **predicted variable** Y (also known as the **criterion variable**) from a value of predictor variable X.

Prediction interval (PI) Interval in which a future value, for example a replication mean, is likely to fall.

Predictor variable Regression provides an estimate for the predicted variable Y from a value of **predictor variable** X.

Preregistered review Peer reviewing by a journal of a full research plan before it is preregistered and before data collection commences.

Preregistration The lodging in advance, at a secure and enduring website and with a date stamp, of a detailed research plan including a data analysis plan. Also known as **registration in advance**.

Probability distribution A graph showing how probability is distributed over the possible values of a variable.

Proportion (P) Fraction of a number of discrete things that have a property of interest. It lies between 0 and 1.

Publication bias Selection of which studies to publish according to the results they obtain. Typically, studies finding statistically significant results are more likely to be published.

p value Probability of obtaining our observed results, or results that are more extreme, IF the null hypothesis is true.

Quartile One of the 25th (first quartile), 50th (median), and 75th (third quartile) percentiles.

Questionable research practices Choices about data analysis or about what to report that are made after seeing the data.

Random assignment Assignment of participants to groups or conditions by means of a random process. It gives the best grounds for a conclusion of causality.

Random effects model Model for meta-analysis that assumes different studies estimate somewhat different values of the population parameter being investigated, for example μ or δ.

Randomized control trial (RCT) A two-way factorial design with one repeated measure. Participants are randomized to treatment and control groups, and data are collected at a number of times, perhaps pretest, posttest, and follow up.

Random sample A sample produced by random sampling from a population.

Random sampling A sampling process in which every data value in the population has an equal chance of being sampled, and values are sampled independently.

Range Interval from the lowest to the highest data point in a data set.

Range restriction If the range of X or Y values in a data set is restricted to less than the full range of X or Y, the correlation of points in the data set is likely to be reduced.

Ratio measurement Same as **ratio level of measurement** and **ratio scaling**. The fourth of the four NOIR levels, which has all the properties of interval measurement and also a true zero. Ratios and percentages can be calculated, as well as the mean and SD. Examples: height, time taken to complete a task.

Rectangular distribution Probability distribution that has the shape of—would you believe—a rectangle, as in Figure 4.9.

Red flag A vital caution about NHST, as described in Chapters 6 and 7.

Reference values Values used to assist interpretation of an ES, when they are judged to be relevant. Cohen, for example, suggested reference values for *d*. Effect sizes should always be interpreted in context.

Registration in advance See **Preregistration**.

Regression The fitting of a regression line of *Y* on *X* to calculate an estimate for the predict*ed* variable *Y* from a value of predict*or* variable *X*.

Regression estimate $\hat{Y}$, which is the value of *Y* calculated from the regression line for a particular value of *X*.

Regression line See **regression**.

Regression weight (*b*) Slope of a regression line.

Repeated measure (also **within-group variable**) An IV all of whose levels are seen by the same group of participants.

Repeated measure design Within-group design, such as the paired design.

Relative risk Risk ratio.

Reliability The repeatability or consistency of a measure. High is good.

The replicability crisis The troubling discovery that a number of published research findings cannot be replicated.

Replication study A study that is a replication of an initial study, usually a close replication.

Replication mean The mean of a close replication study.

Replication p My name for the *p* value given by a replication study.

Research synthesis (also **systematic review**) Review that integrates research evidence, usually by meta-analysis.

Residual In regression, $(Y - \hat{Y})$ is a **residual**, the difference between the value of *Y* for a data point (*X*, *Y*), and $\hat{Y}$, the regression estimate for that value of *X*. It's also known as an **estimation error**.

Right skew Asymmetry of a distribution, with the right hand tail longer and larger than the left. Also called **positive skew**.

Risk Probability, usually but not always of an unwanted event.

Robust techniques **Robust** statistical **techniques** are resistant to departures from some assumptions, for example normality of the population.

Sample A set of *N* data values chosen (often at random) from a population.

Sample ES (also **ES estimate**) ES calculated from data, and usually used as an estimate of the population ES.

Sample statistic A **descriptive statistic**, for example *M* or *s*, that is calculated from sample data and tells us about that data set.

Sampling distribution (also **theoretical sampling distribution**) The distribution of all possible values of a sample statistic.

Sampling variability Extent to which results vary over repeated sampling, or close replications.

Scatterplot Picture of the relation between X and Y, in which each data pair is represented by a dot.

Selective publication Studies not achieving statistical significance are less likely to be published.

Significance Ambiguous term, the "S" word. Write "statistical significance", or avoid it altogether.

Significance level A criterion p value, often .05, .01, or .001, against which an obtained p value is compared.

Simple main effect The effect of one IV at a single level of another IV.

Skew Asymmetry of a distribution, with one tail longer and larger than the other.

Slippery slope of nonsignificance My name for the fallacy that finding a result to be *not* statistically significant is sufficient to justify interpreting it, perhaps in a later section of a report, as zero.

Slippery slope of significance My name for the fallacy that finding a result to be statistically significant is sufficient to justify interpreting it, perhaps in a later section of a report, as important or large.

Slope (b) Gradient of a regression line.

Spread The dispersion or variability within a data set.

Stacked dot plot Dot plot in which the dots representing data points are, where necessary, stacked so all are easily visible. Dots are also moved by tiny amounts along the X axis so they line up neatly in columns, as in Figure 3.3B.

Standard deviation (SD) A measure of the spread of data points.

Standard error (SE) SD of a sampling distribution.

Standardized mean difference (SMD) A term used in medicine for Cohen's d for a difference.

Standardized regression line Regression line of Z_Y on Z_X, which has intercept zero and slope r.

Standardized regression weight (β) Slope of the standardized regression line of Z_Y on Z_X.

Standardized units Units with some generality, such as number of SDs.

Standardizer The SD chosen as the unit of measurement for Cohen's d.

Standard normal distribution Normal distribution with mean of 0 and SD of 1, which is usually displayed on a z axis.

Statistical cognition The empirical study of how people understand and misunderstand statistical concepts and presentations.

Statistical inference A method that uses sample data to draw conclusions about a population.

Statistical model A set of assumptions we make in order to be able to calculate sample or inferential statistics. For example, random sampling is usually one assumption in the statistical model we use to calculate CIs.

Statistical power (also **power**) Probability of rejecting the null hypothesis when the alternative hypothesis is true.

Statistical significance Rejection of the null hypothesis.

Strict NHST NHST with statement in advance of α, the significance level to be used.

Subset contrast The difference between the means of two subsets of group means.

Sum of squares A quantity like $\sum \left(Y - \widehat{Y}\right)^2$, which is the sum of squares of residuals in regression.

Systematic review (also *research synthesis*) Review that integrates all the available research evidence on a topic, almost always by meta-analysis.

Take-home picture A picture that's sufficiently vivid and important to haunt your dreams.

Take-home movie A running simulation that's sufficiently vivid and important to haunt your dreams.

Target effect size, δ Value of δ, the population ES, used in a power calculation.

Target MoE Value of precision specified for calculations of what N we need, when using precision for planning. Target MoE is expressed in units of σ, the population SD.

Test-retest reliability The extent that a measure gives the same result when repeated in the same situation.

Test statistic A statistic with a known distribution, when H_0 is true, that allows calculation of a p value. For example, z and t are often used as test statistics.

The new statistics Statistical techniques, including especially estimation and meta-analysis, that usually provide a better basis for statistical inference than NHST.

Third quartile The 75th percentile.

Time series Data collected at a number of time points, often a large number of time points.

Tragedy of the error bar My name for the unfortunate fact that error bars don't automatically announce what they represent. We need to be told.

Treatment A value that can be taken by the IV. Treatments are also called **levels** or **conditions**.

Trimmed mean Mean calculated after trimming of a data set, often by 20% at each end.

Trimming Removal of a stated percentage, often 20%, of the data points from each end of the distribution.

t test NHST using t as the test statistic.

Two-sided alternative hypothesis An H_1 that includes values that differ in either direction from the null hypothesis value. For example, H_1: $\mu \neq 50$.

Two-tailed p value The p value calculated by including the obtained result and values more extreme in both directions.

Two-way independent groups design Design with two IVs, and a group of participants for every combination of levels of the two IVs.

Type I error Rejection of the null hypothesis WHEN it's true. A false positive.

Type I error rate (α) Probability of rejecting the null hypothesis WHEN it's true.

Type II error Non-rejection of the null hypothesis WHEN it's false. A false negative, a miss.

Type II error rate (β) Probability of not rejecting the null hypothesis WHEN it's false.

Unbiased estimate An estimate of a parameter is **unbiased** if, on average, it equals the parameter. On average it neither underestimates nor overestimates the parameter.

Unimodal distribution A distribution with only one overall peak.

Upper limit (UL) Upper end of a CI.

Validity The extent that a measure actually measures what it's designed to measure. High is good.

Variance The square of the SD.

Weights Relative contributions of different studies in a meta-analysis.

Welch method (or **Welch–Satterthwaite method**) A method for analyzing the independent groups design without needing to assume homogeneity of variance.

Within-group design Design, such as the paired design, in which the IV is a within-group variable.

Within-group variable A variable whose different levels are all seen by a single group of participants. Also known as a **repeated measure**.

z score The distance of a data point or an *X* value from the mean, in standard deviation units.

References

Altman, D. G., Machin, D., Bryant, T. N., & Gardner, M. J. (Eds.) (2000). *Statistics with confidence: Confidence intervals and statistical guidelines* (2nd ed.). London: British Medical Journal Books.

Alvarez, C. (2007). *Does philosophy improve reasoning skills?* Masters thesis, University of Melbourne, Melbourne, Australia. Available from tiny.cc/claudiama

American Psychological Association. (2010). *Publication manual of the American Psychological Association* (6th ed.). Washington, DC: Author.

Aruguete, M. S., Goodboy, A. K., Jenkins, W. J., Mansson, D. H., & McCutcheon, L. E. (2012). Does religious faith improve test performance? *North American Journal of Psychology, 14,* 185–196.

Beek, T., Dijkhoff, L., Wagenmakers, E-J., & Simons, D. J. (2014). Strack replication. Available from osf.io/pkd65

Begley, C. G., & Ellis, L. M. (2012). Raise standards for preclinical cancer research. *Nature, 483,* 531–533. doi:10.1038/483531a

Bem. D. J. (1994). Response to Hyman. *Psychological Bulletin, 115,* 25–27. doi:10.1037/0033-2909.115.1.25

Bem, D. J., & Honorton, C. (1994). Does psi exist? Replicable evidence for an anomalous process of information transfer. *Psychological Bulletin, 115,* 4–18. doi:10.1037/0033-2909.115.1.4

Bennett, C. M., Baird, A. A., Miller, M. B., & Wolford, G. L. (2009). Neural correlates of interspecies perspective taking in the post-mortem Atlantic Salmon: An argument for multiple comparisons correction. *NeuroImage, 47,* S125. doi:10.1016/S1053-8119(09)71202-9 Available from tiny.cc/salmonposter

Bisson, J. I., Roberts, N. P., Andrew, M., Cooper, R., & Lewis, C. (2013). Psychological therapies for chronic post-traumatic stress disorder (PTSD) in adults. *Cochrane Database of Systematic Reviews* 2013, Issue 12. Art. No.: CD003388. doi:10.1002/14651858.CD003388.pub4

Bornstein, M. H., & Bornstein, H. G. (1976). The pace of life. *Nature, 259,* 557–559. doi:10.1038/259557a0

Bosco, F. A., Aguinis, H., Singh, K., Field, J. G., & Pierce, C. A. (2015). Correlational effect size benchmarks. *Journal of Applied Psychology, 100,* 431–449. doi:10.1037/a0038047

Brandt, M. J., IJzerman, H., Dijksterhuis, A., Farach, F. J., Geller, J., Giner-Sorolla, R., ... van 't Veer, A. (2014). The replication recipe: What makes for a convincing replication? *Journal of Experimental Social Psychology, 50,* 217–224. doi:10.1016/j.jesp.2013.10.005

Brethel-Haurwitz, K. M., & Marsh, A. A. (2014). Geographical differences in subjective well-being predict extraordinary altruism. *Psychological Science, 25,* 762–771. doi:10.1177/0956797613516148

Brown, P. C., Roediger III, H. L., & McDaniel, M. A. (2014). *Make it stick: The science of successful learning.* Cambridge, MA: Belknap.

Burgmer, P., & Englich, B. (2012). Bullseye! How power improves motor performance. *Social Psychological and Personality Science, 4,* 224–232. doi:10.1177/1948550612452014

Bushman, B. (2005). Violence and sex in television programs do not sell products in advertisements. *Psychological Science, 16,* 702–708. doi:10.1111/j.1467-9280.2005.01599.x

Button, K. S., Ioannidis, J. P. A., Mokrysz, C., Nosek, B. A., Flint, J., Robinson, E. S. J., & Munafò, M. R. (2013). Power failure: Why small sample size undermines the reliability of neuroscience. *Nature Reviews. Neuroscience, 14,* 365–376. doi:10.1038/nrn3475

Calin-Jageman, R. J., & Caldwell, T. L. (2014). Replication of the superstition and performance study by Damisch, Stoberock, and Mussweiler (2010). *Social Psychology, 45,* 239–245. doi:10.1027/1864-9335/a000190

Carpenter, S. K., Wilford, M. M., Kornell, N., & Mullaney, K. M. (2013). Appearances can be deceiving: Instructor fluency increases perceptions of learning without increasing actual learning. *Psychonomic Bulletin & Review, 20,* 1350–1356. doi:10.3758/s13423-013-0442-z

Carter, T. J., Ferguson, M. J., & Hassin, R. R. (2011). A single exposure to the American flag shifts support toward Republicanism up to 8 months later. *Psychological Science, 22,* 1011–1018. doi:10.1177/0956797611414726

Caruso, E. M., Vohs, K. D., Baxter, B., & Waytz, A. (2013). Mere exposure to money increases endorsement of freemarket systems and social inequality. *Journal of Experimental Psychology: General, 142,* 301–306. doi:10.1037/a0029288

Cash, T. F. (2000). *The multi-dimensional body-self relations questionnaire. Users manual.* Available at www.body-images.com/assessments

Chaix, A., Zarrinpar, A., Miu, P, & Panda, S. (2014). Time-restricted feeding is a preventative and therapeutic intervention against diverse nutritional challenges. *Cell Metabolism, 20,* 991–1005. doi:10.1016/j.cmet.2014.11.001

Chan, D. W. (2007). Components of leadership giftedness and multiple intelligences among Chinese gifted students in Hong Kong. *High Ability Studies, 18,* 155–172. doi:10.1080/13598130701709749

Chervin, R. D., Ruzicka, D. L., Giordani, B. J., Weatherly, R. A., Dillon, J. E., Hodges, E. K., … Guire, K. E. (2006). Sleep-disordered breathing, behavior, and cognition in children before and after adenotonsillectomy. *Pediatrics, 117,* e769–e778. doi:10.1542/peds.2005-1837

Cohen, J. (1977). *Statistical power analysis for the behavioral sciences* (Revised ed.). New York: Academic Press.

Cohen, J. (1988). *Statistical power analysis for the behavioral sciences* (2nd ed.). Hillsdale, NJ: Erlbaum.

Cohen, J. (1994). The earth is round ($p < .05$). *American Psychologist, 49,* 997–1003. doi:10.1037/0003-066X.49.12.997

Conde-Agudelo, A., & Díaz-Rossello, J. L. (2014). Kangaroo mother care to reduce morbidity and mortality in low birthweight infants. *Cochrane Database of Systematic Reviews* 2014, Issue 4. Art. No.: CD002771. doi:10.1002/14651858.CD002771.pub3

Cumming, G. (2012). *Understanding the new statistics: Effect sizes, confidence intervals, and meta-analysis.* New York: Routledge.

Cumming, G. (2014) The new statistics: Why and how. *Psychological Science, 25,* 7–29. doi:10.1177/0956797613504966 Available from tiny.cc/tnswhyhow

Cumming, G. (2016). *ESCI (Exploratory Software for Confidence Intervals)* [Computer software]. Available from www.routledge.com/cw/cumming

Cumming, G., & Finch, S. (2005). Inference by eye: Confidence intervals, and how to read pictures of data. *American Psychologist, 60,* 170–180. doi:10.1037/0003-066X.60.2.170 Available from tiny.cc/inferencebyeye

Cumming, G., & Maillardet, R. (2006). Confidence intervals and replication: Where will the next mean fall? *Psychological Methods, 11,* 217–227. doi:10.1037/1082-989X.11.3.217

Cusack, M., Vezenkova, N., Gottschalk, C., & Calin-Jageman, R. J. (2015). Direct and conceptual replications of Burgmer & Englich (2012): Power may have little to no effect on motor performance. *PLoS ONE, 10*(11): e0140806. doi:10.1371/journal.pone.0140806

Damisch, L., Stoberock, B., & Mussweiler, T. (2010). Keep your fingers crossed! How superstition improves performance. *Psychological Science, 21,* 1014–1020. doi:10.1177/0956797610372631

Deci, E. L., Koestner, R., & Ryan, R. M. (1999). A meta-analytic review of experiments examining the effects of extrinsic rewards on intrinsic motivation. *Psychological Bulletin, 125,* 627–668. doi:10.1037/0033-2909.125.6.627

de Lorgeril, M., Salen, P., Martin, J.-L., Monjaud, I., Boucher, P., & Mamelle, N. (1998). Mediterranean dietary pattern in a randomized trial. *Archives of Internal Medicine, 158,* 1181–1187. doi:10.1001/archinte.158.11.1181

Diekelmann, S., & Born, J. (2010). The memory function of sleep. *Nature Reviews Neuroscience 11,* 114–126. doi:10.1038/nrn2762

Diener, E., & Diener, C. (1996). Most people are happy. *Psychological Science, 7,* 181–186. doi:10.1111/j.1467–9280.1996.tb00354.x

Diener, E., Emmons, R. A., Larsen, R. J., & Griffin, S. (1985). The satisfaction with life scale. *Journal of Personality Assessment, 49,* 71–75. doi:10.1207/s15327752jpa4901_13

Donohue, A., van Gelder, T., Cumming, G., & Bissett, M. (2002). *Reason! project studies, 1999–2002. Reason! project technical report 2002/1.* Melbourne, Australia: University of Melbourne. Available from tiny.cc/tim2002

Ekman, P., Levenson, R., & Friesen, W. (1983). Autonomic nervous system activity distinguishes among emotions. *Science, 221*(4616), 1208–1210. doi:10.1126/science.6612338

Ericsson, K. A., Krampe, R. T., & Tesch-Romer, C. (1993). The role of deliberate practice in the acquisition of expert performance. *Psychological Review, 100,* 363–406. doi:10.1037/0033-295X.100.3.363

Eskine, K. J. (2013). Wholesome foods and wholesome morals? Organic foods reduce prosocial behavior and harshen moral judgments. *Social Psychological and Personality Science, 4,* 251–254. doi:10.1177/1948550612447114

Facione, P. A., & Facione, N. C. (1992). *The California Critical Thinking Skills Test and manual.* Millbrae, CA: California Academic Press.

Floretta-Schiller, S., Berent, B. & Salinas, G. (2015). *The effects of labels on the enjoyment of chocolate.* Unpublished manuscript, Department of Psychology, Dominican University, River Forest, IL.

Flynn, J. R. (2012). *Are we getting smarter? Rising IQ in the twenty-first century.* Cambridge, UK: Cambridge University Press.

Franco, A., Malhotra, N., & Simonovits, G. (2015). Underreporting in psychology experiments: Evidence from a study registry. *Social Psychological and Personality Science, 7,* 8–12. doi:10.1177/1948550615598377

Frenda, S. J., Patihis, L., Loftus, E. F., Lewis, H. C., & Fenn, K. M. (2014). Sleep deprivation and false memories. *Psychological Science, 25,* 1674–1681. doi:10.1177/0956797614534694

Gervais, W. M., & Norenzayan, A. (2012). Analytic thinking promotes religious disbelief. *Science, 336,* 493–496. doi:10.1126/science.1215647

Gigerenzer, G. (2014). *Risk savvy. How to make good decisions.* London: Allen Lane.

Gilbert, R., Salanti, G., Harden, M., & See, S. (2005). Infant sleeping position and the sudden infant death syndrome: Systematic review of observational studies and historical review of recommendations from 1940 to 2002. *International Journal of Epidemiology, 34,* 874–887. doi:10.1093/ije/dyi088

Gladwell, M. (2008). *Outliers: The story of success.* New York: Little Brown.

Godden, D. R., & Baddeley, A. D. (1975). Context-dependent memory in two natural environments: On land and underwater. *British Journal of Psychology, 66*(3), 325–331. doi:10.1111/j.2044–8295.1975.tb01468.x

Gorn, G. J. (1982). The effects of music in advertising on choice behavior: A classical conditioning approach. *Journal of Marketing, 46,* 94. doi:10.2307/1251163

Halagappa, V. K. M., Guo, Z., Pearson, M., Matsuoka, Y., Cutler, R. G., LaFerla, F. M., & Mattson, M. P. (2007). Intermittent fasting and caloric restriction ameliorate age-related behavioral deficits in the triple-transgenic mouse model of Alzheimer's disease. *Neurobiology of Disease, 26,* 212–220. doi:10.1016/j.nbd.2006.12.019

Hattie, J. A. C. (2009). *Visible learning.* Abingdon, UK: Routledge.

Hilgard, J. (2015). *Game violence, game difficulty, and 2D:4D digit ratio as predictors of aggressive behavior.* University of Missouri-Columbia.

Hinkle, D. E., Wiersma, W., & Jurs, S. G. (2003). *Applied statistics for the behavioral sciences* (5th ed.). Boston: Houghton Mifflin.

Hölzel, B. K., Carmody, J., Vangel, M., Congleton, C., Yerramsetti, S. M., Gard, T., & Lazar, S. W. (2011). Mindfulness practice leads to increases in regional brain gray matter density. *Psychiatry Research: Neuroimaging, 191,* 36–43. doi:10.1016/j.pscychresns.2010.08.006

Huff, D. (1954). *How to lie with statistics.* New York: Norton.

References

Hunt, M. (1997). *How science takes stock: The story of meta-analysis.* New York: Russell Sage Foundation.

Hyde, J. S. (2007). New directions in the study of gender similarities and differences. *Current Directions in Psychological Science, 16,* 259–263. doi:10.1111/j.1467-8721.2007.00516.x

Hyman, R. (1994). Anomaly or artifact? Comments on Bem and Honorton. *Psychological Bulletin, 115,* 19–24. doi:10.1037/0033-2909.115.1.19

Ig Nobel Prize in Neuroscience: The dead salmon study. (2012). The scicurious brain, Scientific American blog network. September 25, 2012. Available from tiny.cc/deadsalmon

Ioannidis, J. P. A. (2005). Why most published research findings are false. *PLoS Medicine, 2,* e124. doi:10.1371/journal.pmed.0020124 Available from tiny.cc/mostfalse

Jacowitz, K. E., & Kahneman, D. (1995). Measures of anchoring in estimation tasks. *Personality and Social Psychology Bulletin, 21,* 1161–1166. doi:10.1177/01461672952111004

Johnson, D. J., Cheung, F., & Donnellan, M. B. (2014). Does cleanliness influence moral judgments? A direct replication of Schnall, Benton, and Harvey (2008). *Social Psychology, 45,* 209–215. doi:10.1027/1864–9335/a000186

Kang, S. H. K., & Pashler, H. (2014). Is the benefit of retrieval practice modulated by motivation? *Journal of Applied Research in Memory and Cognition, 3,* 183–188. doi:10.1016/j.jarmac.2014.05.006

Klein, R. A., Ratliff, K. A., Vianello, M., Adams, Jr., R. B., Bahník, Š., Bernstein, M. J., ... Nosek, B. A. (2014a). Data from investigating variation in replicability: A "Many Labs" replication project. *Journal of Open Psychology Data, 2*(1), e4. doi:10.5334/jopd.ad

Klein, R. A., Ratliff, K. A., Vianello, M., Adams Jr., R. B., Bahník, Š., Bernstein, M. J., ... Nosek, B. A. (2014b). Investigating variation in replicability. A "Many Labs" replication project. *Social Psychology, 45,* 142–152. doi:10.1027/1864–9335/a000178

Lakens, D. (2013). Using a smartphone to measure heart rate changes during relived happiness and anger. *IEEE Transactions on Affective Computing, 4,* 238–241. doi:10.1109/T-AFFC.2013.3

Lindsay, D. S. (2015). Replication in psychological science. *Psychological Science, 26,* 1827–1832. doi:10.1177/0956797615616374

Maccoby, E. E., & Jacklin, C. N. (1974). *The psychology of sex differences.* Stanford, CA: Stanford University Press.

Macnamara, B. N., Hambrick, D. Z., & Oswald, F. L. (2014). Deliberate practice and performance in music, games, sports, education, and professions: A meta-analysis. *Psychological Science, 25,* 1608–1618. doi:10.1177/0956797614535810

Mazur, E. (1997). *Peer instruction: A user's manual.* Upper Saddle River, NJ: Prentice Hall.

McCabe, D. P., & Castel, A. D. (2008). Seeing is believing: The effect of brain images on judgments of scientific reasoning. *Cognition, 107,* 343–352. doi:10.1016/j.cognition.2007.07.017

McCarthy, R. J. (2013) *Pre-specified hypotheses and planned analyses.* Avaliable from osf.io/g3kt6

McCarty, M. K., & Kelly, J. R. (2015). When door holding harms: Gender and the consequences of non-normative help. *Social Influence, 10,* 1–10. doi:10.1080/15534510.2013.869252

McDaniel, M. A., Howard, D. C., & Einstein, G. O. (2009). The read-recite-review study strategy. Effective and portable. *Psychological Science, 20,* 516–522. doi:10.1111/j.1467-9280.2009.02325.x

McEldoon, K. L., Durkin, K. L., & Rittle-Johnson, B. (2013). Is self-explanation worth the time? A comparison to additional practice. *The British Journal of Educational Psychology, 83*(4), 615–632. doi:10.1111/j.2044-8279.2012.02083.x

McFerran, B., & Mukhopadhyay, A. (2013). Lay theories of obesity predict actual body mass. *Psychological Science, 24,* 1428–1436. doi:10.1177/0956797612473121

McGuinness, D. (2004). *Early reading instruction: What science really tells us about how to teach reading.* Cambridge, MA: MIT Press.

Messerli, F. H. (2012). Chocolate consumption, cognitive function, and Nobel Laureates. *New England Journal of Medicine, 367,* 1562–1564. doi:10.1056/NEJMon1211064

Michael, R. B., Newman, E. J., Vuorre, M., Cumming, G., & Garry, M. (2013). On the (non) persuasive power of a brain image. *Psychonomic Bulletin & Review, 20,* 720–725. doi:10.3758/s13423-013-0391-6

References

Moery, E., & Calin-Jageman, R. J. (2016). Direct and conceptual replications of Eskine (2013): Organic food exposure has little to no effect on moral judgments and prosocial behavior. *Social Psychology and Personality Science, 7*, 312–319. doi: 10.1177/1948550616639649

Mosley, M., & Spencer, M. (2013). *The FastDiet: Lose weight, stay healthy, and live longer with the simple secret of intermittent fasting*. New York: Atria.

Mueller, P. A., & Oppenheimer, D. M. (2014). The pen is mightier than the keyboard: Advantages of longhand over laptop note taking. *Psychological Science, 25*, 1159–1168. doi:10.1177/0956797614524581

National Reading Panel (2000). *Report*. Washington, DC: National Institute of Child Health and Human Development.

NATSAL (2005). National Centre for Social Research et al., National Survey of Sexual Attitudes and Lifestyles II, 2000–2001 [computer file]. Colchester, Essex: UK Data Archive [distributor], August 2005. SN: 5223. doi:10.5255/UKDA-SN-5223-1

Neville, L. (2012). Do economic equality and generalized trust inhibit academic dishonesty? Evidence from State-level search-engine queries. *Psychological Science, 23*, 339–345. doi:10.1177/0956797611435980

Nosek, B. A., Alter, G., Banks, G. C., Borsboom, D., Bowman, S. D., Breckler, S. J., … Yarkoni, T. (2015). Promoting an open research culture: Author guidelines for journals could help to promote transparency, openness, and reproducibility. *Science, 348* (6242), 1422–1425. doi:10.1126/science.aab2374

Nosek, B. A., Banaji, M. R., & Greenwald, A. G. (2002). Math = male, me = female, therefore math not = me. *Journal of Personality and Social Psychology, 83*, 44–59. doi:10.1037/0022-3514.83.1.44

Open Science Collaboration. (2015). Estimating the reproducibility of psychological science. *Science, 349*(6251), aac4716. doi:10.1126/science.aac4716

O'Reilly, T., Symons, S., & MacLatchy-Gaudet, H. (1998). A comparison of self-explanation and elaborative interrogation. *Contemporary Educational Psychology, 23*, 434–445. doi:10.1006/ceps.1997.0977

O'Rourke, E., Haimovitz, K., Ballwebber, C., Dweck, C. S., & Popović, Z. (2014). Brain points: A growth mindset incentive structure boosts persistence in an educational game. *CHI 2014 Proceedings of the SIGCHI Conference on Human Factors in Computing Systems* (pp. 3339–3348). Toronto, April 2014. New York: ACM. doi:10.1145/2556288.2557157

Ortega, F. B. (2013). The intriguing association among chocolate consumption, country's economy and Nobel Laureates. *Clinical Nutrition, 32*, 874–875. doi:10.1016/j.clnu.2013.05.011

Paille, F. M., Guelfi, J. D., Perkins, A. C., Royer, R. J., Steru, L., & Parot, P. (1995). Double-blind randomized multicentre trial of acamprosate in maintaining abstinence from alcohol. *Alcohol and Alcoholism, 30*(2), 239–247.

Park, L. E., Young, A. F., Troisi, J. D., & Pinkus, R. T. (2011). Effects of everyday romantic goal pursuit on women's attitudes toward math and science. *Personality & Social Psychology Bulletin, 37*(9), 1259–1273. doi:10.1177/0146167211408436

Parris, K. M., & McCarthy, M. A. (2001). Identifying effects of toe-clipping on anuran return rates: the importance of statistical power. *Amphibia-Reptilia, 22*, 275–289. doi:10.1163/156853801317050070

Pinker, S. (2014). *The sense of style*. New York: Viking.

Rattan, A., Good, C., & Dweck, C. S. (2012). "It's ok—Not everyone can be good at math": Instructors with an entity theory comfort (and demotivate) students. *Journal of Experimental Social Psychology, 48*, 731–737. doi:10.1016/j.jesp.2011.12.012

Richard, F. D., Bond, C. F., & Stokes-Zoota, J. J. (2003). One hundred years of social psychology quantitatively described. *Review of General Psychology, 7*, 331–363. doi:10.1037/1089-2680.7.4.331

Richardson, M., Abraham, C., & Bond, R. (2012). Psychological correlates of university students' academic performance: A systematic review and meta-analysis. *Psychological Bulletin, 138*, 353–387. doi:10.1037/a0026838

Ritchie, S. J., & Bates, T. C. (2013). Enduring links from childhood mathematics and reading achievement to adult socioeconomic status. *Psychological Science, 24*, 1301–1308. doi:10.1177/0956797612466268

Robinson, T. N., Borzekowski, D. L. G., Matheson, D. M., & Kraemer, H. C. (2007). Effects of fast food branding on young children's taste preferences, *Archives of Pediatrics & Adolescent Medicine*, *161*, 792–797. doi:10.1001/archpedi.161.8.792

Rohrer, D., Pashler, H., & Harris, C. R. (2015). Do subtle reminders of money change people's political views? *Journal of Experimental Psychology: General*, *144*, e73–e85. doi:10.1037/xge0000058

Rosenthal, R., & Rosnow, R. L. (1985). *Contrast analysis: Focused comparisons in the analysis of variance.* Cambridge, UK: Cambridge University Press.

Rozin, P., Scott, S. E., Zickgraf, H. F., Ahn, F., & Hong, J. (2014). Asymmetrical social Mach bands: Exaggeration of social identities on the more esteemed side of group borders. *Psychological Science, 25*, 1955–1959. doi:10.1177/0956797614545131

Ruffman, T., Perner, J., Naito, M., Parkin, L., & Clements, W. A. (1998). Older (but not younger) siblings facilitate false belief understanding. *Developmental Psychology, 34*(1), 161–174. doi:10.1037/0012-1649.34.1.161

Rugg, D. (1941). Experiments in wording questions: II. *Public Opinion Quarterly, 5*, 91–92. doi:10.1086/265467

Rutledge, T., & Loh, C. (2004). Effect sizes and statistical testing in the determination of clinical significance in behavioral medicine research. *Annals of Behavioral Medicine, 27*, 138–145. doi:10.1207/s15324796abm2702_9

Salsburg, D. (2001). *The lady tasting tea. How statistics revolutionized science in the twentieth century.* New York: W. H. Freeman.

Sanchez C., Sundermeier B., Gray K., & Calin-Jageman R. J. (2016). *Direct replications of Gervais & Norenzayan (2012) provide no evidence that analytic thinking decreases religious belief.* Manuscript submitted for publication.

Schnall, S., Benton, J., & Harvey, S. (2008). With a clean conscience: Cleanliness reduces the severity of moral judgments. *Psychological Science, 19*, 1219–1222. doi:10.1111/j.1467-9280.2008.02227.x

Sedky, K., Bennett, D. S., & Carvalho, K. S. (2014). Attention deficit hyperactivity disorder and sleep disordered breathing in pediatric populations: A meta-analysis. *Sleep Medicine Reviews, 18*, 349–356. doi:10.1016/j.smrv.2013.12.003

Sedrakyan, A., & Shih, C. (2007). Improving depiction of benefits and harms: Analyses of studies of well-known therapeutics and review of high-impact medical journals. *Medical Care, 45*, S23–S28. doi:10.1097/MLR.0b013e3180642f69

Simmons, J. P., Nelson, L. D., & Simonsohn, U. (2011). False-positive psychology: Undisclosed flexibility in data collection and analysis allows presenting anything as significant. *Psychological Science, 22*, 1359–1366. doi:10.1177/0956797611417632

Simonsohn, U. (2015). Small telescopes: Detectability and the evaluation of replication results. *Psychological Science, 26*, 559–569. doi:10.1177/0956797614567341

Spielberger, C. D., Gorssuch, R. L., Lushene, P. R., Vagg, P. R., & Jacobs, G. A (1983). *Manual for the State-Trait Anxiety Inventory.* Palo Alto, CA: Consulting Psychologists Press.

Steiger, J. H. (2004). Beyond the *F* test: Effect size confidence intervals and tests of close fit in the analysis of variance and contrast analysis. *Psychological Methods, 9*, 164–182. doi:10.1037/1082-989X.9.2.164

Stickgold, R., James, L., & Hobson, J. A. (2000). Visual discrimination learning requires sleep after training. *Nature Neuroscience, 3*, 1237–1238. doi:10.1038/81756

Thomason, N. R., Adajian, T., Barnett, A. E., Boucher, S., van der Brugge, E., Campbell, J., … Wilkins, J. (2014). *Critical thinking final report.* The University of Melbourne, N66001-12-C-2004.

Vassallo, S., & Sanson, A. (Eds.) (2013). *The Australian Temperament Project: The first 30 years.* Melbourne: Australian Institute of Family Studies. Available from tiny.cc/atp30

Vermeulen, I., Batenburg, A., Beukeboom, C. J., & Smits, T. (2014). Breakthrough or one-hit wonder? Three attempts to replicate single-exposure musical conditioning effects on choice behavior (Gorn, 1982). *Social Psychology, 45*, 179–186. doi:10.1027/1864–9335/a000182

Weisberg, D. S., Keil, F. C., Goodstein, J., Rawson, E., & Gray, J. R. (2008). The seductive allure of neuroscience explanations. *Journal of Cognitive Neuroscience, 20*, 470–477. doi:10.1162/jocn.2008.20040

Wilcox, R. R. (2009). *Basic statistics: Understanding conventional methods and modern insights.* New York: Oxford University Press.

Wilson, P. H., & McKenzie, B. E. (1998). Information processing deficits associated with developmental coordination disorder: A meta-analysis of research findings. *Journal of Child Psychology and Psychiatry, 39*, 829–840. doi:10.1111/1469–7610.00384

Winokur, M., Holtan, A., & Batchelder, K. E. (2014). Kinship care for the safety, permanency, and well-being of children removed from the home for maltreatment: A systematic review. *Campbell Systematic Reviews* 2014:2. doi:10.4073/csr.2014.2

Zaval, L., Markowitz, E. M., & Weber, E. U. (2015). How will I be remembered? Conserving the environment for the sake of one's legacy. *Psychological Science, 26*, 231–236. doi:10.1177/0956797614561266

Zou, G. Y. (2007). Toward using confidence intervals to compare correlations. *Psychological Methods, 12*, 399–413. doi:10.1037/1082-989X.12.4.399

Author Index

Subject Index

Selected Formulas

CHAPTER 3. PICTURING AND DESCRIBING DATA

Mean: $M = \dfrac{\sum X_i}{N}$ (3.1)

SD and variance: $s = \sqrt{\dfrac{\sum (X_i - M)^2}{N-1}}$ and $V = s^2$ (3.3)

z and X: $z = \dfrac{X - M}{s}$ and $X = M + zs$ (3.4, 3.5)

CHAPTER 4. THE NORMAL DISTRIBUTION AND SAMPLING

For a normal distribution, approximately:

- 95% of the area lies between $z = -2$ and $z = 2$.
- 34% of the area lies between $z = -1$ and $z = 0$, and 34% between $z = 0$ and $z = 1$.
- 2.5% of the area lies above $z = 2$, and 2.5% below $z = -2$.

z and X: $z = \dfrac{X - \mu}{\sigma}$ and $X = \mu + z\sigma$ (4.1, 4.2)

SE: $SE = \sigma/\sqrt{N}$ (4.3)

CHAPTER 5. CONFIDENCE INTERVALS AND EFFECT SIZES

To halve the length of a CI, we need N approximately 4 times as large.
The CI is $[M - \text{MoE}, M + \text{MoE}]$.

MoE for 95% CI on M, σ known: $\text{MoE} = 1.96 \times \sigma/\sqrt{N}$ (5.1)
Two numbers for statistics groupies: $z_{.95} = 1.96$, and $z_{.99} = 2.58$.

z for sample mean M: $z = \dfrac{M - \mu}{\sigma / \sqrt{N}}$ (5.5)

t for sample mean M: $t(N - 1) = \dfrac{M - \mu}{s / \sqrt{N}}$ (5.6)

MoE for 95% CI on M, σ not known: $\text{MoE} = t_{.95}(df) \times s/\sqrt{N}$ (5.9)
For a single group: $df = (N - 1)$

CHAPTER 6. p VALUES, NHST, AND CONFIDENCE INTERVALS

z assuming H_0 is true: $z = \dfrac{(M - \mu_0)}{\sigma / \sqrt{N}}$ (6.1)

t assuming H_0 is true: $t(N - 1) = \dfrac{(M - \mu_0)}{s / \sqrt{N}}$ (6.2)

CHAPTER 7. THE INDEPENDENT GROUPS DESIGN

For two groups: $df = (N_1 + N_2 - 2)$ (7.1)

Pooled SD for independent groups: $s_p = \sqrt{\dfrac{(N_1 - 1)s_1^2 + (N_2 - 1)s_2^2}{N_1 + N_2 - 2}}$ (7.2)

MoE for the difference between independent means:

$$MoE_{diff} = t_{.95}(N_1 + N_2 - 2) \times s_p \times \sqrt{\dfrac{1}{N_1} + \dfrac{1}{N_2}}$$ (7.3)

Cohen's d: $d = \dfrac{\text{Effect size in original units}}{\text{An appropriate standard deviation}} = \dfrac{ES}{SD}$ (7.4)

Cohen's d for independent groups: $d = \dfrac{(M_2 - M_1)}{s_p}$ (7.5)

t for independent groups: $t(N_1 + N_2 - 2) = \dfrac{(M_2 - M_1)}{s_p \times \sqrt{\dfrac{1}{N_1} + \dfrac{1}{N_2}}}$ (7.6)

CHAPTER 8. THE PAIRED DESIGN

MoE for the difference: $MoE_{diff} = t_{.95}(df) \times s_{diff} \times (1/\sqrt{N})$ (8.2)

Standardizer for paired design: $s_{av} = \sqrt{\dfrac{s_1^2 + s_2^2}{2}}$ (8.3)
with $df = (N - 1)$.

d for the paired design: $d = M_{diff} / s_{av}$ (8.4)

t for the paired design: $t(N - 1) = \dfrac{M_{diff}}{s_{diff} \times \left(\dfrac{1}{\sqrt{N}}\right)}$ (8.5)

CHAPTER 11. CORRELATION

z scores for X and Y: $Z_X = \dfrac{X - M_X}{s_X}$ and $Z_Y = \dfrac{Y - M_Y}{s_Y}$ (11.1)

Pearson correlation: $r = \dfrac{\sum Z_X Z_Y}{(N - 1)}$ (11.2)

CHAPTER 12. REGRESSION

SD of residuals: $s_{YX} = \sqrt{\dfrac{\sum(Y - \hat{Y})^2}{(N - 2)}}$ (12.2)

Regression line, Y on X: $\hat{Y} = a + b \times X$ (12.3)

Slope, regression of Y on X: $b = r \times \left(\dfrac{s_Y}{s_X}\right)$ (12.6)

Intercept, regression of Y on X: $a = M_Y - b \times M_X$ (12.7)

Regression line, Y on X: $\hat{Y} = \left[M_Y - r\left(\dfrac{s_Y}{s_X}\right) M_X \right] + \left[r\left(\dfrac{s_Y}{s_X}\right) \right] X$

(12.8)

Regression line, Z_Y on Z_X: $Z_{\hat{Y}} = r \times Z_X$

(12.9)

Variance of residuals: $s_{Y.X}^2 = s_Y^2 \times (1 - r^2)$

(12.12)

and $s_Y^2 = \left[r^2 \times s_Y^2 \right] + s_{Y.X}^2$

(12.13)

CHAPTER 13. FREQUENCIES, PROPORTIONS, AND RISK

Proportion: $P = X / N$
Frequency table:

(13.1)

Expected frequency = Row total × Column total / Grand total

(13.2)

For each main cell: Contribution to $\chi^2 = (\text{Obs} - \text{Exp})^2/\text{Exp}$
Chi-square is the sum of contributions for the four main cells.

(13.3)

Phi coefficient: $\phi = \sqrt{\dfrac{\chi^2}{N}}$

(13.5)

CHAPTER 14. EXTENDED DESIGNS: ONE INDEPENDENT VARIABLE

Pooled SD for three independent groups: $s_p = \sqrt{\dfrac{(n_1 - 1)s_1^2 + (n_2 - 1)s_2^2 + (n_3 - 1)s_3^2}{n_1 + n_2 + n_3 - 3}}$

(14.1)

$df = (n_1 - 1) + (n_2 - 1) + (n_3 - 1) = (N - 3)$

(14.2)

MoE for a single mean: $\text{MoE} = t_{.95}(df) \times s_p \times (1/\sqrt{n_1})$

(14.3)

MoE for a comparison, one-way independent groups design:

$\text{MoE}_{\text{diff}} = t_{.95}(df) \times s_p \times \sqrt{\dfrac{1}{n_1} + \dfrac{1}{n_2}}$

(14.4)

CHAPTERS 14 AND 15. ANOVA

ANOVA: $F = \dfrac{\text{variability of group means}}{\text{variability of data within a group, pooled over all groups}}$

(14.7)

For the main effect of an IV with k levels: $df = (k - 1)$

(15.1)

Taylor & Francis eBooks

Helping you to choose the right eBooks for your Library

Add Routledge titles to your library's digital collection today. Taylor and Francis ebooks contains over 50,000 titles in the Humanities, Social Sciences, Behavioural Sciences, Built Environment and Law.

Choose from a range of subject packages or create your own!

Benefits for you

» Free MARC records
» COUNTER-compliant usage statistics
» Flexible purchase and pricing options
» All titles DRM-free.

Benefits for your user

» Off-site, anytime access via Athens or referring URL
» Print or copy pages or chapters
» Full content search
» Bookmark, highlight and annotate text
» Access to thousands of pages of quality research at the click of a button.

REQUEST YOUR FREE INSTITUTIONAL TRIAL TODAY

Free Trials Available
We offer free trials to qualifying academic, corporate and government customers.

eCollections – Choose from over 30 subject eCollections, including:

Archaeology	Language Learning
Architecture	Law
Asian Studies	Literature
Business & Management	Media & Communication
Classical Studies	Middle East Studies
Construction	Music
Creative & Media Arts	Philosophy
Criminology & Criminal Justice	Planning
Economics	Politics
Education	Psychology & Mental Health
Energy	Religion
Engineering	Security
English Language & Linguistics	Social Work
Environment & Sustainability	Sociology
Geography	Sport
Health Studies	Theatre & Performance
History	Tourism, Hospitality & Events

For more information, pricing enquiries or to order a free trial, please contact your local sales team:
www.tandfebooks.com/page/sales

Routledge
Taylor & Francis Group

The home of Routledge books

www.tandfebooks.com

CPSIA information can be obtained
at www.ICGtesting.com
Printed in the USA
BVHW020432270619
552061BV00002B/2/P